M000106869

Dementia

Dementia

*From Diagnosis to Management –
A Functional Approach*

Michelle S. Bourgeois and Ellen M. Hickey

New York Hove

Psychology Press
Taylor & Francis Group
270 Madison Avenue
New York, NY 10016

Psychology Press
Taylor & Francis Group
27 Church Road
Hove, East Sussex BN3 2FA

Printed in the United States of America on acid-free paper
10 9 8 7 6 5 4 3 2 1

International Standard Book Number-13: 978-0-8058-5606-4 (Hardcover)

Library of Congress Cataloging-in-Publication Data

Bourgeois, Michelle S.
Dementia : from diagnosis to management : a functional approach / Michelle S. Bourgeois, Ellen M. Hickey.
p. ; cm.
Includes bibliographical references and index.
ISBN 978-0-8058-5606-4 (hardcover : alk. paper)
1. Dementia. I. Hickey, Ellen M. (Ellen Mary) II. Title.
[DNLM: 1. Dementia--diagnosis. 2. Dementia--therapy. WM 220 B772d 2009]

RC521.B68 2009
616.8'3--dc22 2008054252

Visit the Taylor & Francis Web site at
http://www.taylorandfrancis.com

and the Psychology Press Web site at
http://www.psypress.com

This book is dedicated to
Dorothy Elvira Smith Planchon and Mary Lou Hickey
and all of the other grandparents and parents
whose love and talents are reflected
in the lives of their children and grandchildren.

Contents

Foreword

Before I started to write this foreword, I went back to one of Michelle Bourgeois' earliest publications concerning the clinical management of people with dementia and memory impairments. This was her first memory aid workbook, published in 1992. She had already amassed four or five preceding publications that developed a research agenda for speech-language pathologists (SLPs) interested in dementia intervention. However, the book on memory aids was her maiden voyage into laying out crystal-clear approaches to management in dementia. It was her first gift to her fellow clinicians, one designed to make their lives a bit easier. Clinicians like Ellen Hickey soon set out to test these ideas with patients in many different nursing homes and clinical settings around the country, learning firsthand what worked and what needed to be modified for more challenging situations. This current book, written by Michelle Bourgeois and Ellen Hickey, is an accumulation of practical experiences and the next gift to their colleagues. It is precisely the appropriate culmination of almost 20 years of work in which they have consistently blended their utterly comprehensive knowledge base with its utterly transparent translation into clinical practice. The beautiful irony in all of this is that I do not believe their purpose was to improve their fellow clinicians' lot in life. Rather, it was aimed at enhancing the lives of individuals with dementia and their families.

In the first chapter of this book, Bourgeois and Hickey quite rightly note that SLPs were beginning to find their way into the study of dementia in the 1980s, largely ignited by the work of Katherine Bayles, Al Kaszniak, and Cheryl Tomoeda. They are also correct in noting that applying the research to treatment of dementia lagged behind. Although Bourgeois and Hickey gracefully avoid saying it, this application actually received the push it needed when Michelle Bourgeois decided to center her life's work on dementia.

That occurred in the mid- to late 1980s at the University of Pittsburgh. I had just become Michelle's doctoral mentor when she said something like the following to me: "I know what I want to do. I want to treat dementia." The skeptic in me managed to stay silent, and I responded by asking how she intended to do it. She proceeded to describe in detail the research question, as well as the study design and analysis that ultimately culminated in the first experimental validation of memory books for use in dementia. This foreword seems to be an appropriate place to use that story to illustrate the trajectory of her career path since that time. It has the additional benefit of permitting me publicly to acknowledge that, just as she has made her mark on the treatment of dementia by making treatment easy, she made my role as a dissertation advisor totally easy as well. I just went along for a wonderful learning experience of a ride ... that continues as I watched her mentor Ellen during her dissertation process and as Ellen carries on the tradition of mentoring her students' research projects, from generation to generation.

Dementia: From Diagnosis to Management—A Functional Approach is also a wonderful learning experience of a ride. It is doubtlessly the most comprehensive compilation of functional and behavioral treatment material available. In addition, Bourgeois and Hickey have embedded all of that intervention material into its scholarly context: the causes of dementia, its neuropsychological manifestations, and its varied medical treatments and complications. They have made their philosophy of treatment clear, and provide solid justification for centering the management of the impairment of dementia squarely on its functional consequences and effects on daily lives. Bourgeois and Hickey speak knowledgeably about the various home and institutional settings that comprise the workplace of clinicians who intervene with dementia, and they seem to have covered every relevant issue from family involvement and staff relationships to interdisciplinary cooperation, environmental manipulations, and reimbursement. It will be apparent to any clinician who has worked in long-term care settings that Bourgeois and Hickey have not locked themselves away in ivory towers of academe, but they have actually worked in the settings they describe. This real-worldliness makes it possible for students encountering the world of dementia for the first time to get a taste of the experience itself, and to realistically weigh their interest in working with this fascinating disorder.

This book is for both seasoned clinicians and beginning students. It is written with the straightforwardness one has come to expect from these writers, and it is evenhanded in its critical analyses. Most chapters have case studies that illustrate important points and issues, as well as appendices that are comprehensive and equally illustrative.

It was not only an honor to have been asked to write the foreword to this comprehensive new text by Michelle Bourgeois and Ellen Hickey, but also a profound pleasure to read it.

Audrey L. Holland, Ph.D.
Regents' Professor Emerita
University of Arizona

Acknowledgments

This book represents the accumulation of knowledge we have gleaned from the many persons with dementia and their caregivers we have attempted to shepherd through the challenges of this disease over the past 18 years. We thank you for your patience and for understanding that we did not always have the answers, but that we were sincere in our efforts to try to find solutions to your difficult situations. It has been an amazing journey, and our lives have been enriched by each family we have come to know. You are our heroes. Thank you for allowing us to share your world.

Everyone who supported us in this endeavor cannot possibly be acknowledged here, but special thanks are extended to the Goldstein, Bourgeois, Hickey, and Hyson families for their unfaltering love and support. Thanks also to the rest of our family and friends, colleagues, and graduate student assistants who supported us throughout this process. We could not have persevered through the writing and editing of this book without your good humor and encouragement. It's payback time!

This book would not have been possible without the support of many agencies and colleagues who made both the funded research and clinical endeavors possible over the years. We would like to acknowledge the Alzheimer's Association and the National Institute on Aging for funding the research. We would like to acknowledge the many research colleagues who helped to conceptualize the research designs and methods, to implement the procedures and collect the data, to analyze and present the results at many national and international conferences, and to write the publications for journals and book chapters. We would also like to thank the many clinicians with whom we have worked and by whom we have been inspired. These communities of scholars and clinicians are unsurpassed in their dedication to the discovery of effective interventions for improving the quality of the lives of our clients with dementia, their families, and caregivers. We would also like to thank Cathleen Petree for her patience, encouragement, and guidance in the process of writing this book. It has been an honor to work with each and every one of you.

The genesis of this work was the love of a grandmother for her granddaughter, the sharing of art, poetry, and needlework from generation to generation… the realization that communication is more than words alone.

1

Introduction
History and Philosophy of Treatment in Dementia

Clinicians from many disciplines have been challenged to provide appropriate and effective interventions for the diverse behavioral symptoms that define the neurologically degenerative condition known as dementia. From the earliest published reference to "being out of one's mind" at the time of the Roman poet Lucretius (50 BCE; Berrios, 1987), and even earlier reports that the ancient Egyptians (2000 BCE) observed major memory disorders to accompany advanced age (Boller & Forbes, 1998), the medical community has described changes in cognitive, psychiatric, and intellectual functioning that were not common features of aging. The first documented use of the term *dementia* by Philippe Pinel (1745–1826), the father of modern psychiatry, coincided with many other terms for similar behavioral symptoms including *amentia, dotage, imbecility, insanity, idiocy, organic brain syndrome,* and *senility* (Boller & Forbes; Torack, 1983). Jean Etienne Esquirol's (1772–1840) description of dementia as "a cerebral disease characterized by an impairment of sensibility, intelligence and will" was eventually documented in the first edition of the *Diagnostic and Statistical Manual of Mental Disorders* (*DSM*; American Psychiatric Association [APA], 1952) to describe dementia as an organic brain syndrome (OBS) that was differentiated from an acute brain syndrome due to its chronic and irreversible nature (Boller & Forbes). Subsequent editions of the *DSM* reflected the evolution of terminology from *OBS* to *senile and presenile dementia* to the current *dementia,* which is defined as "a loss of intellectual abilities of sufficient severity to interfere with social or occupational functioning" (*DSM IV*; APA, 1994).

As early as the 15th and 16th centuries, the cause of "insanity" was attributed to syphilis, a disease that was thought to have been spread by Columbus' sailors, first to Spain and Portugal, then France and Italy. Over time, the term evolved to *general paresis of the insane* or *neurosyphilis.* The late 19th and early 20th centuries brought a more precise and analytic approach to the differentiation of clinical symptoms. As clinicians observed and documented the specific characteristics of individual patients, new diagnostic classifications emerged. Arnold Pick described a "lobar atrophy" that was eventually renamed Pick's disease and Pick's complex; Alois Alzheimer published the first account of Alzheimer's disease in 1906. Kraepelin differentiated "senile" and "presenile" forms of dementia in 1910 (Amaducci, Rocca, & Schoenberg, 1986). The distinction between "cortical" and "subcortical" dementia was first proposed by Von Stockert in the 1930s to describe lesions appearing in the brain stem and deep gray matter. Primary degenerative dementias became the popular nosology in 1980, when the third edition of the *DSM* was published. Advances in neuroimaging and neuropathology, as well as the clinical fields of neuropsychology and speech and language pathology, have revealed the heterogeneity of dementia characteristics and the variety of identifiable subclassifications. Diffuse Lewy body disease, corticobasal degeneration, subcortical gliosis, frontotemporal dementia, primary progressive aphasia, and AIDS dementia complex are some of the most recent types of dementia identified.

The recognition of a disease was soon followed by the identification of treatments to ameliorate the undesirable symptoms. The earliest accounts of intervention for dementia symptoms were the use of a rotating chair, which was suggested for mental conditions related to congested blood in the brain, and the hyperbaric oxygen chamber, thought to reoxygenate brain tissues causing dementia (Cohen, 1983). Julius Wagner von Jauregg, the first psychiatrist to win the Nobel Prize, discovered in 1917 that malaria inoculations improved six of nine patients with neurosyphilis. In the past decade, emergent pharmacologic therapies have provided some hope for effective treatment of dementia symptoms. The cholinesterase inhibitors (Cognex, Aricept, Reminyl, and Exelon) and the N-methyl-D-aspartate receptor antagonist (Namenda) attempt to provide symptomatic improvements. Disease-modifying therapies such as antioxidants, anti-inflammatory agents, and hormone replacement therapies aim to prevent the onset or slow the progression of the disease. When behavioral disturbances including depression, agitation, aggression, and hallucinations require treatment, clinicians can try a variety of neuroleptic, antidepressant, anxiolytic, and anticonvulsant medications (Green, 2005). Nonpharmacological interventions include sensory enhancements; reassurance, distraction, and redirection techniques; social and activity stimulation; environmental modifications; and caregiver education.

The history of the role of speech-language pathologists (SLPs) in the diagnosis and treatment of dementia is relatively short compared to those of other neurological conditions, such as aphasia. SLPs have only begun to develop assessment and treatment approaches for the cognitive and communication deficits that accompany dementia in the past 30 years (Bayles et al., 2005). Bayles and Kaszniak (1987) first documented the cognitive-linguistic deficits and skills of persons with dementia across the stages of brain degeneration. This provided the resources that clinicians needed to assist in the differential diagnosis of patients presenting with dementia symptoms. At that time, when a patient was diagnosed with a degenerative neurological condition, the role of the SLP was to direct the family to supportive services in the community, including nursing homes.

Concurrently, it was recognized that persons with cognitive impairments who resided in long-term care settings required improvements in the care and services provided. Congress passed the Omnibus Budget and Reconciliation Act of 1987 (American Health Care Association, 1990), which mandated physical, cognitive, and communicative evaluations of residents and the development of a care plan upon their admission to a nursing home. In addition, periodic reassessments were required to ensure patient functioning at the highest level possible. Since 1990, long-term care facilities have used a standardized assessment tool, the Resident Assessment Instrument (RAI), composed of the Minimum Data Set (MDS) and the Resident Assessment Protocols (RAPs), to document over 100 behaviors, including cognitive and communicative functioning. When deficits in cognitive and communicative functioning are present, the plan of care should include referral to the SLP for further assessment of treatment needs. However, lack of awareness of potentially effective intervention strategies for cognitive and communicative challenges on the part of nursing personnel often limits referrals (Hopper, Bayles, Harris, & Holland, 2001). Similarly, the pessimistic attitude that persons with degenerative conditions will only lose whatever treatment gains are made often restricts intervention to pharmacological treatment of behavioral symptoms.

From the mid-1980s, when behavioral treatments for the language and cognitive deficits of persons with dementia began to appear, thoughts about therapeutic intervention began to shift from futile to possible. Accumulated evidence from neuroscience and neuropsychology documented the presence of spared skills and abilities that could be used to design effective interventions (Hopper, Bayles, & Kim, 2001). A multitude of intervention approaches either to support and modify patient behaviors directly (Hopper, Bayles, & Kim, 2001) or to assist caregivers to change their own coping strategies (Bourgeois, Schulz, Burgio, & Beach, 2002) have produced positive changes in the quality of the lives of all those affected by the disease. During this same period of time, the World Health Organization (WHO, 2001) developed the International Classification of Functioning, Disability, and Health to guide clinicians in understanding the effects of a medical condition on an individual and facilitating holistic approaches for assessment and treatment of chronic conditions. Figure 1.1 depicts the WHO model components as (a) impairments of body structures and function, (b) activity limitations related to the execution of a task or action by an individual, and (c) participation restrictions that limit involvement in life situations. These components are influenced by a variety of environmental and personal factors.

As will be discussed in the chapter on assessment (chapter 4), the medical conditions that cause dementia produce impairments in structure and function at the level of the brain, resulting in functional activity limitations and participation restrictions. Clinicians have responded by developing assessment instruments to document degree of impairment and the resulting activity limitations and participation restrictions, as well as interventions targeting those specific areas. Impairment-based interventions for dementia are primarily pharmacological interventions, as well as some behavioral interventions. Pharmacological treatments for dementia are designed to remedy the problems with acetylcholinesterase inhibition in the brain cells. Behavioral interventions to address the impairments

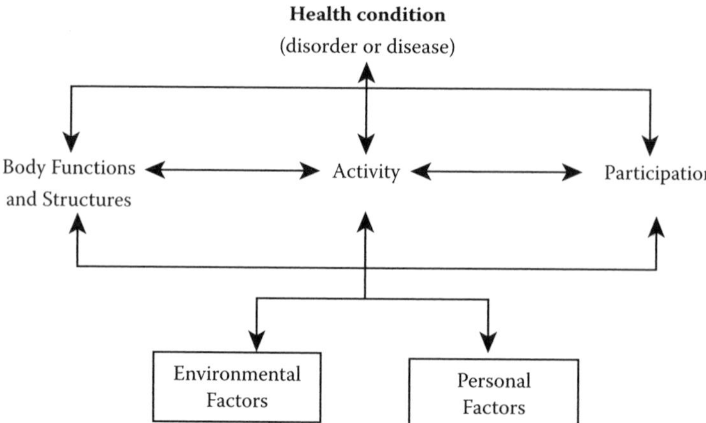

Figure 1.1 The WHO Model of Body Structures/Functions (Impairments), Activities, and Participation (WHO, 2001).

of dementia are performed in the hope of developing new neural connections and pathways to overcome cognitive deficits, such as those relating to memory, sensory perception, language, and motor behaviors. There is little evidence, however, of effects of behavioral treatments at the impairment level, or that improvements will maintain as the degenerative effects of the disease continue to progress. Therefore, the focus of most interventions is to find stimuli or strategies that compensate for the impairments, permitting the individual to function in an adaptive manner. The purpose of these interventions is to maximize participation in daily life at a level that is meaningful and satisfying to the clients, their families, and others in their social environment. Interventions have been developed to promote functional behaviors related to memory, communication, and activities of daily living (ADLs); these will be discussed in chapters 5 and 6.

During the years that clinicians and researchers were beginning to document evidence of treatment efficacy with persons with dementia, SLPs experienced the frustration of Medicare reimbursement claims denials. Claims reviewers had the misconception that the assessment and treatment of cognitive functioning were the responsibilities of psychologists and occupational therapists, not SLPs (Bayles et al., 2005). Various task forces of the American Speech-Language-Hearing Association (ASHA) developed several documents designed to educate claims reviewers and legislators about the cognitive and communicative needs of persons with dementia and the role of the SLP with persons with dementia (ASHA, 1987, 1988, 1991, 1993, 1997, 2005a, 2005b).

The first of these documents was a technical report in which the relationship between cognition and language was defined, the role of the SLP in evaluating and treating persons with dementia was described, and the responsibilities of the SLP on an interdisciplinary cognitive intervention team were outlined (ASHA, 1987). A position paper on the roles of SLPs and audiologists in working with older persons specifically stated that speech and hearing professionals were required to provide services in the areas of needs identification, evaluation, treatment, resource referrals, counseling, discharge planning, services documentation, research, quality assurance, and advocacy (ASHA, 1988). The third document that ASHA published comprised SLP guidelines for serving persons with language, sociocommunicative, and/or cognitive-communicative impairments (ASHA, 1991). In addition to the SLP roles outlined for serving these persons (identification, assessment, intervention, collaboration, case management, education, and advocacy), this document provided specific competencies required to perform each role. In a more general document outlining the preferred practice patterns of SLPs and audiologists (ASHA, 1993), several additional areas of responsibility were outlined for persons providing services to individuals with dementia, including screening for potential language problems. In addition, assessment of cognitive strengths and deficits was recommended, as well as follow-up services to monitor cognitive-communicative status and the maintenance of intervention effects. A second document on preferred practice patterns added additional definitions for the assessment, diagnosis, and treatment of persons with cognitive-communication disorders (ASHA, 1997). Specific procedures for assessing impairments, strengths, deficits, contributing factors, and functional communication were included, as well as advocating for the selection of treatment goals to improve oral and written language and cognitive-communicative behavior.

As the evidence accumulates to justify the involvement of SLPs in the identification, diagnosis, and treatment of persons with cognitive-communication disorders, the above-cited documents have been updated in the areas of the knowledge and skills needed by SLPs (ASHA, 2005a) and their roles in addressing the needs of this population (ASHA, 2005b; see Table 1.1). In addition, leaders in the field have spearheaded efforts to review systematically the published treatment research in order to develop evidence-based practice guidelines for clinicians to manage the cognitive-communication disorders of persons with neurological disorders, including dementia (Golper et al., 2001). The Executive Board of the Academy of Neurological Communication Disorders and Sciences (ANCDS) agreed to develop and publish guidelines referencing research evidence to support clinical decision making in the management of persons with neurological conditions. The determination of practice standards, practice guidelines, and practice patterns will result from the consensus review of all available clinical research literature. The ANCDS Ad Hoc Practice Guidelines Coordinating Committee has directed the individual writing committees to focus on developing practice guidelines instead of practice standards, which require a high degree of certainty based on empirical evidence. Instead, practice guidelines are recommendations for management procedures that have a moderate degree of clinical certainty based on Class II evidence or a strong consensus from Class III evidence (Miller et al., 1999). Class I evidence requires evidence provided by one or more well-designed, randomized, controlled clinical trials; Class II evidence requires one or more well-designed, observational clinical studies with concurrent controls such as single-case or cohort controls; and Class III evidence is provided by expert opinion, case series, case reports, or historical controls (Golper et al.). To date, there are so few Class I studies in the literature that it is unrealistic to attempt to develop practice standards at this time; alternatively, the development of practice guidelines holds the most promise for guiding clinicians and researchers in the development of treatment approaches

TABLE 1.1 American Speech-Language-Hearing Association (ASHA) Position Statement on the Roles of Speech-Language Pathologists Working With Individuals With Dementia-Based Communication Disorders

Identification	Identifying persons at risk for dementia, taking into account the incidence and prevalence of dementia in different culturally and linguistically diverse populations.
Assessment	Selecting and administering clinically, culturally, and linguistically appropriate approaches to the diagnosis and assessment of cognitive-communication disorders of dementia across the course of the underlying disease complex.
Intervention	Selecting and administering clinically, culturally, and linguistically appropriate evidence-based practice techniques for direct intervention with persons with dementia and indirect intervention through their caregivers and environmental modifications.
Counseling	Providing culturally and linguistically appropriate counseling for individuals with dementia and their significant others and caregivers about the nature of their dementia and its course.
Collaboration	Collaborating with individuals with dementia and personal and professional caregivers to develop intervention plans for maintaining cognitive-communication and functional abilities at the highest level throughout the underlying disease course.
Case management	Serving as a case manager, coordinator, or team leader to ensure appropriate and timely delivery of a comprehensive management plan.
Education	Developing curricula; educating, supervising, and mentoring future SLPs in research, assessment, diagnosis, and treatment of cognitive-communication problems associated with dementia; and educating families, caregivers, other professionals, and the public regarding the communication needs of individuals with dementia.
Advocacy	Advocating for services for individuals with dementia, and serving as an expert witness.
Research	Advancing the knowledge base of cognitive-communication problems in the dementias and their treatment through research.

Source: American Speech-Language-Hearing Association (2005b).

that can systematically generate data with more clients with dementia and with more diverse characteristics that will eventually lead to Class I studies. In the subsequent chapters of this volume, we will discuss the degree of evidence provided by each body of research and outline areas of need for stronger evidence.

The field of dementia management is no longer in its infancy; 30 years of attention to diagnostic description and classification, treatment, and management alternatives have generated a scientific base from which clinicians and researchers can proceed to generate evidence for efficacious and effective treatments for the behaviors associated with dementia. We are prepared to guide our clients and their caregivers through the challenges of dementia with the ultimate objective of experiencing the best quality of life possible. This volume aims to serve as a reference manual and the starting point for those who want to provide life-enhancing services to persons with dementia, and to inspire the continued generation of quality research to demonstrate the value of cognitive-communication intervention.

REFERENCES

Amaducci, L., Rocca, W., & Schoenberg, B. (1986). Origin of the distinction between Alzheimer's disease and senile dementia: How history can clarify nosology. *Neurology, 36*, 1497–1499.

American Health Care Association. (1990). *The Long Term Care Survey: Regulations, forms, procedures, guidelines.* Washington, DC: Author.

American Psychiatric Association (APA). (1952). *Diagnostic and statistical manual on mental disorders* (*DSM*). Washington, DC: Author.

American Psychiatric Association (APA). (1980). *Diagnostic and statistical manual on mental disorders* (*DSM-III*: 3rd ed.). Washington, DC: Author.

American Psychiatric Association (APA). (1994). *Diagnostic and statistical manual on mental disorders* (*DSM-IV*; 4th ed.). Washington, DC: Author.

American Speech-Language-Hearing Association (ASHA). (1987). Role of speech-language pathologists in the habilitation and rehabilitation of cognitively impaired individuals. *ASHA, 29*, 53–55.

American Speech-Language-Hearing Association (ASHA). (1988). The roles of speech-language pathologists and audiologists in working with older persons. *ASHA, 30*, 80–84.

American Speech-Language-Hearing Association (ASHA). (1991). Guidelines for speech-language pathologists serving persons with language, socio-communicative, and/or cognitive-communicative impairments. *ASHA, 33*(Suppl. 5), 21–28.

American Speech-Language-Hearing Association (ASHA). (1993). Preferred practice patterns for the professions of speech-language pathology and audiology. *ASHA, 35*(Suppl. 11), i–viii, 1–102.

American Speech-Language-Hearing Association (ASHA). (1997). *Preferred practice patterns for the professions of speech-language pathology and audiology*. Rockville, MD: Author.

American Speech-Language-Hearing Association (ASHA). (2005a). Knowledge and skills needed by speech-language pathologists providing services to individuals with cognitive-communication disorders. *ASHA*(Suppl. 25), 1–9.

American Speech-Language-Hearing Association (ASHA). (2005b). Roles of speech-language pathologists in the identification, diagnosis, and treatment of individuals with cognitive-communication disorders: Position statement. ASHA(Suppl. 25), 1–2.

Bayles, K. A., & Kaszniak, A. W. (1987). *Communication and cognition in normal aging and dementia*. Austin, TX: Pro-Ed.

Bayles, K. A., Kim, E., Azuma, T., Chapman, S. B., Cleary, S., Hopper, T., et al. (2005). Developing evidence-based practice guidelines for speech-language pathologists serving individuals with Alzheimer's disease. *Journal of Medical Speech Language Pathology, 13*(4), xiii–xxv.

Berrios, G. (1987). Dementia during the seventeenth and eighteenth centuries: A conceptual history. *Psychological Medicine, 17*, 829–837.

Boller, F., & Forbes, M. M. (1998). History of dementia and dementia in history: An overview. *Journal of Neurological Sciences, 158*, 125–133.

Bourgeois, M., Schulz, R., Burgio, L., & Beach, S. (2002). Skills training for spouses of patients with Alzheimer's disease: Outcomes of an intervention study. *Journal of Clinical Geropsychology, 8*, 53–73.

Cohen, G. (1983). Historical views and evolution of concepts. In B. Reisberg (Ed.), *Alzheimer's disease: The standard reference* (pp. 29–33). New York: Free Press.

Golper, L. C., Wertz, R. T., Frattali, C. M., Yorkston, K. M., Myers, P., Katz, R., et al. (2001). Evidence-based practice guidelines for the management of communication disorders in neurologically impaired individuals: Project introduction. Retrieved June 24, 2005, from http://www.ancds.duq.edu/guidelines/html

Green, R. (2005). *Diagnostic and management of Alzheimer's disease and other dementias*. Caddo, OK: Professional Communications.

Hopper, T., Bayles, K. A., Harris, F. P., & Holland, A. (2001). The relationship between minimum data set ratings and scores on measures of communication and hearing among nursing home residents with dementia. *American Journal of Speech Language Pathology*, *10*, 370–381.

Hopper, T., Bayles, K. A., & Kim, E. (2001). Retained neuropsychological abilities of individuals with Alzheimer's disease. *Seminars in Speech and Language*, *22*, 261–273.

Miller, R. G., Rosenberg, J. A., Gelinas, D. F., Misumoto, H., Newman, D., Sufit, R., et al. (1999). Practice parameter: The care of the patient with amyotrophic lateral sclerosis (an evidence-based review). *Neurology*, *52*, 1311–1325.

Torack, R. (1983). The early history of senile dementia. In B. Reisberg (Ed.), *Alzheimer's disease: The standard reference* (pp. 23–28). New York: Free Press.

World Health Organization. (2001). International classification of functioning, disability, and health. Retrieved February 21, 2006, from http//www3.who.int/icf/icftemplate.cfm

2

Diagnosis of Dementia

Clinical and Pathophysiological Signs of Various Etiologies

Increasingly, adults who experience a benign memory lapse, such as forgetting where they parked their car in a crowded mall parking lot or forgetting what they went into another room to retrieve, worry that they have Alzheimer's disease. The amount of media airtime devoted to medical findings or personal accounts of Alzheimer-related issues has expanded exponentially in the past decade and has created a heightened awareness and fear of this disease by the general public. When political figures (e.g., Ronald Reagan) share their diagnosis and their families discuss the challenges of the disease, the potential for this disease to strike anyone becomes difficult to ignore. The positive result is that increasing numbers of people are seeking information about dementia from their medical providers and a variety of sources, including the Internet, which often leads to referrals for testing. Increased numbers of individuals being tested leads to a number of benefits: a larger database of clinical cases to analyze, improved methods for more specific and reliable diagnoses, and increased treatment options. Advances in determining the underlying causes of the spectrum of dementia diagnoses are accelerating; the need for accurate and reliable methods for differentiating among diagnostic categories remains a priority for clinicians who are faced with persons and their presenting symptoms. This chapter outlines the range of diagnostic labels in dementia and related conditions, and their associated cognitive, behavioral, neuropsychological, and pathophysiological markers.

The aging process is thought to have three possible cognitive outcomes: (a) normal age-related decline, often described as "normal" and "healthy" aging; (b) age-associated memory impairment, which is not as severe as and does not have all of the features of dementia; or (c) a dementia, which is a clinical syndrome of chronic and progressive symptoms that results from acquired brain disease and includes many types (Christensen & O'Brien, 2000). Although controversial, a new label, *mild cognitive impairment* (MCI), has emerged as a diagnosis; the diagnosis of MCI is reserved for persons demonstrating mild impairments, usually in only one domain (e.g., memory), who do not meet the clinical criteria for a dementia (Green, 2005; Petersen et al., 2001; Winblad et al., 2004). The fourth edition of the *Diagnostic and Statistical Manual of Mental Disorders* (*DSM-IV*; American Psychiatric Association, 1994) defines *dementia* according to three criteria: (a) memory impairment *and* related changes in another cognitive domain such as language, abstract thinking, judgment, or executive functioning, that are (b) sufficiently severe to cause impairment in social and occupational functioning, and that reflect (c) a decline from a previously higher level of functioning (see Box 2.1). Evidence of an organic cause of the memory and intellectual impairments is required as well. There are as many as 75 different disorders that may cause dementias or chronic cognitive impairments. Therefore, a comprehensive medical and neuropsychological evaluation is necessary to distinguish between the potentially reversible and irreversible causes of dementia. The most common medical conditions with possible dementia symptoms are listed in Box 2.2.

BOX. 2.1 DIAGNOSTIC CRITERIA FOR DEMENTIA

1. Memory impairment *and* related changes in another cognitive domain (such as language, abstract thinking, judgment, or executive functioning) that are
   A. sufficiently severe to cause impairment in social and occupational functioning, and
   B. reflect a decline from a previously higher level of functioning.
2. Cognitive and behavioral symptoms
   A. are chronic and progressive,
   B. may be correlated with specific neuropathology of an organic basis,
   C. are differentiated from disturbances of consciousness (e.g., delirium) or psychiatric etiologies (e.g., depression and anxiety disorders) for which there are pharmacological treatments (Ballard, 2000).

Source: American Psychiatric Association (APA; 1994).

BOX 2.2 EXAMPLES OF CONDITIONS THAT MAY CAUSE DEMENTIA SYMPTOMS

1. Metabolic conditions (e.g., thyroid disease, liver disease, and diabetes)
2. Neoplasms
3. Toxins (e.g., alcohol and heavy metals)
4. Infections (e.g., meningitis, neurosyphilis, and HIV)
5. Autoimmune disorders (e.g., multiple sclerosis and lupus)
6. Nutritional disorders (e.g., deficiencies in thiamine, folate, and vitamin B)
7. Pharmaceutical drug effects (e.g., drug interactions)
8. Normal-pressure hydrocephalus

Source: Green (2005).

Dementia is distinguished from other conditions that may be more temporary and/or treatable; for example, other psychiatric conditions (e.g., anxiety and depression) or disturbances of consciousness (e.g., delirium) must be ruled out (Ballard, 2000). Some of these conditions are temporary, given medical treatments. Delirium is an acute disturbance of consciousness that is typically due to a treatable physical condition. For example, urinary tract infections in elders may cause delirium. Psychiatric conditions that may result in cognitive challenges can cause symptoms that mimic dementia, but pharmacological interventions may improve cognition. The term *pseudodementia* has been used to describe such clinical presentations that appear to mimic dementia, but are eventually differentiated due to the subsequent reversal or inconsistency of symptoms (Sachdev & Reutens, 2003). Examples of conditions that may cause pseudodementia include other psychiatric disorders (e.g., depression, mania, schizophrenia, obsessive-compulsive disorder, and generalized anxiety disorder), metabolic disorders (e.g., thyroid disease, diabetes, and renal failure), neoplasms, toxins (e.g., alcohol and heavy metals), infections (e.g., meningitis, neurosyphilis, and HIV), autoimmune disorders (e.g., multiple sclerosis and lupus), nutritional disorders (e.g., thiamine, folate, and B vitamin deficiencies), pharmaceutical drug effects, and normal-pressure hydrocephalus. With identification and appropriate treatment, the effects of most of these conditions can be reversed or improved (Eastley & Wilcock, 2000; Green, 2005). In contrast, neurodegenerative diseases (e.g., Alzheimer's disease, Parkinson's disease, Huntington's disease, frontotemporal dementia, dementia with Lewy bodies, progressive supranuclear palsy, and amyotrophic lateral sclerosis), vascular diseases (e.g., multi-infarct dementia and Binswanger's disease), traumatic events (e.g., dementia pugilistica), and infections (e.g., Creutzfeldt-Jacob disease) may be treated symptomatically, but continue to progress in severity until death. A comprehensive, multidisciplinary clinical assessment of cognitive and noncognitive symptoms is crucial for accurate diagnosis.

THE CLINICAL PRESENTATION

The realization that one's memory and cognitive functioning might be changing is frightening. Most people in this situation monitor their periodic memory lapses and wait until they reach their anxiety threshold to schedule an appointment with their doctor. Others seek out community memory screenings at the earliest sign of a problem. Family members and friends show similar patterns of reluctance or eagerness to investigate increasing cognitive issues. Fears may lead to denial or minimization of symptoms, and hiding symptoms from family and friends. A person who does not drive may believe that it will be safe for the person with cognitive changes to continue driving as long as there is a passenger to monitor performance. At the other end of the continuum, some family members who notice cognitive changes become fearful for the safety of that person and attempt to limit the person's responsibilities, restrict or prohibit driving, and begin to search for alternative living situations before a diagnosis has been made or those limitations become necessary. A thorough medical examination is needed to begin the process of confirming or explaining the underlying causes of the symptoms. Community memory screenings offer a quick and no-cost way to start the process.

Community Memory Screenings

Free memory screenings are frequently offered in the community as a public service by hospitals, geriatric assessment centers, university-affiliated memory disorder clinics, other medical establishments, social service resource centers (e.g., Alzheimer Resource Centers), state-funded agencies (e.g., an Area Agency for the Aging or a Department of Elder Affairs), and national organizations (e.g., the Alzheimer Association or the Alzheimer Foundation of America). Memory-screening events may also be part of a larger community health fair where citizens can obtain free health information and participate in a variety of health screenings (e.g., for blood pressure, cholesterol, bone density, and falls risk). These memory screenings are typically advertised in local newspapers and in public service announcements on the radio and television. The memory screening is designed to provide a quick assessment of cognitive abilities using either memory questionnaires (e.g., the Cognitive Difficulties Scale; McNair & Kahn, 1983) or a screening instrument, such as the Mini Mental State Exam (MMSE; Folstein, Folstein, & McHugh, 1975). Review of the person's medications for potential drug interactions or memory-impairing drugs (i.e., Benadryl used as a sleep aid), screening for depression and other medical and mental health concerns, and the identification of any recent traumatic life events (e.g., the death of a family member or a divorce) are also included in a memory-screening protocol, which usually takes approximately 30 minutes. A compilation of the information gathered in this quick session can be helpful in determining if there appear to be reasonable explanations for the memory symptoms or if more extensive testing is warranted. The person is then counseled to follow up with his or her medical provider. Informational brochures about normal aging and memory, memory-enhancing strategies, and memory loss prevention are available from a variety of sources listed at the end of this chapter.

Medical Assessment

The medical examination begins with a careful documentation of the presenting complaint and history of symptoms in order to identify areas of change in medical condition (e.g., pain, weight, sleep, and activity), cognitive functioning (e.g., language, orientation, initiation and execution of activities, and visuospatial difficulties), and noncognitive functioning (e.g., change in personality, behavioral disturbance, motor functioning, and psychiatric symptoms). Family members or significant others are often very helpful in providing information, particularly if they live with the person. The physician will pay particular attention to the report of symptom onset, rate of progression, and severity of symptoms. A sudden onset will signal the potential for cardiovascular etiology (e.g., transient ischemic attack, or stroke), whereas a gradual insidious onset is expected for an Alzheimer diagnosis. The symptom list will guide the physician in conducting the physical examination and selecting other areas of investigation.

The Physical Examination The physical examination begins with a review of medical conditions. Existing medical conditions may explain impaired cognitive symptoms; for example, cardiovascular disease, diabetes, hypothyroidism, anoxic or hypoxic conditions, liver and renal disease, and other metabolic conditions can all contribute to impaired attention, concentration, and memory. Appropriate treatment of these medical conditions may improve cognition. The physical exam may reveal evidence of cardiovascular-respiratory impairments, as indicated by measuring pulse and blood pressure and listening to the heart, lungs, and abdomen. Chronic hypertension is thought to contribute to a specific type of vascular dementia, Binswanger's disease. The person's current medications for these medical conditions are reviewed and evaluated against self-and family reports of their effectiveness for managing the symptoms of that condition. Sometimes, the addition of a medication or changes in medication dosing can exacerbate cognitive symptoms; reevaluation after a period of adjustment to medications is usually indicated.

Blood Chemistry: Metabolic and Nutritional Factors When the person presents with previously undiagnosed symptoms and an explanatory medical condition is not obvious, blood screening is usually ordered. The recommended routine laboratory analyses include a complete blood count, serum electrolytes, glucose, blood urea nitrogen and creatinine, folate, thyroid-stimulating hormone, and vitamin B_{12} (Knopman et al., 2001). Testing for Lyme disease, syphilis, and HIV is also advisable when risk factors for those conditions are present. Chronic alcoholism is often revealed when nutritional deficiencies are documented from blood chemistries; untreated long-term alcohol abuse is thought to contribute to the dementia symptoms seen in Wernicke-Korsakoff syndrome (Richter & Richter, 2004).

Neurological Examination A focused neurological examination is needed to determine if there are specific neurological conditions that could explain the cognitive complaints. Neurological conditions, such as head trauma and stroke, have known cognitive consequences and must be identified prior to attributing symptoms to dementia. The neurologist will complete a cranial and spinal nerve examination to look for signs of facial weakness; abnormal eye movements; visual field defects; posture, gait, and movement disorders; grasp, sucking, and snout reflexes; and vibratory and proprioceptive sensation deficits that would signal specific neurological conditions. Extrapyramidal signs suggest Lewy body dementia, Parkinson's disease, or Huntington's disease. Cortical sensory signs, primitive reflexes, and an impaired sense of smell are associated with advanced Alzheimer's disease. Ataxia and proprioceptive changes are associated with vitamin B_{12} deficiency. Increased lower-limb tone, brisk reflexes, and apraxic gait are seen in frontal pathologies, such as those from normal-pressure hydrocephalus (Patterson & Clarfield, 2003).

Furthermore, mental status, language functioning, and mood may provide signs that are used to differentiate among focal impairments secondary to vascular lesions, psychotic symptoms related to psychiatric illness, or the gradual deterioration of cognitive functioning in dementia. Neurologists often administer quick screening measures, such as the MMSE (Folstein et al., 1975) and the clock-drawing test (Freedman et al., 1994), to determine global mental status. Age-, culture-, and education-related norms (Crum, Anthony, Bassett, & Folstein, 1993; Grigoletto, Zappala, Anderson, & Lebowitz, 1999) are available for more accurate interpretation of the results. Language and mood are typically assessed informally throughout the evaluation process from responses to direct questioning about the client's symptoms and history.

Family and Psychosocial History The person's psychosocial history is needed for an accurate interpretation of medical and neurological information. Family and social history information includes documentation of relatives with dementia or other high-risk medical conditions, education and occupation, social supports and resources, and living arrangements. When there is evidence that first-degree relatives experienced dementia symptoms, or had medical conditions with known cognitive symptoms, it is more likely the person is at increased risk for dementia. The relationship between educational attainment and dementia risk has received much scrutiny in recent years. Since the publication of Snowdon's (2001) investigation of the cognitive and educational histories of a community of nuns, the potential neuroprotective effects of education have been studied. There is some thought that maintaining social relationships and friendships and participating in social activities (e.g., church, cards and board games, and book clubs) might delay cognitive decline. Some researchers advocate activities that require the client to learn new information (e.g., a second language and a musical instrument) as a way to foster the potential development of new neuronal pathways.

The psychosocial history typically includes determining the extent and composition of the person's social network, including family, friends, care providers, and the resources and support they provide to them. Information about diet, exercise, and alcohol consumption is valuable also for evaluating psychosocial functioning. Accurately determining the needs of a person who lives alone is often difficult, especially if there are few visitors to monitor the physical status of the home and the daily living habits. The presence of a spouse or adult children ensures more accurate and detailed information, although psychological issues, such as grief, anger, and fear, can temper its veracity. An overburdened caregiver puts him or herself and the care recipient at risk for negative physical and emotional outcomes. This interview process is critical for determining the entire range of resources the client and caregiver will need following the medical diagnosis.

Pharmacological Assessment Medication review is an increasingly vital component of the comprehensive dementia evaluation because of the cognition-impairing effects of some common medications and the incidence of polypharmacy in the elderly. Confusion and apathy may be seen in an older person taking over-the-counter sedatives, such as Tylenol PM, or antihistamines, such as Benadryl. Multiple medications for a range of physical illnesses can impact cognitive function and alter drug pharmacokinetics, including prescription and over-the-counter drugs as well as herbal remedies. For example, the prescription drug Coumadin and the over-the-counter medications aspirin and ginkgo biloba are all anticoagulants, which if taken together could thin the blood more than the prescribing physician intended. Many types of medicines have known memory-impairing properties, including analgesics, antipsychotics, anticholinergics, anxiolytics, barbiturates, sedatives, hypnotics, antidepressants, antihistamines, and some urinary agents (Massey & Ghazvini, 2005). Nonprescription drug use should also be reported to the clinician for its potential contribution to impaired cognitive functioning. In addition, noncompliance with medication regimens often exacerbates known medical conditions and can be the result of forgetting or refusing to take the drugs as prescribed. Finally, the neurotoxic effects of drug and alcohol abuse, often overlooked in the elderly, can be reversed if detected and treated appropriately.

Radiological Assessment The most recent evidence-based practice parameters for the diagnosis of dementia (Knopman et al., 2001) include the recommendation that structural neuroimaging with either a noncontrast computed tomography (CT) or magnetic resonance imaging (MRI) scan is appropriate for routine initial assessment. CT provides an X-ray image of intracranial structures to detect brain tumors, subdural hematomas, hydrocephalus, cerebral lesions, cortical atrophy, and ventricular and white matter changes. CT may be useful for recognizing focal lesions when there are few focal neurological signs or when there are psychiatric symptoms; however, findings of cortical atrophy, ventricular enlargement, and reduced CT density may be similar to those seen with age-related changes and psychiatric disorders, such as late-life depression and schizophrenia (Pearlson, Rabins, & Burns, 1991).

Structural MRI is often preferred over CT scans, as MRI uses electromagnetic forces to create a spatial representation of brain tissue and produces improved resolution and superior soft tissue contrast of the images. Furthermore, MRI can be used serially and for the study of normal controls, because it does not use ionizing radiation (Barber & O'Brien, 2000). The differential diagnosis of dementia types is aided by MRI, which is particularly useful for identifying abnormalities in the temporal cortex, determining the recency of a vascular lesion, and highlighting white matter lesions (Foster, 2004). The location and the extent of white matter abnormalities can supplement clinical information about cognitive changes and help confirm a dementia diagnosis, especially in vascular dementia where there is a sudden and stepwise decline in cognitive functioning (Roman et al., 1993). The sensitivity of MRI to detect multiple small lesions due to emboli following open-heart surgery, metastases, and other vascular conditions, such as endocarditis, is important for early treatment and reduction of dementia symptoms (Foster).

In persons with suspected Alzheimer's disease (AD), MRI data reveal generalized atrophy of the whole brain and ventricles, wider cortical sulci, and atrophy of the temporal lobes, hippocampi, and amygdala, with some of these changes evident before dementia symptoms occur. MRI evidence in persons diagnosed with dementia with Lewy bodies includes less medial temporal lobe atrophy than in AD and relative preservation of hippocampal volume. Frontotemporal dementia is characterized by bilateral and symmetrical prefrontal and anterior temporal lobe and basal ganglia atrophy in the absence of focal lesions. In vascular dementia, a wide variety of focal cortical lesions; basal ganglia, thalamus, and white matter changes; generalized cerebral atrophy; and ventricular dilation are seen. MRIs of persons with Huntington's disease reveal reduced basal ganglia volume, and widened frontal horns of the lateral ventricles. White matter and periventricular hyperintensities are seen in most dementias, especially AD, vascular dementia (VaD), dementia with Lewy bodies (DLB), and multiple sclerosis (Barber & O'Brien, 2000). Other forms of MRI, such as diffusion-weighted imaging and fluid-attenuated inversion recovery (FLAIR) imaging, are very sensitive to the increased signal intensities seen in the putamen and caudate with Creuztfeldt-Jakob disease (CJD) and other prion diseases.

A variety of molecular-imaging techniques complement the structural-imaging techniques by depicting cerebral blood flow, the distribution of radioactive-labeled drugs, and biochemical reactions to specific enzymes in the brain. For example, functional MRI (fMRI) detects the modulation of hemoglobin during a task as blood flows through the brain. Magnetic resonance spectroscopy (MRS) studies biochemical changes by measuring radio frequencies (Frederick, Moore, & Renshaw, 2000). Single photon emission computed tomography (SPECT) uses gamma ray–emitting substances to generate images that reflect the biochemical status of cells, including blood flow, synaptic density, and tumor metabolism. Hypoperfusion in the temporal-parietal lobes as measured by SPECT has been associated with an increased likelihood of AD, but the evidence for the value of SPECT in differential diagnosis of dementia is weak (Knopman et al., 2001). Positron emission tomography (PET) measures cerebral glucose metabolism by injecting radio-labeled glucose and recording the gamma rays produced when the isotope decays (Kennedy, 2000). Because PET has been shown to have greater localizing ability and superior spatial resolution, and the tracer can be inserted into natural substances or drugs without altering their biological activity, there is more evidence of diagnostic accuracy for PET than for SPECT. PET is thought to be especially useful for highlighting areas of reduced glucose metabolism that are associated with specific neurodegenerative diseases before they are clinically defined. For example, hypometabolism in the posterior association cortex differentiates AD from frontotemporal dementia (FTD), which presents initially in the anterior association areas. Occipital hypometabolism is seen in DLB and Parkinson's disease. Huntington's disease, progressive supranuclear palsy, and corticobasal degeneration have distinctive patterns of glucose metabolism as well. Although PET imaging is not used in routine dementia evaluation, it shows promise in providing important additional information for unusual or difficult diagnostic situations. Molecular imaging, especially PET, is thought to reflect synaptic activity and, as a result, helps to predict relationships between focal structural lesions and cognitive consequences due to remote projections of neurological pathways (Foster, 2004).

Techniques for measuring the electrical activity of the brain, such as the electroencephalogram (EEG) technique and event-related potentials (ERPs), provide additional diagnostic evidence. EEG often reveals increasing abnormalities with age, usually in temporal regions; the progressive slowing of alpha activity; and an increase in beta, theta, and delta activity in AD. EEG evidence is more normal in VaD than in AD, except where there are focal changes and more severe intellectual decline (Erkinjuntti, 2000). ERPs have been used to measure the processing of stimuli in the auditory and visual cortices, and more recently in the olfactory cortex, in order to supplement the diagnosis of dementia (Murphy & Gilbert, 2004). Although auditory ERPs have shown some delayed latency and small P3 amplitudes in persons with AD, the diagnostic sensitivity and specificity of the olfactory ERP are stronger. Morgan and Murphy (2002) documented significantly longer olfactory ERPs in AD persons than in age- and gender-matched controls, suggesting the potential clinical utility of assessing olfactory performance in a diagnostic battery for dementia.

Neuropsychological Assessment

Another critical component of the diagnosis of dementia is the neuropsychological examination. Neuropsychology is the study of brain, cognitive, affective, and behavioral functioning based on performance in a variety of assessments. The primary function of neuropsychological testing is to determine whether the person's performance is pathological or normal given age, gender, education, and cultural background (Taylor & Monsch, 2004). Age-related changes in vision and hearing may contribute to cognitive changes, including the decline in speed of information processing. These changes must be taken into account in determining whether cognitive changes are consistent with normal cognitive aging, with mild cognitive impairment, or with a dementia diagnosis. Different patterns of performance on tests of cognition (e.g., attention and memory), language, praxis, visuospatial ability, and executive function help to diagnose the different types of dementia. Neuropsychological assessments repeated over time are useful for documenting disease progression and the effects of treatment. These assessments will be described in chapter 4.

THE PATHOPHYSIOLOGY AND GENETICS OF DEMENTIA

Clinical observations need to be correlated with postmortem neuropathological evidence to confirm the degree to which the diagnostic criteria for dementia (e.g., the *DSM-IV*; APA, 1994) are reliable in diagnostic sensitivity and specificity. The neurohistological hallmarks of AD are senile or neuritic plaques and neurofibrillary tangles. Neuritic (i.e., senile) plaques are lesions composed mainly of β-amyloid; neurofibrillary tangles are paired helical filaments, composed of cytoskeletal elements and an abnormally phosphorylated isoform of tau, a glycoprotein (Lantos & Cairns, 2000). One particular variant of β-amyloid, $A\beta_{1-42}$, is significantly decreased in the cerebral spinal fluid (CSF) of 70–90% of persons with AD (Galasko, 2001). Elevated levels of the protein tau are also found in the CSF of 65–90% of persons with AD (Galasko). CSF tau elevations, however, are not unique to AD, but are found in many neurological conditions including acute stroke, encephalitis, and CJD. There is some evidence that the simultaneous measurement of β-amyloid and tau will increase diagnostic sensitivities and specificities (Hulstaert et al., 1999). In addition, abnormal cytoplasmic structures called granulovacuoles, Hirano bodies, decreased neurons (particularly in the hippocampus), abnormal neurites, patterns of gliosis, vascular amyloid, and some white matter changes (leukoaraiosis) are also common in AD (Lantos & Cairns).

The pathology of DLB is similar to that of AD in the expression of senile plaques and β-amyloid, but different in the paucity of tangles and the appearance of a different protein, α-synuclein (Barber, Newby, & McKeith, 2004). DLB also has the additional feature of Lewy bodies in both cortical and subcortical regions (e.g., substantia nigra, as in Parkinson's disease), and minimal plaque (Ince, Perry, & Perry, 2000). FTD is significant for microvacuoles, Pick bodies, and motor neuron abnormalities (Brun et al., 1994). Creutzfeldt-Jakob disease, a rare and rapidly progressive dementia caused by prion protein mutations, is characterized by diffuse neuronal loss in the cortex, basal ganglia, thalamus, brain stem, and spinal cord.

Much research is under way in the areas of genotyping, imaging, and biomarkers in persons with neuropathologically confirmed dementia, to develop accurate and reliable laboratory tests for dementing illnesses and to develop treatments for these illnesses. Progress is being made in identifying specific molecules that are reliably associated with specific diseases through biological fluids such as CSF, plasma, and urine (Diaz-Arrastia & Bastin, 2004). Mutations in the presenilin-1 (on chromosome 14) and presenilin-2 (on chromosome 1) genes are linked to autosomal dominant familial AD (Levy-Lahad & Bird, 1996). Mutations in the amyloid precursor protein (APP) gene on chromosome 21, including enzymes involved in processing APP (β-secretase and γ-secretase), and the existence of the ApoE-ε4 allele encoded by a gene on chromosome 19 are also thought to increase the risk for AD (Wegiel, Wisniewski, Reisberg, & Silverman, 2003). Evidence of mutations of the tau gene on chromosome 17 has been associated with increased tangle formation and neurodegeneration in persons with dementia and parkinsonism (Hardy, 2004). Because there are no reliable medical treatments to cure or slow the progression of dementia, it is not recommended that asymptomatic persons undergo predictive biomarker or genetic testing at this time (Green, 2005).

DIFFERENTIAL DIAGNOSIS

Reversible Conditions

Although there is some controversy about the extent to which the symptoms of dementia might be reversible, the importance of accurate differential diagnosis of conditions that might respond to medical treatment is irrefutable. As discussed

TABLE 2.1 Differentiating the Effects of Normal Aging From Dementia

Classification	Assessment Process
Reversible and/or treatable conditions	• Rule out and treat metabolic and nutritional disorders, depression, other disease processes, and medical conditions.
Age-associated memory impairment	• Rule out depression and dementia. • < 1 standard deviation below mean of young adult scores on cognitive tests. • Slower psychomotor speed; benign forgetfulness. • Preserved occupational and social functioning.
Mild cognitive impairment	• Increased frequency of memory complaints. • Preserved occupational and social functioning. • < 1.5 standard deviations below mean of age and education matched healthy controls on cognitive tests.

earlier, the physician must first rule out metabolic disorders, nutritional disorders, infections and toxins, and drug effects and polypharmacy, among others, as causing the symptoms and then treat the condition with the appropriate pharmaceuticals. When all other potential causes have been ruled out or treated and the cognitive symptoms remain, the possibility that depression, or another psychiatric disorder, is the culprit needs to be addressed. Table 2.1 outlines criteria for differentiating the effects of normal aging from dementia.

The diagnosis of depression can be difficult to make, especially if the person presents with an apathetic demeanor, but does not admit to feelings of regret, sadness, or remorse, and denies fluctuations in mood, memory lapses, or changes in diet, sleep–wake cycles, or libido. Contradictory family reports require investigation into the onset, history, and course of symptoms. When indicated, treatment with antidepressant medication should begin and responsiveness to treatment should be monitored after 6 to 8 weeks. Should affective symptoms improve with treatment, more accurate assessment of cognitive impairment can then be made.

Age-Related Memory Decline

Physicians, clinicians, and researchers struggle with the differentiation of cognitive changes that can be attributed to normal aging processes and those associated with a disease process. Studies of normal elderly individuals without other age-associated medical conditions, such as cardiovascular disease or diabetes, have documented relatively stable cognitive functioning until around 85 years of age (Hickman, Howieson, Dame, Sexton, & Kaye, 2000). There is increasing evidence, however, that even healthy individuals between the ages of 65 and 91 demonstrate significantly slower psychomotor speed than younger adults, as well as evidence of slowing of the electrical activity of the brain as measured by EEG (Salthouse, 1985). The subtle effects on cognition associated with this slower processing have been referred to as "benign forgetfulness" (Kral, 1962) and "age-associated memory impairment" (AAMI; Crook et al., 1986). The formal criteria for AAMI required ruling out depression and dementia, subjective report of memory decline with preserved intellectual ability, and performance on memory testing below one standard deviation from the mean of young adult scores (Crook et al.). The health-maintaining effects of a good diet, regular exercise, social and mental activity, and opportunities for new learning are receiving increased attention in the popular press and in research studies, as the prevention of aging effects are particularly important to the general population.

Mild Cognitive Impairment (MCI)

When memory lapses become more frequent and noticed by family members, the possibility arises that what might have been AAMI may now signal the risk of progression to dementia. Clinicians testing large groups of older persons with subjective memory complaints and their age-matched peers without memory complaints coined the term *mild cognitive impairment* to reflect the increased frequency of memory problems in individuals with otherwise preserved social and occupational functioning (Petersen et al., 2001). The formal criteria for MCI include significant and chronic memory complaints corroborated by an informant and documented to be 1.5 standard deviations below the mean performance of age- and education-matched healthy controls, and otherwise normal cognitive and daily activities functioning (Petersen et al.). In contrast to AAMI, MCI is thought to reflect cognitive changes that are not normal and is possibly a transitional phase between normal aging and dementia (Rivas-Vazquez, Mendez, Rey, & Carrazana, 2002). The estimated incidence of conversion from MCI to dementia has ranged from 10–15% (Petersen et al.) to 80% (Morris et al., 2001). Researchers are currently investigating other factors that might be useful in predicting future conversion to dementia, including the presence of the apolipoprotein E (ApoE)-4 allele (Almkvist & Winblad, 1999), subtle decreases in verbal memory over time (Collie et al., 2001), failure to benefit from cueing at recall (Petersen et al., 1994), and decreased volume of the hippocampus on neuroimaging (Jack et al., 1999; Killiany et al., 2000).

Dementias

Over the past century, clinicians have attempted to organize individual-specific symptom profiles into patterns of functioning. There is a need to distinguish among different dementia etiologies that explain the heterogeneity in the condition. For example, clinicians have identified early-onset and late-onset subgroups of AD to account for persons who presented early with pronounced language impairments, including difficulties with spontaneous speech, naming, repetition, comprehension, reading, and writing (Seltzer & Sherwin, 1983; Sevush, Leve, & Brickman, 1993). Shorter survival times and a more rapid rate of cognitive decline also have been associated with early-onset AD (Mortimer, Ebbit, Jun, & Finch, 1992). Others have suggested that the different symptom patterns reflect stages of deterioration in a more homogeneous view of AD (Reisberg, Ferris, & Crook, 1982). A classification dichotomy between cortical and subcortical dementias emerged to distinguish symptom patterns that resulted in aphasia, apraxia, agnosia, and amnesia from those that included bradyphrenia, mood disturbances, and personality changes (Albert, Feldman, & Willis, 1974). These descriptive categories have been controversial and have changed over time as a result of more sensitive measures including neuropsychological assessment, neurochemistry, brain imaging, and pathology results (Sjögren, Wallin, & Blennow, 2003). Hence, as clusters of symptoms become identified with more persons, new and more specific diagnostic categories emerge. For instance, frontotemporal dementia involves both cortical and subcortical structures. The following descriptions of specific dementia subtypes, therefore, reflect current evidence generated for that classification and the frequency of the diagnosis, and are not an endorsement of any particular classification schema that is subject to change with additional research. Table 2.2 presents common characteristics of the most frequently occurring dementia subtypes.

Alzheimer's Disease (AD) First described by Dr. Alois Alzheimer in 1907, AD is a slowly progressive, degenerative disorder in which memory loss is the hallmark symptom, and language, visuospatial, and executive functioning are impaired. AD is reported to be the most common form of dementia (60–70% of all cases), and to afflict approximately 6–10% of all individuals over the age of 65 and up to 33–40% by age 90 (Ballard, 2000; Cummings, 2003). Annual prevalence prediction studies estimate that there will be over 13 million people with AD in the United States (Hebert, Scherr, Bienias, Bennett, & Evans, 2003), over a half million in Canada (Canadian Study of Health and Aging, 1994), and over 114 million persons worldwide by the year 2050 (Wimo, Winblad, Aguero-Torres, & von Strauss, 2003). The risk factors for AD include age and gender (male–female proportion = 1.2:1.5 respectively); women have higher incidence in Europe, but not reliably in the United States. Other risks may include family history of dementia (and some genetic predispositions, including trisomy 21 and Down's syndrome); lower educational, social, and economic status; being single or living alone; and history of head trauma with loss of consciousness (increases risk by 80%; Jorm, 2000; Munoz, Ganapathy, Eliasziw, & Hachinski, 2000; Richter & Richter, 2004). Studies of potential environmental and neurotoxic factors, such as aluminum, lead, and pesticide exposure, remain inconclusive, as do the effects of oxidative stress, iron deficiencies, chronic alcoholism, and caloric intake (Richter & Richter, 2004). Several genetic factors for AD have been discovered in recent years, including the mutation of the amyloid precursor protein gene on chromosome 21, the presenilin genes on chromosomes 1 and 14, and the Apolipoprotein E (Apo E) gene on chromosome 19. Of the 3 Apo E alleles (e2, e3, and e4), the e4/e4 genotype was associated with 15 times the risk of AD compared to other genotypes (Jorm). Studies suggest that anti-inflammatory and statin medications, replacement estrogen for postmenopausal women, caloric restriction, increased physical and intellectual activities, and the use of antioxidant vitamins (C or E) may have protective effects; however, contradictory studies (Luchsinger, Tang, Shea, & Mayeux, 2003) have been published that render these suggestions inconclusive (Richter & Richter, 2004).

As noted, cognitive changes in AD affect a variety of cognitive processes. In the early stages of AD, lapses in attention and concentration may be present, often with awareness of these occurrences. The most common and earliest symptom of AD, however, is memory impairment. Semantic memory deficits, noted as word-finding

TABLE 2.2 Characteristics of Common Dementia Subtypes

	Alzheimer's Disease (AD)	Vascular Dementia (VaD)	Frontotemporal Dementia (FTD)	Dementia With Lewy Bodies (DLB)	Dementia in Parkinson's Disease (PD)
Prevalence	60–70% of cases 13 million in United States	15–30% of cases	8–20%	20–30%	18–40% of Parkinson's persons
Onset	Slow, gradual progression	Abrupt, stepwise progression	Slow, gradual	Slow, gradual	Slow, gradual, and fluctuating
Cognition	Memory deficits: word finding (early) Short term (mid) Long term (late)	Focal symptoms: Some early; others late	Variable	Intact (early) Gradually fluctuating Similar to AD	Similar to DLB Fluctuating cognition
	Executive dysfunction (early)	Mild executive dysfunction; severe in Binswanger's (early)	Selective and sustained attention deficits (early) Greater deficits than AD	Attention (early) Executive dysfunction (early)	Executive dysfunction (early)
Language	Intact; mild word finding (early) Semantics, pragmatics, reading comprehension, and perseverative (mid) Affective responses only (late)	Focal language deficits variable Co-occurs with extrapyramidal symptoms, gait problems, paresis, and facial weakness	Intact (early) Perseverative, echolalic, and mutism (late) Primary progressive aphasia: early, nonfluent, language deficits Semantic dementia (late), fluent language deficits	Verbal fluency deficits (early) Otherwise intact (early) Similar to AD	Less language impairment than AD Early pragmatic deficits Extrapyramidal symptoms: resting tremor, bradykinesia, and cogwheel rigidity
Visuospatial	Progressive decline	Visual field deficits	Intact (early)	Deficits (early)	
Behavior	Personality and mood changes (early) Delusions, hallucinations, agitation, and repetitive (mid) Ambulation, sleep, and eating (late)	Depression, agitation, anxiety, and apathy (early)	Profound early changes in mood, personality, and social conduct	Visual hallucinations, delusions, and depression (early)	Depression, mood changes Medication-related delusions and hallucinations

problems, may be associated with damage to memory stores or impaired retrieval processes (Hodges & Patterson, 1995). Although working memory remains relatively intact in early AD, central executive function is impaired (Paulesu, Frith, & Frackowiack, 1993). Remote, autobiographical memory gradually deteriorates over time (Greene, Patterson, Xuereb, & Hodges, 1996). These memory changes contribute to the deficits observed in everyday functioning and begin to affect language and communication behaviors. Attention, memory, and central executive functions become severely impaired over the course of the disease.

Language remains relatively intact, compared to memory, in individuals with early-stage AD. Expressive speech is fluent, with no articulation, phonological, or syntactic difficulties, but semantic memory impairments begin to surface as intermittent and subtle problems. They begin to have difficulties with word finding, expressing and comprehending abstract language, and following complex conversation. Reading comprehension, writing, and pragmatic skills remain preserved. As the disease progresses, there is a gradual worsening of semantic abilities, including increased word-finding and naming deficits and surfacing of pragmatic deficits. The result is difficulty comprehending complex instructions and increased production of empty speech indefinite pronouns, as well as difficulty maintaining a topic of conversation, impaired turn taking, and repetitive verbalization of anxious, delusional, and obsessive thoughts. Reading comprehension also begins to decline. Phonology and syntax remain intact, as well as oral reading and simple writing. In the late stages, verbal language becomes severely impaired in expression and comprehension. Ambiguous utterances that are echolalic, perseverative, and paraphasic evolve into incoherent mumbling and eventual mutism. Affective responses (e.g., smiling and pleasant vocalizations) to familiar sensory stimuli, cues, and music may be difficult to distinguish from reflexive behavior (Bayles & Kaszniak, 1987; Lubinksi, 1995). (Language symptoms across stages will be described in more detail in chapter 3.)

Visuospatial abilities have been reported to decline in a progressive fashion over time. Environmental disorientation and route-finding difficulties that occur early in the disease process may foreshadow later difficulties with copying simple and complex figures and the perceptual agnosias. Executive functioning, or the ability to plan, organize, and initiate an action or event, also may be impaired early, but by the middle stages these deficits interfere with everyday functioning. Behavioral symptoms prevalent in 90% of persons with AD include personality changes (disengagement, disinhibition, and apathy); delusions (e.g., theft, persecution, house is not home, infidelity, abandonment, and phantom boarder); hallucinations (visual, auditory, gustatory, olfactory, and haptic); mood disorders (depression, mania, anxiety, and anger); sleep, eating, and sexual disorders; restlessness; pacing; wandering; and repetitive behaviors (Teri & Logsdon, 1994).

Vascular Dementia (VaD) Another frequently occurring form of dementia, accounting for 15–30% of cases, is VaD (Cummings, 2003). Arteriosclerotic changes in the blood supply to the brain, cerebrovascular disorders, and ischemic, hemorrhagic, and/or hypoxic-ischemic cerebral lesions cause VaD. Cerebrovascular risk factors, including hypertension, diabetes, coronary artery disease, smoking, and alcohol abuse, may be exacerbating factors. Subcortical ischemic lesions, particularly in the basal ganglia, thalamus, and subcortical white matter, are typical of VaD. When extensive ischemic injury to the subcortical white matter occurs, usually due to chronic untreated hypertension, it is labeled Binswanger's disease. Multi-infarct dementia (MID) describes the condition of multiple cortical and subcortical vascular lesions (Cummings, 2003).

VaD is distinguished from AD by differences in symptom onset, disease progression, and gait. Persons with VaD may have an abrupt onset of cognitive changes due to a cerebrovascular insult or stroke, and there may be a stepwise progression of symptoms over time due to extensive small-vessel disease with multiple lacunes (Richter & Richter, 2004). Ischemic injury to subcortical white matter is thought to produce gait impairments typical of VaD, including hesitation and diminished stride length and step height (Briley, Wasay, Sergent, & Thomas, 1997). Focal lesions can result in pyramidal symptoms (e.g., hemiparesis, hypertonia, and abnormal reflexes), pseudobulbar affect (e.g., exaggerated emotional responses, dysarthria, dysphagia, and gag reflex), visual field defects, and incontinence. MID and Binswanger's disease may have an abrupt onset of cognitive symptoms and a stepwise, fluctuating, and progressive course.

The cognitive impairments in VaD can be quite variable depending on the region of brain infarcts and the size of the injured area(s). Some persons exhibit signs of early memory loss, executive dysfunction, personality changes, and increased incidence of depression; others show more severe impairment of executive function and less memory impairment than persons with AD (Kertesz & Clydesdale, 1994). Language changes may be focal in nature and coexist with hemiparesis, facial weakness, visual field defects, and extrapyramidal signs (Erkinjuntti, 2000). Persons with Binswanger's disease may have prominent frontal executive dysfunction with loss of insight, apathy, abulia, diminished motivation, variable changes in language and visuospatial skills, diminished speed of mental processing and attention, gait disturbances, and urinary incontinence (Bennett, Wilson, Gilley, & Fox, 1990). Neuropsychiatric symptoms are also prominent in VaD, especially depression, agitation, anxiety, and apathy (Aharon-Peretz, Kliot, & Tomer, 2000). Delusions of jealousy, persecution, and theft (Binetti et al., 1993) are common, as well as disinhibition syndromes, visual hallucinations, and depression.

Frontotemporal Lobar Degeneration Frontotemporal lobar degeneration is a generic term for a group of disorders characterized by atrophy in frontal and anterior temporal lobes without senile plaques, neurofibrillary tangles, or Lewy bodies, but there may be presence of Pick bodies or Tau abnormalities (McKhann et al., 2001; Morris, 2003). This condition was previously known as Pick's disease, and still may be called that when there are pathologically confirmed Pick bodies. Frontotemporal lobar degeneration may result in frontotemporal dementia (FTD) or a primary progressive aphasia (PPA; progressive nonfluent aphasia or semantic dementia). These conditions are characterized by prominent personality or behavioral symptoms that precede memory loss, and are associated with damage to the frontal and/or temporal lobes (McKhann et al.). The specific presentation depends on the location, distribution, and severity of the pathology in the frontal and temporal lobes (Morris, 2003).

FTD occurs when there is bilateral, symmetrical degeneration of the frontal lobes. The prevalence of FTD ranges from 8–20% of cases with degenerative dementia (Gustafson, Brun, & Passant, 1992; Knopman et al., 1990; Ratnavalli et al., 2002). There is a strong family history of FTD, and an estimated 20–40% of cases have autosomal dominant inheritance related to chromosome 17 tau mutations (Kertesz et al., 2000; McKhann et al., 2001; Morris, 2003). FTD frequently occurs in younger adults with a mean age of onset of 53 (Ratnavalli et al.). Persons with FTD may be symptomatic as early as 35 years of age (Franczak, Kerwin, & Antuono, 2004). The onset of FTD is typically signaled by profound early changes in social behaviors (e.g., compulsive lying), personality (e.g., self-centeredness, excessive sentimentality, and inappropriate jocularity), mood (e.g., depression and anxiety), and executive functioning (e.g., loss of insight, disinhibition, and impulsivity), with other cognitive abilities (including memory) remaining relatively intact initially (Franczak et al., 2004; Mirea & Cummings, 2000; Ratnavalli et al.). Thus, these clients are sometimes diagnosed with psychiatric disorders prior to the correct diagnosis of FTD. The presence of greater executive function deficits than memory deficits helps to differentiate FTD from AD, as does the hyperorality, social misconduct, and akinesia (Rosen et al., 2002).

Language changes are mostly in the expressive domain initially, with reduced output, increasing reliance on stereotypical remarks, perseverative and then echolalic responses, and eventual mutism. Comprehension, naming, reading, and written output are usually well preserved, as are visual perception and spatial and motor skills (Franczak et al., 2004). Memory performance is variable; recall is enhanced with specific cues and direct and multiple-choice questions. There is more difficulty with sustained and selective attention and other executive function tasks. Other behavioral disturbances that may develop include high distractibility, hyperorality, hypersexuality, stereotyped and ritualistic behavior, and repetitive behaviors (Mirea & Cummings, 2000).

Progressive aphasias present as either nonfluent progressive aphasia or semantic dementia (SD). Progressive nonfluent aphasia is caused by focal degeneration of the left perisylvian frontotemporal lobe atrophy, whereas SD is caused by bilateral degeneration of the anterior temporal neocortex (Franczak et al., 2004; Neary, 2000). In contrast to FTD, progressive nonfluent aphasia presents initially with a slowly progressive deterioration of language abilities, starting with word-finding difficulties, phonemic paraphasias, and agrammatic errors, but visuospatial and memory skills remain relatively intact and personality and behavioral symptoms are rare (Mesulam, 2001). Expressive language is marked by the repetition of words or phrases that exhibit paraphasic intrusions and apraxic errors; reading and writing also become nonfluent, effortful, and agrammatic (Karbe, Kertesz, & Polk, 1993). Eventually, the person with PPA may develop ideomotor apraxia, progress from nonfluent aphasia to mutism, and display some behavioral symptoms. Other cognitive deficits may present late in the disease process.

Semantic dementia (SD) is another progressive aphasia that is distinguished from PPA by language symptoms that are opposite in nature. That is, persons with SD exhibit a progressively deteriorating fluent aphasia that is well articulated, effortless, and syntactically correct, but anomic and empty of content (Snowden,

Neary, & Mann, 1996). They also have loss of word meaning and/or object identity, which creates difficulty with single-word comprehension and naming, but autobiographical and episodic memory, single-word repetition, reading aloud, and writing are well preserved (Kertesz, Davidson, & McCabe, 1998). Persons with SD also often present with prosopagnosia or associative agnosia, as well as later development of other cognitive deficits. Differential diagnosis of SD versus AD may be challenging; however, visuospatial deficits may be more pronounced in AD, and memory for nonverbal information may be better in SD.

Dementia With Lewy Bodies (DLB) DLB is caused by protein deposits in neuronal cell bodies in the neocortex of the frontal and temporal lobes and basal ganglia. DLB has recently been ranked as the second most commonly occurring cause of dementia with estimates of up to 20–30% of cases exhibiting Lewy bodies at autopsy (Barber, Newby, & McKeith, 2004; Barker et al., 2002). DLB is reported to primarily affect men over the age of 70 years and is characterized by its distinctive pattern of cognitive, psychiatric, and motor symptoms, including early attentional and visuospatial deficits with relatively preserved memory. There is a gradual increase of fluctuating cognition and consciousness with recurrent visual and/or auditory hallucinations, delusions, depression, and falls (McKeith et al., 1996), as well as mood changes, misidentification, and sleep disorders (Galasko, Salmon, Lineweaver, Hansen, & Thal, 1998). These neuropsychiatric deficits are the most salient diagnostic features of DLB, as persons with DLB have significantly higher frequencies of all of these symptoms (except delusions) compared to persons with AD (Ballard et al., 1999). Additionally, persons with DLB are more impaired than persons with AD on verbal fluency, psychomotor speed, executive function (problem solving, abstract reasoning) and visuospatial and constructional ability, but they are similarly impaired on episodic memory and language (Galasko et al., 1998). Approximately half of all persons with DLB exhibit mild extrapyramidal features, which may present as symptoms of parkinsonism, including tremor, rigidity, bradykinesia, gait abnormality, and postural change, as well as procedural memory deficits. The symptomatic treatment of persons with DLB is particularly challenging because of their sensitivity to neuroleptic medications and drugs to treat parkinsonism, which may induce psychosis.

Dementia in Parkinson's Disease (PD) PD is a neurodegenerative extrapyramidal disorder that affects 1.5–2.5% of persons over the age of 70, and is typically most common in White males between the ages of 50 and 79 (Cummings, 2003). The disease is associated with neuronal loss in the substantia nigra, which produces dopamine, an inhibitory neurotransmitter (Papapetropoulos, Gonzalez, Lieberman, Villar, & Mash, 2005; Weintraub & Stern, 2005). Histological evidence—including neuritic plaques, neurofibrillary tangles, loss of pigmented neurons in the substantia nigra, and Lewy body inclusions—suggests multiple pathologies requiring clinical confirmation of symptoms (Assal & Cummings, 2003). The hallmark symptoms of this disease include resting tremor, bradykinesia, rigidity, and postural instability (Weintraub & Stern). These symptoms are responsive to medications (e.g., levodopa and carbidopa), particularly early in the disease process. It should also be noted that deep brain stimulation is becoming a more common treatment for persons with PD (Weintraub & Stern), but this rarely has a positive impact on speech abilities.

Dementia will develop in 18% to 30% of persons with Parkinson's disease; another 30–40% of persons with PD exhibit deficits in executive function without other cognitive signs (Cummings, 2003). Some studies reported cognitive deficits in up to 50% of participants (Libon et al., 2001; Papapetropoulos et al., 2005; Weintraub & Stern, 2005). Persons with PD who had bilateral symptoms and visual hallucinations at diagnosis may be more likely to develop dementia (Aarsland, Andersen, Larsen, & Lolk, 2003; Papapetropoulos et al.); or those who display a prominent akinetic rigid state are reported by some to have a greater incidence of dementia than those with resting tremor (Cummings), but not by others (Papapetropoulos et al.). The pattern of dementia symptoms in PD resembles that of DLB more so than AD. When compared to persons with AD, persons with PD exhibit fluctuating cognition that is markedly slow. They exhibit more executive function impairment, but fewer deficits in verbal and logical memory and less language impairment (Litvan, Mohr, et al., 1991). Although persons with PD and AD are likely to show deficits in working memory, the locus of the deficit is likely to be different, with an inhibitory deficit in PD (Kensinger, Shearer, Locascio, Growdon, & Corkin, 2003). Persons with PD are also likely to display deficits in higher order learning, such as memory for sequences and pairwise learning (Smith & McDowall, 2004).

The common neuropsychiatric symptoms that accompany PD include mood fluctuations, hallucinations, depression, anxiety, agitation, and irritability (Aarsland et al., 1999; Weintraub & Stern, 2005). More severe symptoms of suicidal thoughts, visual hallucinations, delusions, delirium, and sleep disturbances may be related to side effects of treatment with dopaminergic drugs, which have been shown to cause psychosis and nightmares (Lieberman, 1998). These side effects may be reversed with changes in drug types or dosages. Furthermore, the presence of depression and other psychiatric disturbances is correlated with more significant deficits in cognition (Weintraub & Stern, 2005). Furthermore, persons with PD have been observed to present with pragmatic deficits earlier than persons with AD (Litvan, Mohr, et al., 1991). The pragmatic deficits are displayed as difficulty with executive functions and with emotional processing. Persons with PD have difficulty both conveying and understanding emotionality through facial expressions. For example, persons with PD may have difficulty understanding others' facial expressions. These deficits cannot be accounted for by cognitive or neuropsychiatric deficits, or drug side effects, as they can be found in persons with early-stage PD prior to initiation of drug treatments and to diagnosis of these symptoms (Dujardin et al., 2004; Sprengelmeyer et al., 2003). Other researchers, however, have found that some persons with PD have intact ability to comprehend facial expression (Pell & Leonard, 2005).

Progressive Supranuclear Palsy (PSP) PSP is a parkinsonian syndrome that is sometimes confused with PD because of the overlap in symptoms of rigidity, dysarthria, and dementia, but PSP is distinguished by the feature of vertical eye gaze paralysis (Litvan, Agid, Calne, et al., 1996). Similar to PD, executive function impairments are the primary cognitive symptom, with evidence of impaired new learning, reduced verbal fluency, and preserved recognition memory (Litvan, Grafman, Gomez, & Chase, 1989). The neuropsychiatric symptoms of PSP have more characteristics of frontal lobe dysfunction, including high degree of apathy and disinhibition; in comparison to persons with PD, persons with PSP are less depressed and have fewer delusions and hallucinations (Aarsland, Litvan, & Larsen, 2001).

Corticobasal Degeneration (CBD) CBD is another syndrome that may resemble PD due to symptoms of rigidity and cognitive impairment. The distinguishing features of CBD are the asymmetric nature of the rigidity and the presence of dystonia, focal reflex myoclonus, and at least one cortical sign (limb apraxia, cortical sensory loss, or alien limb phenomenon; Litvan, Agid, Goetz, et al., 1997). Speech and language disorders are often the first signs of CBD, with dysarthria (mixed with spastic and/or hypokinetic features), apraxia of speech, or progressive aphasia (nonfluent or anomic) present in 30–40% of cases (Blake, Duffy, Boeve, Ahlskog, & Maraganore, 2003). Frattali, Grafman, Patronas, Makhlouf, and Litvan (2000) also noted aphasic language syndromes in persons with CBD, as well as cognitive deficits that include prominent executive function, verbal fluency, and visuospatial deficits. Severe depression and apathy are the two most common neuropsychiatric symptoms in CBD (Litvan, Cummings, & Mega, 1998).

Dementia in Huntington's Disease (HD) HD is a hereditary and progressive neurodegenerative disorder of the basal ganglia, noted for motor, cognitive, and psychiatric impairments (Cummings, 1995; Paulsen, Ready, Hamilton, Mega, & Cummings, 2001). Neuronal loss occurs in the caudate nucleus, putamen, and globus pallidus, with reduction of neurotransmitters, and frontal lobe atrophy (Thieben et al., 2002). There is also frontal lobe atrophy with disease progression. Klasner and Yorkston (2000) reported that HD symptoms tend to arise in persons between 35 and 42 years old, and that the disease duration is approximately 15 to 17 years; however, there may also be an early or a late onset of the disease. The earliest signs of HD include psychiatric symptoms, such as depression and apathy (Chua & Chiu, 2000; Morris, 1995), as well as personality changes such as low frustration tolerance, impulsivity, and inability to concentrate (Folstein, 1990). Neuropsychiatric symptoms were present in 98% of subjects described by Paulsen et al. (2001). Cognitive deficits in early HD include a selective pattern of attention, executive function, and immediate memory deficits, with relative preservation of semantic memory and delayed recall (Ho et al., 2003).

The behavioral symptoms may predate motor symptoms by up to a decade and seem to be unrelated to the cognitive and motor symptoms (Litvan, Paulsen, et al., 1998; Paulsen et al., 2001). The motor symptoms of HD, such as involuntary movement abnormalities, chorea, akinesia, dyskinesia, gait problems, bradykinesia, and saccadic eye movements, appear later in the disease process, and are sometimes inappropriately treated with neuroleptic medications that can cause cognitive problems (Snowden, Craufurd, Griffiths, & Neary, 1998). Beginning with a generalized cognitive slowing, communication is affected by decreased conversational initiation, diminished topic maintenance, and comprehension of abstract concepts. Over time, deficits in problem-solving abilities, memory skills, executive functioning, and the ability to perceive and interpret emotion in facial expressions interfere with communicative interactions (Lawrence et al., 1996). When the motor symptoms surface, speech production is affected with hyperkinetic dysarthria, characterized by dysprosody, harsh vocal quality, and difficulty timing respiratory support with phonation and articulation. Increased evidence of dysarthria leads to severe reductions in speech intelligibility and the need for alternative modes of communication (Klasner & Yorkston, 2000).

Human Immunodeficiency Virus–Associated Dementia (HIV-D) and AIDS Dementia Complex (ADC) HIV-D is the most common cause of dementia in young and middle-aged persons in the United States (Price & Brew, 1988), and occurs in 7–14% of persons with AIDS (Grant & Martin, 1994). There may be cerebral atrophy in frontal, parietal, and temporal regions, with enlarged ventricles, specifically in the frontal and temporal regions, as well as presence of multinucleated giant cells (MNGCs) and small inflammatory nodules in the white matter and subcortical nuclei (Baldeweg & Gruzelier, 1997). HIV-D presents with cognitive, motor, and behavioral deficits, with the cognitive symptoms usually the first to appear. These include impaired attention and concentration, working memory, and mental speed, and loss of initiation (Price, 2003; Sadek et al., 2004). Language and cognition worsen with disease progression (Price). Sadek et al. also found that persons with HIV-D have a mild retrograde amnesia, similar to the level found in HD, and less severe than that found in AD. Additionally, persons with HIV-D and HD demonstrated a similar level of benefit from cueing. This was interpreted as being indicative of a subcortical pathology in HIV-D, which could be corroborated by the fact that many persons with HIV-D have motor symptoms as well, including gait abnormalities, pathological reflexes, and motor slowing (Price). Early effects on speech are extrapyramidal, including slow, labored, and dysarthric speech. Behavioral and psychological functioning also becomes impaired, with apathy and mood changes that range from depression to marked lability, irritability, and violent outbursts; in the late stages, behavior deteriorates to mutism, immobility, and incontinence (Price). Clinicians should note that the pharmacological treatments for HIV/AIDS might also create increased risk of stroke and heart disease, thereby increasing the likelihood of cognitive deficits even in those without HIV-D or ADC.

Creutzfeldt-Jakob Disease (CJD) CJD is a form of spongiform encephalopathy, resulting in either diffuse or focal injury, with progressive dementia. CJD may be inherited (familial CJD), due to mutations in the prion protein gene on chromosome 20; or it may be transmissible (sporadic CJD) by conversion of normal cellular prion proteins to disease-causing forms (Cummings, 2003). The neuropathological features of CJD include spongiform degeneration, fibrous astrocytes, and microvacuolation of the neocortex with some prion protein–positive plaques (Prusiner, 2001). This rare disorder occurs in one case out of 1 million in the population, with an average age at onset of 60 years, and an average duration of 8 months (Brandel, Delasnerie-Lauprêetre, Laplanche, Hauw, & Alpérovitch, 2000). The presenting symptoms include myoclonus, pyramidal, extrapyramidal, and cerebellar signs, and a distinctive pattern of sharp waves is seen on EEG (Brown et al., 1994; DeSanti, 1997). Cognitive and neuropsychiatric symptoms include progressive memory loss, aphasia, depression, anxiety, delusions, and bizarre or uncharacteristic behavior (Cummings, 2003).

A recent variant of CJD related to the bovine spongiform encephalopathy epidemic in the United Kingdom has been documented to have an earlier age of onset (29 years), prominent early psychiatric symptoms, and a median duration of 14 months (Will et al., 2000). Persons first present with psychiatric symptoms (e.g., depression, social withdrawal, delusions, emotional lability, aggression, and agitation), and the neurological signs of ataxia, myoclonus, involuntary movements, and rapidly progressive cognitive decline follow within 6 months (Zeidler et al., 1997). The slow-wave patterns seen on EEG are not typical of the other variants of CJD, nor are the histological features of numerous prion protein–positive amyloid plaques surrounded by intense spongiform degeneration (Will et al., 2000). There are no known effective treatments for prion diseases; antimalarial and antipsychotic medications have been used symptomatically (Korth, May, Cohen, & Prusiner, 2001).

Pseudodementia

When the diagnostician suspects pseudodementia, there are two general categories to differentiate: (a) disorders that simulate dementia either consciously, such as malingering, or unconsciously, such as hysteria or conversion disorders; and (b) disorders that can be classified as primary psychiatric disorders, such as depression, mania, schizophrenia, obsessive-compulsive disorder, or generalized anxiety disorder, that may present as severe cognitive impairments. The latter category is distinguished from genuine dementias in that they are not progressively degenerative and may be reversible (Sachdev & Reutens, 2003).

To determine if the person is attempting to simulate dementia, or is malingering, clinicians need to find out if the person might be motivated by external incentives, such as financial compensation, avoidance of work or criminal prosecution, or ability to obtain medications. Exaggerated or inconsistent responding on assessment or hysterical and emotional reactions to interview questions may signal simulation of dementia. Reports of sudden onset or rapid progression of symptoms are other red flags. In the case of some degree of medical and psychological sophistication on the part of the subject, simulation or malingering may be difficult to judge. In complex cases, psychological testing should be conducted to rule out personality disorders, factitious disorders (e.g., Munchausen syndrome), or dissociative (hysteria) disorders. Psychiatric consultation is necessary to address primary psychiatric disorders, such as depression, schizophrenia, and mania. In many of these cases, pharmacological treatment can reduce or reverse the presenting cognitive symptoms and confirm a nondementia diagnosis. The high incidence of medical litigation and Medicare fraud in recent years has necessitated that SLPs

BOX 2.3 CASE STUDY

Rebecca Smith, a real estate professional from upstate New York, visits her mother in Florida for a long weekend. When she arrives, her mother is happy to see her and spends the next several hours chatting about family members and the recent events in the neighborhood. Rebecca soon notices that her mother has repeated the same stories about the man across the street watching her from his window and the kids who run through her yard, knocking over the garbage cans, and has asked about her grandson's recent recital several times. She notices piles of mail and magazines on the countertops and newspapers stacked up in the corner of the living room. When Rebecca offers to fix a snack before bedtime, she finds expired and rotting food in the refrigerator. In the bathroom, she notices many pill containers on the counter, some empty and others with pills of various sorts mixed together. Rebecca realizes her mother is more impaired than she thought from her daily telephone conversations. In the morning, she checks in with a neighbor, who expresses relief that she is visiting and confirms her worst fears. She schedules an emergency visit with her mother's physician, whose nurse reviews the contents of the brown bag she has brought with them: 14 medications, and a variety of vitamins and nutritional supplements. To her surprise, her mother readily admits to the nurse that she is having trouble sleeping, does not have much of an appetite or much interest in her usual hobbies and activities, and is afraid to drive her car to the store. When the doctor questions her, she comments that her brain is fuzzy now that she is retired and doesn't have to keep track of daily appointments.

This is a common story, and one that will have a relatively positive outcome. The physician will order a variety of diagnostic tests, blood work, and a CT scan, and refer her for neuropsychological testing. Rebecca will take her mother to visit local assisted living residences and help her to choose an acceptable home. She will arrange to have an agency provide daily meals, an occasional companion, and weekly housekeeping services. In the next month, she will visit more frequently to help her pack and move to her new home. When the dementia diagnosis is eventually made, Rebecca's mother will have made a satisfactory transition to a safe environment.

Not all situations turn out this well … much education is still needed.

prepare themselves to testify as expert witnesses or to document assessment results with an expectation of future subpoena by the courts in such cases.

CONCLUSION

The diagnosis of dementia is a complex process requiring the expertise of many professionals and the observations of those close to the person. From the initial questions about everyday memory lapses, to the medical investigation of metabolic

BOX 2.4 DEMENTIA-SPECIFIC RESOURCES AND WEB SITES

Administration on Aging: http://www.aoa.gov
Alzheimer Disease Education and Referral Center (ADEAR): http://www.alzheim-ers .org
Alzheimer's Association: http://www.alz.org
Alzheimer's Foundation of America: http://www.alzfdn.org
American Geriatrics Society: http://www.americangeriatrics.org
Area Agency on Aging: http://www.n4a.org
Mayo Clinic: http://www.Mayoclinic.com/health/alzheimers-caregivers
Medline Plus: http://www.nlm.nih.gov/medlineplus/alzheimerscaregivers.html
Source for eldercare local community services: http://www.n4a.org/locator
Source for long-term care ombudsmen: http://www.aoa.gov/prof/aoaprog/elder_rights/ LTCombudsman/ltc_ombudsman.asp

systems and the radiological assessment of brain functioning, to the neuropsychological evaluations of cognitive processes, the investigation of all symptoms necessitates the cooperation and communication of a diverse group of practitioners. The diagnostic process will be a lengthy and often frustrating experience for clients and caregivers who would prefer quick and definitive answers to their concerns. Unfortunately, the degenerative nature of many of the dementia etiologies will result in changing symptoms and diagnoses over the course of the person's illness. To the extent that professionals work in an interdisciplinary fashion, using information gathered from multiple sources to inform their decisions, improved diagnostic outcomes will result. This will lead to a better selection of treatment choices and improved quality of life for clients and their families. The following chapters will address in more detail the assessment of cognitive, language, and behavioral symptoms of dementia, and the range of pharmacological and nonpharmacological treatments available.

REFERENCES

Aarsland, D., Andersen, K., Larsen, J. P., & Lolk, A. (2003). Prevalence and characteristics of dementia in Parkinson disease: An 8-year prospective study. *Archives of Neurology*, *60*, 387–392.

Aarsland, D., Larsen, J., Lim, N., Janvin, C., Karlsen, K., Tandberg, E., et al. (1999). Range of neuropsychiatric disturbances in patients with Parkinson's disease. *Journal of Neurology, Neurosurgery, and Psychiatry*, *67*, 492–496.

Aarsland, D., Litvan, I., & Larsen, J. (2001). Neuropsychiatric symptoms of patients with progressive supranuclear palsy and Parkinson's disease. *Journal of Neuropsychiatry and Clinical Neurosciences*, *13*, 43–49.

Aharon-Peretz, J., Kliot, D., & Tomer, R. (2000). Behavioral differences between white matter lacunar dementia and Alzheimer's disease: A comparison on the Neuropsychiatric Inventory. *Dementia and Geriatric Cognitive Disorders*, *11*, 294–298.

Albert, M., Feldman, R., & Willis, A. (1974). The "subcortical dementia": Of progressive supranuclear palsy. *Journal of Neurology, Neurosurgery, and Psychiatry, 37,* 121–130.

Almkvist, O., & Winblad, B. (1999). Early diagnosis of Alzheimer dementia based on clinical and biological factors. *European Archives of Psychiatry and Clinical Neuroscience, 249,* S3–S9.

American Psychiatric Association. (1994). *Diagnostic and statistical manual of mental disorders* (4th ed.). Washington, DC: American Psychiatric Association.

Assal, F., & Cummings, J. (2003). Cortical and frontosubcortical dementias: Differential diagnosis. In V. O. Emery & T. E. Oxman (Eds.), *Dementia: Presentations, differential diagnosis, and nosology* (pp. 239–262). Baltimore: Johns Hopkins University Press.

Baldeweg, T., & Gruzelier, J. (1997). Alpha EEG activity and subcortical pathology in HIV infection. *International Journal of Psychophysiology, 26,* 431–442.

Ballard, C. (2000). Criteria for the diagnosis of dementia. In J. O'Brien, D. Ames, & A. Burns (Eds.), *Dementia* (2nd ed., pp. 29–40). London: Arnold.

Ballard, C., Holmes, C., McKeith, I., Neill, D., O'Brien, J., Cairns, N., et al. (1999). Psychiatric morbidity in dementia with Lewy bodies: A prospective clinical and neuropathological comparative study with Alzheimer's disease. *American Journal of Psychiatry, 156,* 1039–1045.

Barber, R., Newby, J., & McKeith, I. (2004). Lewy body disease. In R. Richter & B. Richter (Eds.), *Alzheimer's disease: A physician's guide to practical management* (pp. 127–135). Totowa, NJ: Humana Press.

Barber, R., & O'Brien, J. (2000). Structural and functional magnetic resonance imaging (MRI). In J. O'Brien, D. Ames, & A. Burns (Eds.), *Dementia* (2nd ed., pp. 115–130). London: Arnold.

Barker, W. W., Luis, C. A., Kashuba, A., Luis, M., Harwood, D. G., Loewenstein, D., et al. (2002). Relative frequencies of Alzheimer disease, Lewy body, vascular and frontotemporal dementia, and hippocampal sclerosis in the State of Florida Brain Bank. *Alzheimer Disease and Associated Disorders, 16,* 203–212.

Bayles, K., & Kaszniak, A. (1987). *Communication and cognition in normal aging and dementia.* Boston: Little, Brown.

Bennett, D., Wilson, R., Gilley, D., & Fox, J. (1990). Clinical diagnosis of Binswanger's disease. *Journal of Neurology, Neurosurgery, and Psychiatry, 53,* 961–965.

Binetti, G., Bianchetti, A., Padovani, A., Lenzi, G., De Leo, D., & Trabucchi, M. (1993). Delusions in Alzheimer's disease and multi-infarct dementia. *Acta Neurologica Scandinavica, 88,* 5–9.

Blake, M., Duffy, J., Boeve, B., Ahlskog, J., & Maraganore, D. (2003). Speech and language disorders associated with corticobasal degeneration. *Journal of Medical Speech-Language Pathology, 11,* 131–146.

Brandel, J., Delasnerie-Lauprêetre, N., Laplanche, J., Hauw, J., & Alpérovitch, A. (2000). Diagnosis of Creutzfeldt-Jakob disease: Effect of clinical criteria on incidence estimates. *Neurology, 54,* 1095–1099.

Briley, D., Wasay, M., Sergent, S., & Thomas, S. (1997). Cerebral white matter changes (Leukoaraiosis), stroke, and gait disturbance. *Journal of the American Geriatrics Society, 45,* 1434–1438.

Brown, P., Gibbs, C., Rodgers-Johnson, P., Asher, D., Sulima, M., Bacote, A., et al. (1994). Human spongiform experimentally transmitted disease. *Annals of Neurology, 35,* 513–529.

Brun, A., Englund, B., Gustafson, L., Passant, U., Mann, D., Neary, D., et al. (1994). Consensus statement: Clinical and neuropathological criteria for fronto-temporal dementia. *Journal of Neurology, Neurosurgery and Psychiatry, 4,* 416–418.

Canadian Study of Health and Aging Working Group. (1994). Canadian Study of Health and Aging: Study methods and prevalence of dementia. *Canadian Medical Association Journal, 150*, 899–913.

Christensen, H., & O'Brien, J. (2000). Age-related cognitive decline and its relationship to dementia. In J. O'Brien, D. Ames, & A. Burns (Eds.), *Dementia* (2nd ed., pp. 15–27). London: Arnold.

Chua, P., & Chiu, E. (2000). Huntington's disease. In J. O'Brien, D. Ames, & A. Burns (Eds.), *Dementia* (2nd ed., pp. 827–843). London: Arnold.

Collie, A., Maruff, P., Shafiq-Antonaci, R., Smith, M., Hallup, M., Schofield, P., et al. (2001). Memory decline in healthy older people: Implications for identifying mild cognitive impairment. *Neurology, 56*, 1533–1538.

Crook, T., Bartus, R., Ferris, S., Whitehouse, P., Cohen, G., & Gershon, S. (1986). Age associated memory impairment: Proposed diagnostic criteria and measures of clinical change: Report of a National Institute of Mental Health work group. *Developmental Neuropsychology, 2*, 261–276.

Crum, R. M., Anthony, J., Bassett, S., & Folstein, M. (1993). Population-based norms for the Mini-Mental State Examination by age and educational level. *JAMA, 69*, 2420–2421.

Cummings, J. L. (1995). Behavioral and psychiatric symptoms associated with Huntington's disease. *Advances in Neurology, 65*, 179–186.

Cummings, J. L. (2003). *The neuropsychiatry of Alzheimer's disease and related dementias*. London: Martin Dunitz.

DeSanti, S. (1997). Differentiating the dementias. In C. T. Ferrand & R. L. Bloom (Eds.), *Introduction to organic and neurogenic disorders of communication: Current scope of practice* (pp. 84–109). Boston: Allyn & Bacon.

Diaz-Arrastia, R., & Baskin, F. (2004). Biological markers in Alzheimer's disease. In R. Richter & B. Richter (Eds.), *Alzheimer's disease: A physician's guide to practical management* (pp. 103–108). Totowa, NJ: Humana Press.

Dujardin, K., Blairy, S., Defebvre, L., Duhem, S., Noël, Y., Hess, U., et al. (2004). Deficits in decoding emotional facial expressions in Parkinson's disease. *Neuropsychologia, 42*, 239–250.

Eastley, R., & Wilcock, G. (2000). Assessment and differential diagnosis of dementia. In J. O'Brien, D. Ames, & A. Burns (Eds.), *Dementia* (2nd ed., pp. 41–47). London: Arnold.

Erkinjuntti, T. (2000). Vascular dementia: An overview. In J. O'Brien, D. Ames, & A. Burns (Eds.), *Dementia* (2nd ed., pp. 623–634). London: Arnold.

Folstein, M., Folstein, S., & McHugh, P. (1975). "Mini-mental state": A practical method for grading the cognitive state of patients for the clinician. *Journal of Psychiatric Research, 12*, 189–198.

Folstein, S. E. (1990). *Huntington disease: A disorder of families*. Baltimore: Johns Hopkins University Press.

Foster, N. (2004). Neuroimaging techniques: CT, MRI, SPECT, PET. In R. Richter & B. Richter (Eds.), *Alzheimer's disease: A physician's guide to practical management* (pp. 89–102). Totowa, NJ: Humana Press.

Franczak, M., Kerwin, D., & Antuono, P. (2004). Frontotemporal lobe dementia. In R. Richter & B. Richter (Eds.), *Alzheimer's disease: A physician's guide to practical management* (pp. 137–143). Totowa, NJ: Humana Press.

Frattali, C., Grafman, J., Patronas, N., Makhlouf, F., & Litvan, I. (2000). Language disturbances in corticobasal degeneration. *Neurology, 54*, 990–992.

Frederick, B., Moore, C., & Renshaw, P. (2000). Magnetic resonance spectroscopy in dementia. In J. O'Brien, D. Ames, & A. Burns (Eds.), *Dementia* (2nd ed., pp. 131–139). London: Arnold.

Freedman, M., Leach, L., Kaplan, E., Winocur, G., Shulman, K., & Delis, D. (1994). *Clock drawing: A neuropsychological analysis*. New York: Oxford University Press.

Galasko, D. (2001). Biological markers and the treatment of Alzheimer's disease. *Journal of Molecular Neuroscience*, *17*, 119–125.

Galasko, D., Salmon, D. P., Lineweaver, T., Hansen, L., & Thal, L. J. (1998). Neuropsychological measures distinguish patients with Lewy body variant from those with Alzheimer's disease. *Neurology*, *50*, A181.

Gant, I., & Martin, A. (Eds.). (1994). *Neuropsychology of HIV infection*. New York: Oxford University Press.

Green, R. C. (2005). *Diagnosis and management of Alzheimer's disease and other dementias*. Caddo, OK: Professional Communications.

Greene, J. D. W., Patterson, K., Xuereb, J., & Hodges, J. R. (1996). Alzheimer's disease and nonfluent progressive aphasia. *Archives of Neurology*, *53*, 1072–1078.

Grigoletto, F., Zappala, G., Anderson, D., & Lebowitz, B. (1999). Norms for the Mini-mental State Examination in a healthy population. *Neurology*, *53*, 315–320.

Gustafson, L., Brun, A., & Passant, U. (1992). Frontal lobe degeneration of non-Alzheimer type. In M. Rossor (Ed.), *Unusual dementias* (pp. 559–582). London: Balliere Tindall.

Hardy, J. (2004). Genetics of Alzheimer's disease and related disorders. In R. Richter & B. Richter (Eds.), *Alzheimer's disease: A physician's guide to practical management* (pp. 3–20). Totowa, NJ: Humana Press.

Hebert, L., Scherr, P., Bienias, J., Bennett, D., & Evans, D. (2003). Alzheimer disease in the US population: Prevalence estimates using the 2000 Census. *Archives of Neurology*, *60*, 1119–1122.

Hickman, S., Howieson, D., Dame, A., Sexton, G., & Kaye, J. (2000). Longitudinal analysis of the effects of the aging process on neuropsychological test performance in the healthy young-old and oldest-old. *Developmental Neuropsychology*, *17*, 323–337.

Ho, A. K., Sahakian, B. J., Brown, R. G., Barker, R. A., Hodges, J. R., Ané, M-N., et al., for the NEST-HD Consortium. (2003). Profile of cognitive progression in early Huntington's disease. *Neurology*, *61*, 1702–1706.

Hodges, J. R., & Patterson, K. (1995). Is semantic memory consistently impaired early in the course of Alzheimer's disease: Neuroanatomical and diagnostic implications. *Neuropsychologia*, *33*, 441–459.

Hulstaert, F., Blennow, K., Ivanoiu, A., Schoonderwaldt, H., Riemenschneider, M., DeDeyn, P., et al. (1999). Improved discrimination of AD patients using beta-amyloid (1-42) and tau levels in CSF. *Neurology*, *52*, 1555–1562.

Ince, P., Perry, R., & Perry, E. (2000). Pathology of dementia with Lewy bodies. In J. O'Brien, D. Ames, & A. Burns (Eds.), *Dementia* (2nd ed., pp. 699–717). London: Arnold.

Jack, C., Petersen, R., Xu, Y., O'Brien, P., Smith, G., Ivnik, R., et al. (1999). Prediction of AD with MRI-based hippocampal volume in mild cognitive impairment. *Neurology*, *52*, 1397–1403.

Jorm, A. F. (2000). Risk factors for Alzheimer's disease. In J. O'Brien, D. Ames, & A. Burns (Eds.), *Dementia* (2nd ed., pp. 383–390). London: Arnold.

Karbe, H., Kertesz, A., & Polk, M. (1993). Profiles of language impairment in primary progressive aphasia. *Archives of Neurology*, *50*, 193–201.

Kennedy, A. (2000). Positron emission tomography in dementia. In J. O'Brien, D. Ames, & A. Burns (Eds.), *Dementia* (2nd ed., pp. 163–177). London: Arnold.

Kensinger, E. A., Shearer, D. K., Locascio, J. J., Growdon, J. H., & Corkin, S. (2003). Working memory in mild Alzheimer's disease and early Parkinson's disease. *Neuropsychology*, *17*(2), 230–239.

Kertesz, A., & Clydesdale, S. (1994). Neuropsychological deficits in vascular dementia vs. Alzheimer's disease. *Archives of Neurology*, *51*, 1226–1231.

Kertesz, A., Davidson, W., & McCabe, P. (1998). Primary progressive semantic aphasia: A case study. *Journal of the International Neuropsychological Society*, *4*, 388–398.

Kertesz, A., Kawarai, T., Rogaeva, E., St. George-Hyslop, P., Poorkaj, P., Bird, T. D., et al. (2000). Familial frontotemporal dementia with ubiquitin-positive, tau-negative inclusions. *Neurology, 54*, 818–827.

Killiany, R., Gomez-Isla, T., Moss, M., Kikinis, R., Sandor, T., Jolesz, F., et al. (2000). Use of structural magnetic resonance imaging to predict who will get Alzheimer's disease. *Annals of Neurology, 47*, 430–439.

Klasner, E. R., & Yorkston, K. M. (2000). AAC for Huntington disease and Parkinson's disease: Planning for change. In D. R. Beukelman, K. M. Yorkston, & J. Reichle (Eds.), *Augmentative and alternative communication for adults with acquired neurologic disorders*. Baltimore: Paul H. Brookes.

Knopman, D., Mastri, A., Frey, W., Sung, J., & Rustan, T. (1990). Dementia lacking distinctive histologic features: A common non-Alzheimer degenerative dementia. *Neurology, 40*, 251–256.

Knopman, D. S., DeKosky, S. T., Cummings, J. L., Chui, H., Corey-Bloom, J., Relkin, N., et al. (2001). Practice parameter: diagnosis of dementia (an evidence-based review). *Neurology, 56*, 1143–1153.

Korth, C., May, B., Cohen, F., & Prusiner, S. (2001). Acridine and phenothiazine derivatives as pharmacotherapeutics for prion disease. *Proceedings of the National Academy of Science USA, 989*, 9836–9841.

Kral, V. (1962). Senescent forgetfulness: Benign and malignant. *Canadian Medical Association Journal, 86*, 257–260.

Lantos, P., & Cairns, N. (2000). The neuropathology of Alzheimer's disease. In J. O'Brien, D. Ames, & A. Burns (Eds.), *Dementia* (2nd ed., pp. 443–459). London: Arnold.

Lawrence, A. D., Sahakian, B. J., Hodges, J. R., Rosser, A. E., Lange, K. W., & Robbins, T. W. (1996). Executive and mnemonic functions in early Huntington's disease. *Brain, 119*, 1633–1645.

Levy-Lahad, E., & Bird, T. (1996). Genetic factors in Alzheimer's disease: A review of recent advances. *Annals of Neurology, 40*, 829–840.

Libon, D. J., Bogdanoff, B., Leopold, N., Hurk, R., Bonavita, J., Skalina, S., et al. (2001). Neuropsychological profiles associated with subcortical white matter alterations and Parkinson's disease: Implications for the diagnosis of dementia. *Archives of Clinical Neuropsychology, 16*, 19–32.

Lieberman, A. (1998). Managing the neuropsychiatric symptoms of Parkinson's disease. *Neurology, 50*, S33–S38.

Litvan, I., Agid, Y., Calne, D., Campbell, G., Dubois, B., Duvoisin, R., et al. (1996). Clinical research criteria for the diagnosis of progressive supranuclear palsy (Steele-Richardson-Olszewski syndrome): Report of the NINDS-SPSP International workshop. *Neurology, 47*, 1–9.

Litvan, I, Agid, Y., Goetz, C., Jankovic, J., Wenning, G., Brandel, J., et al. (1997). Accuracy of the clinical diagnosis of corticobasal degeneration: A clinicopathologic study. *Neurology, 48*, 119–125.

Litvan, I., Cummings, J., & Mega, M. (1998). Neuropsychiatric features of corticobasal degeneration. *Journal of Neurology, Neurosurgery, & Psychiatry, 65*, 717–721.

Litvan, I., Grafman, J., Gomez, C., & Chase, T. (1989). Memory impairment inpatients with progressive supranuclear palsy. *Archives of Neurology, 46*, 765–767.

Litvan, I., Mohr, E., Williams, J., Williams, J., Gomez, C., & Chase, T. (1991). Differential memory and executive functions in demented patients with Parkinson's and Alzheimer's disease. *Journal of Neurology, Neurosurgery, & Psychiatry, 54*, 25–29.

Litvan, I., Paulsen, J., Mega, M., & Cummings, J. (1998). Neuropsychiatric assessment of patients with hyperkinetic and hypokinetic movement disorders. *Archives of Neurology, 55*, 1313–1319.

Lubinski, R. (1995). *Dementia and communication*. San Diego, CA: Singular Publishing Group.

Luchsinger, J., Tang, M., Shea, S., & Mayeux, R. (2003). Antioxidant vitamin intake and risk of Alzheimer disease. *Archives of Neurology, 60*, 203–208.

Massey, A. J., & Ghazvini, P. (2005). Involvement of neuropsychiatric pharmacists in a memory disorder clinic. *Consultant Pharmacist, 20*, 514–518.

McKeith, I., Galasko, D., Kosaka, K., Perry, E., Dickson, D., Hansen, L., et al. (1996). Consensus guidelines for the clinical and pathologic diagnosis of dementia with Lewy bodies (DLB): Report of the consortium on DLB international workshop. *Neurology, 47*, 1113–1124.

McKhann, G. M., Albert, M. S., Grossman, M., Miller, B., Dickson, D., & Trojanowski, J. Q. (2001). Clinical and pathological diagnosis of frontotemporal dementia. *Archives of Neurology, 58*, 1803–1809.

McNair, D., & Kahn, R. (1983). Self-assessment of cognitive deficits. In T. Crook, S. Ferris, & R. Barus (Eds.), *Assessment in geriatric psychopharmacology* (pp. 137–143). New Canaan, CT: Mark Powley.

Mesulam, M. (2001). Primary progressive aphasia. *Annals of Neurology, 49*, 425–432.

Mirea, A., & Cummings, J. (2000). Neuropsychiatric aspects of dementia. In J. O'Brien, D. Ames, & A. Burns (Eds.), *Dementia* (2nd ed., pp. 61–79). London: Arnold.

Morgan, C., & Murphy, C. (2002). Olfactory event-related potentials in Alzheimer's disease. *Journal of the International Neuropsychological Society, 8*, 753–763.

Morris, J., Storandt, M., Miller, J., McKeel, D., Price, J., Rubin, E., et al. (2001). Mild cognitive impairment represents early-stage Alzheimer disease. *Archives of Neurology, 58*, 397–405.

Morris, J. C. (2003). Dementia update 2003. *Alzheimer Disease and Associated Disorders, 17*(4), 245–258.

Morris, M. (1995). Dementia and cognitive changes in Huntington's disease. *Advances in Neurology, 65*, 187–200.

Mortimer, J., Ebbit, B., Jun, S., & Finch, M. (1992). Predictors of cognitive and functional progression inpatients with probable Alzheimer's disease. *Neurology, 42*, 1689–1696.

Munoz, D. G., Ganapathy, G. R., Eliasziw, M., & Hachinski, V. (2000). Educational attainment and SES in patients with autopsy-confirmed AD. *Archives of Neurology, 57*, 85–89.

Murphy, C., & Gilbert, P. (2004). Loss of olfactory function in patients with Alzheimer's disease. In R. Richter & B. Richter (Eds.), *Alzheimer's disease: A physician's guide to practical management* (pp. 165–173). Totowa, NJ: Humana Press.

Neary, D. (2000). Frontotemporal dementia. In J. O'Brien, D. Ames, & A. Burns (Eds.), *Dementia* (2nd ed., pp. 737–746). London: Arnold.

Papapetropoulos, S., Gonzalez, J., Lieberman, A., Villar, J. M., & Mash, D. C. (2005). Dementia in Parkinson's disease: A post-mortem study in a population of brain donors. *International Journal of Geriatric Psychiatry, 20*, 418–422.

Patterson, C. J., & Clarfield, A. M. (2003). Diagnostic procedures for dementia. In V. O. Emery & T. Oxman (Eds.), *Dementia: Presentations, differential diagnosis, and nosology* (pp. 61–88). Baltimore: Johns Hopkins University Press.

Paulesu, E., Frith, C. D., & Frackowiak, R. S. J. (1993). The neural correlates of the verbal components of working memory. *Nature, 362*, 342–345.

Paulsen, J. S., Ready, R. E., Hamilton, J. M., Mega, M. S., & Cummings, J. L. (2001). Neuropsychiatric aspects of Huntington's disease. *Journal of Neurology, Neurosurgery, and Psychiatry, 71*, 310–314.

Pearlson, G. D., Rabins, P. V., & Burns, A. (1991). CT changes in centrum semiovale white matter in dementia of depression. *Psychological Medicine, 21*, 321–328.

Pell, M., & Leonard, C. (2005). Facial expression decoding in early Parkinson's disease. *Cognitive Brain Research*, *23*, 327–340.

Petersen, R., Smith, G., Ivnik, R., Kokmen, E., & Tangalos, E. (1994). Memory function in very early Alzheimer's disease. *Neurology*, *44*, 867–872.

Petersen, R., Stevens, J., Ganguli, M., Tangalos, E., Cummings, J., & DeKosky, S. (2001). Practice parameter: Early detection of dementia: Mild cognitive impairment (an evidence-based review). Report of the Quality Standards Subcommittee of the American Academy of Neurology. *Neurology*, *56*, 1133–1142.

Price, R., & Brew, B. (1988). The AIDS dementia complex. *Journal of Infectious Diseases*, *158*, 1079–1083.

Price, R. W. (2003). Acquired immunodeficiency syndrome dementia complex. In V. O. Emery & T. Oxman (Eds.), *Dementia: Presentations, differential diagnosis, and nosology* (pp. 336–360). Baltimore: Johns Hopkins University Press.

Prusiner, S. (2001). Shattuck lecture: Neurodegenerative diseases and prions. *New England Journal of Medicine*, *344*, 1516–1526.

Ratnavalli, E., Brayne, C., Dawson, K., & Hodges, J. R. (2002). The prevalence of frontotemporal dementia. *Neurology*, *58*, 1615–1621.

Reisberg, B., Ferris, S., & Crook, T. (1982). Signs, symptoms, and course of age-associated cognitive decline. In S. Corkin, K. Davis, J. Growdon, E. Usdin, & R. J. Wurtman (Eds.), *Alzheimer's disease: A report of progress in research* (pp. 177–181). New York: Raven Press.

Richter, R. W., & Richter, B. Z. (Eds.). (2004). *Alzheimer's disease: A physician's guide to practical management*. Totowa, NJ: Humana Press.

Rivas-Vazquez, R., Mendez, C., Rey, G., & Carrazana, E. (2002). Mild cognitive impairment: New neuropsychological and pharmacological target. *Archives of Clinical Neuropsychology*, *19*, 11–27.

Roman, G., Tatemichi, T., Erkinjuntti, T., Cummings, J., Masdeu, J., Garcia, J., et al. (1993). Vascular dementia: Diagnostic criteria for research studies. Report of the NINDS-AIREN International Workshop. *Neurology*, *43*, 250–260.

Rosen, H. J., Hartikainen, K. M., Jagust, W., Kramer, J. H., Reed, B. R., Cummings, J. L., et al. (2002). Utility of clinical criteria in differentiating frontotemporal lobar degeneration (FTLD) from AD. *Neurology*, *58*, 1608–1615.

Sachdev, P., & Reutens, S. (2003). The nondepressive pseudodementias. In V. O. Emery & T. Oxman (Eds.), *Dementia: Presentations, differential diagnosis, and nosology* (pp. 417–443). Baltimore: Johns Hopkins University Press.

Sadek, J. R., Johnson, S. A., White, D. A., Salmon, D. P., Taylor, K. I., DeLaPena, J. H., et al. (2004). Retrograde amnesia in dementia: Comparison of HIV-associated dementia, Alzheimer's disease, and Huntington's disease. *Neuropsychology*, *18*(4), 692–699.

Salthouse, T. (1985). Speed of behavior and its implications for cognition. In J. E. Birren & K. W. Schaie (Eds.), *Handbook of psychology of aging* (pp. 400–422). New York: Van Nostrand.

Seltzer, B., & Sherwin, I. (1983). A comparison of clinical features in early- and late-onset primary degenerative dementia: One entity or two? *Archives of Neurology*, *40*, 143–146.

Sevush, S., Leve, N., & Brickman, A. (1993). Age at disease onset and pattern of cognitive impairment in probable Alzheimer's disease. *Journal of Neuropsychiatry and Clinical Neuroscience*, *5*, 66–72.

Sjögren, M., Wallin, A., & Blennow, K. (2003). Clincial subgroups of Alzheimer disease. In O. Emery & T. Oxman (Eds.), *Dementia: Presentations, differential diagnosis, and nosology* (pp. 139–155). Baltimore: Johns Hopkins University Press.

Smith, J. G., & McDowall, J. (2004). Impaired higher order implicit sequence learning on the verbal version of the serial reaction time task in patients with Parkinson's disease. *Neuropsychology, 18*(4), 679–691.

Snowden, J. S., Craufurd, D., Griffiths, H. L., & Neary, D. (1998). Awareness of involuntary movements in Huntington disease. *Archives of Neurology, 55*, 801–805.

Snowden, J., Neary, D., & Mann, D. (1996). *Fronto-temporal lobar degeneration: Fronto-temporal dementia, progressive aphasia, semantic dementia*. London: Churchill Livingstone.

Snowdon, D. (2001). *Aging with grace*. New York: Bantam.

Sprengelmeyer, R., Young, A. W., Mahn, K., Schroeder, U., Woitalla, D., Buttner, T., et al. (2003). Facial expression recognition in people with medicated and unmedicated Parkinson's disease. *Neuropsychologia, 41*(8), 1047–1057.

Taylor, K., & Monsch, A. (2004). The neuropsychology of Alzheimer's disease. In R. Richter & B. Richter (Eds.), *Alzheimer's disease: A physician's guide to practical management* (pp. 109–120). Totowa, NJ: Humana Press.

Teri, L., & Logsdon, R. G. (1994). Assessment of behavioral disturbance in older adults. In M. P. Lawton & J. A. Teresi (Eds.), *Annual review of gerontology and geriatrics: Focus on assessment techniques* (pp. 107–124). New York: Springer.

Thieben, M., Duggins, A., Good, C., Gomes, L., Mahant, N., Richards, F., McCusker, E., & Frackowiak, R. (2002). The distribution of structural neuropathology in pre-clinical Huntington's disease. *Brain*, 125, 1815–1828.

Wegiel, J., Wisniewski, T., Reisberg, B., & Silverman, W. (2003). The neuropathology of Alzheimer disease. In O. Emery & T. Oxman (Eds.), *Dementia: Presentations, differential diagnosis, and nosology* (pp. 89–120). Baltimore: Johns Hopkins University Press.

Weintraub, D., & Stern, M. B. (2005). Psychiatric complications in Parkinson disease. *American Journal of Geriatric Psychiatry, 13*, 844–851.

Will, R., Zeidler, M., Stewart, G., Macleod, M., Ironside, J., Cousens, S., et al. (2000). Diagnosis of new variant Creutzfeldt-Jacob disease. *Annals of Neurology, 47*, 575–582.

Wimo, A., Winblad, B., Aguero-Torres, G., & von Strauss, E. (2003). The magnitude of dementia occurrence in the world. *Alzheimer Disease and Associated Disorders, 17*, 63–67.

Winblad, B., Palmer, K., Kivipelto, M., Jelic, V., Fratiglioni, L., Wahlund, L., et al. (2004). Mild cognitive impairment—beyond controversies, towards a consensus: Report of the International working group on mild cognitive impairment. *Journal of Internal Medicine, 256*, 240–246.

Zeidler, M., Johnstone, E., Bamber, R., Dickens, C., Risher, C., Francis, A., et al. (1997). New variant Creutzfeldt-Jakob disease: Psychiatric features. *Lancet, 350*, 908–910.

3

Cognitive, Language, and Behavioral Characteristics Across the Stages of Dementia

Changes in cognition, language, and behavior over the degenerative trajectory of most dementias lead to limitations in communication and functional behaviors. Cognitive difficulties, such as forgetting where the car is parked, displaying reluctance to socialize, and expressing anxiety about financial matters, can be the first signs of dementia. The different dementia etiologies are characterized by different patterns of breakdown in these domains. Language and its components, phonology, syntax, semantics, and pragmatics usually remain intact longer, particularly in Alzheimer's disease (AD), masking the underlying cognitive deterioration. Language impairments may not be recognized unless the words are obviously mispronounced, the syntax is not grammatical, or the intent of the communication is not interpretable. Specific language impairments are more likely in semantic dementia, progressive nonfluent aphasia, and possibly vascular dementia (VaD). However, there are subtle changes in language behavior associated with some dementia syndromes that may be signs of underlying memory problems. These changes in language behavior are known as cognitive-communication impairments, may affect ability to convey communicative intent or ability to understand other's communicative intent, and often lead to challenging behaviors. Frequent caregiver complaints include disruptive or repetitive vocalizations, such as repeating questions. Repetitive verbalizations may be due to word-finding–language formulation deficits, comprehension deficits, and/or memory deficits. These cognitive-communication impairments respond well to interventions, such as external memory aids. Thus, clinicians need to understand the deficits in order to design effective interventions.

This chapter will describe the strengths and deficits in cognition (i.e., memory, attention, perception, executive function, and visuospatial skills) and communication (i.e., spoken language production, auditory comprehension, reading and writing, and pragmatic skills) across types of dementia, and how these strengths and deficits are expressed behaviorally. The relationship among cognition, language, and behavior is intertwined, and difficult to discuss as separate phenomena. Problem behaviors, many of which are evident in verbalizations, will be explained based on the type of memory and cognitive-communicative deficits that they reflect. The following discussion will focus on the cognitive, language, and behavioral skills and deficits of the most common dementia etiology, AD, followed by the differences typical of other dementia types. Table 3.1 summarizes the cognitive skills and deficits across dementia etiologies. Assessment procedures and choice of assessment tasks and stimuli will be discussed later in chapter 4. Intervention for memory and communication deficits described in this chapter will be discussed in chapter 5, and interdisciplinary interventions will be discussed in chapter 6.

COGNITIVE SKILLS AND DEFICITS

Memory

Memory problems are typically the first signs of cognitive decline across dementia etiologies, and are the defining feature of AD. These memory problems often result in problem behaviors, which can be explained by failure at different points in memory processing. Thus, the theoretical construct of memory will be reviewed first, followed by a description of memory-processing deficits. Baddeley's (1995) conceptualization of memory consists of three main processing components: encoding and registering information, storing information, and accessing and retrieving information (Baddeley, 1995). Information enters the system through the five senses and becomes encoded in sensory memory. Sensory memories are then held temporarily and manipulated in working memory (which was formerly known as *short-term memory*) in either the phonological "loop" for decoding auditory information or the visuospatial "sketch pad" for interpreting visual images (Baddeley, 1992). If the information is important in the moment, then it is used immediately; if the information will be useful at some later time, it is processed into long-term storage for later retrieval. Long-term storage can be divided into declarative memory (e.g., semantic, episodic, and autobiographical) and procedural memory (e.g., motor learning), as well as explicit (controlled) versus implicit (automatic) memory. The central executive system is believed to control the interaction of memory processes and is particularly vulnerable to the encoding and retrieval difficulties of persons with dementia (Baddeley, 1992). Table 3.2 presents the different types of memory.

Sensory Memory Sensory memory includes information from the senses (i.e., hearing, vision, touch, taste, and smell) that is processed and associated with other behaviors and stimuli, and may be moved to long-term storage for later use in functional behaviors. Vestibular sensation (i.e., body in space) and the somatosenses (i.e., pain, temperature, and proprioception) have been recognized as additional components of sensory memory (Gardner, Martin, & Jessell, 2000). Sensory stimuli must first be perceived by the person through modality-specific perceptual processes and then encoded and stored for later retrieval (Emery, 2000). The accumulation

TABLE 3.1 Cognitive Skills and Deficits Across Dementia Etiologies

	Alzheimer's Disease (AD)	Vascular Dementia (VaD)	Frontotemporal Dementia (FTD)	Dementia With Lewy Bodies (DLB)	Parkinson's Disease (PD)	Huntington's Disease (HD)	Progressive Supranuclear Palsy (PSP)	Multiple Sclerosis (MS)
Memory: sensory and recognition	Impaired	Good	Intact	Intact	Intact	Intact	Intact	Intact
Memory: working and recall	Impaired	Impaired	Impaired	Less impaired	Impaired	Impaired	Impaired	Impaired
Memory: long-term procedural	Impaired late intact	Impaired	Impaired	Less impaired	Less impaired	Impaired	Impaired	Less impaired
Speed of cognitive processing	Normal	Slow	Slow	Fluctuating	Fluctuating		Slow	
Executive functions: plan and shifting	Impaired later	Impaired	Impaired	Impaired	Impaired		Impaired	Impaired
Attention: divided or selective	Impaired early	Impaired		Impaired	Good			Impaired
sustained			Impaired	Fluctuating	Good	Impaired	Impaired	Impaired
Visuospatial	Impaired	Impaired	Less impaired	Impaired	Impaired		Impaired	Impaired
				Hallucinations			vertical gaze	

TABLE 3.2 Types of Memory Processes

I. Sensory memory	Involves attention; alertness; arousal processes; visual, auditory, tactile, taste, and olfactory stimuli; and unconscious awareness
II. Working memory	Involves encoding processes, and temporary storage of limited capacity
III. Long-Term memory	Involves retrieval processes, and permanent storage of unlimited capacity
Declarative (explicit)	Person's knowledge base, conscious awareness
Semantic	Knowledge of the world, facts, and ideas
Episodic	Knowledge of personal experiences (autobiographical)
Nondeclarative (implicit)	Person's knowledge of skills and action patterns, and unconscious awareness
Procedural	Sequenced motor tasks and perceptual tasks

Source: Adapted from Baddeley (1995) and Sohlberg and Mateer (2001).

of sensory information and learned associations has occurred over a lifetime and contributes to the automatic nature of many behavioral responses that are taken for granted. For example, the typical experiences of hearing the doorbell ring or seeing a red traffic signal automatically elicit the motor responses of answering the door or depressing the brake pedal. When these expected behaviors do not occur, two explanations are possible. First, the sensory system might be impaired, causing faulty sensory input or perception; age-related changes in vision and hearing can explain the failure of sensory information to be recognized and understood. For example, not answering the doorbell may be the failure to hear the bell or to recognize the sound as the doorbell. When such deficits are consistent and severe in spite of sensory supports (e.g., hearing aids or glasses), they are known as agnosias (e.g., lack of face recognition is prosopagnosia; other perceptually based agnosias are described later). Second, encoding and related retrieval failures may lead to difficulties in associating the current sensory stimuli with related stimuli in long-term storage. Behaviors, such as fondling objects repeatedly, tapping or patting a tabletop, or staring intently at someone or something, may be signs of difficulty with recognition of everyday objects or persons, or understanding simple instructions. This can create confusion or apathy for individuals with dementia, and frustration on the part of caregivers. For example, lack of cooperation may reflect problems with encoding the auditory information in an instruction, such as "It's time to get ready," which in the past triggered an automatic sequence of bathing, dressing, and grooming behaviors.

Many of the functional deficits that result from sensory problems appear in the later stages of dementia, and evidence exists for preserved sensory processing at early stages of AD. However, there are some inconsistencies in the literature that can be attributed to the types of experimental tasks used to measure sensory processing. For example, in the visual domain, age-matched controls and persons with AD performed similarly on perceptual priming tasks (Salmon & Fennema-Notestine, 1996) and on perceptually based repetition priming tasks (Fleischman et al., 1995). In contrast, poorer performance at earlier stages of AD has been documented using a variety of more complex tasks. For example, subjects with early-stage AD recalled fewer letters in an array than normal controls on a backward-masking task (Miller, 1996); subjects with AD performed significantly worse on visual memory tasks (Kertesz, 1994), visual memory of faces (Damasio, 1999), and visual retention tasks (Massman, Butters, & Delis, 1994) than persons with vascular dementia or Huntington's disease. In fact, recent evidence (Kawas et al., 2003) suggests that poor visual memory performance, as measured by the number of errors on the Benton Visual Retention Test (Benton, 1974), is associated with increased risk of AD.

Studies exploring the vestibular senses have found evidence of impaired sensory function in an investigation of vestibular functioning related to falls; subjects with AD had a decreased ability to suppress incongruent visual stimuli during a balance task, as compared to subjects with PD and normal controls (Chong et al., 1999). This may explain increased falls in the AD group, even before obvious motor deficits appear. Early impairments in olfactory memory in AD have been well documented and correlated with disease severity (Devanand et al., 2000; Nordin & Murphy, 1998). Odor identification tasks (e.g., the 3-item Pocket Smell Test) can discriminate AD from VaD and major depression (MD), as persons with AD display the most difficulty with this test (McCaffrey, Duff, & Solomon, 2000). Thus, changes in the ability to process sensory information require clinicians to attend to stimulus characteristics in planning assessment and intervention.

Clinicians must also attend to the type and the familiarity of tasks used to document sensory memory functioning. Many of the experimental tasks described above were complex and unfamiliar to subjects. Persons with compromised cognitive resources may not understand tasks without functional similarity to everyday behaviors, such as backward masking or visual memory for abstract figures (Kaszniak, Poon, & Riege, 1986). Further research is needed using more functionally relevant behaviors, which would capitalize on more automatic processes and potentially decrease confound that is caused by what appear to be bizarre tasks to persons with dementia. However, with complex tasks, whether functionally relevant or not, there may be multiple explanations for performance failures. This makes it difficult to interpret study results in terms of failures of perception, encoding, or retrieval. Recognition memory tasks have been used to attempt to differentiate success or failure in encoding versus retrieval processes by separating recognition and recall functions. If a person is able to recognize information, then it is assumed to have been encoded, and the deficit is not due to failure of sensory memory. In the later stages of dementia, there is little evidence of information encoding for later retrieval without overt training and external cues to trigger recognition processes.

Working Memory Once perceived, information is encoded, that is, processed and manipulated in working memory and either held for immediate responding or sent to long-term storage for later retrieval. Working memory processes are particularly vulnerable to the effects of dementia, which may be due to failure in the executive control system or, as with sensory memory, due to the types of tasks used to document the process (e.g., digit span forward, word list span, paired associates, and story recall). There is evidence of reduced memory span and short-term memory capacity in AD (Morris, 1986), an increased rate of forgetting (Au, Chan,

& Chiu, 2003) and encoding deficits (Kesner, 1998), and performance deficits on short-term memory tasks with divided attention conditions (Morris, 1996). In addition, speed of information processing decreases over the course of degenerative illnesses, thereby causing decreases in working memory capacity. Thus, lengthy and/or complex auditory or written information may require more time to process and comprehend. Although performance deficits may not be surprising on nonfunctional tasks (e.g., repeating unrelated digits or remembering lists of random words), caregivers report frequent working memory deficits in the everyday lives of persons with dementia (e.g., forgetting what to retrieve from another room or the answer to a question asked repeatedly).

Persons with PD, HD, PSP, and VaD have also demonstrated impairments in the ability to learn and remember new information in immediate and working memory tasks, but with relatively preserved recognition, few intrusions, and improved performance with cueing (Hoppe, Muller, Werheid, Thöne, & von Cramon, 2000; Pillon et al., 1994; Reed et al., 2000). Access to semantic memory has been identified as the cause of working memory deficits in persons with AD, whereas disrupted inhibitory processes are thought to explain working memory deficits in persons with PD (Kensinger, Shearer, Locasio, Growdon, & Corkin, 2003). Gilbert, Belleville, Bherer, and Chouinard (2005) ruled out the limited storage capacity and reduced psychomotor speed theories of working memory deficits in persons with PD; rather, they attributed their deficits to an impaired executive component—that of updating and manipulating information during the task.

In summary, the automatic, unconscious nature of storing relevant information for later retrieval has become disrupted in dementia, and this failure has often been described as an inability to learn new information. However, this myth has been dispelled by Camp and others, who showed that with appropriate training strategies and the use of external cues, persons with dementia can learn new information and retain it for a long time (Camp, 2001; see also Bourgeois et al., 2003). (These training approaches will be discussed in more detail in chapter 5.)

For example, Camp and colleagues have used spaced retrieval, a method of learning and retaining information by successfully recalling that information over increasingly longer periods of time, to attain a variety of functional goals (e.g., remembering their room number, and remembering to use an external memory aid). Similarly, Herlitz, Adolfsson, Bäckman, and Nilsson (1991) documented the ability of subjects with mild dementia to use five types of encoding conditions (verbal + written nouns, verbal + object, object + semantic orienting question, object + self-generated motor cue, and object + experimenter-instructed motor cue) to improve performance on a cued recall test. Persons with moderate dementia utilized all cue types except the verbal + written noun cue, and persons with severe dementia utilized only cues with motor components. These findings suggest, however, that persons with the most severe forms of dementia may still benefit from cues of a motoric nature. Others have confirmed the relative preservation of motoric encoding in dementia (Eslinger & Damasio, 1986; Heindel, Butters, & Salmon, 1988; Rusted & Sheppard, 2002).

Declarative and Explicit Memory: Semantic, Episodic, and Autobiographical Declarative memory, and semantic memory in particular (i.e., the memory for specific words, facts, and ideas), may be somewhat resistant to disease progression because this type of memory may be overlearned or stored for many years. However, access to this store declines noticeably over time. The failure to retrieve words from long-term storage (i.e., word finding or anomia) is the earliest language difficulty across dementia etiologies. Semantic memory impairments have been documented in AD, FTD, DLB (Perry & Hodges, 2000; Lambon Ralph et al., 2001), and HD (van der Hurk & Hodges, 1995). Word-finding difficulty is also common in the conversations of normally aging adults, who occasionally experience the loss of a word or a familiar person's name (Barresi, Nicholas, Connor, Obler, & Albert, 2000; Connor, Spiro, Obler, & Albert, 2004; Craik, Anderson, Kerr, & Li, 1995). The typical response to such a memory lapse is to substitute another word, to describe the word, or to talk around it until the intended meaning is conveyed. The difference between the experience of normal forgetting and memory loss associated with dementia is that individuals with memory impairment do not typically remember the words after a short delay. Consequently, once the word-finding problem interrupts the train of thought, they often digress to another topic, and forget the earlier topic. Over the degenerative course of the disease, word-finding problems become more obvious. The conversations of persons with mid- to late-stage dementia are often described as "content free" or "empty," due to lack of information (Nicholas, Obler, Albert, & Helms-Estabrooks, 1985). When asked a specific question, the answer frequently includes words from the question, indefinite terms, and repetitions.

In contrast, episodic memory is thought to be particularly vulnerable to disease progression because of the need to encode new information frequently when experiencing some event (Caselli & Yanagihara, 1991). Persons with AD have significant difficulty recalling recent and current events, but demonstrate good retrieval of childhood memories. Sartori, Snitz, Sorcinelli, and Daum (2004) found that persons with advanced AD performed in the impaired range on a variety of remote memory measures (i.e., Autobiographical Memory Enquiry, autobiographical fluency, and recognition of remote public events and famous faces) compared to normal controls. Autobiographical fluency for names and remote memory for early public events were better preserved than more recent public events. Remote memory performance was correlated with a measure of semantic fluency (Sartori et al., 2004).

Differences in the type and amount of information retrieved from autobiographical memory have been reported as a function of dementia etiology. Evidence for episodic memory impairments in PD, HD, and PSP have been reported on tasks requiring the learning of new information (Knoke, Taylor, & Saint-Cyr, 1998; Pillon et al., 1994). Persons with subcortical degeneration may have deficits in remote memory, but they are likely to have less difficulty than those with AD, such as in PD (Huber, Shuttleworth, & Paulsen, 1986; Sagar, Cohen, Sullivan, Corkin, & Growdon, 1988), HD, or HIV-D (Sadek et al., 2004). Conversely, persons with semantic dementia are reported to have a loss of early autobiographical memories and a relative sparing of recent memories (Graham & Hodges, 1997). In fact, it has been reported that a striking characteristic of semantic dementia is the ability to remember day-to-day events (e.g., keeping appointments, independent travel, and shopping) concomitant with severe word retrieval deficits (Moss, Kopelman, Cappelletti, Davies, & Jaldow, 2003). There has been some discussion in the literature concerning the nature of the remote memory deficits observed in semantic dementia. Recent studies have documented that when persons with dementia were provided a hierarchy of increasingly specific cues, access to remote memories was comparable to that of healthy controls (Moss et al., 2003). The authors suggest that the word retrieval, or lexical, deficits that characterize semantic dementia can explain the memory retrieval differences found in this population.

There are also differences across dementia etiologies in recognition versus recall tasks. There are reports of intact recognition memory in PD; however, a meta-analysis of recognition memory studies in PD revealed that recognition memory deficits do occur with PD (Whittington, Podd, & Kan, 2000). This was found most often in persons with a dementia diagnosis, as well as those without a dementia diagnosis who were taking PD medications. Recall memory is relatively more impaired than recognition memory across dementias. Prominent retrieval deficits are seen in PD, HD, MS, and PSP (Caine et al., 1986; Knoke et al., 1998; Pillon et al., 1994). However, retrieval from remote memory is more impaired in AD than in PD (Huber et al., 1986), HD, or HIV, despite the relative preservation of older information in AD (Sadek et al., 2004). In addition, cued retrieval was documented to benefit the HIV and HD groups, but not the AD group. In contrast, persons with FTD have demonstrated a retained capacity for storing new information in long-term memory in comparison to persons with AD; their higher free recall, cued recall, and recognition scores are likely due to lack of medial temporal lobe involvement in FTD (Glosser, Gallo, Clark, & Grossman, 2002).

Nondeclarative and Implicit Memory: Procedural Implicit memory is thought to involve the unconscious encoding and recall of information (Schacter, 1987). The evidence for relatively preserved implicit memory functioning in the early stages of dementia comes from priming studies. Morris and Kopelman (1986) documented normal priming effects when persons with AD were asked to name pictures and showed increased naming speed with repeated exposure. Similar preservation of implicit memory functioning for nonverbal tasks was demonstrated when persons with AD became quicker and more accurate with repeated practice in a pursuit rotor task (Heindel, Salmon, Shults, Walicke, & Butters, 1989). In this same study, however, persons with HD did not demonstrate similarly preserved implicit memory skills.

Camp and his colleagues have investigated the potential utility of designing interventions that take advantage of preserved implicit memory functioning to compensate for explicit memory deficits in everyday life (Camp & McKitrick, 1992). They are quick to point out, however, that the effects of repeated exposure alone (i.e., priming), or simply practicing by repeating information, are not sufficient to increase general memory ability in persons with AD. There is some evidence that the act of attempting to retrieve information from memory is what facilitates subsequent retrieval attempts (Bjork, 1988). The spaced retrieval memory-training technique was developed to evaluate the effects of repeatedly retrieving information at increasingly longer intervals, thereby capitalizing on relatively preserved implicit memory skills to teach new information (Camp, 1989; Camp & McKitrick, 1992). This will be described in detail in chapter 5.

Another type of implicit memory, procedural memory, has been described as the best preserved type of memory in AD because the procedures, or skills, involved have been repeated countless times in the person's life, and are thought to be overlearned and not dependent on conscious recall. Procedural memory has been referred to as the "how to" rather than the "what" of information (Schacter & Tulving, 1994). Examples of procedural memory are piano playing and other musical skills, riding a bicycle, cooking, driving, using the telephone, activities of daily living (ADLs; e.g., bathing, eating, and grooming), and ambulation. Procedural memory is relatively preserved in AD, but impaired in PD (Koenig, Thomas-Anterion, & Laurent, 1999; Saint-Cyr, Taylor, & Lang, 1988; Zgaljardic, Borod, Foldi, & Mattis, 2003) and VaD (Libon et al., 1998).

Executive Function

Executive functions include a wide variety of abilities, such as planning, shifting mental sets, inhibiting incorrect responses, and using and manipulating new information (Assal & Cummings, 2003), as well as volition, purposive action, and self-monitoring of effective performance (Lezak, 1995; Ylvisaker & Feeney, 1998). Intact executive functioning allows for successful engagement in social relationships and in independent, purposive, and self-serving behaviors (Lezak; Ylvisaker & Feeney). These include many of the more complex tasks of daily living, such as managing finances, taking medications, shopping, doing housework, using the telephone, preparing meals, and using transportation. Executive dysfunction is observed to some extent in all dementias, and accounts, to some extent, for the difficulty in performing instrumental activities of daily living (IADLs).

Across dementia types, executive functioning for complex tasks and problem solving declines with increasing dementia severity. For example, a significant relationship between performance on the Everyday Problems Test for Cognitively Challenged Elderly (EPCCE; Willis, 1993) and level of severity of cognitive deficits (MMSE score) was documented in a sample of normally aging persons over time (Willis et al., 1998). Furthermore, specific executive function impairments may be revealed by a variety of traditional tests or functional assessments. In many dementias, these deficits may surface early in the course of the disease, although occasionally this may not occur until the middle stages. For example, performance on traditional measures, such as Trailmaking Part B (Reitan & Wolfson, 1985), has revealed executive dysfunction early in AD (Perry & Hodges, 1999) and FTD (Johnson, Head, Kim, Starr, & Cotman, 1999). Results of other tests have differed across types of dementias. For example, on tests of planning (Tower of London; Shallice, 1982) and set shifting (Wisconsin Card Sorting Tests; Heaton, Chelune, Talley, Kay, & Curtiss, 1993), performance is worse in PSP (Grafman, Litvan, Gomez, & Chase, 1990) and MS (Rao, Leo, Bernardin, & Unverzagt, 1991) than in AD. By the middle stages of AD, however, planning deficits are revealed in the Tower of London, and are exhibited as rule-breaking behaviors (Rainville et al., 2002). Furthermore, other studies have found more significant executive function deficits in dementias other than AD. For example, initiation and planning problems are the earliest signs of executive dysfunction in PD (Zagaljardic et al., 2003). The executive function deficits seen early in FTD are also more severe than those in AD (Rosen et al., 2002). Set shifting and response inhibition is more impaired in DLB than AD, which may reflect the observation that executive dyscontrol is associated with frontal lobe damage in DLB (Downes et al., 1998–1999). Persons with DLB show early symptoms of frontal lobe abnormalities such as disinhibition, perseveration, and cognitive inflexibility in decision making (Slachevsky et al., 2004). These behaviors, however, have also been documented in persons with AD (Van Hoesen & Damasio, 1987).

Theory of mind (TOM), or the ability to infer what another person knows by taking his or her perspective, has also been proposed as a component of executive function (Cuerva et al. 2001). Research on TOM in persons with dementia is limited, and findings related to the impact of AD on TOM are inconsistent. Evidence to suggest that TOM knowledge might be present in persons with AD comes from an observational study of nonverbal communicative behaviors between persons with dementia in a day care center (Hubbard, Cook, Tester, & Downs, 2002). Researchers found that these clients actively interpreted others' nonverbal behaviors by taking on the "role" of others and that they acted in the context of shared meanings. However, Cuerva et al. (2001) found TOM deficits concomitant with cognitive impairment in persons with probable mild AD. These discrepant findings may stem from the influence of impairments in general inferencing, executive functions, and working memory on TOM performance. Thus, Youmans (2004) provided visual supports to control for memory deficits in persons with AD; results revealed TOM impairments that were not associated with comprehension, memory, or general inferencing difficulties. Similarly, Gregory et al. (2002) documented TOM deficits in persons with FTD.

Attention and Concentration

Attention is the process of focusing on a specific stimulus (selective attention) for a particular length of time (sustained attention), attending to multiple stimuli at the same time (divided attention), or shifting focus from one stimulus to another (shifting sets) (Norman & Shallice, 1986). Attention and concentration difficulties for simple tasks that require only selective and sustained attention are not typically found in early stages of dementias (Assal & Cummings, 2003). In fact, persons with mild dementia have shown preserved performance on sustained attention tasks, such as digit span tasks or listening for a pattern change in a series of tones (Lines et al., 1991; Perry, Watson, & Hodges, 2000). Certain components of selective attention are relatively intact in the early stages (simple selection processes), but when the physical characteristics of the target and environmental stimuli are similar, discrimination skills become challenged with more errors, increased confusion, and longer response times (Baddeley et al., 2001; Foldi, Jutagir, Davidoff, & Gould, 1992;

Foldi et al., 2005). Similarly, there are early signs of difficulty with more complex tasks that require divided or alternating attention, such as listening for a target word in a list of words while entering digits on a keyboard, or set-shifting tasks requiring persons to perform a task one way and then change when signaled to a different way (e.g., naming fruits and then naming vegetables, or sorting by color and then by shape; Perry & Hodges, 1999). Other complex and functional tasks of divided attention, such as driving and computerized spatial exploration, have also revealed compromised performance early in dementias (Whelihan, DiCarlo, & Paul, 2005).

Clinicians should be aware, however, that performance of complex tasks requires multiple cognitive processes. Thus, differentiating between attention and executive function deficits may be difficult with complex and/or unfamiliar tasks. For example, when multiple and competing demands for attention exceed attentional capacity, reaction time suffers because of the difficulty in deciding which task to attend to; this reflects problems with executive functions, such as inhibitory skills (Baddeley et al., 2001; Foldi, Lobosco, & Schaefer, 2002). Generally, if the task is familiar or practiced, less cognitive effort will be required than for an unfamiliar task, and performance will be better.

Different deficit patterns are observed across dementia types. Greater attention impairments are reported in AD than VaD (Fitten et al 1995). Sustained attention (Huber et al., 1986; Pillon, Dubois, Lhermitte, & Agid, 1986) and selective attention (e.g., finding a symbol in an array; Lee et al., 1999) appear to be intact in PD. However, sustained attention is impaired in PSP (Pillon et al., 1986), in HD (Salmon et al., 1989; Pillon, Dubois, Ploska, & Agid, 1991), and in MS (Rao et al., 1991). There are pronounced attention fluctuations in DLB, with spontaneous periods of impaired alertness and concentration where persons are awake but drowsy and not aware of their environment (Walker et al., 2000). Furthermore, measures of vigilance and complex reaction time corroborate these attention problems in DLB (Ballard et al., 2001).

Foldi and colleagues (2002) suggested that clinicians can facilitate and enhance performance of their clients by attending to how information is presented. Reducing the number of response choices and increasing the differences in physical features of the stimuli can help to alleviate problems with impaired selective attention (decreased inhibition and inefficient search strategies). Presenting materials in a sequential fashion, rather than simultaneously, can help to minimize the problem of resolving competing demands in divided attention tasks. To take advantage of directed and sustained attention skills, clinicians can use familiar cues in routine and expected locations, or novel and emotionally charged cues to enhance attention and everyday functioning. These ideas will be expanded upon later in the intervention chapters.

Perception and Visuospatial Functions

The observation of object and picture recognition and reading difficulties in persons with dementia has led clinicians to suspect changes in perceptual and visuospatial functioning. Likewise, families often ask if visual acuity and eyeglasses need to be evaluated when a family member loses interest in reading. Perceptual problems documented in dementia include auditory agnosias (Hodges, 2001), visual perception deficits (Caselli, 2000), and visuospatial problems, including prosopagnosia (facial recognition), achromatopsia (color perception), and propopagnosia (self-recognition) (Simard, van Reekum, & Myran, 2003). Because perceptual deficits may result in behaviors that compromise activities of daily living, such as misperceiving a trash container for the toilet or mistaking a spouse for a stranger, the identification of perceptual deficits is an important assessment component.

Clinicians must differentiate between acuity deficits and cognitive deficits. Rizzo, Anderson, Dawson, and Nawrot (2000) demonstrated that there was no difference in terms of acuity between the performance of individuals with mild dementia and those without dementia on a battery of vision and cognitive assessments. Significant differences between groups, however, were seen with respect to a variety of cognitive deficits, including visual attention, visuospatial construction, and visual memory tasks. Thus, vision-related cognitive dysfunction should be investigated early in dementias. Many assessment batteries include measures of object size discrimination, form discrimination, overlapping figure identification, visual counting tasks, copying or drawing shapes (e.g., circle, square, or clock), picture arrangement, block design, or object assembly; others include functional visual tasks, such as word and sign reading (Bayles & Tomoeda, 1994). Visual perceptual deficits should also be considered in interpretation of observed reading comprehension deficits. For example, Silveri and Leggio (1996) found that visual perception deficits explained the observed lexical comprehension deficits in participants with AD, which was investigated using word-to-picture matching tasks with foils that shared lexical-semantic, phonological, or visual-perceptual features. Similarly, Glosser, Baker and colleagues (2002) documented reading problems associated with visual-processing deficits.

The impact of perceptual difficulties on other functional behaviors, such as driving, is particularly important for clinicians designing interventions. For example, Uc and colleagues (Uc, Rizzo, Anderson, Shi, & Dawson, 2005) investigated the ability of drivers with mild dementia and normal older adults to detect landmarks and identify traffic signs in an experimental driving task. They found the poor performance of drivers with dementia to be predicted by their performance on measures of visual perception, attention, executive function, and memory. Results revealed that as the cognitive load of the task increased, driving safety worsened.

Different patterns of perceptual problems have been documented by dementia etiology. For example, greater visual perception impairments have been reported in AD than VaD (Fitten et al., 1995). Visuospatial impairments are commonly reported in AD (Assal & Cummings, 2003), in MS (Rao et al., 1991), and in PD with dementia (Assal & Cummings; Stern, Richards, Sano, & Mayeux, 1993). Persons with DLB are reported to have prominent visuospatial deficits, as measured by tests of object size discrimination, form discrimination, overlapping figure identification, and visual counting tasks (Mori et al., 2000; Shimomura et al., 1998). Additionally, Mori et al. and Shimomura et al. found that persons with DLB perform worse than persons with AD on tests of picture arrangement, block design, and object assembly. In comparing persons with AD and PD, persons with

AD perform better on Raven's matrices than those with PD, but persons with PD perform better on tests of block design than those with AD (Huber, Shuttleworth, & Freidenberg, 1989). Similarly, Noe and colleagues (2004) found that persons with DLB performed worse on visual memory tests than subjects with AD and no different than persons with PD. Deficits in visual memory are revealed in persons with AD, VaD, and PD on the Rey-Osterrieth complex figure task, which requires clients to study the figure, and then to draw the figure from memory after it is removed (Freeman et al., 2000); thus, clinicians should ensure that errors are not related to visual perceptual deficits.

Conversely, interpretation of the tasks used to assess perception and visuospatial function may be complicated by memory constraints inherent in visual perceptual tasks. Clinicians must be mindful that poor performance may be related to forgetting the task instructions or not understanding the abstract nature of the task. Some visuospatial tasks require multiple cognitive processes, and it may be difficult to attribute poor performance to one process alone. For example, the clock-drawing task requires attention, memory, executive functions, and visuospatial skills. Similarly, clinicians need to be cautious in predicting poor performance on more functional tasks, such as reading, from poor performance on abstract tasks, such as the Rey-Osterrieth task. In fact, there is evidence of perceptual and visuospatial functioning adequate for reading and responding to familiar written materials and picture stimuli by persons in the later stages of dementia (Bayles et al., 2000; Bourgeois & Mason, 1996; Hoerster, Hickey, & Bourgeois, 2001).

LANGUAGE SKILLS AND DEFICITS

The production of spoken language is a complex process involving the intent to convey information in a form that requires generating multiple phoneme patterns that are recognized as words and are sequenced in a known grammatical order. These phonemes, words, and grammatical forms are learned, stored in memory, and retrieved when the speaker desires to convey a message to another person. These long-term stores are also used in the comprehension of spoken language. Similar processes exist for written language production and comprehension, with the substitution of graphemes for phonemes. The presence of memory impairment, in any form (i.e., recognition, encoding, or retrieval deficit), will interfere with language production and comprehension to some extent, and will vary over the course of the illness. Working memory deficits may explain the diminished performance on language comprehension and production tests by persons with AD. Bayles (2003) argued that the attenuated span capacity, and difficulties with focusing attention, encoding, and activation from long-term storage, did not reflect a loss of linguistic knowledge, particularly when the tasks involved shorter and repeated commands, slower speech rate, and contextual and written supports. Waters and Caplan (2002) have argued that although participants with AD demonstrated lower working memory scores than normal controls on an auditory comprehension task composed of sentences of differing syntactic complexity, they were not impaired in their ability to identify and use syntactic structure to understand sentence meaning.

Although communication is impaired to some degree in all forms of dementia, and by the end stages is virtually nonexistent, there are different patterns of impairment and preserved abilities across the degenerative illness trajectories. Table 3.3 outlines communication and cognitive deficits and strengths across the stages of AD; also, language skills and deficits for other etiologies of dementia are described in more detail below.

TABLE 3.3 Communication and Cognitive Deficits and Strengths of Persons With AD

Communication and Cognitive *Deficits*	Communication and Cognitive *Strengths*
Early Stage	
Mild expressive language deficits related to word-finding problems for names and places	Phonology, syntax, and pragmatics intact Oral reading and writing intact
Receptive language: difficulty comprehending abstract language and complex conversation	Intact comprehension of concrete language Good reading comprehension
Memory: Mild declarative and explicit memory retrieval deficits	Intact nondeclarative, implicit, and sensory memory Aware of language and memory lapses
Executive function: inconsistent problems with IADLs (finances, shopping)	Good sustained attention and concentration
Divided and selective attention lapses	
Mild visuospatial deficits	
Middle Stage	
Increasing expressive language deficits; word-finding problems, lack of content in conversation, and pragmatic difficulties with topic maintenance	Phonology and syntax intact Oral reading for familiar text preserved
Receptive language: difficulty comprehending complex instructions and tasks	Reading comprehension good for familiar words and phrases
Reading comprehension difficulties	Adequate nondeclarative, implicit, and sensory memory
Memory: increasing declarative memory retrieval deficits	
Executive function: lack of inhibition, and planning and set-shifting problems	
Attention: impaired in all domains	
Visuospatial: increasing problems	
Late Stage	
Expression of needs and wants: may be inappropriate verbal or vocal productions; mutism at end stage	Appropriate affective responses to sensory stimuli and music (smiles and pleasant vocalization)
Repetitive vocal and physical behavior	Cooperates with appropriate cues (tactile, visual, and affective)
Severely limited auditory comprehension	Basic needs for attention, communication, and touch present
Severe memory deficits across domains	
Impaired attention, and fluctuating alertness	

Spoken Language Production

Phonology and Neuromotor Speech Production The selection and sequencing of individual phonemes for speech production remain intact throughout most of the duration of AD. Violations of phonotactic constraints of native language and errors in prosody rarely occur (Appell, Kertesz, & Fisman, 1982). Some diseases are associated with neuromotor speech disorders, which occur at a different level of processing than phonological disorders, and are known as apraxia or dysarthria. If changes in motor speech processes are observed in the early stages of the illness, a diagnosis other than AD is indicated. Apraxia of speech is a deficit in motor planning and programming and may occur in degenerative disease, such as in corticobasal degeneration (Blake, Duffy, Boeve, Ahlskog, & Maraganore, 2003; Duffy, 2005). Dysarthrias are a group of motor speech disorders due to deficits in strength, coordination, tone, and/or range of motion of the speech musculature (Duffy). Dysarthrias are common in several degenerative diseases that also may cause dementias, such as PD, HD, PSP, CJD, and ALS, and may be an early sign of a disease (Assal & Cummings, 2003; Campbell-Taylor, 1995; Duffy). For example, in PD, motor speech changes, such as abnormal phonation and respiration with impaired pitch and loudness control, are often early signs of the disease (Campbell-Taylor; Duffy). Estimates suggest that up to 89% of persons with PD will exhibit hypokinetic dysarthria (Liotti et al., 2003), characterized by impaired articulation, rate, and intelligibility, due to paralysis, rigidity, and tremors of the vocal mechanisms (Duffy; Pinto, Thobois, & Costes et al., 2004).

Semantics The most common early symptoms of dementia are word-finding, naming, and verbal description difficulties, due to semantic memory impairment. Initially, individuals experience inconsistent forgetfulness for names, objects, and locations, and mild word-finding difficulties during conversation (Williams, Mack, & Henderson, 1989); there is reduced content, especially abstract content, in discourse (Snowdon, 2001). As the disease progresses, word-finding problems become more frequent, and the flow of conversation is disrupted. Circumlocutions, abandoned phrases, confabulations, word repetitions, paraphasias, and nonspecific words such as *thing* contribute to the perception of "empty" speech (Bayles, 1982; Bayles & Kazniak, 1987; Emery, 2000; Nicholas, Obler, Albert, Helms-Estabrooks, 1985). Echolalia occurs in some cases.

In structured expressive language tasks, such as confrontation naming, anomia is prevalent (Bayles & Kaszniak, 1987; Obler, Dronkers, Koss, Delis, & Friedland, 1986), with naming of nouns more accurate than that of verbs, and naming of natural objects more accurate than that of artifacts (Garrard et al., 1998). As the disease progresses, misperception of items to be named is thought by some to contribute to naming difficulties (Huber et al., 1989; Shuttleworth & Huber, 1988). Other researchers attribute confrontation-naming difficulties experienced by persons with AD, HD, and PD to a semantic features deficit theory (Frank, McDade, & Scott, 1996). On generative naming, or verbal fluency tasks, letter fluency (F, A, S) is better than category fluency (animals, foods) in the earlier stages, but gradually deteriorates equally (Butters, Granholm, Salmon, Grant, & Wolfe, 1987). Sailor and colleagues (Sailor, Antoine, Diaz, Kuslansky, & Kluger, 2004) documented decreased probability of producing atypical exemplars of a common category and the slowed rate at which memory was searched in persons with AD compared with elderly controls.

Several explanatory theories have arisen to help understand the nature of naming difficulties in AD. Kempler (1995) believed that a lexical access impairment explains the semantic retrieval difficulties instead of a deterioration of underlying lexical representations for several reasons. First, persons with AD use circumlocution in confrontation-naming tasks and often produce the intended word after saying something similar or describing it (Bayles & Tomoeda, 1983). Second, comprehension is better than production of the same words, and persons with AD often use gestures to indicate the function of an unnamed object (Kempler, 1988). Finally, phonemic cues can help in word retrieval (Neils, Brennan, Cole, Boller, & Gerdeman, 1988). Semantic priming evidence also supports the lexical access hypothesis (Nebes, 1989), but there is conflicting evidence of lack of priming, subgroup differences, and hyperpriming that would suggest disrupted semantic representations (Chertkow, Bub, & Seidenberg, 1989). Others have suggested that naming deficits are related to attention and concentration problems (Cannatà, Alberoni, Franceschi, & Mariani, 2002; Selnes, Carson, Rovner, & Gordon, 1988).

Chenery, Murdoch, and Ingram (1996) provided some evidence that the nature of the naming deficit seen in AD may change over the course of the disease progression. They suggested that, in the early stages, persons with AD have difficulty with procedural routines for obtaining semantic details from memory; in the middle stages, the semantic store is reduced; and eventually naming ability is eroded because of semantic structure degradation. Snowden and colleagues, in their study of the deterioration of semantic memory in dementia, found consistently better name recall for personally relevant people, places, and objects than nonpersonal names and places (Snowden, Griffiths, & Neary, 1994).

Some subtle differences on naming and verbal fluency tasks have been reported as a function of etiology. For example, Bayles and Tomoeda (1983) reported that persons with HD do not exhibit difficulty on the Boston Naming Test until later in the disease. Similarly, persons with PD have milder naming deficits and lack paraphasic errors throughout their disease course (Huber et al., 1989). Verbal fluency is worse overall in PSP, PD, HD, and VaD than in AD (Huber et al.; Lafosse et al., 1997; Pillon et al., 1986); however, category fluency is worse in AD, whereas letter fluency is better in PSP and HD than AD (Rosser & Hodges, 1994) and better in AD than VaD (Duff Canning, Leach, Stuss, Ngo, & Black, 2004).

Syntax Grammatical knowledge appears to be resilient in the face of semantic declines in AD. In later stages of the disease, when semantic deficits interfere to such an extent that only single words or short phrases are uttered, syntactic forms appear to deteriorate. Jorm (1986) suggested that grammatical ability may be an example of an automatic function that may be preserved in dementia. In fact, persons with mild to moderate dementia produce language similar in grammatical complexity to persons with normal cognition (Heir, Hagenlocker, & Shindler,

1985; Kempler, Curtiss, & Jackson, 1987). Syntactic ability appears intact in a range of tasks, including spontaneous utterance production (Kempler et al., 1987), sentence comprehension (Schwartz, Marin & Saffran, 1979), and writing to dictation (Kempler et al.). There have not been any reports of agrammatism in the AD literature (Kempler, 1995). There are, however, some subtle reductions in grammatical complexity associated with the general cognitive decline in AD; declines in sentence length, grammatical complexity, verbal fluency, and propositional content were seen in the interview transcripts of persons with mild dementia compared to persons without dementia (Lyons, Kemper, LaBarge, & Ferraro, 1994).

Pragmatics Pragmatics is assessed through discourse production, by eliciting a language sample using one or more genres of discourse. Discourse is a series of connected utterances, such as picture description, monologue, debate, topic-prompted conversation, and more typical conversation. Deficits in all other aspects of spoken language production, listed above, can also be assessed in discourse tasks. Early cognitive-linguistic changes in discourse might be useful for the preclinical identification of dementia. In picture description tasks, persons with probable AD and MCI were significantly impaired when compared to normal controls on measures of gist and details (Chapman et al., 2002), and subtle differences in lexical semantic processing, such as semantic paraphasias, word-finding delays, fewer error repairs, and fewer themes identified (Forbes, Venneri, & Shanks, 2002). However, Hopper, Bayles, and Kim (2001) reported that individuals in the mild stages of AD produced meaningful and relevant descriptive and figurative statements using accurate sentence structure and grammar in a picture description task. Of note, the complexity of the stimuli used to elicit discourse may influence performance. For example, Ehrlich, Obler, and Clark (1997) systematically varied the amount of content and format of picture stimuli; persons with AD performed better when the picture contained less information, but they still produced less content, shorter sentences, more sentence fragments, and more errors than normal controls.

During conversation, there may be some evidence of irrelevant or vague comments, and repetition. Early discourse deficits are attributed to word-finding problems (Nicholas, Obler, Albert, & Helms-Estabrooks, 1985) and memory-encoding deficits (Kempler, 1995). Many language strengths, however, are also displayed, as the apparently typical exchange of social pleasantries can mask the lack of information conveyed. This language strength often contributes to the uncertainty of the seriousness of the person's memory deficits on the part of family and medical providers. In the middle stages of the disease, changes in language production are evident and pragmatic deficits, such as topic maintenance and knowledge of the listener's perspective, are impaired (Kempler, 1995; Nicholas et al., 1985; Ripich & Terrell, 1988). Utterances become increasingly irrelevant and inaccurate and contain unnecessary repetitions, irrelevant content, and lack of information. Yet, social conventions, such as turn taking, remain largely intact. In the late stages, responsiveness to one's name or to social greetings may persist even when expressive output is mostly unintelligible or incoherent (Bayles, Tomoeda, Cruz, & Mahendra, 2000).

Discourse can be measured also in terms of coherence and cohesion. The coherence of the discourse is based on how well sentences and ideas are related in a conversation. The logical sequence and thematic nature of coherent discourse reflects cognitive processes such as organization and planning (Ulatowska & Chapman, 1995). Ripich and Terrell (1988) documented impaired coherence related to missing information in topic-directed discourse. Intrusions of irrelevant and incorrect information have also been reported as characteristics of impaired coherence (Ulatowska, Allard, & Donnell, 1988). In contrast, *cohesion* refers to the relatedness of words and concepts within the sentence, and processes at the linguistic level (Ulatowska & Chapman). Measures of cohesion in discourse have included linguistic devices such as reference, connectors, and verb tense (Ulatowska & Chapman). In addition, referential errors, greater use of pronouns, and vague terms (e.g., "thing, that, or somebody") have been associated with cohesion impairments in discourse (Dijkstra, Bourgeois, Petrie, Burgio, & Allen-Burge, 2002; Hier, Hagenlocker, & Shindler, 1985; Obler, 1983; Ripich & Terrell, 1988).

Finally, persons with dementia may also be described as having pragmatic difficulties due to emotional processing deficits. For example, persons with PD often have difficulty with both expression and comprehension of emotionality in facial expressions. These deficits cannot be accounted for by cognitive or neuropsychiatric deficits, or drug side effects, as they can be found in persons with early-stage PD prior to initiation of drug treatments and to diagnosis of these symptoms (Dujardin et al., 2004; Sprengelmeyer et al., 2003). Other researchers, however, have found that some persons with PD have intact ability to comprehend facial expression (Pell & Leonard, 2005).

Oral Reading The ability to read aloud remains relatively intact until the later stages of AD. For example, single-word reading ability was evident on the Functional Linguistic Communication Inventory (Bayles & Tomoeda, 1994), even in individuals with late-stage AD. Reading is likely to be most impaired in persons with semantic dementia, as some theorists have suggested that the process of reading involves the interaction of orthographic, phonologic, and semantic systems (Patterson, Graham, & Hodges, 1994). Thus, when the semantic system is disordered, the other systems will be affected. Patterson et al. (1994) found intact oral reading ability for high-frequency words and words with regular spelling-to-sound correspondence in persons with semantic dementia, and difficulties with irregularly spelled words and pseudowords. Noble, Glosser, and Grossman (2000), however, did not find this same pattern of oral reading in participants with other types of dementia (AD, frontotemporal dementia, and progressive aphasia). Other researchers have theorized that differences in anatomic location of disease expression can explain contradictory findings. For example, it has been proposed that lesions in the occipital lobe are related to difficulties with orthography, but lesions in the left inferior temporal region are seen with semantic processing difficulties (Noble et al., 2000).

Written Language Production

The expression of thoughts and ideas through writing generally mirrors what the person is able to express verbally, unless there is a significant difference in limb versus speech motor abilities. Writing severity has been correlated with dementia severity across a variety of tasks: spelling performance (Aarsland, Høien, & Larsen, 1995), single-written-sentence performance (Kemper et al., 1993), and narrative performance (Horner, Heyman, Dawson, & Rogers, 1988). Aarsland et al. (1995) revealed evidence of both lexical and phonological strategy impairments in persons with AD. On single-word tasks, spelling and writing of regular words and nonwords are preserved, but poor spelling of irregular words is common (Rapcsak, Arthur, Bliklen, & Rubens, 1989), and high-frequency words are written better than low-frequency words (Hughes, Graham, Patterson, & Hodges, 1997).

In writing at the sentence level, Kemper et al. (1993) found that as dementia progressed, information content, sentence length, number of clauses, and use of verb forms and conjunctions declined. The syntax of persons with moderate and severe dementia, however, was relatively preserved, though simple in form and reduced in content. Furthermore, on more complex, narrative-writing tasks, several investigators have documented impaired ability to retrieve information from semantic and long-term memory (Henderson, Buckwalter, Sobel, Freed, & Diz, 1992; LaBarge, Smith, Dick, & Storandt, 1992). Horner et al. (1988) found that the mechanics of writing remain intact, but difficulties in retrieving words were reflected in written text that was shorter and syntactically simpler than would be predicted by the premorbid educational and occupational status of the individuals. By the middle stages of the disease, a marked reduction in the ability to generate written text is evident, and perseveration in words and letters may be common. In the late stages, scribbling and random marks on the paper may be the only behaviors remaining.

Auditory Comprehension

The comprehension of spoken language, or auditory comprehension, is gradually impacted by the cognitive deficits experienced by the person. Reclusive or social isolation behaviors may be the first signs of difficulties in this area. Auditory comprehension appears intact for simple, structured, and concrete language, but impaired for abstract language, even in early stages, due to a lack of attention or concentration, encoding, or working memory deficits (Code & Lodge, 1987; Kempler, Van Lancker, & Read, 1988). On a picture–sentence matching task, in which the syntactic complexity of the sentences ranged from simple active to center-embedded object relative sentences, persons with mild cognitive impairment demonstrated only slight difficulties in syntactic processing compared with the healthy controls (Bickel, Pantel, Eysenbach, & Schröder, 2000). Waters and Caplan (2002) found similarly preserved syntactic comprehension even though working memory deficits were documented in persons with early-stage AD. Furthermore, the comprehension of simple three-stage commands may remain relatively intact through middle stages of dementia (Bayles & Tomoeda, 1993).

In a study of discourse comprehension, Welland, Lubinski, and Higginbotham (2002) found that persons with early- and middle-stage AD demonstrated poorer comprehension of narratives than persons without brain damage, but had similar patterns of better comprehension for main ideas than details, and better comprehension for stated than implied information. As the disease progresses, comprehension is enhanced when the ideas conveyed are short, syntactically simple, and personally relevant. In the severe stages, comprehension performance declines for one-step commands, multiple-choice and yes–no questions (Bayles & Tomoeda, 1993), and sentence–picture matching tasks (Bickel et al., 2000). Small, Kemper, and Lyons (1997) systematically evaluated the effects of grammatical complexity, presentation rate (normal versus slow), and repetition type (verbatim versus paraphrase) on sentence comprehension in AD and found no effects for a slow speech rate. The decline in comprehension as a function of increasing grammatical complexity was improved, however, with either verbatim or paraphrased repetition. Comprehension of nonverbal language, such as tone of voice and facial expression, appears to remain intact throughout the disease progression. Therefore, caregivers may have to be trained to recognize that their own nonverbal behaviors may elicit responses different from what they intended to convey verbally.

Reading Comprehension

The comprehension of written text mirrors auditory comprehension abilities and deficits, with a gradual decline in ability to understand text at premorbid complexity levels. Reading deficits may be attributed to memory-encoding deficits, difficulty keeping multiple ideas in mind and making inferences, or long-term and semantic memory deficits. These memory and inferencing deficits may cause the person to reread the same material, to have difficulty understanding the gist of the material, or to lose interest in familiar types of reading materials, which are often the first signs of reading difficulty. Some persons abandon pleasure reading out of frustration; others are more persistent in their continuing attempts to maintain a lifelong interest.

Determining the extent to which reading comprehension is impaired in dementia has been difficult because of the differences in difficulty and complexity of the many tasks used to assess comprehension (Mathias, 1996). Furthermore, the interaction of semantic, lexical, and visual recognition systems complicates matters, particularly on irregular and nonword reading tasks where most persons with AD demonstrated preserved skills in comparison to reading comprehension deficits on sentence level tasks (Rapcsak et al., 1989). Bayles et al. (1991) evaluated semantic memory loss longitudinally with 11 different word-reading tasks; they concluded that a person had to miss all possible tasks related to a single concept to determine it is lost from semantic memory.

Working memory deficits are thought to account for deficits in reading comprehension of sentences (Kempler et al., 1998). In an experimental task evaluating the effects of semantic versus syntactic cues on sentence comprehension, written sentences were either paired with a picture (to decrease the demands on working memory) or removed from view before the test pictures were presented (Grober & Bang, 1995). Comprehension improved when the semantic cues were available and storage demands were minimized, suggesting a syntactic deficit unrelated to semantic or working memory impairments.

There is some evidence from studies of the use of written cues to mediate problem behaviors that rudimentary reading abilities remain throughout the disease progression (e.g., Bourgeois, Burgio, Schulz, Beach, & Palmer, 1997) and to improve conversation regarding personally relevant topics (e.g., Bourgeois, 1992, 1993; Bourgeois & Mason, 1996; Hoerster, Hickey, & Bourgeois, 2001). Written text that is personally relevant to the individual and that triggers associated memories may hold the greatest promise of maintaining communication with the person throughout the illness.

Summary

To date, researchers and clinicians have documented the many changes in communicative functions in dementia as a function of disease severity and etiology. Although much is now known about the course of language skills and deficits in dementia, the heterogeneity of symptom expression across individuals with neurodegenerative diseases necessitates continued research efforts. For example, in one study, persons with early-onset AD presented with more language deficits than those with late-onset AD, and these deficits correlated with rapid progression of the disease (Faber-Langendoen et al., 1988). Yet, others have failed to find a similar correlation; severity of language and severity of dementia may be correlated, but not age of onset and degree of language involvement (Bayles, 1991; Cummings, Benson, Hill, & Read, 1985). Language deficits clearly support certain diagnoses (i.e., SD, Pick's disease, and PPA), whereas language abilities are relatively preserved in others, such as PSP (Albert, Feldman, & Willis, 1974) and MS (Rao et al., 1991). Clearly, the clinician planning intervention for the person with dementia will need to determine the specific areas of language deficit and preserved ability of each client, one's cognitive strengths and weaknesses, as well as how these cognitive-communication changes are reflected as problem behaviors.

BEHAVIOR PROBLEMS

Characteristics of Behavior Problems

Behavior problems may stem from relatively benign forgetfulness to more significant memory loss, and may result in a range of challenges from disorientation and confusion, to repetitive verbal and physical behaviors, to aggressiveness, and to apathy. The frequency, intensity, severity, and pattern of problem behaviors vary as a function of the individual, the stage and etiology of disease, and a variety of environmental variables, including others' responses to the behaviors. In early stages, memory lapses begin to interfere with everyday functioning; some common complaints include getting lost or disoriented while driving, forgetting appointments, repeating questions, irritability, and uncharacteristic personality and mood swings. Persons experiencing these symptoms often become fearful of having dementia and hide or deny the existence, frequency, or severity of their symptoms. Arguments with family members over memory-related problems become increasingly frequent and disruptive, precipitating a visit to the physician.

As dementia progresses, problem behaviors can become more diverse, more frequent, and more difficult to manage. In the middle stages of disease progression, the impact of cognitive deterioration is seen in the repetitive nature of many problem behaviors, especially repeated questions. When a caregiver has repeatedly answered the same question, it becomes painfully obvious that the person is not processing information as expected. Uncharacteristic behaviors, such as hoarding, overly friendly interactions with strangers, hallucinations or delusions, or angry outbursts, challenge caregivers to find strategies other than trying to reason with the individual to deescalate a volatile situation. Fortunately for the caregiver, the pattern of problem behaviors changes as the disease progresses further. In the later stages, the more agitated and challenging behaviors subside; as cognition deteriorates, behaviors slow down, become more repetitive, and reflect decreasing stimulus recognition and comprehension. Apathy and lethargy; loss of overlearned behaviors such as grooming, eating, toileting, and ambulation; and unintelligible vocalizations characterize the final stages of dementia. Caregivers often mention that this period, when more physical or nursing care is required, can be less stressful to them because the behaviors are more predictable and manageable.

Cohen-Mansfield (2000) has developed a taxonomy of problem behaviors in dementia along two dimensions (physical and verbal, and aggressive and nonaggressive), as shown in Figure 3.1. Problem behaviors that are verbally aggressive include yelling, screaming, cursing, making strange noises, and making sexual advances. Problem behaviors that are verbally nonaggressive include repetitive requests, demands, questions, complaining, and negativism. In the physical domain, aggressive behaviors include hitting, scratching, biting, kicking, grabbing, pushing, throwing and tearing things, hurting self or others, and sexual advances. Nonaggressive physical behaviors include hoarding and hiding things, pacing and

verbal/vocal

nonaggressive	aggressive
verbally nonaggressive	**verbally aggressive**
complaining negativism repetitive sentences or questions constant, unwarranted requests for attention or help	cursing and verbal aggression making strange noises verbal sexual advances screaming
physically nonaggressive	**physically aggressive**
performing repetitious mannerisms inappropriate robing and disrobing eating inappropriate substances handling things inappropriately trying to get to a different place pacing, aimless wandering intentional falling general restlessness hoarding things hiding things	physical sexual advances hurting self or others throwing things leaning things scratching grabbing pushing spitting kicking biting hitting

physical

Figure 3.1 Behaviors in the CMAI Organized by Dimensions. Reprinted with permission from J. Cohen-Mansfield.

aimless wandering, inappropriately disrobing, eating inappropriate substances, and repetitive physical behaviors or mannerisms.

The various dementia etiologies may present with different patterns of behavior problems. In early AD, memory impairments predominate, resulting in progressive changes in mood and depression, anxiety, agitation, and aggression. In more severe AD, frontal lobe damage results in hallucinations, delusions, and apathy; as well, changes in sexual behavior, abnormal nighttime behaviors, and hoarding behaviors are common. DLB presents with defining features of visual hallucinations, delusions, mood changes, and sleep disorders (Cummings, 2003). Similarly, PD commonly results in mood changes, hallucinations, anxiety, apathy, depression, and irritability (Aarsland, Litvan, & Larsen, 2001; Cummings, 1995). VaD results in depression, agitation, and anxiety that are often more common and more severe than in AD (Aharon-Peretz, Kliot, & Tomer, 2000). VaD may also cause delusions, personality changes, disinhibition, and symptoms associated with specific areas of focal damage (e.g., anosagnosia from right parietal lesion or aphasia from left hemisphere lesions; Cummings, 2003). FTD results in prominent behavioral symptoms early in the disease process, most notably disordered personal conduct and disinhibition (Cummings, 2003). Additionally, FTD often causes distractibility, indifference, apathy, or repetitive, stereotypic, and compulsive behaviors. The lack of depressive symptoms and later onset of memory impairments distinguishes FTD from AD (Levy et al., 1998). Based on an analysis of the Clinical Dementia Rating Scale (Morris, 1993), after matching for age and MMSE score, FTD caused more severe impairments than AD or SD in the following functional areas: judgment, problem solving, community affairs, home and hobbies, and personal care (Rosen et al., 2004).

Problem behaviors have been explained by the theory of unmet needs—the "Need-Driven Compromised Behavior Model" (Algase et al., 1996, Beck et al., 1998), as displayed in Figure 3.2. Persons with dementia have a range of personal, social, environmental, physical, and emotional needs that they may not be able to communicate in an effective way due to the changes in language and cognition related to their medical condition. Often, these behavioral expressions of needs are misinterpreted as maladaptive behaviors that need intervention. Unfortunately, many interventions are overly restrictive. Physical and/or chemical restraints may eliminate certain problem behaviors, but they may also cause lethargy and apathy or other problem behaviors. Furthermore, the interventions do not often meet the need that the person was trying to communicate.

Relationships Among Language, Memory, and Behavior in Dementias

Language and the many facets of cognition, particularly memory, are so intertwined that it is difficult to consider one separate from the other when describing their attributes. The specific language and memory deficits that result in problem behaviors can be difficult to tease apart given their considerable overlap (e.g., a person may have both semantic deficits and difficulty interpreting cues in the environment, which may both result in confused language or aggressive behaviors). Potkins and colleagues (2003) have documented strong associations between

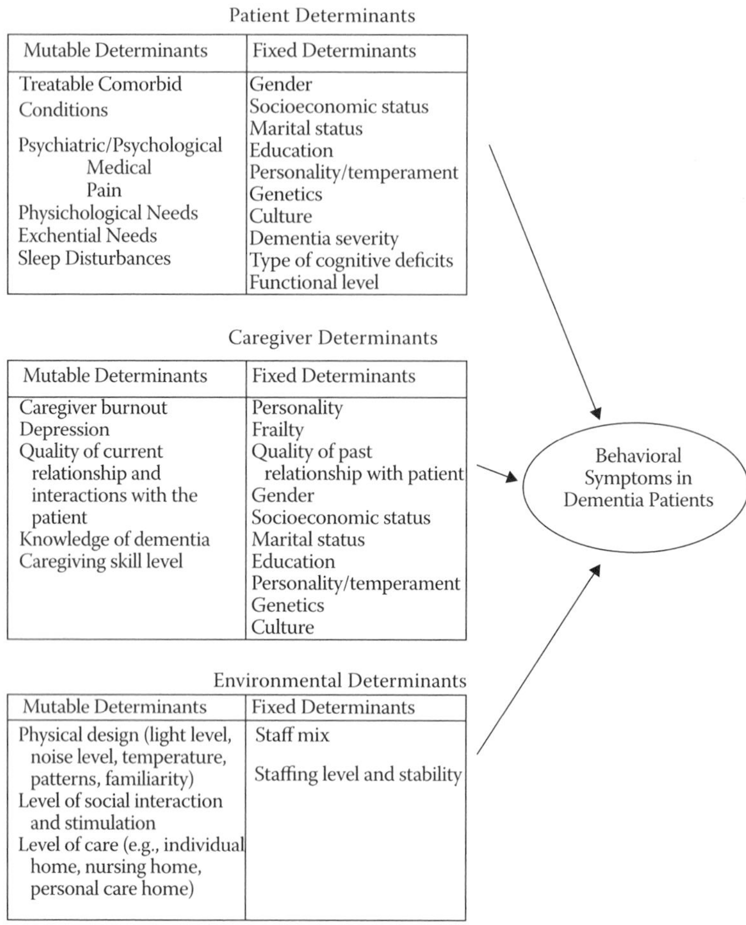

Figure 3.2 Determinants of Behavioral Symptoms in Dementia Patients. (Kunik et al., 2003).

expressive language impairments and delusions, and between receptive language difficulties and aberrant motor behaviors. Furthermore, decreased participation in activities correlated with expressive and receptive language difficulties, but social withdrawal correlated more strongly with receptive language deficits (Potkins et al.). Thus, we must understand the relationships between language, cognitive, and behavioral deficits associated with dementias in order to prescribe appropriate interventions for the resulting functional limitations.

Table 3.4 classifies the continuum of language deficits and related problem behaviors as exemplars of failure of a particular memory system: (a) sensory memory, (b) working memory, or (c) long-term memory. This proposed classification scheme does not, however, preclude the possibility of alternate explanations. On the contrary, multiple theories should be considered when attempting to develop an effective intervention for a particular problem. For example, a sound clinical

TABLE 3.4 Classifying Language Deficits and Problem Behaviors by Memory Subsystem

Sensory memory: problems with registration, recognition, and identification	**Short-term, temporary working memory**: problems with encoding and decoding	**Long-term, semantic, episodic, and procedural memory**: problems with retrieval
Visual agnosia: does not recognize common objects; puts objects in wrong places	Repetitive questions; failure to encode answer	Word-finding problems: specific words, facts, and names of familiar persons, places, and events; uses wrong name
Sundowning: does not recognize his or her home	Follows caregiver; forgets caregiver is temporarily in the other room	States erroneous information: lying and accusations
Repetitive tactile manipulation; does not recognize object Delusions; misidentifies people, objects, and places	Uncooperative, may not follow directions or instructions: failure to encode or decode verbal stimuli	Disruptive vocalization: inability to access words to express wants and needs Forgets how to dress, bathe, feed, and toilet self
Hallucinations: sees people and objects that are not there Distracted by competing sensory stimuli; sensory overload	Agitation, pacing: failure to encode responses to anxiety-induced behavior	Forgets how to use telephone and other familiar implements Does not complete tasks Apathy: forgets what to do Wandering: forgets where to go

approach to determining how to reduce a resident's disruptive vocalization would involve assessing for potential sources of the problem, such as inability to identify environmental cues, inability to remember what was just told about a situation, or inability to retrieve the words needed to express a need. With time and practice, clinicians should be able to accumulate sufficient experience with their clients' unique expressions of needs to become accurate in hypothesis testing to interpret their meaning. The majority of behaviors categorized as memory related in Table 3.4 would also be classified along Cohen-Mansfield's nonaggressive agitation dimension.

Problem behaviors that can be explained as deficits in sensory memory include not recognizing or misidentifying common objects, people, or locations. Working memory problems result in failure to encode information or instructions related to a particular situation (e.g., the answer to a repeated question). Failures to retrieve, or loss of storage of, words and familiar routines from long-term memory can lead to errors in communication and activities of daily living. Consider, however, behaviors such as wandering, lack of initiation and cooperation, and sundowning. These behaviors could be explained as problems with the integration of sensory input, encoding, *and* retrieval processes, not just one process alone, as illustrated in Box 3.1.

Sundowning behaviors might also be considered problems with several memory systems simultaneously. When persons say they need to go home, pack a suitcase or shopping bag, or seek an exit, they may not remember that they are in their own home because the once-familiar visual cues have lost their salience. Alternatively,

BOX 3.1 CASE STUDY

Mr. Smith asks his wife to get the broom from the kitchen closet so that he can sweep the leaves off the front porch. She does not return in a timely fashion. He finds her holding a watering can and wandering the hallway. The stressed caregiver might think she was deliberately disregarding his request. More likely, however, she fully intended to get the broom, but became distracted by the watering can, which replaced her intended plan. When asked to recall the original request, she may not remember the request, nor would she be able to say what she was holding or what she intended to do with it. The cause of this change of plans may be that the original request to get the broom may well have been understood but not encoded into long-term memory, and when an interesting new cue appeared, it triggered a new behavior, preventing retrieval of the original request.

they may not be able to remember the words to express the need to become actively engaged in a desired purposeful activity. The housecleaner who always finished her work at 5 p.m., changed into her street clothes, and then took the bus to her own home to cook dinner for her family may exhibit behaviors reminiscent of her former routine unless she is engaged in an activity in the late afternoon.

In late stages of dementia, when access to vocabulary is severely limited, caregivers must interpret maladaptive behaviors and disruptive vocalizations as communicative attempts, albeit unsuccessful ones, and must attempt strategies to address their clients' needs. If one adopts the view that these problems are communicative attempts, then understanding and meeting their needs would appear to be the responsibility of the speech-language pathologists (SLP). The SLP would facilitate the development of an intervention plan that would involve the use of alternative modes of expression to convey these unmet needs. Psychologists and behavior analysts, however, are more likely to receive referrals to address these problems.

Clinicians can develop interventions to modify problem behaviors with communication-related techniques, such as visual and auditory cues, especially when the behaviors are expressed verbally (e.g., repeated requests, or complaints). If physically nonaggressive behaviors, such as wandering or restlessness, are interpreted as memory impairments (i.e., forgets destination, or forgets what to do), SLPs may attempt interventions to increase awareness of place and activities. Verbally and physically aggressive behaviors, however, may never have been identified as viable targets for cognitive-communicative intervention, especially from an SLP. It is important to consider that these difficult behaviors are, in fact, attempts to communicate an unmet need and, when ignored or misinterpreted, result in increasing frustration and escalating intensity of the behavior. Physically aggressive behaviors directed at others (i.e., hitting, pushing, and kicking) might be expressions of extreme displeasure or discomfort. Alternatively, these aggressive behaviors may simply be inappropriate attempts to gain attention and interaction with others.

Efforts to discern the cause or triggers of problem behaviors will involve soliciting information from the person or others in the environment, and/or observing the person and the situation. Both internal and external causes must be investigated. Sometimes, there are reasons external to the individual that are offensive, such as loud noises or uncomfortable room temperatures. In other cases, the person is in pain or is anxious, fearful, or bored. The insight of a knowledgeable caregiver is often needed to understand the problem. The clinician who is an occasional visitor, however, may observe potential causes that have gone unnoticed by the typical caregivers. A variety of environmental factors that are routine and familiar to the staff may create confusion or frustration for the residents with dementia: the constant discordant interruptions of loudspeaker announcements, unfamiliar contemporary music or television programs, the visual similarity of every resident's doorway, or long facility hallways with exit signs at the end.

In addition, the clinician needs to assess the client's physical and social environment for clues about what might be causing or reinforcing negative behaviors. For example, if someone is sitting too close to another person whose repeated attempts to move away elicit countermoves to remain close, then one could predict frustration with this behavior, leading to pushing away the offender. It would not be appropriate to punish the person sitting too close to the other or the person doing the pushing, as these were both attempts to communicate. Instead, the challenge is to find ways to enhance appropriate communicative interactions. Similarly, it would not be appropriate to refer these clients for more intrusive intervention, such as medications, when personal and social needs are obvious in the problem behaviors exhibited. The following chapters will review an extensive array of interventions that have been applied to problem behaviors that reflect impaired communication.

REFERENCES

Aarsland, D., Høien, T., & Larsen, J. (1995). Alexia and agraphia in dementia of the Alzheimer type. In M. Bergener & S. Finkel (Eds.), *Treating Alzheimer's and other dementias* (pp. 298–308). New York: Springer.

Aarsland, D., Litvan, I., & Larsen, J. (2001). Neuropsychiatric symptoms of patients with progressive supranuclear palsy and Parkinson's disease. *Journal of Neuropsychiatry and Clinical Neurosciences, 13*, 43–49.

Albert, M., Feldman, R., & Willis, A. (1974). The "subcortical dementia" of progressive supranuclear palsy. *Journal of Neurology, Neurosurgery and Psychiatry, 37*, 121–130.

Algase, D. L., Beck, C., Kolanowski, A., Whall, A., Berent, S., Richards, K., et al. (1996). Need-driven dementia-compromised behavior: An alternative view of disruptive behavior. *American Journal of Alzheimer's Disease, 11*, 10–19.

Appell, I., Kertesz, A., & Fisman, M. (1982). A study of language functioning in Alzheimer patients. *Brain and Language, 17*, 73–91.

Assal, F., & Cummings, J. (2003). Cortical and frontosubcortical dementias: Differential diagnosis. In V. O. Emery & T. E. Oxman (Eds.), *Dementia: Presentations, differential diagnosis, and nosology* (pp. 239–262). Baltimore: Johns Hopkins University Press.

Au, A., Chan, A., & Chiu, H. (2003). Verbal learning in Alzheimer's dementia. *Journal of the International Neuropsychological Society, 9*, 363–375.

Baddeley, A. (1992). Working memory. *Science*, *255*, 556–569.

Baddeley, A. (1995). The psychology of memory. In A. D. Baddeley, B. A. Wilson, & F. N. Watts (Eds.), *Handbook of memory disorders* (pg. 3–26). New York: John Wiley.

Baddeley, A., Baddeley, H., Bucks, R., & Wilcock, G. (2001). Attentional control in Alzheimer's disease. *Brain*, *124*, 1492–1508.

Ballard, C., O'Brien, J., Gray, A., Cormack, F., Ayre, G., Rowan, E., et al. (2001). Attention and fluctuating attention in patients with dementia with Lewy bodies and Alzheimer disease. *Archives of Neurology*, *58*, 977–982.

Barresi, B. A., Nicholas, M., Connor, L. T., Obler, L. K., & Albert, M. L. (2000). Semantic degradation and lexical access in age-related naming failures. *Aging, Neuropsychology, and Cognition*, *7*, 1–10.

Bayles, K. (1982). Language function in senile dementia. *Brain and Language*, *16*, 265–280.

Bayles, K. (1991). Age at onset of Alzheimer's disease: Relation to language dysfunction. *Archives of Neurology*, *48*, 155–159.

Bayles, K. (2003). Effects of working memory deficits on the communicative functioning of Alzheimer's dementia patients. *Journal of Communication Disorders*, *36*, 209–219.

Bayles, K., & Kaszniak, A. (1987). *Communication and cognition in normal aging and dementia*. Boston: College Hill Press.

Bayles, K., & Tomoeda, C. (1983). Confrontation naming impairment in dementia. *Brain and Language*, *19*, 98–114.

Bayles, K., & Tomoeda, C. (1993). *The Arizona Battery of Communication Disorders of Dementia*. Austin, TX: Pro-Ed.

Bayles, K., & Tomoeda, C. (1994). *Functional Linguistic Communication Inventory*. Austin, TX: Pro-Ed.

Bayles, K., Tomoeda, C., Cruz, R., & Mahendra, M. (2000). Communication abilities of individuals with late-state Alzheimer disease. *Alzheimer Discourse and Associated Disorders*, *14*, 176–181.

Bayles, K., Tomoeda, C., Kaszniak, A., & Trosset, M. (1991). Alzheimer's disease effects on semantic memory: Loss of structure or function. *Journal of Cognitive Neuroscience*, *3*, 166–182.

Beck, C., Frank, L., Chumbler, N. R., O'Sullivan, P, Vogelpohl, T. S., Rasin, J., et al. (1998). Correlates of disruptive behavior in severely cognitively impaired nursing home residents. *The Gerontologist*, *38*, 189–198.

Benton, A. L. (1974). *Revised visual retention test: Clinical and experimental application* (4th ed.). New York: Psychological Corporation.

Bickel, C., Pantel, J., Eysenbach, K., & Schröder, J. (2000). Syntactic comprehension deficits in Alzheimer's disease. *Brain and Language*, *71*, 432–448.

Bjork, R. A. (1988). Retrieval practice and the maintenance of knowledge. In M. M. Gruneberg, P. Morris, & R. Sykes (Eds.), *Practical aspects of memory* (Vol. 2, pp. 396–401). London: Academic.

Blake, M., Duffy, J., Boeve, B., Ahlskog, J., & Maraganore, D. (2003). Speech and language disorders associated with corticobasal degeneration. *Journal of Medical Speech-Language Pathology*, *11*, 131–146.

Bourgeois, M. (1992). Evaluating memory wallets in conversations with patients with dementia. *Journal of Speech and Hearing Research*, *35*, 1344–1357.

Bourgeois, M. (1993). Effects of memory aids on the dyadic conversations of individuals with dementia. *Journal of Applied Behavior Analysis*, *26*, 77–87.

Bourgeois, M., Burgio, L., Schulz, R., Beach, S., & Palmer, B. (1997). Modifying repetitive verbalization of community dwelling patients with AD. *The Gerontologist*, *37*, 30–39.

Bourgeois, M., Camp, C., Rose, M., White, B., Malone, M., Carr, J., et al. (2003). A comparison of training strategies to enhance use of external aids by persons with dementia. *Journal of Communication Disorders*, *36*, 361–378.

Bourgeois, M., & Mason, L. A. (1996). Memory wallet intervention in an adult day care setting. *Behavioral Interventions: Theory and Practice in Residential and Community-Based Clinical Programs*, *11*, 3–18.

Butters, N., Granholm, E., Salmon, D., Grant, I., & Wolfe, J. (1987). Episodic and semantic memory: A comparison of amnesic and demented patients. *Journal of Clinical and Experimental Neuropsychology*, *9*, 479–497.

Caine, E., Bamford, R., Schiffer, R., Shoulson, I., & Levy, S. (1986). A controlled neuropsychological comparison of Huntington's disease and multiple sclerosis. *Archives of Neurology*, *43*, 249–254.

Camp, C. J. (1989). Cognitive aging: Issues in research and application; introduction. *Educational Gerontology*, *15*(6), R3–R5.

Camp, C. J. (2001). From efficacy to effectiveness to diffusion: Making the transitions in dementia intervention research. *Neuropsychological Rehabilitation*, *11*(3–4), 4955–517.

Camp, C. J., & McKitrick, L. A. (1992). Memory interventions in Alzheimer's-type dementia populations: Methodological and theoretical issues. In R. L. West & J. D. Sinnott (Eds.), *Everyday memory and aging: Current research and methodology* (pp. 155–172). New York: Springer-Verlag.

Campbell-Taylor, I. (1995). Motor speech changes. In R. Lubinski (Ed.), *Dementia and communication* (pp. 70–82). San Diego, CA: Singular.

Cannatà, A., Alberoni, M., Franceschi, M., & Mariani, C. (2002). Frontal impairment in subcortical ischemic vascular dementia in comparison to Alzheimer's disease. *Dementia and Geriatric Cognitive Disorders*, *13*, 101–111

Caselli, R. (2000). Visual syndromes as the presenting feature of degenerative brain disease. *Seminars in Neurology*, *20*, 139–144.

Caselli, R., & Yanagihara, T. (1991). Memory disorders in degenerative neurological diseases. In T. Yanagihara & R. Peterson (Eds.), *Memory disorders* (pp. 369–396). New York: Marcel Dekker.

Chapman, S., Zientz, J., Weiner, M., Rosenberg, R., Frawley, W., & Burns, M. (2002). Discourse changes in early Alzheimer's disease, mild cognitive impairment, and normal aging. *Alzheimer Discourse and Associated Disorders*, *16*, 177–186.

Chenery, H., Murdoch, B., & Ingram, J. (1996). An investigation of confrontation naming performance in Alzheimer's dementia as a function of disease severity. *Aphasiology*, *10*, 423–441.

Chertkow, H., Bub, D., & Seidenberg. M. (1989). Priming and semantic memory loss in Alzheimer's disease. *Brain and Language*, *36*, 420–446.

Chong, R., Horak, F., Frank, J., & Kaye, J. (1999). Sensory organization for balance: specific deficits in Alzheimer's but not in Parkinson's disease. *Journals of Gerontology*, *54*(3), M122–M128

Code, C., & Lodge, B. (1987). Language in dementia of recent referral. *Age and Ageing*, *16*, 366–372.

Cohen-Mansfield, J. (2000). Approaches to the management of disruptive behavior. In M. P. Lawton & R. Rubenstein (Eds.), *Interventions in dementia care: Toward improving quality of life* (pp. 39–65). New York: Springer.

Connor, L. T., Spiro, A., III, Obler, L. K., & Albert, M. L. (2004). Change in object naming ability during adulthood. *Journal of Gerontology, Psychological Sciences*, *59B*(5), P203–P209.

Craik, F., Anderson, N., Kerr, S., & Li, K. (1995). Memory changes in normal ageing. In A. D. Baddeley, B. A. Wilson, & F. N. Watts (eds.), *Handbook of memory disorders* (pg. 211–242). Chichester, UK: Wiley.

Cuerva, A., Sabe, L., Kuzis, G., Tiberti, C., Dorrego, F., & Starkstein, S. (2001). Theory of mind and pragmatic abilities in dementia. *Neuropsychiatry, Neuropsychology and Behavioral Neurology, 14*, 153–158.

Cummings, J. L. (1995). Behavioral and psychiatric symptoms associated with Huntington's disease. *Advances in Neurology, 65*, 179–186.

Cummings, J. L. (2003). *The neuropsychiatry of Alzheimer's disease and related dementias*. London: Martin Dunitz.

Cummings, J., Benson, D., Hill, M., & Read, S. (1985). Aphasia in dementia of the Alzheimer type. *Neurology, 35*, 394–397.

Damasio, A. (1999). *The feeling of what happens: Boday and emotion in the making of consciousness*. New York: Harcourt, Brace.

Devanand, D., Michaels-Marston, K., Liu, X., Pelton, G., Padilla, M., Marder, K., et al. (2000). Olfactory deficits in patients with mild cognitive impairment predict Alzheimer's disease at follow-up. *American Journal of Psychiatry, 157*, 1399–1405.

Dijkstra, K., Bourgeois, M. S., Petrie, G., Burgio, L., & Allen-Burge, R. (2002). My recaller is on vacation: Discourse analysis of nursing home residents with dementia. *Discourse Processes, 33*(1), 53–76

Downes, J., Priestly, N., Doran, M., Ferran, J., Ghadiiali, E., & Cooper, P. (1998–1999). Intellectual, mnemonic, and frontal functions in dementia with Lewy bodies: A comparison with early and advanced Parkinson's disease. *Behavioral Neurology, 11*, 173–183.

Duff Canning, S., Leach, L., Stuss, D., Ngo, L., & Black, S. (2004). Diagnostic utility of abbreviated fluency measures in Alzheimer disease and vascular dementia. *Neurology, 62*, 556–562.

Duffy, J. (2005). *Motor speech disorders: Substrates, differential diagnosis, and management* (2nd ed.). Toronto: Mosby.

Dujardin, K., Blairy, S., Defebvre, L, Duhem, S., Noël, Y., Hess, U., et al. (2004). Deficits in decoding emotional facial expressions in Parkinson's disease. *Neuropsychologia, 42*, 239–250.

Duke, L., & Kaszniak, A. (2000). Executive control functions in degenerative dementias: a comparative review. *Neuropsychology Review, 10*, 75–99.

Ehrlich, J., Obler, L., & Clark, L. (1997). Ideational and semantic contributions to narrative production in adults with dementia of the Alzheimer's type. *Journal of Communication Disorders, 30*, 79–99.

Emery, O. V. (2000). Language impairment in dementia of the Alzheimer type: A hierarchical decline? *International Journal of Psychiatry in Medicine, 30*, 145–164.

Eslinger, P., & Damasio, A., (1986). Preserved motor learning in Alzheimer's disease: Implications for anatomy and behavior. *Journal of Neuroscience, 6*, 3006–3009.

Faber-Langendoen, K., Morris, J., Knesevich, J., LaBarge, E., Miller, J., & Berg, L. (1988). Aphasia in senile dementia of the Alzheimer type. *Annals of Neurology, 23*, 365–370.

Fitten, L., Perryman, K., Wilkinson, C., Little, R., Burns, M., Pachana, N., et al. (1995). Alzheimer and vascular dementias and driving. *Journal of the American Medical Association, 273*, 1360–1365.

Fleischman, D., Gabrieli, J., Reminger, S., Rinaldi, J., Morrell, F., & Wilson, R. (1995). Conceptual priming in perceptual identification for patients with Alzheimers-disease and a patient with right occipital lobectomy. *Neuropsychology*, 9(2), 187–197.

Foldi, N., Jutagir, R., Davidoff, D., & Gould, T. (1992). Selective attention skills in Alzheimer's disease: Performance on graded cancellation tests varying in density and complexity. *Journal of Gerontology*, *47*, P146–P153.

Foldi, N., Lobosco, J., & Schaefer, L. (2002). The effect of attentional dysfunction in Alzheimer's disease: Theoretical and practical implications. *Seminars in Speech and Language*, *23*, 139–150.

Foldi, N., Schaefer, L., White, R., Johnson, R., Berger, J., Carney, M., et al. (2005). *Neuropsychology*, *19*, 5–17.

Forbes, K., Venneri, A., & Shanks, M. (2002). Distinct patterns of spontaneous speech deterioration: An early predictor of Alzheimer's disease. *Brain & Cognition*, *48*, 356–361.

Frank, E., McDade, H., & Scott, W. (1996). Naming in dementia secondary to Parkinson's, Huntington's, and Alzheimer's diseases. *Journal of Communication Disorders*, *29*, 183–197.

Freeman, R., Giovannetti, T., Lamar, M., Cloud, B., Stern, R., Kaplan, E., et al. (2000). Visuocontructional problems in dementia: Contributions of executive systems functions. *Neuropsychology*, *14*, 415–426.

Gardner, E., Martin, J., & Jessell, T. (2000). The bodily senses. In E. Kandel, J. Schwartz, & T. Jessell (Eds.), *Principles of neural science* (pp. 430–450). New York: McGraw-Hill.

Garrard, P., Patterson, K., Watson, P., & Hodges, J. (1998). Category specific semantic loss in dementia of Alzheimer's type: Functional-anatomical correlations from cross-sectional analyses. *Brain*, *121*, 633–646.

Gilbert, B., Belleville, S., Bherer, L., & Chouinard, S. (2005). Study of verbal working memory in patients with Parkinson's disease. *Neuropsychology*, *19*, 106–114.

Glosser, G., Baker, K., de Vries, J., Alavi, A., Grossman, M., & Clark, C. (2002). Disturbed visual processing contributes to impaired reading in Alzheimer's disease. *Neuropsychologia*, *40*, 902–909.

Glosser, G., Gallo, J., Clark, C., & Grossman, M. (2002). Memory encoding and retrieval in frontotemporal dementia and Alzheimer's disease. *Neuropsychology*, *16*, 190–196.

Grafman, J., Litvan, I., Gomez, C., & Chase, T. (1990). Frontal lobe function in progressive supranuclear palsy. *Archives of Neurology*, *47*, 553–558.

Graham, K., & Hodges, J. (1997). Differentiating the roles of the hippocampal complex and the neocortex in long-term memory storage: Evidence from the study of semantic dementia and Alzheimer's disease. *Neuropsychology*, *11*(1), 77–89.

Gregory, C., Lough, S., Stone, V., Erzinclioglu, S., Martin, L., Baron-Chen, S., et al. (2002). Theory of mind in patients with frontal variant frontotemporal dementia and Alzheimer's disease: Theoretical and practical implications. *Brain*, *125*, 752–764.

Grober, E., & Bang, S. (1995). Sentence comprehension in Alzheimer's disease. *Developmental Neuropsychology*, *11*, 95–107.

Heaton, R. K., Chelune, G., Talley, J. L., Kay, G. G., & Curtiss, G. (1993). *Wisconsin card sorting test, Revised and expanded*. Lutz, FL: Psychological Assessment Resources.

Heindel, W., Butters, N., & Salmon, D. (1988). Impaired learning of a motor skill in patients with Huntington's disease. *Behavioral Neuroscience*, *102*(1), 141–147.

Heindel, W., Salmon, D., Shults, C., Walicke, P., & Butters, N. (1989). Neuropsychological evidence for multiple implicit memory systems :A comparison of Alzheimers, Huntingtons, and Parkinsons-disease patients. *Journal of Neuroscience*, 9(2), 582–587.

Heir, D., Hagenlocker, K., & Shindler, A. (1985). Language disintegration in dementia on a picture description task. *Brain and Language*, *25*, 117–133.

Henderson, W., Buckwalter, J., Sobel, E., Freed, D., & Diz, M. (1992). The agraphia of Alzheimer's disease. *Neurology*, *42*, 777–784.

Herlitz, A., Adolfsson, R., Bäckman, L., & Nilsson, L-G. (1991). Cue utilization following different forms of encoding in mildly, moderately, and severely demented patients with Alzheimer's disease. *Brain and Cognition*, *15*, 119–130.

Hodges, J. R. (2001). Frontotemporal dementia (Pick's disease): Clinical features and assessment. *Neurology*, *56* (11), S6–S10.

Hoerster, L., Hickey, E., & Bourgeois, M. (2001). Effects of memory aids on conversations between nursing home residents with dementia and nursing assistants. *Neuropsychological Rehabilitation*, *11*, 399–427.

Hoppe, C., Muller, U., Werheid, K., Thöne, A., & von Cramon, D. (2000). Digit Ordering Test: Clinical, psychometric, and experimental evaluation of a verbal working memory test. *The Clinical Neuropsychologist*, *14*, 38–55.

Hopper, T. (2003). "They're just going to get worse anyway": Perspectives on rehabilitation for nursing home residents with dementia. *Journal of Communication Disorders*, *36*, 345–359.

Hopper, T., Bayles, K., & Kim, E. (2001). Retained neuropsychological abilities of individuals with Alzheimer's disease. *Seminars in Speech and Language*, *22*, 261–273.

Horner, J., Heyman, A., Dawson, D., & Rogers (1988). The relationship of agraphia to the severity of dementia in Alzheimer's disease. *Archives of Neurology*, *45*, 760–763.

Hubbard, G., Cook, A., Tester, S., & Downs, M. (2002). Beyond words: Older people with dementia using and interpreting nonverbal behaviour. *Journal of Aging Studies*, *16*, 155–167.

Huber, S., Shuttleworth, E., & Freidenberg, D. (1989). Neuropsychological differences between the dementias of Alzheimer's and Parkinson's disease. *Archives of Neurology*, *46*, 1287–1291.

Huber, S., Shuttleworth, E., & Paulsen, G. (1986). Dementia in Parkinson's disease. *Archives of Neurology*, *43*, 987–990.

Hughes, J., Graham, N., Patterson, K., & Hodges, J. (1997). Dysgraphia in mild dementia of Alzheimer's type. *Neuropsychologia*, *35*, 533–545.

Johnson, J., Head, E., Kim, R., Starr, A., & Cotman, C. (1999). Clinical and pathological evidence for a frontal variant of Alzheimer's disease. *Archives of Neurology*, *56*, 1233–1239.

Jorm, A. (1986). Controlled and automatic information processing in senile dementia: A review. *Psychological Medicine*, *16*, 77–88.

Kaszniak, A., Poon, L., & Riege, W. (1986). Assessing memory deficits: An information processing approach. In L. Poon (Ed.), *Handbook for clinical memory assessment of older adults* (pp. 168–189). Washington, DC: American Psychological Association.

Kawas, C., Corrada, M., Brookmeyer, R., Morrison, A., Resnick, S., Zonderman, A., et al. (2003). Visual memory predicts Alzheimer's disease more than a decade before diagnosis. *Neurology*, *60*, 1089–1093.

Kemper, S., LaBarge, E., Farraro, R., Cheung, H., Cheung, H., & Storandt, M. (1993). On the preservation of syntax in Alzheimer's disease. *Archives of Neurology*, *50*, 81–86.

Kempler, D. (1988). Lexical and pantomime abilities in Alzheimer's disease. *Aphasiology*, *2*, 147–159.

Kempler, D. (1995). Language changes in dementia of the Alzheimer type. In R. Lubinski (Ed.), *Dementia and communication* (pp. 98–114). Philadelphia: Decker.

Kempler, D., Curtiss, S., & Jackson, C. (1987). Syntactic preservation in Alzheimer's disease. *Journal of Speech and Hearing Research*, *30*, 343–350.

Kempler, D., Van Lancker, D., & Read, S. (1988). Proverb and idiom interpretation in Alzheimer disease. *Alzheimer Disease and Associated Disorders*, *2*, 38–49.

Kensinger, E., Shearer, D., Locascio, J., Growdon, J., & Corkin, S. (2003). Working memory in mild Alzheimer's disease and early Parkinson's disease. *Neuropsychology*, *17*, 230–239.

Kertesz, A. (1994). Language deterioration in dementia. In V. O. B. Emery & T. E. Oxman (Eds.), *Dementia: Presentations, differential diagnosis, and nosology* (pp. 108–122). Baltimore: Johns Hopkins University Press.

Kesner, R. (1998). Neurobiological views of memory. In J. Martinez & R. Kesner (Eds.), *Neurobiology of learning and memory* (pp. 361–416). San Diego, CA: Academic Press.

Knoke, D., Taylor, A., & Saint-Cyr, J. (1998). The differential effects of cueing on recall in Parkinson's disease and normal subjects. *Brain and Cognition*, *38*, 261–274.

Koenig, O., Thomas-Anterion, C., & Laurent, B. (1999). Procedural learning in Parkinson's disease: Intact and impaired components. *Neuropsychologia*, *37*, 1103–1109.

Kunik, M., Martinez, M., Snow, A., Beck, C., Cody, M., Rapp, C., et al. (2003) Determinants of behavioral symptoms in dementia patients. *Clinical Gerontologist*, *26*(3–4), 83–89.

LaBarge, E., Smith, D., Dick, L., & Storandt, M. (1992). Agraphia in dementia of the Alzheimer type. *Archives of Neurology*, *49*, 1151–1156.

Lafosse, J., Reed, B., Mungas, D., Sterling, S., Wahbeh, H., & Jagust, W. (1997). Fluency and memory differences between ischemic vascular dementia and Alzheimer's disease. *Neuropsychology*, *11*, 514–522.

Lambon Ralph, M., Powell, J., Howard, D., Whitworth, A., Garrard, P., & Hodges, J. (2001). Semantic memory is impaired in both dementia with Lewy bodies and dementia of Alzheimer's type: A comparative neuropsychological study and literature review. *Journal of Neurology, Neurosurgery, and Psychiatry*, *70*, 149–156.

Lee, S., Wild, K., Hollnagel, C., & Grafman, J. (1999). Selective visual attention in patients with frontal lobe lesions or Parkinson's disease. *Neuropsychologia*, *37*, 595–604.

Levy, M., Cummings, J., Fairbanks, L., Masterman, D., Miller, B., Craig, A., et al. (1998). Apathy is not depression. *Journal of Neuropsychiatry and clinical neurosciences*, *10*(3), 314–319.

Lezak, M. D. (1995). *Neuropsychological assessment* (3rd ed.). Oxford: Oxford University Press.

Libon, D., Bogdanoff, B., Cloud, B., Skalina, S., Giovannetti, T., Gitlin, H., et al. (1998). Declarative and procedural learning, quantitative measures of the hippocampus, and subcortical white alterations in Alzheimer's disease and ischemia vascular dementia. *Journal of Clinical and Experimental Neuropsychology*, *20*, 30–41.

Lines, C., Dawson, C., Preston, G., Reich, S., Foster, C., & Traub, M. (1991). Memory and attention in patients with senile dementia of the Alzheimer type and in normal elderly subjects. *Journal of Clinical and Experimental Neuropsychology*, *13*, 691–702.

Liotti, M., Ramig, L., Vogel, D., Cook, C., Ingham, R., Ingham, J., et al. (2003). Hypophonia in Parkinson disease: Neural correlates of voice treatment revealed by PET. *Neurology*, *1–2*, 432–440.

Lyons, K., Kemper, S., LaBarge, E., & Ferraro, F. (1994). Oral language and Alzheimer's disease: A reduction in syntactic complexity. *Aging & Cognition*, *1*, 271–281.

March, E., Wales, R., & Pattison, P. (2003). Language use in normal ageing and dementia of the Alzheimer type. *Clinical Psychologist*, *7*, 44–49.

Massman, P., Butters, N., & Delis, D. (1994). Some comparisons of verbal deficits in Alzheimer dementia, Huntington disease, and depression. In V. O. B. Emery & T. E. Oxman (Eds.), *Dementia: Presentations, differential diagnosis, and nosology* (pp. 232–248). BaltimoreD: Johns Hopkins University Press.

Mathias, J. (1996). Reading disorder in Alzheimer-type dementia. In R. Morris (Ed.), *The cognitive neuropsychology of Alzheimer-type dementia* (pp. 149–165). Oxford: Oxford University Press.

McCaffrey, R., Duff, K., & Solomon, G. (2000). Olfactory dysfunction discriminates probably Alzheimer's dementia from major depression. *Journal of Neuropsychiatry and Clinical Neurosciences*, *12*, 29–33.

Miller, E. (1996). The assessment of dementia. In R. Morris (Ed.), *The cognitive neuropsychology of Alzheimer-type dementia* (pp. 291–309). Oxford: Oxford University Press.

Mori, E., Shimomura, T., Fujimori, M., Hirono, N., Imamura, T., Hashimoto, M., et al. (2000). Visuoperceptual impairment in dementia with Lewy bodies. *Archives of Neurology, 57*, 489–493.

Morris, J. C. (1993). The Clinical Dementia Rating (CDR): Current version and scoring rules. *Neurology, 43*, 2412–2414.

Morris, R. G. (1986). Short-term forgetting in senile dementia of the Alzheimer's type. *Cognitive Neuropsychology, 3*, 77–97.

Morris, R. G. (1996). Attentional and executive dysfunction. In R. Morris (Ed.), *The cognitive neuropsychology of Alzheimer-type dementia* (pp. 49–70). Oxford: Oxford University Press.

Morris, R. G., & Kopelman, M. D. (1986). The memory deficits in Alzheimer-type dementia: a review. *Quarterly Journal of Experimental Psychology, 38*(4), 575–602.

Moss, H., Kopelman, M., Cappelletti, M., Davies, P., & Jaldow, E. (2003). Lost for words or loss of memories? Autobiographical Memory in semantic dementia. *Cognitive Neuropsychology, 20*, 703–732.

Nebes, R. (1989). Semantic memory in Alzheimer's disease. *Psychological Bulletin, 106*, 377–394.

Neils, J., Brennan, M., Cole, M., Boller, F., & Gerdeman, B. (1988). The use of phonemic cueing with Alzheimer's disease patients. *Neuropsychologia, 26*, 351–354.

Nicholas, M., Obler, L., Albert, M., & Helms-Estabrooks, N. (1985). Empty speech in Alzheimer's disease and fluent aphasia. *Journal of Speech and Hearing Research, 28*, 405–410.

Noble, K., Glosser, G., & Grossman, M. (2000). Oral reading in dementia. *Brain and Language, 74*, 48–69.

Noe, E., Marder, K., Bell, K., Jacobs, D., Manly, J., & Stern, Y. (2004). Comparison of dementia with Lewy bodies to Alzheimer's disease and Parkinson's disease with dementia. *Movement Disorders, 19*, 60–67.

Nordin, S., & Murphy, C. (1998). Odor memory in normal aging and Alzheimer's disease. *Annals of the New York Academy of Sciences, 855*, 686–693.

Norman, D. A., and Shallice, T. (1986). Attention to action: Willed and automatic control of behaviour. In R. J. Davidson, G. E. Schwartz, & D. Shapiro (Eds.), *Consciousness and self-regulation* (Vol. 4, pp. 1–18). New York: Plenum.

Obler, L. (1983). Language and brain function in dementia. In S. Segalowitz (Ed.), *Language functions and brain organization*. New York: Academic Press.

Obler, B., Dronkers, N., Koss, E., Delis, D., & Friedland, R. (1986). Retrieval from semantic memory in Alzheimer-type dementia. *Journal of Clinical Experimental Neuropsychology, 8*, 75–92.

Patterson, K., Graham, N., & Hodges, J. (1994). Reading in dementia of the Alzheimer type: A preserved ability? *Neuropsychology, 8*, 395–407.

Pell, M., & Leonard, C. (2005). Facial expression decoding in early Parkinson's disease. *Cognitive Brain Research, 23*, 327–340.

Perry, R., & Hodges, J. (1999). Attention and executive deficits in Alzheimer's disease. A critical review. *Brain, 122*, 383–404.

Perry, R., & Hodges, J. (2000). Differentiating frontal and temporal variant frontotemporal dementia from Alzheimer's disease. *Neurology, 54*, 2277–2284.

Perry, R., Watson, P., & Hodges, J. (2000). The nature and staging of attention dysfunction in early (minimal and mild) Alzheimer's disease: Relationship to episodic and semantic memory impairment. *Neuropsychologia, 38*, 252–271.

Pillon, B., Deweer, B., Michon, A., Malapani, C., Agid, Y., & DuBois, B. (1994). Are explicit memory disorders of progressive supranuclear palsy related to damage to striatofrontal circuits? Comparison with Alzheimer's, Parkinson's, and Huntington's diseases. *Neurology, 44*, 1264–1270.

Pillon, B., Dubois, B., Lhermitte, F., & Agid, Y. (1986). Heterogeneity of cognitive impairment in progressive supranuclear palsy, Parkinson's disease, and Alzheimer's disease. *Neurology, 36*, 1179–1185.

Pillon, B., Dubois, B., Ploska, A., & Agid, Y. (1991). Severity and specificity of cognitive impairment in Alzheimer's, Huntington's, and Parkinson's, and progressive supranuclear palsy. *Neurology, 41*, 634–643.

Pinto, S., Thobois, S., Costes, N., Le Bars, D., Benabid, A., Broussolle, E., et al. (2004). Subthalamic nucleus stimulation and dysarthria in Parkinson disease: A PET study. *Brain: A Journal of Neurology, 127*(3), 602–625.

Potkins, D., Myint, P., Bannister, C., Tadros, G., Chithramohan, R., Swann, A., et al. (2003). Language impairment in dementia: impact on symptoms and care needs in residential homes. *International Journal of Geriatric Psychiatry, 18*, 1002–1006.

Rainville, C., Amieva, H., Lafont, S., Dartigues, J-F., Orgogozo, J-M., & Fabrigoule, C. (2002). *Archives of Clinical Neuropsychology, 17*, 513–530.

Rao, S., Leo, G., Bernardin, L., & Unverzagt, F. (1991). Cognitive dysfunction in multiple sclerosis. I. Frequency, patterns, and prediction. *Neurology, 41*, 685–691.

Rapcsak, S., Arthur, S., Bliklen, D., & Rubens, A. (1989). Lexical agraphia in Alzheimer's disease. *Archives of Neurology, 46*, 65–68.

Reed, B., Eberling, J., Mungas, D., Weiner, M., & Jagust, W. (2000). Memory failure has different mechanisms in subcortical stroke and Alzheimer's disease. *Annals of Neuroloogy, 48*, 275–284.

Reitan, R., & Wolfson, D. (1985). The Halstead-Reitan Neuropsychological Test Battery: Theory and clinical interpretation. Phoenix, AZ: Neuropsychology Press.

Ripich, D., & Terrell, B. (1988). Cohesion and coherence in Alzheimer's disease. *Journal of Speech and Hearing Disorders, 53*, 8–14.

Rizzo, M., Anderson, S., Dawson, J., & Nawrot, M. (2000). Vision and cognition in Alzheimer's disease. *Neuropsychologia, 38*, 1157–1169.

Rosen, H. J., Hartikainen, K. M., Jagust, W., Kramer, J., Reed, B., Cummings, J., et al. (2002). Utility of clinical criteria in differentiating frontotemporal lobar degeneration (FTLD) from AD. *Neurology, 58*, 1608–1615.

Rosen, H., Pace-Savitsky, K., Perry, R., Kramer, J., Miller, B., & Levenson, R. (2004). Recognition of emotion in the frontal and temporal variants of frontotemporal dementia. *Dementia and Geriatric Cognitive Disorders, 17*, 277–281.

Rosser, A., & Hodges, J. (1994). Initial letter and semantic category fluency in Alzheimer's disease, Huntington's disease, and progressive supranuclear palsy. *Journal of Neurology, Neurosurgery, and Psychiatry, 57*, 1389–1394.

Rusted, J., & Sheppard, L. (2002). Action-based memory in Alzheimer's disease: a longitudinal look at tea making. *Neurocase, 8*(1–2), 111–126.

Sadek, J., Johnson, S., White, D., Salmon, D., Taylor, K., DeLaPena, J., et al. (2004). Retrograde amnesia in dementia: Comparison of HIV-associated dementia, Alzheimer's disease, and Huntington's disease. *Neuropsychology, 18*, 692–699.

Sagar, H., Cohen, N., Sullivan, E., Corkin, S., & Growdon, J. (1988). Remote memory function in Alzheimer's disease and Parkinson's disease. *Brain, 111*, 185–206.

Sailor, K., Antoine, M., Diaz, M., Kuslansky, G., & Kluger, A. (2004). The effects of Alzheimer's disease on item output in verbal fluency tasks. *Neuropsychology, 18*, 306–314.

Salmon, D., & Fennema-Notestine, C. (1996). Implicit memory. In R. G. Morris (Ed.), *The cognitive neuropsychology of Alzheimer-type dementia* (pp. 105–127). Oxford: Oxford University Press.

Salmon, D., Kwo-on-Yuen, P., Heindel, W., Butters, N., & Thal, L. (1989). Differentiation of Alzheimer's disease and Huntington's disease with Dementia Rating Scale. *Archives of Neurology, 46*, 1204–1208.

Saint-Cyr, J., Taylor, A., & Lang, A. (1988). Procedural learning and neostriatal dysfunction in man. *Brain, 111*, 941–959.

Sartori, G., Snitz, B., Sorcinelli, L., & Daum, I. (2004). Remote memory in advanced Alzheimer's disease. *Archives of Clinical Neuropsychology, 19*, 779–789.

Schacter, D. (1987). Implicit memory: History and current status. *Journal of Experimental Psychology, 13*, 501–518.

Schacter, D., & Tulving, E. (1994). *Memory systems 1994*. Cambridge, MA: MIT Press.

Schwartz, M., Marin, O., & Saffran, E. (1979). Dissociations of language function in dementia: A case study. *Brain and Language, 7*, 277–306.

Selnes, O., Carson, K., Rovner, B., & Gordon, B. (1988). Language dysfunction in early- and late-onset possible Alzheimer's disease. *Neurology, 38*, 1053–1056.

Shallice, T. (1982). Specific impairments of planning. *Philosophical Transactions of the Royal Society B: Biological Sciences, 298*, 199–209.

Shimomura, T., Mori, E., Yamashita, H., Imamura, T., Hirono, N., Hashimoto, M., et al. (1998). Cognitive loss in dementia with Lewy bodies and Alzheimer disease. *Archives of Neurology, 55*, 1547–1552.

Shuttleworth, E., & Huber, S. (1988). The naming disorder of dementia of Alzheimer type. *Brain and Language, 34*, 222–234.

Silveri, M., & Leggio, M. (1996). Influence of disorders of visual perception in word-to-picture matching tasks in patients with Alzheimer's disease. *Brain and Language, 54*, 326–334.

Simard, M., van Reekum, R., & Myran, D. (2003). Visuospatial impairment in dementia with Lewy bodies and Alzheimer's disease: a process analysis. *International Journal of Geriatric Psychiatry, 18*, 387–391.

Slachevsky, A., Villalpando, J., Sarazin, M., Hahn-Barma, V., Pillon, B., & Dubois, B. (2004). Frontal assessment battery and differential diagnosis of frontotemporal dementia and Alzheimer disease. *Archives of Neurology, 61*, 1104–1107.

Small, J., Kemper, S., & Lyons, K. (1997). Sentence comprehension in Alzheimer's disease: Effects of grammatical complexity, speech rate, and repetition. *Psychology & Aging, 12*, 3–11.

Snowden, J., Griffiths, H., & Neary, D. (1994). Semantic dementia: Autobiographical contribution to preservation of meaning. *Cognitive Neuropsychology, 11*, 265–288.

Snowdon, D. (2001). *Aging with grace*. New York: Bantam.

Sohlberg, M. M., & Mateer, C. (2001). *Introduction to cognitive rehabilitation: Theory and practice*. New York: Guilford.

Sprengelmeyer, R., Young, A. W., Mahn, K., Schroeder, U., Woitalla, D., Buttner, T., et al. (2003). Facial expression recognition in people with medicated and unmedicated Parkinson's disease. *Neuropsychologia, 41*(8), 1047–1057.

Stern, Y., Richards, M., Sano, M., & Mayeux, R. (1993). Comparison of cognitive changes in patients with Alzheimer's and Parkinson's disease. *Archives of Neurology, 50*, 1040–1045.

Uc, E., Rizzo, M., Anderson, W., Shi, Q., & Dawson, J. (2005). Driver landmark and traffic sign identification in early Alzheimer's disease. *Journal of Neurology, Neurosurgery, and Psychiatry, 76*, 764–768.

Ulatowska, H., Allard, L., & Donnell, A. (1988). Discourse performance in subjects with dementia of the Alzheimer type. In H. Whitaker (Ed.), *Neuropsychological studies in nonfocal brain damage* (pp. 108–131). New York: Springer-Verlag.

Ulatowska, H., & Chapman, S. (1995). Discourse studies. In R. Lubinski (Ed.), *Dementia and communication* (pp. 115–132). Philadelphia: Decker.

Van der Hurk, P., & Hodges, J. (1995). Episodic and semantic memory in Alzheimer's disease and progressive supranuclear palsy: A comparative study. *Journal of Clinical and Experimental Neuropsychology, 17*, 459–471.

Van Hoesen, G., & Damasio, A. (1987). Neural correlates of the cognitive impairment in Alzheimer's disease. In F. Plum (Ed.), *Handbook of physiology: The nervous system* (pp. 871–898). Baltimore: Williams & Wilkins.

Walker, M., Ayre, G., Cummings, J., Wesnes, K., McKeith, I., O'Brien, J., et al. (2000). Quantifying fluctuation in dementia with Lewy bodies, Alzheimer's disease, and vascular dementia. *Neurology, 54*, 1616–1624.

Waters, G., & Caplan, D. (2002). Working memory and online syntactic processing in Alzheimer's disease: Studies with auditory moving window presentation. *Journal of Gerontology, 57B*, P298–311.

Welland, R., Lubinski, R., & Higginbotham, D. (2002). Discourse Comprehension Test performance of elders with dementia of the Alzheimer type. *Journal of Speech, Language, & Hearing Research, 45*, 1175–1187.

Whelihan, W., DiCarlo, M., & Paul, R. (2005). The relationship of neuropsychological functioning to driving competence in older persons with early cognitive decline. *Archives of Clinical Neuropsychology, 20*(2), 217–228.

Whittington, C., Podd, J., & Kan, M. (2000). Recognition memory impairment in Parkinson's disease: power and meta-analyses. *Neuropsychology, 14*, 233–246.

Williams, B., Mack, W., & Henderson, V. (1989). Boston Naming Test in Alzheimer's disease. *Neuropsychologia, 27*, 1073–1079.

Willis, S. (1993). *Test manual for the Everyday Problems Test for Cognitively Challenged Elderly*. University Park: Pennsylvania State University.

Willis, S. L., Allen-Burge, R., Dolan, M., Bertrand, R., Yesavage, J., & Taylor, J. (1998). Everyday problem solving among individuals with Alzheimer's disease. *The Gerontologist, 38*, 569–577.

Ylvisaker, M., & Feeney, T. (1998). A Vygotskyan approach to rehabilitation after TBI: A case illustration. *Special Interest Division 2: Neurophysiology and Neurogenic Speech and Language Disorders Newsletter, 8*, 14–18.

Youmans, G. (2004). *Theory of mind performance of individuals with Alzheimer-type dementia profiles*. Unpublished doctoral dissertation, Florida State University, Tallahassee.

Zgaljardic, D., Borod, J., Foldi, N., & Mattis, P. (2003). A review of the cognitive and behavioral sequelae of Parkinson's disease: Relationship to frontostriatal circuitry. *Cognitive and Behavioral Neurology, 16*, 193–210.

4

Assessment

Cognitive, Communicative, and Behavioral Characteristics

The specific cognitive, communicative, and functional strengths and deficits associated with dementia are important to assess for appropriate functional management. According to the American Speech-Language-Hearing Association (ASHA; 2005), "[S]peech-language pathologists (SLPs) play a primary role in the assessment, diagnosis, and treatment of ... adults with cognitive-communicative disorders" (p. 3; see also ASHA, 2004). Factors to consider in planning for assessment, types of assessment procedures to consider, and specific tools will be described. This chapter will briefly outline the assessment of dementia, from a global dementia-rating perspective, to a more comprehensive diagnostic perspective; the focus will be on assessment for treatment planning and treatment potential.

FACTORS TO CONSIDER IN PLANNING FOR ASSESSMENT

First, the type of information the referral source seeks to gain will dictate the purpose and nature of an assessment. Examples of potential referral sources include physicians, other rehabilitation professionals, family caregivers, or the client themselves. The type of information the referral source seeks may vary according to level of care being provided, such as acute care, subacute rehabilitation, long-term care, or home care. Referral sources may want to know if the client shows signs of a disease or injury, the level of care needed for discharge planning, if the client demonstrates a change in condition (increase or decrease in function), if the client has benefited from treatment, or if the client shows potential to benefit from treatment. Various types of assessment will be used for these purposes, with some overlap when dealing with functional management issues (e.g., assessment for functional outcomes of treatment will overlap with determining level of care needed upon discharge).

Second, a clinician's assumptions and knowledge of the effects of normal aging on cognition and communication will influence the choice of assessment tasks and interpretations. Although dementia is not a result of normal aging, cognitive processes do slow with age, which may affect a variety of communicative processes. Many standardized tests of language and cognition do not include elderly persons in the normative samples. Thus, test norms must be interpreted cautiously if normative data for upper age ranges are limited or nonexistent. In addition, examiners must be able to recognize and accommodate age-related sensory limitations to ensure optimal test performance. Elders may need larger print size or a modified background (e.g., a yellow background with large black print) to enhance processing of written or picture stimuli; or they may have marked difficulty attending to auditory stimuli in a noisy testing environment. In addition, if the purpose of assessment is to determine appropriate service needs, practitioners should be aware that recommendations for rehabilitation might be biased by one's perception of an older person's potential for treatment success.

Furthermore, given the limitations of standardized tests, decisions about rehabilitation and placement should be based on the functional and realistic needs of the individual derived from a variety of assessments, and not solely from standardized test results. Thus, given the focus of dementia management on functional needs, functional assessment is imperative. ASHA describes functional assessment of communication as measurement of the ability to communicate in daily living contexts, taking into consideration environmental modifications, adaptive equipment, the time required to communicate, and the listener's familiarity with the client (ASHA, 2004). The focus of functional communication assessment should be to identify communication strengths, or abilities, while taking into consideration the severity of the communication problem and the client's premorbid lifestyle and future wants and needs.

Finally, there are a variety of tools available for assessment, including formal and informal measures, and observational and interview protocols. Various tools are more likely to be used by specific members of the interdisciplinary team (e.g., the physician or neurologist, neuropsychologists, nurse, and/or the SLP). Specific tools should be chosen in accordance with the purpose of the assessment and the level of the client's functioning that is being assessed, as defined by the World Health Organization's (WHO) International Classification of Functioning, Disability, and Health (ICF; WHO, 2001). Assessment can take place at any of the ICF levels: structures and functions, activities and participation, quality of life, and contextual factors. Regardless of the tools used, individual characteristics of a client must be considered when interpreting assessment results.

Types of Assessment

The purpose of the assessment will determine the type of evaluation procedures used, such as screenings, diagnostic evaluations, and assessments for treatment planning and functional outcomes. Screenings are designed to determine if there is a problem or a change in condition (at any ICF level) that warrants a more detailed evaluation. Diagnostic evaluations are designed to identify specific impairments in structures and functions that may contribute to a differential diagnosis, and are often part of a larger medical team evaluation with neurology and neuropsychology. Assessment for treatment planning is designed to identify the client's functional needs and limitations, as well as areas of strength that will assist in maintaining or improving functional behaviors, usually at the levels of activities and participation and/or quality of life. Assessment for treatment planning includes a careful examination of contextual factors that influence behavior. In planning for functional outcomes, the clinician will identify how treating the cognitive, language, and communication deficits will affect the client's functioning.

Screening procedures will vary depending on the type of facility and its policies. The Omnibus Budget Reconciliation Act of 1987 called for periodic reassessments of long-term care residents to ensure that they are functioning at their maximum potential (American Health Care Association, 1990). In most facilities, these screenings are conducted on a quarterly basis, or minimally twice per year. In a screening, the clinician seeks evidence to identify a change in condition, which may be either an increase or decrease in body structure and function, and/or activities and participation. In many nursing homes, screening procedures include only a chart review and possibly an interview with caregivers; hands-on assessment with the resident is not permitted unless a referral for a full evaluation is received. The medical record must include evidence for change in condition, as documented by nurses, physicians, or other therapists. This evidence may be in the professionals' notes, but important data are often found in the Resident Assessment Instrument (RAI), which is the standardized assessment tool used in long-term care facilities. The RAI is composed of the Minimum Data Set (MDS) and the Resident Assessment Protocols (RAPs), which document over 100 behaviors including cognitive and communicative functioning (Hawes et al., 1997).

BOX 4.1 EXAMPLES OF A CHANGE IN CONDITION

1. Indicating an increase in body functions, activities, and/or participation

   The nurses' notes indicate, "Mrs. Jones is much more alert than she has been since admission, and is beginning to demonstrate agitated behaviors." This increased alertness would indicate that she may be better able to participate in rehabilitation efforts, whereas the increased agitation would indicate a new functional need.
2. Indicating a decrease in body functions, activities, and/or participation

   The nurses' notes indicate that a client has been refusing to eat solid foods, has lost weight, has not been participating in social activities, and has significantly decreased interaction with staff in the past month. This would indicate a decrease in functional status, as well as decreases in activities and participation that may benefit from rehabilitation services.

In community settings, a screening usually includes brief formal and/or informal assessments, including an interview with the client and caregiver and brief depression, discourse, orientation, memory task, and/or global cognitive measures (e.g., the Mini-Mental State Exam [MMSE]; Folstein, Folstein, & McHugh, 1975). Community screenings may have the benefit of earlier detection and referral for dementia diagnosis than traditional methods of referral, such as primary care physician referral (Barker et al., 2005). Regardless of the location or format of screening, if a change in condition or a disease process is suspected or identified, then a referral for a full evaluation should be obtained from the physician.

The type of evaluation that follows the screening will depend on whether there has been an evaluation to determine medical diagnosis. For example, someone who had suspected deficits identified at a community memory screening should be referred for a medical exam, which should lead to referrals for complete evaluations by neurology, neuropsychology, and speech-language pathology. If the purpose of the evaluation is medical diagnosis, then the clinician may help to identify a disease process or course of a disease, or may help to pinpoint the location of the lesion (e.g., cortical versus subcortical signs). During the process of diagnostic evaluations that result in the person's diagnosis of dementia, a full complement of language and cognitive assessment batteries should be completed. In terms of cognitive-communicative diagnosis, the clinician will determine the type and severity of communication disorders, as well as communication strengths. For someone who already has a medical diagnosis of dementia (e.g., a nursing home resident), the purpose will more often be assessment for treatment planning, which should focus on identifying problem areas as well as strengths. After identifying the purpose and type of assessment to conduct, the clinician then collects information, forms hypotheses, tests those hypotheses, and then revises those hypotheses, as needed, by acquiring additional information.

Assessment Procedures

The clinician immediately formulates, tests, and revises hypotheses using formal and informal testing procedures. See Table 4.1 for a summary of the pros and cons of various types of assessment procedures used in treatment planning and for examples of commonly used measures. Regardless of the setting, functional assessment tools may include interview protocols, observations, checklists, and formal and informal tests. The clinician first collects case history data from any available medical records and interviews with the client and/or caregiver(s). The interview is designed to gather information regarding specific client and caregiver concerns and personal and medical history, and (if for the purpose of treatment planning) the client's and caregiver's preferred treatment goals, and desired treatment outcomes. Other aspects to cover in the case history include the client's previous and current activities and interests, the level of current and future participation, and supports and barriers to participation. Specific assessment and trial therapy tasks can then be chosen based on known sensory needs and case history information. Persons who live in residential facilities may have more caregivers and different treatment needs than persons living in their own homes.

TABLE 4.1 Advantages and Disadvantages of Common Assessment Tools for Treatment Planning

Types and Tests	Advantages	Disadvantages
Standardized global cognitive measures:		
• Mini-Mental State Examination (Folstein, Folstein, & McHugh, 1975) • Burns Brief Inventory of Communication and Cognition (Burns, 1997) • Montreal Cognitive Assessment (Nasreddine et al., 2003) • Global Deterioration Scale (Reisberg, Ferris, deLeon, & Crook, 1982)	Obtain ballpark idea of functioning and severity level	Not specific enough to determine individual's strengths and weaknesses
Standardized test battery for impairments:		
• Arizona Battery for Communication Disorders in Dementia (Bayles & Tomoeda, 1993)	Comprehensive measure that documents impairments; may identify relative strength areas	Too lengthy to give in one sitting; may not help identify successful, functional treatment domains; and not sensitive to changes due to treatment
Standardized test batteries for activities:		
• Functional Linguistic Communication Inventory (Bayles & Tomoeda, 1994) • Rivermead Behavioural Memory Test (Wilson, Cockburn, & Baddeley, 1985)	More functional tasks; may indicate types of cues and stimuli to use for treatment	Tasks may be too decontextualized to give indicator of everyday communication abilities; and not sensitive to changes due to treatment
Functional assessment tools:		
• Bourgeois Oral Reading Screen (Bourgeois, 1992b; see Appendix 4.4) • Spaced Retrieval Screen (Brush & Camp, 1998; see Appendix 4.5)	Determines expectation for effectiveness of cues and learning potential; brief	Stimuli may not be personally relevant
Assessment of problem behaviors:		
• Behavioral Pathology in Alzheimer's Disease Rating Scale (BEHAVE-AD; Reisberg et al., 1987) • Cohen-Mansfield Agitation Inventory (Cohen-Mansfield, 1986)	Important for identifying treatment goals based on specific behaviors to increase or decrease	Requires input from others (family and professionals)

(*Continued*)

TABLE 4.1 (Continued)

Types and Tests	Advantages	Disadvantages
• The Nursing Home Behavior Problem Scale (Ray, Taylor, Lichtenstein, & Meador, 1992)		
• Caregiver interview and forms (behavior diary and behavior log; Bourgeois & Hopper, 2005, Tables 3–5)		
Observational protocols:		
• Functional Goals Screening Protocol: Community Clients With Dementia (Bourgeois, & Rozsa, 2006; see Appendix 4.1)	Important for identifying treatment goals, cueing strategies, and setting specifics (partners, activities, and locations)	Requires observation over time, different locations, and multiple informants
• Screening Protocol to Monitor Residents With Dementia (Rozsa & Bourgeois, 2006; see Appendix 4.6)		
Interview protocols:		
• Personal Wants, Needs, and Safety Assessment Form (Bourgeois, in press; see Appendix 4.1)	Necessary for personalized treatment materials and appropriate goal planning	Requires input from others (family and professionals)
• Memory Aid Information Form (community version) (Bourgeois, 1992b; see Appendix 4.2)		
• Memory Aid Information Form—Nursing Home Version (Bourgeois, 1992b; see Appendix 4.3)		

There are pros and cons of formal and informal assessment procedures. These procedures may also be described as static versus dynamic assessment procedures (Turkstra et al., 2005). Static assessment involves the use of standardized tests according to administration protocol. Formal tests of language and cognitive functioning may help to establish a diagnosis, make a prognosis, and ensure a thorough survey of all dimensions of language and/or cognition. An advantage is that they may simplify the process of communicating with other professionals if there is mutual familiarity with the instruments. Over time, a skilled clinician will acquire vast amounts of information from administration of a familiar battery to interpret the client's performance on these tests; however, clinicians must be aware of the many biases that exist in standardized measures, particularly with regard to the age, education, and cultural background of the person being assessed (Crum, Anthony, Bassett, & Folstein, 1993; Dufouil et al., 2000; Jones & Gallo, 2002; Mungas, Marshall, Weldon, Haan, & Reed, 1996; Sloan & Wang, 2005).

Other potential limitations include over- or undertesting, lack of sensitivity, lack of specificity, lack of ecological validity, and failure to uncover reasons for difficulties or to uncover strategies or factors that may improve performance (Turkstra et al.; Ylvisaker & Feeney, 1998; Ylvisaker, Szekeres, & Feeney, 2001). Thus, in assessment for treatment planning, hypotheses generated by standardized instruments should also be tested in more ecologically valid contexts.

Dynamic testing involves manipulation of formal or informal test procedures to determine what accounts for success or failure in tasks (e.g., changing length, complexity, or physical characteristics of stimuli, or providing feedback or other types of support; Turkstra et al., 2005; Ylvisaker & Feeney, 1998; Ylvisaker et al., 2001). Informal or dynamic assessment can be invaluable in tailoring assessments for individual needs and for treatment planning. Carefully designed interviews, observations, and experiments in natural settings can make up for most of the concerns of formal testing. Limitations of informal assessment include biased interpretations of results due to lack of norms. Inexperienced clinicians may have difficulty interpreting findings if the behaviors observed are not extreme or do not fit into an obvious pattern. Furthermore, replication of informal assessment procedures to compare performance over time or across clients can be challenging, due to a lack of standardized procedures. Despite these challenges, dynamic assessment is useful to identify factors that can be manipulated to improve performance, and to determine how strengths can be used to compensate for cognitive and communicative needs (Ylvisaker & Feeney). The clinician may identify the starting point for a treatment plan and develop a hierarchy of difficulty for the individual, which may vary from client to client.

ASSESSMENT OF BODY STRUCTURES AND FUNCTIONS (IMPAIRMENT)

Differential diagnosis usually involves assessment of body structures and functions (i.e., their impairments and strengths; WHO, 2001), with identification of strengths and weaknesses in cognitive, linguistic, and motor skills. Clinicians should keep in mind that diagnostic assessment tends to be impairment oriented, which may encourage impairment-oriented intervention. This is often *not* the most effective approach for individuals with dementia, for whom cognitive processing treatments are not recommended (Holland, 2003). Thus, identification of both deficits and strengths is particularly important in assessment for treatment planning, as the clinician seeks to develop compensatory strategies for impairments by capitalizing on strengths. Assessment of body structures and functions can identify strengths in reading comprehension and oral reading abilities in persons with Alzheimer's disease (AD), which can be used to develop written cues for conversation and memory (Bourgeois, 1992a). Specific types of impairment-based assessment procedures are described below. Tools that were designed specifically for persons with dementia will be described in the most detail. It should be noted that clinicians do often use other standardized instruments that were developed to assess cognition in general, or that were designed for other populations. A thorough discussion of these tools is beyond the scope of this chapter, as many neuropsychological measures were designed to measure discrete domains of behavior to quantify and localize brain damage (Farah & Feinberg, 2000; Lezak, Howieson, & Loring, 2004). The focus of this chapter is functional assessment for treatment planning. Thus, impairment-based measures that lack ecological validity are not often the most useful tools in assessment for treatment planning or for measuring functional outcomes. There are other valuable resources for comprehensive overviews of such tools that assess impairments, such as Lezak et al.'s (2004) *Neuropsychological Assessment*, 4th ed., which is used widely by neuropsychologists.

Sensory Screening

Regardless of the purpose for assessment, procedures should include screenings of sensory functioning (i.e., hearing and vision). This will ensure that the cues delivered for functional and compensatory treatment strategies are appropriate for the sensory abilities of the client. The Minimum Data Set (MDS; Hawes et al., 1997) includes general, functional items regarding hearing and vision (Box 4.2). In addition, an SLP should conduct a pure-tone audiometric screening, conduct word recognition testing, and check hearing aids. Vision screening should include checking the condition of the client's glasses and functional visual recognition. Simply washing the client's glasses and making sure that they are worn properly may influence a client's ability to perform on a test. Vision screening can also include the client's recognition of signs in the environment and ability to read one's name utilizing a variety of print sizes. The clinician should also make observations regarding the client's scanning and attention to right and left visual fields.

Global Dementia Rating Scales

Interview-Based Rating Scales Mental status rating scales are used to translate cognitive impairments into global stages of diseases, or severity of cognitive deficits. This can be useful for classifying clients and predicting relative treatment outcomes (Albert, 1994). There are two types of mental status rating scales: interview based and client administered. Interview-based protocols include measures such as the Clinical Dementia Rating Scale (CDR; Morris, 1993), the Global Deterioration Scale for Age-Related Cognitive Decline and Alzheimer's Disease (GDS; Reisberg, Ferris, deLeon, & Crook, 1982), the Clinician Interview-Based Impression of Change—Plus Caregiver Information (CIBIC+; Schneider & Olin, 1997), and the Symptoms of Dementia Screener (SDS; Mundt, Freed, & Greist, 2000). These protocols are designed to be administered to a caregiver informant by a skilled clinician (e.g., the CDR, GDS, and CIBIC+) or by a layperson (e.g., the SDS). The caregivers provide information regarding behavioral functioning, from which the clinician subjectively evaluates clients' cognitive skills (e.g., memory, orientation, judgment, problem solving, community affairs, home and hobbies, personal care, psychiatric symptoms, and performance on psychometric tests). Jorm (1996) reported that there is ample evidence for the reliability and

BOX 4.2 HEARING AND VISION SCREENING QUESTIONS FROM THE MINIMUM DATA SET (MDS)

Hearing (with hearing appliance, if used):
- Hears adequately: normal talk, TV, phone
- Minimal difficulty when not in quiet setting
- Hears in special situations only—speaker has to adjust tonal quality and speak distinctly
- Highly impaired, or absence of, useful hearing

Communication devices and techniques (check all that apply during last 7 days):
- Hearing aid, present and used
- Hearing aid, present and not used regularly
- Other reception communication techniques used (e.g., lip reading)

Vision (ability to see in adequate light and with glasses, if used):
- Adequate: sees fine detail, including regular print in newspapers and books
- Impaired: sees large print, but not regular print in newspapers and books
- Moderately impaired: limited vision; not able to see newspaper headlines, but can identify objects
- Highly impaired: object identification in question but eyes appear to follow objects
- Severely impaired: no vision or sees only light, colors, or shapes; eyes do not appear to follow objects

Visual limitations or difficulties:
- Side vision problems: decreased peripheral vision (e.g., leaves food on one side of tray, difficulty traveling, bumps into people and objects, and misjudges placement of chair when seating self)
- Experiences: sees halos or rings around lights, sees flashes of light, sees "curtains" over eyes

Visual appliances: Glasses, contact lenses, magnifying glass

validity of informant-based scales for assessing cognitive impairment and decline in dementia.

The CDR involves interviews with both the client and the caregiver. There are seven domain scores: memory, orientation, judgment, problem solving, community activities, home and hobbies, and personal care. Each item is scored on a

5-point scale from 0 (no impairment) to 3 (severe dementia). The CDR differentiates the types of impairment profiles seen in AD, frontotemporal dementia (FTD), and semantic dementia (SD) (Rosen et al., 2004). The GDS rates seven severity levels, or stages, of dementia: for example, 1 (normal), 3 (early confusion), 5 (middle dementia), and 7 (late dementia). Clinicians determine the GDS score using all sources of available information, which might include a structured interview regarding cognitive, behavioral, and functional abilities, including memory, orientation, judgment, problem solving, community affairs, home and hobbies, personal care, psychiatric symptoms, and performance on psychometric tests. Clinicians should be aware that the GDS might underestimate the communicative abilities of persons with severe dementia (Bayles, Tomoeda, Cruz, & Mahendra, 2000). The CIBIC+ is used often in clinical trials, with scores based on interviews with both the participants and their caregivers. The CIBIC+ evaluates four domains: general, cognitive, behavioral, and activities of daily living (ADLs). The SDS consists of 11 questions regarding memory, psychiatric symptoms, ADLs, and instrumental ADLs (IADLs). Three or more caregiver responses of "yes" signify a positive dementia screen. Advantages of the SDS are ease of use by nonclinical personnel, administration by mail or by telephone, simplicity of comprehension by caregivers, and potential anonymity of responses (Mundt et al., 2000). The SDS developers (Mundt et al.) also suggested that persons who are concerned about onset of dementia or cognitive decline could respond to the questions themselves.

Client-Administered Scales The best-known client-administered mental status rating scale is the MMSE (Folstein et al., 1975). This tool is used widely in long-term care settings as well as physicians' offices and other health care settings because it is quick to administer, and gives a broad idea of a client's cognitive functioning. The MMSE screens orientation to time and place, language (name two objects, repeat a sentence, follow a three-step command, read aloud and follow a written command, and write a sentence), visuospatial construction (design copy), immediate and delayed verbal memory (three-word recall), and mental control (count backward from 100 by 7, or spell *world* backward). Severity levels are determined by criterion scores. Because it is used so frequently, the MMSE simplifies communication across health care providers who are familiar with the interpretation of its scores and cognitive severity levels; however, several problems have been identified with its use. First, scores are influenced by a variety of variables (e.g., education, race, sex, and age; Crum et al., 1993; Dufouil et al., 2000; Jones & Gallo, 2002; Mungas et al., 1996; Sloan & Wang, 2005). Crum and colleagues suggested different cutoff scores for normal performance based on education: 29/30 for persons with 9 to 12 years of education; 26/30 for persons with 5 to 8 years of schooling, and 22/30 for persons with 0 to 4 years of schooling. Second, the tasks are highly dependent on language abilities, so persons with focal language disturbances will likely appear to be more cognitively impaired than they are. In addition, the sensitivity of the MMSE is not adequate to identify early symptoms of AD and mild cognitive impairment (MCI). Yet, the sensitivity of the MMSE to cognitive change in drug trials has been demonstrated (Mohs, 2006).

Due to the problems with the MMSE, particularly the narrow range of possible scores and ceiling effects, researchers have developed a Modified MMSE, known as the 3MS (Jones et al., 2002). In addition to the items in the MMSE, the 3MS includes items for date and place of birth, word fluency, similarities, and delayed recall of words. Scores may range from 0 to 100, and may also yield an MMSE score, if desired. The psychometric characteristics have been studied, and normative data are provided for a sample of elderly Canadians who have lower education (Tombaugh, McDowell, Kristjansson, & Hubley, 1996), and for an elderly American sample with a broad range of education by Jones et al. An advantage of the 3MS, with use of the Jones et al. norms, is that education-adjusted scores can be obtained (e.g., adding raw score points for low education). A weakness of both normative studies is the lack of racial and ethnic diversity in the samples. Jones et al. reported that the 3MS has better reliability and sensitivity than the MMSE.

Researchers have worked to construct brief tests that have adequate sensitivity and specificity for detecting dementia. One such test is the 7-minute screen, or 7MS (Solomon et al., 1998), which is a combination of items from other existing tests: temporal orientation (Benton, 1983), enhanced cued recall (Grober & Buschke, 1988), verbal fluency, and clock drawing. A total score can be calculated, but if the person scores in the abnormal range on at least two subtests, then dementia is likely. The 7MS has higher sensitivity than the MMSE for detecting cognitive deficits from early AD and other dementias, as well as MCI, but poorer specificity with regard to other psychiatric diagnoses, such as depression (Meulen et al., 2005). Meulen and colleagues also reported that the 7MS is possibly more susceptible than the MMSE to biases due to education, age, and culture.

Likewise, the Montreal Cognitive Assessment (MoCA; Nasreddine et al., 2005) is a reliable global cognitive measure that is more sensitive than the MMSE in detecting early AD and MCI. The MoCA screens a variety of cognitive and language processes: attention (trails, digit span, and serial 7s), orientation, visuoconstructional skills (cube and clock draw), delayed word recall, and language (confrontation naming, repetition, verbal fluency, and abstraction). There are 30 possible points on the MoCA, with the cutoff score for "normal" at 26.

The Brief Kingston Standardized Cognitive Assessment—Revised (*Brief*KSCA-R; Hopkins, Kilik, Day, Rows, & Hamilton, 2005) was developed as a screening tool that can be administered by professionals without expertise in cognitive testing. The eight subtests assess memory with four tasks (orientation, word recall, delayed recall, and word recognition), visual-motor abilities with three tasks (clock drawing, spatial reversal, and perseveration), and verbal abilities with one task (abstract thinking). This test also provides rating scales to assess the quality of behaviors observed during testing. The *Brief*KSCA-R can be administered in about 15 minutes. The maximum score is 62, and the tool is sensitive to early cognitive impairments by comparing the client's score to distribution curves of typical adults and those with dementias, rather than a single cutoff score. Psychometric properties are adequate.

The Alzheimer's Quick Test (AQT; Wiig, Nielsen, Minthon, & Warkentin, 2002) is another test that is sensitive to early cognitive decline of persons with MCI or dementia. The AQT can be administered in approximately 5 to 10 minutes.

The AQT includes five sets of timed naming tasks, with scoring for both accuracy and timing of responses, which results in criterion-referenced scores that fall in ranges of normal, less accurate or slower than normal, nonnormal, and pathological. Advantages of the AQT are good reliability for repeated administration, sensitivity to early parietal lobe dysfunction, and utility with a broad range of ages and cultural backgrounds. The AQT has been standardized on persons aged 15 to 72. Results can be interpreted according to various dementia profiles.

Another brief screening to detect early dementias includes just two tasks: a memory recall task and a verbal fluency task (Kilada et al., 2005). The memory task is a repetition task of the phrase, "John Brown 42 Market Street Chicago," and the verbal fluency task is the generation of animal names for one minute. Use of these two tasks was found to be more sensitive and specific than the MMSE in individuals with memory complaints.

A screening test developed specifically for use by SLPs, but not specifically for dementia, is the Cognitive-Linguistic Quick Test (CLQT; Helm-Estabrooks, 2001). The CLQT can be completed in less than 30 minutes, and assesses orientation, attention, verbal and visual memory, confrontation naming, auditory comprehension, and executive functions. The CLQT includes the clock-drawing task (Freedman et al., 1994), which is sensitive to attention, memory, executive functions, and visuospatial construction deficits, and is particularly well suited to persons with lower education levels (Barrie, 2002; Royall, Cordes, & Polk, 1998). The CLQT provides subscale scores and severity levels for attention, memory, language, and executive functions, as well as a global score and severity level. The CLQT also provides a separate perseveration score, which is a sensitive indicator of brain injury (Helm-Estabrooks). Norms are provided for persons 18–89 years old, and the nonclinical standardization samples included African American, Latino, and White participants. The clinical standardization sample had fewer minorities, and included persons with right-, left-, and bilateral hemisphere strokes, closed head injury, and AD. The CLQT is also available in Spanish. Test–retest reliability is adequate for most tasks; interrater reliability and validity are adequate.

Some other reliable standardized cognitive measures that are used frequently include the Blessed Dementia Scale (BDS; Blessed, Tomlinson, & Roth, 1968), which consists of functional and mental status assessment components, and the Cambridge Cognitive Examination (CAMCOG; Blessed, Block, Butters, & Kay, 1991), which is the neuropsychological component of the Cambridge Mental Disorders of the Elderly Examination (CAMDEX; Roth et al., 1986) and includes items from the MMSE, but is more effective in detecting dementia of different types (Lazaro et al., 1995). More thorough reviews of these measures are found in Kane and Kane (2000).

Comprehensive Dementia Assessment Batteries

There exist a variety of comprehensive assessment batteries of cognitive and behavioral functioning that assess the client at the body structure and function levels. SLPs and/or neuropsychologists assess structure and function in terms of cognition and language. Cognitive domains include attention, perception, memory, and executive functions (e.g., insight, inhibition, initiation, and planning). Language domains include spoken and written language production and auditory and reading comprehension. Global measures of cognition are preferable to specific cognitive assessment for severely impaired persons because they are generally brief, and can be completed by persons with shorter attention spans; furthermore, many of the tasks on specific cognitive assessments are decontextualized, making it even more difficult for persons with severe deficits to understand the tasks (Mungas, Reed, & Kramer, 2003). A brief description of some of the commonly used comprehensive batteries in dementia diagnosis follows.

The Dementia Rating Scale—2 (DRS-2; Jurica, Leitten, & Mattis, 2001) evaluates attention, initiation, construction, conceptualization, perseveration, praxis, abstraction, and verbal and nonverbal recent memory, with scores ranging from 0 to 144 (cutoff for mild impairment is 123). The DRS-2 can be used with adults ranging from 56 to 105 years old to sensitively measure and characterize degree of dementia, with performance profiles that differentiate AD from Parkinson's disease (PD) and Huntington's disease (HD) (Johnson-Greene, 2004; Mungas et al., 2003; Salmon, Kwo-on-Yuen, Heindel, Butters, & Thal, 1989). Advantages of the DRS-2 include its usefulness with persons with lower levels of cognitive function and as a longitudinal measure. A disadvantage of the DRS-2 is that it does not provide normative data for persons who have less than 8 years of education, or for ethnic minorities; however, it does provide age- and education-corrected normative data (Johnson-Greene).

The Consortium to Establish a Registry for Alzheimer's Disease Neuropsychological Assessment (CERAD; Welsh, Butters, & Mohs, 1994) battery includes subtests for language (e.g., verbal fluency and confrontation naming), constructional praxis, memory (free recall, and delayed recall and recognition), and the MMSE. When used with the CDR and the DRS, the CERAD battery can be used to obtain a diagnostic impression of AD alone, AD associated with other disorders, or non-AD dementia.

The Kaplan Baycrest Neurocognitive Assessment (KBNA; Leach, Kaplan, Rewilak, Richards, & Proulx, 2000) assesses attention and concentration, memory (immediate and delayed recall, and delayed recognition), verbal fluency, spatial processing, and reasoning and conceptual shifting. The KBNA provides standard scores and percentiles for each index and percentile categories (i.e., a low, medium, or high risk of cognitive impairment) for the process scores for persons 20 to 89 years. It requires approximately 1 hour to administer.

The Repeatable Battery for the Assessment of Neuropsychological Status (RBANS; Randolph, 1998) includes 12 subtests yielding six indices, such as visuospatial, memory, attention, and language abilities. Norms for standard scores are available for persons from 20 to 89 years old. Parallel forms were designed for repeated test administration to prevent learning effects. Test administration takes up to 30 minutes. The RBANS was designed to identify abnormal cognitive decline in older adults, and can be used in differentiating dementia types, including AD, HD (Randolph, Tierney, Mohr, & Chase, 1998), and PD (Beatty et al., 2003). Yet, Beatty and colleagues warned that the diagnosis of dementia should not be made using the RBANS alone. The RBANS can also be used to screen for cognitive deficits in younger adults with greater sensitivity than the MMSE and DRS (Randolph et al., 1998), as well as in older adults (Duff et al., 2005). Caution should be used in interpreting results for persons with lower education levels (Gontkovsky, Mold, & Beatty, 2002).

The Alzheimer's Disease Assessment Scale—Cognitive (ADAS-cog; Rosen, Mohs, & Davis, 1984) is a cognitive testing instrument widely used in clinical drug trials. The ADAS-cog consists of 11 items that measure memory (recognition and recall), language (comprehension and production), praxis (constructional and ideational), and orientation, and takes approximately 30 minutes to administer. There are 70 points possible, with an expected mean decline of 9 points per year in untreated persons with AD, and an increase of 3–4 points is likely to reflect clinical improvement (Mohs, 2006). Versions of the ADAS are also available in French, German, Spanish, Italian, Finnish, Korean, Danish, Greek, Hebrew, and Japanese.

The Severe Impairment Battery (SIB; Saxton, McGonigle-Gibson, Swihart, Miller, & Boller, 1990; see also Saxton, McGonigle, Swihart, & Boller, 1993) was developed specifically for persons with severe cognitive deficits, for whom other neuropsychological instruments are not sensitive to change or result in "floor" effects. The SIB allows these persons to participate in testing through use of gestural cues and by capitalizing on preserved skills. The SIB has norms for persons 51 to 91 years old, with strong psychometric properties and good reliability on repeated administration (Saxton et al., 1990; Schmitt et al., 1997). Thus, the SIB is useful in drug trials for participants with severe dementia. The SIB was designed to be administered by SLPs, occupational therapists, or neuropsychologists in approximately 30 minutes. For persons with very severe deficits, this testing may not be possible, so a short form was developed (SIB-S), which takes approximately 10 to 15 minutes to administer (Saxton et al., 2005). The SIB-S is as sensitive to change, and assesses the same nine cognitive domains, as the original SIB: expressive language, memory (verbal and nonverbal), social interaction, color naming, praxis, reading, writing, fluency, and attention. An advantage of the SIB is that standardized translations are available in German, French, and Italian. The SIB-S was tested in English and French.

Due to the many limitations on the use of many cognitive-linguistic measures with clients with dementia, Bayles and Tomoeda (1993) developed a comprehensive assessment battery, the Arizona Battery of Communication in Dementia (ABCD). The ABCD includes 4 screening tasks (speech discrimination, visual perception, visual field, and visual agnosia) and 14 subtests in the areas of mental status, concept definition, verbal learning and memory, linguistic comprehension and expression, and visuospatial construction, and is therefore used extensively in diagnostic settings. The benefits of the ABCD are that it is standardized with an extensive population of clients across the cognitive continuum, and that it is thorough for assessing a variety of cognitive domains. The ABCD differentiates Alzheimer's dementia from normal functioning and from aphasia. It also can be used to determine severity of cognitive deficits. A challenge in using the ABCD is that it is quite lengthy and time consuming. Thus, the full battery is rarely administered in its entirety, but clinicians may choose specific subtests to probe further specific cognitive domains.

Another cognitive-linguistic battery not developed specifically for dementia but often used by SLPs is the Ross Information Processing Assessment—Geriatric (RIPA-G; Ross-Swain & Fogle, 1996). The RIPA-G assesses attention; orientation; working, recent, and remote memory; verbal organization and reasoning; and auditory and reading comprehension. The standardization sample included residents of skilled nursing facilities who were 65 to 98 years old and had cognitive-linguistic deficits from a variety of medical conditions (e.g., chronic obstructive pulmonary disease, Alzheimer's, and stroke), as well as healthy control subjects who were 65 to 94 years old. The RIPA-G is a variation of the original test, which is often used with younger clients (i.e., under 72 years): the Ross Information Processing Assessment—2 (RIPA-2; Ross-Swain, 1996). The standardization sample of the RIPA-2 included persons with traumatic brain injury, ages 15 to 77 years old. There are some psychometric limitations to be aware of with the RIPA versions, but the revisions have stronger reliability and validity than the original RIPA. The internal consistency and interrater reliability of the RIPA-2 are adequate.

Domain-Specific Assessment Tools

Clinicians often use a variety of other measures to thoroughly assess domains of concern. Memory and executive function assessments are particularly useful in characterizing deficits and documenting decline in persons with mild cognitive impairment and early dementia (Mungas et al., 2003). These are only two of the domains of cognitive processing that can be assessed at the impairment level. Many of these instruments are designed specifically to be used by (neuro)psychologists. Because the focus of this text is on functional management of communication and behaviors in persons with dementia, a complete review of impairment-oriented language measures will not be provided. There are many other resources available for such information (e.g., Bayles & Kaszniak, 1987; Lezak, Howieson, & Loring, 2004; Lubinski, 1991; Ripich, 1991). See Table 4.2 for a list of frequently used impairment-oriented, domain-specific cognitive tests.

If SLPs are particularly interested in impairment-oriented assessment of various language functions, aphasia measures may be administered to clients with dementia. Such comprehensive aphasia assessments as the Boston Diagnostic Aphasia Examination—3 (BDAE-3; Goodglass, Kaplan, & Barresi, 2000) and the Western Aphasia Battery (WAB; Kertesz, 1982) are often used to document impairments in specific language domains, such as semantics, syntax, and phonology, pragmatics, and discourse. Comprehensive assessment tools are important in the differential diagnosis of language impairments due to brain damage because they sample a wide range of behaviors efficiently. For example, the BDAE-3 includes more than 40 subtests divided into the following sections: fluency, conversation and expository speech, auditory comprehension, articulation, recitation and music, repetition, naming, paraphasia, reading, and writing. It also has extended subtests that include narrative speech and fables, auditory comprehension, repetition, naming, reading, writing, and praxis. The severity of aphasia can be rated on a scale from 1 to 7. Despite the availability of these measures, the administration of an entire comprehensive measure to clients with dementia is not often possible in one sitting,

TABLE 4.2 Examples of Domain-Specific, Impairment-Oriented Standardized Tests

Attention

Brief Test of Attention (Schretlen, 1997)
Letter Cancellation (Lezak, 1983)
Trail Making Test (subtest of Halstead-Reitan Neuropsychological Test Battery; Reitan & Wolfson, 1985)
Behavioral Inattention Test (Wilson, Cockburn, & Halligan, 1987)

Memory

Revised Wechsler Memory Scale (WMS-R; Russell, 1975; Wechsler, 1987)
Benton Revised Visual Retention Test (BVRT-R; Benton, 1974)
Fuld Object Memory Evaluation (Fuld, 1981)
Pyramids and Palm Trees Test (Howard & Patterson, 1992)
Recognition Span Test (Moss, Albert, Butters, & Payne, 1986)
The Autobiographical Memory Interview (AMI; Kopelman, Wilson, & Baddeley, 1990)
Doors and People (Baddeley, Emslie, & Nimmo-Smith, 1994)

Language

Revised Boston Naming Test (Huff, Collins, Corkin, & Rosen, 1986)
National Adult Reading Test (Nelson, 1982)
Token Test (DeRenzi & Vignolo, 1962)
The Speed and Capacity of Language-Processing Test (Baddeley, Emslie, & Nimmo-Smith, 1992)

Executive Function

Delis Kaplan Executive Function System (D-KEFS; Delis, Kaplan, & Kramer, 2001)
Executive Interview (EXIT; Royall, Mahurin, & Gray, 1992)
Wisconsin Card Sort Test, revised and extended (WCST; Heaton, Chelune, Talley, Kay, & Curtiss, 1993)
Raven's Standard Progressive Matrices (Raven, 1958)

Visuospatial

Benton Facial Recognition Test (Benton, Sivan, Hamsher, Varney, & Spreen, 1983)
Hooper Test of Visual Organization (Hooper, 1958)
Rey-Osterrieth Complex Figure (Bernstein & Waber, 1994)
The Visual Object and Space Perception Battery (Warrington, 1991)

and is rarely necessary. A good use of comprehensive aphasia measures for assessment of persons with dementia is to administer specific tasks of interest in dynamic assessment; this may determine specific linguistic characteristics that account for success or failure in communication.

ASSESSMENT OF ACTIVITIES AND PARTICIPATION

In predicting the level of care needed for a client, or in determining a client's level of need for and outcomes of rehabilitative services, procedures should be targeted toward activities and participation, which involve the daily functional status of clients with dementia. A variety of functional behaviors should be assessed, particularly during assessment for treatment planning and for measuring treatment outcomes. This type of assessment examines a variety of functional behaviors related to communication, ADLs, IADLs, and problem behaviors. Examples of cognitive-communicative abilities and limitations include the client's ability to converse with significant others, to request basic needs, to read prescription labels, to write checks and manage money, to prepare meals and do housework, and to use the telephone. Both activity abilities and limitations should be noted, with limitations characterized in terms of nature, duration, and quality (WHO, 2001). For instance, a client may be able to make requests, but the nature of the requests may reflect poor pragmatic abilities or inappropriate behaviors; or a client may be able to complete simple meal preparation, but may take an excessive amount of time to do so.

Dementia-Specific Measures

ADL and IADL Tests If a client's deficits are limiting the ability to perform one or more ADLs or IADLs, then the clinician needs to identify strengths that may be used in designing compensatory strategies, so that the client may continue to perform these activities. ADL and IADL measures that include communication skills (e.g., telephone use) and higher-order cognitive skills (e.g., money management) may be used in treatment planning, as well as for measuring the outcomes of speech-language pathology treatments. These ADL and IADL tools have better ecological validity than impairment-oriented assessment tools, as they address everyday needs of the client. There are a variety of ADL and IADL tools that were developed specifically for persons with dementia: the Functional Assessment Scale (FAST; Reisberg, 1988), the Alzheimer Disease Cooperative Study—Activities of Daily Living Scale (ADCS-ADL; Galasko et al., 1997), the Disability Assessment in Dementia Scale (DADS; Gelinas et al., 1999), and the Activities of Daily Living Questionnaire Scale (ADLQ; Johnson, Barion, Rademaker, Rehkemper, & Weintraub, 2004; Oakley, Lai, & Sunderland, 1999). The FAST (Reisberg) assesses physical and instrumental ADLs, with 16 items. The FAST was designed to provide a valid and reliable assessment of the progression of functional loss through the course of the degenerative illness, and is based on caregiver interview. Clinicians should be aware that the FAST may underestimate the communicative abilities of persons with late-stage dementia (Bayles et al., 2000).

The ADCS-ADL was developed for use in clinical trials of drug treatments for AD. The ADCS-ADL measures basic ADLs (e.g., eating, dressing, grooming, and bathing), as well as a wide variety of IADLs related to leisure interests (e.g., watching television, reading a magazine, and pursuing a hobby), household chores (e.g., making a meal or snack, clearing dishes, and using appliances), and community activities (e.g., shopping, and going to appointments). The ADCS-ADL may be a better measure of distinct functional abilities than cognitive assessments (Galasko, Kershaw, Schneider, Zhu, & Tariot, 2004).

The DADS (Gelinas et al., 1999) can be completed as either a questionnaire or an interview with the caregiver. The caregiver is asked to identify the client's ability to initiate and perform basic ADLs and IADLs, and consists of 46 items that can be categorized into three domains: initiation, planning and organization, and performance. The DADS was developed for use in clinical trials, and has been shown to be sensitive to change over time, with good reliability and validity (Feldman et al., 2001; Gelinas et al.). Despite this, the utility of this test is questionable for typical clinical populations. Consequently, the ADLQ variation was developed for use in more typical outpatient settings (Johnson et al., 2004; Oakley et al., 1999). The ADLQ is based on an interview with a caregiver, and measures functioning in six areas of ADLs: self-care, household care, employment and recreation, shopping and money, travel, and communication. The ADLQ has good reliability and validity and is sensitive to change over time.

Communication Tests In addition, there are tools for SLPs to assess communication activities, designed specifically for administration with persons with dementia. A commonly used reliable test is the Functional Linguistic Communication Inventory (FLCI; Bayles & Tomoeda, 1994). The FLCI tests more functional communication skills than the ABCD. The FLCI subtests include greeting and naming, comprehension of signs, object to picture matching, word reading and comprehension, following commands, and pantomime. Another tool, which was developed for assessing persons with dementia in long-term care environments, is the Communication Outcome Measure of Functional Independence (COMFI; Santo Pietro & Boczko, 1997). The COMFI scale measures psychosocial interaction, communication and conversation, mealtime independence, and cognition, based on observation during mealtimes. The clinician rates 20 behaviors on scales from 0 (never occurs) to 5 (always occurs); its psychometric properties have not been tested widely.

General Measures

ADL and IADL Tests Additionally, ADL and IADL tools that were not developed specifically for persons with dementia are sometimes used to assess functional cognitive and communication abilities. Several of these tools assess performance in simulated everyday activities. The Rivermead Behavioral Memory Test—II (RBMT-II; Wilson, Cockburn, & Baddeley, 2003) is a measure of everyday memory functioning, which has a variety of simulated everyday tasks (e.g., recalling faces, routes, and stories). The RBMT-II is more ecologically valid than the impairment-based memory tests, but some of the tasks still seem odd when decontextualized (e.g., route finding). The RBMT-II is a performance-based assessment of lexical, semantic, and verbal priming; orientation; and immediate and delayed verbal, visual, procedural, and prospective memory. This test has norms extending up to 96 years, which is an advantage for use in dementia management. The standardization sample included persons with right- and left-hemisphere strokes, traumatic brain injury, subarachnoid hemorrhage, and other forms of brain damage. Four parallel forms are available to prevent practice effects.

Similarly, tests of attention and executive functions that are based on simulations have been developed. The Test of Everyday Attention (TEA; Robertson, Ward, Ridgeway, & Nimmo-Smith, 1994) is a performance-based test of attention that simulates functional activities, such as using the elevator or telephone, listening for lottery numbers, and searching a map. Sustained, selective, divided, and alternating attention can be measured in a variety of tasks using these everyday functional behaviors. In addition to the ecological validity provided through use of everyday behaviors, other advantages include parallel forms of the TEA so that repeated measurement does not result in learning effects, and standardization on adults with hearing impairments (Robertson et al., 1994) and those with dementia (Robertson, Ward, Ridgeway, & Nimmo-Smith, 1996).

The Biber Cognitive Estimation Test (BCET; Bullard et al., 2004) is an experimental tool that can be used to assess abilities related to everyday functional needs. This test has 15 items that involve estimating time, distance, weight, and quantity (e.g., What is the distance an adult can walk in an afternoon? How much do a dozen, medium-sized apples weigh? What is the age of the oldest living person in the United States? How many slices of bread are there in a one-pound loaf?). Responses require a variety of cognitive abilities, including working memory, semantic memory, planning, mental control, self-monitoring, and self-correction. In typical adults, the results are not impacted by age or education. The psychometric properties of the BCET have been tested with typical adults of a variety of ages, as well as small samples of adults with Alzheimer's and Parkinson's disease. The BCET differentiated between adults with typical cognitive abilities and those with dementia, and demonstrated adequate reliability and validity for dementia assessment. Thus, the BCET is a test that is easy to administer and may provide useful information for predicting a person's independence in everyday activities.

The Behavioral Assessment of the Dysexecutive Syndrome (BADS; Wilson, Alderman, Burgess, Emslei, & Evans, 1996) has seven subtests that simulate everyday tasks to assess cognitive flexibility, problem solving, planning, and self-monitoring. The BADS has norms that extend to 87 years for healthy adults and 76 years for adults with brain injury. The BADS does not have psychometric data for test–retest reliability; otherwise, it does have adequate psychometric properties. Likewise, the Behavioral Dyscontrol Scale (BDS; Belanger et al., 2005) can be used with persons with AD. The BDS contains nine items that require motor responses in the following areas: alternating hand sequences, inhibition, learning complex motor sequences, alphanumeric sequencing, and awareness of deficit or insight. The BDS is scored using a 3-point scale. Reliability and validity were demonstrated with elders. The BDS discriminates between persons with AD and MCI, but not between those with MCI and typical elders (Belanger et al.). In addition, the BDS predicts performance in ADLs, after controlling for severity of memory deficits.

Other assessment tools score the client on performance of actual ADLs or IADLs, rather than simulated activities. These performance-based measures have been designed to evaluate adults' everyday competence in actual IADLs: the Everyday Problems Test (EPT; Willis & Marsiske, 1993), the Everyday Problems Test for Cognitively Challenged Elderly (EPCCE; Willis, 1993), and the Revised Observed Tasks of Daily Living (OTDL-R; Diehl et al., 2005). The EPT is an 84-item test measuring older adults' cognitive competencies for managing IADLs, including food preparation, medication use, telephone use, financial management, shopping, housekeeping, and transportation use. Similarly, the EPCCE is a shorter, 32-item measure of the ability of individuals to solve problems of daily living encountered in everyday tasks such as meal preparation, medication use, telephone use, shopping, financial management, household maintenance, and transportation.

In the OTDL-R, the client performs three tasks in each of three domains of IADLs: telephone use, medication use, and financial management; each task has subtasks or steps that yield a total of 28 items that are scored. The OTDL-R showed good reliability and validity and may be more useful in outpatient and home care settings than paper-and-pencil tests, which are more subject to biases related to education and literacy (Diehl et al., 2005).

Communication Tests The Communicative Activities of Daily Living, 2nd ed. (CADL-2; Holland, Frattali, & Fromm, 1999), measures performance in a variety of simulated communication activities (e.g., visit to the doctor, telephone use, and checkbook and pill bottle comprehension). The CADL-2 was designed for use with adults with acquired neurological disorders. The standardization sample included primarily persons with right- and left-hemisphere strokes, and a smaller number of persons with traumatic brain injury and other neurological diagnoses. The participants were mostly White, with a few representatives from racial and ethnic minorities. The CADL-2 has good psychometric properties, but requires further testing with persons with dementia.

Similarly, a tool was developed for use by SLPs to examine everyday communication needs of adults with a wide variety of acquired neurological communication disorders. The Functional Assessment of Communication Skills for Adults (ASHA-FACS; Frattali, Thompson, Holland, Wohl, & Ferketic, 1995) includes rating scales of the client's ability to perform everyday communication activities such as using the telephone, reading television guides and newspapers, and having a conversation in four domains: social communication; communication of basic needs; reading, writing, and number concepts; and daily planning. The ASHA-FACS manual provides information on the adequacy of its psychometric properties.

Another communication domain that has particular relevance for the development of functional treatment goals is reading. Reading comprehension can be assessed using either formal or informal reading comprehension measures. In the absence of dementia-specific standardized reading measures, those that have been constructed for persons with aphasia can be used, such as the Reading Comprehension Battery for Aphasia, 2nd ed. (RCBA-2; LaPointe & Horner, 1998); the Measure of Cognitive-Linguistic Abilities (MCLA; Ellmo, Graser, Krchnavek, Calabrese, & Hauck, 1995); and subtests of the Communication Activities of Daily Living (CADL-2; Holland et al., 1999), Western Aphasia Battery (Kertesz, 1982), and BDAE-3 (Goodglass et al., 2000), among others. Many of these assessments include functional reading items, such as common traffic signs, medication labels, telephone directories, and menus, and performance on these items may reflect better preserved abilities than assessments using single words, abstract concepts, or generic topics. Informal and personalized reading assessment using the client's name, address, and other functional words and phrases provides direct evidence of functional reading ability.

Rating Scales

ADL and IADL Scales

Other ADL and IADL rating scales were developed for rehabilitation populations in general: the Functional Activities Questionnaire (FAQ; Pfeffer, Kurosaki, Harrah, Chance, & Filos, 1982), the Functional Independence Measure (FIM) Uniform Data System for Medical Rehabilitation (State University of New York at Buffalo, 1993), the Functional Assessment Measure (FAM; Hall, 1997; Hall, Hamilton, Gordon, & Zasler, 1993), and the Rehabilitation Institute of Chicago Functional Assessment Scale—Version II (RIC-FAS II; Heinemann, 1989). These are all rating scales used by clinicians to indicate level of assistance in functional activities, for example, dressing, bathing, grooming, money management, meal preparation, and communication. The client is given a score from 7 (independent) to 1 (dependent) for each behavior on each of the scales.

A scale that was developed for use by nurses in long-term care is the Nursing Home Disabilities Instrument (NHDI; Valk, Post, Cools, & Schrijvers, 2001). In the NHDI, the nurse scores the resident on 24 behaviors in the domains of mobility, ADLs, alertness, resistance, cognition, and incontinence. Scores are based on observations of everyday functioning in the nursing home. Psychometric properties of the NHDI are adequate (Valk et al., 2001).

Communication Rating Scales

Because many of the available scales did not address communication abilities in detail, the Functional Communication Measures (FCM; Frattali et al., 1995) were developed by the ASHA Task Force on Treatment Outcome and Cost Effectiveness. This tool was designed to measure change in FCM rating to demonstrate achievement of functional outcomes resulting from clinical intervention. The clinician rates the client for 13 different communication variables on a 7-point scale, before and after treatment. The FCM scales can be used with any population. In addition, the Communication Effectiveness Index (CETI; Lomas et al., 1989), a rating scale developed for use with persons with aphasia, can be used for persons with dementia. On the CETI, a communication partner is asked to rate the client on a variety of everyday communication situations (e.g., reading the newspaper and talking in a group). Another observation-based rating scale that can be used for measuring functional outcomes is the Communication Assessment Scale for the Cognitively Impaired (CAS; Friedman & Tappen, 1991). The 30 items are rated on a scale of 1 (absence of function) to 3 (full function) after 15 minutes of interaction with the individual.

Discourse Assessment

Persons with dementia often display discourse production and comprehension deficits. Discourse production samples are obtained using a variety of monologue and/or dialogue tasks, and analyzed with quantitative and/or qualitative techniques (e.g., Chapman et al., 2002; Ehrlich, Obler, & Clark, 1997; Glosser, 1991; Tompkins, 1995). Monologues may be composed of narrative (i.e., picture description) or procedural tasks (i.e., activity description). Microlinguistic analyses of monologues can include measures of the components of language (i.e., phonology, semantics, syntax, and morphology) and productivity (e.g., number of words or information units produced per minute). Macrolinguistic analyses of monologues may include measures of story structure, such as cohesion and coherence, or accuracy and completeness of main concepts (Nicholas & Brookshire, 1993, 1995). Disadvantages of these structured monologue samples are the decontextualized nature of the tasks, which may be confusing for a person with cognitive deficits and may not elicit a typical discourse sample, and the time-consuming nature of the analyses. An advantage is that the structure allows the procedures to be easily replicated to examine change over time.

Dialogue samples may be collected through interview, conversation, or debate tasks, and analyzed for the microlinguistic aspects above, or for pragmatics. The Discourse Abilities Profile (Terrell & Ripich, 1989) assesses the presence or absence of discourse features in a variety of tasks, including narrative discourse ("Tell me something interesting that happened to you when you were growing up"), procedural discourse ("Tell me how to make toast and jelly"), and spontaneous conversation. Discourse features coded range from specific narrative features (i.e., abstract, setting, and episode), procedural features (i.e., essential and optional steps), turn taking, and types of speech acts to general discourse behaviors (i.e., stress, intonation, rote, eye contact, gestures, and coherence).

Measures of specific pragmatic features may examine speech acts, topic control, social skills, and conversational repair (Hartley, 1995; Perkins, Whitworth, & Lesser, 1998; Prutting & Kirchner, 1987; Small, Geldart, & Gutman, 2000). A variety of pragmatic checklists that have been developed for use with clients with traumatic brain injury also could be used with persons with dementia, such as the Pragmatic Protocol (Prutting & Kirchner) and the Conversational Skills Rating Scale and the Social Skills Checklist (Hartley). These rating scales and checklists can be used much more efficiently than the more thorough micro- or macrolinguistic analyses.

More recently, a pragmatic assessment has been designed specifically to examine persons with dementia: the Profile of Pragmatic Impairment in Communication (PPIC; Hays, Niven, Godfrey, & Linscott, 2004). The PPIC allows the clinician to assess the client's production and comprehension of literal content as well as intended meaning, or implicature. The PPIC was developed using Gricean principles of cooperation (e.g., interaction has an implicitly agreed upon purpose) and conversational maxims (e.g., exchanges should end at a mutually agreed point, and contributions should be expressed clearly, be true and relevant, and contain neither too little nor too much information; Hays et al., 2004). In addition, Hays and colleagues developed items that assess other rules of conversation, including social style, subject matter, and aesthetics. These constructs relate to cultural norms for communication, such as appropriateness of topics. The PPIC demonstrated good reliability and validity, and results relate to cognitive abilities.

Qualitative analyses can be conducted on discourse samples to describe, in rich detail, specific behaviors or their functions in natural contexts (Damico, Oelschlaeger, & Simmons-Mackie, 1999; Damico & Simmons-Mackie, 2003; Damico, Simmons-Mackie, Oelschlaeger, Elman, & Armstrong, 1999; Perkins, 1995; Perkins et al., 1998;

Small et al., 2000; Tetnowski & Franklin, 2003; Togher, 2001). Togher described Systemic Functional Linguistics (SFL), a procedure that examines discourse genres, the expected behaviors for each genre, and discrepancies between genres. SFL takes into account the power structure inherent in different discourse genres (e.g., information-giving versus -receiving roles) that may explain the client's discourse behaviors. Damico and Simmons-Mackie described the ethnographic procedure known as Conversation Analysis (CA; Sacks, Schegloff, & Jefferson, 1974), which has strong ecological validity. CA seeks evidence of communicative success or failure in the sequential context of interaction, keeping in mind the principle of collaborative achievement of conversation. CA can be used to examine influences on the sharing of conversational turns, such as shared knowledge of interlocutors, manifestations of cognitive impairments in conversation, and individual discourse styles (Perkins; Perkins et al.).

The results of CA can be combined with results of cognitive-neuropsychological findings for comprehensive treatment planning (Damico & Simmons-Mackie, 2003; Tetnowski & Franklin, 2003). The benefit of using either of these qualitative analyses is the strong ecological validity of the results. A significant disadvantage is the time-consuming nature of such analyses, if done thoroughly. Thus, we recommend that an experienced clinician learn the principles of qualitative analyses to enhance observations between a client and a typical communication partner (e.g., family and/or staff caregiver). Of note, production of written narratives can be assessed in a similar fashion, with the expectation that similar micro- and macrolinguistic deficits would be seen.

Formal and informal measures of discourse comprehension may be used to document difficulties comprehending lengthy, complex, and/or abstract discourse. These deficits are due to attention, memory, reasoning, and/or language deficits. An example of a formal measure of discourse comprehension includes the Discourse Comprehension Test, 2nd ed. (DCT-2; Brookshire & Nicholas, 1997). This test was standardized on persons with aphasia and right-brain damage, but does not have adequate psychometric properties; only content validity and concurrent validity were assessed in the standardization process. Welland, Lubinski, and Higginbotham (2002) used the first edition of the DCT (Brookshire & Nicholas, 1993) in a study of persons with early and middle Alzheimer's dementia. Both groups of participants with AD performed significantly worse than typical age-matched controls, but not significantly different than each other. On such measures, persons with dementia are expected to have greater difficulty with comprehension of abstract language and/or details than with main ideas.

As noted above, subtests can be taken from comprehensive aphasia measures to assess particular aspects of language, such as discourse comprehension. The Complex Ideational subtest of the BDAE-3 can be used to informally assess comprehension of complex yes–no questions and inferential abilities of persons with dementia. Other informal measures can be constructed by the clinician to examine inferential abilities, and comprehension of the details versus gist of a story (Chapman et al., 2002). There are a variety or resources available that are not dementia specific but that provide comprehensive reviews of such measures (e.g., Meyers, 1999; Tompkins, 1995).

Checklists used to examine communication in the natural environment may be more realistic. Observation protocols have been established to determine the range of behaviors and factors that affect behaviors in the natural environment with other residents as well as with staff, family, visitors, or volunteers, including the Checklist of Communicative Environment (Armstrong & Woodgates, 1996), the Communication/Environment Assessment and Planning Guide (Lubinski, 1991), and the Communication Assessment Scale (Friedman & Tappen, 1991). For persons with severe communication impairments who communicate only through nonverbal expressions of affect, the Philadelphia Geriatric Center Affect Rating Scale (Lawton, Van Haitsma, & Klapper, 1996) can be used. This tool is completed by a clinician based on a 10-minute observation period, during which the duration of affective states (pleasure, anger, anxiety and fear, sadness, interest, and contentment) is rated on a 5-point scale.

Problem Behavior Assessment

Cognitive and communication deficits can often result in problem behaviors (e.g., repetitive questions, disruptive vocalizations, wandering, or passivity) that affect everyday functional status. Thus, another important aspect of assessment for treatment planning and for treatment outcomes is the measurement of problem behaviors. Kennedy (2002) recommended describing behaviors in a systematic fashion with quantitative measures of the presence or absence of a desired behavior, such as the frequency, rate, magnitude, and duration of behaviors, and the situations in which they occur. Thus, the clinician should identify, describe, and count the frequency of caregiver and client complaints, seeking answers to questions such as the following: What are the specific problems? Where do they occur, and at what time of day? How often do they occur? What is the consequence of the problem, who says and does what, and does it work? What is causing the activity limitation or participation restriction? What impact does this problem have on quality of life?

Several protocols have been developed to identify problem behaviors and care needs from the perspective of caregivers, including family and/or staff caregivers. Some of the more popular rating scales include the Behavioral Pathology in Alzheimer's Disease Rating Scale (BEHAVE-AD; Reisberg et al., 1987); the Cohen-Mansfield Agitation Inventory (CMAI; Cohen-Mansfield, 1986); the Nursing Home Behavior Problem Scale (NHBPS; Ray, Taylor, Lichtenstein, & Meador, 1992); the Multidimensional Observation Scale for Elderly Subjects, which also measures cognitive and psychosocial functioning (MOSES; Helmes, Csapo, & Short, 1987); and the ADAS Non-Cognitive Functions Test (ADAS-noncog; Rosen et al., 1984). The BEHAVE-AD (Reisberg et al., 1987) is used to rate the severity of seven areas of behaviors on a scale of 0 (not present) to 3 (present in most severe form): paranoid and delusional ideations, anxieties and phobias, activity disturbances, hallucinations, aggressiveness, diurnal rhythm disturbances, and affective disturbance. The CMAI (Cohen-Mansfield) is used to rate 29 agitated behaviors on a scale of 1 (never) to 7 (several times per hour), based on four factors: aggressive, physically nonaggressive, verbally agitated, and hiding and hoarding behaviors. Nursing assistants often provide information for nurses to score this assessment in long-term care settings. The NHBPS (Ray et al., 1992) is a 29-item rating of severe problem behaviors that have occurred in the past 3 days (0 = never to 4 = always). This measure correlates highly with the CMAI, mental impairment, and the use of sedative drugs or restraints, and has been used in research studies. The MOSES (Helmes et al., 1987) measures five areas of cognitive and psychosocial functioning (self-care, disoriented behavior, depressed and anxious mood, irritable behavior, and withdrawn behavior) with 40 items in a forced-choice format. The ADAS also includes a noncognitive functions test, with 10 items and a total possible of 50 points. The ADAS-noncog measures tearfulness, depression, concentration, uncooperativeness, delusions, hallucinations, pacing, motor activity, tremors, and appetite on a 6-point severity scale. As noted previously, versions of the ADAS are also available in French, German, Spanish, Italian, Korean, Finnish, Danish, Greek, Hebrew, and Japanese. Regardless of the particular tool used to document problem behaviors, the clinician should be aware that subjective reporting measures, such as the NHBPS, may be subject to bias by the staff member completing it, and that observations by the clinician should supplement such measures (Vance et al., 2003).

Finally, clinicians should seek not only to identify and describe problem behaviors but also to determine the source of the behaviors, keeping in mind that problem behaviors represent some attempt to interact in the environment or to communicate an unmet need (Algase et al., 1996; Kunik et al., 2003). Clinicians should describe the contextual variables that impact a client's behaviors and functioning, categorized by client, caregiver, and environmental variables, with each category identified by both fixed (i.e., not changeable) and mutable (i.e., changeable) variables (Kunik et al.). Many of the contextual variables could be altered to resolve a difficult situation. See Figure 3.1 for the model developed by Kunik and colleagues. An illustrative example was provided by Zgola and Bordillon (2002), who described the problems frequently observed at mealtime, including several factors that are unfamiliar and/or undesirable, such as mealtime schedules, food and drink options, presentation of food (e.g., the use of trays with numerous items that make the meal visually confusing), and table mates. Persons with dementia cope with these unfamiliar or undesirable variables as best they can, but their actions are often described as resistance, aggression, withdrawal, manipulation, or generally disruptive behavior. Many of the variables that were listed in this example of mealtime challenges represent mutable variables. Staff needs to consider changing these variables, rather than just deeming the residents "uncooperative" or "difficult."

Treatment goals should be based on the most frequent or most disruptive problem behaviors. A family caregiver may report that the most frequent problem behavior is repetitive questions, but the most problematic behavior is wandering and leaving the house at night. The clinician should conduct an assessment for treatment planning to determine the cause of the problem behaviors and plan strategies that capitalize on the client's strengths. Strategies to prevent the client's behavior of leaving the house at night should be suggested first, and then strategies to decrease repetitive questions can be reviewed. A nursing home caregiver is likely to report that a resident's most problematic behaviors are refusals to bathe and disruptive vocalizations. The clinician would conduct assessment for treatment planning to determine the cause of these behaviors and then design strategies to increase compliance and decrease disruptive vocalizations, thereby increasing functional communication. In either case, treatment outcome measures should be specific to the target behaviors and assess their frequency and magnitude. Use of standardized measures in these cases would not be valid as outcome measures, as it is not reasonable to expect changes on a standardized test when the treatment goal modified a specific functional behavior. Rather, the frequency and magnitude of target behaviors can be measured by enlisting the assistance of family and staff caregivers in taking data on these behaviors. See Figure 4.1 for examples of behavior diaries and logs on which to record problem behaviors.

Of note, these behavior diaries and logs can have a treatment effect with both the client and the caregiver. The simple act of recording the data can break the cycle of the antecedent–behavior–consequence by providing a different consequence. For example, a caregiver who typically tries to reason with the person about a repetitive question might leave the situation to record the behavior in the diary. When the caregiver is out of view, the person does not repeat the question, thereby eliminating reinforcement or attention for the problem behavior and eliminating the behavior itself. Furthermore, some caregivers have reported that their own perceptions of the frequency or intensity of a particular problem have changed based on keeping these data. For instance, a problem that *seems* to happen 10 times a day may *actually* happen only once a day, which may not seem as troublesome when the objective data are reviewed.

Observations and interviews should be used in establishing treatment goals. A variety of informants can be interviewed (e.g., clients, and family and staff caregivers), and the client can be observed in a variety of contexts (e.g., dining room, lounge, and activities room) to obtain relevant information. Caregivers should describe expected outcomes for activities and participation that will help

Behavior Diary

Date	**Time**	**Describe the Behavior**	**How Often?**

Behavior Log

Day	Count Problem: Cannot find room	Count Problem: Asks what time it is.
Monday		
Tuesday		
Wednesday		
Thursday		
Friday		
Saturday		
Sunday		

Figure 4.1 Behavior Diary and Behavior Log.

to determine treatment goals and to set criteria for desired treatment outcomes. Figure 4.2 illustrates an example of a form completed by a caregiver to indicate the client's daily schedule and routine, and Figure 4.3 illustrates a form completed by a caregiver to indicate desired participation in activities. Such forms, along with the interview, will provide information on the client's wants and needs, interests, and hobbies. Protocols have been developed to gather such information, as well as safety information and memory aid content (Bourgeois, 1992a, 2007; see Appendices 4.1–3). For many residents of long-term care facilities, the individual, family, recreation staff, and/or pastoral staff may have already completed similar forms, which are kept in the medical record.

Interpretation of assessment results must be considered within the context of relevant background information, including the level of caregiver support, which impacts the client's participation in the home and community, or residence. Participation should be characterized in terms of the nature, duration, and quality of actual participation or restrictions. Additionally, supports and barriers that are already in place for the client's participation in a variety of relationships and roles in society should be identified. This may include the client's own reactions and caregivers' reactions to the disease and deficits that impact on societal participation, as well as the current situation and projections for the future (e.g., living arrangement and health status). For example, attention and working memory deficits may limit the person's ability to comprehend conversational language, which may then restrict the person's ability to comprehend complex conversations and result in withdrawal from social situations. The support (or lack thereof) provided

	Monday	Tuesday	Wednesday	Thursday	Friday	Saturday	Sunday
8 am	Breakfast Dressed	Dressed	Dressed	Dressed	Dressed	Dressed	Dressed
9 am							
10 am	Senior Center		Senior Center				Church
11 am							
Noon	Lunch	Lunch	Lunch	Lunch	Lunch	Lunch	Lunch
1 pm							
2 pm							
3 pm							
4 pm							
5 pm	Dinner	Dinner	Dinner	Dinner		Dinner	Dinner
6 pm	TV News				Dinner at Son's house		
7 pm		Choir Practice					
8 pm							
9 pm							
10 pm							
11 pm	Bed	Bed	Bed	Bed	Bed	Bed	Bed

Figure 4.2 Daily Schedule and Routine Form.

Environment/Activity	People	Frequency of Contact	Problems
Home	Me Wife, Mary	24-7	Lots of arguments Loss of intimacy
Church	Minister, Friends: Bob & Jane Smith, H. Jones, many others	Sunday, Tuesday Choir Practice	Can't remember names
Senior Center	Men's Group	Wednesday	Names, following conversation
Grocery Store	Clerk	varies	Giving correct money
Son's home	Son, Spouse T.(6 yrs), M. (2 yrs)	Once/week	Yells at kids

Figure 4.3 Desired Participation Form.

by frequent communication partners will impact whether or not this withdrawal occurs, such as the availability, willingness, and supportiveness of communication partners, and communication demands and expectations.

ASSESSMENT OF TREATMENT POTENTIAL

Assessment for treatment potential can be one of the most important aspects of an evaluation when considering reimbursement issues. To obtain reimbursement for services, many third-party payers require that clinicians report on prognosis for improvement with treatment and document a statement of reasonable expectation for achieving the desired treatment outcomes. Observation and informal assessment procedures can be used in trial therapy, which is conducted to determine the client's responsiveness to treatment techniques. Many clients with dementia have preserved oral reading and reading comprehension abilities that can be capitalized on in designing compensatory strategies; thus, documentation of responsiveness to written cues is useful for stating reasonable expectation for progress in treatment. The Bourgeois Oral Reading Screen (Bourgeois, 1992a) is an informal tool that can be used for this purpose (see Appendix 4.4). Asking the client to read aloud and comment on each page provides valuable information about the size of the type that is read with ease and the length and syntactic complexity of the text that is understood. Difficulty with this task does not necessarily dictate that a client cannot use written cues. Dynamic assessment should be used to determine if the client is able to respond to enlarged or enhanced cues. If the client does not read the sentences as instructed, the clinician can manipulate the physical characteristics of the stimuli (e.g., increasing font size, copying onto yellow paper, or showing one sentence and picture at a time). If the client attends to the stimuli, but appears confused by the task, then the clinician should use personally relevant information to determine if the client can use written cues for conversations about personal information. Furthermore, comprehension of the written cues can be determined by attending to other comments that the client makes about the sentences (e.g., "My wife is not Mary" or "Where is Swissvale? I never heard of that!").

Another useful trial therapy tool is the Spaced Retrieval Screen (Brush & Camp, 1998; see Appendix 4.5), which determines learning potential and documents expectation for structured training to improve targeted behaviors. In this task, the client learns the clinician's name. If the client can recall the name at a 1-minute delay in three trials, there is expectation that spaced retrieval training will be a successful tool for training other facts and strategies with this client. Again, if the client does not seem motivated by the task, then a different target can be used, particularly one that the clinician knows is problematic (e.g., the client's room number).

Finally, the client's stimulability for treatment should be assessed through observation of the client in everyday routines. The client is observed in the natural environment to establish the types of cues and stimuli that evoke a response, as well as describing the types of behaviors the client produces. This information is used to design stimuli and tasks that will provide opportunities for the client to perform the target behaviors in the natural setting. Bourgeois has developed several forms

CASE 4.1: ILLUSTRATION OF A FUNCTIONAL ASSESSMENT FOR TREATMENT PLANNING IN HOME CARE

Mr. Fitzpatrick, an 82-year-old retired teacher, was referred to speech therapy through a home health care agency following his discharge from cardiac rehabilitation. His medical records documented a prior diagnosis of vascular dementia, with increased confusion and agitation. His wife was adamant about caring for him at home, though the medical team questioned whether this would be possible. During the SLP's first meeting with Mr. Fitzpatrick, she screened his cognitive function (Montreal Cognitive Assessment [MoCA]), hearing and vision function, functional reading ability (Bourgeois Oral Reading Screen [BORS]), and ability to learn her name (Spaced Retrieval Screen). Assessments revealed moderate cognitive-linguistic deficits, adequate hearing for one-on-one communicative interactions, adequate vision to read 14-font print, and ability to recall new information after a 1-minute delay. Interviews and interest inventories conducted with Mr. Fitzpatrick and his wife revealed that he wanted to return to his hobbies of taking care of his plants, preparing simple meals, and reading. His wife was concerned about his safety awareness and outbursts when he got frustrated, and he complained, "My wife mixes everything up whenever I try to do anything, and there's nothing interesting in the newspaper anymore." The SLP developed a plan of treatment using visual reminder cards for the sequences of steps in Mr. Fitzpatrick's hobbies, and worked with his wife to design memory books and boxes related to his interests instead of reading the newspaper. Treatment also included training his wife to prompt Mr. Fitzpatrick to use the written cue cards for his hobbies.

to assist clinicians in documenting the types of behaviors that would be conducive to functional goal development. See Appendices 4.6 and 4.7 for the Screening Protocol to Monitor Residents With Dementia (Rozsa & Bourgeois, 2006) and the Functional Goals Screening Protocol: Community Clients With Dementia (Bourgeois & Rozsa, 2006), respectively. These forms are used to document cognitive and communication behaviors, and attention and receptivity to a variety of sensory stimuli and environmental variables. The clinician should observe the client's responsiveness to visual stimuli (e.g., pictures, colors, and signs), auditory cues (e.g., talking or music), and tactile stimuli (e.g., materials with a variety of textures). The clinician also should use the procedures described previously to provide an indication of the client's attempts and desire to interact with others or engage with the environment (e.g., frequency of initiation, and active versus passive participation). This will allow the clinician to observe whether the client interacts with others, engages in activities, and either actively or passively participates in the home and community, or residential, settings.

CASE 4.2: ILLUSTRATION OF ASSESSMENT FOR TREATMENT PLANNING IN LONG-TERM CARE

Mrs. Seinfeld is admitted to long-term care after her husband, who was her primary caregiver at home, dies. The SLP routinely screens all new admissions. Based on a brief interview with the nursing staff and a review of Mrs. Seinfeld's medical records, the SLP requests a referral for cognitive-linguistic evaluation and treatment. Nursing staff report that they do not always understand what Mrs. Seinfeld is requesting, especially when she becomes agitated. Problem behaviors reported by nursing staff include refusal to bathe or change her clothes, repetitive questions regarding the whereabouts of her husband, and wandering into other residents' rooms. The SLP conducts an evaluation using the MoCA to determine current level of impairment, and the Bourgeois Oral Reading Screen and Spaced Retrieval Screen to determine potential to benefit from written cues and to learn new skills and strategies. Mrs. Seinfeld has moderate cognitive deficits, with preserved reading ability and good responsiveness to the spaced retrieval technique. The SLP obtains information from the case history and the activities department interest inventory that are in the medical record. She also obtains photos and additional information from Mrs. Seinfeld's granddaughter, who lives nearby. Functional goals include the use of graphic cue cards to increase compliance with bathing and dressing, a memory wallet for increased quality and satisfaction with conversational interactions, and interest books for engagement during alone times. Nursing staff will be included in the training, so that they will learn to use effective communication techniques and cueing systems in care routines, and activities staff will be included so that they will use cueing systems to enhance social interaction and participation in facility programs.

ASSESSMENT OF FUNCTIONAL OUTCOMES

Because most interventions for dementia are not designed to remedy the impairments of dementia, impairment-based measures are not recommended for measuring functional outcomes. Rather, measures of activities and participation, such as those described above, are often used to assess functional outcomes. There are limitations even with these measures, as they may not be related to the behaviors being treated. Thus, clinicians may measure the specific behaviors that are being treated, rather than standard disability measures (Bourgeois, 1998). Clinical researchers who have designed behavioral interventions to improve activities and participation in persons with dementia often measure the specific behaviors that were modified by the intervention at pre- and post treatment (as well as during treatment in many instances). For example, persons with dementia who received memory aids (collections of picture and sentence stimuli in a book or wallet format) used significantly more statements of fact (including novel statements) and fewer ambiguous utterances during conversations (Bourgeois, 1990, 1992b, 1993; Bourgeois & Mason, 1996). Furthermore, disruptive vocalization (i.e., repetitive questions and demands) were reduced by using written stimulus cues in the form of index cards, memo boards, and memory book pages (Bourgeois, Burgio, Schulz, Beach, & Palmer, 1997). Other conversational behaviors that were measured in a behavioral intervention, "Breakfast Club," included questioning, use of each other's names, eye contact, and topic maintenance (Santo Pietro & Boczko, 1998). More information on these interventions and their outcomes will be described in chapter 5.

REFERENCES

Albert, M. S. (1994). Brief assessments of cognitive function in the elderly. In M. P. Lawton & J. A. Teresi (Eds.), *Annual review of gerontology and geriatrics focus on assessment techniques* (Vol. 4, pp. 93–106). New York: Springer.

Algase, D. L., Beck, C., Kolanowski, A., Whall, A., Berent, S., Richards, K., et al. (1996). Need-driven dementia-compromised behavior: An alternative view of disruptive behavior. *American Journal of Alzheimer's Disease*, *11*(6), 10, 12–19.

American Health Care Association. (1990). *The long term care survey: Regulations, forms, procedures, guidelines*. Washington, DC: Author.

American Speech-Language-Hearing Association. (2004). Evaluating and treating communication and cognitive disorders: Approaches to referral and collaboration for speech-language pathology and clinical neuropsychology [Technical report]. *ASHA Supplement*, *23*, 47–58.

American Speech-Language-Hearing Association. (2005). *The roles of speech-language pathologists working with individuals with dementia-based cognitive-communicative disorders: Technical Report*. Rockville, MD: Author.

Armstrong, L., & Woodgates, S. (1996). Using quantitative measure of communicative environment to compare two psychogeriatric day care settings. *European Journal of Disorders of Communication*, *31*, 309–317.

Baddeley, A. D., Emslie, H., & Nimmo-Smith, I. (1992). *The Speed and Capacity of Language-processing Test.* Bury St. Edmunds, UK: Thames Valley Test Company.

Baddeley, A., Emslie, H., & Nimmo-Smith, I. (1994). *Doors and people*. Bury St. Edmunds, UK: Thames Valley.

Barker, W., Luis, C., Harwood, D., Loewenstien, D., Bravo, M., Ownby, R., et al. (2005). The effects of a memory screening program on the early diagnosis of Alzheimer disease. *Alzheimer Disease & Associated Disorders*, *19*, 1–7.

Barrie, M. A. (2002). Objective screening tools to assess cognitive impairment and depression. *Topics in Geriatric Rehabilitation*, *18*, 28–46.

Bayles, K. A., & Kaszniak, A. W. (1987). *Communication and cognition in normal aging and dementia*. Boston: College-Hill.

Bayles, K. A., & Tomoeda, C. K. (1993). *Arizona battery for communication disorders in dementia*. Austin, TX: Pro-Ed.

Bayles, K. A., & Tomoeda, C. K. (1994). *Functional linguistic communication inventory*. Tucson, AZ: Canyonlands.

Bayles, K. A., Tomoeda, C. K., Cruz, R. F., & Mahendra, N. (2000). Communication abilities of individuals with late-stage Alzheimer disease. *Alzheimer Disease and Associated Disorders*, *14*(3), 176–181.

Beatty, W., Ryder, K., Gontkovsky, S., Scott, J. G., McSwan, K., & Bharucha, K. (2003). Analyzing the subcortical dementia syndrome of Parkinson's disease using the RBANS. *Archives of Clinical Neuropsychology*, *18*(5), 509–520.

Belanger, H. G., Wilder-Willis, K., Malloy, P., Salloway, S., Hamman, R. F., & Grigsby, J. (2005). Assessing motor and cognitive regulation in AD, MCI, and controls using the Behavioral Dyscontrol Scale. *Archives of Clinical Neuropsychology*, *20*, 183–189.

Benton, A. L. (1974). *Revised visual retention test: Clinical and experimental application* (4th ed.). New York: Psychological Corporation.

Benton, A. L. (1983). *Contributions to neuropsychological assessment*. New York: Oxford University Press.

Benton, A. L., Sivan, A. B., Hamsher, K. De S., Varney, N. R., & Spreen, O. (1983). *Contribution to neuropsychological assessment*. New York: Oxford University Press.

Bernstein, J. H., & Waber, D. (1994). *Rey-Osterrieth complex figure*. Lutz, FL: Psychological Assessment Resources.

Blessed, G., Block, S., Butters, T., & Kay, D. (1991). The diagnosis of dementia in the elderly: A comparison of CAMCOG (the Cognitive Section of the CAMDEX), the AGE-CAT Program, DSM-II, the Mini-Mental State examination and some short rating scales. *British Journal of Psychiatry*, *159*, 193–198.

Blessed, G., Tomlinson, B., & Roth, M. (1968). The association between quantitative measures of dementia and of senile change in the cerebral gray matter of elderly subjects. *British Journal of Psychiatry*, *114*, 797–811.

Bourgeois, M. (1990). Enhancing conversation skills in Alzheimer's Disease using a prosthetic memory aid. *Journal of Applied Behavior Analysis*, *23*, 29–42.

Bourgeois, M. (1992a). *Enhancing the conversations of memory-impaired persons: A memory aid workbook*. Gaylord, MI: Northern Speech Services.

Bourgeois, M. (1992b). Evaluating memory wallets in conversations with patients with dementia. *Journal of Speech and Hearing Research*, *35*, 1344–1357.

Bourgeois, M. (1993). Effects of memory aids on the dyadic conversations of individuals with dementia. *Journal of Applied Behavior Analysis*, *26*, 77–87.

Bourgeois, M. S. (1998). Functional outcomes assessment of adults with dementia. *Seminars in Speech and Language*, *19*, 261–279.

Bourgeois, M. S. (2007). *Memory books and other graphic cuing systems*. Baltimore: Health Professions Press.

Bourgeois, M., Burgio, L., Schulz, R., Beach, S., & Palmer, B. (1997). Modifying repetitive verbalization of community dwelling patients with AD. *The Gerontologist*, *37*, 30–39.

Bourgeois, M., & Hopper, T. (2005, February). *Evaluation and treatment planning for individuals with dementia*. Proceedings of the American Speech Language Hearing Association Health Care Conference, Palm Springs, CA.

Bourgeois, M., & Mason, L. A. (1996). Memory wallet intervention in an adult day care setting. *Behavioral Interventions*, *11*, 3–18.

Bourgeois, M., & Rozsa, A. (2006). Functional Goals Screening Protocol: Community Clients with Dementia. In D. Beukelman, K. Garrett, & K. Yorkston (Eds.), *AAC interventions for adults in medical settings: Integrated assessment and treatment protocols*. Baltimore: Brookes.

Brookshire, R., & Nicholas, L. (1993). *Discourse comprehension test*. Minneapolis, MN: BRK.

Brookshire, R., & Nicholas, L. (1997). *Discourse comprehension test—revised*. Minneapolis, MN: BRK.

Brush, J., & Camp, C. (1998). Using spaced-retrieval as an intervention during speech-language therapy. *Clinical Gerontologist*, *19*(1), 51–64.

Bullard, S. E., Fein, D., Gleeson, M. K., Tischer, N., Mapou, R. L., & Kaplan, E. (2004). The Biber cognitive estimation test. *Archives of Clinical Neuropsychology*, *19*, 835–846.

Chapman, S. B., Zientz, J., Weiner, M., Rosenberg, R., Frawley, W., & Burns, M. H. (2002). Discourse changes in early Alzheimer disease, mild cognitive impairment, and normal aging. *Alzheimer Disease and Associate Disorders*, *16*(3), 177–186.

Cohen-Mansfield, J. (1986). Agitated behaviors in the elderly. II. Preliminary results in the cognitively deteriorated. *Journal of the American Geriatrics Society*, *34*, 722–727.

Crum, R., Anthony, J., Bassett, S., & Folstein, M. (1993). Population-based norms for the Mini-Mental State Examination by age and educational level. *Journal of the American Medical Association*, *269*, 2386–2391.

Damico, J. S., Oelschlaeger, M., & Simmons-Mackie, N. (1999). Qualitative methods in aphasia research: Conversation analysis. *Aphasiology*, *13*, 667–680.

Damico, J. S., & Simmons-Mackie, N. (2003). Qualitative research and speech-language pathology: A tutorial for the clinical realm. *American Journal of Speech-Language Pathology*, *12*(2), 131–143.

Damico, J. S., Simmons-Mackie, N., Oelschlaeger, M., Elman, R., & Armstrong, E. (1999). Qualitative methods in aphasia research: Basic issues. *Aphasiology*, *13*, 651–665.

Delis, D. C., Kaplan, E., & Kramer, J. H. (2001). *Delis-Kaplan executive function system: Examiner's manual*. San Antonio, TX: Psychological Corporation.

DeRenzi, E., & Vignolo, L. A. (1962). Token Test. *Brain*, *85*, 665–678.

Diehl, M., Marsiske, M., Horgas, A. L., Rosenberg, A., Saczynski, J. S., & Willis, S. L. (2005). The Revised Observed Tasks of Daily Living: A performance-based assessment of everyday problem solving in older adults. *Journal of Applied Gerontology*, *24*(3), 211–230.

Duff, K., Schoenberg, M., Patton, D., Paulsen, J., Bayless, J., Mold, J., et al. (2005). Regression-based formulas for predicting change in RBANS subtests with older adults. *Archives of Clinical Neuropsychology*, *20*(3), 281–290.

Dufouil, C., Clayton, D., Brayne, C., Chi, L. Y., Dening, T. R., Paykel, E. S., et al. (2000). Population norms for the MMSE in the very old: Estimates based on longitudinal data. *Neurology*, *55*, 1609–1613.

Ehrlich, J. S., Obler, L. K., & Clark, L. (1997). Ideational and semantic contributions to narrative production in adults with dementia of the Alzheimer's type. *Journal of Communication Disorders*, *30*, 79–99.

Ellmo, W. J., Graser, J. M., Krchnavek, E. A., Calabrese, D. B., & Hauck, K. (1995). *Measure of cognitive-linguistic abilities*. Vero Beach, FL: Speech Bin.

Farah, M. J., & Feinberg, T. E. (Eds.). (2000). *Patient-based approaches to cognitive neuroscience*. Cambridge, MA: MIT Press.

Feldman, H., Sauter, A., Donald, A., Gelinas, I., Gautier, S., Torfs, K., et al. (2001). The Disability Assessment for Dementia Scale: A 12-month study of functional ability in mild to moderate severity Alzheimer's disease. *Alzheimer Disease and Associated Disorders*, *15*, 89–95.

Folstein, M. F., Folstein, S. E., & McHugh, P. R. (1975). "Mini-mental state": A practical method for grading the cognitive state of clients for the clinician. *Journal of Psychiatry Research*, *12*, 189–198.

Frattali, C., Thompson, C., Holland, A., Wohl, C., & Ferketic, M. (1995). The FACS of life: ASHA FACS—a functional outcome measure for adults. *ASHA*, *37*, 40–46.

Freedman, M., Leach, L., Kaplan, E., Winocur, G., Shulman, K. I., & Delis, D. C. (1994). *Clock drawing: A neuropsychological analysis*. New York: Oxford University Press.

Friedman, R., & Tappen, R. (1991). The effect of planned walking on communication in Alzheimer's disease. *Journal of the American Geriatrics Society*, *39*, 650–654.

Fuld, P. A. (1981). *The Fuld object memory evaluation*. Chicago: Stoelting Instrument.

Galasko, D., Bennett, D., Sano, M., Ernesto, C., Thomas, R., Grundman, M., et al. (1997). An inventory to assess activities of daily living for clinical trials in Alzheimer's disease. *Alzheimer's Disease Cooperative Study; Alzheimer Disease & Associated Disorders*, *11*(Suppl. 2), S33–S39.

Galasko, D., Kershaw, P. R., Schneider, L., Zhu, Y., & Tariot, P. (2004). Galantamine maintains ability to perform activities of daily living in patients with Alzheimer's disease. *Journal of the American Geriatrics Society*, *52*, 1070–1076.

Gelinas, I., Gauthier, L., McIntyre, M., & Gautier, S. (1999). Development of a functional measure for persons with Alzheimer's disease: the Disability Assessment for Dementia. *American Journal of Occupational Therapy*, *53*, 471–481.

Glosser, G. (1991). Patterns of discourse production among neurological patients with fluent language disorders. *Brain and Language*, *40*(1), 67–88.

Gontkovsky, S. T., Mold, J. W., & Beatty, W. W. (2002). Age and educational influences on RBANS index scores in a nondemented geriatric sample. *Clinical Neuropsychologist*, *16*(3), 258–263.

Goodglass H., Kaplan, E., & Barresi, B. (2000). *The Boston diagnostic aphasia examination* (3rd ed.). San Antonio, TX: Psychological Corporation.

Grober, E., & Buschke, H. (1988). Screening for dementia by memory testing. *Neurology*, *38*, 900–903.

Hall, K. M. (1997). The Functional Assessment Measure (FAM). *Journal of Rehabilitation Outcomes*, *1*(3), 63–65.

Hall, K. M., Hamilton, B., Gordon, W. A., & Zasler, N. D. (1993). Characteristics and comparisons of functional assessment indices: Disability rating scale, functional independence measure and functional assessment measure. *Journal of Head Trauma Rehabilitation*, *8*(2), 60–74.

Hartley, L. L. (1995). *Cognitive-communicative abilities following brain injury: A functional approach*. San Diego, CA: Singular.

Hawes, C., Morris, J., Phillips, C., Fries, B., Murphy, K., & Mor, V. (1997). Development of the nursing home Resident Assessment Instrument in the USA. *Age and Ageing*, *26*(Suppl. 2), 19–25.

Hays, S-J., Niven, B. E., Godfrey, H. P. D., & Linscott, R. J. (2004). Clinical assessment of pragmatic language impairment: A generalizability study of older people with Alzheimer's disease. *Aphasiology*, *18*(8), 693–714.

Heaton, R. K., Chelune, G., Talley, J. L., Kay, G. G., & Curtiss, G. (1993). *Wisconsin card sorting test, Revised and expanded*. Lutz, FL: Psychological Assessment Resources.

Heinemann, A. W. (1989). *Rehabilitation Institute of Chicago: Functional assessment scale—revised.* Chicago: Rehabilitation Institute of Chicago.

Helm-Estabrooks, N. (2001). *Cognitive linguistic quick test*. San Antonio, TX: Psychological Corporation.

Helmes, E., Csapo, K. G., & Short, J. A. (1987). Standardization and validation of the Multidimensional Observation Scale for Elderly Subjects (MOSES). *Journal of Gerontology*, *42*, 395–405.

Holland, A. (2003). Improving communication skills in individuals with dementia. *Journal of Communication Disorders*, *36*(5), 325–326.

Holland, A., Frattali, C., & Fromm, D. (1999). *Communicative activities of daily living* (2nd ed.). Austin, TX: Pro-Ed.

Hooper, E. (1958). *Hooper visual organization test*. Los Angeles: Western Psychological Services.

Hopkins, R. W., Kilik, L. A., Day, D. A. J., Rows, C. P., & Hamilton, P. F. (2005). The brief Kingston standardized cognitive assessment—revised. *International Journal of Geriatric Psychiatry*, *20*, 227–231.

Howard, D., & Patterson, K. (1992). *Pyramids and palm trees*. Bury St. Edmunds, UK: Thames Valley.

Johnson, N., Barion A., Rademaker, A., Rehkemper, G., & Weintraub, S. (2004). The Activities of Daily Living Questionnaire: A validation study in patients with dementia. *Alzheimer Disease Associated Disorders*, *18*(4), 223–230.

Johnson-Greene, D. (2004). Test review: Dementia Rating Scale-2 (DRS-2). *Archives of Clinical Neuropsychology*, *19*(1), 145–147.

Jones, R. N., & Gallo, J. J. (2002). Education and sex differences in the Mini-Mental State Examination: Effects of differential item functioning. *Journal of Gerontology: Series B: Psychological Sciences and Social Sciences*, *57B*(6), 548–558.

Jones, T., Schinka, J. A., Vanderploeg, R. D., Small, B. J., Graves, A., & Mortimer, J. A. (2002). 3MS normative data for the elderly. *Archives of Clinical Neuropsychology*, *17*(2), 171–177.

Jorm, A. F. (1996). Assessment of cognitive impairment and dementia using informant reports. *Clinical Psychology Review*, *16*(1), 52–73.

Jurica, P. J., Leitten, C. L., & Mattis, S. (2001). *Dementia Rating Scale-2*. Lutz, FL: Psychological Assessment Resources.

Kane, R. L., & Kane. R. A. (Eds.). (2000). *Assessing older persons: Measures, meaning, and practical applications*. New York: Oxford University Press.

Kaplan, E., Leach, L., Rewilak, D., Richards, B., & Proulx, G. (2000) *Kaplan Baycrest Neurocognitive Assessment*. San Antonio, TX: Psychological Corporation.

Kennedy, M. (2002). Principles of assessment. In R. Paul (Ed.), *Introduction to clinical methods in communication disorders*. New York: Brookes.

Kertesz, A. (1982). *Western aphasia battery*. New York: Harcourt Brace Jovanovich.

Kilada, S., Gamaldo, A., Grant, E. A., Moghekar, A., Morris, J. C., & O'Brien, R. J. (2005). Brief screening tests for the diagnosis of dementia: Comparison with the Mini-Mental State Exam. *Alzheimer Disease and Associated Disorders*, *19*, 8–16.

Kopelman, M., Wilson, B., & Baddeley, A. (1990). *The autobiographical memory interview*. Bury St. Edmunds, UK: Thames Valley.

Kunik, M. E., Martinez, M., Snow, A. L., Beck, C. K., Cody, M., Rapp, C. G., et al. (2003). Determinants of behavioral symptoms in dementia patients. *Clinical Gerontologist*, *26*(3/4), 83–89.

LaPointe, L. & Horner, J. (1998). *Reading comprehension battery for aphasia (RCBA-2)*. Austin, TX: Pro-Ed.

Lawton, M. P., Van Haitsma, K., & Klapper, J. (1996). Observed affect in nursing home residents with Alzheimer's disease. *Journal of Gerontology: Psychological Sciences*, *51B*, P3–P14.

Lazaro, L., Marcos, T., Pujol, J., & Valdes, M. (1995). Cognitive assessment and diagnosis of dementia by CAMDEX in elderly general hospital patients. *International Journal of Geriatric Psychiatry, 10*(7), 603–609.

Leach, L., Kaplan, E., Rewilak, D., Richards, B., & Proulx, G. (2000). *Kaplan Baycrest neurocognitive assessment (KBNA)*. San Antonio, TX: Psychological Corporation.

Lezak, M. D. (1983). *Neuropsychological assessment*. New York: Oxford University Press.

Lezak, M. D., Howieson, D. B., & Loring, D. M. (2004). *Neuropsychological assessment* (4th ed.). New York: Oxford University Press.

Lomas, J., Pickard, L., Bester, S., Elbard, H., Finlayson, A., & Zogharb, C. (1989). The Communicative Effectiveness Index: Development and psychometric evaluation of a functional communication measure for adult aphasia. *Journal of Speech and Hearing Disorders*, *54*, 1113–1124.

Lubinski, R. (Ed). (1991). *Dementia and communication*. Philadelphia: Decker.

Mattis, S. (2001). *Dementia rating scale* (DRS-2; 2nd ed.). Lutz, FL: Psychological Assessment Resources.

Meulen, E., Schmand, B., van Campen, J. P., de Koning, S. J., Ponds, R. W., Scheltens, P., et al. (2005). The seven minute screen: a neurocognitive screening test highly sensitive to various types of dementia. *Journal of Neurology, Neurosurgery, and Psychiatry*, *75*, 700–705.

Meyers, P. S. (1999). *Right hemisphere damage: Disorders of communication and cognition*. Stamford, CT: Thomson Learning.

Mohs, R. (2006). *ADAS-Cog: What, why and how?* Retrieved on May 13, 2006, from http://www.alzheimer-insights.com/insights/vol3no1/vol3no1.htm

Morris, J. C. (1993). The Clinical Dementia Rating (CDR): Current version and scoring rules. *Neurology*, *43*, 2412–2414.

Moss, M. B., Albert, M. S., Butters, N., & Payne, M. (1986). Differential patterns of memory loss among patients with Alzheimer's disease, Huntington's disease, and alcoholic Korsakoff's syndrome. *Archives of Neurology*, *43*, 239–246.

Mundt, J. C., Freed, D. M., & Greist, J. H. (2000). Lay person-based screening for early detection of Alzheimer's disease: Development and validation of an instrument. *Journals of Gerontology: Series B: Psychological Sciences and Social Sciences*, *55B*(3), 163–170.

Mungas, D., Marshall, S. C., Weldon, M., Haan, M., & Reed, B. R. (1996). Age and education correction of Mini-Mental State Examination for English- and Spanish-speaking elderly. *Neurology*, *46*, 700–706.

Mungas, D., Reed, B., & Kramer, J. (2003). Psychometrically matched measures of global cognition, memory, and executive function for assessment of cognitive decline in older persons. *Neuropsychology*, *17*(3), 380–392.

Nasreddine, Z., Phillips, N., Bédirian, V., Charbonneau, S., Whitehead, V., Collin, I., et al. (2005). The Montreal Cognitive Assessment (MOCA): A brief screening tool for mild cognitive impairment. *Journal of the American Geriatrics Society*, *53*, 695–699.

Nelson, H. (1982). *National adult reading test.* Swindon, UK: NFER-Nelson.

Nicholas, L. E., & Brookshire, R. H. (1993). A system for quantifying the informativeness and efficiency of the connected speech of adults with aphasia. *Journal of Speech and Hearing Research*, *36*, 338–350.

Nicholas, L. E., & Brookshire, R. H. (1995). Presence, completeness, and accuracy of main concepts in connected speech of non-brain-damaged adults and adults with aphasia. *Journal of Speech and Hearing Research*, *38*, 145–156.

Oakley, F., Lai, J. S., & Sunderland, T. (1999). A validation study of the Daily Activities Questionnaire: An activities of daily living assessment for people with Alzheimer's disease. *Journal of Outcome Measures*, *3*, 297–307.

Perkins, L. (1995). Applying conversation analysis to aphasia: Clinical implications and analytic issues. *European Journal of Disorders of Communication, 30*, 372–383.
Perkins, L., Whitworth, A., & and Lesser, R. (1998). Conversing in dementia: a conversational analytic approach. *Journal of Neurolinguistics, 11*(1/2), 33–53.
Pfeffer, R. T., Kurosaki, C., Harrah, J., Chance, S., & Filos, S. (1982, May). Measurement of functional activities of older adults in the community. *Journal of Gerontology, 37*, 323–329.
Prutting, C., & Kirchner, D. M. (1987). A clinical appraisal of the pragmatic aspects of language. *Journal of Speech and Hearing Disorders, 52*, 105–119.
Randolph, C. (1998). *Repeatable Battery for the Assessment of Neuropyschological Status*. San Antonio, TX: Psychological Corporation.
Randolph, C., Tierney, M. C., Mohr, E., & Chase, T. (1998). The Repeatable Battery for the Assessment of Neuropsychological Status (RBANS): Preliminary clinical validity. *Journal of Clinical Experimental Neuropsychology, 20*(3), 310–319.
Raven, J. C. (1958). *Ravens standard progressive matrices*. Oxford: J. C. Raven.
Ray, W. A., Taylor, J. A., Lichtenstein, M. J., & Meador, K. G. (1992). The Nursing Home Behavior Problem Scale. *Journals of Gerontology: Medical Sciences, 47*, M9–M16.
Reisberg, B. (1988). Functional assessment staging (FAST). *Psychopharmacology Bulletin, 24*(4), 653–659.
Reisberg, B., Borenstein, J., Salob, S. P., Ferris, S. H., Franssen, E., & Georgotas, A. (1987). Behavioral symptoms in Alzheimer's disease: Phenomenology and treatment. *Journal of Clinical Psychiatry, 48*(Suppl.), 9–15.
Reisberg, B., Ferris, S. H., de Leon, M. J., & Crook, T. (1982). The global deterioration scale for assessment of primary degenerative dementia. *American Journal of Psychiatry, 139*(9), 1136–1139.
Reitan, R. M., & Wolfson, D. (1985). Trail making test. In *The Halstead-Reitan neuropsychological test battery*. Tucson, AZ: Neuropsychology Press.
Ripich, D. (1991). Language and communication in dementia. In D. Ripich (Ed.), *Geriatric Communication Disorders* (pp. 255–292). Austin, TX: Pro-Ed.
Robertson, I. H., Ward, T., Ridgeway, V., & Nimmo-Smith, I. (1994). *The Test of Everyday Attention*. Gaylord, MI: Northern Speech Services.
Robertson, I. H., Ward, T., Ridgeway, V., & Nimmo-Smith, I. (1996). The structure of normal human attention: The Test of Everyday Attention. *Journal of the International Neuropsychological Society, 2*, 525–534.
Rosen, H. J., Narvaez, J. M., Hallam, B., Kramer, J., Wyss-Coray, C., Gearhart, R., et al. (2004). Neuropsychological and functional measures of severity in Alzheimer disease, frontotemporal dementia, and semantic dementia. *Alzheimer Disease and Associated Disorders, 18*, 202–207.
Rosen, W. G., Mohs, R. C., & Davis, K. L. (1984). A new rating scale for Alzheimer's disease. *American Journal of Psychiatry, 141*, 1356–1364.
Ross-Swain, D. (1996). *Ross Information Processing Assessment–2*. Austin, TX: Pro-Ed.
Ross-Swain, D., & Fogle, P. (1996). *Ross Information Processing Assessment–Geriatric (RIPA-G)*. Austin, TX: Pro-Ed.
Roth, M., Tym, E., Mountjoy, C.Q., Huppert, F. A., Hendrie, H., Verma, S., & Goddard, R. (1986). CAMDEX. A Standardised instrument for the diagnosis of mental disorder in the elderly with special reference to the early detection of dementia. *The British Journal of Psychiatry, 149*, 698–709.
Royall, D. R., Cordes, J. A., & Polk, M. (1998). CLOX: An executive clock drawing task. *Journal of Neurology, Neurosurgery, and Psychiatry, 64*, 588–594.
Royall, D. R., Mahurin, R. K., & Gray, K. F. (1992). Bedside assessment of executive dyscontrol: The Executive Interview (EXIT). *Journal of the American Geriatrics Society, 40*, 1221–1226.

Rozsa, A., & Bourgeois, M. (2006). Screening Protocol to Monitor Residents with Dementia. In D. Beukelman, K. Garrett, & K. Yorkston (Eds.), *AAC Interventions for Adults in Medical Settings: Integrated assessment and treatment protocols*. Baltimore: Brookes.

Russell, E. W. (1975). A multiple scoring method for the assessment of complex memory functions. *Journal of Consulting & Clinical Psychology*, *43*, 800–809.

Sacks, H., Schegloff, E., & Jefferson, G. (1974). A simplest systematics for the organization of turn-taking for conversation. *Language*, *50*(4), 696–735.

Salmon, D. P., Kwo-on-Yuen, P. F., Heindel, W. C., Butters, N., & Thal, L. J. (1989). Differentiation of Alzheimer's disease and Huntington's disease with the Dementia Rating Scale. *Archives of Neurology*, *46*, 1204–1208.

Santo Pietro, M. J., & Boczko, R. (1997). *Communication outcome measure of functional independence (COMFI Scale)*. Vero Beach, FL: Speech Bin.

Santo Pietro, M. J., & Boczko, F. (1998). The Breakfast Club: Results of a study examining the effectiveness of a multi-modality group communication treatment. *American Journal of Alzheimer's Disease*, *13*, 146–158.

Saxton, J., Kastango, K., Hugonot-Diener, L., Boller, F., Verny, M., Sarles, C., et al. (2005). Development of a short form of the Severe Impairment Battery. *American Journal of Geriatric Psychiatry*, *13*(11), 999–1005.

Saxton, J., McGonigle, K. L., Swihart, A. A., & Boller, F. (1993). *Severe impairment battery*. Bury St. Edmunds, UK: Thames Valley.

Saxton, J., McGonigle-Gibson, K., Swihart, A. A., Miller, V. J., & Boller, F. (1990). Assessment of the severely demented patient: Description and validation of a new neuropsychological test battery. *Psychological Assessement*, *2*, 298–303.

Schmitt, F., Ashford, W., Ernesto, C., Saxton, J., Schneider, L., Clark, C. M., et al. (1997). The severe impairment battery: concurrent validity and the assessment of longitudinal change in Alzheimer's disease. *Alzheimer Disease and Associated Disorders*, *11*(Suppl. 2), S51–S56.

Schneider, L. S., & Olin, J. T. (1997). Eligibility of Alzheimer's disease clinic patients for clinical trails. *Journal of the American Geriatrics Society*, *45*(8), 923–928.

Schretlen, D. (1997). *Brief test of attention*. Lutz, FL: Psychological Assessment Resources.

Shipley, K., & McAfee, J. (1998). *Assessment in speech-language pathology* (2nd ed.). San Diego, CA: Singular.

Sloan, F. A., & Wang, J. (2005). Disparities among older adults in measures of cognitive function by race or ethnicity. *Journal of Gerontology: Psychological Sciences*, *60B*(5), P242–P250.

Small, J. A., Geldart, K., & Gutman, G. (2000). Communication between individuals with dementia and their caregivers during activities of daily living. *American Journal of Alzheimer's Disease and Other Dementias*, *15*(5), 291–302.

Solomon, P. R., Hirschoff, A., Kelly, B., Rolin, M., Brush, M., Deveaux, R., et al. (1998). A 7 minute neurocognitive screening battery highly sensitive to Alzheimer's disease. *Archives of Neurology*, *55*, 349–355.

State University of New York at Buffalo, Research Foundation. (1993). *Guide for use of the Uniform Data Set for Medical Rehabilitation: Functional independence measure*. Buffalo, NY: Author.

Terrell, B., & Ripich, D. (1989). Discourse competence as a variable in intervention. *Seminars in Speech Language Disorders*, *10*, 282–297.

Tetnowski, J. A., & Franklin, T. C. (2003). Qualitative research: Implications for description and assessment. *American Journal of Speech-Language Pathology*, *12*(2), 155–164.

Togher, L. (2001). Discourse sampling in the 21st century. *Journal of Communication Disorders*, *34*(1/2), 131–150.

Tombaugh, T. N., McDowell, I., Kristjansson, B., & Hubley, A. M. (1996). Mini-Mental State Exam (MMSE) and the Modified MMSE (3MS): a psychometric comparison and normative data. *Psychological Assessment*, *8*, 48–59.

Tompkins, C. A. (1995). *Right hemisphere communication disorders: Theory and management*. San Diego, CA: Singular.

Turkstra, L., Ylvisaker, M., Coelho, C., Kennedy, M., Sohlberg, M., & Avery, J. (2005). Practice guidelines for standardized assessment of persons with traumatic brain injury. *Journal of Medical Speech-Language Pathology*, *13*(2), ix–xxviii.

Valk, M., Post, M. W. M., Cools, H. J. M., & Schrijvers, G. A. J. P. (2001). Measuring disability in nursing home residents: Validity and reliability of a newly developed instrument. *Journal of Gerontology*, *56B*, P187–191.

Vance, D. E., Burgio, L. D., Roth, D. L., Stevens, A. B., Fairchild, J. K., & Yurick, A. (2003). Predictors of agitation in nursing home residents. *Journal of Gerontology*, *58B*(2), P129–P137.

Warrington, E. (1991). *Visual object and space perception battery (VOSP)*. Los Angeles: Western Psychological Services.

Watson, C. M., Chenery, H. J., & Carter, M. S. (1999). An analysis of trouble and repair in the natural conversations of people with dementia of the Alzheimer's type. *Aphasiology*, *13*(3), 195–218.

Wechsler, D. (1987). *Wechsler Memory Scale–R*. San Antonio, TX: Psychological Corporation.

Welland, R. J., Lubinski, R., & Higginbotham, D. J. (2002). Discourse comprehension test performance of elders with dementia of the Alzheimer type. *Journal of Speech-Language-Hearing Research*, *45*(6), 1175–1187.

Welsh, K., Butters, N., & Mohs, R. (1994). The Consortium to Establish a Registry for Alzheimer's Disease (CERAD): V.A normative study of the neuropsychological battery. *Neurology*, *44*(4), 609–614.

Wiig, E. H., Nielsen, N. P., Minthon, L., & Warkentin, S. (2002). *Alzheimer's Quick Test: Assessment of Parietal Function*. San Antonio, TX: Psychological Corporation.

Willis, S. L. (1993). *Test manual for the Everyday Problems Test for Cognitively Challenged Elderly*. University Park: Pennsylvania State University.

Willis, S. L., & Marsiske, M. (1993). *Manual for the Everyday Problems Test*. University Park: Pennsylvania State University.

Wilson, B. A., Alderman, N., Burgess, P., Emslei, H., & Evans, J. J. (1996). *Behavioral assessment of the dysexecutive syndrome (BADS)*. Bury St. Edmunds, UK: Thames Valley.

Wilson, B. A., Cockburn, J., & Baddeley, A. (1985). *The Rivermead Behavioural Memory Test*. Titchfield, UK: Thames Valley.

Wilson, B. A., Cockburn, J., & Baddeley, A. (2003). *The Rivermead Behavioural Memory Test—Revised*. Bury St. Edmunds, UK: Thames Valley.

Wilson, B. A., Cockburn, J., & Halligan, P. W. (1987). *Behavioral Inattention Test*. Titchfield, UK: Thames Valley.

World Health Organization. (2001). *International classification of functioning, disability, and health*. Retrieved February 21, 2006, from http//www3.who.int/icf/icftemplate.cfm

Ylvisaker, M., & Feeney, T. (1998). *Collaborative brain injury intervention: Positive everyday routines*. San Diego, CA: Singular

Ylvisaker, M., Szekeres, S., & Feeney, T. (2001). Communication disorders associated with traumatic brain injury. In R. Chapey (Ed.), *Language intervention strategies in aphasia and related neurogenic communication disorders* (4th ed., pp. 745–808).

Zgola, J. M., & Bordillon, G. (2002). Four guys at the table. *Alzheimer's Care Quarterly*, *3*(4), 279–288.

APPENDIX 4.1: PERSONAL WANTS, NEEDS, AND SAFETY ASSESSMENT FORM

<table>
<tr><td colspan="2">Assessing the Wants, Needs, and Safety of: (name)</td></tr>
<tr><td colspan="2">Environment: Home Hospital Assisted Living Nursing Home (circle one)</td></tr>
<tr><td colspan="2">Wants: The expression of personal preferences, likes, and dislikes</td></tr>
<tr><td>Likes:</td><td>Dislikes:</td></tr>
<tr><td colspan="2">Needs: The satisfaction of physical comforts and emotional needs</td></tr>
<tr><td>Physical:

Pain:</td><td>Emotional:</td></tr>
<tr><td colspan="2">Safety: The prevention of harm to one's self or others</td></tr>
<tr><td colspan="2">Medication:

Falls prevention:

Eating:

Personal hygiene:</td></tr>
<tr><td colspan="2">Environmental constraints:</td></tr>
<tr><td colspan="2">Emergency contacts:</td></tr>
</table>

APPENDIX 4.2: MEMORY AID INFORMATION FORM

© Michelle S. Bourgeois, Ph.D.

Please complete this biographical information for:
(Name): ______
(Nickname): ______

Family Information

Mother:
Name: ______
Date of Birth: ______
Birthplace: ______
Date of Death: ______

Father:
Name: ______
Date of Birth: ______
Birthplace:
Date of Death:

Brothers:
Names: ______
______

Sisters:
Names: ______
______

Wife/Husband
Name: ______ Date of Birth: ______
Birthplace: ______ Date of Marriage: ______
Location of Marriage (city, state): ______
Date of Death (if applicable): ______

Children:
Names:
1. ______ 2. ______ 3. ______ 4. ______

Spouse: (include married name for daughters)
1. ______ 2. ______ 3. ______ 4. ______

Grandchildren:
1. ______ 2. ______ 3. ______ 4. ______
1. ______ 2. ______ 3. ______ 4. ______
1. ______ 2. ______ 3. ______ 4. ______

What are the current occupations of these children?
1. ______ 2. ______ 3. ______ 4. ______

Where are the children and grandchildren currently living (city, state)?
1. ______ 2. ______ 3. ______ 4. ______

Your Family Member's Life History
Date of birth: ______ Place of birth: ______
Childhood home (city, state): ______
High school: ______ College: ______

Military Service:
Branch: ______________________ When: ______________________
Occupation(s): When:
______________________ ______________________
______________________ ______________________
______________________ ______________________

Special Honors/awards:
____
____
____

Hobbies, favorite leisure activities (past and/or present):
____

Places lived as an adult: When:
______________________ ______________________
______________________ ______________________

Clubs, social organizations: ______________________
Held office? ______________________
Church or temple: ______________________
Church- or temple-related activities or involvements (for example, deacon, choir, etc.) ______________________
____

Favorite pets (past and/or present):
______________________ ______________________

Memorable vacations:
Where: ______________________
When: ______________________
With whom: ______________________
Best friends: ______________________
____

Any other memorable events, details: ______________________
____

Problem Behaviors: Describe any other specific problems you are having and how often they occur (example: My mother asks to go to church every 10 minutes).

____
____
____
____
____
____

Daily Schedule: Please complete a daily schedule for your family member including all routine activities.

Usual Daily Schedule Special Activities

7:00 a.m. __________
7:30 a.m. __________
8:00 a.m. __________
9:00 a.m. __________
9:30 a.m. __________
10:00 __________
10:30 __________
11:00 __________
11:30 __________
12 Noon __________
12:30 p.m. __________
1:00 p.m. __________
1:30 __________
2:00 __________
2:30 __________
3:00 __________
3:30 __________
4:00 __________
4:30 __________
5:00 __________
5:30 __________
6:00 __________
6:30 __________
7:00 __________
7:30 __________
8:00 __________
8:30 __________
9:00 __________
9:30 __________
10:00 __________
10:30 __________
11:00 __________
11:30 __________
12 Midnight __________

Any other activities that your family member participates in during his/her spare time but which is not part of the daily schedule? __________

____

____

APPENDIX 4.3: MEMORY AID INFORMATION FORM: NURSING HOME VERSION

Name: ______________________________

Room #: __________

Roommate: ____

Friends: ____

Breakfast: time: ____________ favorite foods: ____________________

Lunch: time: ____________ favorite foods: ____________________

Dinner: time: ____________ favorite foods: ____________________

Location of meals: ____

Daily activities (what activity, with whom, location, who takes client to the activity, and any other information pertaining to daily schedule):

Approximate morning wake-up time: ___________________________________

Approximate bedtime: ____

Everyday: ____

____

____

Monday: ____

Tuesday: ____

Wednesday: ____

Thursday: ____

Friday: ____

Saturday: ____

Sunday: ____

Family who visit: ____

____

____

Other family: ____

____

____

Staff members: (name and activity):

____

____

____

____

Other Information: ______________________________

____

____

Likes	**Dislikes**
______________	______________
______________	______________
______________	______________
______________	______________

Interests and Hobbies

____

____

____

APPENDIX 4.4: BOURGEOIS ORAL READING MEASURE

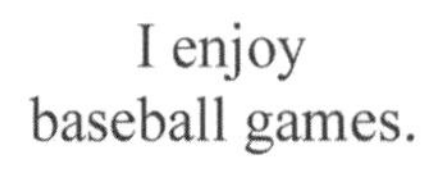

The dog's name is Rover.

I live in Swissvale.

My sister is 75 years old.

My wife's name is Mary.

Source: Bourgeois (1992a).

APPENDIX 4.5: SPACED RETRIEVAL SCREEN

1. *(NO DELAY)* "Today we are going to practice remembering my name. My name is __________________. What is my name?"
   Correct: "That's right. I am glad that you remembered."
2. *(SHORT DELAY)* "Good. I will give you more opportunities to practice as I am working with you today. Let's try again. What is my name?"
   Correct: "That's right. I am glad that you remembered."
3. (*LONG DELAY*) "You are doing well remembering my name for a longer period of time, and that's the idea. I would like you to always remember my name. I will be practicing this with you during therapy by asking you often. What is my name?"
   Correct: "That's right; you are remembering for a longer period of time. You did a great job remembering my name."

If the client is incorrect at any level three times in a row, this client is not appropriate for SR training; say, "Thanks for trying so hard. Let's work on something else now."
Source: Brush and Camp (1998).

APPENDIX 4.6: SCREENING PROTOCOL TO MONITOR RESIDENTS WITH DEMENTIA

Resident's Name: ______________________
Date of Screening: ______________________
Medical Diagnosis: ______________________
Date of Birth: __________ Age: __________ Sex: __________

PART 1: RESIDENT INTERVIEW

A. Personal Information

Family		Occupation	
Hobbies		Dislikes	

Premorbid Basic Reading Ability	Yes	No	Unable to answer
Premorbid Basic Writing Ability	Yes	No	Unable to answer
Wears Hearing Aid	Yes	No	
Wears Glasses	Yes	No	For some activities
Other Languages Spoken	Yes	No	Other: __________

B. MMSE Score: __________ Mild = 20–23; Moderate = 12–19; Severe = < 12
Strengths: __________ Weaknesses: __________

C. Conversational Sample:

Tell me about your stay here at (name of facility).

Discourse Features	Present	Absent	No Opportunity
Takes turns	______	______	______
Relinquishes turn	______	______	______
Maintains topic	______	______	______
Initiates new topic	______	______	______
Transitions from topic	______	______	______
Requests clarification	______	______	______
Clarifies	______	______	______

D. Orientation to Environment:

Show me to your room	Able	Requires assistance (Mild Mod Max)	Not able
Show me to the dining area	Able	Requires assistance (Mild Mod Max)	Not able

Show me the activities room	Able	Requires assistance (Mild Mod Max)	Not able
Show me the activities board	Able	Requires assistance (Mild Mod Max)	Not able

E. Memory Book Use: (Use clinician's memory book if resident does not have one)

If resident has book:

Does resident have memory book?	Yes	No
Is book readily available for resident's use?	Yes	No
Does resident engage in conversation about book?	Yes	No
Does resident maintain topic?	Yes	No
Does resident make novel comments?	Yes	No
Does resident make error statements (false comments)?	Yes	No
Does resident transition from page to page?	Yes	No

Observations:

F. Reading Screening (Based on memory book)**:** Pass Fail **Level:** Full sentence Short phrase Single word

G. Spaced-Retrieval Screening: Pass Fail

Observations:

PART 2: RESIDENT OBSERVATION

A. Social Communication Observation (direct or from staff):

Resident communicates wants and needs in various settings	Able	Requires assistance	Not able
Resident makes likes/ dislikes known	Able	Requires assistance	Not able
Resident converses with staff	Able	Requires assistance	Not able
Resident initiates conversations with others	Able	Requires assistance	Not able

B. Presence of Problem Behaviors:

Behavior	According To	Description (including time of day)

C. Swallowing:

Presence of dysphagia Yes No If applicable: Oral Pharyngeal Esophageal

Date of most recent evaluation: ______

Alternative means for nutrition/hydration: Yes No If yes: ______

CURRENT DIET (Check)

Regular diet	Thin liquids	Sips from cup
Mechanical Soft	Nectar thick	No straw
Puree	Honey thick	Cueing required
Clear liquids	No liquids	Other:
Full liquids	Nothing by mouth	

D. Activities of Daily Living: Assistance Requirements (Circle)

Mobility	Independent	Cane	Walker	Wheelchair
Meals/eating	Independent	Minimal assistance	Moderate assistance	Dependent
Grooming	Independent	Minimal assistance	Moderate assistance	Dependent
Dressing	Independent	Minimal assistance	Moderate assistance	Dependent
Toileting	Independent	Minimal assistance	Moderate assistance	Dependent

APPENDIX 4.7: FUNCTIONAL GOALS SCREENING PROTOCOL: COMMUNITY CLIENTS WITH DEMENTIA

Name: ______________________ Date of Screening: ______________
Medical Diagnosis: ____
Date of Birth: ______________ Age: __________ Gender: __________

PART 1: CLIENT INTERVIEW

A. Personal Information

Family		Occupation	
Lives with:		Hobbies	
Friends		Activities	
Preferences		Dislikes	

Premorbid Basic Reading Ability	Yes	No	Unable to answer
Premorbid Basic Writing Ability	Yes	No	Unable to answer
Wears Hearing Aid	Yes	No	
Wears Glasses	Yes	No	For some activities
Other Languages Spoken	Yes	No	Other: __________

B. MMSE Score: __________ Mild = 20–23; Moderate = 17–19; Severe = < 17
Strengths: ______________ Weaknesses: ______________

C. Conversational Sample:

Tell me about your family (or what you did for a living):

Discourse Features	Present	Absent	No Opportunity
Takes turns	______	______	______
Relinquishes turn	______	______	______
Maintains topic	______	______	______
Initiates new topic	______	______	______
Transitions from topic	______	______	______
Requests clarification	______	______	______
Clarifies	______	______	______

D. Orientation to Environment:

Show me where the bathroom is?	Able	Requires assistance (Mild Mod Max)	Not able
Show me where your telephone is?	Able	Requires assistance (Mild Mod Max)	Not able
Show me where I can get a glass of water?	Able	Requires assistance (Mild Mod Max)	Not able

E. Auditory and Tactile Behaviors:

Is attentive when others are talking?	Yes	No
Holds, squeezes, manipulates objects?	Yes	No
Is bothered by noises (radio, TV)?	Yes	No
Rubs, smoothes, explores surface with hands?	Yes	No
Is attentive to or participates in music, singing?	Yes	No
Hits, bangs, slaps objects or surfaces?	Yes	No

F. Visual and Functional Reading Behaviors: (Use newspaper, magazine, other written materials in the home)

Prompt client to "Tell me something interesting from this paper (magazine, mail, etc.)

Does client read aloud from the materials?	Yes	No
Does client make comments about the topic?	Yes	No
Does client engage others with the materials (ask questions, point)?	Yes	No
Does client turn pages to find another topic?	Yes	No
Does client notice objects in the near/far distance?	Yes	No

Observations:

G. Reading Screening (Bourgeois, 1992):

Print: Small __/24 correct Large __/24 correct

Observations:

H. Spaced-Retrieval Screening (Camp et al., 1998):

Immediate 30 sec 60 sec Pass Fail

Repeat after me (short statement):

Observations:

PART 2: CLIENT OBSERVATION

A. **Social Communication Observation** (direct or from caregiver):

Client communicates wants and needs in various settings	Able	Requires assistance	Not able
Client makes likes/dislikes known	Able	Requires assistance	Not able
Client converses with others	Able	Requires assistance	Not able
Client initiates conversations with others	Able	Requires assistance	Not able

B. Presence of Problem Behaviors:

Behavior	According To	Description (including time of day)

C. Swallowing:

Presence of dysphagia	Yes	No	If applicable:	Oral	Pharyngeal	Esophageal

Date of most recent evaluation: ____________________
Alternative means for nutrition/hydration: Yes No If yes: ______________

CURRENT DIET (Check)

Regular diet	Thin liquids	Sips from cup
Mechanical soft	Nectar thick	No straw
Puree	Honey thick	Cueing required
Clear liquids	No liquids	Other:
Full liquids	Nothing by mouth	

D. Activities of Daily Living: Assistance requirements (Circle)

Mobility	Independent	Cane	Walker	Wheelchair
Meals/eating	Independent	Minimal assistance	Moderate assistance	Dependent
Grooming	Independent	Minimal assistance	Moderate assistance	Dependent
Dressing	Independent	Minimal assistance	Moderate assistance	Dependent
Toileting	Independent	Minimal assistance	Moderate assistance	Dependent

5

Treatment
Solutions to Cognitive- and Communication-Based Problems

As discussed in chapter 1, the philosophy of dementia management has evolved substantially over the past few decades. Prior to the late 1990s, the therapeutic potential of persons with dementia had been rather pessimistic due to the degenerative nature of dementia. Clinicians provided supportive services only to the families of persons diagnosed with dementia because there were no known effective interventions for reversing the inevitable decline in cognitive and behavioral symptoms. Two of the driving forces for the changes in philosophical approaches to the management of dementia include the World Health Organization's (WHO) development of the *International Classification of Impairment, Disability, and Handicap* (ICIDH; WHO, 1980), now the *International Classification of Functioning, Disability, and Health* (WHO, 2001) and the Omnibus Budget and Reconciliation Act of 1987 (OBRA; American Health Care Association, 1990). These influences sparked a new attitude toward working with persons with dementia, with an increased focus on maintaining independent functioning for as long as possible and enhancing the quality of life of persons with dementia as well as their caregivers.

There has been an explosion in development, evaluation, and publication of behavioral interventions over the past two decades, which has changed the outlook of clinicians in many disciplines. Effectiveness has been documented for specific behavioral intervention approaches that reduce the activity limitations or participation restrictions resulting from impairments. Although these treatments will not reverse the impairments caused by the neurological damage, they may facilitate the maintenance of a quality lifestyle. In addition, treatments that target compensatory strategies to circumvent impairments may also allow the person to participate in his or her social milieu in a meaningful way. Now that there is a substantial number of published treatment studies, clinical researchers must evaluate the effects of these treatments and provide recommendations for their use with specific subgroups of the population. In 2001, the Academy of Communication Disorders and Sciences (ANCDS) began the process of reviewing the literature, documenting the evidence for each intervention, and making recommendations for further research (Bayles et al., 2005). This has been done with the support of the American Speech-Language-Hearing Association (ASHA) and the Department of Veteran's Affairs. To date, six manuscripts outlining evidence-based practice guidelines for working with persons with dementia have been published (Bayles et al.; Hopper et al., 2005; Mahendra et al., 2005, 2006; Bayles et al., 2006; Kim et al., 2006; Zientz et al., 2007). This chapter will review the many interventions designed and evaluated for treating the cognitive and communicative problems associated with dementia, indicating which treatments have credible evidence. Suggestions will follow for how these interventions can be used to address the principles of functional intervention, which are described below.

SOME GUIDING PRINCIPLES FOR FUNCTIONAL INTERVENTION

Clinicians must keep in mind that the interventions to be discussed in the following chapters have not been shown to change brain function or the impairment resulting from dementia. Rather, they have documented changes in behaviors that support engagement and participation in everyday life. The following three principles of dementia intervention are proposed as guidelines for selecting functional treatment goals and outcomes. The primary goals of intervention should be (a) to maintain independent functioning for as long as possible, (b) to maintain quality of life through supported participation and engagement in desired activities, and (c) to achieve these goals through procedures that are personally relevant to the client and are trained within functional contexts. See the details of each principle as follows.

Maintain Independent Functioning as Long as Possible

Intervention should begin in the earliest stages of the degenerative condition. This way, the individual is aware of his or her own deficits and remaining skills, can communicate desired goals and personal preferences, can identify effective memory strategies currently used, and can participate in planning and implementing compensatory strategies for future functional losses. An ideal approach is to enhance areas of strength and to reduce demands on impaired systems. As dementia symptoms progress, external communication and memory aids should be modified accordingly in order to promote maximal function. This way, the person can maintain as high a level of independence as long as possible across the early and middle stages of the disease.

Maintain Quality of Life via Supported Participation and Engagement

Activities that define the individual's lifestyle and personality must be identified in order to match compensatory strategies and the potential need for caregiver or partner training with specific activities. A variety of life activities ranging from employment to volunteer jobs to leisure activities can be analyzed for potential compensatory supports that can be implemented by the individual or by trained caregivers or peers. Arkin (1996, 2001) described a supported volunteer program in which college students were paired with adults with dementia and accompanied them to their volunteer activities (e.g., an animal shelter or a hospital) for enhanced socialization and cognitive support to complete the activities.

Emphasize Personal Relevance and Contextual Training

The importance of selecting treatment targets and activities based on the person's lifelong interests and habits is paramount in addressing motivation and treatment adherence issues. As clinicians, we know that the client who is motivated and has participated in the selection of treatment targets and activities will be most likely to carry out the treatment plan; likewise, we usually do not have much optimism for those who must be cajoled and convinced to attempt a specific protocol or strategy. Therefore, it is ideal to be planning treatment and compensatory strategy implementation with early-stage, motivated persons; however, when that window of opportunity has closed, the next best option is to know what interests and activities are held in high regard by the client and to plan modifications and supports that will facilitate the maintenance of those activities. Eisner (2001) has developed an approach for the selection of interest-appropriate materials and activities that is based on the personal strengths and interests of the individual. Camp and colleagues (1997, 2004) have also developed successful interventions for persons with dementia who maintain previous skills and strengths, are personally relevant, and seem to contribute to a positive self-perception. For example, persons with early-stage dementia were trained to be leaders of a small-group activity for persons with more advanced dementia and demonstrated effective leader skills and increased engagement, satisfaction, and pleasure in comparison to those participating in standard activity programming (Camp & Skrajner, 2004). These treatments will be described in chapter 6.

The principle of providing treatment in the context where the desired behavior is to be displayed is particularly important with degenerative conditions where the expectation for generalization to other situations and contexts may be limited. To the extent possible, it is necessary to provide training and practice in the specific environment where the behavior is to occur. When the desired task is trained in the desired location, there is no need to plan (and hope) for generalization to the desired location. Additionally, modifications to the visual support or other aspects of the situation can also be made on the spot, preventing failure or the acquisition of incomplete or erroneous components of the procedure. If a more traditional training venue is used (e.g., the SLP's office or therapy room), there is an increased potential for delayed training effects (at best) or failure to use the compensatory strategy.

COGNITIVE AND COMMUNICATIVE INTERVENTION: PHARMACOLOGICAL VERSUS NONPHARMACOLOGICAL APPROACHES

Pharmacological Approaches

Common practice has come to be to expect the availability of a medication to alleviate any new physical symptom. Thus, not surprisingly, individuals experiencing cognitive symptoms request a pill to improve their memory loss as well. The pharmaceutical industry has recognized this increasing market potential and has produced a variety of medications designed to treat the cognitive and behavioral symptoms associated with dementia. The therapeutic agents that have been developed in the past 20 years have either been shown to demonstrate some symptomatic improvements, such as the cholinesterase inhibitors and the NMDA receptor antagonists, or to have potential disease-modifying effects, such as the antioxidant, hormone replacement, and anti-inflammatory therapies. At this time, there are no therapies that have proven to reverse or halt the progressive downward trajectory of the degenerative diseases that cause dementia.

The discovery of cholinergic cell abnormalities in the brains of persons with AD in the 1980s led to the cholinergic hypothesis of geriatric memory dysfunction and the development of pharmaceuticals designed to stimulate cholinergic neurotransmitter functioning (Bartus, Dean, Beer, & Lippa, 1982). Tacrine (Cognex) was the first cholinesterase-inhibiting drug approved for the treatment of AD to show significant improvements over placebo on cognitive testing (Knapp et al., 1994). Serious liver function and gastrointestinal side effects, however, led to the development of several other variant compounds, including donepezil (Aricept), rivastigmine (Exelon), and galantamine (Reminyl). These drugs have addressed many of the problems with side effects, dosing frequency, and tolerability, and have shown increased efficacy on measures of cognitive functioning and activities of daily living (ADLs; Farlow, 2004; Hsuing & Feldman, 2004; Ismail & Tariot, 2004). The outcome measures used to document the effects of the drugs in these studies have ranged from a global measure of cognitive, behavioral, and daily functioning to a performance-based assessment. The global measure was the Clinician's Interview-Based Impression of Change with caregiver input (CIBIC+; Knopman, Knapp, Gracon, & Davis, 1994), which asked if the person had improved, stayed the same, or worsened overall. The performance-based measure was the Alzheimer's Disease Assessment Scale—Cognitive Subscale (ADAS-cog; Mohs, Rosen, & Davis, 1983).

Donepezil, rivastigmine, and galantamine have all been shown to be effective for persons with mild–moderate AD in improving cognition and ADL functioning, with effects maintained for up to 1 year (Feldman et al., 2001; Feldman, Spiegel, & Quarg, 2003; Wilcock, Lilienfeld, & Gaens, 2000). In addition, rivastigmine and galatamine have been reported to improve or maintain function and to improve or delay neuropsychiatric and behavioral symptoms, such as apathy, delusions, hallucinations, and agitation, for about 1 year (Blesa, 2004). Galantamine may also delay the need for full-time care (FTC), thereby decreasing the length of FTC usage as well as health care costs (Getsios, Caro, Caro, & Ishak, 2001). Persons with VaD and PD have demonstrated improvements with donepezil and galantamine (Aarsland, Laake, Larsen, & Janvin, 2002; Black et al., 2003). Unfortunately, the positive effects of these drugs do not last for very long, so alternative strategies are also required. Winblad and Jelic (2004) have published a study of the long-term effects (4 years) of the four acetylcholinesterase-inhibiting compounds and found a common response pattern. There is an initial improvement in cognition that maintains above baseline levels for approximately 1 year, but cognition continues to decline after 1 year. Results also revealed some support for continuous long-term treatment, rather than delayed treatment, using these drugs. The combined effects of donepezil and cognitive-communicative interventions have been reported to produce better outcomes than drug treatment alone (Chapman, Weiner, Rackley, Hynan, & Zientz, 2004), suggesting even more avenues of treatment opportunities to explore when the drug alone does not result in adequate or desired level of change.

The most recent treatment approach is memantine (Namenda), which is the first noncholinergic approach. Memantine is an NMDA receptor antagonist that addresses a different neurotransmitter, glutamate. This has been the first drug to demonstrate significant improvements in moderate to severe AD and VaD (Reisberg et al., 2003; Wilcock, Mobius, & Stoffler, 2002), and to be used in conjunction with donepezil (Tariot et al., 2004).

A variety of other medications including antipsychotics, anxiolytics, sedatives, and antidepressants are used to ameliorate the many difficult behavioral symptoms of dementia, including mood disturbance, altered perception, agitation, aggression, anxiety, and sleep and appetite disturbances (Rosenquist, Tariot, & Loy, 2000). Paradoxically, many of these drugs can improve one problem while creating another. For example, neuroleptic medications can have sedating effects and cause problems with gait and posture (Green, 2005). Clinical trials and efficacy data are very limited for these psychoactive drugs used for a variety of target behaviors. Therefore, clinicians are advised to use pharmacological interventions as a last resort (American Geriatrics Society and American Association for Geriatric Psychiatry, 2003; Doody et al., 2001; Howard et al., 2001; Tilly & Reed, 2004). A variety of environmental and/or behavioral techniques should be implemented first for the treatment of agitation, aggression, and depression. If these interventions are not effective and the person has the potential to cause harm or the condition has not improved within 30 days, then pharmacological approaches should be tried using the following practice guidelines: Start with low doses of psychoactive medications, increase dosage slowly, consider nonneuroleptics first, avoid the use of multiple medications, and monitor target behaviors and signs of toxicity frequently (Green).

The search for strategies to prevent or slow the progression of cognitive symptoms led to theories about the relationships among stress, diet, inflammation, and hormones and dementia, with these theories leading to subsequent therapeutic recommendations. Based on the premise that neurons are susceptible to oxidative stress that can cause the formation of free radicals and lead to neuronal degeneration, attempts have been made to reverse these negative effects with antioxidant compounds, such as vitamin supplements and specific foods, with contradictory findings (Luchsinger & Mayeux, 2004; Luchsinger, Tang, Shea, & Mayeux, 2003). Currently, large-scale multicenter prevention trials are being conducted to evaluate the efficacy of vitamin E and ginkgo biloba, two alleged antioxidants, in preventing or slowing the progression of dementia. Similarly, federally funded dementia prevention studies to determine the effects of anti-inflammatory medications (Martin, Meinert, & Breitner, 2002), hormone replacement therapy (Shumaker et al., 2004), and statins (Li et al., 2004) are under way. Smaller studies of experimental compounds, such as the APP β and γ secretase inhibitors and β-amyloid vaccine, are promising as well (Robinson, Bishop, & Munch, 2003). These pharmacological interventions are impairment-based interventions for dementia, designed to remedy the problems with acetylcholinesterase inhibition in the brain cells. Until scientists discover the underlying causes and effective cures for these diseases, clinicians and families will need to rely on behavioral, nonpharmacological interventions to address the many symptoms of dementia that interfere with daily life.

Nonpharmacological Behavioral Treatment Approaches

Behavioral approaches to treating the challenging symptoms of dementia have also been the subject of much study over the past few decades. These can be used in combination with, or instead of, pharmacological treatments, particularly when the pharmacological treatments do not modify symptoms to the satisfaction of persons with dementia or their caregivers, or when persons are reluctant to use, or are noncompliant in their use of, medications. Behavioral interventions that target the impairments in body structures and functions in dementia are designed to develop new neural connections and pathways to overcome cognitive deficits, such as memory, sensory perception, language, and motor behaviors, among others. There is little evidence, however, for the effectiveness of behavioral treatments at the impairment level, or that improvements maintain as the degenerative effects of the disease continue to progress. Therefore, the focus of most interventions is to find stimuli or strategies that compensate for the impairments, permitting the individual to function in an adaptive manner during activities of daily living. The purpose of these interventions is to maximize participation in daily life at a level that is meaningful and satisfying to the clients, their families, and others in their social environment. Interventions have been developed to promote functional behaviors related to memory, communication, ADLs, and instrumental ADLs (IADLs).

A virtual explosion of interest and publications in these interventions has been witnessed in recent years. Professionals in a variety of disciplines—including speech-language, physical, occupational, music, and recreation therapists; nurses; social workers; psychologists; and psychiatrists—have produced a plethora of therapeutic strategies and approaches, some with empirical support, and others steeped in "clinical lore" (Bird, 2000). A more holistic and humanistic approach, intended to maintain function and prevent excess disability, has replaced the pessimistic attitude that "nothing could be done for the person so only focus on the caregiver" (Clark, 1995). The result is an increase in the development of nonpharmacological treatment programs designed to improve the quality of life of these individuals and their families by enhancing communication and affect, improving performance of activities of daily living, maintaining functional behavior, and reducing problem behaviors and psychotic symptoms (Cohen-Mansfield, 2005).

Prior to the mid-1980s, the behavioral treatment literature in dementia consisted of single studies on diverse approaches representing the continuum of disciplines that were struggling to figure out how to manage the problematic symptoms of their clients with dementia. Bourgeois' (1991) review of the treatment literature categorized the approaches as focused on (a) environmental, (b) stimulus control, (c) reinforcement, or (d) group therapy. The effects of these interventions were mostly noted in the areas of engagement, social interaction, and cooperation, with some anecdotal effects on specific communication behaviors. These effects, however, were not compelling to professionals or families who wanted to see a return to previous behavior patterns as a result of treatment. Without evidence that robust changes in problem behaviors could result from direct treatment, many professionals advocated an indirect approach, focusing on providing support and coping mechanisms to the caregiver (Clark, 1995; Rau, 1993). Bourgeois (1991) challenged clinicians to develop specific interventions for persons designed to (a) address functional skills important in daily life and likely to recruit naturally occurring reinforcement, (b) choose intervention procedures that built on preserved skill abilities, and (c) select goals to match the constraints and opportunities of the environment. Since then, a dramatic increase in therapeutic strategies has emerged to address the needs for direct intervention on the continuum of dementia-related problem behaviors. As the ASHA Position Statement, "Role of Speech-Language Pathologists in the Identification, Diagnosis, and Treatment of Individuals With Cognitive-Communication Disorders" (ASHA, 2005) suggests, SLPs should provide intervention in the form of "training discrete cognitive processes, teaching specific functional skills, and developing compensatory strategies and support systems" (p. 2). The extent to which the clinical research literature supports the efficacy of these forms of intervention, through the publication of evidence-based reviews of specific treatments, will be addressed in the following chapters.

Memory and Cognitive Stimulation Approaches

The direct treatment of memory impairment at the neuronal level through pharmacological treatments has yielded less than satisfactory results. The amelioration of memory, cognitive, and behavioral symptoms is modest at best, and temporary in all cases. The direct treatment of memory impairments through behavioral, nonpharmacological interventions has been more promising. Yet the effects of treatment are still modest and temporary, with little evidence of generalization outside of the treatment setting. A multitude of techniques and strategies to teach, reteach, or support memory processes that have been damaged by illness or injury have been published in the cognitive rehabilitation literature. Studies exploring interventions for specific memory systems or processes (e.g., explicit, implicit, declarative, nondeclarative, autobiographical, and episodic) have compared performance in younger and older adults, with and without memory deficits (e.g., Baddeley, 1999; Kausler, 1994). It is beyond the scope of this chapter to review all of these areas of memory rehabilitation; however, there are many comprehensive reviews of this literature published elsewhere (e.g., Parenté & Herrmann, 1996; Yanagihara & Petersen, 1991). This chapter will focus on the memory rehabilitation literature that addresses memory impairments of persons with dementia, particularly declarative memory deficits.

Treatment strategies for the declarative memory deficits of persons with dementia have been described as either internal (to the individual) or external in focus (Bourgeois, 1991) (see Table 5.1). Internal strategies involve some mental manipulation of the information to be remembered, such as mnemonic techniques, rehearsal, and visual association strategies. There is an extensive literature that documents the successful use of these types of strategies for a myriad of remembering tasks by young adults and older adults (Dixon, de Frias, & Bäckman, 2001; Kapur, Glisky, & Wilson, 2004; Petro, Herrmann, Burrows, & Moore, 1991). Some of these studies have shown that even older persons with significant memory impairments can learn these strategies, but the effects are quite modest and transient (e.g., Cavallini, Pagnin, & Vecchi, 2002). For example, Hofmann, Hock, Kühler, and Müller-Spahn (1996) trained persons with mild to moderate AD to practice everyday tasks using computer-based simulations and found no evidence of cognitive improvement or transfer of training to real-life situations. Similarly, Davis, Massman, and Doody (2001) evaluated a program of cognitive intervention including face–name associations, spaced retrieval, and cognitive stimulation techniques with 37 persons with AD and found small gains in learning personal information but no generalization to overall neuropsychological functioning or quality of life. Thus, internal strategies may be more useful for people experiencing normal memory changes due to aging than for individuals with dementia.

The internal strategies require recognition of their purpose, conscious rehearsal, and the ability to apply them at the relevant time. These types of strategies have become popular in the lay press; there has been a proliferation of books

TABLE 5.1 Examples of Internal and External Memory Strategies and Demands

Examples of Internal Strategies	Examples of External Strategies
Mnemonics	Calendar, diary
Face–name associations	Multifunctional watch, timers
Mental retracing of events	Shopping lists, string on finger
First-letter associations	Putting things in a special place
Memory games and drills	Signs and labels
Rehearsal	Audio recording and memory aids
Internal Strategies Require:	**External Strategies Require:**
Effortful, conscious processing	Automatic processing
Active memory search to recall information	Recognition of information based on experience and practice
Internal monitoring of information	External monitoring of information
Mental representation inside the brain	Physical, permanent products in the environment

for the general public on memory enhancement (e.g., Mason, Kohn, & Clark, 2001; Nelson, 2005; Small, 2002). Fogler and Stern (1988) presented 16 different memory strategies, mostly internal, including visual imagery, mnemonics, story method, chunking, and first-letter cues. The lay public has been particularly interested in attending programs such as MemAerobics (Winningham et al., 2003) and Memory 101 (Weinstein & Sachs, 2000) designed to teach memory strategies and improve memory abilities. Although it is relatively easy to document improved memory knowledge and satisfaction with these sorts of educational programs (Troyer, 2001), it is more challenging to determine the extent to which cognitively stimulating activities might be protective or serve as a buffer against cognitive decline. Explorations of the "use it or lose it" hypothesis have yielded conflicting results (Mackinnon, Christensen, Hofer, Korten, & Jorm, 2003); for example, Hultsch, Hertzog, Small, and Dixon (1999) found that changes in intellectual activities were related to cognitive changes, but they also found that cognitive declines in high-ability individuals limited their activities.

Even in the early stages, however, persons with dementia might not have the learning ability or motivation to use internal memory techniques; instead, external strategies, which aim to reduce the demand on a person's memory and compensate for the impairment, may be more effective (Camp, Bird, & Cherry, 2000). External memory strategies take advantage of cues in the environment to trigger recall and retrieval from long-term memory storage. For example, verbal reminders, beepers, announcements, written reminders, calendars, memo boards, notepads, sticky notes, and designated places for objects can help persons to remember important facts, to do a task, or to keep an appointment.

The literature on external memory strategies ranges from studies that document the usefulness of specific auditory, visual, or other sensory cues to enhance recognition and recall of important information needed in a specific situation to those that provide a multitude of cues thought to stimulate multiple memory systems simultaneously in order to effect changes in functional behaviors (Bourgeois, 2007; Sohlberg & Mateer, 2001). The earliest memory rehabilitative approaches, such as reality orientation (RO; Folsom, 1968), and the more recent cognitive stimulation approaches (e.g., Elder Rehab; Arkin, 2001) attempt to modify multiple functional behaviors using a variety of cues and rehearsal strategies together. Other rehabilitative strategies have focused on the expression of factual memory and related behaviors through language interventions that are similarly multifaceted in the presentation of cues and procedures to elicit functional behaviors, for example validation therapy (VT; Feil, 1992a, 1992b) and Breakfast Club (Santo Pietro & Boczko, 1997).

Reality Orientation Reality orientation was the first therapeutic intervention specifically designed to address the memory and cognitive deficits of persons with dementia (Folsom, 1968). The purpose of RO is to maintain previously acquired skills by providing prompts and cues, rather than to teach new skills. Prompts and cues are usually in the form of a standard set of orientation facts, representing the date, location, next anticipated holiday, and outside weather conditions. These facts are often printed in large type and posted in a common area. Applications of RO involve training in one of the following contexts: minimal daily exposure to these facts in a group therapy format, reality-based conversation with staff at every opportunity in a continuous 24-hour format, or a combined group therapy and 24-hour program. Reviews of the extensive literature on this technique and its many variations evaluated the effectiveness of presenting orientation and memory information to persons in a structured and consistent way (Holden & Woods, 1995; Spector, Davies, Woods, & Orrell, 2000). In general, this type of cognitive stimulation has produced increased scores on measures of verbal orientation when compared to no-treatment control groups, and inconsistent conclusions about changes in other related behaviors (Woods, 1996).

Despite these lackluster outcomes, RO has been adopted as a standard practice in most nursing homes, typically in the form of an RO board posted in a common area thought to be accessible to all. There is little evidence that staff is encouraged to use the board in any systematic way; consequently, this potentially useful technique is often little more than the standard nursing home decoration. One should not assume residents will attend to and understand posted information without staff assistance and periodic review of the information. In addition, the information on the board is often of little importance to the residents, or is not available when needed. For example, if the facts on the RO board are important to a discussion that is occurring in the dining room, a board in the hallway near the nurses' station will not provide useful cues. To maximize the potential for a person to use relevant RO information, it might be wise to ensure that the RO facts are important and functional for the individual, that he has opportunities to practice using the information, and that the cues are portable. For example, knowing the current year may be irrelevant to a person with dementia who thinks it is 1950. Instead, there may be some specific information that the person is having trouble remembering that causes anxiety, such as not knowing when her son will visit next. A memory wallet or cue cards that the person can carry are useful ways to have important information with him when needed (Bourgeois, Burgio, Schulz, Beach, & Palmer, 1997; Bourgeois, Dijkstra, Burgio, & Allen-Burge, 2001). The salience of the RO stimuli may be enhanced with training, or with routine and repetitive exposure. Suggestions for such training are discussed below, under the discussion on spaced retrieval training.

Validation Therapy Naomi Feil developed an intervention approach, validation therapy, in response to reality orientation, which she found to be overly confrontational, thereby contributing to social withdrawal and hostility on the part of the person with dementia (Feil, 1992a, 1992b). Instead of orienting the person to the present reality, validation therapy is a way of communicating with the persons with dementia in whatever time or location they think it is, such that their feelings and views of reality are acknowledged. Based on the belief that persons with dementia may have a need to resolve personal conflicts before the end of their life, this technique involves recognizing and acknowledging the person's expression of feelings in verbal and nonverbal ways. Feil proposed that persons with dementia progress through four stages of the resolution phase of life: malorientation, time confusion, repetitive motion, and vegetation.

Experimental validation of these stages and a person's progression through them is lacking; in fact, there appear to be considerable overlap and fluctuation in the behaviors associated with this resolution continuum. Alternatively, Feil has suggested the use of specific techniques for particular situations, with an emphasis on nonverbal communication (e.g., touch, eye contact, and tone of voice). Most of the evidence for this technique is anecdotal; one of the few published experiments investigated the effects of a validation group for five persons with dementia that was held for one hour once a week for 20 weeks (Morton & Bleathman, 1991). Contradictory patterns were seen among the residents, with two increasing their verbal interactions, one decreasing verbalizations, and two not completing the study. Benjamin's (1995) review of the literature emphasized the potential positive effects of VT on affective and communicative behaviors in persons in the advanced stages of dementia, and the need for more experimental research with larger populations of persons with dementia.

Cognitive Stimulation In an effort to prevent or slow down the expected deterioration of cognition in dementia, clinicians have documented the effectiveness of cognitive remediation for specific tasks, such as memory for word lists (Zarit, Zarit, & Reever, 1982), category and alphabet cues for object memory (Bird & Luszcz, 1993), and practical problem solving (Quayhagen & Quayhagen, 1989). Multifaceted, comprehensive cognitive remediation approaches have also been evaluated. Quayhagen, Quayhagen, Corbeil, Roth, and Rodgers (1995) reported the long-term effects of a three-component cognitive remediation program including memory, problem solving, and conversation activities delivered by a trained family caregiver. Using an instruction workbook that included activities of graded complexity in the areas of word fluency, immediate and long-term verbal recall, verbal recognition, nonverbal recall and recognition, problem solving and planning, and categorization and conceptualization, caregivers implemented the protocol 6 days a week for 60 minutes a session over a 12-week period. When compared to placebo (passive activity) or wait-list control groups, the active cognitive stimulation group demonstrated significant posttreatment improvements in overall cognitive functioning, word fluency, and recall of nonverbal material. These effects returned to baseline levels by the 9-month follow-up, whereas the placebo and control groups demonstrated declines below baseline levels on some outcomes.

The challenge to clinicians is to develop interventions that will sustain remediation gains while there is continued cognitive decline due to the disease process. This requires robust treatment effects on tasks with credible content and social validity; unfortunately, the evidence of this is largely unreported to date. In addition, the evidence for generalization of treatment effects from practice and training tasks to real-world activities remains elusive. For example, Schreiber, Schweizer, Lutz, Kalveram, and Jancke (1999) used a computerized virtual reality memory-training program to train object–location and walking routes to individuals with dementia, measuring posttherapy improvements on several subtests of the Rivermead Behavioral Memory Test (Wilson, Cockburn, & Baddeley, 1985). They did not indicate, however, that these gains transferred to real-life tasks.

Elder Rehab Arkin (2001) has addressed the issue of maintenance of cognitive remediation gains in her research program. Her initial work was designed to identify the relative effectiveness of two different learning strategies (quiz versus repetition) on fact recall in persons with Alzheimer's disease (Arkin, 1997). She demonstrated that participants who listened to audiotapes of a narrative, including questions in a quiz format, learned more and retained the information longer than participants who listened to audiotapes narrating the information twice. Although this study is limited in generalizability due to the small number of subjects, the clinical implications of an active rehearsal strategy to maintain important information are promising.

Arkin has expanded her investigation of the effects of cognitive stimulation, first with an approach called the Volunteers in Partnership program (VIP; Arkin, 1996), in which university student volunteers participated in community activities (e.g., museum visits, bicycling, shopping, or volunteer work) and structured language stimulation (e.g., verbal fluency and conversation) with persons with AD. This was expanded into Elder Rehab, which was developed to compensate for the limited cognitive-linguistic services provided to maintain or improve the abilities of persons with mild to moderate dementia residing in the community (Arkin, 1999; Mahendra & Arkin, 2003). In Elder Rehab, the students continue to deliver a variety of memory and language stimulation activities, as well as participate in physical exercise and a weekly volunteer service task.

Arkin has demonstrated maintenance or improvements in discourse and memory abilities of Elder Rehab participants. At the end of the academic semester, 7 of 12 participants improved on posttest discourse, picture description, and proverb interpretation tasks. In order to evaluate the potential contribution of attention and physical activity to the effects seen in that study, a follow-up study compared the effects of the intervention with and without structured language stimulation, with both experimental and control groups receiving the same amount of the other components (physical exercise, memory training, and supervised volunteer work; Mahendra & Arkin, 2003). Although the treatment group demonstrated performance maintenance on 13 of the 14 measures of language and cognition, and improvements in physical fitness and mood, the control group participants who were engaged in unstructured conversation instead of the language stimulation activities performed similarly on postintervention language testing. In an investigation of the discourse of four participants who participated in the program for 4 years, Mahendra and Arkin found that they maintained or improved performance on all discourse measures compared to pretreatment testing. Additional research with a larger population of subjects is needed to understand the relative contributions of the different intervention components. Although Arkin's programs have utilized university student volunteers, Mahendra and Arkin suggested that staff, family caregivers, or other volunteers could also fill this role.

Breakfast Club The Breakfast Club (Santo Pietro & Boczko, 1997) is a communication stimulation approach consisting of a group treatment protocol delivered by a speech-language pathologist to a small group of residents. Multisensory cues are provided to facilitate communication during the preparation, serving, and eating of a breakfast meal. The purposes of the treatment are to maintain conversational, pragmatic, organizational, and decision-making skills through the stimulation of all senses (auditory, visual, olfactory, gustatory, and tactile) and procedural memories (including linguistic, motor, and reading) in order to prevent isolation, learned helplessness, and the deterioration of communication skills. This structured treatment approach incorporates many therapeutic principles specifically designed to facilitate communicative interactions, including the use of a structured routine or format for the session; a variety of stimuli to trigger associations with previously learned verbal, social, and motor behaviors; and individualized verbal cueing strategies to optimize the participation of each group member. There is a wide variety of language facilitation procedures: a continuum of question formats from open-ended to paired-choice to yes–no; the use of a cueing hierarchy (visual, semantic); the use of carrier phrases; and direct modeling of responses. Table 5.2 shows the 10-step protocol for a 1-hour session.

Evaluation of the Breakfast Club protocol delivered over a 12-week period to 20 persons with midstage dementia revealed improvements in psychosocial interaction, communication, conversation, mealtime independence, and cognitive function as measured by a 20-point functional independence scale, the Communication Outcome Measure of Functional Independence (COMFI; Boczko, 1994). When compared to control subjects who participated in small conversation groups, the Breakfast Club participants demonstrated significant increases in independence scores on the COMFI. In addition, anecdotal reports of increased attention, use of other participants' names during the session, decreased distractibility, fewer off-topic comments and interruptions, increased humorous remarks, reduced agitation and anxiety, and increased social interaction in other areas of the facility were indicative of the potential usefulness of this protocol in maintaining skills necessary for

TABLE 5.2 Examples of Breakfast Club Procedures

1. Group assembly, greeting, and nametag distribution
2. Facilitated discussion of juice
   "Can you read the name of this juice?" (visual cue)
   "This one has lots of vitamin C." (semantic cue)
   "You want a cold glass of ________." (carrier phrase)
3. Facilitated discussion of coffee
   Facilitator shows coffee pot and ground coffee (visual cue)
   Facilitator passes coffee around for members to smell (olfactory cue)
   "What's something hot to drink in the morning?" (semantic cue)
   "Do you want your coffee black or with milk?" (paired choice)
4. Facilitated discussion and selection of breakfast choice for the day
5. Facilitated discussion of food preparation
6. Facilitated execution and sequencing of food production
7. Facilitated distribution of prepared food
8. Facilitated discussion of another beverage option
9. Facilitated conversation on a variety of general-interest topics during meal
10. Group termination protocol, including cleanup, nametag return, and goodbyes

Source: Adapted from Santo Pietro and Boczko (1997).

quality of life. Originally designed to be implemented by speech-language pathologists, this program has been used by nursing assistants, occupational therapists, and others (Santo Pietro & Boczko, 1998). In chapter 6, we will discuss how this type of intervention can also be used in cotreatment with other disciplines.

Reminiscence Therapy Another verbal therapeutic approach that has existed since the 1960s is reminiscence therapy. Originally used with persons with depression, reminiscence therapy has two common variations: life review therapy and reminiscence therapy discussion groups. Life review therapy was described as a normal life process through which older persons come to terms with how they have lived their lives through recalling and evaluating specific experiences (Butler, 1963, 1980). Life review has a more therapeutic purpose than reminiscence therapy, and is conducted privately with a trained therapist in order to understand difficult or painful past experiences (Garland, 1994). In contrast, the goals of reminiscence therapy may include increased communication and social interaction for the purpose of entertainment or pleasure; when conducted in a group, the facilitator encourages a positive atmosphere and may redirect sad or painful memories to a more private session.

There has been a considerable body of empirical research on reminiscence therapy published in the past decade, with equivocal outcomes. Reminiscence therapy groups have been directly compared to other therapeutic approaches, such as support groups (Goldwasser, Auerbach, & Harkins, 1987), RO groups (Baines, Saxby, & Ehlert, 1987), and other types of group activities (Head, Portnoy, & Woods, 1990). Outcome measures documented improvements during group activities on variables such as depression, pleasure and engagement in the group, cognition and orientation, and problem behaviors, but little evidence of generalization of the effects to other times or locations, or of maintenance of treatment effects. Involving nursing staff with reminiscence therapy activities has been shown to change staff perceptions of residents (Baines et al., 1987; Gibson, 1994). Another recent, and promising, modification of reminiscence therapy was reported by Alm et al. (2004), who conducted reminiscence therapy sessions with visual supports in the form of a multimedia, LCD touch-panel display. They reported qualitative outcomes of enjoyment, ease of use, and desire to participate in additional sessions by nine participants with dementia (MMSE scores between 8 and 22).

Kim et al.'s (2006) evidence-based review of six published reminiscence therapy studies concluded that there is Class II evidence for the use of group RT to produce positive effects on communication and cognition of persons with dementia. Methodological shortcomings of the reviewed studies, however, require cautious acceptance of the suggested clinical practice guidelines. More rigorous evaluation of RT in future studies should include random assignment, larger number of participants, procedural similarities among studies, and sufficient treatment details reported to allow for replication and fidelity of treatment application.

External Memory Aids and Graphic Cueing Strategies

External Aids to Enhance Long-Term Memory Retrieval The retrieval of factual, conceptual, and procedural information thought to be stored in long-term memory becomes increasingly impaired as dementia progresses. Anomia, or word-finding difficulty, a failure to retrieve words from long-term storage, is typically the earliest, and most specific, language and memory symptom in dementia. Because normally aging adults compensate for word-finding problems by substituting similar words or talking around the missing word, it is often overlooked as one of the early warning signs of the pervasive loss of semantic information in dementia (Craik, Anderson, Kerr, & Li, 1995). The difference between the experience of normal forgetting and memory loss associated with dementia is that once the retrieval problem interrupts their train of thought, individuals with memory impairment often digress to another topic, and forget the earlier topic. Over the degenerative course of the disease, word-finding and other semantic retrieval problems become more obvious and in need of specific strategies that provide alternate access routes to the information. One of the most common manifestations of retrieval from long-term memory storage occurs in conversations. Typically, in a satisfying conversational exchange, there is reciprocity of information giving and receiving on the parts of two conversationalists. When one of these persons has a memory impairment that impedes the retrieval of declarative memory information, the success of the interaction is in jeopardy from lack of informative content exchange. External memory aids in print and electronic formats have been developed to access semantic storage via alternate pathways.

Bourgeois (1990, 1992a, 1992b) explored the use of written and picture cues, in the form of memory wallets and memory books, to assist in the retrieval of personal information necessary to maintain conversations between persons with AD and their caregivers. Figure 5.1 presents a variety of memory wallets and memory books used to stimulate conversation and memory. These external memory aids contain simple declarative sentences and a relevant photograph or illustration (one per page). The information to be included in a memory aid is solicited from the person with dementia and his or her family or caregivers; important biographical information (e.g., date and location of birth, parents, siblings, spouse, and educational milestones), daily activity information (e.g., meal times and details, bathing and grooming, and leisure activities), and other relevant personal information (e.g., answers to repeated questions) are among the facts included in the memory aid. When personal photographs are not available, a variety of clip art, magazine pictures, and line drawings can be used to illustrate the written statements. Bourgeois (2007) has published a manual detailing the possible types and formats of memory aids; in addition, instructions for making the memory aids wearable and portable are included.

The positive effects of memory wallets and memory books on the conversations of persons with dementia have been well documented. In an initial study, Bourgeois (1990) explored the effects of memory wallets on the conversational interactions between persons with moderate dementia and their caregivers. In baseline conversations without a memory wallet, subjects with moderate dementia provided limited and repetitive information when prompted to talk about their family, their life, and their daily schedule. Access to the memory wallet during the treatment condition enabled them to read aloud each sentence and then elaborate about the topic, increasing the number of factual statements significantly and decreasing repetitiveness and ambiguity.

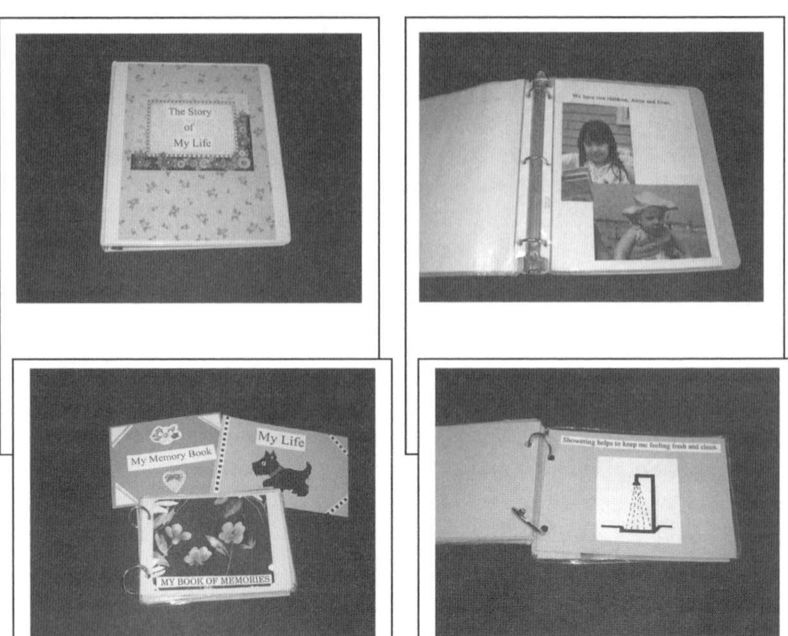

Figure 5.1 Memory Wallets and Memory Books.

Systematic replications of this study with persons with greater cognitive and sensory deficits revealed the efficacy of this approach, as long as the visual stimulus characteristics of the memory aid matched the persons' deficits (Bourgeois, 1992a). That is, the font size of the type was increased until it was read easily, and the size of the memory aid was prescribed for ease of physical manipulation. Some persons required 8- × 11-inch pages and plastic page protectors to improve page turning, and others required lightweight, laminated 3- × 5-inch pages in a portable format (i.e., on a book ring and lanyard, necklace, wristband, or belt). Also, the number of pages varied depending on the extent of the content to be included in the aid; persons with more severe impairments required fewer pages (i.e., 10–15). The effects of these studies have been replicated with subjects with severe dementia (Andrews-Salvia, Roy, & Cameron, 2003; McPherson et al., 2001).

These studies raise the possibility that reading, generally thought to be one of the language deficits by the middle stages of dementia, is actually relatively preserved. There is increasing evidence that the written modality may be relatively spared in dementia and that orthographic information can access semantic information that is not accessible by other auditory or verbal input modalities (Bourgeois, 2001). Psycholinguistic theories of reading suggest an interdependency of orthographic, phonologic, and semantic processes (Patterson & Hodges, 1992). Similarly, autobiographical memory may contribute to maintaining meaning and access to specific words, particularly personally relevant names and places (Snowden, Griffiths, & Neary, 1994).

CASE 5.1: USE OF MEMORY BOOK AS DISEASE PROGRESSES

Mrs. Jones, who attended an adult day care facility and was diagnosed with early-stage dementia, was given a memory wallet consisting of 30 pages of biographical information made by a friendly visitor with the assistance of his daughter. At the second visit, when Mrs. Jones came to the page that stated, "I was a high school teacher 30 years before retiring," she paused before reading the statement, turned over the page, and said, "I bet you didn't know that I taught just about every grade and subject in all those years. My first teaching job was a fifth grade social studies class." She had written a list of schools, grade levels, and subjects on the back of the page.

Nine months later, when Mrs. Jones was asked to tell the visitor about her life using the memory wallet, she started reading at the first page, continuing until she reached the last page, and then she started over from the beginning and read until the visitor suggested they get a snack. A year later, Mrs. Jones smiled when asked to talk about her life, held the memory wallet, but did not start reading. When the visitor read aloud the first page, she smiled and patted the picture. As the visitor continued reading each page and commenting about the pictures, Mrs. Jones continued smiling and patting the pictures, and on occasion would repeat a word that the visitor had said.

This example illustrates the changing nature of the communicative interaction as the disease progresses. In the early stage, Mrs. Jones was aware that the visitor had heard that she was a retired schoolteacher, and she planned to elaborate on that idea by making notes for herself about her different jobs during her career. Mrs. Jones, at this stage, was capable of an equitable conversation; her pragmatic awareness was intact, and her language and memory skills allowed her to plan for a more satisfying second conversation. As the disease progressed, Mrs. Jones lost that pragmatic awareness, and the conversational interaction became one-sided. When she finished reading her memory wallet, she started over; this reflected her desire to maintain the social closeness with the visitor, and the only way she could remember how to do that was by rereading her memory wallet. And by the time the disease had progressed to an advanced stage, Mrs. Jones had lost her verbal abilities as well, but not her desire to communicate, which she did by smiling, patting the wallet, and echoing an occasional word. The visitor, at this point, was entirely responsible for carrying on the conversation by reading and elaborating on the wallet content.

A variety of positive outcomes have been found with the use of external memory aids. Increased turn-taking and topic maintenance and reduced partner prompting and conversational dominance were found with the use of memory aids (Bourgeois, 1993; Hoerster, Hickey, & Bourgeois, 2001). Subsequent research (Bourgeois et al., 1997) demonstrated that specific problem behaviors, such as repetitive questions about a deceased relative or the status of a pension check, were reduced by including a page in the memory book that answered the question (e.g., "Mary died in 1994 and is buried in Westlawn Cemetery" and "My pension checks are deposited in the bank on Monday"). Similarly, other repetitive verbalizations were reduced by training spouses to use written cueing strategies (e.g., cue cards and memo boards). Furthermore, nursing assistants were successfully trained to use portable, laminated memory books to increase comprehension and cooperation with care activities, such as bathing and grooming, by residents with dementia in nursing homes (Bourgeois et al., 2001). Residents in the experimental group (memory books + staff intervention) had more positive verbalizations with staff and peers when memory books were present. These staff-training techniques will be discussed in more detail in chapter 10.

In summary, the use of memory wallets and books has evolved over the years. Originally, they served as a cueing strategy designed to support retrieval of factual information from long-term memory to improve conversations. They have also been shown to enhance retrieval of a variety of information that impacts the daily lives of persons with dementia and their caregivers, including increased cooperation with care routines and reduced problem behaviors.

Other memory retrieval strategies have attracted the attention of the general public, who are acutely aware and afraid of the memory lapses they experience with increasing age. The electronics industry has gotten into the long-term memory retrieval business with the development of devices to store information, to prompt owners to attend to the information with a variety of alarm and messaging features, and to retrieve the relevant or desired information. Devices such as calculators, planners (e.g., Daytimers and Dayrunners), personal data storage devices, watches, and cell phones can address memory and organizational needs (Harrell, Parenté, Bellingrath, & Lisicia, 1992; Kapur, 1995; Parenté & Herrmann, 1996). Handheld computers and cell phones with their memory storage and signaling features (e.g., Palm Pilots) provide many memory-enhancing functions (Glisky, 1995; Sohlberg & Mateer, 2001).

Although there are limited efficacy data on the usefulness of these devices with persons with dementia, the available data generated with persons with memory impairments due to other neurological conditions are encouraging (Bourgeois, 2005; Kapur, 1995). Some important considerations for the use of memory aids include the person's premorbid familiarity with and use of such aids, the amount of training required in the use of the aid, and the costs associated with the aid and with training. Obviously, familiar and simpler aids would be the more feasible choices for persons with dementia. In fact, information pendants, medic alert devices, and safe-return bracelets containing personal information (i.e., name and address) and medical information (i.e., diagnosis and allergies) (Alzheimer's Association, 2003) require little effort on the part of the person with dementia to have access to important personal and safety information.

External Aids to Enhance Sensory Memory The importance of the senses of vision, hearing, smell, and touch to recognition and recall of information is undisputable. When the senses begin to fail due to disease or the aging process, everyday functioning is compromised, requiring supports or substitutes for the degraded information. External aids can enhance the sensory features of stimuli, making them more salient, visible, heard, and felt.

The concept of a prosthetic environment to overcome the physical and cognitive limitations of old age was first suggested by Lindsley (1964). Attention to the stimulus characteristics of the environment, such as physical design and sensory features, and the social environments in dementia-specific units of nursing homes has created living environments that are minimally challenging and especially supportive for the person with dementia (Cohen, 1994). Important associations between auditory, visual, or tactile features and past experiences of the person with memory impairment are triggered by enhanced sensory cues (Garrett & Yorkston, 1997; Sohlberg & Mateer, 2001). For example, the auditory cue of a whistling teakettle may trigger longheld memories for the process of making a cup of tea. A door alarm that emits a loud, noxious sound whenever the person with dementia touches the door handle can signal a dangerous situation and reduce exit-seeking behaviors. In contrast, listening to soothing "white noise" (waterfall and nature sounds) via headphones may help to recall a previous nature walk and reduce anxieties or fears expressed as disruptive vocalizations (Burgio, Scilley, Hardin, Hsu, & Yancy, 1996). Auditory cueing systems can also provide important information required to maintain everyday functioning. Telephone-reminding systems such as voice mail and pill dispensers with timed alarms help persons to remember the content of phone messages and to take their medications at appropriate times (Azrin & Powell, 1969; Leirer, Morrow, Pariante, & Doksum, 1988; Leirer, Morrow, Tanke, & Pariante, 1991). Simple verbal reminders at regularly scheduled intervals have been effective at reducing incontinence in nursing home residents (prompted voiding technique; Schnelle, 1990).

It is important to note, however, that certain auditory cues may remind the person that *something* needs to be remembered, but not *what* (Woods, 1996). In addition, the person's hearing status may compromise the adequate processing and comprehension of certain types of auditory cues. For example, the alarms used for persons who are not supposed to get out of a bed or chair alone may be ineffective due to memory or hearing deficits. A person with dementia can be taught that the alarm is a signal to sit or lie back down; however, if the person cannot hear the alarm, then this cue will be useless. In both cases, additional cues or cue enhancement may be required to prevent confusion and impaired comprehension; other sensory modalities may be enlisted to provide the appropriate information to maintain function.

Visual cues are thought to trigger associated long-term memories that have accumulated over years of sensory experiences. Objects in the environment, photographs, and traffic signs can cue long-term memories for iconic symbols that are recognized with little effort. The use of a routine place and location for specific objects, such as hanging the car keys by the door to the garage, keeping a note pad for messages by the telephone, and placing bills to be paid in a specific letter tray on the desk, comprises commonsense visual cueing strategies used by many individuals without confirmed memory impairments (Harris, 1980). Written visual cues, such as labels on drawers, nametags, Post-It notes, grocery lists, activity schedules, wall calendars, orientation and message boards, medication organizers, maps, and floor plans, take advantage of the unconscious, automatic, and relatively preserved processes involved in reading comprehension (Bourgeois, 2001). Visual enhancements such as enlarging the print, using a light background with dark text (e.g., pale yellow with navy print is recommended for elders' eyes), creating high-contrast situations, or using personal objects can increase a person's attention to the importance of the cue. Certain organizational strategies similarly address the visual salience of objects in specific locations; for example, silverware trays, desk supply organizers, and closet organizers for shoes facilitate finding and recognizing desired objects.

Simple visual cues have frequently been the basis of effective interventions for a variety of problem behaviors in the home and institutional environments. Stop signs, directional signs, grid lines on the floor, murals, or nature posters have been used as visual barriers to prevent exit seeking and to promote safe wandering (Hussian & Brown, 1987; Kincaid & Peacock, 2003; Namazi, Rosner, & Calkins, 1989). Placing a particular object or materials along the pacing route of an individual can cue him or her to engage in an alternate activity (i.e., a laundry basket with towels to be folded). A vase of bright red flowers cued a person to her assigned table in the dining room (Leseth & Meader, 1995). Personal photographs and large-print nameplates helped nursing home residents to find their own rooms and prevent unwanted access to other resident rooms (Nolan, Mathews, & Harrison, 2001). The simplicity and effectiveness of these kinds of visual cues have led to the adoption of color schemes, street signs, and personalized front doors and mailboxes as a popular marketing strategy for residential facilities (Zeisel, Hyde, & Shi, 1999).

The use of written text as memory cues expands the utility of this technique to more complex everyday behaviors. For example, caregivers have been taught to write messages and activity suggestions on an erasable memo board magnetically attached to the refrigerator for persons whose pacing route included the kitchen in order to decrease anxiety (e.g., "I'll be home for dinner") and to increase desired behaviors (e.g., "Please water the plants") (Bourgeois et al., 1997). Medication adherence problems have been addressed with a variety of visual and written cueing systems, such as 7-day medication organizers (Park & Kidder, 1996). Visual aids in the form of a tear-off calendar (MacDonald, MacDonald, & Phoenix, 1977), a check-off chart (Gabriel, Gagnon, & Bryan, 1977), and pill containers used in combination with a visual organizational chart (Park, Morrell, Frieske, & Kincaid, 1992) were found to increase adherence by elderly users.

Visual cues by themselves, even if they are in the direct path of the intended recipient, do not guarantee that they are seen, recognized, and responded to as desired. It may be necessary to point out, identify, and rehearse the cue with the person to make it noticeable and to keep it salient. When staff routinely identified environmental cues with persons, the signs, signposts, and labels on drawers and cupboards were found to be effective cues (Gilleard, Mitchell, & Riordan, 1981; Hanley, 1981; Josephsson et al., 1993; Lam & Woods, 1986). Enhanced stimuli alone, however, cannot be expected to produce desired changes in a person's functioning without training or routine and repetitive exposure (Cohen & Weisman, 1991; Zeisel et al., 1999).

Other sensory cues, such as tactile, olfactory, and gustatory cues, have also been effective in triggering memory and maintaining functional behaviors (specific interventions that address this strategy will be discussed in more detail in chapter 6). Tangible stimuli in the form of dolls and stuffed animals improved the meaningfulness and relevance of conversations of persons with dementia (Hopper, Bayles, & Tomoeda, 1998). Positive alternative behaviors were prompted by tactile aids in the form of dolls in persons who exhibited troublesome behaviors (Ehrenfeld, 2003; Godfrey, 1994). Similarly, decreased agitation and improved family visiting were documented when a variety of handmade, therapeutically based sensorimotor recreational items (e.g., an activity apron, an electronic busy box, a look-inside purse, and squeezies) were given to nursing home residents with dementia (Buettner, 1999). Smells, such as the burning of candles with a pine scent or gingerbread and vanilla scents, may trigger memories of Christmas trees and baking cookies with their mother, and lead to satisfying conversational interactions.

Sensory aids that combine multiple sensory features may have increased salience. The keyless car door opener that beeps and causes the headlights of the car to flash when you lock and unlock the car remotely is an effective car-finding device for a vehicle lost in a large parking lot. Medication organizers with auditory alarms signal the person to take the appropriate medication at that time; cell phones can be programmed to alert the owner to read a text message medication reminder. Similarly, the NeuroPage device is an auditory pager that signals the user to look at the message screen for the next written appointment prompt (Hersch & Treadgold, 1994). Table 5.3 provides a hierarchy of sensory cues to consider in developing effective interventions.

External Aids for Memory Encoding

The hallmark memory symptom in dementia is working memory, or encoding deficits. Caregivers report frequent repetitive questions or demands and having to remind persons repeatedly of what to do, where to go, and what they were saying. Typically, desired information is conveyed verbally, is recognized and acknowledged as the answer to a question or a reassuring statement of fact, but is not processed and stored for later retrieval. The information has to be presented repeatedly, often because the amount of information to be processed or encoded exceeds the processing capacity. Complex auditory information may require even more time to process and comprehend. If urged to respond before having processed the instruction completely, the person may provide a negative response, reflecting frustration, anger, and lack of comprehension. Reducing the amount of verbal information presented at a time, altering caregivers' expectations for quick responses, and training caregivers to use facilitative methods to encode the desired information are strategies that should improve these interactions. Compensatory memory strategies can facilitate the transfer of new information from working to long-term memory or circumvent the encoding process by providing access to the desired information in such a way that it becomes part of the environment and does not need to be stored for later retrieval.

TABLE 5.3 A Hierarchy of Sensory Cues

Auditory	
Speech: Sentences	Open-ended questions, general directions, statements
	Either-or questions, commands, specific directions
	Close technique, one-step directions
	(Books on tape; radio talk shows, conversation)
Phrases:	Multiword phrase (command, statement)
Words:	Single word (command, statement)
Music: General:	Performance (concerts, recitals)
	General: background (television, radio, cassette player)
	Familiar songs (without lyrics); seasonal, age-appropriate
	Familiar songs (with lyrics); seasonal, age-appropriate
Environment:	Unfamiliar sounds and noises
	Familiar sounds: doorbells, telephone, sirens, and animal sounds
	Unfamiliar voices: strangers
	Familiar voices: family and friends
Visual	
Gestures:	Formal sign language system
	Pantomime
	Single gesture
Graphic:	Written text: Books and newspapers (multiparagraph, storyline)
	Written text: Multiple sentences (single paragraph)
	Written text: Single sentence
	Written text: Phrase
	Written text: Single word
	Complex picture (photographs, and multiple objects and persons)
	Simpler picture (photographs, single subject, and environmental signs and symbols)
Picture:	Photograph
	Color drawing: realistic or abstract art
	Black and white; line drawing
Colors	Color coding; environmental (wallpaper, carpeting, etc.)
	Color icons: red = stop, and green = go
Physical and Tactile	
Physical	Shadowing
	Physical guidance and prompting (minimal)
	Physical guidance and prompting (maximal)
	Full assistance
Textural	Texture coding; environmental (wallpaper, carpeting, etc.)
	Texture icons; sandpaper = rough, and silk = smooth
Objects	Actual three-dimensional objects, and abstract two-dimensional objects
Olfactory	
Familiar smells	Comfort foods (bread, cookies, and baby powder)
	Familiar smells (wet animal, flowers, new car, fresh-mowed grass, etc.)
Environmental	Familiar places (bakery, gas station, etc.)
	Dangerous smells (fire, smoke, gas, etc.)

The primary way to address an encoding deficit is to provide a structured and consistent procedure for insuring that the information to be remembered is encoded. Rehabilitation therapists have a long history of training persons with memory impairments due to brain injuries to use written strategies, such as memory notebooks, diaries, note taking, appointment calendars, and planners (Harrell et al., 1992; Sohlberg & Mateer, 2001). If important information that is presented verbally is written down immediately, the odds of being able to remember that information because one can read it are increased. This commonsense approach is a typical strategy reported by young and older respondents without diagnosed memory impairments (Harris, 1980). When the frequency of note taking becomes extreme to the point that family members find handfuls of notes on scraps of paper, memory concerns are voiced. Persons in the early stages of dementia can be aware of their deficits and use this strategy on their own to mask their symptoms. These written notes become external memory aids for important information that needs to be remembered; having a concrete, tangible written note obviates the need to encode and store it internally. Busy professionals, students, and almost anyone faced with a myriad of facts to remember in their daily life use appointment calendars and planners routinely to circumvent the need to encode and store all of that information. Audiotape recorders, telephone answering machines, voice message devices, and speech compression tape recorders, several of which use a tape loop feature for continuous reminders, are used for a similar purpose: to record information to be remembered later in a form external to the person. Woods (1983) taught a person with severe memory impairment to use a diary (appointment book) to retrieve personal information; Hanley and Lusty (1984) taught another person to use a diary and a watch to retrieve orientation information that improved her appointment keeping.

Even though these types of memory aids are commonly used by people in their daily lives, and some people instinctively develop a system that meets their individual needs, there are many others who may require some training to design and implement an efficient and effective system. For example, elders with clinically significant memory impairments may need structured training to use a simple calendar reliably. Camp, Foss, O'Hanlon, and Stevens (1996) demonstrated positive outcomes when training persons with dementia to incorporate calendar use into their daily routine via a spaced retrieval training protocol. Anecdotal reports of overly complex and cumbersome routines (e.g., multiple bell timers to remember several steps in a task or overly detailed computer calendars) that become the focus of one's daily life to the detriment of other activities suggest the need for memory strategy classes or counseling sessions for the general public as well as those with diagnosed memory impairments.

When the person with dementia can no longer write down information reliably for him or herself, caregivers can use external aids in the form of written notes for a variety of encoding-related problem behaviors. Bourgeois (1994) reported decreasing the repetitive questions of a father to his daughter concerning the whereabouts of his wife with a page in his memory book that said, "My wife, Lillian, died of heart disease in 1967." In another study, Bourgeois and colleagues taught caregivers to use a variety of written cues (i.e., memory book pages, cue cards, and dry erase memo boards) for reducing the repetitive verbalizations of their spouse with dementia (Bourgeois et al., 1997). Repeated requests to leave the house, to answer a question, and to go home were reduced by having the caregivers redirect their spouse to the memory aid by saying, "The answer is in your memory book (or memo board, or card)," or "Read this ______" (handing her a written instruction for an alternate activity). The frequency of repetitive questions was reduced significantly after treatment. Caregivers reported generalizing the use of reminder cards to a variety of situations; one wife kept index cards in the car on which to write the answer to the constant query, "Where are we going?" Others used cards in church and on a bus trip; another caregiver designed a "fake" letter from the Internal Revenue Service to remind her husband that he had submitted his tax return and that his refund check had been deposited in his bank account. Figure 5.2 illustrates a variety of graphic cueing systems for encoding information to be remembered at a later time (e.g., cue cards and memo boards).

Practical applications of these external aids in the nursing home with persons with advanced dementia were reported (Bourgeois et al., 2001). Nursing aides were trained to use communication, or reminder, cards with their resident with dementia when they were providing care, such as showering or feeding. Each resident had a collection of personalized cards that addressed problems identified by their nursing aide, such as "Showering makes me feel warm and clean," "My nurse Betty helps me get dressed every day," or "Eating helps me stay strong and healthy." Nursing aides presented the appropriate card to the resident, asked them to read it, and then asked them to proceed with the activity. Nursing aides reported increased compliance and cooperation with care activities and decreased negative reactions subsequent to using the cards. Additionally, an interactive CD-ROM training program for reminder card use by nursing aides in the nursing home has been demonstrated to increase nursing aide knowledge of and intention to use the strategy and perceived self-efficacy in managing resident problem behaviors (Irvine, Bourgeois, & Ary, 2003). Figure 5.3 illustrates examples of reminder cards used in long-term care settings.

When written cues are found to be successful with the person with dementia and the caregiver has many cards and written notes around the house, it may

Figure 5.2 Graphic Cueing Systems: Reminder Cards and Memo Board.

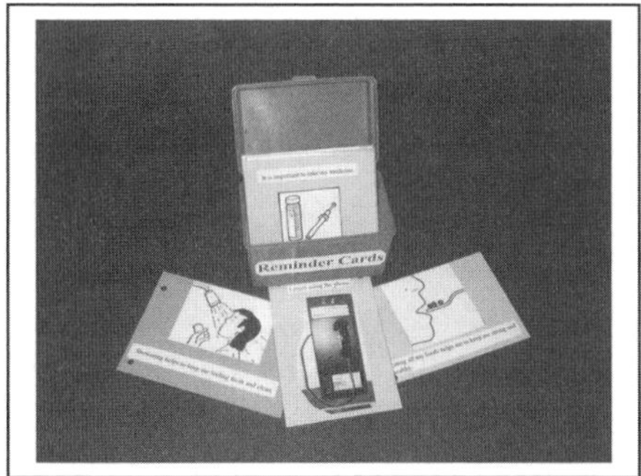

Figure 5.3 Reminder Cards Used in Long-Term Care Settings.

TABLE 5.4 Examples of External Memory Aid Strategies for Various Types of Memory

Strategies to Enhance Long-Term Memory Retrieval
Signs, labels, cue cards, diaries, calendars, and message boards
Memory wallets, books, and notebooks
Electronic planners (PDAs)
Computers, cell phones, and watches
Strategies to Enhance Sensory Memory
Visual
Enlarged print, bright colors, high contrast, highlighting, and color coding
Personal objects
Nametags, pillboxes, Post-It notes, and cards
Auditory
Doorbells, telephone ringers, alarms, and timers
Hearing aids and assistive listening devices
Strategies to Enhance Memory Encoding
Memory book pages, cue cards, and memo boards
Memory notebooks and planners
Electronic voice organizers and voice message devices
Tape recorders
Training: repetition, practice, and routine use

become important to organize the individual statements or cards into a memory wallet or memory book for more efficient access whenever desired (Bourgeois, 1990, 1992a, 2007). At this point, the collection of facts to be remembered serves an external memory storage function for the retrieval of information that may be or should be stored in long-term memory. Table 5.4 lists the examples of external memory strategies that enhance the various types of memory processes.

The obvious overlap in function of the various memory aids discussed above underscores the complexity and interrelatedness of memory processes. For example, a written cue card can serve as a sensory aid (i.e., visual stimulus), a trigger of long-term memories, and an encoding strategy (i.e., rereading the card). Memory aids alone, however, may not serve an encoding function without additional prompts or training. The person with dementia may need to be exposed to the memory cue repeatedly for its use or salience to become incorporated into daily use; training the person to attend to or use the salient cues in the environment may be a necessary component of the intervention strategy. Training, as discussed in the next section, can take many forms and has been the topic of much research.

TRAINING CONSIDERATIONS

Many of the above described external memory aids may require training to ensure their routine use and to retain their recognition, organizational, and memory-supporting value. Unless the person previously used some type of electronic or written organizational aid, a significant amount of time might be required for them to learn how to use and to incorporate such a system into daily life. Even simple environmental aids, such as signs and labels, may need periodic practice in identifying, reading, and discussing them to maintain their salience and intended function. The deterrent to the use and training of many memory aids, however, is the belief that persons with dementia who have encoding memory deficits are unable to acquire new information and demonstrate new learning. This belief, however, has been challenged by Camp (1999) and others with evidence that persons with dementia can learn new information, or relearn "forgotten" information, using appropriate training strategies, such as spaced retrieval, a memory-training strategy described below.

Factors to consider before selecting an external memory aid and a potential training regimen include the individual's level of literacy, prior experience with reminding systems, degree and severity of cognitive impairment, and level of self-awareness of his or her memory problems and motivation to compensate for them. Intervention targets and training techniques will vary depending on the stage and severity of the cognitive deficits. Persons with a mild cognitive impairment may begin to reactivate formerly useful reminding systems independently (e.g., the retired businessman who starts to use a planner again or the retired college professor who keeps a small notebook to record people's names and words he has forgotten recently). Persons with mild memory impairment usually request memory rehabilitation efforts and participate in the development and evaluation of their own functional systems.

As memory deficits worsen, successful memory-enhancing systems require premorbid familiarity, multisensory salient features, or specific training protocols (e.g., spaced retrieval training). When introducing a novel cueing system, such as an enlarged plate switch with a picture of a nurse taped to it as an alternative call button, training the person with dementia "to touch the picture when you need a nurse" would be necessary (Garrett & Yorkston, 1997). Many examples of successful training of external memory aids have been reported in the literature, including the use of a handheld computer to get to scheduled appointments and take medication (Kim, Burke, Dowds, & George, 1999), and a portable paging and text screen system, the NeuroPage (Hersch & Treadgold, 1994). Enwefa (1999) trained 10 persons with dementia to use communication wallets and the Alpha Talker, an augmentative communication device with preprogrammed phrases, and measured more conversational content with the electronic device. Lekeu, Wojtasik, Van der Linden, and Salmon (2002) used cue cards and spaced retrieval to teach two persons with dementia to use a mobile phone; although both eventually learned to use their phones correctly, one person required much more training than the other.

Not all efforts at training in the use of electronic memory aids have been successful, however. Kapur (1995) detailed efforts to train persons with a range of memory disorders to use electronic organizers; two of the five subjects failed to learn, and two others only reduced their memory lapses by 50%. The only successful user was a bank clerk who learned to use a Tandy organizer in two training sessions and used it daily in performing the duties of her job. The educational level of the participants, degree of impairment and motivation to use the devices, and appropriateness of the training techniques were thought to contribute to the difficulties encountered by the unsuccessful participants.

Sohlberg and Mateer (2001) have suggested the use of training protocols that incorporate a variety of effective instruction techniques, including functional task selection, task analysis, errorless instruction, prompting, cueing, feedback, and reinforcement. In addition, the role of the caregiver as a facilitator of external aids cannot be overlooked. Many of the reports of successful aid use have involved family and nursing aides who ensured that the aids were available and prompted their use at appropriate times (Bourgeois et al., 1997, 2001). Much of the literature on training use of external aids has been with persons who have sustained memory loss due to traumatic brain injury or other etiologies. Thus, more research is needed to find efficacious ways to enable persons with memory loss due to degenerative dementias to use external aids effectively.

Although additional research is still needed, this emerging literature is encouraging in the diversity of evidence that is accumulating to debunk the myths that persons with cognitive deficits could not learn new information or maintain treatment effects over the long term. It should be clear from this chapter that the maintenance of functional memory skills is possible when persons are provided with the appropriate system of external cues and training procedure for their condition.

Spaced Retrieval

Spaced retrieval (SR), a memory-training procedure, involves the systematic recall of information over successively longer intervals and the retention of the information for long time periods (Brush & Camp, 1998). SR is a shaping paradigm applied to memory (Bjork, 1988; Camp & McKitrick, 1992; Landauer & Bjork, 1978). The "spacing effect" phenomenon has been researched extensively, and practice distributed over time has been shown to be superior to consecutive learning trials (or massed practice; Ebbinghaus, 1964). Based on the principles of classical conditioning and repetition priming, spaced retrieval takes advantage of the relatively preserved skills of reading, motor learning, and procedural memory to help persons remember specific facts (e.g., family members' names and their room number) and functional strategies (e.g., the use of a memo board or scheduled activities card, or safe swallowing strategies).

SR is also considered an errorless training technique, in that the timing of the prompt and response is strictly monitored to prevent the person from producing an incorrect response (Wilson, Baddeley, Evans, & Shiel, 1994). In a spaced retrieval training session, the therapist begins the training by stating the purposes of the session: "Today I am going to help you remember where your room is; your room number is written on this card. When you want to remember where your room is, I want you to look at your card." The therapist then prompts the person with dementia to produce the target response by saying, "How do you remember where your room is?" The person with dementia responds, "I look at my card." The therapist replies, "That's correct, and I want you to remember that because I will be asking you again in a few minutes." After a specified time interval, the therapist repeats the prompt, "How do you remember where your room is?" Each correct response results in doubling the time interval before the next prompt. Incorrect responses elicit the modeling and repetition of the correct response. The expectation of an immediate correct response is important in preventing incorrect responses; any hesitation should elicit the therapist's modeled response and the person's immediate repetition. This can initially feel unnatural to most clinicians, who have been trained in a cueing protocol that allows the person several seconds to produce a response before providing increasingly informative cues in order for the person to eventually produce the correct response. This counterintuitive procedure, however, results in rapid and durable acquisition of the target response (Bourgeois et al., 2003; Camp, Foss, O'Hanlon, et al., 1996).

SR has been shown in previous case studies to be effective across a variety of conditions, including AD (Camp, Foss, Stevens, & O'Hanlon, 1996; McKitrick, Camp, & Black, 1992), dementia associated with Parkinson's Disease (PD; Hayden & Camp, 1995), dementia associated with Korsakoff's syndrome (Camp & Schaller, 1989), vascular and mixed dementia (e.g., Abrahams & Camp, 1993; Bird, Alexopoulos, & Adamowicz, 1995), and postanoxia dementia (Bird et al., 1995). For example, Hayden and Camp demonstrated that persons with dementia associated with PD could learn new motor activities through SR when, under ordinary conditions, they could not.

Spaced retrieval has been used to teach persons with dementia to remember the names of common objects (Abrahams & Camp, 1993), to remember to perform a future action (Camp, Foss, Stevens, et al., 1996), face–name and object–location associations (Camp & Stevens, 1990), to use a strategy (e.g., "look at the calendar"; Camp, Foss, O'Hanlon, et al., 1996), and to use external memory aids (Bourgeois et al., 2003). Because the primary focus of SR is to teach a verbal response to an auditory prompt, it is important to end each SR training session with the execution of the trained strategy. For example, in teaching a client to look at a card to remember her room number, the clinician should say at the end of the SR training, "Great, now let's go find your room," and walk with the client to the room. This ensures that the trained verbal response is associated with the actual desired task, correct room finding. Camp (1999) explained the effectiveness of pairing verbal and motor behaviors to be due to the nondeclarative nature of the conditioned association of verbal and motor behaviors. Additionally, with certain motor behaviors, the client produces the behavior in addition to the verbal response all through the training (e.g., Clinician: "What should you do before you stand up?" Client: "Lock my wheelchair brakes," while reaching to lock brakes; clinician will provide hand-over-hand modeling of the behavior if client does not give immediate response). Table 5.5 provides examples of typical SR prompts and responses.

TABLE 5.5 Examples of Typical SR Prompts and Responses

Remembering Names and Facts

T: "If you can't think of the name of something, I want you to describe it or tell what you do with it. Now what should you do if you cannot think of the name of something?"

C: "I should describe it, or I should tell what I do with it."

Compensatory Swallow Technique

T: "After you swallow your food, I want you to take a sip of liquid. What should you do after you swallow your food?"

C: "I should take a sip of liquid."

Safety: Sitting

T: "Make sure you feel the back of the chair on your legs before you sit down. What should you do before you sit down?"

C: "I should feel the back of the chair on my legs."

Safety: Walker

T: "When you walk with your walker, please stay inside it like this. How do you walk with your walker?"

C: "I stay inside it like this."

Safety: Foot Rests

T: "In order for your hip to heal properly, keep your feet on the foot rests. Where should you put your feet?"

C: "On the foot rests."

Repetitive Questions

T: "You live at Menorah Park. Where do you live?"

C: "I live at Menorah Park."

Use of External Cues

T: "If you want to know what activities we have planned today, you can come over here and read this schedule. Where can you look to find out what is planned for the day?"

C: "I can go here to read this schedule."

T: "When you get up in the morning, please go to the refrigerator and read the message I left for you. What should you do when you get up in the morning?"

C: "I go to the refrigerator and read the message."

Note: T = Therapist C = Client.

The neuropsychological rehabilitation principle of "errorless learning" is based on the interaction of two types of memory: declarative (explicit) and nondeclarative (implicit or procedural) memory (Squire, 1992, 1994). Declarative memory involves the conscious learning and retrieval of personal or autobiographical facts. Deficits in retrieval from declarative memory are the most frequent and obvious problems demonstrated by persons in the early stages of dementia. Nondeclarative memory involves the use of well-learned processes and the unconscious, relatively effortless acquisition and retrieval of new information. Reading, singing, playing a musical instrument, walking, and eating are considered well-learned, nondeclarative memory skills. Therefore, the person who cannot recall the name of a family member (declarative memory deficit), but reads the name written in a memory book (nondeclarative memory ability) and recounts the latest news of this person, is demonstrating the interaction of these two memory systems. Most new learning demonstrated by persons with dementia takes advantage of the unconscious or effortless nature of the nondeclarative memory system and circumvents declarative memory; in addition, repetition priming is thought to be the component of nondeclarative memory that involves the ability to improve performance with practice, which can occur without effort and unconsciously (Camp, Foss, O'Hanlon, et al., 1996; Camp & Stevens, 1990; Cherry, Simmons, & Camp, 1999; Schacter, Rich, & Stampp, 1985; Vanhalle, Van der Linden, Belleville, & Gilbert, 1998).

To learn and retain new information, persons with memory deficits should engage in "errorless" practice with the new information. Declarative memory deficits prevent self-monitoring and self-correcting of responses during training, so inaccurate learning can occur. Therefore, errors during training must be inhibited by not allowing a time delay before the response or by prompting with a succession of cues. One clinician had the frustrating experience of trying to teach her name, Angela, to her client with dementia. On the first training trial, she provided the prompt, "What is my name?" and paused. The client responded, "I'm not sure; I think it starts with an A; is it Andrew?" Because the clinician did not interrupt her after her expression of uncertainty, and provide her with the correct name for her immediate repetition, this client persisted in responding, "Andrew," to the prompt on future trials. Although she did eventually learn the correct name, 4 months later when asked for her name at follow-up, she responded, "Andrew" (Bourgeois et al., 2003).

Errorless learning and practice have been used in the treatment of memory deficits due to other neurological conditions, such as traumatic brain injury, and for a variety of tasks such as the names of objects and people, use of an electronic memory aid, general knowledge and orientation information (Wilson et al., 1994), the use of a word-processing program (Glisky, 1995; Hunkin, Squires, Aldrich & Parkin, 1998), cued- and free-recall name generation (Evans et al., 2000; Hunkin, Squires, Parkin, & Tidy, 1998), and word list learning (Hillary et al., 2003). Several of these studies have directly compared the effects of error*less* and error*ful* (i.e., trial-and-error) learning and conclude that errorless learning is more efficient and produces more accurate learning than errorful conditions. Conflicting results have been reported, however; for example, Evans et al. could not replicate Wilson et al.'s findings of the benefits of errorless learning for the use of an electronic organizer.

Sohlberg and Mateer (2001) suggested that these discrepancies in the literature may be related to the nature of the trained tasks (e.g. experimental versus functional), differences in task demands, and training conditions (e.g., short training and testing delays). Hopper et al.'s (2005) review of the evidence supporting the use of SR as an effective training paradigm evaluated 15 studies of SR that provide Class II and Class III evidence of training cue behavior and face– and object–name associations to persons with dementia. Most of the studies (12/15) documented strong maintenance of trained behaviors, and some studies (6/15) reported generalized training effects to functional daily living tasks.

Vanishing Cues

Another way to conduct errorless learning is the method of vanishing cues (Glisky, Schacter, & Tulving, 1986). In this technique, which is designed for more complex information or behaviors, the client is provided with enough information to provide the correct response on the initial trial. Over subsequent trials, the information is gradually withdrawn and the client is required to respond with fewer cues. Some procedural differences in the technique have been reported in the literature, such as withholding the first letter of the word to be recalled (Wilson, 1992) and combining this priming technique with SR (Hunkin, Squires, Aldrich, et al., 1998). More research is needed to better understand the application and outcomes of these techniques with procedural variations designed to address the individual learning styles of clients with memory impairment.

Cueing Hierarchies

The most common teaching strategy employed by speech-language pathologists is the use of cueing hierarchies to elicit desired behaviors (for a review, see Patterson, 2001). Cueing hierarchies are used frequently for teaching individuals with acquired neurological communication impairments to perform certain communication behaviors, such as word finding. Cueing hierarchies (CH) are a systematic and graded sequence of cues that have increasing power. Treatment protocols have been established using CHs to guide the selection and sequencing of cues. Clinicians evaluate an individual's response to each cue type and design a unique training hierarchy based on the relative strength or power of each cue to elicit the desired response. Bollinger and Stout (1976) described this procedure as response-contingent small-step treatment that can be accomplished in an ascending or descending sequence in order to elicit the desired response with the least powerful cue. In her review of CHs in word retrieval studies, Patterson (2001) found two common ways to implement this technique: traditional CHs using descending and ascending movement, and modified CHs using descending cues only.

Bourgeois and colleagues (2003) directly compared the use of SR and CH to train fact and strategy goals with persons with dementia. The CH used included semantic cues ("Something to look at"), phonemic cues ("ac" first syllable of the target Activity List), visual cues (point to list), and tactile cues (touch and hold list), followed by imitation ("I look at my activity list"). The study found that persons with dementia learned goals using both strategies within a similar time frame, but at the 4-month follow-up, more goals learned through SR were remembered.

Prospective Memory Training

Similar to spaced retrieval, prospective memory training is a systematic procedure for training a client to remember to carry out a specific task in the future (Sohlberg & Mateer, 2001). As the client demonstrates success at remembering to do the task, the time interval for task recall is increased. Originally designed for persons with brain injuries, the training paradigm varies multiple variables in order to obtain generalization to functional everyday activities. For example, the type of task can vary from a one-step motor command to a multistep functional task. The time interval between prompts (or time delay) for task execution is systematically increased with successful performance. The activity engaged in during the intervals between executed tasks can range from quiet monitoring of the passage of time to conversation with the clinician or completion of other therapy tasks such as worksheets. Finally, the type of prompt used to signal task initiation can vary from the use of an alarm to the independent monitoring of the passage of time by the client. The effectiveness of this training paradigm was evaluated in several studies with brain-injured clients (Furst, 1986; Raskin & Sohlberg, 1996; Sohlberg, White, Evans, & Mateer, 1992); prospective memory performance increased on training tasks, with evidence of generalization to real-world tasks for some clients. Research is needed on the effectiveness of this technique for persons with dementia.

CRITICAL VARIABLES

In an effort to determine the most efficient training paradigm, clinicians have begun to question which variables are the most critical determinants of efficient learning in individuals with cognitive disorders. Camp and colleagues have described the critical components of the SR technique to be (a) the doubling or halving of time intervals between prompts, (b) the exact wording of the task prompt, (c) the nature of the interval activity (unrelated to the task), and (d) training to a time criterion. Sohlberg and Mateer (2001) recommended conducting prospective memory training with (a) repeated and fixed time intervals, (b) different tasks for each trial, and (c) various interval activities. To date, however, these two training paradigms have not been compared directly.

Other researchers have investigated the relative effects of specific variables on training outcomes. For example, Hochhalter, Bakke, Holub, and Overmier (2004) trained participants with AD or alcohol-induced dementia to learn pill names with adjusted interval or uniform interval spaced retrieval procedures. None of the participants learned with the uniform interval (30 seconds between each training trial) procedures, even with additional training trials. Morrow and Fridriksson (2005) compared strict versus randomized SR intervals in treating anomia in persons with mild to moderate aphasia and found a small but insignificant difference when the typical SR protocol was used compared with the randomized interstimulus (RSS) interval procedure. Fewer training sessions and somewhat better maintenance of training effects were shown for the SR condition compared with the RSS condition.

These findings were similar to an earlier study comparing SR with a cueing hierarchy training approach, where SR training was more efficient and longer lasting than CH training for persons with anomic aphasia (Fridrikssen, Holland, Beeson, & Morrow, 2005). Training schedules (fixed versus variable sessions) have been compared, with better effects revealed for the group that received the most sessions compared to the group that received a fixed number (six) of sessions on alternate days over a 2-week period (Cherry & Simmons-D'Gerolamo, 2004). In an effort to provide daily training, Joltin, Camp, and McMahon (2003) delivered SR treatment over the telephone to persons with dementia with encouraging results. In a related study, Melton and Bourgeois (2005) provided SR training over the telephone to seven persons with chronic memory problems related to TBI and found evidence for generalization of trained goals to everyday tasks for all participants.

CONCLUSION

This chapter reviewed a variety of memory-, cognition-, and language-enhancing interventions for persons with dementia. Although there are an impressive number of treatment studies in the current literature, and the intervention outcomes are encouraging, there is still a great need for evidence documenting their efficacy. It is largely just a matter of time until clinicians have designed and implemented treatments, documented the effects, and published the results of a sufficient number of well-designed and controlled studies that these efforts will be justified. In the meantime, the clinician who plans to select intervention techniques to improve the functional status of a client with dementia would be well advised to consider the guiding principles of functional goal and treatment selection that were described earlier in the chapter. The primary goals of intervention should be (a) to maintain independent functioning for as long as possible, (b) to maintain quality of life through supported participation and engagement in desired activities, and (c) to achieve these goals through procedures that are personally relevant to the client and are trained within functional contexts. In this age of increasing constraints on reimbursement, it is imperative that the most efficient treatment models are implemented. The careful collection of data to document progress and the effectiveness of interventions with each individual client is also imperative, and will be discussed more in chapter 11.

REFERENCES

Aarsland, D., Laake, K., Larsen, J., & Janvin, C. (2002). Donepezil for cognitive impairment in Parkinson's disease: A randomized controlled study. *Journal of Neurology, Neurosurgery and Psychiatry*, *72*, 708–712.

Abrahams, J. P., & Camp, C. J. (1993). Maintenance and generalization of object naming training in anomia associated with degenerative dementia. *Clinical Gerontologist*, *12*, 57–72.

Alm, N., Astell, A., Ellis, M., Dye, R., Gowans, G., & Campbell, J. (2004). A cognitive prosthesis and communication support for people with dementia. *Neuropsychological Rehabilitation*, *14*, 117–134.

Alzheimer's Association. (2003). *Safe return*. Retrieved August 18, 2003, from http://www.alz.org/ResourceCenter/Programs/SafeReturn.htm

American Geriatrics Society and American Association for Geriatric Psychiatry. (2003). Consensus statement on improving the quality of mental health care in U.S. nursing homes: Management of depression and behavioral symptoms associated with dementia. *Journal of the American Geriatrics Society*, *51*, 287–298.

American Health Care Association. (1990). *The Long Term Care Survey: Regulations, forms, procedures, guidelines*. Washington, DC: Author.

American Speech-Language-Hearing Association. (2005). Roles of speech-language pathologists in the identification, diagnosis, and treatment of individuals with cognitive-communication disorders: Position statement (ASHA Supplement No. 25), Rockville, MD: Author.

Andrews-Salvia, M., Roy, N., & Cameron, R. (2003). Evaluating the effects of memory books for individuals with severe dementia. *Journal of Medical Speech-Language Pathology*, *11*, 51–59.

Arkin, S. (1996). Volunteers in partnership: An Alzheimer's rehabilitation program delivered by students. *American Journal of Alzheimer's Disease*, *11*, 12–22.

Arkin, S. (1997, July/August). Alzheimer memory training: Quizzes beat repetition, especially with more impaired. *American Journal of Alzheimer's Disease*, 147–158.

Arkin, S. (1999). Elder rehab: A student-supervised exercise program for Alzheimer's patients. *The Gerontologist*, *39*, 729–735.

Arkin, S. (2001). Alzheimer rehabilitation by students: Interventions and outcomes. *Neuropsychological Rehabilitation*, *11*, 273–317.

Azrin, N., & Powell, J. (1969). Behavioral engineering: The use of response priming to improve prescribed self-medication. *Journal of Applied Behavior Analysis*, *2*, 39–42.

Baddeley, A. (1999). *Essentials of human memory*. East Sussex, UK: Psychology Press.

Baines, S., Saxby, P., & Ehlert, K. (1987). Reality orientation and reminiscence therapy: A controlled cross-over study of elderly confused people. *The British Journal of Psychiatry*, *151*, 222–231.

Bartus, R., Dean, R., Beer, B., & Lippa, A. (1982). The cholinergic hypothesis of geriatric memory dysfunction. *Science*, *217*, 408–417.

Bayles, K., Kim, E., Azuma, T., Chapman, S., Cleary, S., Hopper, T., et al. (2005). Developing evidence-based practice guidelines for speech-language pathologists serving individuals with Alzheimer's dementia. *American Journal of Medical Speech Language Pathology*, *13*(4), xiii–xxv.

Benjamin, B. (1995). Validation therapy: An intervention for disoriented patients with Alzheimer's disease. *Topics in Language Disorders*, *15*, 66–74.

Bird, M. (2000). Psychosocial rehabilitation for problems arising from cognitive deficits in dementia. In R. Hill, L. Backman, & A. Stigsdotter-Neely (Eds.), *Cognitive rehabilitation in old age*. Oxford: Oxford University Press.

Bird, M., Alexopoulos, P., & Adamowicz, J. (1995). Success and failure in five case studies: Use of cued recall to ameliorate behaviour problems in senile dementia. *International Journal of Geriatric Psychiatry*, *10*, 305–311.

Bird, M., & Luszcz, M. (1993). Enhancing memory performance in Alzheimer's disease: Acquisition assistance and cue effectiveness. *Journal of Clinical and Experimental Neuropsychology*, *15*, 921–932.

Bjork, R. A. (1988). Retrieval practice and the maintenance of knowledge. In M. M. Gruneberg, P. Morris, & R. Sykes (Eds.), *Practical aspects of memory* (Vol. 2, pp. 396–401). London: Academic Press.

Black, S., Roman, G. C., Geldmacher, D. S., Salloway, S., Hecker, J., Burns, A., et al. (2003). Efficacy and tolerability of donepezil in vascular dementia: Positive results of a 24-week, multicenter, international, randomized, placebo-controlled clinical trial. *Stroke*, *34*, 2323–2330.

Blesa, R. (2004). Noncognitive symptoms and long-term treatment expectations for Alzheimer disease. *Alzheimer Discourse and Associated Disorders, 18*, S9–S14.

Boczko, F. (1994, July/August). The breakfast club: A multi-modal language stimulation program for nursing home residents with Alzheimer's disease. *The American Journal of Alzheimer's Care and Related Disorders and Research*, 35–38

Bollinger, R. L., & Stout, C. E. (1976). Response-contingent small-step treatment: Performance-based communication intervention. *Journal of Speech and Hearing Disorders, 41*, 40–51.

Bourgeois, M. (1990). Enhancing conversation skills in Alzheimer's disease using a prosthetic memory aid. *Journal of Applied Behavior Analysis, 23*, 29–42.

Bourgeois, M. (1991). Communication treatment for adults with dementia. *Journal of Speech and Hearing Research, 34*, 831–844.

Bourgeois, M. S. (1992a). *Conversing with memory impaired individuals using memory aids: A memory aid workbook*. Gaylord, MI: Northern Speech Services.

Bourgeois, M. (1992b). Evaluating memory wallets in conversations with patients with dementia. *Journal of Speech and Hearing Research, 35*, 1344–1357.

Bourgeois, M. (1993). Effects of memory aids on the dyadic conversations of individuals with dementia. *Journal of Applied Behavior Analysis, 26*, 77–87.

Bourgeois, M. (1994). Teaching caregivers to use memory aids with patients with dementia. *Seminars in Speech and Language, 15*(4), 291–305.

Bourgeois, M. (2001). Is reading preserved in dementia? *The ASHA Leader, 6*(9), 5.

Bourgeois, M. (2005). Dementia. In L. LaPointe (Ed.), *Aphasia related neurogenic language disorders* (3rd ed., pp. 199–212). New York: Thieme.

Bourgeois, M. (2007). *Memory books and other graphic cuing systems*. New York: Health Professions Press, Brookes.

Bourgeois, M., Burgio, L., Schulz, R., Beach, S., & Palmer, B. (1997). Modifying the repetitive verbalization of community dwelling patients with AD. *The Gerontologist, 37*, 30–39.

Bourgeois, M., Camp, C., Rose, M., White, B., Malone, M., Carr, J., et al. (2003). A comparison of training strategies to enhance use of external aids by persons with dementia. *Journal of Communication Disorders, 36*, 361–378.

Bourgeois, M., Dijkstra, K., Burgio, L., & Allen-Burge, R. (2001). Memory aids as an AAC strategy for nursing home residents with dementia. *Augmentative and Alternative Communication, 17*, 196–210.

Brush, J., & Camp, C. (1998). Using spaced-retrieval training as an intervention during speech-language therapy. *Clinical Gerontologist, 19*(1), 51–64.

Buettner, L. (1999, January/February). Simple Pleasures: A multilevel sensorimotor intervention for nursing home residents with dementia. *American Journal of Alzheimer's Disease*, 41–52.

Burgio, L., Allen-Burge, R., Roth, D., Bourgeois, M., Dijkstra, K., Gerstle, J., et al. (2001). Come talk with me: Improving communication between nursing assistants and nursing home residents during care routines. *The Gerontologist, 41*, 449–460.

Burgio, L., Schilley, K., Hardin, J. M., Hsu, C., & Yancey, J. (1996). Environmental "white noise": An intervention for verbally agitated nursing home residents. *Journal of Gerontology, 51B*(6), 364–373.

Butler, R. (1963). The life review: An interpretation of reminiscence in the aged. *Psychiatry, 26*, 65–76.

Butler, R. (1980). The life review: An unrecognized bonanza. *International Journal of Aging and Human Development, 12*, 35–38.

Camp, C. (1999). Memory interventions for normal and pathological older adults. In R. Schulz, G. Maddox, & M. P. Lawton (Eds.), *Annual review of gerontology and geriatrics: Focus on interventions research with older adults* (pp. 155–189). New York: Springer.

Camp, C. J., Bird, M. J., & Cherry, K. E. (2000). Retrieval strategies as a rehabilitation aid for cognitive loss in pathological aging. In R. D. Hill, L. Bäckman, & A. S. Neely (Eds.), *Cognitive rehabilitation in old age* (pp. 224–248). New York: Oxford University Press.

Camp, C. J., Foss, J. W., O'Hanlon, A. M., & Stevens, A. B. (1996). Memory interventions for persons with dementia. *Applied Cognitive Psychology, 10*, 193–210.

Camp, C. J., Foss, J. W., Stevens, A. B., & O'Hanlon, A. M. (1996). Improving prospective memory task performance in persons with Alzheimer's disease. In M. A. Brandimonte, G. Einstein, & M. McDaniel (Eds.), *Prospective memory: Theory and applications* (pp. 351–367). Hillsdale, NJ: Lawrence Erlbaum.

Camp, C. J., Judge, K. S., Bye, C. A., Fox, K. M., Bowden. J., Bell, M., et al. (1997). An intergenerational program for persons with dementia using Montessori methods. *The Gerontologist*, 5(37), 688–692.

Camp, C. J., & McKitrick, L. A. (1992). Memory interventions in Alzheimer's-type dementia populations: Methodological and theoretical issues. In R. L. West & J. D. Sinnott (Eds.), *Everyday memory and aging: Current research and methodology* (pp. 155–172). New York: Springer-Verlag.

Camp, C. J., & Schaller, J. R. (1989). Epilogue: Spaced-retrieval memory training in an adult day-care center. *Educational Gerontology, 15*, 641–648.

Camp, C., & Skrajner, M. J. (2004). Resident-assisted Montessori programming (RAMP): Training persons with dementia to serve as group activity leaders. *The Gerontologist*, 44, 426–431.

Camp, C. J., & Stevens, A. B. (1990). Spaced-retrieval: A memory intervention for dementia of the Alzheimer's type (DAT). *Clinical Gerontologist, 10*, 658–661.

Cavallini, E., Pagnin, A., & Vecchi, T. (2002). The rehabilitation of memory in old age: Effects of mnemonics and metacognition in strategic training. *Clinical Gerontologist, 26*, 125–132.

Chapman, S., Weiner, M., Rackley, A., Hynan, L., & Zientz, J. (2004). Effects of cognitive-communication stimulation for Alzheimer's disease patients treated with donepezil. *Journal of Speech-Language-Hearing Research, 47*, 1149–1163.

Cherry, K. E., Simmons, S. S., & Camp, C. J. (1999). Spaced-retrieval enhances memory in older adults with probable Alzheimer's disease. *Journal of Clinical Geropsychology*, 5, 159–175.

Cherry, K., E., & Simmons-D'Gerolamo, S. S. (2004). Spaced-retrieval with probably Alzheimer's. *Clinical Gerontologist, 27*(1/2), 139–157.

Clark, L. (1995). Interventions for persons with Alzheimer's disease: Strategies for maintaining and enhancing communicative access. *Topics in Language Disorders, 15*, 50–69.

Cohen, G. (1994). Foreword: Towards new models of dementia care. *Alzheimer Disease and Associated Disorders, 8*, 2–4.

Cohen, U., & Weisman, G. (1991). *Holding on to home: Planning environments for the elderly and the confused*. Owings Mills, MD: National Health Publishing.

Cohen-Mansfield, J. (2005). Nursing staff members' assessments of pain in cognitively impaired nursing home residents. *Pain Management Nursing, 6*(2), 68–75.

Craik, F., Anderson, N., Kerr, S., & Li, K. (1995). Memory changes in normal ageing. In A. D. Baddeley, B. A. Wilson, & F. N. Watts (Eds.), *Handbook of memory disorders* (pp. 211–242). Chichester, UK: Wiley.

Davis, R., Massman, P., & Doody, R. (2001). Cognitive intervention in Alzheimer disease: A randomized placebo-controlled study. *Alzheimer Disease and Associated Disorders, 15*, 1–9.

Dixon, R., de Frias, C., & Bäckman, L. (2001). Characteristics of self-reported memory compensation in older adults. *Journal of Clinical and Experimental Neuropsychology, 23*, 650–661.

Doody, R., Stevens, J., Beck, C., Dubinsky, R., Kaye, J., Gwyther, L., et al. (2001). Practice parameter: Management of dementia (an evidence-based review): Report of the Quality Standards Subcommittee of the American Academy of Neurology. *Neurology, 56*, 1154–1166.

Ebbinghaus, H. (1964). *Memory: A contribution to experimental psychology*. New York: Dover.

Ehrenfeld, M. (2003). Using therapeutic dolls with psychogeriatric patients. In C. E. Schaefer (Ed.), *Play therapy with adults* (pp. 291–297). New York: John Wiley.

Eisner, E. (2001). *Can do activities for adults with Alzheimer's disease*. Austin, TX: Pro-Ed.

Enwefa, R. L. (1999). An investigative study of the efficacy of an external aid (conversation wallet) and augmentative communication (alpha talker device) on the communicative functions of middle stage Alzheimer's disease populations. *Dissertation Abstracts International*, 59(11-B), 5801.

Evans, J. J., Wilson, B. A., Schuri, U., Andrade, J., Baddeley, A. D., Bruna, O., et al. (2000). A comparison of "errorless" and "trial-and-error" learning methods for teaching individuals with acquired memory deficits. *Neuropsychological Rehabilitation, 10*, 67–101.

Farlow, M. (2004). Rivastigmine for treatment of AD. In R. Richter & B. Richter (Eds.), *Alzheimer's disease: A physician's guide to practical management* (pp. 187–192). Totowa, NJ: Humana.

Feil, N. (1992a). *Validation: The Feil method*. Cleveland, OH: Edward Feil.

Feil, N. (1992b). Validation therapy. *Geriatric Nursing, 13*, 129–133.

Feldman, H., Gautier, S., Hecker, J., Vellas, B., Subbiah, P., & Whalen, E. (2001). Donepezil MSAD Study investigators Group. A 24-week, randomized, double-blind study of donepezil in moderate to severe Alzheimer's disease. *Neurology, 57*, 613–620.

Feldman, H., Spiegel, R., & Quarg, P. (2003). An evaluation of the effects of rivastigmine on daily function in Alzheimer's disease at different levels of cognitive impairment. *Neurology, 60*, A412.

Fogler, J., & Stern, L. (1988). *Improving your memory*. Baltimore.: Johns Hopkins University Press.

Folsom, J. C. (1968). Reality orientation for the elderly mental patient. *Journal of Geriatric Psychiatry, 1*, 291–307.

Fridrikssen, J., Holland, A., Beeson, P., & Morrow, L. (2005). Spaced retrieval treatment of anomia. *Aphasiology, 19*, 99–109.

Furst, C. (1986). The memory derby: Evaluating and remediating intention memory. *Cognitive Rehabilitation, 4*, 24–26.

Gabriel, M., Gagnon, J. P., & Bryan, C. K. (1977). Improved patient compliance through use of a daily drug reminder chart. *American Journal of Public Health*, *67*, 968–969.

Garland, J. (1994). What splendour, it all coheres: Life-review therapy with older people. In J. Bornat (Ed.), *Reminiscence reviewed: Perspectives, evaluations, achievements*. Buckingham, UK: Open University Press.

Garrett, K., & Yorkston, K. (1997). Assistive communication technology for elders with cognitive and language disabilities. In R. Lubinski & D. J. Higginbotham (Eds.), *Communication technologies for the elderly* (pp. 203–234). San Diego, CA: Singular.

Getsios, D., Caro, J. J., Caro, G., & Ishak, K. (2001). Assessment of health economics in Alzheimer's disease (AHEAD): Galantamine treatment in Canada. *Neurology, 57*, 972–978

Gibson, F. (1994). What can reminiscence contribute to people with dementia? In J. Bornat (Ed.), *Reminiscence Reviewed: perspectives, evaluations, achievements*. Buckingham, UK: Open University Press.

Gilleard, C., Mitchell, R. G., & Riordan, J. (1981). Ward orientation training with psychogeriatric patients. *Journal of Advanced Nursing, 6*, 95–98.

Glisky, E. L (1995). Computers in memory rehabilitation. In A. D. Baddeley, B. A. Wilson, & F. N. Watts (Eds.), *Handbook of memory disorders* (pp. 557–575). New York: John Wiley.

Glisky, E. L., Schacter, D. L., & Tulving, E. (1986). Learning and retention of computer-related vocabulary in amnesic patients: Method of vanishing cues. *Journal of Clinical and Experimental Neuopsychology*, *8*, 292–312.

Godfrey, S. (1994). Doll therapy. *Australian Journal on Ageing*, *13*, 46.

Goldwasser, A. N., Auerbach, S. M., & Harkins, S. W. (1987). Cognitive, affective, and behavioral effects of reminiscence group therapy on demented elderly. *International Journal of Aging and Human Development*, *25*(3), 209–222.

Green, R. (2005). *Diagnostic and management of Alzheimer's disease and other dementias*. Caddo, OK: Professional Communications.

Hanley, I. G. (1981). The use of signposts and active training to modify ward disorientation in elderly patients. *Journal of Behavior Therapy and Experimental Psychiatry*, *12*, 241–247.

Hanley, I. G., & Lusty, K. (1984). Memory aids in reality orientation: A single-case study. *Behavior Research Therapy*, *22*, 709–712.

Harrell, M., Parenté, F., Bellingrath, E. G., & Lisicia, K. (1992). *Cognitive rehabilitation of memory: A practical guide*. Gaithersburg, MD: Aspen.

Harris, J. E. (1980). Memory aids people use: Two interview studies. *Memory & Cognition*, *8*, 31–38.

Hawley, K. S., & Cherry, K. E. (2004). Spaced-retrieval effects on name-face recognition in older adults with probable Alzheimer's disease. *Behavior Modification*, *28*, 276–296.

Hayden, C. M., & Camp, C. J. (1995). Spaced-retrieval: A memory intervention for dementia in Parkinson's disease. *Clinical Gerontologist*, *16*(3), 80–82.

Head, D., Portnoy, S., & Woods, R. (1990). The impact of reminiscence groups in two different settings. *International Journal of Geriatric Psychiatry*, *5*, 295–302.

Hersch, N., & Treadgold, L. (1994). NeuroPage: The rehabilitation of memory dysfunction by prosthetic memory and cueing. *Neuropsychological Rehabilitation*, *4*, 187–197.

Hillary, F. G., Schultheis, M. T., Challis, B. H., Millis, S. R., Carnevale, G. J., Galshi, T., et al. (2003). Spacing of repetitions improves learning and memory after moderate and severe TBI. *Journal of Clinical and Experimental Neuropsychology*, *25*, 49–58.

Hochhalter, A., Bakke, B., Holub, R., & Overmier, J. B. (2004). Adjusted spaced retrieval training: A demonstration and initial test of why it is effective. *Clinical Gerontologist*, *27*, 159–168.

Hoerster, L., Hickey, E., & Bourgeois, M. (2001). Effects of memory aids on conversations between nursing home residents with dementia and nursing assistants. *Neuropsychological Rehabilitation*, *11*, 399–427.

Hofmann, M., Hock, C., Kühler, A., & Müller-Spahn, F. (1996). Interactive computer-based cognitive training in patients with Alzheimer's disease. *Journal of Psychiatric Research*, *30*, 493–501.

Holden, U., & Woods, R. (1995). *Positive approaches to dementia care* (3rd ed.). Edinburgh: Churchill Livingstone.

Hopper, T., Bayles, K., & Tomoeda, C. (1998). Using toys to stimulate communicative function in individuals with Alzheimer's disease. *Journal of Medical Speech-Language Pathology*, *6*, 73–80.

Hopper, T., Mahendra, N., Kim, E., Azuma, T., Bayles, K., Cleary, S., et al. (2005). Evidence-based practice recommendations for working with individuals with dementia: Spaced-retrieval training. *American Journal of Medical Speech-Language Pathology*, *13*(4), xxvii–xxxiv.

Howard, R., Ballard, C., O'Brien, J., & Burns, A. (2001). Guidelines for the management of agitation in dementia. *International Journal of Geriatric Psychiatry*, 16, 714–717.

Hsuing, G., & Feldman, H. (2004). Donepezil in treatment of AD. In R. Richter & B. Richter (Eds.), *Alzheimer's disease: A physician's guide to practical management* (pp. 179–186). Totowa, NJ: Humana.

Hultsch, D., Hertzog, C., Small, B., & Dixon, R. (1999). Use it or lose it: Engaged lifestyle as a buffer of cognitive decline in aging? *Psychology & Aging, 14*, 245–263.

Hunkin, N. M., Squires, E. J., Aldrich, F. K., & Parkin, A. J. (1998). Errorless learning and the acquisition of word processing skills. *Neuropsychological rehabilitation, 8*, 433–449.

Hunkin, N. M., Squires, E. J., Parkin, A. J., & Tidy, J. A. (1998). Are the benefits of errorless learning dependent on implicit memory? *Neuropsycologia, 36*, 25–36.

Hussian, R. A., & Brown, D. C. (1987). Use of two-dimensional grid patterns to limit hazardous ambulation in demented patients. *Journal of Gerontology, 42*, 558–560.

Irvine, A. B., Bourgeois, M., & Ary, D. V. (2003). An interactive multi-media program to train professional caregivers. *Journal of Applied Gerontology, 22*, 269–288.

Ismail, M., & Tariot, P. (2004). Galantamine in treatment of AD. In R. Richter & B. Richter (Eds.), *Alzheimer's disease: A physician's guide to practical management* (pp. 193–202). Totowa, NJ: Humana.

Joltin, A., Camp., C., & McMahon, C. (2003). Spaced-retrieval over the telephone: An intervention for persons with dementia. *Clinical Psychologist, 7*, 50–55.

Josephsson, S., Backman, L., Borell, L., Bernspang, B., Nygard, L., & Ronnberg, L. (1993). Supporting everyday activities in dementia: an intervention study. *International Journal of Geriatric Psychiatry, 8*, 395–400.

Kapur, N. (1995). Memory aids in the rehabilitation of memory disordered patients. In A. D. Baddeley, B. A. Wilson, & F. N. Watts (Eds.), *Handbook of memory disorders* (pp. 534–556). Chichester, UK: Wiley.

Kapur, N., Glisky, E., & Wilson, B. (2004). Technological memory aids for people with memory deficits. *Neuropsychological Rehabilitation, 14*, 41–60.

Kausler, D. H. (1994). *Learning and memory in normal aging*. San Diego, CA: Academic Press.

Kim, H. J., Burke, D. T., Dowds, M. D., & George, J. (1999). Utility of a microcomputer as an external memory aid for a memory impaired head injury patient during in-patient rehabilitation. *Brain Injury, 13*, 147–150.

Kincaid, C., & Peacock, J. (2003). The effect of a wall mural on decreasing four types of door-testing behaviors. *Journal of Applied Gerontology, 22*, 76–88.

Knapp, M., Knopman, D., Solomon, P., Pendlebury, W., Davis, C., & Gracon, S. (1994). A 30-week randomized controlled trial of high-dose tacrine in patients with Alzheimer's disease. The Tacrine Study Group. *JAMA, 271*, 985–991.

Knopman, D., Knapp, M., Gracon, S., & Davis, C. (1994). The Clinician Interview-Based Impression (CIBI): A clinician's global change rating scale in Alzheimer's disease. *Neurology, 44*, 2315–2321.

Lam, D. H., & Woods, R. T. (1986). Ward orientation training in dementia: A single-case study. *International Journal of Geriatric Psychiatry, 1*, 145–147.

Landauer, T. K., & Bjork, R. A. (1978). Optimal rehearsal patterns and name learning. In M. M. Gruneberg, P. Morris, & R. Sykes (Eds.), *Practical aspects of memory* (pp. 625–632). London: Academic Press.

Lawton, M. P., & Rubinstein, R. L. (Eds.). (2000). *Interventions in dementia care: Toward improving quality of life*. New York: Springer.

Leirer, V. O., Morrow, D. G., Pariante, G. M., & Doksum, T. (1988). Increasing influenza vaccination adherence through voice mail. *Journal of the American Geriatric Society, 37*, 1147–1150.

Leirer, V. O., Morrow, D. G., Tanke, E. D., & Pariante, G. M. (1991). Elders' nonadherence: Its assessment and medicaiton reminding by voice mail. *The Gerontologist, 31*, 514–520.

Lekeu, F., Wojtasik, V., Van der Linden, M., & Salmon, E. (2002). Training early Alzheimer patients to use a mobile phone. *Acta Neurologica Belgica*, *102*, 114–121.

Leseth, L., & Meader, L. (1995). Utilizing an AAC system to maximize receptive and expressive communication skills of a person with Alzheimer's disease. *ASHA AAC Special Interest Division Newsletter*, *4*, 7–9.

Li, G., Higdon, R., Kukull, W., Peskind, E., Van Valen Moore, K., Tsuang, D., et al. (2004). Statin therapy and risk of dementia in the elderly: A community-based prospective cohort study. *Neurology*, *63*, 1624–1628.

Lindsley, O. R. (1964). Geriatric behavioral prosthetics. In R. Kastenbaum (Ed.), *New thoughts on old age* (pp. 41–60). New York: Springer.

Luchsinger, J. A., & Mayeux, R. (2004). Dietary factors and Alzheimer's disease. *Neurology*, *3*, 579–587.

Luchsinger, J. A., Tang, M., Shea, S., & Mayeux, R. (2003). Antioxidant vitamin intake and risk of Alzheimer disease. *Archives of Neurology*, *60*, 203–208.

Lund, D., Hill, R., Caserta, A., & Wright, S. (1995). Video respite: An innovative resource for family, professional caregivers, and persons with dementia. *The Gerontologist*, *35*, 683–687.

MacDonald, E. T., MacDonald, J. B., & Phoenix, M. (1977). Improving drug compliance after hospital discharge. *British Medical Journal*, *2*, 618–621.

Mackinnon, A., Christensen, H., Hofer, S., Korten, A.,& Jorm, A. (2003). Use it and still lose it? The association between activity and cognitive performance established using latent growth techniques in a convenience sample. *Aging, Neuropsychology, & Cognition*, *10*, 215–229.

Mahendra, N., & Arkin, S. (2003). Effects of four years of exercise, language, and social interventions on Alzheimer discourse. *Journal of Communication Disorders*, *36*, 395–422.

Mahendra, N., Kim, E., Bayles, K., Hopper, T., Cleary, S., & Azuma, T. (2005). Evidence-based practice recommendations for working with individuals with dementia: Computer-assisted cognitive interventions (CACIs). *Journal of Medical Speech-Language Pathology*, *13*(4), xxxv–xliv.

Martin, B. K., Meinert, C. L., & Breitner, J. C. (2002). Double placebo design in a prevention trial for Alzheimer's disease. *Controlled Clinical Trials*, *23*(7), 93–99.

Mason, D., Kohn, M., & Clark, K. (2001). *The memory workbook: Breakthrough techniques to exercise your brain and improve your memory*. Oakland, CA: New Harbinger.

McPherson, A., Furniss, F. G., Sdogati, C., Cesaroni, F., Tartaglini, B., & Lindesay, J. (2001). Effects of individualized memory aids on the conversation of persons with severe dementia. *Aging & Mental Health*, *5*, 289–294.

McKitrick, L. A., Camp, C. J., & Black, F. W. (1992). Prospective memory intervention in Alzheimer's disease. *Journal of Gerontology*, *47*(5), 337–343.

Melton, A., & Bourgeois, M. (2005). Training compensatory memory strategies via the telephone for persons with TBI. *Aphasiology*, *19*, 353–364.

Mohs, R., Rosen, W., & Davis, K. (1983). The Alzheimer's disease assessment scale: An instrument for assessing treatment efficacy. *Psychopharmacological Bulletin*, *19*, 448–450.

Morrow, K. L., & Fridriksson, J. (2005) Comparing fixed- and randomized-interval spaced retrieval in anomia treatment. *Journal of Communication Disorders*, *39*, 2–11.

Morton, I., & Bleathman, C. (1991). The effectiveness of validation therapy in dementia: A pilot study. International *Journal of Geriatric Psychiatry*, *6*, 327–330.

Namazi, K., Rosner, T., & Calkins, M. (1989). Visual barriers to prevent ambulatory Alzheimer's patients from exiting through an emergency door. *The Gerontologist*, *29*, 699–702.

Nelson, A. (2005). *The Harvard Medical School guide to achieving optimal memory*. New York: McGraw-Hill.

Nolan, B., Mathews, M., & Harrison, M. (2001). Using external memory aids to increase room finding by older adults with dementia. *American Journal of Alzheimer's Disease, 16*, 251–154.

Parenté, R., & Herrmann, D. (1996). *Retraining cognition: Techniques & applications*. Gaithersburg, MD: Aspen.

Park, D. C., & Kidder, D. P. (1996). Prospective memory and medication adherence. In M. A. Brandimonte, G. Einstein, & M. McDaniel (Eds.), *Prospective memory: Theory and applications* (pp. 369–390). Hillsdale, NJ: Lawrence Erlbaum.

Park, D. C., Morrell, R. W., Frieske, D., & Kincaid, D. (1992). Medication adherence behaviors in older adults: Effects of external cognitive supports. *Psychology & Aging, 7*, 252–256.

Patterson, J. P. (2001). The effectiveness of cueing hierarchies as a treatment for word retrieval impairment. *American Speech-Language-Hearing Association, Division 2, Neurophysiology and Neurogenic Communication Disorders, 11*(2), 11–18.

Patterson, K., & Hodges, J. R. (1992). Deterioration of word meaning: Implications for reading. *Neuropsychologia, 30*, 1025–1040.

Petro, S., Herrmann, D., Burrows, D., & Moore, C. (1991). Usefulness of commercial memory aids as a function of age. *International Journal of Aging and Human Development, 33*, 295–309.

Quayhagen, M., & Quayhagen, M. (1989). Differential effects of family-based strategies on Alzheimer's disease. *The Gerontologist, 29*, 150–155.

Quayhagen, M., Quayhagen, M., Corbeil, R., Roth, P., & Rodgers, J. (1995). A dyadic remediation program for care recipients with dementia. *Nursing Research, 44*, 153–159.

Raskin, S. A., & Sohlberg, M. (1996). The efficacy of prospective memory training in two adults with brain injury. *Journal of Head Trauma Rehabilitation, 11*, 32–51.

Rau, M. (1993). *Coping with communication challenges in Alzheimer's disease*. San Diego, CA: Singular.

Reisberg, B., Doody, R., Stoffler, A., Schmitt, F., Ferris, S., & Mobius, H. (2003). Memantine study group: Memantine in moderate-to-severe Alzheimer's disease. *New England Journal of Medicine, 348*, 1333–1341.

Robinson, S., Bishop, G., & Munch, G. (2003). Alzheimer vaccine: Amyloid-beta on trial. *Bioessays, 25*, 283–288.

Rosenquist, K., Tariot, P., & Loy, R. (2000). Treatments for behavioral and psychological symptoms in Alzheimer's disease and other dementias. In J. O'Brien, D. Ames, & A. Burns (Eds.), *Dementia* (2nd ed., pp. 571–601). London: Arnold.

Santo Pietro, M. J., & Boczko, F. (1997). The Breakfast Club and related programs. In B. Shadden & M. A. Toner (Eds.), *Aging and communication* (pp. 341–359). Austin, TX: Pro-Ed.

Santo Pietro, M. J., & Boczko, F. (1998). The Breakfast Club: Results of a study examining the effectiveness of a multi-modality group communication treatment. *American Journal of Alzheimer's Disease, 13*, 146–158.

Schacter, D. L., Rich, S. A., & Stampp, M. S. (1985). Remediation of memory disorders: Experimental evaluation of the spaced-retrieval technique. *Journal of Clinical and Experimental Neuropsychology, 7*, 79–96.

Schnelle, J. F. (1990). Treatment of urinary incontinence in nursing homepatients by prompted voiding. *Journal of the American Geriatrics Society, 38*, 356–360.

Schreiber, M., Schweizer, A., Lutz, K., Kalveram, K., & Jancke, L. (1999). Potential of an interactive computer-based training in the rehabilitation of dementia: An initial study. *Neuropsychological Rehabilitation, 9*(2), 155–167.

Shumaker, S., Legault, C., Kuller, L. Rapp, S. R., Thal, L., Lane, D. S., et al. (2004). Conjugated equine estrogens and incidence of probable dementia and mild cognitive impairment in postmenopausal women. *JAMA, 291*, 2947–2958.

Small, G. (2002). *The memory bible*. New York: Hyperion.

Smith, W. L. (1988, May). Behavioral interventions in gerontology: Management of behavior problems in individuals with Alzheimer's disease living in the community. Paper presented at the Association for Behavior Analysis Convention, Philadelphia.

Snowden, J., Griffiths, H., & Neary, D. (1994). Semantic dementia: Autobiographical contribution to preservation of meaning. *Cognitive Neuropsychology, 11*, 265–288.

Sohlberg, M., & Mateer, C. (2001). *Cognitive rehabilitation: An integrative neuropsychological approach*. New York: Guilford.

Sohlberg, M., White, O., Evans, E., & Mateer, C. (1992). An investigation into the effects of prospective memory training. *Brain Injury, 6*, 139–154.

Spector, A., Davies, S., Woods, B., & Orrell, M. (2000). Reality orientation for dementia: A systematic review of the evidence of effectiveness from randomized controlled trials. *The Gerontologist, 40*, 206–212.

Squire, L. R. (1992). Memory and the hippocampus: A synthesis from findings with rats, monkeys, and humans. *Psychological Review, 99*, 195–231.

Squire, L. R. (1994). Declarative and nondeclarative memory: Multiple brain system supporting learning and memory. In D. L. Schacter & E. Tulving (Eds.), *Memory systems 1994* (pp. 203–232). Cambridge, MA: MIT Press.

Tariot, P., Farlow, M., Grossberg, G., Graham, S., McDonald, S., & Gergel, I. (2004). Memantine Study Group: Memantine treatment in patients with moderate to severe Alzheimer disease already receiving donepezil: A randomized controlled trial. *JAMA, 291*, 317–324.

Tilly, J., & Reed, P. (2004). *Evidence on interventions to improve quality of care for residents with dementia in nursing and assisted living facilities*. Alzheimer's Association. Retrieved March 3, 2006, from http://www.alz.org

Troyer, A. (2001). Improving memory knowledge, satisfaction, and functioning via an education and intervention program for older adults. *Aging, Neuropsychology and Cognition, 8*, 256–268.

Vanhalle, C., Van der Linden, M., Belleville, S., & Gilbert, B. (1998, December). Putting names on faces: Use of a spaced retrieval strategy in a patient with dementia of the Alzheimer's type. *Neurophysiologyo and Neurogenic Speech and Language Disorders*, 17–21.

Volicer, L., & Bloom-Charette, L. (1999). Assessment of quality of life in advanced dementia. In L. Volicer & L. Bloom-Charette (Eds.), *Enhancing the quality of life in advanced dementia* (pp. 3–20). Philadelphia: Taylor & Francis.

Weinstein, B. E. (1991). Auditory testing and rehabilitation of the hearing impaired. In R. Lubinski (Ed.). *Dementia and Communication* (pp. 223–237). Philadelphia: Decker.

Weinstein, C., & Sachs, W. (2000). Memory 101: A psychotherapist's guide to understanding and teaching memory strategies to patients and significant others. *Journal of Geriatric Psychiatry, 33*, 5–26.

Wilson, B. A. (1992). Rehabilitation and memory disorders. In L. R. Squire & N. Butters (Eds.), *Neuropsychology of memory*. New York: Guilford.

Wilson, B. A., Baddeley, A., Evans, J., & Sheil, A. (1994). Errorless learning in the rehabilitation of memory impaired people. *Neuropsychological Rehabilitation, 4*, 307–326.

Wilcock, G., Lilienfeld, S. & Gaens, E. (2000). Efficacy and safety of galantamine in patients with mild to moderate Alzheimer's disease: Multicentre randomized controlled trial. Galantamine International-1 Study Group. *BMJ, 321*, 1445–1449.

Wilcock, G., Mobius, H., & Stoffler, A. (2002). A double-blind, placebo-controlled multicentre study of memantine in mild to moderate vascular dementia (MMM500). *International Clinical Psychopharmacology, 17*, 297–305.

Wilson, B., Cockburn, J., & Baddeley, A. (1985). *The Rivermead Behavioral Memory Test*. Titchfield, UK: Thames Valley.

Winblad, B., & Jelic, V. (2004). Long-term treatment of Alzheimer disease: Efficacy and safety of acetylcholinesterae inhibitors. *Alzheimer Disease and Associated Disorders*, *18*, S2–S8.

Winningham, R., Anunsen, R., Hanson, L., Laux, L., Kraus, K., & Reifers, A. (2003). MemAerobics: A cognitive intervention to improve memory ability and reduce depression in older adults. *Journal of Mental Health & Aging*, *9*, 183–192.

Woods, R. T. (1983). Specificity of learning in reality orientation sessions: A single-case study. *Behaviour Research and Therapy*, *21*, 173–175.

Woods, R. T. (1996). Psychological "therapies" in dementia. In R. T. Woods (Ed.), *Handbook of the clinical psychology of ageing* (pp. 575–600). New York: John Wiley.

World Health Organization. (1980). *International classification of impairment, disabilities, and handicaps*. Geneva, Switzerland: Author.

World Health Organization. (2001). *International classification of functioning, disability and health (ICF)*. Geneva, Switzerland: Author.

Yanagihara, T., & Petersen, R. (Eds.). (1991). *Memory disorders: Research and clinical practice*. New York: Marcel Dekker.

Zarit, S. H., Zarit, J. M., & Reever, K. E. (1982). Memory training for severe memory loss: Effects on senile dementia patients and their families. *The Gerontologist*, *22*, 373–377.

Zeisel, J., Hyde, J., & Shi, L. (1999). Environmental design as a treatment for Alzheimer's disease. In L. Volicer & L. Bloom-Charette (Eds.), *Enhancing the quality of life in advanced dementia* (pp. 206–222). Philadelphia: Taylor & Francis.

6

Management
An Interdisciplinary Focus

Increasingly, rehabilitation scientists have evidence that intervention can improve the daily functional skills and decrease problem behaviors of persons with dementia. As discussed in chapters 4 and 5, we can achieve such functional outcomes for activities and participation through development of compensatory strategies that capitalize on preserved skills. The purpose of this chapter is to identify how the interdisciplinary team can implement specific behavioral or environmental interventions. In the previous chapter, pharmacological approaches and behavioral interventions that addressed communication and memory skills from the perspectives of speech-language pathology and psychology were reviewed. These interventions largely addressed communication and memory deficits at the levels of impairments of cognitive functioning (e.g., pharmacological treatments) and compensatory strategies for the impairments and activity limitations of dementia (e.g., use of communication cards and spaced retrieval memory training). This chapter explores the wealth of treatments that have been developed from the traditions of other disciplines, such as recreation therapy, music and art therapy, occupational therapy, nursing, and spiritual care, among others, to reduce activity limitations and participation restrictions (e.g., use of written cue cards to promote participation in activities, and attention to furniture arrangement and lighting in residential facilities) of persons with dementia. Each rehabilitation discipline has contributed various sensory-based and activity-focused techniques to enhance positive skills and to reduce problem behaviors in persons with dementia (e.g., Arkin, 1998; Eisner, 2001; Hellen, 1998; Lawton, 1999; Tappen, 1997; Volicer & Bloom-Charette, 1999). This chapter will focus on adaptations to the physical and sensory environment, daily leisure activities, and social environments, as both environmental design and programming are important in caring for persons with dementia (Forrest & Cohen, 2004).

The efficacy of each approach will be discussed relative to the strength of the research evidence available in the literature. For example, Gitlin and colleagues (Gitlin, Liebman, & Winter, 2003) conducted a systematic review of environmental interventions; the majority (i.e., 10 of 11 randomized controlled trials) of these studies revealed outcomes of decreased problem behaviors and/or increased functional abilities in the participants with dementia. However, few interventions have undergone randomized controlled trials, and unfortunately, most of the available studies have methodological flaws. Despite the fact that further research is needed, clinicians can build the case for providing interdisciplinary intervention to persons with dementia by using the available studies and by documenting functional outcomes to justify the provision of services; thus, suggestions will be made for measuring functional outcomes. Finally, the consultative and/or collaborative roles of the SLP on the interdisciplinary rehabilitation team will be outlined. Other rehabilitation professionals address many of the same patient behaviors as the SLP, albeit from different theoretical viewpoints and therapeutic perspectives.

THE INTERDISCIPLINARY TEAM

The goal of dementia management is to maintain or to increase functional behaviors, even as the disease progresses, in order to maintain or increase activities, participation, and quality of life. All team members need to work together, preferably in an interdisciplinary or transdisciplinary fashion, to maximize treatment outcomes for our clients. Team members may come from nursing, speech-language pathology, occupational therapy, physical therapy, recreation therapy and leisure activities, music therapy, social workers, clergy, and physicians. In long-term care and some day care settings, nurses and nursing assistants are often responsible for most aspects of the client's daily care, from supervising or assisting with activities of daily living to giving medications. Because nurses are most often the professionals attending to the client throughout the day, in comparison to other team members, they often have essential information and tips on caring for the client. Occupational therapists may deal with a client's activities of daily living and positioning needs, as well as cognitive abilities. Physiotherapists may also work on the client's positioning, as well as overall strength and mobility. In some facilities, occupational therapists work more on upper-extremity strength and activities, and physiotherapists work more on lower-extremity strength and activities. Recreation therapists and leisure activities staff may develop strategies and tools for the client to participate in favorite pastimes; and in long-term care, they often direct the programming of activities. Social workers are often case managers who deal with the legal and financial aspects of the client's care. Some social workers will also provide counseling services for clients and their family members. Clergy attend to the client's spiritual well-being and assist the client in attending religious ceremonies or receiving sacraments. Physicians are responsible for overseeing all of the client's care, although they often spend the least time with the client and rely on information from the whole team. Regardless of how many team members work with a client, communication across disciplines is essential for maximizing functional outcomes. Rehabilitation professionals from each discipline are responsible for educating other team members about the particular strategies that are developed, and for training caregivers to use these strategies. Additionally, clinicians must conduct ongoing assessment to determine if progress toward functional outcomes is being made, or if the treatment plan needs to be modified.

In the development of strategies and a treatment plan, we recommend that rehabilitation professionals adopt the three general principles of intervention that were discussed in chapter 4: (a) maintenance of independent functioning as long as possible, (b) maintenance of quality of life via supported participation and engagement, and (c) emphasis on personal relevance and contextual training. Specific interventions that follow these principles, and the evidence available to support these interventions, will be described in this chapter.

BARRIERS TO ACTIVITIES, PARTICIPATION, AND ENGAGEMENT

Given that dementia management often takes place in the context of day cares or residential care facilities, this section will focus primarily on research in institutional settings. Lubinski (1995) described nursing home environments as "communication impaired environments" due to the limited opportunities for successful, meaningful communication. Many other researchers have also found that the physical and social settings of most nursing homes are not conducive to social interaction (Grainger, 1995; Jacelon, 1995; Kaakinen, 1992, 1995; Liukkonen, 1995; Lubinski, Morrison, & Rigrodsky, 1981; Retsinas & Garrity, 1985). This often leads to social isolation of residents, particularly those with cognitive and communication deficits. There are many factors that contribute to this predicament: resident, staff, and physical environment factors. Physically, social interaction is discouraged by the lack of private areas, poor lighting, noise, and the arrangement of furniture. The beauty shop may be the only area of a nursing home that encourages social interaction regarding personal topics (Sigman, 1985).

Resident factors include few partners and topics of choice, and institutional rules that limit interaction possibilities. Residents of nursing homes are more likely to be unmarried and childless than elders who remain in their own homes (Jacelon, 1995). Consistent with the phenomena of institutions (Goffman, 1961), organizational rules may prevent people with disabilities from being integrated into the social interaction and activities of the nursing home (Lubinski, 1995; Lubinski et al., 1981). Residents have reported implicit rules regarding the type and amount of talk that is acceptable in nursing homes (Kaakinen, 1992, 1995; Lubinski et al., Sigman, 1985), including beliefs that they should not bother the staff unnecessarily with conversation, talk too much, talk about loneliness, talk to those who are senile or difficult to communicate with, have private conversations in front of others, or complain. Likewise, physical and cognitive impairments are positively correlated with decreased engagement and increased conflict and distress in nursing home residents (Mor et al., 1995; Schroll, Jonsson, Mor, Berg, & Sherwood, 1997). Disabled residents' efforts at social integration are often met with rejection because of this conflict and distress, propagating the social isolation in a cyclical manner. Only one third of residents are comfortable talking with other residents (Schroll et al., 1997). Many alert residents do not want to reside with cognitively impaired residents (Levesque, Cossette, & Potvin, 1993). Furthermore, lucidity, speech, and sight are key determinants in making friends in a nursing home (Retsinas & Garrity, 1985).

There are also many staff issues that contribute to social isolation in nursing homes. These will be discussed in the staff caregiving chapter (chapter 10). Overall, in nursing homes, there are few communication partners and topics of choice, and few reasons to engage in conversation. Given these environmental barriers, environmental interventions are necessary to improve the daily functional skills and well-being of persons with dementia.

ENVIRONMENTAL INTERVENTIONS

Overall well-being and functioning of persons with dementia can be impacted by the physical environment in which they live. Zeisel et al. (2003) found that there were many aspects of the environment that were significantly correlated with behavioral correlates of health. Thus, the environment is one of the resources that clinicians may capitalize upon to promote maximum functioning and quality of life in persons with dementia. This section will discuss the design and structure of care facilities, object arrangement within units, and sensory-enhancing adaptations. There is little research that systematically examines specific environmental interventions; thus, most of the evidence comes from expert opinion, anecdotes, and noncontrolled observational studies. The few controlled studies that do exist include multicomponent interventions so that the specific features of environmental interventions cannot be determined. Gitlin et al. (2003) and Day, Carreon, and Stump (2000) conducted literature reviews to determine the evidence for various therapeutic environment designs. The goals of adaptations to the physical environment include the following: (a) to decrease agitation, (b) to increase well-being, (c) to provide safety and reduce exiting behaviors, (d) to improve privacy and dignity issues (Gitlin et al.), and (e) to increase activities, participation, and engagement. As such, the recommended environmental interventions target everyday functional behaviors, rather than abstract underlying cognitive skills, as recommended by Holland (2003).

Gitlin et al. (2003) found three general principles across studies involving successful environmental interventions. First, the interventions sought to decrease environmental complexity. This was accomplished by relaxing the rules and the expectations for residents and by minimizing distractions for residents. Second, the successful interventions sought to increase orientation and awareness through the use of sensory stimuli and cues. Finally, the interventions created a low-stimulation and comfortable environment for residents. Gitlin and colleagues stated that the priority of the strategies used should be to provide predictability, familiarity, and structure in the daily life of persons with dementia; however, the facility design must also meet the needs of the staff.

Many day care, assisted living, and long-term care facilities are being designed now based on research that suggests that environmental factors, such as plants, animals, artwork, adequate lighting, and furniture arrangements, have a significant influence on persons with dementia (e.g., Brawley, 2002b; Calkins, 2005; Danes, 2002; Day et al., 2000; Forrest & Cohen, 2004; Gitlin et al., 2003; Gotestam & Melin, 1987; Kincaid & Peacock, 2003; Moore, 2002; Nagy, 2002; Noell-Waggoner, 2002; Noreika, Kuhoth, & Torgrude, 2002; Sloane, Zimmerman, Gruber-Baldini,

& Barba, 2002; Teresi, Holmes, & Ory, 2000; Zeisel et al., 2003). These newer facilities often try to create more home-like environments, rather than institutional or medical-looking settings. More often, however, a building already exists and must be used as well as possible. Although many buildings are not ideal, many modifications can be made that will enhance functioning, for example, changing the furniture arrangement and décor or camouflaging exits.

Building Design and Structure

When planning a new facility or making facility modifications, there are four principles of building design: (a) planning principles, (b) general attributes, (c) building organization, and (d) specific rooms and activity spaces (Day et al., 2000). The planning of buildings should be done to capitalize on features that will enhance the safety and well-being of residents with dementia. Some structural characteristics of the building to be considered include the following: the size of the units; the size, shape, and pattern of hallways; the size and structure of doorways; the availability and location of common versus private spaces; the freedom of residents to move around the facility; and entrances and exits to buildings or floors (Day et al.; Gitlin et al., 2003; Zeisel et al., 2003). Day et al. reviewed 71 empirical studies regarding the design for dementia facilities. Given the limitations of these studies, which were similar to other studies concerning dementia interventions (e.g., small sample sizes, poor subject and intervention description, and limited experimental control due to lack of control groups or settings), tentative recommendations were provided. Zeisel et al. conducted a longitudinal study of 15 assisted living facilities and nursing homes to determine the environmental factors that influenced the behavioral correlates of health. Based on their findings and the reviews by Day et al. and Gitlin et al., therapeutic design and planning of environments for persons with dementia should include small size, segregated units (cognitively impaired separated from noncognitively impaired), a noninstitutional design (especially in dining rooms), moderate levels of environmental stimulation, higher light levels with exposure to bright light, covers for panic bars and doorknobs to decrease exit behaviors, outdoor areas with therapeutic design, more visible toilets, and reduced environmental stress factors that increase stress in bathing (Day et al.).

Forrest and Cohen (2004) described a building that was designed to control agitation by using circular designs to allow the residents to wander without reaching a dead end. The building had many curves and circular shapes so that residents could walk without being obstructed, but it also had many rest areas so that residents could stop and sit as needed. Similarly, Danes (2002) described a model facility, Woodside Place, which had many design features that contributed to the residents' well-being and sense of community. Woodside Place was one of the first dementia special care facilities and was designed with a focus on maintaining independence, autonomy, and well-being of its residents. There was also an emphasis on retaining individuality and premorbid lifestyles as well as on community. When compared to more traditional nursing homes, the residents of Woodside Place engaged in social behavior three times more often. Thus, Danes examined the features of several buildings that used the Woodside Place model to determine what design features contributed to this sense of community. Each facility was divided into small units, with 12 to 18 residents per unit. Residents had freedom of movement within the units and facilities, and movement around the common areas was encouraged.

Additionally, Danes (2002) revealed that the informal, common areas were just as important as, if not more important than, the formal areas for structured activities. Within the informal common areas, residents tended to congregate and socialize in a more natural way, such as sitting on couches or at kitchen tables to talk. The architectural features that contributed to the creation of a sense of community at Woodside Place and affiliated facilities included familiar and welcoming residential settings. These settings allowed for shared daily activities, "social walking," greeting others, and "porch sitting." *Social walking* was walking in pairs or groups while interacting socially, which was encouraged by the freedom of movement in common areas. *Porch sitting* was sitting near entrances and exits of the buildings, and it was postulated that these were areas of interest given the opportunity to observe the activity of people coming and going.

Danes (2002) also found that the connective spaces in the building were particularly important for the chance for residents to engage in self-initiated activities and social interaction. There were three key design features that promoted this social activity in the connective spaces. The connective spaces were a common link between major activity centers of the facility (e.g., craft rooms, hair salon, courtyard, and offices). The connective spaces were pleasant, with natural lighting in the daytime and soft lighting at night, and attractive décor. The connective spaces were open to both interior and exterior spaces that allowed the residents to see what is going on in the next space, and to either observe or join in activities of interest. Furthermore, facilities with a residential character (versus institutional) and common spaces that varied in ambiance were associated with reduced social withdrawal and depression (Gotestam & Melin, 1987; Zeisel et al., 2003).

In addition to these important common areas, residents of facilities also need private and personalized spaces (Morgan & Stewart, 1998; Sigman, 1985; Zeisel et al., 2003). As noted above, the lack of private spaces in care facilities restricts residents' opportunities for meaningful conversation with family and other visitors. Buildings need to be designed to provide private spaces, either by offering private bedrooms or by having other rooms that residents may use, particularly with visitors so that they may have private, personal conversations. Privacy and personalized spaces reduce anxiety, aggression, and psychotic problems, and improve sleep (Morgan & Stewart; Zeisel et al.). Zeisel et al. found that privacy and personalized space were particularly important features that were related to behavioral health outcomes.

Visual Barriers and Cues

Visual barriers and stimuli can be used to either attract or distract residents. Doors between rooms can be removed or added depending on the need for the space; for example, removing a door may facilitate room finding, such as finding the bathroom. Covering doorknobs with a cloth and/or disguising doors can be used to prevent residents from using a door (Namazi, Rosner, & Calkins, 1989).

On the other hand, creative visual stimuli can be used to disguise exits to prevent escaping. For example, Kincaid and Peacock (2003) studied the effectiveness of using wall murals to prevent door testing. Twelve residents were observed over a 12-week period, before and after a wall mural was used to disguise a door and elevator, to determine if wall murals changed typical door-testing behaviors. The door and wall murals resulted in a significant decrease in overall door-testing behavior. Out of the 12 residents, only three continued to test the doors after the mural was painted across the elevator and door, and two of these residents also decreased their behavior. Only one resident, with higher mental status, increased door-testing behavior with the wall mural. The wall mural may have also contributed to decreasing the institutionalized feeling and increasing the impact of the circular design of the building. Kincaid and Peacock suggested that wall murals can be an effective way to reduce agitation and/or potentially harmful situations for residents. This type of visual stimuli can also decrease stress for the staff, as they do not have to worry as much about the residents' "escape" behaviors, their interactions with residents may become more positive when they are not constantly focused on redirecting the residents, and the residents are spending more time interacting with one another. However, staff must not overly rely on the wall mural, and they must remain vigilant in attending to the residents' attempts to escape. In the Kincaid and Peacock study, one resident did leave the unit three times by following family members or staff when they opened the door. Dickinson and McLain-Kark (1998) also found that camouflaged exits reduce elopement attempts. On the other hand, tape grids on the floor in front of doors have had mixed results in reducing door-testing behaviors (Chafetz, 1990; Hussian & Brown, 1987; Namazi et al., 1989). Facilities should use strategies to camouflage exits, possibly with the addition of silent electronic locks, as these features were associated with less depression than facilities with alarmed exits (Zeisel et al., 2003). Another strategy identified by Zeisel et al. to decrease exit and door-testing behaviors is putting doors on the sides of hallways, not at the end. This may decrease the residents' attention to the exits by taking them out of the residents' direct view as they walk down the halls.

Object Arrangement

The objects in the environment should be age, gender, and culturally appropriate (Mahendra, 2001). Objects should also facilitate the residents' mood and recall of fond memories, and provide a sense of security. Some of these objects were already discussed in chapter 5, in the discussion of external aids that support the ability to recall past memories and focus the communication context (e.g., toys and memory wallets). Here, objects will be discussed in terms of providing interest areas and stimuli to engage the resident and to decrease wandering behavior, as well as furniture and its arrangement. Many facilities contain long hallways with a nursing station located somewhere on the hall. Residents are often lined up facing into the hallway, rather than facing each other. Modifications can be made to such a hallway by arranging furniture so that residents may sit and face each other, which may encourage interaction.

Interest areas could be set up so that residents may find an activity of interest in which to engage. Some facilities use artwork in the hallways to give the residents and their visitors something to talk about. For example, if the facility has a rotating display of artwork, then the visitors can ask the resident to look at the exhibit and talk about it with them, perhaps making visits more enjoyable. Cohen-Mansfield and Werner (1998) found that walking paths with multisensory activity centers resulted in decreased exit seeking, better mood, and better engagement with family members. Similarly, Forrest and Cohen (2004) described a building that was designed to control agitation. The facility also had home-like themed living areas and smaller activity centers that were designed to encourage the residents to linger and become engaged in an activity (e.g., music, reading, games, or congregating with other residents). The results of such design features resulted in a greater community sense and more interaction and engagement.

BOX 6.1 ENVIRONMENTAL DESIGN

A multilevel care facility was designed with the changing levels of needs of persons with dementia in mind. On the dementia unit, there was a kitchen and a living room with a fireplace. There was also a courtyard that the residents could freely access, as it was enclosed, with only one door from the dementia unit. The SLP observed that the residents seemed at home in this setting and would invite her to sit in their kitchen or by their fireplace to talk. They would also congregate together, sitting at the family-style kitchen table. Once they needed a higher level of skilled care, the residents were moved to a skilled nursing unit. Here, the residents could congregate in a lounge area. This time, the lounge area was across from the nurses' station, enclosed in glass, so that the nurses could keep an eye on the residents at all times. The lounge was designed with several different interest areas, including a variety of sensorimotor activities and tactile stimuli that residents with severe cognitive deficits could enjoy. The SLP observed that there seemed to be more interaction among residents and fewer incidents of agitated behaviors or repetitive questions directed at the nurses, as the residents were not lined up facing the nurses' station, and they had interesting things to do.

Outdoor Environments and Therapeutic Gardens

Persons with dementia, particularly those who live in care facilities, often do not get adequate exposure to the outdoors. Several researchers have suggested that increasing free access to the outside, including to therapeutic gardens, may increase the quality of life of persons with dementia (Brawley, 2002; Day et al., 2000). Access to therapeutic gardens would increase exposure to light and sun, which has several health benefits, including improving circadian rhythms and sleep-wake cycles, reducing depression, and improving vitamin D synthesis. Therapeutic gardens with safe, secure outside spaces may offer many other benefits as well, including encouraging walking and other forms of exercise, providing opportunities for socialization and sensory stimulation, as well as providing other fun and meaningful activities (Brawley, 2002). Furthermore, Stewart (1995) found that access to therapeutic gardens reduced elopement attempts and improved sleep. Brawley (2002) suggested a number of factors to consider in planning for therapeutic garden designs, including making the space highly visible to residents, selecting appropriate plants, creating interesting walking paths, ensuring smooth paving surfaces that curtail glare and walking surfaces that are slip resistant, creating clearly distinguishable borders of the pathway, using uniform texture and color on the pathway, and providing spaces for privacy as well as activities. Outdoor spaces can include open spaces for exercise, nooks for solitude or visits with family, and porches for doing activities, resting, or eating. If residents have access to outdoors, they may also engage in other purposeful, physical activities, such as raking, mowing, gardening, or hanging clothes on a line. These activities may be enjoyable and stimulating for residents who were accustomed to completing them previously. Brawley (2002) also suggested that having the opportunity to engage with natural sensory stimuli, such as plants, flowers, trees, and wildlife, can enhance the quality of life of persons with dementia.

On the other hand, Sloane et al. (2002) conducted a longitudinal study of 193 residential care and assisted living facilities and 40 nursing homes in four states, following nearly 3,000 residents for one year. They found that the presence of plants may actually be detrimental to residents. When plants were found sometimes in common areas and extensively in residents' rooms in nursing homes, there was a correlation with increased hospitalization and mortality. When plants were found often in common areas of assisted living facilities, there was a correlation with increased hospitalization and greater ADL decline. Conclusions cannot be drawn from this study, despite the large size, as the study was observational in nature and had many flaws. A controlled intervention study is needed to determine if plants do put residents at increased risk for hospitalization and mortality.

Sensory-Enhancing Adaptations

Sensory overstimulation and understimulation can both contribute to confusion and agitation in persons with dementia, so caregivers need to strike a careful balance in the level of stimulation (Day et al., 2000; Gitlin et al., 2003). For example, Day et al. recommended removing unnecessary clutter, eliminating overstimulating televisions and alarms, and providing tactile stimulation in surfaces and wall hangings. Another source of overstimulation and confusion can be overhead paging systems, which should be reduced to the greatest extent possible. Zeisel et al. (2003) found that one of the most significant factors in behavioral correlates of health is understandable and controlled sensory stimuli. Residents' ability to comprehend sensory stimuli is related to less verbal aggression and agitation, and fewer psychotic problems (Burgio, Scilley, Hardin, Hsu, & Yancey, 1996; Cohen-Mansfield & Werner, 1997; Zeisel et al.). Thus, clinicians should attend to all types of sensory deficits and stimuli of residents.

Visual Changes take place in aging persons' eyes that gradually reduce the eyes' ability to receive light, to adapt to changes in light, to tolerate glare, and to discriminate color (Noell-Waggoner, 2002). These changes in vision make it difficult for older adults to distinguish objects in, and therefore to understand, the environment. Furthermore, inadequate light is one of the most common reasons for falls in older adults. Researchers have suggested that contrast becomes more important in the design features of buildings, as well as in visual stimuli for older adults (Noell-Waggoner; Teresi et al., 2000). In addition to the problems from aging, persons with dementia may have visual perceptual deficits that may vary depending on the type of dementia (e.g., Alzheimer's versus Parkinson disease). Thus, clinicians should be aware of the visual deficits and abilities of residents and how the types of stimuli in the environment may affect the residents' functional abilities. Visual characteristics that should be considered in design features include quality and quantity of light, colors and color contrasts, and size of stimuli. These features should be considered not just for building design but also for other stimuli such as types of signs and décor. Noell-Waggoner reported that older adults need more light exposure with less glare, and also suggested that lighting in facilities be set up using the standards of the Engineering Society of North America to establish the quantity and quality of light needed. These standards are available for all three countries in North America: Mexico, the United States, and Canada.

With respect to quality of light, Noell-Waggoner (2002) emphasized that glare be controlled, both directly from light sources and from reflective surfaces. Noell-Waggoner also recommended having flicker-free lighting, uniformity in ambient lighting, and a balance of daylight and artificial light. For example, some facilities use room-darkening drapes to prevent the glare from natural light, but this eliminates too much light; rather, sheers should be used to reduce glare while letting light in. Furthermore, Noell-Waggoner instructed that light should be oriented toward the visual task of interest and not into the person's eyes, and she suggested that for the best color rendition, lamps with a high rating on a color-rendering index (scale of 100) should be used. With respect to quantity of light, Noell-Waggoner reported that older adults require three to five times more light than younger adults. Again, facilities must ensure that an adequate amount of light is provided, without creating glare. Noell-Waggoner suggested use of energy-efficient indirect lighting systems with the provision of additional task lighting where it is needed. Such a system would direct both artificial and natural light toward the ceiling and walls to diffuse light throughout the room. When planning for task lighting, planners should ensure that task lights (e.g., a desk lamp) are in reach and easy to use. Rather than having lamps with small switches that are hard to find underneath the lampshade, the facility should use lamps that turn on and off by touching the base. Finally, Teresi et al. (2000) suggested the use of yellow rather than blue fluorescent or incandescent lighting to reduce glare.

Because of the lower levels of light that are received into an older person's eyes, color may not be discriminated properly. High-contrast color usage can be used to compensate for this, such as black on white backgrounds or blue on yellow backgrounds (Teresi et al., 2000). Teresi et al. advised against the use of blue and green together, as these colors will not be discriminated from each other properly.

However, Noell-Waggoner (2002) suggested that although contrast is important, color lightness versus darkness is more important than color contrast. She suggested that the use of colors with medium tone is good because those that are darker than medium are seen as gray or black (e.g., navy or burgundy). In order to maximally plan colors, clinicians can obtain a gray scale from an art supply store to ensure the most useful contrasts. Noell-Waggoner reported that good value contrasts will enhance the residents' ability to see in both low- and bright-light conditions, indoors and outdoors, and day or night. Some specific recommendations that were made include wall colors that are a medium tone with a light color on ceilings (Noell-Waggoner), or in a neutral color with contrasting colors to highlight thresholds, and extra light and contrasting colors to underline the presence of obstacles (Teresi et al.). Noell-Waggoner also pointed out that paint colors absorb or reflect light, so dark paint colors should be avoided, as they absorb too much light.

Some additional lighting strategies include instructing caregivers to allow elders extra time to adjust to differences in outdoor and indoor lighting by putting a seat just inside and outside doors so that the person can sit while adjusting to the light change (Noell-Waggoner, 2002). In addition, designers should avoid white or light-colored surfaces outside because they reflect too much light and cause glare, which can impose a safety hazard and increases the risk of falls. Signs used to increase orientation should be large, but in addition, residents need to be trained to use the signs, as signs alone may not impact residents' orientation (Day et al., 2000). Finally, Teresi et al. (2000) suggested that clinicians need to consider the overall fit of the person in the physical and social environment, as each discrete variable is not likely to result in much difference in residents' functioning.

Acoustics and Auditory Stimuli The acoustic atmosphere of most facilities is not conducive to residents' functional abilities. For example, Sloane, Mitchell, Calkins, and Zimmerman (2000) measured sound pressure levels of 60 to 70 decibels in dining rooms and at nursing stations; this is the level of loud conversation. Teresi et al. (2000) reported that there is a relationship between noise and negative functional outcomes. Given that most residents have hearing disabilities, environmental planners should consider the auditory stimulation and acoustics of each space, and efforts should be made to create a good acoustic environment or to improve the acoustic properties of the space. This can be achieved by providing a physical space that dampens acoustic stimuli, such as with curtains and carpet. Many residential facilities, however, avoid the use of carpets because they are harder to keep clean.

Auditory interventions can be used to reduce agitation and to increase functional behaviors. For example, Burgio et al. (1996) reported the positive effects of environmental "white noise" (e.g., water sounds) audiotapes on verbal agitation in nursing home residents with severe dementia. In the Gitlin et al. (2003) review, eight studies involved some form of auditory stimulation (e.g., soothing music, natural sounds, or white noise), and three studies evaluated music in combination with other sensory-based strategies. (Music-based interventions will be discussed later, under combination strategies.) Gitlin et al. found that 10 out of 11 studies reported improvements after auditory interventions. There were many methodological inconsistencies, however, that made it difficult for Gitlin et al. to make specific recommendations based on the findings. For example, the amount and type of exposure to auditory stimulation differed across studies, outcome measures differed, and different interventions did not always result in different results. Gitlin et al., however, did note that it appears that some form of soothing auditory sounds reduces agitation.

Another aspect of auditory intervention that is often overlooked or not attended to adequately is that of hearing aid usage by residents with dementia. Palmer, Adams, Bourgeois, Durrant, and Rossi (1999) studied the impact of hearing aid usage on problem behaviors in eight persons with Alzheimer's disease and their caregivers. The participants resided at home with a family caregiver who completed pre- and posttreatment outcome measures. Results revealed that participants wore their hearing aids for 4 to 13 hours per day, and that, after hearing aid treatment, one to four problem behaviors were significantly reduced for all of the participants. Based on a hearing handicap instrument, nearly all of the caregivers indicated that hearing handicap had been significantly reduced. Palmer et al. (1999) also noted that those with the lowest cognitive function received the least benefit from wearing hearing aids. The care plan for residents with hearing impairment should include that nursing staff ensure that hearing aid batteries are working and the hearing aids are worn consistently.

Multisensory Stimuli Sensory cues, such as tactile, olfactory, and gustatory cues, have also been effective in triggering memory and maintaining functional behaviors. Tangible stimuli in the form of dolls and stuffed animals improved the meaningfulness and relevance of conversations of persons with dementia (Hopper, Bayles, & Tomoeda, 1998). Similarly, decreased patient agitation and improved family visiting were documented when a variety of handmade, therapeutically based sensorimotor recreational items (e.g., an activity apron, an electronic busy box, an look-inside purse, and squeezies) were given to nursing home residents with dementia (Buettner, 1997, 1999). Smells, such as the burning of candles with a pine scent or gingerbread and vanilla scents, may trigger memories of Christmas trees and baking cookies with their mother, and lead to satisfying conversational interactions. Foods that have sweet or salty tastes are often preferred by the person with dementia, and the use of sweeteners, such as honey or sugar, can encourage the reluctant eater. These eating behaviors will be discussed further in chapter 7. Multisensory stimulation for persons in the late stages of dementia, such as Snoezelen, will be discussed in chapter 11.

Problems and Future Research Needs

Gitlin et al. (2003) reported that there does not appear to be one single strategy that is more effective than another, and different interventions may result in similar results, but methodological flaws do not allow us to make specific conclusions. However, the strategies that have been reviewed do seem to result in outcomes of high clinical relevance. Many of these recommended environmental strategies are simple, low-cost environmental changes that could easily be implemented and result in cost-effective, clinically significant changes in behavior and quality of life (Gitlin et al.).

Teresi et al. (2000), however, identified difficulties in implementation of therapeutic design recommendations. For example, they cited a study (Schnelle, Alessi, Al-Samarrai, Fricker, & Ouslander, 1999) in which staff members refused to reduce noise levels to criterion at night (below 50 dB); thus, administrators' and regulators' awareness of environmental issues in dementia care must be increased. Teresi et al. recommended a move away from observational research toward intervention research, while recognizing that nursing homes present many methodological challenges, such as lack of random assignment of residents. However, they do recommend that differences in characteristics of individuals in different settings be controlled for, as residents of special care units (SCUs) differ from those of non-SCUs. A significant need that was identified was caregiver training (family or staff) and appropriate adaptations of the environment according to the client's needs at various stages of the illness.

Day et al. (2000) and Teresi et al. (2000) pointed out that we need to consider both the physical and social environments of care facilities. Furthermore, environmental modifications need to match the cognitive level of the persons in the environment, as interventions that are appropriate for persons at the middle stages of dementia may not be appropriate for those in the later stages. Day et al. reported that studies of discrete environmental elements be conducted so that designers can determine the impact of individual design elements. Zeisel et al. (2003) identified many needs for future research, including therapeutic gardens, soothing colors, nondisorienting carpeting patterns, higher lighting levels, and alternative bathing settings. Methodological issues, such as larger sample size, more diverse samples, interactive and cumulative effects of environmental conditions, and organizational factors, need to be examined. Additionally, drug treatments, supportive environments, and focused caregiving strategies should be investigated in various combinations using interdisciplinary approaches in order to find the approaches most likely to result in significant improvements in functioning of persons with dementia (Zeisel et al.).

INDIVIDUALIZED AND GROUP ACTIVITIES INTERVENTIONS

Importance of Pleasurable Activities and Engagement

Clinicians and families should ensure that persons with dementia are able to maintain participation in the pleasurable and satisfying activities of one's daily life through individualized care plans. It is the enjoyment and gratification from particular activities that contribute to our uniqueness as individuals. Unfortunately, many activities based on premorbid hobbies and interests are complex and require the skills that are deteriorating due to dementia. A classic example of decreased participation is when the avid poker player's friends ask his wife to plan alternate activities for the usual poker day so they can avoid confronting him with the fact that he can no longer play competitively. Another example is when the devoted letter writer deflects questions about her much shorter and simpler letters with comments like "I'm so busy lately, I can hardly keep up with my writing." Another example of symptomatic behaviors is the lay reader who begins to decline invitations to participate in the church service with the excuse, "I need to get my glasses checked." This change in participation often occurs too slowly to be noticed by others and is rarely attributed to memory impairment. However, the avoidance of familiar activities and social withdrawal do, in fact, signal the individual's emerging awareness that cognitive skills are not as sharp as they once were. A complete list of familiar and pleasurable hobbies and activities, past and current levels of participation in those activities, and a rank ordering of the most important activities to maintain for future enjoyment should be obtained. With this information, the interdisciplinary team can focus on designing supportive strategies for the most important activities.

Social and Participation Barriers

As the language and cognitive skills of persons with dementia deteriorate with advancing disease, their social partners develop increasingly negative impressions of their ability to maintain social competence and independence (Lubinski, 1995). This is particularly problematic in the nursing home environment, where caregivers' lowered expectations of the residents contribute to activity limitations and the condition of premature "learned helplessness." It is also a problem in home and community settings, when caregivers and families assume the duties and responsibilities of the person with dementia (e.g., managing finances) and relieve them of others (e.g., driving). Social withdrawal, depression, and decreasing participation in favorite activities are signs of the need for intervention. Researchers have begun to document the types of preserved language and cognitive abilities that can help adults with dementia maintain a socially interactive life. Quality of life among adults with dementia depends in part on the frequency and quality of verbal interactions they have with their caregivers (Bourgeois, Dijkstra, & Hickey, 2005).

Thus, clinicians should also attend to social groups, particularly in day care or long-term care facilities. Professionals can identify the organization and composition of social groups, as well as the interactions within these groups (Gitlin et al., 2003). Some examples of strategies for increasing socialization include the simulated presence of family members via audio or video recordings (e.g., Woods & Ashley, 1995), structured group programs (e.g., Camp & Skrajner, 2004), pet therapy (e.g., Batson, McCabe, Baun, & Wilson, 1998; Erickson, 1985), and intergenerational programs (e.g., Aday et al., 1991a, b; Chamberlain, Fetterman, & Maher, 1994). There are reports that these and other types of activities for persons with dementia, at various levels of cognitive function, contribute to increased socialization, but the evidence is not that strong (e.g., Nissenboim & Vroman, 1998). Clinicians should also consider the theory, or the principles, behind the intervention, particularly when there is no scientific evidence available for an intervention (i.e., the intervention is based only on expert opinion). The interventions recommended here apply learning principles to dementia management and target everyday functional behaviors, rather than abstract underlying cognitive skills (Holland, 2003).

Maintaining Self-Identity Through Social Roles and Adapted Work

Successful communicative interaction allows adults with dementia to remain part of social networks and to maintain their roles in these networks. Certain roles, such as a teacher, advice giver, or nurturer, are some of the common ways that people interacted with each other throughout their lifetime; these familiar interactions tend to follow script-like sequences. Camp and Skrajner (2004) demonstrated that adults with early-stage dementia were able to function as group leaders for a small-group activity of memory bingo. They were able to learn procedures involved in leading a group and were able to engage in this role effectively. Similarly, Camp et al. (1997) reported on the preserved teaching role behaviors demonstrated by residents with severe dementia when asked to interact with toddlers using Montessori materials.

Fulfilling a helping or teaching role may have additional psychological benefits, such as higher self-esteem and well-being (Liang, Krause, & Bennett, 2001). Dijkstra, Bourgeois, Youmans, and Hancock (2006) examined the effects of two different information-providing roles, an advice-giving role and a teacher role, to assess whether preserved knowledge in community-dwelling adults with moderate dementia could be activated, resulting in qualitatively different conversational content as a function of assigned roles. Study 1 examined differences in language production for a social conversation versus an advice-giving role. Participants were asked, in counterbalanced sessions with the experimenter, to converse about or to provide advice about three topics (marriage, children, and church). Study 2 assessed the extent to which adults with dementia were able to assume a teacher role and to demonstrate preserved knowledge of action sequences and instructive language during a cooking task. In both studies, participants were expected to fulfill these roles by drawing from previous experiences in the remote past as a parent, sibling, or friend, when they gave advice or taught others how to make a recipe. The results confirmed that adults with moderate dementia were able to fulfill role-specific tasks notwithstanding deficits in short-term memory, working memory, and episodic memory, as long as these tasks took place in an appropriate social and communicative context and as long as the role to be fulfilled was adequately triggered. These findings suggest that preserved discourse and role-related abilities in adults with dementia may allow these individuals to engage in interactions involving active, established social roles. Successfully assuming specific roles may also contribute to a better quality of life and more rewarding social interactions with peers and caregivers.

In another study of community-dwelling persons with early to moderate dementia, Maddox and Burns (1999) described the development and evaluation of the Adapted Work Program (AWP), a sheltered workshop for male veterans attending a day care program. This work program was based on conceptual models from occupational therapy (i.e., the Allen cognitive disabilities framework; Allen, 1988) and from nursing (i.e., the progressively lowered stress threshold; Hall & Buckwalter, 1987). The AWP provides structured work activities at different performance levels to enhance self-esteem and meaningful roles. The types of work tasks included collating and stapling print materials, labeling envelopes, inspecting and sorting surgical towels, folding blankets, and portioning and wrapping food for the cafeteria. To allow for continued success, demonstrations, visual cues, and other strategies and adaptations were provided for the more moderately impaired participants. Results of a pilot study of 12 individuals who attended the 4-hour-per-day program 3 days a week for a full year revealed positive effects on participants' mood, as measured by the Geriatric Depression Scale (Yesavage et al., 1983), and some improvement on a self-esteem measure (Rosenberg, 1965); control subjects showed declining scores on the same measures. Furthermore, participants and caregivers reported feelings of success in task performance, and of satisfaction with the work role and the maintenance of social relationships.

Maintaining Participation in Social Groups

Question-Asking Reading Activity programming for long-term care residents and adult day clients may include a "current events" group or newspaper reading by a staff member. However, for persons with dementia, this type of activity often leads to disruptive behaviors or passivity due to the length and/or complexity of stories read, or the lack of familiar context for the stories. For persons with dementia who have strengths in reading skills, Question-Asking Reading (QAR) is an alternative intervention that can promote participation in newsgroup activities through the use of written cues (Stevens, Camp, King, Bailey, & Hsu, 1998; Stevens, King, & Camp, 1993). QAR utilizes external prompts to encourage active participation and to facilitate increased comprehension of the text that is read. The suggested routine for the group activity involves the following steps: (a) orientation, (b) distribute cue cards, (c) distribute two-paragraph text, (d) group reading of paragraph 1, (e) question asking, (f) group reading of paragraph 2, and (g) question asking. Orientation involves talking about the day's activity as well as general orientation information, such as the day, date, and surroundings, then introduction to the passage. Once this discussion is complete, the cards with written cues for questions are distributed. These written cues are designed to prompt discussion about the story that will be read in the group: for example, "Ask about a word that is hard to say," "Ask about the main idea," "Ask about what happens next," "Ask about a specific detail in the story," and "Ask if anyone knows additional information on this topic." After distributing cue cards, a two-paragraph text is distributed. The group reads the passage, with one group member reading the first paragraph, and then group members taking turns asking questions, using their cue cards to think of questions about the text. Results of a QAR study revealed that participants interacted more with each other and with staff, and exhibited better text comprehension and better retention of the information, as compared to typical reading groups. It is important to note that the role of the leader is significant in engaging the participants in the QAR procedure initially, but with repeated exposure to the QAR procedures, participants require fewer prompts to read in turn, ask and answer questions, and offer novel insights on the topic.

This type of activity could be modified to meet the cognitive needs and abilities of the group members, for example, modifying the passage length and complexity, and/or the specificity of the cue cards. The idea is to have the group members actively engaged in a reading and discussion activity, rather than passively listening to a staff member or volunteer read to them. See Case 6.1 for an illustration of such activities.

CASE 6.1 ILLUSTRATION OF MAINTAINING PARTICIPATION

An SLP began working in a long-term care facility in the fall of 2001. Each day she would walk past the activity room, often hearing an activity assistant reading the newspaper to a group of residents. There were few stories in the newspaper that the SLP felt were appropriate to read to the residents (e.g., stories about anthrax in mailings, terror threats, and the war in Afghanistan). She was concerned that the residents were not actively engaged, and that those who were attending to the stories may be negatively impacted by hearing such bad news every day, while possibly not fully understanding what was happening in the world. The SLP worked with the activities assistant to teach her to use the Question-Asking Reading technique to engage the residents in reading stories of interest that would encourage them to use their intact remote memories and interests in discussions about the readings.

Poetry-Writing Groups Other reading-related interventions, such as book clubs and poetry-writing groups, have been developed to enhance communication and reminiscence and to prevent the negative predicament of excess social disability (Ryan, Meredith, MacLean, & Orange, 1995). Poetry-writing groups evolved from reminiscence sessions where a group leader would stimulate conversation on a specific topic (e.g., spring, the beach, and school days), write down the memories and feelings of participants, and then read aloud the phrases as poetry. (Hagens, 1995; Koch, 1977; Schuster, 1998). Hagens, Beaman, and Ryan (2003), in their review of this literature, found that family and nursing home staff reported improved self-esteem of residents and improved relationships with staff and family after reading the writings of the group. In an effort to expand on this enhanced social environment model, the investigators implemented a "reminisce and write" group (Hagens), in which they wrote down participants' words into a poetry format, and solicited objects related to the poem from family members in order to construct a remembering box. These boxes contained photographs and other personally relevant objects from the person's past life that elicited memories and conversation when shared with staff and family. The remembering box, a framed copy of their poem, and a large photograph of the resident were displayed in the resident's room; the authors conducted staff in-services and encouraged staff to use the materials with residents over a 14-month period. Staff reported using the boxes and poems as communication tools, to learn the histories of the residents, and to redirect residents during periods of agitation or sadness.

Maintaining Lifelong Interests Through Modified Activities

Strength-Based Programming Eisner (2001) has developed an approach for the selection of interest-appropriate materials and activities that is based on the

TABLE 6.1 Strength-Based Programming Based on Theory of Multiple Intelligences

Intelligence Types	Examples of Activities
Verbal-linguistic	Communication cards, memory wallets, and word games
Logical-mathematical	Card and board games, jigsaw puzzles, and organizational tasks
Visual-spatial	Crafts and picture games
Tactile-kinesthetic	Dance, exercise, ball games, and dolls and plush toys
Auditory-musical	Music, sound games, and toys with sound effects
Interpersonal	Discussions, drama, storytelling, group games, and dolls and toys
Intrapersonal	Writing journals, collages of personal items, and solitaire
Naturalistic	Picnics, nature walks, gardening, animals, nature shows and videos, and science games and activities

Source: For strength-based programming, Eisner (2001); and for theory of multiple intelligences, Gardner (1993).

CASE 6.2 ILLUSTRATION OF MODIFYING AN ACTIVITY—SCRABBLE

- **Level 1.** In the game of Scrabble, participants select seven random tiles with letters of the alphabet and attempt to formulate words with the letters for the maximum possible points using a game board. Words are placed on the game board in a crossword puzzle format, to intersect with existing words on the board. The game continues until participants' tiles no longer form words to add to the board. The winner has accumulated the most points from the added values of his or her individual word plays. This game requires good vocabulary, spelling, attention, prediction, and working memory skills.
- **Level 2.** To simplify the rules of the game, Scrabble could be played without the game board, eliminating the crossword puzzle aspect of the game. Players can select randomly seven letter tiles and attempt to formulate a word with the letters. On each player's turn, he or she can place the word in the middle of the table for all to see; scores can be accumulated by adding the values of each letter tile for each word played. If no word can be formulated, players can use a turn to trade in tiles.
- **Level 3.** Scrabble letter tiles can be used for a word- and/or letter-matching game. Word cards can be prepared in advance on topics of interest (e.g., school days: pencil, paper, teacher, math, science, spelling, etc.), and players uncover tiles from the pile in the middle of the table to match the letters on their card. As a group activity, players can take turns picking a tile and matching it to their card; as a solitary activity, a person can match tiles to letters on the word card for as long as this activity is engaging.

personal strengths and interests of the individual. This intervention approach was developed using the theory of multiple intelligences (Gardner, 1983, 1993). This theory states that all persons have individual strengths and weaknesses, and that their areas of strength can be identified in the types of activities and the career path that they have chosen. In addition, persons with dementia continue to demonstrate areas of relative strength, often reflecting premorbid interests, which should be used to develop appropriate activities. These strengths and interests need to be identified and capitalized on in programming activities for them. Eisner developed a manual of "can-do" activities that capitalize on each of the multiple intelligences. The manual includes a chapter on modifying activities according to cognitive needs (Bourgeois, 2001). Examples of activities that can be conducted across each domain of multiple intelligences are displayed in Table 6.1. See Case 6.2 for an example of how a favorite activity can be modified as cognitive deterioration progresses. This intervention is supported by Level IV evidence, or expert opinion.

Montessori-Based Activities Maria Montessori developed the Montessori approach to educating children, with an emphasis on self-paced learning and developmentally appropriate activities (Camp, 1999; Camp et al., 1997). Montessori-based activities provide learners with cognitive stimulation and opportunities to interact successfully and meaningfully with their environment. These activities contain explicit cues about how to complete the activity; they also focus on recognition, rather than recall, making them ideal activities for persons with dementia to promote maintenance of previous skills and strengths. Camp and colleagues developed successful interventions that use Montessori principles for persons with dementia in adult day programs (Judge, Camp, & Orsulic, 2000) and long-term care settings (Camp et al.; Orsulic-Jeras, Judge, & Camp, 2000; Vance, Camp, Kabacoff, & Greenwalt, 1996). Participants have included persons with dementia interacting with each other (e.g., Camp & Skrajner, 2004), with preschool children (e.g., Camp et al.), with staff (e.g., Schneider, Diggs, Orsulic, & Camp, 1999), or with family members (Schneider & Camp, 2002). These well-designed, controlled, and quasi-experimental studies provide Level IIa evidence (well-designed controlled study without randomization) and Level IIb evidence (well-designed quasi-experimental studies) in support of the use of Montessori activities with persons with dementia.

In this manual of Montessori activities for persons with dementia, Brush and Camp (1999) described a series of activities that involve the active manipulation of concrete materials in purposeful, personally relevant ways. Montessori activities provide learning tasks in sensory, motor, and abstract domains that encourage independence, confidence, and contributions to society. Each activity is started at a simple level and gradually increases in complexity while providing structured repetition, immediate feedback, and a high probability of success to promote unconscious learning. This type of learning is based on priming, motor learning, and implicit memory, which are relatively spared in AD and related dementias (Camp, 1999). Some examples of the types of activities are tool use and scooping for fine and gross motor skills; sound, scent, color, and shape identification and sorting for sensory skills; and counting and conceptual sorting for abstract cognitive skills. See Table 6.2 for further examples of activities.

TABLE 6.2 Examples of Montessori Activities

Type of Activities	Examples
Motor	Scooping Polishing objects Cylinder blocks Dressing frames
Sensory	Sound cylinders Scent identification Tactile sorting Color and shape matching
Abstract	Number rods and counting Sandpaper letters Sorting tasks (e.g., emotions, or plant versus animal) Geography activities

Source: Camp (1999) and Camp et al. (1997).

When elders with dementia were asked to show preschool children how to complete Montessori tasks, they were able to do so easily and without prompting (Camp et al., 1997). Participants appeared to have a positive self-perception and increased sense of self-worth, reduced behavior problems, and more functional behaviors when serving in this teacher role (Camp et al.). Furthermore, Montessori activities resulted in significantly more constructive engagement, less passive engagement, and more pleasure (Orsulic-Jeras et al., 2000). Camp and Skrajner (2004) found that training persons with early-stage dementia to be leaders of a small-group activity for persons with more advanced dementia resulted in effective leader skills and increased engagement, satisfaction, and pleasure in comparison to standard activity programming. Schneider and Camp (2002) reported positive benefits of training family visitors to use Montessori activities; residents had significantly more active and less passive engagement with visitors, and the visitors reported that they felt significantly less burden in their visits and that they saw positive changes in their loved ones.

Pleasant Events Pleasant Events interventions were first applied to elders with depression (Zeiss & Lewinsohn, 1986), and then to home-dwelling persons with dementia and their caregivers, based on the premise that engaging in desired pleasant activities would reduce feelings of depression. Using the Pleasant Events Schedule–AD (Teri & Logsdon, 1991) to identify a comprehensive list of desirable activities, Teri, Logsdon, Uomoto, and McCurry (1997) first trained caregivers to increase the frequency of these specific Pleasant Events in the daily routine of the person with dementia. They then trained caregivers to use problem-solving strategies, using a Behavior Therapy–Problem-Solving intervention, to overcome the barriers preventing the implementation of increased pleasant events. Results revealed that Pleasant Events–Problem-Solving interventions are correlated with lower levels of reported depression in persons with dementia. More recently, nursing assistants (NAs) were trained to perform individualized activities with residents of a dementia special care unit (Lichtenberg, Kemp-Havican, MacNeill, & Johnson, 2005). The activities were identified on each resident's Pleasant Events Schedule–AD (Teri & Logsdon) or were suggested by the NAs. A mixed design was used to examine the effects of this intervention on residents' well-being. For residents in the experimental group, the program involved an explanation of the relationship between daily activities and one's feelings, relaxation exercises, mood ratings (on a scale of 1–10) before and after the activities, and a 15–20-minute individual activity. Examples of activities included engaging with correspondence (e.g., cards and letters), reminiscing, socializing, pampering, bird watching, reading, walking, and fixing things. See Case 6.3 for an example of the need for Pleasant Events for residents with dementia. Results for the experimental group revealed a significant improvement in the Behave—AD (Reisberg et al., 1987), as well as fewer troublesome and dangerous behaviors after treatment and higher mood ratings immediately after the activities; in contrast, the control group displayed more troublesome behaviors after the study. Thus, Pleasant Events interventions can reduce problem behaviors and increase opportunities for positive engagement in home-dwelling or long-term care residents with dementia. This intervention is supported by Level Ib evidence, or randomized controlled trials.

CASE 6.3 ILLUSTRATION OF PLEASANT ACTIVITIES

A woman moved into a nursing home after her husband died. Her children suddenly realized how much their father had been compensating for her memory deficits. The woman appeared to be quite depressed after the loss of her husband, and this exacerbated her cognitive deficits. The facility staff discovered that a former church friend of this woman was living in the facility and decided to put them in the same room. The women were often found together, wandering the facility looking for something to do. Sometimes one woman would begin to cry and ask when she could go home, and the other would then either try to console her or also become upset. The facility administrator found the women trying to leave the building one day, so he asked them to help out with a task. He gave one woman a ball of yarn, and handed the other woman the end of the yarn and asked her to unroll the ball and make a new one. When the SLP saw the women sitting near the front door, engaged in this activity, she asked what they were doing. One woman answered, "Somebody asked us to make a new ball of yarn out of a perfectly good ball of yarn. They must think we're 'cuckoo' or something!" The SLP then walked the women to the activities room and asked them to assist with folding placemats that had been laundered. The women were much more pleased with this activity, and as the staff began giving them more pleasant and meaningful activities to do, the women had fewer crying episodes and escape attempts.

Simple Pleasures Simple Pleasures is a therapeutic recreation activity that is designed to reduce isolation, inactivity, and agitation (Buettner, 1999; Kolanowski, Buettner, Costa, & Litaker, 2001). The idea behind Simple Pleasures is to provide age- and stage-appropriate recreational items for nursing home residents and to teach staff, families, and volunteers how to make and to use the items to interact with the residents. Simple Pleasures items consist of a variety of handmade, therapeutically based sensorimotor recreational items (e.g., an activity apron, an electronic busy box, a look-inside purse, and squeezies). The types of Simple Pleasures designed by the investigators reflected the Need-Driven Dementia Compromised Behavior Model (Algase et al., 1996), which was the precursor to the conceptual model of behavioral problems (Kunik et al., 2003) discussed in chapter 4. See Table 6.3 for examples of Simple Pleasures, and see Case 6.4 for an example of a client for whom a toolbox was used to increase engagement and decrease problem behaviors.

In a study using a crossover design, Buettner (1999) found decreased agitation, increased engagement and interaction, and increased frequency of and satisfaction with family visits when Simple Pleasures were given to nursing home residents with dementia. Additionally, Simple Pleasures interventions can be very economical, as Buettner recommended that volunteers (e.g., church auxiliaries or guilds) make them. In Buettner's project, 450 volunteers were trained to make the items.

TABLE 6.3 Simple Pleasures

Type of Activity/Stimulation	Examples
Sensori-motoractivities	• Squeezies (balloons filled with bird seed) • Sensorimotor activities • Patchwork sewing cards • Wave machines: starry nights or ocean waves (plastic bottle filled with mineral oil, glitter, star shaped sequins, or seashells) • Stuffed fish, butterfly • Sensory stimulation box: push buttons to light LEDs and activate buzzers
Reminiscence, language, cognitive	• Look-inside purses, briefcases, and tackle boxes • Home decorator kits: book of wallpaper, carpet, fabric, and paint swatches • Message magnets: words and phrases on magnet strips • Picture dominoes and bingo
Tactile manipulation; sensorimotor	• Table ball game: roll tennis ball into wooden box with holes • Latchbox: wooden board with various latches, hinges, and locks to manipulate • Activity aprons
Heat	• Muff: for hand warming • Hot water bottle cover
Ambulatory	• Wanderer's cart (made with PVC pipe)

Source: Buettner (1999).

CASE 6.4 CASE ILLUSTRATION OF A MEMORY BOX FOR ENGAGEMENT

Mr. Pearson, who worked as a mechanic for over 70 years, entered a long-term care facility. Mr. Pearson was not able to discuss details of his work. He did not initiate interactions with other residents, and often wandered around the facility looking for something to do. He often physically manipulated objects and seemed to be looking for things to "fix." An activities assistant made a memory box constructed from a toolbox, labeled with the name of the auto body shop where the resident worked for all those years. Inside, she put toy cars, pictures of cars and car parts, tools, and other memorabilia that would allow the resident to reminisce about his time as a mechanic. The staff were instructed to place the toolbox near the resident whenever he began wandering and looking for something to do. Mr. Pearson's troublesome behaviors decreased, and the staff were able to enjoy interactions with the resident related to his favorite topic.

In a small treatment study, Kolanowski et al. (2001) selected Simple Pleasures to enrich the physical and social environment and also matched the activities to each individual's style of interest and premorbid personality traits (e.g., extraversion and openness). Results revealed that mean time on task was significantly higher during the treatment than control condition, but there was no significant difference in degree of participation between conditions. Additionally, there was increased positive affect during the treatment condition, but no difference in level of negative affect, mood, or dementia behaviors across treatment or control. However, during the treatment condition, the participants had more days when no dementia behaviors were exhibited, as compared to during the control condition. Simple Pleasures are supported by Level IIb evidence.

Maintaining Connections and Interactions

Simulated Presence Family or staff caregivers often use radio, television, and/or movies to try to occupy or entertain persons with dementia. Sometimes a person may enjoy listening to a favorite radio program, or watching a favorite movie or the same televised football game repeatedly. Eventually, however, people with dementia often lose interest, even for familiar movie classics or favorite sporting events. This is often due to under- or overstimulation with this type of activity, leading to passivity or agitation for some persons, particularly as cognitive deficits become more severe. Radio or video programs may have too much complex dialogue, and too little or too much action; there may be too much visual and/or auditory stimulation, making it difficult to understand what is happening.

Interventionists have, therefore, sought an alternative to radio, movies, and television. One such alternative is homemade audiotapes or videotapes made specifically for the individual with dementia; for example, family members may tape themselves talking to their relative, which provides a "simulated presence" (Woods & Ashley, 1995). This intervention is useful when regular radio and television programs become too overstimulating and/or too difficult to comprehend. In this intervention, a family member fills out a memory inventory form about topics that typically elicit positive emotions in the resident during visits. The family member then makes a personalized, interactive audiotape that contains references to preserved memories. Each audiotape concentrates on two to three themes, repeated in different ways (e.g., important life events, loved ones, hobbies, and interests). Family members are encouraged to use phrases of affection. The tape is edited and silent pauses are added, so the resident has the opportunity to respond to the tape. This provides some form of social contact, while capitalizing on preserved long-term memories to engage the individual in reminiscing and to elicit positive emotions. Woods and Ashley reported decreased social isolation and agitation in the residents who participated, and recommended "simulated presence" for nursing home residents who respond well to family and other familiar people. In a series of four studies, researchers have documented that SimPres audiotapes made by family members or nursing home staff reduced agitation at a rate 14% greater than usual care and 46% greater than the placebo condition, and reduced withdrawn behavior 25% more often than with usual care and double the rate of the placebo conditions (Camberg, Woods, & McIntyre, 1999). Alternatively, videotapes could be made by family members, and may also include stories, songs, or activities. A family video could be a useful tool for staff to use to comfort or redirect a confused or agitated resident.

Video Respite There are commercially available videotapes for persons with dementia who do not have family to make personalized videotapes (Lund, Hill, Caserta, & Wright, 1995), or they may also provide more variety in videotapes. Video Respite videos are highly interactive and engage the person with dementia in a variety of therapeutic activities (e.g., reminiscence, music, and exercise). Individuals are encouraged to follow along and participate with the activities and conversations on the videotapes. Lund et al. (1995) demonstrated that the Video Respite tapes engage persons with dementia (e.g., smiling, laughing, and commenting) for longer periods of time than other video presentations (e.g., classic movies and television shows). Other findings included a reduction in problem behaviors, such as complaining, withdrawing, wandering, and asking repetitive questions; reduced depression; and increased self-esteem and self-awareness. This intervention can be very useful for family members caring for a person with dementia at home, so that the caregiver can prepare dinner or take a shower without worrying about entertaining the person with dementia; staff caregivers can use Video Respite as an individual or group activity.

Maintaining Spirituality and Religious Practices

There is little scientific research into interventions that use spiritual or religious practices with persons with dementia, and those that do exist are small-scale studies (e.g., Khouzam, Smith, & Bissett, 1994). There are, however, a number of anecdotal reports on persons with dementia who are able to continue to participate in singing hymns or reciting prayers long after one would expect the person to be able to do so (e.g., in advanced stages of dementia, when the person has become predominantly nonverbal; e.g., Roff & Parker, 2003; Stuckey, Post, Ollerton, FallCreek, & Whitehouse, 2002). There are also some correlational studies that investigate the impact of religious identity and/or religious attendance on cognitive function in older adults (e.g., Van Ness & Kasl, 2003). Stuckey et al. (2002) conducted a qualitative study by holding a community dialogue about the importance of spirituality and religion in dementia care with persons with dementia and their caregivers. The literature that is available, as well as clinical common sense, suggests that holistic care plans for persons with dementia include meeting their spiritual and religious needs in addition to their physical, cognitive, and social and emotional needs (Abramowitz, 1993; Bell & Troxel, 2001; Clayton, 1991; Everett, 1996; Khouzam et al., 1994; Richards, 1990; Roff & Parker; Stuckey et al.). The consensus is that spiritual and religious practices are meaningful activities that can offer a person a way to remain engaged; to connect with family, friends, and caregivers; and to stimulate mental activity. Because clinicians may not be familiar with or comfortable with a person's spiritual or religious practices, they should collaborate with family caregivers as well as the faith community to promote participation in spiritual and religious practices for as long as possible (Roff & Parker).

Stuckey and colleagues (2002), as well as several other experts, recommended that spiritual activities be a multisensory experience (Bell & Troxel, 2001; Everett, 1996). Likewise, Van Ness and Kasl (2003) suggested that religious practices can stimulate cognitive activity because they use many domains of intelligence (e.g., verbal, musical, and emotional) and because religious services require both perception and production activities (e.g., listening to sermons, reciting prayers, and singing songs). Clayton (1991) recommended that a "right-brain approach" be used in spiritual activities. Such a multisensory approach would focus on a variety of experiences, such as music, aroma, touch, and nature in spirituality, rather than just on the verbal and intellectual aspects of worship practices.

Prayers can connect persons with dementia to their sacred spiritual or religious beliefs (Abramowitz, 1993; Richards, 1990; Roff & Parker, 2003; Stuckey et al., 2002). Because people with dementia have preserved long-term memories, these strengths can be used in planning spiritual activities. For example, most people learned religious prayers and songs in childhood; hence, these became overlearned and rote through ongoing practice and rehearsal. Thus, singing hymns and reciting prayers are often more automatic verbal behaviors than engaging in more spontaneous topics of conversation. Roff and Parker suggested that these long-remembered rituals and prayers may provide comfort and reassurance to persons with dementia. Marston (2001) described a case study of a woman who was admitted to a nursing home for physical deficits; she reduced conflict with the staff after psychotherapy that also included a discussion of spirituality and the importance of her ritual with a prayer list. Marston suggested that persons with cognitive deficits would also benefit from staff recognition of the importance of spiritual activities in the care plan. Marston's recommendations for development and use of a prayer list could be used with persons in the early stages of dementia and modified for those in later stages. He described three steps: (a) exploring the meaning of prayer and how prayer is most effective, (b) reviewing how a prayer list would work, and (c) developing and using the prayer list.

Inclusion of spiritual needs in the care plan also dignifies the person with dementia by recognizing the need to feel connected, loved, and hopeful, and to feel valued as a person and not just a patient or resident (Bell & Troxel, 2001). Furthermore, Bell and Troxel suggested that even persons with advanced dementia may have spiritual needs that must be attended to at the end of life, a time when spiritual experiences may be the most profound for an individual. Persons with dementia and their caregivers reported that they used religious or spiritual explanations to cope and to come to peace with the dementing illness. They also reported being able to use their spirituality or religion to find "gifts amid loss" (Stuckey et al., 2002, p. 204), and that it allowed them to live in the moment and to appreciate the blessings they did have. Furthermore, attention to relationships as spiritual connections assisted the persons with dementia and their caregivers in coping, as they felt that they were "all in this together" (Stuckey et al., p. 204) through their shared humanity. To promote continued participation in the faith community, Roff and Parker (2003) described a model of a spiritual team, called a Care Team. Such support is necessary when the disease process is long term, and when people can be excluded due to a lack of understanding and inclusion in the faith community and due to embarrassment of family members who may not be willing to bring persons with dementia to worship services. The Care Team model, thus, trains the volunteers on ways to provide service for persons with dementia and their caregivers, and to promote their spiritual growth and practice. Where such a service is not available, clinicians can train members of the faith community to use compensatory strategies, such as those described in chapter 5, which will allow persons with dementia to continue to participate in spiritual and religious practices. Another suggestion is to incorporate spiritual or religious content into Montessori activities, as described earlier. For example, a Montessori activity could be sorting names of Bible characters into those from the Old or the New Testament, or to arrange the verses of a hymn or prayer into the proper order.

Although many experts have advocated the inclusion of spirituality in the care plan, there is a lack of evidence to support any particular intervention recommendation. Further research is needed that builds on these ideas and provides evidence of the clinical outcomes. For example, in a small study, Khouzam et al. (1994) demonstrated that reading Bible passages reduced agitation in persons with Alzheimer's disease. Additional studies could build the strength of this evidence. Evidence is also needed from a variety of religious and ethnic traditions, and clinicians need to be sensitive to the diversity of needs across their clients from various backgrounds (Stuckey et al., 2002). Future research should also investigate the impact of the clinician's own beliefs about spiritual and religious practices on the clinical outcomes (Marston, 2001).

INTERGENERATIONAL PROGRAMMING

Intergenerational programming can be used in residential facilities or within elderly persons' homes. When combined with service learning, intergenerational programs can provide benefits to students as well as to the persons with dementia. Many intergenerational programs were prompted by federal policies and academic initiatives (Aday, Rice, & Evans, 1991; Aday, Sims, & Evans, 1991; Baecher-Brown, 1997; Chamberlain et al., 1994; Wilson & Simson, 1991). The rise of intergenerational programs also coincided with the increased emphasis on service learning in colleges and universities throughout the country (Campus Compact, 1994). Service learning incorporates community service into higher education. Intergenerational programs have been utilized across disciplines, including social work (Gesino & Siegel, 1995; Wilson & Simson), occupational therapy (Greene, 1998), psychology (Fretz, 1979), sociology and anthropology (McGowan, 1994; McGowan & Blankenship, 1994), and speech-language pathology (Arkin, 1998). Intergenerational programs and service learning have common requirements of reciprocity of benefits for both the recipient and provider of services (Greene, 1998). Benefits for both groups of participants may include a sense of being part of a larger society, improved self-esteem, and increased awareness of progress in one's own life (Aday et al., 1991; Chamberlain et al.). Additional benefits for elders may include receiving needed services; and for the students, decreasing ageism, gaining practical experience, and increasing interest in gerontology careers.

The efficacy of intergenerational programs for persons with dementia is unclear at this point. The intergenerational service-learning literature is largely descriptive or quasi-experimental, lacking methodological rigor (Kocarnik & Ponzetti, 1991). A problem with some intergenerational programs was the lack of adequate training for the students to communicate with the elders. For example, many of the initial negative reactions of students in the Gesino and Siegel (1995) program were related to not knowing how to communicate with the residents. Thus, training and aging education appear to be important components of intergenerational programs (Friedman, 1997; Savishinsky, 1992). Despite the many methodological flaws, intergenerational programs appear to be a valuable mechanism to decrease social isolation and to improve societal integration of youth and elders. Qualitative reports of college students' journals (McGowan & Blankenship, 1994) and reaction worksheets (Gesino & Siegel) showed that the students modified their self-identity and decreased ageism as a result of their experiences with elders.

In addition, some of the programs already described above have included an intergenerational component, for example the roles study by Dijkstra et al. (2006), the Montessori program conducted between preschool children and residents with dementia (Camp et al., 1997), and the Volunteers in Partnership program (Arkin, 1998). Other activity-based interventions could also be easily carried out within an intergenerational context (e.g., strength-based programming, Pleasant Events, and music and art therapy programs). Benefits of music and art therapy programs will be discussed in the next section.

COMBINED ACTIVITY-BASED AND ENVIRONMENTAL INTERVENTIONS

Music Therapy

Music is an important part of most, if not all, cultures, so much so that it permeates many aspects of daily life. Given its importance, music can be used as an intervention for persons with dementia. Music therapy has been identified as being a combined environmental and interpersonal strategy (Clair, 1996). Many persons with dementia are deprived of meaningful musical experiences, and may be particularly susceptible in some long-term care facilities that may not offer the genre of music that they appreciate (Chavin, 2002). Music should be chosen that is relevant and appropriate to the individual. There may be general preferences according to age, gender, religion, ethnicity, or culture, and music that is provided should be age, gender, and culturally appropriate. For example, Runci, Doyle, and Redman (1999) reported that an Italian woman with dementia who resided in a nursing home in Australia responded better to music therapy when delivered in her original language than her second language. Gibbons (1977) found that most older adults prefer music that they enjoyed during the time period of their young adulthood, and also prefer stimulating to sedating music. These factors should be considered in developing music therapy and in planning music to be played in the background; however, caregivers must not make assumptions about musical preferences based on an individual's demographic characteristics (Chavin).

As well, it is important to consider background music and its influences on the sensory environment. For example, music can be used as part of the environment in dining halls to decrease confusion and to increase meal consumption and social interaction (Denney, 1997; Ragneskog, 1996). Likewise, Goddaer and Abraham (1994) found that introduction of soothing music at lunch resulted in reduced agitation among nursing home residents with dementia. In a review of the use of background music to modify the mood of the listening audience, Taylor (1981) concluded that altering the tempo and dynamics of music can have a more stimulating or sedating effect on the listener. Hanser (1997) experimentally manipulated various musical elements (e.g., tempo and loudness) and measured physiological responses (galvanic skin response, heart rate, and blood pressure) with no differential effects. However, subjects who liked the music had lower mean heart rate and blood pressure than those who did not like the music. This finding supports the importance of personal preference in musical selection. Therefore, Hanser (1999) found it surprising that several studies reported significant effects of prerecorded music on agitation and disruptive behavior (Gaebler & Hemsley, 1991; Sambandham & Schirm, 1995).

Experts (e.g., Chavin, 2002) have suggested that persons with dementia should be actively involved in music making, not just listening. Persons with dementia have been found to have intact remote procedural memory for making music, such as preserved piano-playing ability (Crystal, Grober, & Masur, 1989) and preserved rhythmic abilities in individuals in the later stages who have lost other functional skills (Clair, Bernstein, & Johnson, 1995). Furthermore, music triggers functional activities and positive emotions in advanced dementia (Clair & Bernstein, 1990).

Small studies have been conducted to examine the effects of music therapy on persons with dementia, generally with positive effects, such as decreased agitation (Bright, 1986; Tabloski, 1995) and increased engagement with decreased disruptive verbalizations (Casby & Holm, 1994). However, other research had variable results. Music therapy resulted in decreased disruptive behaviors for a person with Alzheimer's but caused increased agitation in a person with chronic cognitive deficits from traumatic brain injury followed by stroke (Gardiner, Furois, Tansley, & Morgan, 2000); thus, individual programming is very important in determining the type of music therapy activities used and whether music has the desired effect for each person with dementia.

Mahendra (2001) reported that the pairing of a preferred musical stimulus and related questions resulted in increased verbal communication and increased nonverbal engagement. Likewise, Clair (1996) found that singing increased alert responses by persons with late-stage dementia; however, these responses also increased later during the control visits that involved the experimenter sitting in silence. Clair postulated that singing might have been an unusual stimulus that was able to elicit the attention of the participants, followed by increased responsiveness even during silence, due to familiarity. Given limitations in the study, further research is needed.

A meta-analysis of music therapy studies found that there was an improvement in social behaviors, a possible reduction in wandering and restlessness during meals, and a reduction in agitated behaviors during bathing (Koger, Chapin, & Brotons, 1999). In a review of the literature on music therapy, Chavin (2002) reported that music therapy, when used correctly, can positively influence persons with dementia in a number of ways, including improvements in mood, behavior, speech, interaction, and activities of daily living performance. Furthermore, persons with dementia may be able to express their individuality through musical activities, even if nonverbal. Lou (2001) agreed, in a review of the music therapy literature, that this type of intervention may have positive effects on persons with dementia; six of seven studies reviewed demonstrated reduced agitated behaviors in persons with dementia when they were given music therapy. For example, a music therapy protocol that included listening to preferred musical selections along with exercise, facial massage, and progressive relaxation resulted in reduced depression, distress, and anxiety in older adults compared to a no-contact control group (Hanser & Thompson, 1994). However, Lou warned that the available studies have significant methodological weaknesses that limit the generalizability of the findings, including problems with the theoretical framework, design, outcome measures, description of interventions, and use of standardized protocols.

Given the available evidence, it appears that music therapy shows promise for managing the challenging behaviors of persons with dementia and for increasing their quality of life. Clair and Ebberts (1997) found that caregivers reported more satisfaction in their visits after the onset of a music therapy program during visits with persons with dementia. This is similar to the effect of the Montessori activities described above. Chavin suggested the following options for setting up music programs for persons with dementia in long-term care: (a) Develop a music therapy program with a board-certified music therapist; (b) develop a specialized music program with a music therapist; (c) develop a one-on-one or small-group music program within the activity programming; or (d) bring in professional musicians to perform on a regular basis. Chavin also suggested that we keep in mind that music may change a person's mood for the better or for the worse, and that it may affect a person positively or negatively; in addition, remember that not everyone enjoys music, and some people are particularly selective in the music that is enjoyable. Finally, clinicians should evaluate the successfulness of music programs by considering a variety of issues, such as the size of the group, the response of each individual, and the appropriateness of the music selections and activities. Music therapy is supported by Levels IIb and III evidence, quasi- and nonexperimental studies.

Pet Therapy

Some activity programming and/or environmental interventions include the presence of either stuffed or live animals. Researchers have suggested that animals may stimulate past memories and/or promote engagement in persons with dementia, possibly by providing a shared, tangible context for communication (Erickson, 1985; Hopper et al., 1998; Lubinski, 1995; Mahendra, 2001; Thomas, 1994). Hopper and colleagues (1998) used toys, including a stuffed dog, in the environment of four long-term care residents with dementia during a conversational task. Results revealed increased information units when conversing in the presence of the toys; however, for three out of four participants, total words and frequency of verbal initiations did not change significantly in the presence or absence of toys. Results also revealed that there was no effect of how realistic the toys were. Other researchers have demonstrated that stuffed animals increased alertness, smiling, and nodding and decreased agitation (Bailey, Gilbert, & Herweyer, 1992) and that they increased life satisfaction, psychosocial function, social competence, and personal neatness and decreased depression (Francis & Baly, 1986).

Likewise, real animals may increase the socialization, mood, and verbal and nonverbal expression of persons with dementia (Batson et al., 1998; Damon & May, 1997; Kongable, Buckwalter, & Stolley, 1989). More residential facilities are including live animals as part of the environment, often cats, birds, or dogs, as the underlying philosophy is changing to make residential facilities more home-like (Thomas, 1994). Dogs are often used for pet therapy, and may live at the facility, may assist in occupational or physical therapy goals, or may visit the residents with volunteers. Anecdotally, persons with dementia have been observed to respond very well to animals, with increased responsiveness and communication when the animal enters the room. Also, some residents with dementia benefit from having a role to fulfill in caring for animals (e.g., feeding, providing water, brushing, or cleaning cages). However, facilities must also attend to residents' allergies and other health concerns with live animals. One study found minimal impact of stuffed versus live animals on an individual with dementia, but did report anecdotal evidence for qualitative differences in the resident's affect and type of communication with the live animal over the stuffed animal (Curtright & Turner, 2002). This was a case study with many methodological issues, and it needs to be replicated, particularly given the more positive results noted above. Sloane et al.

(2002) reported reduced mortality in nursing homes with at least one cat, reduced hospitalization in assisted living facilities with at least three animals and/or at least one dog, and an inverse relationship of functional decline and presence of animals in nursing homes.

These quasi-experimental and nonexperimental studies, as well as expert opinion, provide evidence at Levels II to IV, and suggest that use of stuffed or live animals may improve the quality of life of persons with dementia. Clinicians should determine whether pets were an important part of a person's life and provide such treatments in cases where animals and pets may be soothing. Even for those who were not pet owners, animals may improve quality of life and increase opportunities for interaction. The positive findings of stuffed animals are encouraging, given concerns about animal allergies or any other hygienic concerns that may arise in care facilities. Clinicians may introduce such interventions and make careful observations to provide evidence for each of their clients.

COTREATMENT AND CONSULTATION: "PLAYING WELL WITH OTHERS"

For the most effective interventions, the members of the interdisciplinary team must work together effectively and efficiently. This requires good communication, both oral and written, and cooperation among team members. The speech-language pathologist should advocate for communication intervention for persons with cognitive-communicative deficits. Below, you will find suggestions for building caseloads. This section will address the ways that the SLP can collaborate with other team members using the interventions above. Both authors have frequently heard comments or been asked questions such as "Isn't this the job of the OT?" There is overlap among the roles of the OT and the SLP, as well as the SLP and the psychologist, the social worker, the recreation therapist, and others. The idea of a well-oiled machine comes to mind in addressing this issue. The team must work together for a common goal, but should not duplicate efforts. Communication is the oil that keeps the machine running. By communicating with each other, the SLP can ensure that he or she is not duplicating the efforts of other team members. In addition, cotreatment is often beneficial for the client and may make the other team members' work more efficient by enhancing communication with the client, or by training the team members how to use memory strategies that will enhance goal achievement.

An example of an intervention that is very suitable for cotreatment is the Breakfast Club, which was described in chapter 5. Occupational therapists may cotreat within this intervention to enhance instrumental activities of daily living related to cooking and homemaking, or to enhance functional mobility. Physiotherapists may also cotreat to address mobility issues within the Breakfast Club. Likewise, clients who previously enjoyed cooking as a hobby may benefit from having a recreation therapist involved in the group. In general, the Breakfast Club is not something that the SLP could carry out on a long-term basis with clients; the SLP can train nursing assistants and/or activities assistants to use these procedures for long-term maintenance of the goals of Breakfast Club.

Mahendra and Arkin (2003) recommended that a role of SLPs could be as trainers and supervisors of nonprofessional rehab partners (e.g., caregivers, students, and volunteers) for persons with dementia. They provided preliminary evidence that persons with mild to moderate dementia improved discourse and communication measures after participating in a 4-year Elder Rehab program with university students that involved health-enhancing and esteem-building community-based activities (physical fitness and supervised volunteer work). Based on this work, they also recommended that SLPs collaborate with activity programmers at long-term care and day care settings to support the maintenance of language and cognitive skills and social communication through group cognitive stimulation activities. Finally, they recommended that SLPs regularly educate other professionals on the variables that facilitate learning in individuals with dementia. See Appendix 6.1 for an example of how the first author became involved in the "Sunset Club," an activities program for residents with dementia who suffered from sundowning behaviors. This plan was put into place to enhance the participation and engagement of the group members by tailoring the activities to each person's strengths and language and cognitive levels.

WHAT IF I DO NOT GET REFERRALS FOR CLIENTS WITH DEMENTIA?

As we have delineated in this book thus far, the SLP's role is to work with persons with cognitive-communication disorders, even if those disorders result from degenerative diseases. The SLP can educate professional and family caregivers regarding the role of the SLP and can solicit these referrals. Yet, many SLPs simply go along with usual practice in their workplace and are kept busy enough with dysphagia referrals, so they do not go out of their way to look for communication-related referrals. Thus, the needs of many individuals with reduced communication abilities are not being met. Below are some tips for increasing the caseload of clients with cognitive-communicative disorders, based on the second author's clinical experience in a wide variety of nursing homes and hospitals.

First, try to get one referral for a person for whom you think you can make a significant change in activities, participation, and/or quality of life. This way, you can demonstrate that improvements can be made with one case, which may increase your credibility with the rest of the team. As other team members begin to see how much an SLP can do for persons with dementia, further educate them on cognitive-communication disorders and the role of SLPs. Remember to include nursing assistants and family members as integral team members who can advocate for appropriate services for persons with dementia. A good way to demonstrate techniques and to increase understanding of SLP treatments is to co-treat with OT and PT. Another excellent way to increase understanding of treatment techniques and enhance carryover of goals is to treat within leisure activity programs. This allows you to demonstrate techniques and train activities staff, and will likely increase your referrals for other residents with whom they are having difficulty. Finally, an excellent way to gain acceptance of your role is to educate staff from the top down—if you get support from "higher up" (e.g., the director of nursing or the nursing home administrator), you are very likely to start receiving referrals for your services.

CASE 6.5 ILLUSTRATION OF GAINING SUPPORT FOR SERVICES

An SLP started a new job in a nursing home. She was eager to implement the strategies she had learned about in her training. The SLP whom she replaced, however, worked only with residents with dysphagia or dysarthria. After a few weeks, the SLP's caseload had decreased and she had time to screen other residents. One resident of interest to the SLP was Mrs. Franklin, who sat in the hallway and spit at, kicked, punched, and called names to people walking by. The SLP spoke to the nursing staff about Mrs. Franklin's problem behaviors and her lack of positive interactions with others, and requested a referral for intervention. The social worker and nursing staff stated, "Why would you see her? What could you possibly do with her?" The SLP did a chart review, and found that this was actually a change of condition—Mrs. Franklin previously did not initiate any interaction and was very lethargic most of the time. Based on the ability to document this change in condition, and Mrs. Franklin's increased potential to participate in treatment given her increased alertness, the SLP was able to obtain the referral. The SLP learned that Mr. Franklin lived in the independent apartments next to the facility. When he visited, Mrs. Franklin was quiet and content, but they rarely talked. Mr. Franklin was skeptical but more than happy to have someone attempt to help his wife to communicate. The SLP went to his apartment and worked with Mr. Franklin to select pictures of Mrs. Franklin's life and family, and to make a memory wallet. This couple had a tremendously interesting life together! Mrs. Franklin was very pleased to read the memory wallet and converse about the topics. She told stories of living in Europe; recalled her daughter, who had died at the age of 18; and was proud to discuss her accomplishments as a teacher. Her husband sat and watched, with tears rolling down his face, as he discovered that his wife had not forgotten all these important details of their life—she just needed assistance to recall them and to converse about them. Furthermore, the staff began to surround Ms. Franklin, rather than avoid her, because they wanted to know more about the amazing things this woman had done in her life. The problem behaviors quickly disappeared because Mrs. Franklin now had a way to initiate positive interaction with many conversation partners. The memory wallet also kept her mind stimulated when she was alone. The SLP soon had such a big caseload (including many residents with cognitive-communication disorders) that she had a waiting list and the rehab company had to send in an extra SLP to help her catch up with all the referrals!

REFERENCES

Abramowitz, L. (1993). Prayer as therapy among the frail Jewish elderly. *Journal of Gerontological Social Work*, *19*, 69–75.

Aday, R. H., Rice, C., & Evans, E. (1991a). Intergenerational Partners Project: A model linking elementary students with senior center volunteers. *The Gerontologist*, *31*(2), 263–266.

Aday, R. H., Sims, C. R., & Evans, E. (1991b). Youth's attitudes toward the elderly: The impact of intergenerational partners. *The Journal of Applied Gerontology*, *10*(3), 372–384.

Algase, D. L., Beck, C., Kolanowski, A., Whall, A., Berent, S., Richards, K., et al. (1996). Need-driven dementia-compromised behavior: An alternative view of disruptive behavior. *American Journal of Alzheimer's Disease*, *11*, 10–19.

Allen, C. K. (1988). Occupational therapy: Functional assessment of the severity of mental disorders. *Hospital and Community Psychiatry*, *39*, 140–142.

Arkin, S. M. (1998). Volunteers in partnership: An Alzheimer's rehabilitation program delivered by students. *American Journal of Alzheimer's Disease*, *11*(1), 12–22.

Baecher-Brown, D. (1997). Why a geriatric center? *Journal of Gerontological Social Work*, *28*(1/2), 163–170.

Bailey, J., Gilbert, E., & Herweyer, S. (1992). To find a soul. *Nursing*, *22*, 63–64.

Batson, K., McCabe, B., Baun, M., & Wilson, C. (1998). The effect of a therapy dog on socialization and physiological indicators of stress in persons diagnosed with Alzheimer's disease. In C. Wilson & D. C. Turner (Eds.), *Companion animals in human health* (pp. 203–215). Thousand Oaks, CA: Sage.

Baum, C., & Edwards, D. F. (2002). What persons with Alzheimer's disease can do: A tool for communication about everyday activities. *Alzheimer's Care Quarterly*, *4*(2), 108–118.

Bayles, K. A., & Kim, E. S. (2003). Improving the functioning of individuals with Alzheimer's disease: emergence of behavioral interventions. *Journal of Communication Disorders*, *36*, 327–343.

Bayles, K. A., Kim, E. S., Azuma, T., Chapman, S. B., Cleary, S., Hopper, T. et al. (2005). Developing evidence-based practice guidelines for speech-language pathologists serving individuals with Alzheimer's dementia. *Journal of Medical Speech-Language Pathology*, *13*(4), xiii–xxv.

Bell, V., & Troxel, D. (2001). Spirituality and the person with dementia: A view from the field. *Alzheimer's Care Quarterly*, *2*, 31–45.

Bourgeois, M. S. (2001). Matching activity modifications to the progression of functional changes. In E. Eisner (Ed.), *Can do activities for adults with Alzheimer's disease* (pp. 101–107). Austin, TX: Pro-Ed.

Bourgeois, M., Dijkstra, K., & Hickey, E. (2005). Impact of communicative interaction on measuring quality of life in dementia. *Journal of Medical Speech Language Pathology*, *13*, 37–50.

Brawley, E. C. (2002a). Bathing environments: How to improve the bathing experience. *Alzheimer's Care Quarterly*, *3*(1), 38–41.

Brawley, E. C. (2002b). Therapeutic gardens for individuals with Alzheimer's disease. *Alzheimer's Care Quarterly*, *3*(1), 7–11.

Bright, R. (1986). The use of music therapy and activities with dementia patients who are deemed "difficult to manage." *Clinical Gerontologist*, *6*, 131–144.

Brush, J. A., & Camp, C. J. (1998). *A therapy technique for improving memory: Spaced retrieval*. Beachwood, OH: Menorah Park Center for Senior Living.

Buettner, L. (1997). *Simple Pleasures: A multi-level sensory motor intervention for nursing home residents with dementia*. Binghamton, NY: Binghamton University Press.

Buettner, L. (1999, January-February). Simple Pleasures: a multilevel sensorimotor intervention for nursing home residents with dementia. *American Journal of Alzheimer's Disease*, 41–52.

Burgio, L., Scilley, K., Hardin, M. J., Hsu, C., & Yancey, J. (1996). Environmental "white noise": An intervention for verbally agitated nursing home residents. *Journal of Gerontology: Psychological Sciences*, *51B*, P364–P373.

Calkins, M. P. (2005). Environments for late-stage dementia. *Alzheimer's Care Quarterly*, 6(1), 71–75.

Calkins, M. P., Namazi, K. H., Rosner, T. T., Olson, A. & Brabender, B. A. (1988). *Home modifications: Responding to dementia*. Chardon, OH: Corrine Dolan Alzheimer Center.

Camberg, L., Woods, P., & McIntyre, K. (1999). SimPres: A personalized approach to enhance well-being in persons with Alzheimer's disease. In L. Volicer & L. Bloom-Charette (Eds.), *Enhancing the quality of life in advanced dementia* (pp. 126–139). Philadelphia: Brunner/Mazel.

Camberg, L., Woods, P., Ooi, W. L., Hurley, A., Volicer, L., Ashley, J., et al. (1999). Evaluation of simulated presence: A personalized approach to enhance well-being in persons with Alzheimer's disease. *Journal of American Geriatrics Society*, *47*, 446–452.

Camp, C. J. (1999). *Montessori-based activities for persons with dementia* (Vol. 1). Beachwood, OH: Menorah Park Center for the Aging.

Camp, C. J., Judge, K. S., Bye, C. A., Fox, K. M., Bowden, J., Bell, M., et al. (1997). An intergenerational program for persons with dementia using Montessori methods. *The Gerontologist*, *37*, 688–692.

Camp, C. J., & Skrajner, M. J. (2004). Resident-assisted Montessori programming (RAMP): Training persons with dementia to serve as group activity leaders. *The Gerontologist*, *44*, 426–431.

Campus Compact. (1994). *Annual report*. Providence, RI: Brown University.

Casby, J. A., & Holm, M. B. (1994). The effect of music on repetitive disruptive vocalizations of persons with dementia. *American Journal of Occupational Therapy*, *48*, 883–889.

Chafetz, P. K. (1990). Two-dimensional grid is ineffective against demented patients exiting through glass doors. *Psychology and Aging*, *5*, 146–147.

Chamberlain, V. M., Fetterman, E., & Maher, M. (1994). Innovation in elder and child care: An intergenerational experience. *Educational Gerontology*, *19*, 193–204.

Chavin, M. (2002). Music as communication. *Alzheimer's Care Quarterly*, 3(2), 145–156.

Clair, A. A. (1996). The effect of singing on alert responses in persons with late stage dementia. *Journal of Music Therapy*, *33*, 234–247.

Clair, A., & Bernstein, B. (1990). A preliminary study of music therapy programming for severely regressed persons with Alzhiemer's type dementia. *Journal of Applied Gerontology*, *9*, 299–311.

Clair, A., Bernstein, B., & Johnson, G. (1995). Rhythm playing characteristics in persons with severe dementia including those with probable Alzheimer's type. *Journal of Music Therapy*, *32*, 113–131.

Clair, A., & Ebberts, G. (1997). The effects of music therapy on interactions between family caregivers and their care receivers with late stage dementia. *Journal of Music Therapy*, *34*, 148–164.

Clayton, J. (1991). Let there be life: An approach to worship with Alzheimer's patients and their families. *Journal of Pastoral Care*, *45*, 177–179.

Cohen-Mansfield, J., & Werner, P. (1997). Management of verbally disruptive behaviors in nursing home residents. *Journal of Gerontology: Medical Sciences*, 52A, M369–M377.

Cohen-Mansfield, J., & Werner, P. (1998). The effects of an enhanced environment on nursing home residents who pace. *The Gerontologist*, *38*, 199–208.

Crystal, H., Grober, E., & Masur, D. (1989). Preservation of musical memory in Alzheimer's disease. *Journal of Neurology, Neurosurgery, and Psychiatry*, 52, 1415–1416.

Curtright, A., & Turner, G. S. (2002). The influence of a stuffed and live animal on communication in a female with Alzheimer's dementia. *Journal of Medical Speech-Language Pathology*, *10*(1), 61–71.

Damon, J., & May, R. (1997). The effects of pet facilitative therapy on patients and staff in an adult day care center. *Activities, Adaptation, & Aging*, *8*, 117–131.

Danes, S. (2002). Creating an environment for community. *Alzheimer's Care Quarterly*, *3*(1), 61–66.

Day, K., Carreon, D., & Stump, C. (2000). The therapeutic design of environments for people with dementia: A review of the empirical research. *The Gerontologist*, *40*(4), 397–416.

Denney, A. (1997). Quiet music: An intervention for mealtime agitation? *Journal of Gerontological Nursing*, *23*, 16–23.

Dickinson, J. I., & McLain-Kark, J. (1998). Wandering behavior and attempted exits among residents diagnosed with dementia-related illnesses: A qualitative approach. *Journal of Women and Aging*, *10*, 23–35.

Dijkstra, K., Bourgeois, M., Youmans, G., & Hancock, A. (2006). Implications of an advice giving and teacher role on language produce in adults with dementia. *The Gerontologist*, *46*, 357–366.

Eisner, E. (2001). *Can do activities for adults with Alzheimer's disease*. Austin, TX: Pro-Ed.

Erickson, R. (1985). Companion animals and the elderly. *Geriatric Nursing*, *6*, 92–96.

Everett, D. (1996). *Forget me not: The spiritual care of persons with Alzheimer's*. Edmonton, AB: Inkwell Press.

Forrest, M. M., & Cohen, J. (2004). Marrying design/organization and programming to create a home and community for Alzheimer's residents. *Alzheimer's Care Quarterly*, *5*(1), 9–12.

Francis, G., & Baly, A. (1986). Plush animals: Do thy make a difference? *Geriatric Nursing*, *74*, 140–143.

Fretz, B. R. (1979). College students as paraprofessionals with children and the aged. *American Journal of Community Psychology*, *7*(3), 357–360.

Friedman, B. (1997). The integration of pro-active aging education into existing educational curricula. *Journal of Gerontological Social Work*, *28*(1/2), 103–110.

Gaebler, H., & Hemsley, D. (1991). The assessment and short-term manipulation of affect in the severely demented. *Behavioural Psychotherapy*, *19*, 145–156.

Gardiner, J. C., Furois, M., Tansley, D. P., & Morgan, B. (2000). Music therapy and reading as intervention strategies for disruptive behavior in dementia. *Clinical Gerontologist*, *22*(1), 31–46.

Gardner, H. (1983). *Frames of mind: The theory of multiple intelligences*. New York: Basic.

Gardner, H. (1993). *Multiple intelligences: The theory in practice*. New York: Basic.

Gesino, J. P., & Siegel, E. (1995). Training gerontological social workers for nursing home practice. *Gerontology & Geriatrics Education*, *15*(4), 69–82.

Gibbons, A. C. (1977). Popular music preferences of elderly people. *Journal of Music Therapy*, *14*, 180–189.

Gitlin, L. N., Liebman, J., & Winter, L. (2003). Are environmental interventions effective in the management of Alzheimer's disease and related disorders? *Alzheimer's Care Quarterly*, *4*(2), 85–107.

Goddaer, J., & Abraham, I. J. (1994). Effects of relaxing music on agitation during meals among nursing home residents with severe cognitive impairment. *Archives of Psychiatric Nursing*, *3*, 150–158.

Goffman, E. (1961). *Asylums*. Harmondsworth, UK: Penguin.

Gotestam, K. G., & Melin, L. (1987). Improving well-being for patients with senile dementia by minor changes in the ward environment. In L. Levi (Ed.), *Society, stress, and disease* (pp. 295–297). Oxford: Oxford University Press.

Grainger, K. (1995). Communication and the institutionalized elderly. In J. F. Nussbaum & J. Coupland (Eds.), *Handbook of communication and aging research* (pp. 417–436). Mahwah, NJ: Lawrence Erlbaum.

Greene, D. (1998). Reciprocity in two conditions of service learning. *Educational Gerontology*, *24*, 411–424.

Hagens, C. (1995). Reminisce and write: A creative writing program for the nursing home. *Long Term Care Journal*, *5*(2), 9–10.

Hagens, C., Beaman, A., & Ryan, E. (2003). Reminiscing, poetry writing, and remembering boxes: Personhood-centered communication with cognitively impaired older adults. *Activities, Adaptation, and Aging*, *27*, 97–112.

Hall, G. R., & Buckwalter, K. C. (1987). Progressively lowered stress threshold: A conceptual model for care of adults with Alzheimer's disease. *Archives of Psychiatric Nursing*, *1*, 399–406.

Hanser, S. (1997). Music therapy for Alzheimer's patients and families. In *Proceedings of the 1997 annual meeting of the American Psychiatric Association*. San Diego, CA: APA.

Hanser, S. (1999). Music therapy with individuals with advanced dementia. In L. Volicer & L. Bloom-Charette (Eds.), *Enhancing the quality of life in advanced dementia* (pp. 141–166). Philadelphia: Brunner/Mazel.

Hanser, S., & Thompson, L. (1994). Effects of a music therapy strategy on depressed older adults. *Journal of Gerontology*, *49*, 265–269.

Hellen, C. R. (1998). *Alzheimer's disease: Activity-focused care*. Boston: Butterworth-Heinemann.

Holland, A. (2003). Improving communication skills in individuals with dementia. *Journal of Communication Disorders*, *36*, 325–326.

Hopper, T. L. (2003). "They're just going to get worse anyway": Perspectives on rehabilitation for nursing home residents with dementia. *Journal of Communication Disorders*, *36*, 345–359.

Hopper, T., Bayles, K A., & Tomoeda, C. K. (1998). Using toys to stimulate communication function in individuals with Alzheimer's disease. *Journal of Medical Speech-Language Pathology*, *6*(2), 73–80.

Hussian, R. A., & Brown, D. C. (1987). Use of two-dimensional grid to limit hazardous ambulation in demented patients. *Journal of Gerontology*, *42*, 558–560.

Jacelon, C. S. (1995). The effect of living in a nursing home on socialization in elderly people. *Journal of Advanced Nursing*, *22*, 539–546.

Judge, K. S., Camp, C. J., & Orsulic, S. (2000). Use of Montessori-based activities for clients with dementia in adult day care: Effects on engagement. *American Journal of Alzheimer's Disease*, *15*(1), 42–46.

Kaakinen, J. R. (1992). Living with silence. *The Gerontologist*, *32*(2), 258–264.

Kaakinen, J. (1995). Talking among elderly nursing home residents. *Topics in Language Disorders*, *15*(2), 36–46.

Khouzam, H. R., Smith, C. E., & Bissett, B. (1994). Bible therapy: A treatment of agitation in elderly patients with Alzheimer's disease. *Clinical Gerontologist*, *15*, 71–74.

Kincaid, C., & Peacock, J. R. (2003). The effect of a wall mural on decreasing four types of door-testing behaviors. *The Journal of Applied Gerontology*, *22*(1), 76–88.

Kocarnik, R. A., & Ponzetti, J. J. (1991). The advantages and challenges of intergenerational programs in long term care facilities. *Journal of Gerontological Social Work*, *16*(1/2), 97–107.

Koch, K. (1977). *I never told anybody: Teaching poetry writing in a nursing home*. New York: Random House.

Koger, S., Chapin, K., & Brotons, M. (1999). Is music therapy an effective intervention for dementia? A meta-analytic review of literature. *Journal of Music Therapy*, *36*, 2–15.

Kolanowski, A., Buettner, L., Costa, P., & Litaker, M. (2001). Capturing interests: Therapeutic recreation activities for persons with dementia. *Therapeutic Recreation Journal*, *35*, 220–235.

Kongable, L. G., Buckwalter, K. C., & Stolley, J. M. (1989). The effects of pet therapy on the social behavior of institutionalized Alzheimer's clients. *Archives of Psychiatric Nursing*, *3*, 191–198.

Kunik, M. E., Martinez, M., Snow, A. L., Beck, C. K., Cody, M., Rapp, C. G., et al. (2003). Determinants of behavioral symptoms in dementia patients. *Clinical Gerontologist*, *26*(3/4), 83–89.

Lawton, M. P. (1999). Environmental design features and the well-being of older persons. In M. Duffy (Ed.), *Handbook of counseling and psychotherapy with older adults* (pp. 350–363). Hoboken, NJ: John Wiley.

Levesque, S., Cossette, S., & Potvin, L. (1993). Why alert residents are more or less willing to cohabit with cognitively impaired peers: An exploratory model. *The Gerontologist*, *33*(4), 514–522.

Liang, J., Krause, N. M., & Bennett, J. M. (2001). Social exchange and well-being: Is giving better than receiving? *Psychology and Aging*, *16*(3), 511–523.

Lichtenberg, P. A., Kemp-Havican, J., MacNeill, S. E., & Johnson, A. S. (2005). Pilot study of behavioral treatment in dementia care units. *The Gerontologist*, *45*(3), 406–410.

Liukkonen, A. (1995). Life in a nursing home for the frail elderly: Daily routines. *Clinical Nursing Research*, *4*(4), 358–370.

Lou, M. (2001). The use of music to decrease agitated behaviour of the demented elderly: The state of the science. *Scandinavian Journal of Caring Science*, *15*, 165–173.

Lubinski, R. (1995). State-of-the-art perspectives on communication in nursing homes. *Topics in Language Disorders*, *15*(2), 1–19.

Lubinski, R., Morrison, E., & Rigrodsky, S. (1981). Perception of spoken communication by elderly chronically ill patients in an institutional setting. *Journal of Speech and Hearing Disorders*, *46*, 405–412.

Lund, D., Hill, R., Caserta, A., & Wright, S. (1995). Video Respite: An innovative resource for family, professional caregivers, and persons with dementia. *The Gerontologist*, *35*, 683–687.

Maddox, M., & Burns, T. (1999). Adapted Work Program: A sheltered workshop for patients with dementia. In L. Volicer & L. Bloom-Charette (Eds.), *Enhancing the quality of life in advanced dementia* (pp. 56–77). Philadelphia: Brunner/Mazel.

Mahendra, N. (2001). Direct interventions for improving the performance of individuals with Alzheimer's disease. *Seminars in Speech and Language*, *22*(4), 291–303.

Mahendra, N., & Arkin, S. (2003). Effects of four years of exercise, language, and social interventions on Alzheimer disease. *Journal of Communication Disorders*, *36*, 395–422.

Mandel, S. (1993). The role of the music therapist on the hospice/palliative care team. *Journal of Palliative Care*, *9*, 37–39.

Marston, D. C. (2001). Prayer as a meaningful activity in nursing homes. *Clinical Gerontologist*, 173–178.

McGowan, T. G. (1994). Mentoring-reminiscence: A conceptual and empirical analysis. *International Journal of Aging and Human Development*, *39*(4), 321–336.

McGowan, T. G., & Blankenship, S. (1994). Intergenerational experience and ontological change. *Educational Gerontology*, *20*, 589–604.

Moore, K. D. (2002). Observed affect in a dementia day center: Does the physical setting matter? *Alzheimer's Care Quarterly*, *3*(1), 67–73.

Mor, V., Branco, K., Fleishman, J., Hawes, C., Phillips, C., Morris, J., et al. (1995). The structure of social engagement among nursing home resident. *Journal of Gerontology: Psychological Sciences, 50B*(1), P1–P8.

Morgan, D. G., & Stewart, M. J. (1998). Multiple occupancy versus private rooms on dementia care units. *Environment and Behavior, 30*, 487–504.

Nagy, J. W. (2002). Kitchens that help residents reestablish home. *Alzheimer's Care Quarterly, 3*(1), 74–77.

Namazi, K. H., Rosner, T. T., & Calkins, M. P. (1989). Visual barriers to prevent ambulatory Alzheimer's patients from exiting through an emergency door. *The Gerontologist, 29*, 699–702.

Nissenboim, S., & Vroman, C. (1998). *The positive interactions program of activities for people with Alzheimer's disease*. Baltimore: Health Promotions Press.

Noell-Waggoner, E. (2002). Light: An essential intervention for Alzheimer's disease. *Alzheimer's Care Quarterly, 3*(4), 343– 352.

Noreika, J., Kuhoth, J., & Torgrude, S. (2002). Using a post occupancy evaluation to guide bathroom design in a dementia specific, assisted-living facility. *Alzheimer's Care Quarterly, 3*(1), 32–37.

Orsulic-Jeras, S., Judge, K., & Camp, C. (2000). Montessori-based activities for long-term care residents with advanced dementia: Effects on engagement and affect. *The Gerontologist, 40*, 107–111.

Palmer, C. V., Adams, S. W., Bourgeois, M., Durant, J., & Rossi, M. (1999). Reduction in caregiver-identified problem behaviors in patients with Alzheimer disease post-hearing-aid fitting. *Journal of Speech, Language, and Hearing Research, 42*, 312–328.

Ragneskog, H. (1996). Influence of dinner music on food intake and symptoms common in dementia. *Scandinavian Journal of Caring Science, 10*, 11–17.

Reisberg, B., Borenstein, J., Salob, S., Ferris, S., Franssen, E., & Georgotas, A. (1987). Behavioral symptoms in Alzheimer's Disease: Phenomenology and treatment. *Journal of Clinical Psychiatry, 48*, 9–15.

Retsinas, J., & Garrity, P. (1985). Nursing home friendships. *The Gerontologist, 25*, 376–381.

Richards, M. (1990). Meeting the spiritual needs of the cognitively impaired. *Generations, 14*, 63–64.

Roff, L. L., & Parker, M. W. (2003). Spirituality and Alzheimer's disease care. *Alzheimer's Care Quarterly, 4*(4), 267–270.

Rosenberg, M. (1965). *Society and the adolescent self-image*. Princeton, NJ: University Press.

Runci, S., Doyle, C., & Redman, J. (1999). An empirical test of language-relevant interventions for dementia. *International Psychogeriatrics, 11*(3), 301–311.

Ryan, E., Meredith, S., MacLean, M., & Orange, J. (1995). Changing the way we talk with elders: Promoting health using the Communication Enhancement Model. *International Journal of Aging and Human Development, 41*(2), 87–105.

Sambandham, M., & Schirm, V. (1995). Music as a nursing intervention for residents with Alzheimer's disease in long-term care. *Geriatric Nursing, 16*, 79–83.

Savishinsky, J. S. (1992). Intimacy, domesticity, and pet therapy with the elderly: expectation and experience among nursing home volunteers. *Social Science and Medicine, 34*(12), 1325–1334.

Schneider, N. M., & Camp, C. J. (2002). Use of Montessori-based activities by visitors of nursing home residents with dementia. *Clinical Gerontologist, 26*(1/2), 71–84.

Schneider, N. M., Diggs, S., Orsulic, S., & Camp, C. J. (1999, March). Nursing assistants teaching Montessori activities. *Journal of Nurse Assistants*, 13–15.

Schnelle, J., Alessi, G., Al-Samarrai, N., Fricker, R., & Ouslander, J. (1999). The nursing home at night: effects of an intervention on noise, light, and sleep. *Journal of the American Geriatrics Society, 47(4)*, 430–438.

Schroll, M., Jonsson, P. V., Mor, V., Berg, K., & Sherwood, S. (1997). An international study of social engagement among nursing home residents. *Age and Aging*, *26*(S2), 55–59.

Schuster, E. (1998). A community bound by words: Reflections on a nursing home writing group. *Journal of Aging Studies*, *12*(2), 137–147.

Sigman, S. (1985). Conversational behavior in two health care institutions for the elderly. *Institutional Journal of Aging and Human Development*, *21*, 147–163.

Sloane, P. D., Mitchell, C. M., Calkins, M., & Zimmerman, S. I. (2000). Light and noise levels in Alzheimer's disease special care units. *Research and Practice in Alzheimer's Disease*, *4*, 241–249.

Sloane, P. D., Zimmerman, S., Gruber-Baldini, A. L., & Barba, B. E. (2002). Plants, animals, and children in long-term care: How common are they? Do they affect clinical outcomes? *Alzheimer's Care Quarterly*, *3*(1), 12–18.

Stevens, A., Camp, C., King, C., Bailey, E., & Hsu, C. (1998). Effects of a staff implemented therapeutic group activity for adult day care clients. *Aging & Mental Health*, *2*(4), 333–342.

Stevens, A., King, C., & Camp, C. (1993). Improving prose memory and social interaction using question asking reading with adult day care clients. *Educational Gerontology*, *19*, 651–662.

Stewart, J. T. (1995). Management of behavior problems in the demented patient. *American Family Physician*, *52*, 2311–2320.

Stuckey, J. C., Post, S. G., Ollerton, S., FallCreek, S. J., & Whitehouse, P. J. (2002). Alzheimer's disease, religion, and the ethics of respect for spirituality: A community dialogue. *Alzheimer's Care Quarterly*, *3*(3), 199–207.

Tabloski, P. A. (1995, Spring). Using music to calm agitated nursing home residents. *Travelers Center on Aging Newsletter*, *9*(3), 1–2.

Tappen, R. M. (1997). *Interventions for Alzheimer's disease: A caregiver's complete reference*. Baltimore: Health Promotions Press.

Taylor, D. (1981). Music in general hospital treatment from 1900 to 1950. *Journal of Music Therapy*, *18*, 62–73.

Teresi, T. A., Holmes, D., & Ory, M. G. (2000). The therapeutic design of environments for people with dementia: Further reflections and recent findings from the National Institute on Aging Collaborative Studies of Dementia Special Care Units. *The Gerontologist*, *40*(4), 417–421.

Teri, L., & Logsdon, R. G. (1991). Identifying pleasant events for Alzheimer's disease patients: The Pleasant Events Schedule-AD. *The Gerontologist*, *31*, 124–127.

Teri, L., Logsdon, R., Uomoto, J., & McCurry, S. (1997). Behavioral treatment of depression in dementia patients: A controlled clinical trial. *Journal of Gerontology: Psychological Sciences*, *52B*, P159–P166.

Thomas, W. (1994). *The Eden alternative: Nature, hope, and nursing homes*. Columbia: University of Missouri.

Vance, D. Camp, C., Kabacoff, M., & Greenwalt, L. (1996, Winter). Montessori methods: Innovative interventions for adults with Alzheimer's disease. *Montessori Life*, *8*, 10–12.

Van Ness, P. H., & Kasl, S. V. (2003). Religion and cognitive dysfunction in an elderly cohort. *Journal of Gerontology*, *58B*(1), S21–S29.

Volicer, L., & Bloom-Charette, L. (Eds.). 1999. *Enhancing the quality of life in advanced dementia*. Philadelphia: Brunner/Mazel.

Wilson, L. B., & Simson, S. (1991). The role of social work in intergenerational programming. *Journal of Gerontological Social Work*, *16*(1/2), 87–96.

Woods, P., & Ashley, J. (1995). Simulated presence therapy: Using selected memories to manage problem behaviors in Alzheimer's disease patients. *Geriatric Nursing, 16*, 9–14.
Yesavage, J. A., Brink, T., Rose, R., Lum, D., Huang, V., Adey, M., et al. (1983). Development and validation of a geriatric depression screening scale: A preliminary report. *Journal of Psychiatric Research, 17*, 37–49.
Zeisel, J., Silverstein, N. M., Hyde, J., Levkoff, S., Lawton, M. P., & Holmes, W. (2003). Environmental correlates to behavioral health outcomes in Alzheimer's special care units. *The Gerontologist, 43*(5), 697–711.
Zeiss, A. M., & Lewinsohn, P. M. (1986). Adapting behavioral treatment for depression to meet the needs of the elderly. *The Clinical Psychologist, 39*, 98–100.

APPENDIX 6.1: SPEECH THERAPY INVOLVEMENT WITH THE SUNSET CLUB

Ellen Hickey, Ph.D., CCC-SLP
October 12, 2001

Goals of speech therapy involvement: increase verbal participation and interaction among residents, and increase use of recognition cues for memory deficits.

Use strength-based programming: idea of multiple intelligence theory....

- Determine each person's strengths, and build on those strengths (e.g., Mrs. Jones = verbal; Mrs. Smith = motor).
- Provide necessary support in areas of weakness....

  For example, Mrs. Smith: strengths in motor skills and weakness in verbal skills; when doing verbal activities, provide written cues for her participation, and link verbalizations to motor behaviors; and provide much positive reinforcement and opportunities for her to feel proud during motor activities.

Increasing verbal participation: whether a strength or weakness, most residents with dementia will have word-finding deficits to some extent ... need to emphasize strengths and not highlight weaknesses in this area....

- Ask open-ended questions that do not have right or wrong answers, but have many possible answers ("What do you think about...?").
- Encourage interaction for the sake of personal connection rather than to obtain right or wrong answers.
- Avoid yes–no questions if you are trying to get the residents discussing—if yes or no will answer the question, that is all you are likely to get, especially from those with weakness in verbal skills.
- Provide written cues, such as...

  - For example, if doing a naming activity, use cards that have the name printed on the picture, change the task from naming to oral reading, and then ask the resident to elaborate on it.
  - For example, if discussing current events:
    - use a poster board, dry-erase board, or easel to write names of people, places, and events.
    - give index cards to each resident with written cues related to the topic, such as "I am registered Democrat. I voted for Jimmy Carter."
    - read a brief story related to current events, give residents with lower verbal ability index cards with a question to pose to the group that is related to the story, and allow residents with greater verbal ability to answer the questions (provide them written cues as needed, such as on the dry-erase board, etc.).
- Use pictures, drawing, gestures, and pointing to supplement verbal input and output to enhance communication. Have scrap paper available near each resident to write cues or draw, or cue them to use other communication modalities to get their message across.
- Use memory books and communication cards in small-group conversation (2–3 residents)—allow residents to look at each other's books
- Use themes to tie activities together—music, discussion, motor games, and so on.

7

Management of Eating and Swallowing Challenges

Given the many diseases that cause dementia, the presence and severity of eating and swallowing problems in persons with dementia are determined by the specific neuropathological process. Eating and swallowing problems are of the utmost concern in the care of persons with dementia, particularly in nursing home settings, due to the impact of these problems on overall health (e.g., nutrition, hydration, and respiratory health). Malnutrition and dehydration may exacerbate further cognitive deficits, in addition to causing other medical problems. This chapter will outline the range of problems and assessment procedures related to eating and swallowing as dementia progresses, as well as the variety of treatment approaches useful for enhancing the dining experience.

The purpose of this chapter is to describe the role of the SLP in managing eating and swallowing problems in persons with dementia. The lay public, as well as many in the medical and rehabilitation arena, are only aware that SLPs address dysphagia (i.e., swallowing disorders) with the dementia population. Even persons who do not have a disease that causes a specific oral-pharyngeal dysphagia will likely have needs in the areas of eating and swallowing that can be treated best with the expertise of the SLP. A variety of treatment approaches useful for improving nutrition and enhancing the dining experience will be discussed. Although eating is traditionally seen within the purview of occupational therapists, it is important for SLPs to be involved in the assessment and treatment of eating and swallowing problems because of the impact of cognitive-linguistic deficits on these functional abilities. Thus, in order to accomplish the best outcomes for persons with dementia, the SLP usually works in collaboration with other team members, such as nurses, activities staff, occupational therapists, dieticians and nutritionists, physical therapists, respiratory therapists, and physicians. By working in collaboration and recognizing individual needs, the team can nurture the person and improve nutrition and quality of life.

DESCRIPTION OF EATING AND SWALLOWING CHALLENGES

Eating is one of the last functional behaviors to be lost in the course of dementia, and there is a predictable course of deterioration of these skills (Njegovan, Man-Son-Hing, Mitchell, & Molnar, 2001). In the early stages, there may be difficulty with grocery shopping and preparing meals as cognitive deficits progress, and persons with dementia may not remember to eat. As the later stages ensue, problems with chewing and swallowing develop, which cause the aspiration of food or saliva, coughing or choking, and sometimes pneumonia. Perceptual and cognitive impairments result in failure to recognize food and eating implements or how to use them (Brush, Meehan, & Calkins, 2002). Thus, there are a wide variety of issues to be concerned about when a person with dementia has difficulty eating and swallowing. Caregivers should be aware that these problems extend beyond simple oral-pharyngeal dysphagia that SLPs typically deal with in persons with dementia (Brush et al., 2002). Below is a description of some challenges and concerns related to eating and swallowing.

Beyond the fact that proper nutrition and hydration are critical for well-being (Amarantos, Martinez, & Dwyer, 2001), rituals surrounding sharing meals are often a part of one's cultural identity, past memories, and quality of life (Brush et al., 2002; Hellen, 2002; Kofod & Birkemose, 2004; Zgola & Bordillon, 2002). Caregivers must keep in mind that eating is not just a nutritional activity but a social one as well (Calkins & Brush, 2003), and the presence of eating and swallowing problems may contribute to social isolation (Layne, 1990). Moreover, mealtimes are just one area in which persons with dementia experience loss of control, particularly as they enter residential care (Zgola & Bordillon). Thus, providing nutrition and enjoyable mealtimes is a common concern in caring for elders, particularly for those with dementia (Gillick & Mitchell, 2002; Njegovan et al., 2001). Caregivers should use mealtime as an opportunity to make residents feel like a part of the community and to recognize them as dignified adults (Bowlby Sifton, 2002). Finally, given the likelihood of eating challenges as dementia progresses, caregivers must consistently monitor food and fluid intake, as well as signs of malnutrition and dehydration, whether in the home or residential setting.

Appetite Regulation

Many people with dementia experience decreased appetite regulation (Morley & Silver, 1995; Simmons & Schnelle, 2003). Furthermore, persons with dementia often have decreased activity levels, which can further exacerbate their decreased appetite. Their frequent depression and confusion can contribute to failure to thrive (Groom, 1993; Morley, 1997; Roberts & Durnbaugh, 2002; Simmons, Osterweil, & Schnelle, 2001). Others have also noted that mood disturbance may contribute to decreased appetite (e.g., Silver, 1993; Simmons & Schnelle; Morley). Neuroimaging studies have revealed deficits in cortical processing in areas that may be involved in appetite regulation and eating behaviors, such as the anterior cingulate cortex (Hu et al., 2002) and the mesial temporal lobe (Grundman, Corey-Bloom, Jernigan,

Archibald, & Thal, 1998). Hu and colleagues postulated that lesions in this area may be implicated in the poor nutritional regulation and weight problems in persons with AD, as lesions in this area are known to cause reduced appetite and apathy and decreases in goal-directed behaviors (Devinsky, Morrell, & Vogt, 1995). Gillick and Mitchell (2002), however, suggested that there may be a number of other causes of decreased eating that must be ruled out before proceeding with interventions, such as medications (e.g., antidepressants), biochemical abnormalities (e.g., overactive thyroid, liver problems, and kidney failure), and infections (e.g., bladder infections).

Despite decreased appetite regulation, persons in the early to middle stages of dementia may actually eat too much due to memory deficits that cause one to forget whether he or she has eaten. Other problems for persons in the early stages, however, may moderate such effects. For example, cognitive deficits in persons who are trying to maintain independent functioning may interfere with grocery shopping and meal planning and preparation, which may lead to not eating enough. As the disease progresses, problems with decreased appetite, reduced recognition of thirst, and forgetting to eat and drink often lead to malnutrition and dehydration and their associated complications (Roberts & Durnbaugh, 2002; Simmons et al., 2001). For many, as the disease progresses and the body slows due to severe changes in physiology, the body does not process enough calories, even if provided with tube feedings (Gillick & Mitchell, 2002; Groom, 1993).

Weight Loss

Spindler (2002) reviewed the literature on nutritional considerations in dementia and found that persons with AD tend to weigh less than other elders, that olfactory dysfunction in AD is associated with dementia severity, and that weight loss is most often associated with inadequate food intake and not with increased energy expenditure. There is some controversy in the literature, however, about whether weight loss occurs before or after onset of AD (Barret-Connor, Edelstein, Corey-Bloom, & Wiederholt, 1998; Cronin-Stubbs, Beckett, Field, & Evans, 1998; Guyonnet et al., 1998). There are several measurement problems that contribute to contradictory findings in the literature; thus, Spindler made the following recommendations for more accurate measurement: weigh people at the same time of day, with the same type and amount of clothes, and on the same scale over time. In exploring when to be concerned about weight loss, Huffman (2002) cautioned that a loss of 5–10% of usual body weight in a 1–12-month period is not within normal limits.

Malnutrition and Dehydration Elderly persons are at increased risk of malnutrition, with prevalence estimates of those in ambulatory care as high as 40% (Silver, 1993). Silver also reported that there is a lack of accepted nutritional standards for this age group, and that poor nutrition leads to prolonged hospital stays, and is a factor in institutionalization. Low body mass index and malnutrition are significant problems among nursing home residents, with malnutrition affecting 30 to 85% of nursing home residents (Landi et al., 1999; Saletti, Lindgren, Johansson, & Cederholm, 2000; Simmons & Reuben, 2000) and dehydration affecting as many as 60% of residents (Holben, Hassell, Williams, & Helle, 1999). Consumption of less than 75% of the served meal is considered to be a clinically significant eating problem according to the Minimum Data Set (MDS; Simmons & Reuben). Simmons and Schnelle (2003) reported that the majority of nursing home residents have low oral food and fluid intake, according to the MDS criterion, and that those with cognitive deficits are at particularly high risk for malnutrition. Others have argued that behavioral disturbances (e.g., irritability, agitation, and disinhibition), rather than severity of cognitive deficits, are related to altered food selection that may contribute to malnutrition (Greenwood et al., 2005). Beyond poor appetite regulation, persons with AD tend to display a preference for carbohydrates, especially sweets, rather than proteins (Greenwood et al.). Some signs of poor nutrition and hydration are weight loss, skin changes and breakdown, increased confusion, increased falls, and mortality (Groom, 1993; Kofod & Birkemose, 2004; Morley, 1997; Roberts & Durnbaugh, 2002; Simmons et al., 2001). Additional signs of malnutrition are incontinence, weakness, and increased susceptibility to infections. Additional signs of dehydration include dry mouth and cracked lips, sunken eyes, dark-colored urine, constipation, lethargy, and dizziness. These negative health effects can result in decreased quality of life.

BOX 7.1 MALNUTRITION AND DEHYDRATION WARNING SIGNS

- Signs of malnutrition and dehydration:
  - weight loss, skin changes, skin breakdown (e.g., pressure sores), increased confusion, increased falls, and mortality
- Additional signs:
  - Malnutrition: incontinence, weakness, and increased susceptibility to infections.
  - Dehydration: dry mouth and cracked lips, sunken eyes, dark-colored urine, constipation, lethargy, and dizziness.

Source: Groom, 1993; Kofod & Birkemose, 2004; Morley, 1997; Roberts & Durnbaugh, 2002; Simmons et al., 2001.

There are general age-related physiological changes that put one at risk of malnutrition, such as changes in body composition with decreased lean muscle mass, hypodipsia, and diminished palatability (Silver, 1993). In addition, a variety of diseases put elders at risk for malnutrition, such as cerebrovascular disease, Parkinson disease, cancer, cardiomyopathy, diabetes, arthritis, esophagitis, acute or chronic infections, congestive heart failure, and chronic obstructive pulmonary disease (Silver; Simmons & Schnelle, 2003). Additionally, limited physical activity, depression, and other mood disturbances contribute to diminished appetite (Morley & Silver, 1995; Silver; Simmons & Schnelle). Physical stressors, such as pain, chronic illnesses, constipation, lack of dentures or poorly fitting dentures, and medications that decrease the appetite or reduce saliva, also interfere with eating (Roberts & Durnbaugh, 2002; Silver). Other risks for malnutrition in nursing homes include having physical and cognitive impairments, being a non–English speaker, and having no family to assist at mealtime (Kayser-Jones, 2000).

Types of Eating Challenges

Cognitive Based As noted above, persons with dementia are likely to have increasing difficulties with eating as the severity of dementia progresses. The effects of dementia (e.g., lack of recognition of environment or tablemates, delusions, and hallucinations) complicate the dining experience, particularly in nursing homes. In a study of 349 nursing home residents, 87% of the residents exhibited mealtime difficulties due to impairments that included dysphagia, poor oral intake, positioning problems, or challenging behaviors (Steele, Greenwood, Ens, Robertson, & Seidman-Carlson, 1997). The problems related to dysphagia will be discussed below. Whether or not a person has dysphagia, there are likely to be other eating challenges, many related to cognitive deficits. For example, Zgola and Bordillon (2002) described the types of problems with eating in nursing homes and found that many are related to cognition. Results revealed several early-stage memory deficits that interfere with eating, including difficulty finding the dining room, remembering when meals are served, making food choices, and maintaining socially appropriate conversations and manners. Attention deficits and perceptual difficulties increase with disease progression, making it difficult for the person to stay seated through the entire meal, resist distractions, and manipulate utensils and condiment packets (e.g., creamer, sugar, and salt).

Inability to remain seated or to self-feed because of memory or praxic problems signals the advanced disease state (Zgola & Bordillon, 2002). There may be variability through the disease process in refusal to eat and disruptive behavior during mealtimes. Blandford, Watkins, Mulvihill, and Taylor (1998) examined feeding behaviors in persons with end-stage dementia and found both active and passive aversive feeding behaviors. The active behaviors largely included problem behaviors, such as mixing and playing with food without eating, throwing food, eating nonedible items, holding the hand in front of the mouth, as well as grabbing, hitting, or biting the feeder. These behaviors were more common in middle stages, with a trend to decrease in end stages. The severity of these eating and swallowing challenges was correlated with cognitive status.

Sensory Based Sensory factors also put one at risk for limited eating and drinking (Briller, Proffitt, Perez, & Calkins, 2001). Hearing loss and difficulty hearing in noisy environments interfere with the social interactions possible in dining situations; for some, wearing hearing aids creates discomfort due to the amplification of environmental sounds as well as sounds of their own chewing (Baucom, 1996; Roberts & Durnbaugh, 2002). There are several age-related physical changes in vision that contribute to eating problems, including decreases in pupil size and reaction time, reduced contrast and color saturation and discrimination, loss of peripheral vision, and difficulties with depth perception and spatial orientation (Brush et al., 2002; Rizzo, Anderson, Dawson, & Nawrot, 2000). Sensory changes in smell and taste may be related to age, medications, and AD (Schiffman, 1997).

Environmental Factors A variety of external factors also put older persons at risk of malnutrition and dehydration. For example, even for those living at home, the environment may not be conducive to adequate food and liquid intake, possibly due to isolation (social or geographic) or limited income (Silver, 1993). Those with dementia are particularly at risk for malnutrition and dehydration, especially in institutional settings. For example, the external stressors of loud noises or music, bland food on institutional trays, and staff-to-staff conversations impact dining in institutional settings (Roberts & Durnbaugh, 2002). Brush et al. (2002) identified several environmental factors that SLPs should include in assessment, including lighting and noise levels, behavior of tablemates, and number of staff in the dining room. Inadequate staffing in the dining room is often related to another external factor that puts nursing home residents at risk of malnutrition and dehydration: inadequate feeding assistance (e.g., no verbal prompts, food bites are too large, and residents are fed too quickly; Amella, 1999; Kayser-Jones, 1996; Kayser-Jones & Schell, 1997; Simmons & Schnelle, 2003). Some have suggested that food exchange behaviors are more common among nursing home residents with dementia, but Silver and Albert (2000) did not find significant differences in these behaviors between those with and without dementia. They did find, however, that staff intercepted only approximately one quarter of these occurrences, which may put residents at risk of malnutrition, as well as of choking and aspiration and other complications from receiving inappropriate food choices or giving away their own food.

Staff Factors There are a wide variety of staff problems that may put residents at risk for malnutrition and dehydration, including inaccurate documentation of oral food and fluid consumption and nutritional supplementation, failure to identify residents in need of intervention, inadequate staff training in individualized feeding assistance, overestimation of feeding assistance provided, and no routine assessment of food preferences (Simmons, Babinou, Garcia, & Schnelle, 2002; Kayser-Jones et al., 1998; Simmons & Schnelle, 2003). Nursing assistants often use a task-oriented approach to mealtime with residents. This approach often leads to an "assembly-line" style of care, causing stress to both staff and residents (Roberts & Durnbaugh, 2002). Similarly, Simmons and Schnelle noted that staff often use physical assistance with those who could self-feed if given the appropriate cueing and encouragement.

For those who are not eating and drinking adequate amounts, there are risks of simply beginning to feed them. For example, some persons with dementia may become agitated, aggressive, or protective, thus resisting caregivers' efforts to hand-feed (Talerico & Evans, 2000). These problems are likely to occur particularly in the middle stages of dementia. If the person is able to self-feed, staff efforts to feed create excess disability and result in threats to dignity. The care team must ensure that all suitable procedures and strategies have been attempted before beginning the more invasive feeding by staff, and staff must be trained to provide such care in ways that will protect the persons' autonomy and dignity (Zgola & Bordillon, 2002). Furthermore, once staff begin to feed residents, they are often placed in segregated dining areas, putting them at risk for social isolation (Layne, 1990).

Thus, staff must make every effort to allow residents to continue to self-feed and to eat in their favored dining areas. Reed and colleagues (Reed, Zimmerman, Sloane, Williams, & Boustani, 2005) conducted an observational study of the food and fluid intake of 407 residents with dementia in 45 assisted living facilities and nursing homes; this revealed that 54% of the observed residents had low food intake and 51% of them had low fluid intake. The factors that contributed to greater food and fluid intake included staff monitoring of residents, having meals in a public dining area, and the presence of noninstitutional features, such as tablecloths and not eating off trays.

Simmons and Schnelle (2003) recommended a 2-day assessment process to improve the staffing situation in nursing homes so that residents may receive adequate assistance with food and fluid intake, and so that staff may accurately monitor these issues. Data to be collected in the 2-day assessment included the number of residents who need feeding assistance and have low oral intake, the type of assistance needed, and how much staff time it will take (e.g., group versus one-on-one). The assessment included examination of resident behavior that may be impacting eating, such as mood disturbance, behavioral problems, and dysphagia. An important recommendation was that nursing home staff spend significantly more time on quality feeding assistance than they currently do, a recommendation that requires creative problem solving. Furthermore, they recommended that the staff prioritize residents at highest risk for weight loss.

TYPES OF SWALLOWING CHALLENGES

In the presence of dementia, dysphagia decreases one's ability to enjoy meals and to consume the necessary food and liquid necessary for adequate nutrition and hydration (Brush et al., 2002). Swallowing difficulties are likely to increase in severity over the course of dementing illnesses; usually in Alzheimer's, the presence of dysphagia signals the end stage of the disease (Zgola & Bordillon, 2002). In other diagnoses, dysphagia will often occur earlier due to the neuromuscular deficits that present earlier in these diseases, for example, Parkinson disease (Volonté, Porta, & Comi, 2002) and Huntington disease (Kagel & Leopold, 1992). A complete description of these disorders is beyond the scope of this chapter. Regardless of diagnosis, many persons in nursing homes who have dementia will also have dysphagia. Steele and colleagues (1997) found that 87% of 349 nursing home residents had mealtime difficulties, including 68% of residents who presented with dysphagia. Swallowing disorders, or dysphagia, may be classified as oral, pharyngeal, or esophageal. SLPs most often deal with oral and pharyngeal deficits, and occasionally esophageal deficits. Symptoms of oral and pharyngeal dysfunction include difficulty initiating swallowing, nasal regurgitation, drooling and difficulty managing secretions, choking and coughing episodes while feeding, and food sticking in the pharynx and/or larynx (Buchholz, 1994). If not properly diagnosed and managed, these deficits often lead to serious medical concerns, such as dehydration, malnutrition, laryngospasm, bronchospasm, aspiration pneumonia, or asphyxia.

The most common deficits in many persons with Alzheimer dementia occur during the oral stage; these deficits often result from cognitive deficits, such as not attending to food in the mouth or not remembering to chew and swallow. As noted previously, Blandford and colleagues (1998) studied the aversive feeding behaviors of persons with dementia. They found several passive aversive problems in feeding behaviors that were divided into two groups: those that directly interfered with the act of eating (oropharyngeal dysphagia and selective feeding behaviors) and those that indirectly impair eating (resistive behaviors and apraxia or agnosia). These behaviors were associated with severe and end-stage dementia (MMSE = 0–5). Examples of oropharyngeal dysphagia symptoms included neuromuscular incoordination in the oral stage of eating that prevented adequate mouth and tongue control for mastication, bolus formation, and transfer of bolus to the pharynx. Selective feeding behaviors were related to the quality of the food that persons were willing to eat (e.g., textures, tastes, temperatures, and quantities). Resistive behaviors included those that prevented food from getting into the mouth, such as puckering the lips and failing to open the mouth or spilling food from the mouth. Behaviors that were due to apraxia or agnosia reflected a lack of cognitive or mechanical abilities, which required general prompting or cueing (Blandford et al.). Behaviors such as closing the mouth tightly to bite the feeding utensil (i.e., fork or spoon) may fall under the category of apraxic behaviors, but they may also be due to resistive efforts. Overall, the data from this study suggest a pattern of progressive change in feeding behaviors consistent with the decline in cognition and other functional activities. The continuous involuntary failure to accept oral feeding is thought to be the cause of death in dementia when there is not an additional comorbidity (Ahronheim, 1996).

ASSESSMENT OF EATING AND SWALLOWING CHALLENGES

Given the wide variety of these problems, the SLP must thoroughly address eating and swallowing in the assessment process. For example, any changes in mealtime behaviors, the physiology of the swallow, cognition and communication, and sensory loss must all be assessed (Logemann, 2003). Brush et al. (2002) stated that SLPs should become accustomed to assessing environmental factors that impact eating and swallowing (e.g., noise and lighting, staff numbers, and behavior of tablemates), as "the scope of practice of SLPs includes addressing environments that affect communication and swallowing" (p. 331). Roberts and Durnbaugh (2002) suggested examination of a wide range of factors related to meals, such as those described above, but through the use of a comprehensive model for dementia care, such as the Need-Driven Dementia-Compromised Behavior model (Algase et al., 1996), as described in chapter 3, as a way to look at the reason for compromised eating behaviors (e.g., internal versus external stressors).

The goal of assessment is to identify the nature and severity of eating and swallowing deficits, to identify factors that contribute to these deficits, and to determine the capacity for improving safety and the potential to benefit from skilled SLP services. The components of eating and swallowing assessment overlap with those of cognitive-communicative assessment by SLPs, such as chart review, case history, and observation; additional procedures include positioning, structural-functional examination of the swallowing mechanism, and specific evaluation of eating and swallowing behaviors. There are problems with the reliability and validity of bedside clinical swallow evaluations, with fewer than 50% having adequate reliability (McCullough et al., 2000). Those measures that McCullough and colleagues found to have adequate reliability include chart review and case history for pneumonia, gastrointestinal disorder, medications, the presence of a feeding tube, and the need for suctioning; structural-functional examination for saliva production and management, strength and range of motion for lips and tongue, and volitional cough; prolonged total swallow duration, presence of oral stasis after the swallow, and overall swallowing function in trial swallows; and wet voice or coughing up to 1 minute after the swallow in a 3-ounce swallow test. Specific procedures will be discussed further below.

Chart Review and Case History

The chart review and case history are important for determining a history of eating and swallowing problems, as well as a history of medical conditions that are likely to cause such problems. For example, the SLP must find out if there is a diagnosis of dementia and a specific neurological illness, and be aware of the likelihood of neuromuscular swallowing problems with various illnesses (e.g., Parkinson disease, Huntington disease, and amyotrophic lateral sclerosis). The SLP must review physicians' and/or nurses' notes for evidence of a history of dysphagia, or of signs or symptoms of dysphagia, such as decreased food and liquid intake, weight loss, fever, chest congestion, and/or *pneumonia*; orders for current diet and liquid intake must also be noted, not just for dysphagia recommendations but also for allergies and medical restrictions (e.g., low-salt diet or diabetic diet). Other aspects of health status or care to note include *gastrointestinal disorder, medications, the presence of a feeding tube*, and *the need for suctioning* (McCullough et al., 2000). The nurses' or nutritionists' notes should also be reviewed for observations of coughing or choking while eating or drinking, assistance with feeding, and food preferences. Other important information in the medical record may also include results of chest X-rays and swallowing studies (e.g., videofluoroscopy).

With respect to the context of eating, the clinician should obtain information regarding where, when, what, how often, how much, and with whom a person is accustomed to eating (Calkins & Brush, 2003). Other considerations include whether the client enjoyed doing other activities (e.g., TV, radio, or newspaper) while eating, and whether the client is a slow or fast eater. Any changes to that familiar context of eating may contribute to eating and/or swallowing problems. The SLP should also conduct an interview with the client if possible, asking questions related to the above information. The SLP must determine the client's perception and awareness of any eating or swallowing problems. If the client is unfamiliar to the SLP, the interview is also an opportunity to gather information regarding cognitive-communicative status. The clinician can also verify or add to these findings with observation of habitual mealtime behaviors, including eating or feeding behaviors.

Positioning

The client's typical positioning during meals is important to note. This includes whether the person eats in bed or up in a chair, in a wheelchair or armchair, and so on. The SLP should note the body posture and head posture of the client, as well as his or her ability to modify positioning given instructions or spontaneously. The ideal position for eating and swallowing, for most persons, is sitting upright in a chair with knees and hips at 90-degree angles, with the head positioned straight over the spine. Compensatory positioning strategies can be examined as needed, such as flexing the head with a "chin tuck." Often in the late stage of dementia, the head will be chronically flexed or hyperextended, and the focus of the assessment will be on determining the use of adaptive feeding equipment for that position (Hellen, 2002). Postural supports and alternative seating should also be considered.

Structural-Functional Examination of the Swallowing Mechanism

The structural-functional examination of the oral-pharyngeal mechanisms will not likely be as thorough for a client with dementia as it would be for those without cognitive deficits, due to difficulty understanding the procedures and following instructions (see Yorkston, Beukelman, Strand, & Bell, 1999; or see Duffy, 1995). The clinician should start with visual observations, such as evidence of the client's *saliva production and saliva management* (e.g., drooling, excessive saliva in the mouth, or xerostomia, or dry mouth); visual inspection should also include the face, *lips, tongue* for symmetry, *strength, range of motion*, the health of tissues and the like, and of respiratory patterning (e.g., the respiratory rate, and abdominal versus thoracic breathing). One strategy for observing movements is to engage the client in an imitation "game" in order to get the person to imitate various oral-motor behaviors, such as lip pursing, jaw opening, and other typical behaviors on such an assessment. Furthermore, sensory assessment will be limited by cognitive abilities, but the SLP may note any positive or negative behaviors related to various types of tastes, temperatures, and textures.

If possible, the structural-functional exam should include assessment of the strength and quality of the *volitional cough* and swallowing on command. If the person is unable to respond to commands, the clinician should note reflexive coughs and swallows, observing laryngeal elevation and voice quality after a cough or swallow. It should be noted that reliability of the assessment of the gag reflex was poor; given the fact that this is not necessarily a meaningful sign in detecting dysphagia (McCullough et al., 2000), and given the likelihood of upsetting a confused client with this procedure, clinicians should consider whether this is a worthwhile procedure in dysphagia assessment for those with dementia.

The SLP should also note the client's speech production abilities, including the presence or absence of dysarthria, and intelligibility of speech (McCullough et al., 2000). Other aspects of the integrity of the swallowing mechanism that can be determined from the speech sample include *voice quality* (e.g., dysphonia, breathy, harsh, or wet and gurgly). Judgments of dysphonia and wet and gurgly voice quality may also be reliably obtained from sustained phonation.

Clinical ("Bedside") Evaluation of Eating and Swallowing Behaviors

Eating Several assessment tools have been developed for use with persons with dementia, and/or for use in the nursing home setting, and will be described further below. In general, the tools designed for eating assessment examine the ability of the person to get the food and drink from dish to mouth, and the tools designed for swallowing assessment examine the ability of the person to manage the food and liquid within the oral cavity and to swallow the bolus safely. Regardless of the tool used, the clinician should collect data on a number of factors that may influence the client's ability to eat.

One of the first issues to be considered is the context of eating. Eating and swallowing behaviors should be assessed under habitual conditions as well as ideal conditions to determine current problems and potential for improvement. The clinician should note the effect of sensory variables and social variables in the environment on the ability of the client to eat. Visual stimuli to be considered include amount of distraction (e.g., people coming and going), lighting (quantity and quality), and visual contrasts between table and dishes and between dishes and food (Koss & Gilmore, 1998). The clinician should observe the amount and types of auditory stimuli, including the background noise from machines and cooking (e.g., ice machine, and dishes and silverware clanging) and people talking, as well as the ability of the client to attend to conversations or verbal instructions at his or her table (Calkins & Brush, 2003).

Assessment of eating should include the use of a variety of utensils and dishes to eat and drink liquids and solids. The clinician should note the client's attention to items placed in front of him or her (e.g., is there left neglect?) and ability to identify food and liquid items and utensils appropriately (e.g., is there an agnosia?). In addition, the clinician should evaluate the client's ability to initiate eating and to manipulate the utensils in order to self-feed (e.g., is there an executive function problem or an apraxia?). Occupational therapists (OTs) often conduct this portion of the assessment, perhaps in collaboration with the SLP; OTs assess range of motion, strength, and endurance of the upper extremities; grasp and release ability; and visual-motor integration abilities that impact use of utensils (Hellen, 2002). If caregivers feed the person, the clinician should assess the client's response to feeding. In any case, the clinician should also note any feeding aversive behaviors (as described above; Blandford et al., 1998).

Some assessment tools have been developed to determine the need for feeding assistance for nursing home residents. For example, the Feeding Assistance Observational Protocol—Dining Room (Simmons & Schnelle, 2003) was developed so that nursing supervisors could monitor the quality of feeding assistance provided and the accuracy of oral intake documentation. The general categories of behaviors monitored include nursing assistants' abilities to accurately identify residents with clinically significant low oral food and fluid intake, to provide assistance to at-risk residents, to provide feeding assistance to residents identified on the MDS as needing assistance, and to provide verbal prompts to those who need assistance.

The Meal Assistance Screening Tool (MAST; Steele, 1996) was developed to identify the types and severity of mealtime difficulties experienced by nursing home residents, in eight categories: mealtime prerequisites (e.g., alert or drowsy), seating and positioning problems, dentition and oral hygiene, type of diet provided, type of assistance provided, intake, challenging behaviors (e.g., yelling and hoarding), and eating problems (e.g., dysphagia). Steele et al. (1997) used the MAST to assess 349 nursing home residents. They documented problems in 87% of the residents, including dysphagia (68%), poor oral intake (46%), positioning problems (35%), and challenging behaviors (40%) such as drowsiness, interfering body movements, distractibility, and hostility. Better oral intake was seen for residents with severe cognitive impairment than those with mild to moderate cognitive impairment due to the fact that many of the residents with severe impairments received partial or total feeding assistance.

Other tools that were developed to assess residents' feeding behaviors include the Feeding Behavior Inventory (FBI; Durnbaugh, Haley, & Roberts, 1996), the Feeding Dependency Scale (FDS) and the Aversive Feeding Behavior Inventory (AFBI; Blandford et al., 1998), and the Eating Behavior Scale (EBS; Tully, Lambros Matrakas, & Musallam, 1998). The FBI (Durnbaugh et al., 1996) was developed to record the challenging behaviors displayed by persons with midstage dementia. The FBI includes 33 specific behaviors in four categories: resistive and disruptive behaviors, style of eating, pattern of intake, and oral behaviors. Total eating time and percentage of food and protein consumed are also recorded during a 30–40-minute observation period. This tool was developed so that it could be administered by anyone who is professionally trained to assess resident behaviors. Durnbaugh and colleagues found evidence of good external validity and good interrater reliability. The authors also developed a Mealtime Interventions protocol (Durnbaugh, Haley, & Roberts, 1993) that suggested specific interventions for each of the 33 behaviors identified on the FBI. The intervention protocol will be discussed in the interventions section of this chapter, "Treatment of Eating and Swallowing Challenges."

Similarly, the FDS and the AFBI were developed to enhance feeding strategies in late-stage dementia (Blandford et al., 1998). The results of a qualitative study and factor analysis of abnormal feeding behaviors in dementia revealed two distinct groups: active aversive feeding behaviors and passive aversive feeding behaviors, as described above. Likewise, the Eating Behavior Scale (Tully et al., 1998) was developed to assess functional abilities during eating. This tool allows caregivers to identify behaviors that either directly or indirectly impair eating. A pilot test of the measure was conducted with 30 subjects to evaluate the psychometric properties of the EBS. Significant correlations were reported with all neuropsychological measures (e.g., the MMSE, Mattis Dementia Rating Scale, and Ravens Matrices); estimates of reliability (average percent agreement = 95.5%) and content validity (CVI = 1.0) were acceptable.

Swallowing There are a wide variety of swallowing behaviors that should be assessed, noting difficulties within the oral and/or pharyngeal stages. The swallowing assessment often begins with just a sip of water so that if there are significant concerns about swallowing safety and aspiration, the person will not have ingested any food or liquid that is more likely to cause infection. From there, the clinician administers a variety of foods and liquids with varying textures and consistencies, in both controlled trials and habitual self-feeding trials. Oral stage difficulties include such issues as difficulty chewing, forming a bolus, manipulating the bolus within the mouth, and/or moving the bolus from anterior to posterior oral cavity for transfer to the pharyngeal cavity. With respect to chewing, the clinician should note the type of chewing pattern (e.g., a rotary pattern or a suck-swallow pattern) and adequacy of chewing different types of foods (e.g., crunchy versus soft foods). With respect to manipulation and movement of the bolus, the clinician should note the effect of textures on the person's ability to form a cohesive bolus versus the food falling apart into various parts of the mouth, and the ability to hold food in the mouth. As cognitive deficits and/or motor deficits begin to interfere with the oral stage, some clients will need altered food textures and food restrictions (e.g., soft foods only, and no combinations of liquids and solids, such as in soups) to ensure safety of forming and manipulating a bolus. This will be discussed further under the treatment section, below.

In the pharyngeal stage, the clinician should note the speed and adequacy of laryngeal excursion. The swallowing process happens very quickly. By placing four fingers on the front of the client's neck, in the laryngeal and base of tongue areas, the clinician should be able to palpate immediate movement of the laryngeal structures up and forward. Signs and symptoms of difficulty in the pharyngeal stage include suspected delayed and/or inadequate laryngeal excursion, coughing, throat clearing, and/or wet voice quality immediately or shortly after swallowing, or complaints of food feeling "stuck in the throat." Clinicians were found to reliably judge trial swallows of thin and thick liquids and puree consistencies for the following measures: *prolonged total swallow duration, presence of oral stasis after the swallow*, and *overall swallowing function* (McCullough et al., 2000). Finally, clinicians were able to accurately determine *wet voice or coughing up to 1 minute after the swallow in a 3-ounce swallow test*. McCullough and colleagues, however, cautioned clinicians that the safety of the 3-ounce swallow test is questionable and may unnecessarily put clients at risk.

Instrumental Assessments

In acute or out-patient settings, if there are any suspicions of pharyngeal swallowing difficulty, clients are referred for instrumental swallowing assessment (e.g., a modified barium swallow or videofluoroscopy swallow study, or fiberendoscopic evaluation of swallowing [FEES]) with a physician's order. Many have suggested that these procedures are necessary in all cases, given the low reliability of many clinical bedside evaluation measures (McCullough et al., 2000), as well as their lack of ability to detect silent aspiration or to fully evaluate the efficacy of compensatory strategies (e.g., Leder, Sasaki, & Burrell, 1998). Thus, many third-party payers require instrumental assessment if pharyngeal dysphagia is suspected, in order to determine whether the person can benefit from swallowing treatment and the best treatment procedures to use (Logemann, 2003). For example, certain intense tastes or bolus temperatures can trigger the pharyngeal phase of the swallow faster, or use of a chin tuck position may prevent aspiration; these are patient specific and require the clinician to report treatment efficacy data from an instrumental assessment. (See chapter 11 for additional information on documentation and reimbursement issues.)

When working with persons with dementia in the nursing home setting, however, there is controversy regarding the referral for instrumental assessment of swallowing, based on a number of factors. These factors range from logistical and financial concerns (e.g., transportation) to the complications of removing a person with dementia from the habitual setting for assessment. Persons with dementia often do not respond well to such changes in environment, becoming more confused. In combination with cognitive and behavioral deficits that interfere with ability to follow instructions and fully participate in the assessment, these problems may limit the validity of the results (Broniatowski, 1998). Thus, the SLP must consider these issues in requesting an instrumental assessment in an unfamiliar environment. On the other hand, if the SLP is able to conduct FEES in the natural environment, then this is highly recommended for those clients who would be able to cooperate with the procedure (Broniatowski; Leder et al., 1998). There are several advantages of FEES: It detects silent aspiration at bedside, using minimally invasive procedures without contrast material or radiation, which allows this assessment to be administered as often as necessary.

TREATMENT OF EATING AND SWALLOWING CHALLENGES

The goals of eating and swallowing interventions are generally to increase safety, to enhance nutrition and hydration, to decrease excess disability, to enhance independence, and to preserve dignity. As stated by Hellen (2002),

> The challenge becomes one of opening opportunities for diners to participate in the warmth of a pleasant meal, to feel surrounded by caring persons, and, most importantly, to experience a sense of being included, being connected to self and others. (p. 304)

Thus, the goals are not simply to ensure adequate intake, but to enhance overall physical, mental, and emotional well-being. There are a variety of approaches that can be used to improve eating and swallowing in persons with dementia. As noted above, many of the challenges are related to environmental factors, sensory changes, cognitive-communicative deficits, and staff factors that make it difficult for persons with dementia to engage in safe intake of the proper quantity and quality of food and liquids, let alone to maintain independence and dignity.

There are a variety of strategies that can improve mealtimes and nutritional intake in persons with dementia, as well as enhance quality of life. Clinicians may use the tools described in the assessment section (above) to determine the most effective and/or efficient interventions to use. For example, after use of the Feeding Behavior Inventory (Durnbaugh et al., 1996) to identify which of the 33 behaviors are in need of intervention, clinicians may use the accompanying Mealtime Interventions protocol (Durnbaugh et al., 1993) to determine specific interventions to be used. Roberts and Durnbaugh (2002) suggested that caregivers use the Need-Driven Dementia-Compromised Behavior model (Algase et al., 1998) to first reduce stressors; once disruptive behaviors are reduced, then the clinician may address self-care deficits and intervene to promote nutrition (Roberts & Durnbaugh). The interventions to be discussed below are grouped into three overarching categories meant to enhance the dining experience: food selection and environmental factors, cognitive and memory strategies and training, and caregiver interventions. Regardless of the types of interventions used, Silver (1993) stated that starting early is the key to success in intervening with, or preventing, malnourishment.

FOOD SELECTION AND ENVIRONMENTAL FACTORS

When elders move into assisted living or long-term care, they often have to adjust to changes in the context of eating. This is to be expected, as facilities cannot possibly accommodate every individual's eating preferences. However, some accommodation for the needs and deficits of individuals must be taken into consideration in order to promote optimal nutrition, hydration, and quality of life. Satisfaction with mealtime is impacted by the food quality, quantity, and social context. The health care team can implement positive changes in the food offerings and social context of the mealtime in order to maximize nutrition and quality of life, such as lower environmental distractions and social interactions during meals. Experts often recommend introducing a more home-like or more naturalistic setting to improve the overall dining experience for persons with dementia (e.g., Altus, Engelman, & Mathews, 2002; Bowlby Sifton, 2002; Brush et al., 2002; Calkin & Brush, 2003; Kofod & Birkemose, 2004; Laurenhue, 2002; Zgola & Bordillon, 2002). Suggestions for enhancing these aspects of the dining experience will be described herein.

First, caregivers should be aware of appropriate goals for food and fluid intake for persons with dementia, who will need fewer calories as the disease advances into later stages. Spindler et al. (1996) suggested that adequate energy intake should be measured in kilocalories and adjusted by body weight; they recommended a daily intake of 30–35 kcal/kg of body weight to ensure weight maintenance. Furthermore, Spindler and colleagues reported that this requires a focus on the energy content of foods offered, not just the volume; diets should include foods that are high in energy (e.g., butter, oil, nuts, sauces and gravy, ice cream, and cheese), as well as foods that are rich in nutrients, such as cereals that are fortified (with folate and vitamin B12), fruits and vegetables (vitamin C), and oils (vitamin E). Strong sweet or salty tastes are often preferred by the person with dementia, and the use of sweeteners, such as honey or sugar, can encourage the reluctant eater (Spindler, 2002). In addition, increasing sensory stimulation through food odors and flavor enhancement improves appetite (Yen, 1996), and providing food that looks and smells appealing in adequate (not overwhelming) portions also improves appetite (Roberts & Durnbaugh, 2002). An additional suggestion to increase appetite is to provide regular exercise (Hellen, 2002; Silver, 1993).

In addition, improvements in oral food and fluid intake have been found with improvements in the dining environment, food service, social stimulation, and staff attention (Lange-Alberts & Shott, 1994; Musson et al., 1990). Roberts and Durnbaugh (2002) suggested a fine dining approach, either restaurant or buffet style, to improve choices and opportunity for more of residents' favored foods. Hellen (2002) suggested that successful mealtimes require a personalized approach, with knowledge of individual food preferences; when food intake is poor at meals, the person may be encouraged to eat by providing choices or by providing the person's "comfort food." For those who are concerned about saving some of their food for later, caregivers may offer food that is wrapped and does not spoil (Hellen). Provision of "finger foods" increases nutrient intake, decreases weight loss, and reduces the need for high-calorie and protein supplements (Jean, 1997). Others have suggested the use of nutritional supplements, along with food texture and volume adjustments, to support mealtime independence without compromising adequate nutritional intake (Morris & Volicer, 2001). A between-meal snack intervention (Simmons & Schnelle, 2003) was useful for 82% of residents who did not improve with feeding assistance. Hellen suggested slowing down the pace of meals and offering finger foods to increase food intake. As the disease progresses, many persons require chopped or pureed foods, but caregivers may continue to offer finger foods by putting the food in an ice cream cone. Serving one food or course at a time may also improve food intake by simplifying the meal and making the amount of food less overwhelming (Gillick & Mitchell, 2002; Hellen).

In addition to attending to the foods served, the overall dining environment should be maximized for enhanced nutrient intake and quality of life. Roberts and Durnbaugh (2002) suggested that the dining room milieu should be quiet and small with limited activity, and have small tables with armchairs designed not to tip; additionally, there should be adequate staff with proper training to assist residents to eat in a timely manner so that they do not have to wait. In their review of the literature, Zgola and Bordillon (2002) revealed several improvements in dining features that resulted in benefits to residents: the quality of food, the environment and setting for dining, the timing and delivery of meals, mealtime activities, and several issues related to staff attitude, assistance, and training. They recommended that facilities find sustainable ways to incorporate global changes in the ways meals are offered, embracing a holistic approach to dining and nutrition. Their program will be described further below, as an example of a multicomponent program. Next, specific environmental strategies will be described.

Visual and Auditory Stimuli Several simple environmental modifications for increasing dining success include limiting extraneous stimulation (e.g., removing nonfood items from table before serving food), increasing the lighting (e.g., add lights to the corners and perimeter of the dining room), decreasing glare (e.g., use of window sheers and tablecloths), and increasing the visual contrast of the food and place setting (e.g., dark tablecloth and light dishes) (Brush et al., 2002; Calkins & Brush, 2003; Hellen, 2002; Koss & Gilmore, 1998; Roberts & Durnbaugh, 2002). Koss and Gilmore reported that older adults require three times as much light as younger ones; they utilized enhanced lighting and maximum visual contrasts in table settings to increase food intake and to reduce negative behaviors for 13 residents with AD in long-term care. Brush and colleagues increased the lighting and enhanced table-setting contrasts, with the use of tray liners and tablecloths, for 25 residents of two long-term care facilities for 4 weeks. Results revealed improvements in oral intake in 23 of 25 residents. In both facilities, there were group differences in functional behaviors, such as increased frequency of conversations with staff, initiating conversation, responding appropriately to questions, and increased ability to find and use napkin and to follow simple directions (facility 1), and reduced distractibility, anxiety, and assistance needed, and improved ability to follow simple directions (facility 2). Brush et al. noted that some of the increases in functional communication behaviors may have been related to the increased numbers of staff in that facility's dining room, which was not under the researchers' control.

Other visual and auditory distracters to decrease include the number of people coming and going and staff shouting and talking to each other (Calkins & Brush, 2003). In order to absorb as much of the background noise as possible, the dining room should contain furniture and drapes made of fabric, such as fabric-covered acoustic panels that drape down from the ceiling and on the walls (Calkins & Brush). Another strategy to decrease environmental noise is to put up wall partitions with high-rated acoustic material to block out noise from the kitchen, ice machine, and tray service areas. Unfortunately, many residential facilities limit the use of fabrics and textiles for ease of cleaning and enhanced sanitation, but the resulting hard surfaces also serve to increase acoustic energy. Finally, caregivers should ensure that residents' hearing aids and glasses are in place for meals, unless the noise of the environment and of their own chewing is distressing with hearing aids (Hellen, 2002; Roberts & Durnbaugh, 2002).

Music Ragneskog, Brane, Karlsson, and Kihlgren (1996) implemented a dinner music intervention and documented increased food intake and decreased depression, irritability, and restlessness in residents with dementia. These results were thought to reflect the effect of the music intervention on the staff; they served the patients more food during music conditions than nonmusic conditions. Different types of music were shown to produce different effects on residents; one resident became calm when soothing music was played; other residents spent more time eating and ate more (Ragneskog, Kihlgren, Karlsson, & Norberg, 1996). Hicks-Moore (2005) also documented the calming effects of music in a quasi-experimental, ABAB design with 30 residents with severe cognitive impairment and agitation behaviors. During weeks 2 and 4 when music was introduced, reductions in agitated behavior were observed.

Social Context For persons who have lived alone for many years, a move to a residential facility, where expectations include eating in a group setting, may be stressful. For others who may have been lonely after a spouse died or friends moved away, this move to a group setting may be a welcome change. As noted previously, the person's eating history should include whether meals were eaten alone or with others, and this information should be considered in determining the most functional context for eating. Using a behavioral communication intervention designed to address the physiological and social interaction needs of residents with dementia, Beattie, Algase, and Song (2004) documented decreased wandering, increased sitting, greater food consumption, and stable weight in three residents with dementia. Hellen (2002) recommended that the optimal context to increase function and well-being is a low-stimulus environment with small groups and compatible tablemates. Family members or other visitors may either encourage or inhibit functional eating and swallowing behaviors. For those who have always prayed before meals, the rushed context of many residential dining rooms may be prohibitive; offering a prayer or moment of silence before meals may reduce this problem (Hellen). Finally, staff should encourage conversation among residents.

Cognitive and Memory Strategies and Training Given that most of the eating challenges in persons with early stages of Alzheimer's disease are due to cognitive deficits, cognitive strategies can be devised to improve eating and swallowing behaviors, and the overall dining experience. In the early stage of dementia, the person may still be attempting to live at home, and may need assistance with shopping and meal preparation. Some creative external cognitive strategies can be used to help maintain this level of independence. For example, shopping lists can be organized according to the organization of one's grocery store by making columns in accordance with the aisles of the grocery store. See Figure 7.1 for an example. Additionally, strategies to identify food that is out of date and to organize refrigerators and cupboards can be developed through the use of written cues and labels. Calendars can be made to list the meals that will be eaten each day, and crossed off to help the person remember whether or not he or she has eaten. Cooking can also be maintained through the use of written cues and timers, or simplified with the use of a microwave. When the person is unable to prepare hot meals, "Meals on Wheels" may be arranged to serve one hot meal per day. This sometimes has the added benefit of a little bit of socialization with the person delivering the meal. When the disease is one that also causes more specific oral-pharyngeal dysphagia, the person may benefit from the use of spaced retrieval training and written cue cards to recall safe swallowing strategies, as will be illustrated below.

In the middle stages, cognitive, psychiatric, and behavioral disturbances may affect eating and swallowing. For example, some residents refuse to go to the dining hall due to fears of being poisoned or of not being able to pay for their meals. Hellen (2002) recommended several creative strategies for dealing with such problem behaviors. For example, a take-out box can be used if there is concern about being poisoned; a letter can be provided stating that the person has paid his or her "dues," which includes meals. As cognitive deficits increase, mealtime becomes more confusing and simplification is needed, such as using multisensory cues to foster recall of mealtime memories, and using a task analysis to simplify the components of eating and to sequence eating activities consistently, offering one item at a time and using one-step directions (Calkins & Brush, 2003; Gillick & Mitchell, 2002; Hellen).

As discussed in chapters 5 and 6, SLPs can develop use of external strategies to improve functional behaviors. For example, written reminder cards can be made for safe swallowing during meals, or for the multiple instructions in a swallowing evaluation. For persons with severe cognitive deficits, cards can be made for each step in the eating and swallowing process: Open your mouth, chew, and swallow. Reminder cards may also be used to facilitate use of specific swallowing

Aisle 1: Produce	Aisle 2: Bread, crackers	Aisle 3: Cereals
Aisle 4: Cleaning products	**Aisle 5: Health care products**	**Aisle 6: Soda, chips, snack foods**
Aisle 7: Frozen vegetables, dinners	**Aisle 8: Frozen desserts**	**Aisle 9: Dairy and eggs (milk, cheese, yogurt)**

Figure 7.1 Example of Grocery Shopping List, Organized by Store Aisles.

strategies, such as chin tuck positioning, or alternating liquids and solids. These strategies may help to maintain independence over a longer period of time, or to minimize the amount of cueing and assistance needed. See Figure 7.2 for examples of reminder cards.

Brush and Camp (1998) described the successful training of an 86-year-old resident of a long-term care facility to use a compensatory strategy for his dysphagia, which was trained with the spaced retrieval training procedure. After a thorough swallowing assessment (bedside and radiographic) revealed that the resident needed to alternate bites of food with sips of liquid to clear the food from the

1. Food labels for items in refrigerator

Chicken, Feb. 1, 2006

Green Beans, Feb. 1, 2006

2. Food labels for cupboards

Canned soups and vegetables

Pasta, rice, cereals

3. Meal menu

Today's Meal

Green Beans
Mashed Potatoes
Chicken
Brownie
Coffee

4. Eating Sequence

1. Pick up my spoon
2. Scoop my food
3. Open my mouth
4. Put food in mouth
5. Chew food
6. Swallow food

5. Safe Eating/Swallowing

1. Sit up straight
2. Take a small sip
3. Chin down
4. Swallow

Take a bite.
Chew and chew.
Swallow.
Take a sip.
Start over.

6. Swallowing evaluation

Take a sip/bite.
Keep it on my tongue.
Wait.
Swallow.

7. Oral Hygiene: Dentures

1. Get denture box
2. Remove dentures
3. Put dentures in box
4. Fill box with water
5. Put denture tablet in water
6. Close denture box
7. Get cup
8. Put water in cup
9. Rinse mouth with water

Figure 7.2 Written Cues for Eating and Swallowing Challenges.

valleculae, the clinician began training with a visual cue card ("After you swallow your food, take a sip of liquid"). Using the spaced retrieval technique, the clinician prompted, "What do you do after you swallow your food?" The resident responded, "I take a sip of liquid," and the clinician prompted him to take a sip. During training, the visual prompt was changed to read, "Chew-swallow-sip," and then removed when the resident was remembering to take a sip 83% of the time. At the 8-week follow-up session, the resident completed the compensatory technique 95% of the time, requiring only one reminder per meal to use the safe swallowing technique. Also note the strategies in Table 7.1 for a variety of cognitive-related eating and swallowing challenges.

TABLE 7.1 Cues for Cognitive-Based Eating and Swallowing Challenges

Challenge	Strategies
Shopping and Preparing Meals	
Shopping	Use organized lists
Storing food	Write labels and dates on foods in refrigerator
	Write category labels in pantry and cupboards.
Cooking	Timers
	Simplified written recipes
	Microwave
	Help prepare foods: Put on sauces and dressing, butter bread, and cut food
	"Meals on Wheels"
Loss of Interest in Eating, or Poor Appetite	
	Emphasize meal routines
	Assist with meal preparation to get multisensory stimulation
	Provide a limited number of immediate choices (show menu or food pictures)
	Provide frequent small meals and snacks
	Provide small portions, individually
	Provide foods that look like real food, and use real dishes and silverware
Overeating	
	Provide distractions and alternative activities
	Limit access, and provide low-calorie snacks
	Use checklist of meals—check off after each meal eaten
Safety	
Impulsive eating	Supervise eating rate
	Remind person to take small bites and sips
	Use written reminder card for small bites and sips
Food preparation	Cut into bite size, and serve at a safe temperature

(Continued)

TABLE 7.1 (Continued)

Challenge	Strategies
Memory Deficits	
Forgets to eat	Use a schedule card and alarms
	Use reminder cards: For example, "Eating keeps me strong and healthy"
Forgets how to eat	Use reminder cards with steps: multiple steps per card, or one step per card (e.g., "Open mouth," "Chew," and "Swallow")
	Imitation (you eat!)
	Verbal and gestural cues
	Written cues: "I am eating green beans"
	Physical assistance—get them started
Perceptual Deficits	
Smell and taste	Throw out spoiled food—use labels
	Enhance foods—use salt substitutes, sugar substitutes, and sweet versus sour (contrasts)
	Use a mixture of temperatures and textures (if not orally defensive)
Vision	Enhance presentation: color contrast among placemat, bowl, and food
	Remove tray and all nonfood items
	Provide items that look like real food
	Maximize lighting
Agitation and Pacing	
	Need extra calories
	Reduce distractions (e.g., eat at the table, not in front of the TV)
	Eat one-on-one (then join in family meal)
	Eat one item at a time
	"Cocktail party" approach—eat "by the way" with finger foods
	Use a calm, slow approach in providing assistance
	Allow the person to eat alone as necessary
Mechanics of Eating	
	Accept and accommodate messiness: Use plastic tablecloths, napkins, and shirt protectors
	Use plateguard and weighted utensils.
	Use bowls and "scoopable" foods that require a spoon only
	Use finger foods
Supplements and Enhancers	
	Add protein (e.g., soy) powders to milk
	Provide shakes as snacks

TABLE 7.1 (Continued)

Challenge	Strategies
	Add fiber using wheat germ
	Load on sauces, gravy, butter, shredded cheese, and so on to increase calories
	Put sweet supplements on foods (chocolate syrup and jellies)
	Use salts (or salt substitutes) and spices
Dehydration	
(Note: Dehydration exacerbates cognitive deficits!)	Note if person is not accurately perceiving thirst
	Frequently offer drinks
	Provide easily accessible drinks (e.g., individual servings such as juice boxes)
	Avoid asking yes–no questions (i.e., "Do you want a drink?")
Swallowing Disorders (i.e., dysphagia)	
Choking hazards	Avoid hot dogs, popcorn, crackers, and "mixed" textures
	Crush pills (consult pharmacist first)
Need modified diets	**Regular**: bacon, chicken, broccoli, salad
	Soft: toast, hamburger, cooked vegetables
	Ground: banana, baked fish, scrambled eggs
	Puree: applesauce, cream of wheat, grits, yogurt, pudding, thin mashed potato, ice cream (if no thin liquid restriction)
Need thickened liquids	**Nectar**
	Honey
	Pudding
Warning signs Contact your doctor for a referral to a speech-language pathologist if you notice	**ANY of the following**: Holding food in mouth, requires cues to swallow Food left in mouth (collected in cheek) Throat clearing during and after meals Coughing during and after meals Wet or gurgly voice Rapid *or* gradual change in weight Fever Pneumonia
End Stage: Severely Limited Eating	
Changes to expect	Swallowing problems, not chewing food, refusing to eat, not recognizing food, and eating nonedibles
Limited intake	Provide comfort tray: selection of fluids, Jell-O, ice cream, and the like

(*Continued*)

TABLE 7.1 (Continued)

Challenge	Strategies
Oral Hygiene Problems (Note: Changes should not be sudden.)	
Signs	Food avoidance (toast, meat, etc.), mouth ulcers, thrush medications, and sensitive gums
Dentures	Provide assistance in cleaning (visual support and verbal cues)
	Obtain adjustment by dentist if weight changes
Oral cleaning	Use written reminder cards for tooth brushing
	Use glycerin swabs
	Ensure that mouth is clear of all food after each meal and snack

Source: Adapted from Melton and Bourgeois (2004).

CAREGIVER INTERVENTIONS

Caregivers are responsible for monitoring and providing cueing or assistance for safe eating and swallowing, adapting interventions along with the progression of cognitive deficits. Unfortunately, staff training is often not sufficient for use of the most effective and efficient procedures (Simmons & Schnelle, 2003). Thus, researchers have developed training programs designed to help staff to understand eating and swallowing problems in persons with dementia, and the best ways to assist their residents. In addition to the environmental and cognitive strategies already suggested in the above sections, optimal ways for staff to cue or to feed residents will be discussed. Staff training should emphasize a person-centered, rather than a task-oriented, approach for mealtime with residents (Hellen, 2002; Roberts & Durnbaugh, 2002), so as to reduce the stress of both staff and residents. The care team must ensure that all suitable procedures and strategies have been attempted before beginning the more invasive feeding by staff; and staff must be trained to provide such care in ways that will protect the persons' autonomy and dignity (Simmons & Schnelle; Zgola & Bordillon, 2002). This also requires having enough staff available to follow through with a person-centered approach (Hellen).

Hellen (2002) recommended that caregiver training include some basic information about various diseases that cause dementia, as well as those that are likely to affect eating and swallowing in elders, such as Parkinson's disease, strokes, and arthritis. Some simple recommendations can often help residents to maintain autonomy, such as with the use of adaptive equipment for self-feeding. Postural supports or adapted seating options may be necessary (Hellen). Dishes should be nonskid and sturdy to promote as much independence as possible (Roberts & Durnbaugh, 2002). For some, weighted utensils or other adaptive utensils may be required. Due to visual-perceptual deficits, it is often helpful to remove the tray and place food items on the table. As noted above, visual contrasts, such as dark tablecloths and white plates, facilitate self-feeding. Staff should reposition the food on the plate or tray as needed. As deficits progress, cueing and other assistance may be needed. Staff should be trained in techniques to provide hands-on assistance (e.g., bridging, chaining, and hand over hand), as well as in a communication style that will enhance cueing (e.g., the use of a calm, slow style and short sentences) (Hellen). Staff should offer reinforcement and encouragement for self-feeding efforts, and should sit in front of the person when providing cueing or assistance. Some other suggestions for safe swallowing include ensuring that residents receive the proper diet ordered by the physician (e.g., the correct textures, amounts, and nutrients), adding unsalted broth to foods that appear too thick for swallowing, and alternating liquids and solids (Hellen).

When cueing and other assistive techniques (e.g., finger foods) no longer work, caregivers assume the feeding responsibility (Gillick & Mitchell, 2002). In such cases, nurse supervisors need to provide training and supervision to ensure that the staff consistently use appropriate person-centered feeding techniques, such as cut meat, remove nonfood items from the tray, do not force feed, do not mix pureed foods, open cartons, offer fluids throughout the meal, wipe crumbs and dribble from the mouth, move slowly, touch and speak gently, use simple sentences, and make eye contact (Kayser-Jones & Schell, 1997; Roberts & Durnbaugh, 2002; Simmons et al., 2001). Staff should also be consistent with the use of adaptive equipment to assist with feeding, as cognitive decline affects simple procedures, such as taking food from a spoon. In this case, caregivers should avoid using plastic utensils; rather, rubber-coated utensils will increase safety for persons who begin to bite too hard on the spoon when being fed (Hellen, 2002).

Roberts and Durnbaugh (2002) developed a program to train staff to use the tool Mealtime Interventions. The strategies identified in the Mealtime Interventions protocol were based on results of the FBI. After completing the FBI, the clinician pushes a pencil through boxes corresponding to the problem eating behaviors; on the reverse side of the tool, a hole appears next to the recommended intervention. Staff received a training program, composed of an instructor's manual, quizzes, and video vignettes of challenging situations, with five goals: (a) to improve their observational assessment skills in mealtime, (b) to increase awareness of nutritional needs of persons with Alzheimer's disease, (c), to develop intervention skills for mealtimes, (d) to practice use of these tools, and (e) to apply the skills to simulations of persons with challenging mealtime behaviors. In a 3-week pre- and posttraining pilot study with 26 residents with midstage AD and 52 staff, Roberts and Durnbaugh found that staff were able to identify appropriate interventions significantly more often in posttraining than in pretraining. Whereas overall food consumption did not differ, food selection included more nutritious and less nonnutritious foods.

Simmons and Schnelle (2003) investigated the effects of a 2-day trial of feeding assistance on residents' oral food and fluid intake during meals. Results revealed that 50% of the participants significantly increased their mealtime intake in response to the intervention; and a higher level of cognitive and physical impairment was associated with a higher increase in oral intake in response to the intervention. Many of the residents who did not improve intake did respond when given staff attention for snacks between meals. Likewise, Chang and Lin (2005) evaluated the effects of a comprehensive feeding skills training program for nursing assistants on their knowledge and attitude and on residents' total eating time, food intake, and feeding difficulty. Sixty-seven nursing assistants were randomly assigned to either a treatment group (n = 31), who received 3 hours of in-service training and 1 hour of hands-on training, or a control group (n = 36), who did not receive any training. Significant improvements in the knowledge and attitude of trained nursing assistants, but not control group nursing assistants, were reported, as well as significantly longer total eating time and more feeding difficulties for the treatment group residents. There were no group differences in food intake as a result of treatment.

Altus and colleagues (2002) used an ABAB design to evaluate the effects of using family-style meals to increase participation and communication in five persons with dementia in a nursing home. Rates of participation and communication doubled when residents were presented with serving bowls and empty plates (B) compared to the baseline condition of prepared food trays (B^1). After a brief period of instruction on the use of prompts and praise during meals, participation increased to 65% of tasks and appropriate communication increased to 18% of observations. In addition, three of the five residents gained weight during the intervention period, and the CNA who participated in the study rated her satisfaction with resident participation (5 = *very satisfied*), communication (4 = *somewhat satisfied*), and the overall program (5 = *very satisfied*). She indicated that she definitely will continue using family-type meals, was very satisfied with the amount of work she had to do during family-style meals, and believed they resulted in the most independent resident behavior. Similarly, Ruigrok and Sheridan (2006) documented improved food intake, nutritional status, and quality of life in long-term care residents who received assistance during home-style dining where personal choice and independence were supported.

Others have investigated the effectiveness and benefits of training volunteers to feed residents. Lipner, Bosler, and Giles (1990) reported increased socialization, communication, and patient safety when trained and supervised volunteers fed residents. Similarly, the Dining With Dignity program was designed to improve nursing home residents' nutritional intake through an intervention that trained volunteers to provide one-on-one assistance during meals (Marken, 2004). These results are promising given the frequent problems with staffing in nursing homes. Staff caregivers could be assigned to feed more complex residents, whereas volunteers could provide cueing and assistance to those who need less skilled care.

CASE 7.1 ILLUSTRATION OF A CAREGIVER INTERVENTION

Cleary (2006) reported a case study in which a variety of strategies were utilized to increase independence and safety in eating/swallowing for a man with Parkinson's disease. The staff members were trained to implement the following strategies: seat him at a consistent place and follow a predictable routine in the dining room, place a Plexiglas barrier around his eating area to prevent him from eating extraneous items (e.g., sugar packets), and provide one food item at a time. This client reportedly was very distractible at meals, ate independently only 20% of the time, had severe weight loss due to poor intake, and experienced two choking episodes before intervention. After the intervention, he reportedly ate independently 70% of the time and gained nine pounds in the first 45 days of intervention.

Multicomponent Interventions

Zgola and Bordillon (2002) developed a program, Bon Appetit!, to provide a comprehensive program to address all of the necessary elements for a positive dining experience, including the food, its flavor and texture, the environment and setting, the timing of meals, the manner of service or delivery, activities related to mealtimes, staff attitudes and training, assistive techniques, assessment and documentation, and organizational structure. The mission of the program is to "enable the kind of dining experience that preserves each person's dignity, identity, and connections with family and culture while accommodating his or her changing needs throughout the course of his or her life" (p. 280). Furthermore, the program is meant to incorporate the mealtime experience into normal daily routines, for example, inviting residents to help set tables and clean up, and combining news group activities and breakfast meals. This is accomplished by organizing a team of department heads (the Dining Enhancement Committee) to guide the implementation of the program, and unit-based teams of direct care staff (the Action Team) to implement the program and to give feedback to the committee. There is a staff-training program that includes six core topics: (a) the value of meals; (b) how age and physical and cognitive impairments interfere with the enjoyment of meals; (c) how to interact socially with residents at the table; (d) how to present meals in an attractive manner and ensure the dining room is pleasant and comfortable; (e) how to offer graded assistance with eating; and (f) how to feed residents who are dependent.

Zgola and Bordillon (2002) conducted an effectiveness study, in a typical nursing home with typical staff, and conducted retrospective interviews and rating scales 12 months after the program had been implemented. Both staff and administration reported many improvements in the dining environment and their interactions with residents, but no improvement in the residents' ability to sit still or to concentrate on the meal. Staff did, however, feel more confident in their ability to positively respond to challenging behaviors; they also reported increases in feeling relaxed and observations of residents being more calm and sociable than before program implementation (Zgola & Bordillon). Furthermore, families were pleased with their perceptions of better dining care and a more pleasant dining environment.

Without the proper role models and staff supervision, staff are more likely to use a task approach to feeding residents (Kayser-Jones & Schell, 1997). Thus, Simmons and Schnelle (2003) recommended the use of staff management programs by supervisory-level staff to ensure care delivery; they recommended the use of standardized direct observational protocols of staff feeding assistance. Both of the multicomponent programs described above utilized staff management systems, as recommended by Burgio and Stevens (1999), to maintain the quality and effectiveness of the programs. Zgola and Bordillon (2002) used the different levels of organizational management to empower the staff and make them accountable, as well as to provide a system for the administration to ensure proper delivery of the program. Staff management should ensure that intervention programs will not be utilized only while researchers are present, but are sustainable over the long term.

CASE 7.2 ILLUSTRATION OF A MULTICOMPONENT INTERVENTION

An SLP joined the team in a multilevel care facility in a rural area, working primarily in the acute rehabilitation and transitional living units with young persons with traumatic brain injury. She received a referral for dysphagia services for a resident in the long-term care unit. She was dismayed to find out that there were only occasional SLP services in the long-term care unit, and that the persons living there were considered "low priority" by the team. Given the difficulty in maintaining adequate rehabilitation professional staffing, the team members did not feel they could spare the time for people who were "unable to benefit from treatment." The SLP went to conduct the swallowing assessment and found the resident in the hall, lined up among many other residents who were all facing into the hallway. There were a few nursing assistants who were feeding the residents by squeezing pureed food into their mouths with a large syringe. The staff were talking amongst themselves, and the residents were either passively taking the food or acting out. The SLP stated that she wanted to attempt to feed the resident using real dishes and silverware. The staff obtained the requested items, but stated that it was pointless. They were quite surprised when the resident was able to eat her whole tray without signs of unsafe swallowing! The SLP used the following strategies: remove distracting items, offer one item at a time, talk to the resident in a calm voice, give one-step directions, and use written reminder cards for each step (open your mouth, chew, and swallow). The SLP then offered to do some in-service training and demonstrations for the nursing staff so that they may improve their mealtime care for all residents. The administration and families were delighted; the direct care staff initially were apprehensive, but soon learned that the strategies did not increase their workload and that, in fact, some residents became much easier to feed.

Eating Issues in End-Stage Dementia

As noted previously, eating is one of the last functional behaviors to be lost in the course of dementia (Njegovan et al., 2001). In the late stages, persons with dementia are fed by staff. This period can last from a few months to several years, but when the person consistently spits out food, pushes away the spoon, and gags on or refuses to drink liquids, it becomes necessary to decide on either a palliative care approach or tube feeding. Although many people seem to think that not feeding a person is cruel, there is not sufficient evidence that tube feeding improves quality of life for persons with end-stage dementia. The SLP can provide families and other caregivers with information as they make decisions about whether the focus of eating and hydration will be to maximize comfort in the final stage of life, or to attempt to prolong life.

The goal of palliative care is the best quality of life for patients and their families by providing care that is life affirming, does not hasten or postpone death, provides relief from pain, addresses psychological and spiritual needs, and supports both patients and families (Pollens, 2004). Palliative, or comfort, care involves offering food and drink only to the extent the person continues to accept and enjoy them. Studies have documented that patients at the end of life experience little to no hunger or thirst, and the potential discomfort of a dry mouth can be alleviated with mouth swabs or ice chips (Gillick & Mitchell, 2002; McCann, Hall, & Groth-Juncker, 1994). In some facilities, "comfort trays" are used at the end of life to offer hydration, consisting of items such as water, Jell-O, and ice cream.

The fact that fewer than 1% of patients with dementia participated in palliative care programs (Luchins & Hanrahan, 1993) was thought to be related to the lack of indicators for the final stages of the disease. Alvarez-Fernández and colleagues (Alvarez-Fernández, Garcia-Ordonez, Martinez-Manzanares, & Gomez-Huelgas, 2005) conducted a prospective observational study of 67 community-dwelling patients with advanced dementia and discovered that artificial nutrition via a nasograstic tube, pneumonia, and hypoalbuminemia (from malnutrition) were associated with shortened survival. Clinicians, therefore, have developed tools to aid families and medical professionals in the decision-making process (Eggenberger & Nelms, 2004; Mitchell, Tetroe, & O'Connor, 2001). More information about end-of-life decision making and advance directives can be found in chapter 11.

Tube feeding requires either the insertion of a tube via the nasal passages, through the esophagus and into the stomach (nasogastric), or the insertion of a percutaneous endoscopic gastrostomy (PEG) tube from the mouth, through the esophagus, into the stomach, and through an incision in the stomach wall and skin. This latter procedure is performed by giving the person a mild sedative and a local anesthetic to numb the skin, and is well tolerated by most (Gillick & Mitchell, 2002). Persons with advanced dementia, however, may become agitated by the feeding tube and attempt to pull it out. The use of restraints and sedating drugs to maintain the tube placement can cause other health problems, and may not prevent aspiration, malnutrition, or mortality (Mitchell, Kiely, & Lipsitz, 1997). In fact, in their review of the evidence-based literature, Finucane, Christmas, and Travis (1999) did not find better outcomes for persons with advanced dementia who received artificial nutrition or hydration. Aspiration continues to occur in many persons who are tube-fed, particularly if they have dysphagia, and this contributes significantly to their mortality (Chouinard, Lavigne, & Villeneuve, 1998; Dharmarajan & Unnikrishnan, 2004; Knelb, Feinberg, & Tully, 1989); and yet, physicians persist in providing enteral nutrition to patients with advanced dementia, even when the patient had an advance directive to forgo feeding tube placement (Shega, Hougham, Stocking, Cox-Hayley, & Sachs, 2003). Tube feeding does not seem to improve well-being in those with severe neurological deficits and functional impairments (e.g., dysphagia or pneumonia), even when patients are provided with adequate calories (Chouinard et al., 1998). Chouinard and colleagues hypothesized that this may indicate a decreased ability to synthesize protein, resulting in a failure-to-thrive syndrome. Sanders and colleagues (Sanders et al., 2000) found that persons with dementia, as compared to those with other diagnoses, had higher mortality rates with gastrostomy tube feedings, leading these researchers to suggest that health practitioners may want to advise against the use of gastrostomy feedings with persons with dementia. Gillick (2000) also reported an increasing attitude that feeding tubes are not advisable in end-stage dementia.

Irwin (2006) reviewed the current thinking on the role of the speech-language pathologist in making end-of-life decisions, particularly with regard to the feeding of patients with advanced dementia. Although SLPs often participate in the development and implementation of nutrition care plans in long-term care facilities (White, 2005), some studies have shown that they may not have adequate knowledge about the operation and consequences of tube feeding or safe oral intake to be a strong advocate for the patient's preferences (Davis & Conti, 2003). Few SLPs are reported to be members of the palliative or hospice care team in spite of the fact that patients with advanced dementia may experience dysphagia and require recommendations and precautions for food and liquid consistencies, and oral intake facilitation techniques. In some cases, however, SLPs have contributed significantly to management decisions reducing tube placements (Monteleoni & Clark, 2004). Eggenberger and Nelms (2004) suggested that SLPs who want to enhance the ability of family members to make informed nutritional and end-of-life decisions for their loved one should integrate the current best practice evidence and their clinical expertise when providing feeding recommendations.

REFERENCES

Ahronheim, J. C. (1996). Nutrition and hydration in the terminal patient. *Clinics in Geriatric Medicine*, *12*, 379–391.

Algase, D. L., Beck, C., Kolanowski, A., Whall, A., Berent, S., Richards, K., et al. (1996). Need-driven dementia-compromised behavior: An alternative view of disruptive behavior. *American Journal of Alzheimer's Disease, 11*, 10–19.

Altus, D., Engelman, K., & Mathews, M. (2002). Using family-style meals to increase participation and communication in persons with dementia. *Journal of Gerontological Nursing*, *28*(9), 47–53.

Alvarez-Fernández, B., Garcia-Ordonez, M. A., Martinez-Manzanares, C., & Gomez-Huelgas, R. (2005). Survival of a cohort of elderly patients with advanced dementia: Nasogastric tube feeding as a risk factor for mortality. *International Journal of Geriatric Psychiatry*, *20*, 363–370.

Amarantos, E., Martinez, A., & Dwyer, J. (2001). Nutrition and quality of life in older adults. *Journal of Gerontology*, *56A*(11), 54–64.

Amella, E. J. (1999). Factors influencing the proportion of food consumed by nursing home residents with dementia. *Journal of the American Medical Society*, *47*, 879–885.

Barret-Connor, E., Edelstein, S., Corey-Bloom, J., & Wiederholt, W. (1998). Weight loss precedes dementia in community-dwelling older adults. In B. Vellas, S. Riviere, & J. Fitten (Eds.), *Research and practice in Alzheimer's disease: Weight loss and eating behaviour in Alzheimer's patients* (pp. 19–21). New York: Springer.

Baucom, A. (1996). *Hospitality design for the graying generation: Meeting the needs of a growing market*. New York: John Wiley.

Beattie, E., Algase, D., & Song, J. (2004). Keeping wandering nursing home residents at the table: Improving food intake using a behavioral communication intervention. *Aging & Mental Health*, *8*, 109–116.

Blandford, G., Watkins, L., Mulvihill, M., & Taylor, B. (1998). Assessing abnormal feeding behavior in dementia: A taxonomy and initial findings. In B. Vellas, S. Rivieres, & J. Fitten (Eds.), *Research and practice in Alzheimer's disease: Weight loss and eating behaviour in Alzheimer's patients* (pp. 47–64). New York: Springer.

Bowlby Sifton, C. (2002). Eating and nutrition: Nurturing, food, and community life. *Alzheimer's Care Quarterly*, *3*(4), iv–v.

Briller, S., Proffitt, M., Perez, K., & Calkins, M. (2001). *Creating Successful dementia care settings: Vol. 1. Understanding the environment through aging senses*. Baltimore: Health Professions.

Broniatowski, M. (1998). Editorial: Fiberoptic endoscopic evaluation of dysphagia and videofluoroscopy. *Dysphagia*, *13*, 22–23.

Brush, J. A., & Camp, C. J. (1998). Spaced retrieval during dysphagia therapy: A case study. *Clinical Gerontologist*, *19*, 96–99.

Brush, J. A., Meehan, R. A., & Calkins, M. P. (2002). Using the environment to improve intake for people with dementia. *Alzheimer's Care Quarterly*, *3*(4), 330–338.

Buchholz, D. W. (1994). Dysphagia associated with neurological disorders. *Acta oto-rhino-laryngologica belgica*, *48*, 143–155.

Burgio, L., & Stevens, A. (1999). Behavioral interventions and motivational systems in the nursing home. In R. Schulz, G. Maddox, & M. Lawton (Eds.), *Annual review of gerontology and geriatrics: Vol. 18. Focus on interventions research with older adults* (pp. 284–320). New York: Springer.

Calkins, M. P. & Brush, J. A. (2003). Designing for dining. *Alzheimer's Care Quarterly*, *4*(1), 73–76.

Chang, C., & Lin, L. (2005). Effects of a feeding skills training programme on nursing assistants and dementia patients. *Journal of Clinical Nursing*, *14*, 1185–1192.

Chouinard, J., Lavigne, E., & Villeneuve, C. (1998). Weight loss, dysphagia, and outcome in advanced dementia. *Dysphagia*, *13*, 151–155.

Cleary, S. (2006). Shifting paradigms: Treating swallowing and eating problems in dementia. *Communiqué*, *20*(2), 4–7.

Cronin-Stubbs, D., Beckett, L., Field, T., & Evans, D. (1998). Alzheimer's disease and loss of weight in community-dwelling older adults. In B. Vellas, S. Riviere, & J. Fitten (Eds.), *Research and practice in Alzheimer's disease: Weight loss and eating behaviour in Alzheimer's patients* (pp. 13–18). New York: Springer.

Davis, L. A., & Conti, G. J. (2003). Speech-language pathologists' roles and knowledge levels related to non-oral feeding. *Journal of Medical Speech-Language Pathology*, *13*(1), 15–30.

Devinsky, O., Morrell, M. J., & Vogt, B. A. (1995). Contributions of anterior cingulate cortex to behavior. *Brain*, *118*, 279–306.

Dharmarajan, T., & Unnikrishnan, D. (2004). Tube feeding in the elderly. The technique, complications, and outcome. *Postgraduate Medicine*, *115*, 51–54.

Duffy, J. (1995). *Motor speech disorders: Substrates, differential diagnosis, and management*. Toronto: Mosby.

Durnbaugh, T., Haley, B., & Roberts, S. (1993). Feeding behaviors in mid-stage Alzheimer's disease: A review. *Alzheimer Care Related Disorders Research*, *8*, 22–27.

Durnbaugh, T., Haley, B., & Roberts, S. (1996). Assessing problem feeding behaviors in mid-stage Alzheimer's disease. *Geriatric Nursing*, *17*, 63–67.

Eggenberger, S., & Nelms, T. (2004). Artificial hydration and nutrition in advanced Alzheimer's disease: Facilitating family decision-making. *Journal of Clinical Nursing*, *13*, 661–667.

Finucane, T., Christmas, C., & Travis, K. (1999). Tube feeding in patients with advanced dementia: A review of the evidence. *JAMA*, *282*, 1365–1370.

Gillick, M. (2000). Rethinking the role of tube feeding in patients with advanced dementia. *New England Journal of Medicine*, *342*, 206–210.

Gillick, M. R., & Mitchell, S. L. (2002). Facing eating difficulties in end-stage dementia. *Alzheimer's Care Quarterly*, *3*(3), 227–232.

Greenwood, C. E., Tam, C., Chan, M., Young, K. W. H., Binns, M. A., & van Reekum, R. (2005). Behavioral disturbances, not cognitive deterioration, are associated with altered food selection in seniors with Alzheimer's disease. *Journal of Gerontology: Medical Sciences*, *60A*(4), 499–505.

Groom, D. (1993). A diagnostic model for failure to thrive. *Journal of Gerontological Nursing*, *19*(6), 12–16.

Grundman, M., Corey-Bloom, J., Jernigan, T., Archibald, S., & Thal, L. (1998). Low body mass index and mesial temporal cortex atrophy in Alzheimer's disease. In B. Vellas, S. Riviere, & J. Fitten (Eds.), *Research and practice in Alzheimer's disease: Weight loss and eating behaviour in Alzheimer's patients* (pp. 37–38). New York: Springer.

Guyonnet, S., Nourhashemi, F., Ousset, P., Micas, M., Ghisolfi, A., Vellas, B., et al. (1998). Factors associated with weight loss in Alzheimer's disease. In B. Vellas, S. Riviere, & J. Fitten (Eds.), *Research and practice in Alzheimer's disease: Weight loss and eating behaviour in Alzheimer's patients* (pp. 7–11). New York: Springer.

Hellen, C. R. (2002). Doing lunch: A proposal for a functional well-being assessment. *Alzheimer's Care Quarterly*, *3*(4), 302–315.

Hicks-Moore, S. (2005). Relaxing music at mealtime in nursing homes: Effects on agitated patients with dementia. *Journal of Gerontological Nursing*, *31*(12), 26–32.

Holben, D. H., Hassell, J. T., Williams, J. L., & Helle, B. (1999). Fluid intake compared with established standards and symptoms of dehydration among elderly residents of a long term care facility. *Journal of the American Dietetic Association*, *99*, 1447–1450.

Hu, X., Okamura, N., Arai, H., Higuchi, M., Maruyama, M., Itoh, M., et al. (2002). Neuroanatomical correlates of low body weight in Alzheimer's disease: A PET study. *Progress in Neuropsychopharmacology and Biological Psychiatry*, *26*, 1285–1289.

Huffman, G. (2002). Evaluating and treating unintentional weight loss in the elderly. *American Family Physician*, *65*, 640–650.

Irwin, W. (2006). Feeding patients with advanced dementia: The role of the speech-language pathologist in making end-of-life decisions. *Journal of Medical Speech-Language Pathology*, *14*, xi–xiii.

Jean, L. A. (1997). Finger-food menu restores independence in dining. *Health Care Food Nutrition Focus*, *14*(1), 4–6.

Kagel, M. C., & Leopold, N. A. (1992). Dysphagia in Huntington's disease: A 16 year retrospective. *Dysphagia*, *7*, 106.

Kayser-Jones, J. (1996). Mealtime in nursing homes: The importance of individualized care. *Journal of Gerontological Nursing*, *22*(3), 26–31.

Kayser-Jones, J. (2000). Improving the nutritional care of nursing home residents. *Nursing Homes*, *49*(10), 56.

Kayser-Jones, J., & Schell, E. S. (1997, March/April). Staffing and the mealtime experience of nursing home residents on a special care unit. *American Journal of Alzheimer Disease*, 67–72.

Kayser-Jones, J., Schell, E. S., Porter, C., Barbaccia, J. C., Steinbach, C., Bird, W. F., et al. (1998). A prospective study of the use of liquid oral dietary supplements in nursing homes. *Journal of the American Geriatrics Society*, *46*, 1378–1386.

Knelb, J., Feinberg, M., & Tully, J. (1989). The relationship of pneumonia and aspiration in an elderly population. *Gerontologist*, *29*, 195A.

Kofod, J., & Birkmose, A. (2004). Meals in nursing homes. *Scandinavian Journal of Caring Sciences*, *18*, 128–134.

Koss, E., & Gilmore, C. G. (1998). Environmental interventions and functional abilities of AD patients. In B. Vellas, J. Filten, & G. Frisoni (Eds.), *Research and practice in Alzheimer's disease* (pp. 185–191). New York: Serdi/Springer.

Landi, F., Zuccala, G., Gambassi, G., Incalzi, R. A., Manigrasso, L., Pagano, F., et al. (1999). Body mass index and mortality among old people living in the community. *American Journal of the Geriatrics Society, 47*, 1072–1076.

Lange-Alberts, M. L., & Shott, S. (1994). Nutritional intake: Use of touch and verbal cueing. *Journal of Gerontological Nursing, 20*, 36–40.

Laurenhue, K. (2002). From dietary to dining: Bon appetit! *Alzheimer's Care Quarterly, 3*(4), 339–342.

Layne, K. L. (1990). Feeding strategies for the dysphagic patient: A nursing perspective. *Dysphagia, 5*, 84–88.

Leder, S. B., Sasaki, C. T., & Burrell, M. I. (1998). Fiberoptic endoscopic evaluation of dysphagia to identify silent aspiration. *Dysphagia, 13*, 19–21.

Lipner, H., Bosler, J., & Giles, G. (1990). Volunteer participation in feeding residents: Training and supervision in a long-term care facility. *Dysphagia, 5*(2), 89–95.

Logemann, J. (2003, February 18). Dysphagia and dementia: The challenge of dual diagnosis. *The ASHA Leader*, 1.

Luchins, D., & Hanrahan, P. (1993). What is appropriate health care for end-stage dementia? *Journal of the American Geriatrics Society, 41*, 25–30.

Marken, D. (2004). Enhancing the dining experience in long-term care: Dining With Dignity program. *Journal of Nutrition for the Elderly, 23*(3), 99–109.

McCann, R., Hall, W., & Groth-Juncker, A. (1994). Comfort care for terminally ill patients: The appropriate use of nutrition and hydration. *JAMA, 274*, 1236–1246.

McCullough, G. H., Wertz, R. T., Rosenbek, J. C., Mills, R. H., Ross, K. B., & Ashford, J. R. (2000). Inter- and intrajudge reliability of a clinical examination of swallowing in adults. *Dysphagia, 15*, 58–67.

Melton, A., & Bourgeois, M. (2004, February). Feeding and swallowing issues in dementia. Invited presentation at the Pilot Club's Annual Alzheimer Update, Tallahassee, FL.

Mitchell, S., Kiely, D., & Lipsitz, L. (1997). The risk factors and impact on survival of feeding tube placement in nursing home residents with severe cognitive impairment. *Archives of Internal Medicine, 157*, 327–332.

Mitchell, S., Tetroe, J., & O'Connor, A. (2001). A decision aid for long-term tube-feeding in cognitively impaired older persons. *Journal of the American Geriatrics Society, 49*, 313–316.

Monteleoni, C., & Clark, E. (2004). Using rapid-cycle quality improvement methodology to reduce feeding tubes in patients with advanced dementia: Before and after study. *British Medical Journal, 329*, 491–494.

Morley, J. E. (1997). Anorexia of aging. *American Journal of Clinical Nutrition, 66*, 760–773.

Morley, J. E., & Silver, A. J. (1995). Nutritional issues in nursing home care. *Annals of Internal Medicine, 123*, 850–859.

Morris, J., & Volicer, L. (2001). Nutritional management of individuals with Alzheimer's disease and other progressive dementias. *Nutrition in Clinical Care, 4*, 148–155.

Muller, J., Wenning, G. K., Verny, M., McKee, A., Chaudhuri, K. R., Jellinger, K., et al. (2001). Progression of dysarthria and dysphagia in postmortem-confirmed Parkinsonsian disorders. *Archives of Neurology, 58*, 260–264.

Musson, N. D., Kincaid, J., Ryan, P., Glussman, B., Varone, L., Gamarra, N., et al. (1990). Nature, nurture, nutrition: Interdisciplinary programs to address the prevention of malnutrition and dehydration. *Dysphagia, 5*, 96–101.

Njegovan, V., Man-Son-Hing, M., Mitchell, S., & Molnar, F. (2001). The hierarchy of functional loss associative with cognitive decline in older persons. *Journal of Gerontology A: Biological Science & Medical Science, 56*, M638–M643.

Pollens, R. (2004). Role of the speech-language pathologist in palliative hospice care. *Journal of Palliative Medicine*, 7, 694–702.

Ragneskog, H., Brane, G., Karlsson, I., & Kihlgren, M. (1996). Influence of dinner music on food intake and symptoms common in dementia. *Scandinavian Journal of Caring Sciences*, *10*(1), 11–17.

Ragneskog, H., Kihlgren, M., Karlsson, I., & Norberg, A. (1996). Dinner music for demented patients: Analysis of video-recorded observations. *Clin Nurs Res*, *5*(3), 262–277.

Reed, P., Zimmerman, S., Sloane, P., Williams, C., & Boustani, M. (2005). Characteristics associated with low food and fluid intake in long-term care residents with dementia. *The Gerontologist*, *45*, 74–80.

Regnard, C., Matthews, D., Gibson, L., & Clark, S. (2004). Current learning in palliative care. Retrieved January 9, 2006, from http://www.hth.org.uk/elearning/pdf/hprhn-5.pdf

Richards, K., Lambert, C., & Beck, C. (2000). Deriving interventions for challenging behaviors from the need-driven, dementia-compromised behavior model. *Alzheimer's Care Quarterly*, *1*(4), 62–76.

Rizzo, M., Anderson, S. W., Dawson, J., & Nawrot, M. (2000). Vision and cognition in Alzheimer's disease. *Neuropsychologia*, *38*(8), 1157–1169.

Roberts, S., & Durnbaugh, T. (2002). Enhancing nutrition and eating skills in long term care. *Alzheimer's Care Quarterly*, *3*(4), 316–329.

Ruigrok, J., & Sheridan, L. (2006). Life enrichment programme: Enhanced dining experience, a pilot project. *International Journal of Health Care Quality Assurance Incorporating Leadership in Health Services*, *19*(4/5), 420–429.

Saletti, A., Lindgren, E. Y., Johansson, L., & Cederholm, T. (2000). Nutritional status according to Mini Nutritional Assessment in an institutionalised elderly population in Sweden. *Gerontology*, *46*, 139–145.

Sanders, D. S., Carter, M. J., D'Silva, J., James, G., Bolton, R. P., & Bardhan, K. D. (2000). Survival analysis in percutaneous endoscopic gastrostomy feeding: A worse outcome in patients with dementia. *American Journal of Gastroenterology*, *95*, 1472–1475.

Schiffman, S. (1997). Taste and smell losses in normal aging and disease. *JAMA*, *278*, 1357–1362.

Shega, J., Hougham, G., Stocking, C., Cox-Hayley, D., & Sachs, G. (2003). Barriers to limiting the practice of feeding tube placement in advanced dementia. *Journal of Palliative Medicine, 6*, 885–893.

Silver, A. J. (1993). The malnourished older patient: When and how to intervene. *Geriatrics*, *48*(7), 70–74.

Silver, S. A., & Albert, S. M. (2000). Dementia and food exchange in nursing home dining areas. *Journal of Applied Gerontology*, *19*(4), 476–483.

Simmons, S. F., Babinou, S., Garcia, E., & Schnelle, J. F. (2002). Quality assessment in nursing homes by systematic direct observations: Feeding assistance. *Journal of Gerontology: Medical Sciences*, *57A*(10), M1–M7.

Simmons, S., Osterweil, D., & Schnelle, J. (2001). Improving food intake in nursing home residents with feeding assistance: A staff analysis. *Journal of Gerontology*, *56A*(12), M790–M794.

Simmons, S. F., & Reuben, D. (2000). Nutritional intake monitoring for nursing home residents: A comparison of staff documentation, direct observation, and photography methods. *Journal of the American Geriatrics Society*, *48*, 209–213.

Simmons, S. F., & Schnelle, J. F. (2003). Implementation of nutritional interventions in long-term care. *Alzheimer's Care Quarterly*, *4*(4), 286–296.

Spindler, A. A. (2002). Nutritional considerations for persons with Alzheimer's disease. *Alzheimer's Care Quarterly*, *3*(4), 289–301.

Spindler, A., Renvall, M., Nichols, J., & Ramsdell, J. (1996). Nutritional status of patients with Alzheimer's disease: A one-year study. *Journal of the American Dietetic Association, 96*, 1013–1018.

Steele, C. (1996). *Meal assistance screening tool*. Ontario: Steele.

Steele, C., Greenwood, C., Ens, I., Robertson, C., & Seidman-Carlson, R. (1997). Mealtime difficulties in a home for the aged: Not just dysphagia. *Dysphagia, 12*, 45–50.

Talerico, K. A., & Evans, L. K. (2000). Making sense of protective behaviors in persons with dementia. *Alzheimer Care Quarterly, 1*(4), 77–86.

Tully, M., Lambros Matrakas, K., & Musallam, K. (1998). The eating behavior scale: A simple method of assessing functional ability in patients with Alzheimer's disease. In B. Vellas, S. Riviere, & J. Fitten (Eds.), *Research and practice in Alzheimer's disease: Weight loss and eating behaviour in Alzheimer's patients* (pp. 65–69). New York: Springer.

Volonté, M. A., Porta, M., & Comi, G. (2002). Clinical assessment of dysphagia in early phases of Parkinson's disease. *Neurological Sciences, 23*, S121–S122.

White, H. (2005). Nutrition in advanced Alzheimer's disease. *North Carolina Medical Journal, 66*, 307–312.

Yen, P. (1996). When food doesn't taste good anymore. *Geriatric Nursing, 17*, 44–45.

Yorkston, K. M., Beukelman, D. R., Strand, E. A., & Bell, K. R. (1999). *Management of motor speech disorders in children and adults* (2nd ed.). Austin, TX: Pro-Ed.

Zgola, J. M., & Bordillon, G. (2002). Four guys at the table. *Alzheimer's Care Quarterly, 3*(4), 279–288.

8

Quality of Life Issues

The ultimate objective in providing services to persons with dementia is life enhancement. Increasingly, researchers and clinicians are using quality of life (QoL) measures as outcome measures across a wide variety of interventions and diseases. The degree to which dementia symptoms influence the quality of life of persons with dementia and those in their environments has been the focus of much research in the past 2 decades. This chapter reviews the current thinking about definitions of QoL in persons with dementia and about whose perspective is important in assessment and treatment. Considerable difficulty exists in defining a construct like QoL, which has such different meanings to different individuals and groups. QoL has been conceptualized as the modern counterpart to the notion of "the good life" (George & Bearon, 1980). Significant measurement issues also exist when considering elders with degenerative neurological disorders causing cognitive and communicative deficits that make test administration difficult. Suggestions for obtaining valid and reliable measurements will be provided.

Generally, older adults have often been faced with a number of losses, but most are able to maintain their QoL by maintaining current activities, replacing current activities with adaptive ones, and/or adapting to changes by filtering out incongruous information (Brandstadter & Greve, 1994; Volicer & Bloom-Charette, 1999). Persons with dementia may need assistance in using such strategies to maintain quality of life. Therefore, specific treatments for improving and/or maintaining the QoL of persons with late stages of dementia are reviewed. Finally, information that will be useful to SLPs and other health care professionals regarding advance directives and palliative care, and suggestions for having end-of-life conversations, will be provided.

ASSESSING QUALITY OF LIFE IN PERSONS WITH DEMENTIA

Defining Quality of Life

Conceptualization of QoL Quality of life is a concept that evades explicit definition. Researchers around the globe have been struggling with the conceptualization of QoL for elders over the past few decades, recognizing that QoL for elders may be different than for younger adults. There have been problems with inconsistency in definitions, and in determining specific domains to include in the conceptualization and assessment tools, as well as in developing reliable procedures for the measurement of subjective experiences of individuals (Dempster & Donnelly, 2000; Volicer & Bloom-Charette, 1999). In the 1960s and 1970s, QoL was defined as a subjective perception of emotions, such as life satisfaction and happiness (Wyller et. al., 1997, 1998). Since then, a variety of models has been proposed. Some conceptualizations of QoL involve perceptions of life satisfaction in general, or broad dimensions of physical and mental well-being or satisfaction. Life satisfaction has been conceptualized by some as satisfaction with life progression, current situations, future prospects, and general senses of happiness and well-being (George & Bearon, 1980). For elders, life satisfaction is also related to lifetime exposure to trauma (Krause, 2004). Life satisfaction has been equated with QoL by some researchers (e.g., Wyller et. al., 1997, 1998), whereas other researchers consider this to be just one domain of QoL (e.g., Adkins, 1993; Lundh & Nolan, 1996).

Other conceptualizations include specific dimensions of QoL, which may involve a variety of overlapping factors, such as global impression of QoL, emotional and behavioral functioning and well-being, feelings and mood, intellectual and cognitive functioning, awareness of self, self-esteem, social functioning and well-being, the existence of a support network, the ability to pursue and enjoy interests and recreations, energy and vitality, physical well-being, functional well-being, response to surroundings, as well as environmental, occupational, and financial factors (Albert, 1997; Howard & Rockwood, 1995; Kane, 2003; Lundh & Nolan, 1996; Rabins, Kasper, Kleinman, Black, & Patrick, 1999; Silberfeld, Rueda, Krahn, & Naglie, 2002; Volicer & Bloom-Charette, 1999). Given the large number of factors to consider, variability among subgroups may also be important. For example, social relationships were more important to elderly women than men in their opinions of life satisfaction (Cheng & Chan, 2006). Some researchers recommend the conceptualization of QoL as a dynamic construct with interaction between the conditions of an individual's life and his or her perceptions of those conditions (Allison, Locker, & Feine, 1997; Noro & Aro, 1996; Radomski, 1995). The World Health Organization (WHO; World Health Organization Quality of Life [WHOQOL] Group, 1993, 1995) defined *quality of life* as "an individual's perception of their position in life, in the context of the culture and value systems in which they live and in relation to their goals, expectations, standards, and concerns."

Cultural Issues Saxena, O'Connell, and Underwood (2002) reported that "social and cultural factors play an important role in people's perceptions and expectations of how they see their health and quality [of] life" (p. 82). Gender, race, ethnicity, and religion should be considered when assessing quality of life, and when making decisions about providing care (Cunningham, Burton, Hawes-Dawson, Kington, & Hays, 1999; Saxena et al., 2002). Also, the types of health conditions that are prevalent tend to vary to some extent across racial, ethnic, and socioeconomic groups (e.g., the prevalence of diabetes, hypertension, and heart disease; Smith & Kington, 1997). Cunningham et al. (1999) reported that African American participants rated items relating to spirituality, weight-related concepts, and hopefulness as very relevant in QoL measurement; meanwhile, the items that are on many standard health-related QoL measures (e.g., SF-36 and SF-12; Ware, Kosinski, & Keller, 1996; Ware & Sherbourne, 1992) were ranked in the lower two thirds. In cultures where elders are valued and respected (e.g., many Asian cultures), QoL issues may differ from those where elders are devalued and patronized (e.g., many Western cultures).

In the development of the WHOQOL-100, the WHOQOL Group (1998b) found that there are six domains of health-related quality of life that are important throughout the world: physical health, psychological health, level of independence, social health, environmental health, and spirituality, religiousness, and personal beliefs (SRPB). The group then developed a supplementary module, the WHOQOL SRPB. Through focus groups and pilot testing held around the world, they found eight facets that were of importance across cultural groups that had good psychometric properties: spiritual connection, meaning and purpose in life, awe, wholeness and integration, spiritual strength, inner peace, hope and optimism, and faith. Additional facets were important around work, but did not have adequate psychometric properties in testing: kindness to others, code to live by, acceptance of others, forgiveness, death and dying, miscellaneous (e.g., control over one's life, detachment and attachment), and freedom to practice beliefs and rituals.

QoL in Elders Lawton (1991) proposed one of the first comprehensive conceptualizations of QoL for elders, including four domains: objective environment (physical attributes of the environment), perceived QoL (subjective life satisfaction), psychological well-being (emotional state), and behavioral competence (physical health, functional competence, cognition, time use, and social behavior). This model was later applied to persons with dementia (Lawton, 1994). Maintaining a sense of self is an important aspect of QoL for older persons (Lundh & Nolan, 1996; Roos & Havens, 1991). Lawton's model does not specify sense of self or self-esteem; however, this may be particularly important for persons with dementia. Self-esteem has been conceptualized as a general sense of self-worth or a feeling of personal value. George and Bearon (1980) recognized the significance of the relationship between intervention and self-esteem, acknowledging that some interventions may actually be detrimental to an individual's self-esteem and others may enhance self-esteem. Whatever the model used, QoL is an essential construct to be concerned about in elders, who were found to have lower QoL than younger adults in an international study (Saxena et al., 2002). Among those over 65 years old, results also revealed poorer quality of life for persons with less education and for women.

Health-Related QoL (HR-QoL) Many investigations of QoL in elders focus on health-related QoL issues (HR-QoL), which refers to physical, emotional, and social aspects of life that may be affected by changes in an individual's health status (Williams, 1998). Health has been conceptualized by the World Health Organization (1946) as a state of complete physical, mental, and social well-being, and not simply the absence of disease, discomfort, and disability. *Functional status* refers to the ability to complete activities of daily living (ADLs) independently. HR-QoL measurement often includes measures of physical and/or mental functions, including ADL measures. Wyller and colleagues (1997, 1998) suggested that QoL theory has suffered from the expansion of the construct to include physical function and ADL abilities. This concern recognizes that health status does not necessarily equate with health satisfaction. QoL is not necessarily dependent on objective physical ability, although individuals with more severe deficits do frequently have lower self-reported QoL. Studies have shown that physical health may not be as important as emotional health for subjective well-being (Browne et al., 1994; Dorman, Waddell, Slattery, Dennis, & Sandercock, 1997a; Nordeson, Engstrom, & Norberg, 1998; Siu, Reuben, Ouslander, & Osterweil, 1993). Albert (1997) criticized narrow definitions of HR-QoL that included only dimensions intrinsic to a person and excluded external influences such as environment and social support. Albert described four domains of QoL that should be included in generic (as opposed to disease-specific) health-related QoL assessment: physical and occupational function, psychological function, social interaction, and somatic symptoms.

The mental health aspects of HR-QoL may involve issues such as depression and anxiety, which can present problems in assessing the factors that contribute to outcome in elders with health problems. Depression and medical conditions had additive effects on decreased physical function and well-being in late-middle-aged and older people (Ormel et al., 1998). No medical conditions (e.g., back pain, stroke, or degenerative neurological diseases) accounted for more variance than depression did. Depressive symptoms were both a unique risk and a unique contribution to decreased well-being. Medical conditions that did show some interaction with depression included diabetes, hearing problems, vision problems, and cognitive impairment. All of these conditions are likely to be comorbid with dementia in the elderly. Careful attention should be paid to the contributions of both medical conditions and depression on the perceived health of persons with dementia, and neither should be used in isolation to determine QoL. Furthermore, those with disease and disability may be able to maintain life satisfaction through social engagement (social networks and social activity), which seems to be more important for elders with both disease and disability than for their healthier peers (Jang, Mortimer, Haley, & Graves, 2004).

QoL for Institutionalized Elders Environmental considerations should be taken into account for those who are living at home versus institutionalized elderly, who reportedly have poorer QoL (Noro & Aro, 1996). In addition to the above dimensions of HR-QoL, dimensions of QoL that have been examined for institutionalized elderly are choice, control, individuality, privacy, involvement, engagement, and the quality of the environment and staff morale (Coons & Mace, 1996; Philp, Mutch, Devaney, & Ogston, 1989). A longitudinal study revealed that depressive symptoms increased over 3–6 years of long-term care, whether in residential care facilities or at home (Pot, Deeg, Twisk, Aartjan, & Beekman, 2005), and this could not be accounted for by health condition.

The issues of social functioning, social engagement, and social isolation come up repeatedly when considering QoL of nursing home residents. In assisted living, regression analyses revealed social cohesion to be the greatest predictor of QoL, with other predictors including having fewer health conditions, participation in social activities, monthly family contact, and an environment low in conflict (Mitchell & Kemp, 2000). There are many causes of social isolation in residential facilities. Residents of nursing homes are more likely to be unmarried and childless than elders who remain in their own homes (Jacelon, 1995), and those who do have families are likely to have less contact upon admission (Port et al., 2001). Only one third of residents are comfortable talking with other residents (Schroll et al., 1997). In addition, environmental barriers and organizational rules of the institutions may prevent people with disabilities from being integrated into the social interaction and activities of the nursing home (Goffman, 1961; Lubinski, 1995; Lubinski, Morrison, & Rigrodsky, 1981). Additionally, as noted in chapter 6, the physical and social settings of most nursing homes are not conducive to social interaction (Grainger, 1995; Jacelon; Liukkonen, 1995; Lubinski; Lubinski et al., 1981; Retsinas & Garrity, 1985). Social interaction is discouraged by the lack of private areas, poor lighting, noise, and the arrangement of furniture. There are few communication partners and topics of choice, and few reasons to engage in conversation. The beauty shop may be the only area of a nursing home that encourages social interaction regarding personal topics (Sigman, 1985). Consistent with the phenomena of institutions (Goffman), residents have reported implicit rules regarding the type and amount of talk that is acceptable in nursing homes (Kaakinen, 1992, 1995; Lubinski et al.; Sigman), including beliefs that they should not bother the staff unnecessarily with conversation, talk too much, talk about loneliness, talk to those who are senile or difficult to communicate with, have private conversations in front of others, or complain. Furthermore, staff are frequently perceived by residents to be too busy to engage in social interaction (Jacelon; Kaakinen, 1992, 1995; Liukkonen; Lubinski et al.; Sigman). Staff–resident interaction is infrequent and poor in quality (Grainger). When staff members do have the opportunity to talk, they more frequently talk to each other than to the residents (Sigman).

In a literature review of frameworks of QoL for nursing home residents, Gerritsen, Steverink, Ooms, and Ribbe (2004) determined that the most appropriate framework was the theory of social production functions, which states that human behavior is aimed at being well through the achievement of a hierarchy of goals, with subjective well-being at the top of the hierarchy. This is reportedly achieved through physical and social well-being (Ormel, Lindenberg, Steverink, & Verbrugge, 1999). The following instrumental goals are lower in the hierarchy: stimulation, comfort, affection, behavioral confirmation, and status (Ormel et al., 1999). The goals are achieved by using resources; lower goals become resources as they are achieved. Everyone is assumed to need some level of both physical and social well-being, but older persons may have fewer resources and may discard some goals (Steverink, 2001).

Kane (2003) stated that the issue of domains to measure will depend on the budget for assessment in addition to the theory of QoL being used; additionally, cultural differences would affect the important domains in different countries and cultures. Actual QoL for long-term care residents is often reduced by policies, such as building codes (e.g., lack of privacy), federal and state mandates (e.g., limits to choice and control), and cost-cutting measures (e.g., staffing reductions) (Kane, 2001, 2003; Volicer & Bloom-Charette, 1999). Suggestions for improving QoL of persons with dementia will be provided in the treatment section, "Interventions Designed to Improve Quality of Life."

QoL for Persons With Dementia There is no widely agreed upon definition of QoL for persons with dementia at this point. Brod (1998) defined *quality of life* as "a multidimensional concept encompassing social, psychological, and physical domains" (p. 26). In focus groups, persons with dementia reported that they valued reminiscing about the past and "making the best of it" "one day at a time" (Thorgrimsen et al., 2003). Woodend, Nair, and Tang (1997) reported that individuals with dementia indicated that social aspects of life had a great impact on their overall quality of life. Among the most important aspects were internal control over social life, and interpersonal relationships. Given the importance of social relationships in quality of life in general, and for persons with dementia in particular, clinicians should be quite concerned about the QoL of persons in nursing homes.

Residents with depression or cognitive deficits are commonly found to have poor social engagement (Achterberg et al., 2003). Mor et al. (1995) found that social engagement was a critical factor in QoL of nursing home residents; those with physical and cognitive impairments were more likely to have decreased engagement and increased conflict and distress (Mor et al.; Schroll, Jonsson, Mor, Berg, & Sherwood, 1997). Disabled residents' efforts at social integration are often met with rejection because of this conflict and distress, propagating the social isolation in a cyclical manner. Furthermore, cognitively intact residents do not want to live with cognitively impaired residents (Levesque, Cossette, & Potvin, 1993), and lucidity, speech, and sight are key determinants in making friends in a nursing home (Retsinas & Garrity, 1985). Finally, a significant factor in decreased family contact upon admission to a nursing home was the presence of dementia (Port et al., 2001); factors that were related to less reduction in family contact included kinship closeness, support network proximity, and White race.

Selwood, Thorgrimsen, and Orrell (2005) investigated longitudinal changes in quality of life over 1 year in 40 persons with dementia who had previously participated in a larger study (Thorgrimsen et al., 2003). Although there was no mean change in the group, approximately half of the participants had changes in their QoL. Initial quality of life was the only significant predictor of QoL one year later; other variables that were correlated with QoL were depression and anxiety, but not cognition. Logsdon, Gibbons, McCurry, and Teri (1999) also found that depression and QoL scores were correlated. Zank and Leipold (2001) found that people with more severe dementia had fewer depressive symptoms and better life satisfaction than those with less severe dementia. Similarly, Albert and colleagues (1996) found less positive affect as dementia severity increased, but only to a point, when there was an increase in positive affect in those with the most severe stages of dementia. However, Albert and colleagues (2001) found that more severe dementia was related to lower QoL, but this may be due to use of proxy informants. Lyketsos and colleagues (2003) examined longitudinal QoL in long-term care residents with dementia using the Alzheimer's Disease-Related Quality of Life (ADRQL) scale. Half of the participants did not demonstrate a decline in QoL over 2 years. The only predictor of greater decline was having lower QoL at baseline; sociodemographic variables, cognitive function, ADL impairment, behavioral impairment, and depression were not related to decline in QoL. These are interesting findings, given that many professionals and laypersons alike assume that cognitive decline is an important factor in QoL. Much remains to be understood about the longitudinal effects of dementia on QoL. To identify relevant aspects of QoL for elders, including those with dementia, some gerontology researchers have argued for the use of individualized definitions of QoL that may vary depending on individual and cultural values and definitions of health and disability (Browne et. al., 1994; Browne, O'Boyle, McGee, McDonald, & Joyce, 1997; Dempster & Donnelly, 2000; Howard & Rockwood, 1995).

Measurement Issues

Assessing QoL in persons with dementia is problematic, due to difficulty expressing their physical and emotional health, social and financial status, and other factors that contribute to their definition of a quality life. Although new tools have been developed specifically for measuring QoL in persons with dementia (e.g., Brod, Steward, Sands, & Walton, 1999; Logsdon et al., 1999; Rabins et al., 1999; Selai, Trimble, Rossor, & Harvey, 2000), interpreting the responses of persons with communication and cognitive deficits remains a challenge. Given frequent fatigue, distractibility, or misunderstanding during assessment, researchers and clinicians often question the validity and reliability of responses by persons with dementia. However, QoL evaluation is very important, as it may be used in policy development, and in outcomes measurement for intervention research or clinical practice. Thorgrimsen and colleagues (2003) reported that there are currently over 1,000 generic and health-related QoL instruments available, many of them with poor validity (Gill & Feinstein, 1994). Valid and reliable measurement procedures are essential. Given the ominous problems of conceptualization, it is no surprise that the development of valid and reliable tools has been a challenge for researchers of QoL. Various measurement issues arise in developing measures and methods to assess QoL: subjective versus objective procedures, single versus multiple domains or mixed instruments, self-report versus proxy report procedures, and generic and disease-specific instruments.

Subjective Versus Objective Procedures Problems arise in measuring subjective dimensions of QOL, such as life satisfaction. Life satisfaction can be measured globally or specifically (e.g., satisfaction with overall life or with family roles, or overall well-being versus physical well-being). It is difficult to determine to what exactly participants are responding when providing self-reports of life satisfaction; this problem is greater for general life satisfaction measurement than domain-specific satisfaction. Most tools are constructed of several items that the test developers determined would capture life satisfaction (e.g., Life Satisfaction

Index-Z; Wood, Wylie, & Sheafor, 1969). Many of the tools that were developed for healthy adults cannot be used with persons with dementia due to the cognitive and/or communicative deficits that are present.

Objective measurement of general health and functional status has been researched extensively. Functional status is an area that is most likely to change with intervention, making it an attractive domain for outcomes measurement (George & Bearon, 1980). However, the extent to which objective measures of functional status are actually QoL measures is questionable, as they are activity or ability measures. Furthermore, despite the extant literature on general health and functional status measures, there is still no simple or straightforward way to measure general health or HR-QoL. Again, questions arise regarding objective health and abilities versus subjective self-perceptions of physical, mental, and social well-being. Although the two concepts are intertwined, they are different.

Individualized Assessment Browne and colleagues (1997) identified three essential elements to any QoL instrument: the domains measured, the criteria to determine higher and lower QoL, and the weight, or importance, to be placed on different domains. They disagreed with developers of typical measures that do not allow for this weighting procedure, as these instruments are based on a needs approach to assessment that assumes that these needs are common across all individuals and are more important than wants. Allowing individuals to indicate their own definition of QoL may be more meaningful and valid, but poses other problems for evaluation methods, particularly difficulty with completion of the necessary weighting or ranking procedures. Even healthy elders have difficulty completing the "weighting" procedures used in individualized QoL measurement (Browne et al., 1994; Dempster & Donnelly, 2000), and most of those with dementia cannot or will not complete the weighting procedure (Coen et al., 1993). Dempster and Donnelly found that older persons were able to consistently rank order the importance of various domains of QoL, but that the oldest participants had much difficulty converting these rankings into weightings. Thus, researchers and clinicians could use rankings of individual importance rather than more complicated weighting procedures. Browne et al. (1997) examined a direct weighting procedure, which is less complicated than a judgment analysis weighting procedure, to determine its reliability and validity with typical young adults. Results were promising, as the direct procedure had better reliability and was quicker to administer than the judgment analysis. Another study found that the direct weighting procedure was useful with persons with HIV/AIDS (Hickey et al., 1996). Further research is needed to determine its utility for older persons and for those with cognitive impairment.

Single Versus Multiple Domains, or Mixed The wide breadth of domains in QoL assessment is both its strength and its weakness (Albert, 1997). Even within HR-QoL assessment, there are many domains that could be assessed, leading to problems with scoring and quantification of results. Some measures have only one global score, some have only domain scores, whereas others have both global and domain scores. Comparison of results across measures is extremely difficult given these differences in scoring procedures.

Mode of Administration Another issue in QOL assessment in elders, particularly those with neurological disorders, is mode of administration (e.g., independent self-report questionnaires versus an interview-based approach). Some have suggested that, for persons with dementia, QoL instruments must be completed in an interview with an examiner (Novella, Jochum, et al., 2001). A way to simplify the assessment procedures for individuals who have cognitive and communicative disorders is to use a visual analogue scale for either a single subjective rating of overall global health satisfaction or items with scales for multiple domains (e.g., Kwa, Limburg, & de Haan, 1996). As people progress through the early to middle stages of dementia, assumptions are often made that with increasing memory loss and dementia, people have compromised insight into their condition, making their responses to QoL assessment unreliable (e.g., Selai, Vaughan, Harvey, & Logsdon, 2001; Thorgrimsen et al., 2003). Yet, persons with mild to moderate cognitive impairment can provide consistent responses to questions about their preferences, their choices, and their involvement in decisions regarding their daily lives (Feinberg & Whitlatch, 2001).

As persons progress into late stages of dementia, self-report in either interview or questionnaire administration becomes more difficult. Evaluation of these persons may depend on the examiner's observations and interpretations of their cues and behaviors, as they become unable to overtly express feelings about their lives and changes in the quality of their lives (Lawton, 1994, 1997; Volicer & Bloom-Charette, 1999). Albert (1997) generated a list of behaviors that are assumed to have positive or negative emotional valence, and that have been used to judge QoL, although he cautioned against interpreting the behaviors as positive or negative without other evidence to support the judgment (e.g., confabulation). Albert and colleagues (1996) suggested that whether or not a person has dementia, one's subjective experience is not observable or directly accessible to others.

Proxy Informants Due to the frequent assumption that persons with cognitive impairments are unreliable informants, proxy informants have often been recruited to complete QoL assessments. Proxy informants can be family members, friends, or professional caregivers who know the client well. Proxy informants are asked to report what they believe to be true for the individual's QoL. The equivalence of proxy ratings and self-reports has been studied with samples of individuals with a variety of diseases and neurological disorders; proxies are consistently found to be more negative than the person with the disease (Andersen, Vahle, & Lollar, 2001; Dorman, Waddell, Slattery, Dennis, & Sandercock, 1997b; Epstein, Hall, Tognetti, Son, & Conant, 1989; Hays et al., 1995; Justice, Rabeneck, Hays, Wu, & Bozzette, 1999; Magaziner, Simonsick, Kashner, & Hebel, 1988; Novella, Jochum, et al., 2001; Pierre, Wood-Dauphinee, Korner-Bitensky, Gayton, & Hanley, 1998; Sneeuw, Aaronson, de Haan, & Limburg, 1997; Spranger & Aaronson, 1992; Viitanen, Fugl-Meyer, Bernspang, & Fugl-Meyer, 1988; Wu et al., 1997). Epstein and colleagues (1989) found that proxies tend to give more weight to negative information than to positive information. Unfortunately, proxy informants tend to overestimate the cognitive abilities of persons with dementia and to underestimate their emotional well-being (Bourgeois, Dijkstra, & Hickey, 2005a; Burke, Rubin,

Morris, & Berg, 1998; Hickey & Bourgeois, 2000; Miller, 1980). Teri and Wagner (1991) found that family caregivers rated persons with dementia as more depressed than clinicians, and both proxy groups rated the persons with dementia as more depressed than the care recipients rated themselves. Similar results were found in nursing homes (Berlowitz, Du, Kazis, & Lewis, 1995; Thapa & Rowland, 1989). On the other hand, proxy informants are fairly accurate in their estimate of physical abilities of persons with neurological disorders (Dorman et al., 1997; Hays et al., 1995; Sneeuw et al., 1995; Wu et al.). Consequently, greater patient–proxy concordance has been reported for objective QoL domains, such as health and functional status, than for subjective ones, such as self-esteem, life satisfaction, and emotional well-being (Novella, Ankri, et al., 2001; Sanifort, Becker, & Diamond, 1996).

More recently, Kane et al. (2005) found that family proxy reports were statistically significantly correlated with nursing home residents' reports of QoL on the domains of comfort, functional competence, privacy, dignity, meaningful activity, security, and autonomy, but not enjoyment or relationships. Staff proxy reports were statistically significantly correlated with resident reports on all domains except dignity and relationships. Despite these statistically significant results, the low correlations suggest that proxy reports should not be used as a substitute for self-report. Additionally, family member proxies and clinician proxies provide different responses. Cheng and Chan (2006) found that family members provide more valid responses on items related to less observable items of the QoL-AD (e.g., usual activities, and anxiety and depression), whereas clinicians provide more valid responses on more observable items of the QoL-AD (e.g., mobility and self-care). Novella and colleagues (Novella, Ankri, et al., 2001) found a less clear-cut discrepancy between family and staff proxies; spouses' and nurses' responses showed more agreement with participants than children's and nursing assistants' responses. Thus, one must consider the type of tool being used, or the type of proxy available, and choose the tool and proxy accordingly, or use more than one type of proxy in order to obtain a broader perspective on the individual's QoL.

There are a number of proxy factors to consider in QoL assessment. The health status, education, and understanding of the proxy must be considered. Additionally, the nature of the relationship and amount of time spent between the proxy and the person with dementia must be considered (Thorgrimsen et al., 2003; Zimmerman & Magaziner, 1994). The lack of concordance between patient and proxy ratings in nursing home settings may be related to the amount and quality of their verbal and social interactions. Communication difficulties impede social interaction and constrain participation in self-reported QoL measurements (Brod et al., 1999). When residents do not express themselves clearly, caregivers often misinterpret what they are trying to communicate. Thus, caregivers often do not understand the subtleties of the persons' feelings (Zimmerman & Magaziner). This lack of concordance may also be compounded by the lack of insight into deficits often seen in persons with dementia (Reed, Jagust, & Coulter, 1993; Sevush & Leve, 1993).

Some elderly family members may not be good proxy raters secondary to their own failing health. Other problems with proxy reports in intervention studies include increased random error and reduced power, increased bias, and decreased outcomes (Dorman et. al., 1997b). However, the bias would not be expected to affect the direction of the treatment effect or its statistical significance, but it may affect the clinical significance of outcome measures (Sneeuw et. al., 1997). Proxy reports should be used conservatively secondary to the substantially different information provided (Dorman et. al., 1997b; Hays et. al., 1995). One possible solution to the problem of proxy bias is calibration of proxy measures (Wu et. al., 1997). Another suggestion, which needs to be evaluated, is to train proxies to find out about their care recipients' perceived QoL through structured conversations prior to completing QoL measures (Bourgeois, Dijkstra, & Hickey, 2005b). Kane (2005) reported that proxy reports should not be used in place of self-report, but as additional information.

Generic Versus Disease-Specific Measures Elders have been noted to not respond to items that do not pertain to them, and this is particularly the case for those items having to do with strenuous physical activity (Hobson & Meara, 1997). Individuals who have severe physical disabilities are noted to have more missing data in their self-reports of HR-QOL (van Straten et al., 1997). Furthermore, it is questionable if the studies on the healthy elderly can be generalized to the neurologically impaired population because many studies exclude those with cognitive and/or communicative impairments (e.g., Hobson & Meara, 1997; van Straten et al.; Viitanen et al., 1988; Wyller et al., 1997, 1998). Because many instruments assume intact cognitive abilities, their utility in assessing persons with dementia is questionable (Albert, 1997). Floor effects in measurement instruments are common for this population because of the severely reduced activity of individuals with moderate to severe dementia. In some research (Novella, Jochum, et al., 2001), however, persons with dementia have successfully completed generic health-related quality of life measures, such as the Duke Health Profile (Parkerson, Broadhead, & Tse, 1990).

Specific problems arise in assessment of QOL in elders when considering the institutionalized population, such as response bias due to social desirability, missing data due to irrelevant items, and the aforementioned issues related to the cognitive and communicative deficits that are so prevalent in the institutionalized population (Philp et. al., 1989). Particularly when using self-report, it is difficult to know if a participant misunderstood an item or deemed it irrelevant, or if he or she did not respond because the item relates to an ability that cannot be conducted at all. This has been a problem for instruments that were developed for the younger adult population and then used on the elderly population, particularly in the areas of work and physical exertion (Hobson & Meara, 1997). Several researchers have favored disease-specific tools for the increased specificity (Hobson & Meara; Howard & Rockwood, 1995; Williams, 1998).

The ideal dementia-specific QoL instrument would have appropriate validity, reliability, and sensitivity. In addition, sensitivity to changing status is important in order to determine if persons with dementia perceive their QoL to change with declining physical and/or cognitive abilities, or with interventions designed to improve participation, engagement, and QoL. Recently, a few instruments have been developed for use with persons with cognitive and communicative disorders, which has allowed for comparison of self-report versus proxy report with persons with dementia and their caregivers (e.g., Brod, 1998; Logsdon et al., 1999; Rabins et al., 1999; Selai et al., 2000). However, interpreting the responses of persons with communication and cognitive deficits remains a challenge. The validity and reliability of responses are often questioned, as patients may demonstrate fatigue, distractibility, or misunderstanding during assessment.

QoL Instruments for Persons With Dementia

There are an overwhelming number of QoL assessment tools. See Table 8.1 for a listing of some examples of instruments. For the past decade, researchers have focused on developing QoL assessment instruments specifically for persons with dementia so that they may provide self-report responses; several clinical researchers have emphasized that the individual's perspective is essential in QoL

TABLE 8.1 Examples of Generic and Dementia-Specific Quality of Life Instruments That Measure Single or Multiple Domains

Generic Instruments

Single Domain

Duke Health Profile (Parkerson, Broadhead, & Tse, 1990)
Pleasant Events Schedule (MacPhillamy & Lewinsohn, 1982; Teri & Lewinsohn, 1982)
Unpleasant Events Schedule (Lewinsohn, Mermeistein, Alexander, & MacPhillamy, 1985; Teri & Lewinsohn, 1982)
Geriatric Depression Scale (GDS; Yesavage et al., 1983); GDS-4, GDS-15 (Bohac, Smith, & Rummans, 1996; Isella, Villa, & Appollonio, 2005; Sheikh & Yesavage, 1986)
Satisfaction With Life Scale (Diener, Emmons, Larson, & Griffin, 1985)
Quality of Communication Life Scale (Paul-Brown, Frattali, Holland, Thompson, & Caperton, 2004)

Multiple Domains

Life Satisfaction Index A and B (Neugarten, Havighurst, & Tobin, 1961)
Life Satisfaction in the Elderly (Salamon, 1988)
Life Satisfaction Instrument–Z (Wood, Wylie, & Sheafor, 1969)
Philadelphia Geriatric Center Morale Scale (Lawton, 1975)
Quality of Well-Being Scale (Kaplan, Bush, & Berry, 1976)
MOS Functioning and Well-Being Profile (Stewart et al., 1992)
Functional Status Questionnaire (Jette et al., 1986)
Multidimensional Functional Multilevel Assessment Instrument (Lawton, Moss, Fulcomer, & Kleban, 1992)
EuroQoL–5D (EQ-5D; EuroQoL Group, 1990)
WHOQOL–Brief (WHOQOL Group, 1998a)
WHOQOL–100 (WHOQOL Group, 1998b)

Individualized Instruments

Schedule for the Evaluation of Individual Quality of Life (SEIQoL; O'Boyle et al., 1993)
Patient Generated Index (PGI; Ruta, Garratt, Leng, Russell, & MacDonald, 1994)
Subjective Domains of Quality of Life Measure (SDQLM; Amir, Bar-On, & Penso, 1996; Coen et al., 1993)

Dementia Specific

Self-Report

Quality of Life–AD (QOL–AD; Logsdon, Gibbons, McCurry, & Teri, 2000)

TABLE 8.1 (Continued)

Generic Instruments
Dementia Specific
Quality of Life Assessment Schedule (QOLAS; Selai, Trimble, Rossor, & Harvey, 2000)
Dementia Quality of Life Scale (DQoL; Brod, Steward, Sands, & Walton, 1999)
Proxy Report
Alzheimer Disease Related Quality of Life (ADRQL; Rabins, Kasper, Kleinman, Black, & Patrick, 2000)
Clinical Dementia Rating Scale (CDR; Sano, Albert, Tractenberg, & Schittini, 2000)
Observational Tools
Philadelphia Geriatric Center Affect Rating Scale (Lawton, Van Haitsma, & Klapper, 1996)
Apparent Affect Rating Scale (AARS; Lawton, Van Haitsma, Perkinson, & Ruckdeschel, 1999)
Multidimensional Observational Scale for Elderly Subjects (MOSES; Helmes, Csapo, & Short, 1987)
Vienna List (Porzsolt et al., 2004)
Pleasant Events Schedule–AD (PES-AD; Teri & Logsdon, 1991)
Dementia Care Mapping (Bradford Dementia Group, 1997)

measurement (e.g., Whitehouse, Patterson, & Sami, 2003). Given that there is not yet a "gold standard" measure for persons with dementia, researchers often choose instruments from a variety of dementia-specific tools and generic tools available for the elderly population. The specific choice of instrument is dependent upon the purpose for assessment, the examiner's perspective on QoL conceptualization, and the characteristics of participants. Regardless, the above factors must be considered in choosing QoL assessment tools: single versus multiple domains, subjective versus objective judgments, self-report versus proxy report, individual versus common, and generic versus disease specific.

Dementia-Specific Tools Several of the instruments that have been developed to obtain self-report from persons with dementia may also be used for proxy report, such as the Dementia Quality of Life Scale (DQoL; Brod et al., 1999), the Quality of Life–Alzheimer's Disease Scale (QoL-AD; Logsdon et al., 1999), and the Quality of Life Assessment Schedule (QOLAS; Selai et al., 2000). Other scales were developed as proxy measures, for example, the Alzheimer Disease Related Quality of Life Scale (ADRQL; Rabins et al., 1999), which results in a global score for QoL by summing five domain scores: social interaction, awareness of self, enjoyment of activities, feelings and mood, and response to surroundings.

The QoL-AD (Logsdon et al., 1999) was based on a literature review of quality of life in dementia, and contains 13 items that are scored on a 4-point Likert-type scale: physical health, energy, mood, living situation, memory, family, marriage, friends, chores, fun, money, self, and life as a whole. The developers for this scale reported acceptable reliability and validity for both self-report and proxy report. Reliability and validity were further investigated by Thorgrimsen and colleagues (2003) by comparing the QoL-AD with the DQoL (Brod et al., 1999), the EQ-5D (EuroQoL Group, 1990), and well-being observations during dementia care mapping (DCM; Bradford Dementia Group, 1997), as well as gathering perspectives of persons with dementia and caregivers (family and staff) in focus groups. Results revealed that the QoL-AD has good validity and reliability, even for persons with severe cognitive deficits (MMSE < 10). The QoL-AD has also demonstrated sensitivity to change (Selwood et al., 2005; Thorgrimsen et al.). Furthermore, results were consistent with previous research on QoL in persons with dementia: QoL is highly subjective, but persons with dementia are able to provide self-report, and this self-report is generally more positive than caregivers' proxy reports. QoL scores were also significantly correlated with depression scores, but not with cognitive scores. Given its ease of administration over a wide range of dementia severity and its strong psychometric properties, the QoL-AD has become a very popular tool in clinical research internationally (Whitehouse et al., 2003).

The DQoL was based on results of three caregiver focus groups who identified domains that are important to persons with dementia. The DQoL contains 29 items that are scored on a 5-point Likert scale that result in an overall score and 5 subscale scores: self-esteem, positive affect, negative affect, feelings of belonging, and sense of aesthetics. The DQoL has acceptable reliability and validity for persons with mild to moderate cognitive deficits (MMSE > 11). Thorgrimsen and colleagues (2003) found that participants with MMSE scores below 10 had difficulty completing the DQoL, although they did pass the screening tool provided with the instrument. In a follow-up study of those participants, Selwood and colleagues (2005) again found that the DQoL was more difficult for participants to complete than the QoL-AD was.

Observational Measures Observational measures have their own limitations. The Philadelphia Geriatric Center Affect Rating Scale (Lawton, Van Haitsma, & Klapper, 1996) is completed by a clinician after a 10-minute observation period, during which the duration of affective states (pleasure, anger, anxiety or fear, sadness, interest, and contentment) is rated on a 5-point scale. Using this tool, Lawton and colleagues found that persons with dementia express less positive affect than other nursing home residents. Later, Lawton, Van Haitsma, Perkinson, and Ruckdeschel (1999) refined this tool to develop the Apparent Affect Rating Scale, in which residents' facial expressions and body language are rated during structured 5-minute observations for evidence of happiness, anger, anxiety, and engagement. A measure of behaviors that have the potential to contribute to pleasant experiences of patients with dementia is the Pleasant Events Schedule–AD (PES-AD; Teri & Logsdon, 1991). This caregiver-completed inventory of pleasant experiences rates each of 54 items on their frequency, availability, and enjoyability during the past month. The Multidimensional Observational Scale for Elderly Subjects (MOSES; Helmes, Csapo, & Short, 1987) is an observational tool in which a caregiver reports the frequency, over the past one week, of several items (e.g., how often the resident speaks of being sad, looks sad, shows signs of sadness like tears, expresses interest in the outside world, responds to contact from other residents, and initiates contacts with other residents).

Dementia Care Mapping (Bradford Dementia Group, 1997) was developed to provide observational ratings of articulation, feeding, social withdrawal, passive engagement, walking, and a number of indicators of well-being. Porzsolt et al. (2004) developed the Vienna List, a 41-item observational checklist to assess persons with severe dementia in the following domains: communication, aggression, expression of negative feelings, mobility, and possibilities of bodily contact. Trained raters complete the checklist based on a maximum 2-minute observation period, using a 5-point Likert scale. The Vienna List reportedly has satisfactory validity and reliability (Porzsolt et al., 2004; Richter, Schwarz, Eisemann, & Bauer, 2003). In addition, Richter, Schwarz, Eisemann, and Bauer (2004) found that the Vienna List was useful in documenting outcomes of a geriatric rehabilitation unit; they also found that it was less time-consuming and more practical than some instruments.

Observational measures have the potential to document change in patients' positive affect and/or experiences and may be useful outcome measures for interventions. However, Kane (2003) warned that this approach is difficult to implement due to staffing considerations and the possible rarity of the behaviors being observed. Observers require training to provide valid and reliable ratings, and the likelihood of observing the target behaviors during a brief observation period may be quite low. Furthermore, Kane stated that "observation of QOL cannot be limited to the working day and week; residents' lives are shaped by what happens or does not happen in the long stretches of time when outsiders are absent" (p. 35).

Generic Tools Some tools that were developed for generic use may be useful, but others may be too difficult or may not discriminate well enough for use with persons with dementia. Use of the EQ-5D with persons with dementia does not appear to be recommended, given poor discrimination among those with varying QoL scores (Thorgrimsen et al., 2003) and difficulty completing the measure (Silberfeld et al., 2002). Despite this difficulty, persons with dementia are able to identify QoL domains that are lacking in generic QoL instruments.

The Geriatric Depression Scale (GDS; Yesavage et al., 1983) is frequently used in nursing homes. Given the relationship of depression and QoL, clinicians may use this as a single-domain QoL instrument. Several short forms of the GDS have been developed with variable psychometric properties (Aikman & Oehlert, 2000; Almeida & Almeida, 1999; Bohac, Smith, & Rummans, 1996; Sheikh & Yesavage, 1986). Isella, Villa, and Appollonio (2005) examined the utility of the short forms to screen and quantify depression in persons with mild to moderate dementia. Results supported the use of the GDS-4 for screenings and the GDS-15 for evaluation of severity. Some researchers caution that there may be a positive response bias in persons with MMSE scores less than 18 (Bédard et al., 2003).

Finally, there is one quality of communication life scale, the Quality of Communication Life Scale (QCL; Paul-Brown, Frattali, Holland, Thompson, & Caperton, 2004), available that has been preliminarily tested with persons with dementia. The QCL measures "the extent to which a person's communication acts, as constrained within the boundaries drawn by personal and environmental factors, allow meaningful participation in life situations" (Paul-Brown et al., 2004, p. 8). Because communication disorders are a reality of dementia, it is important to assess how communication difficulties may affect the resident's quality of life. The QCL was designed to be completed independently by adults with acquired neurological communication disorders. Bourgeois, Dijkstra, and Hickey (2005b) found that persons with dementia were able to reliably complete the instrument when the examiner sat with the residents, read the instructions, gave sufficient time for residents to respond, and gave appropriate prompts for the resident to respond, as needed; ongoing research is investigating the relationship of proxy and resident responses.

INTERVENTIONS DESIGNED TO IMPROVE QUALITY OF LIFE

Interventions are called for that promote dignity and respect, and improve quality of life by enhancing quality of interactions and activities, not just quantity (Butler, 2002; Calkins, 2003; Kane, 2001, 2003; Seman, 2005). (See Seman's article for a detailed discussion of the definition of dignity and suggestions for providing care that focuses on dignity.) In designing intervention, clinicians should make efforts to understand clients' and caregivers' perspectives on quality of life and quality of care. Using the methods described above, clinicians can gain this understanding for treatment planning and use quality of life outcomes for documentation of treatment goals. Unfortunately, persons in the late stages of dementia are rarely able to participate in goal setting; caregivers must use knowledge about persons' likes and dislikes from past history. A clinician who is new to a person with late-stage dementia should rely on as many sources of information as possible: family, friends, and staff at all levels. For instance, in the second author's clinical experience, the cleaning and maintenance staff often have astute observations about a resident whom they have known for long periods of time, and may be able to provide insights that other staff are not. Interventions in the late stage of dementia should be designed to increase quality of life. The findings that depression and anxiety were related to QoL (Selwood et al., 2005) and that persons with more severe dementia have lower QoL (Albert et al., 2001) could be important for justifying interventions that aim to improve QoL; we cannot change cognition, but we may be able to increase pleasant events, decrease depression and anxiety, increase comfort and decrease pain, and provide emotional and spiritual support.

Several clinical researchers suggest policy changes to improve the environment of residential facilities. Such intervention strategies will be discussed (e.g., staff training). Some of the interventions to be described in this chapter have been discussed previously in chapter 6. Whereas the focus in that chapter was largely on increasing activities and participation, the focus here will be on implementation in the late stages of dementia to increase quality of life. Intervention strategies such as multisensory stimulation and environmental approaches are also relevant for those in late stages of dementia, but may need to be modified so as not to be overly stimulating or complex. Snoezelen, Simple Pleasures, and Simulated Presence are interventions that were discussed previously, and will be discussed further here. See chapter 6, however, for information on aromatherapy, music therapy, and spirituality for persons in the late stages of dementia.

Policy and Staff Approaches

Several clinicians and researchers have suggested that institutional changes are needed in policy, staff training, and staff support in order to provide care that is person centered, so that we may enhance quality of life and treat each person with dementia with dignity (Calkins, 2003; Coon, Mace, & Weaverdyck, 1996; Kane, 2003; Mitchell & Kemp, 2000; Seman, 2005). Seman emphasized the importance of examining our own values and definition of dignity, as well as considering others' values and definitions. A shared understanding may promote staff selection of creative interventions for each individual's strengths and needs. Seman also suggested that staff efforts should focus not on managing a person's behaviors but on meeting needs and, ultimately, supporting dignity. Coon et al. (1996) suggested that federal and state regulations and building codes and mandates need to be changed to increase choice, control, and individuality, thereby improving QoL, in long-term care.

Kane (2001, 2003) reported that institutional policies often conflict with providing an atmosphere for improved QoL, and that a priority shift is needed in nursing home care. She suggested that new staff configurations and more staff training related to QoL assessment and intervention are needed. Kane (2001) identified a number of areas in which quality of care could be improved to enhance quality of life, many of which are currently low priority due to current regulations: (a) sense of safety, security, and order; (b) physical comfort; (c) enjoyment; (d) meaningful activity; (e) relationships; (f) functional competence; (g) dignity; (h) privacy; (i) individuality; (j) autonomy and choice; and (k) spiritual well-being. Some suggestions to target these areas that are relevant in late-stage dementia care included breaking down the rigidity of routines, fostering more normal and natural relationships between staff and residents, permitting spontaneity, individualizing end-of-life care and rituals to mark death, and empowering nursing assistants.

Likewise, Mitchell and Kemp (2000) made many suggestions that could improve the atmosphere of institutions, thereby improving the QoL of residents. Specifically, a more homelike and warm environment with less conflict and more family and social involvement were the keys to contented residents and QoL. They suggested that this requires one-on-one time between staff and residents. Suggestions for administrators included hiring staff with good interpersonal skills and warm personalities, and communicating the message that spending time with residents is indeed part of a staff member's job. In order to create an atmosphere in which staff feel comfortable in fulfilling this role, Mitchell and Kemp suggested the following:

> (a) developing training and educational programs that emphasize the role of the social environment and how to create it; (b) developing and providing manuals of best practices that illustrate how social climates have been created in other facilities; (c) encouraging facilities to build smaller homes, or clusters of homes in a large facilities, instead of one large facility, as increased bed size was correlated with higher levels of conflict; and (d) including a statement about developing QOL in the licensing requirements similar to those statements that emphasize the importance of resident autonomy. (p. P125)

Although their research focused on assisted living facilities, these suggestions could be just as important in caring for persons with late-stage dementia who are less mobile and less communicative, therefore requiring staff to initiate one-on-one contact.

Recommendations for staff training have also been proposed by Bourgeois, Dijkstra, and Hickey (2005a). Training caregivers to improve their communicative interactions with residents with dementia has the potential to change quality of life perceptions of both residents and caregivers (e.g., Bourgeois, Dijkstra, Burgio, & Allen-Burge, 1999; McCallion, Toseland, Lacey, & Banks, 1999). As will be noted in chapter 10, a communication training program resulted in increases in the quantity and quality of communicative interactions between residents with dementia and staff (Allen-Burge, Burgio, Bourgeois, Sims, & Nunnikhoven, 2001; Bourgeois et al., 1999, 2001). Trained skills were maintained by nursing aides in the treatment group throughout the postintervention and 3-month follow-up phases (Bourgeois et al., 2004). There were no effects of the communication intervention on residents' self-rating of depression, but the proxy depression scores decreased from pre- to post intervention in the treatment group only. Staff talked more in common areas and in one-on-one conversations with residents with lower MMSE scores. Increased talking on the part of the nursing aide was thought to be related to their own level of comfort in a conversation with someone with a communication impairment; when residents had difficulty expressing themselves, spoke in a confused manner, or did not initiate conversation, nursing aides took control of the conversation and spoke more than the residents. These findings are consistent with those of Hoerster, Hickey, and Bourgeois (2001), who found that staff talked more and asked more questions of residents who were less able to communicate effectively due to greater cognitive impairments. This may then lead to the misinterpretation of impaired communication as a reflection of depression. It appears, however, that when trained staff members have better opportunities for communicative interactions under conditions of increased social closeness, they have an increased awareness of their residents' feelings. Bourgeois et al., (2005b) presented preliminary evidence that providing opportunities to converse about quality of life topics, using written prompts, improved nursing aides' ratings of the quality of life of their residents. Similarly, McCallion et al. (1999) found significant differences between treatment and control nursing aide ratings of resident depression following a communication skills program.

Sensory Stimulation Approaches

Snoezelen® Appropriate environmental stimulation for persons in the late stages of dementia is the core of Snoezelen®. This intervention stems from the belief that all individuals need stimulation and recreation (Baker et al., 2001; Baker, Dowling, Wareing, Dawson, & Assey, 1997; Brown, 1999; Verkaik, van Weert, & Francke, 2005). Snoezelen® is a multisensory experience combining stimuli such as soft lighting, mirror balls, spot lights, optic fiber sprays or panels, bubble machines, gentle music, a variety of tactile surfaces and aromatherapy, vibrating pads, and comfortable cushions. Snoezelen® is designed to achieve several goals: to gently stimulate the primary senses (sight, touch, hearing, and smell), to provide a secure and unrestrained environment, and to allow relaxation. The role of staff in Snoezelen® is to facilitate physical contact or other interaction with the stimuli, based on the individual's preferences and pace. The idea is to provide pleasurable activities without any pressure.

Snoezelen® reportedly improves quality of life of residents with severe dementia by providing a meaningful activity without requiring intellectual reasoning or verbal responses (Brown, 1999). Verkaik et al. (2005) suggested that it is the noncognitive theory and individualized approach to clients' needs that make this treatment successful in improving clients' well-being. Literature reviews that included use of Snoezelen® for persons with dementia (Lancioni, Cuvo, & O'Reilly, 2002; Livingston, Johnston, & Katona, 2005; Verkaik et al.) revealed that Snoezelen® often has immediate within-session effects on aspects of improved QoL; however, better quality research is needed to determine longer-term effects. People in the late stages of dementia demonstrated increased engagement and reduced apathy during Snoezelen® sessions, as compared to baseline (Holtkamp, Kragt, Van Dongen, Van Rossum, & Salentijn, 1997; Hope, 1998; Kragt, Holtkamp, Van Dongen, Van Rossum, & Salentijn, 1997; Moffat, Barker, Pinkney, Garside, & Freeman, 1993; Pinkney, 1997; Spaull, Leach, & Frampton, 1998). There have also been reports of positive immediate postsession effects on social and emotional measures, with inconclusive evidence for generalized long-term outcomes (Moffat et al., 1993; Spaull et al., 1998). Baker et al. reported immediate within-session effects of Snoezelen® on language and memory and attentiveness to the environment, as well as positive longer-term effects on social and emotional measures, as compared to persons with dementia who received typical activities programs. However, Lancioni et al. (2002) cautioned clinicians that several of the studies (Baker et al.; Hope; Moffat et al.) also reported that some persons actually had behavioral deterioration and had to be removed from the Snoezelen® intervention program. Baillon, van Diepen, and Prettyman (2005) also found individual differences in responses to Snoezelen®. Lancioni et al. drew three conclusions from their review of Snoezelen®: There may be positive within-session effects on the withdrawal behaviors of persons with dementia, a stimulus-preference screening may further increase within-session effects and decrease negative effects, and increasing within-session effects may be important for improving postsession outcomes.

Lancioni et al. (2002) suggested that many facilities may not be able to provide a complete Snoezelen® room, due to cost and space limitations; however, the preference screening may allow staff to provide "mini-Snoezelen" experiences in a more practical way. A preference screening (i.e., sensory likes/dislikes) was used in combination with staff training (i.e., four weekly training sessions plus homework, and provision of a Snoezelen® manual) in a 24-hour Snoezelen® approach to dementia care in several nursing homes (van Weert, van Dulmen, & Spreeuwenberg, 2005c). Results revealed many positive, generalized benefits in terms of decreases in problem behaviors. This study and others by van Weert and colleagues have revealed many positive benefits of the use of Snoezelen® during morning care routines, with significant changes in indicators of residents' well-being and communication, as well as nursing assistants' job satisfaction and quality of care. Results revealed that staff used a person-centered approach to care when they implemented Snoezelen® (van Weert, Janssen, & van Dulmen, 2006). In addition, trained CNAs demonstrated improved communication behaviors with residents (e.g., increased resident-directed gaze, affective touch, smiling, and amount of social conversation), and residents also demonstrated increased smiling and CNA-directed eye gaze, and less negative verbal behaviors after trained CNAs began using Snoezelen® during morning care (van Weert, van Dulmen, & Spreeuwenberg, 2005a). Finally, nursing assistants who use Snoezelen® during morning care, as compared to those providing routine care, reported many improvements in work quality in areas such as time pressure, perceived problems, stress reactions and emotional exhaustion, contact with residents, and overall job satisfaction (van Weert, van Dulmen, & Spreeuwenberg, 2005b). As was suggested by Kane (2001), policy and organizational changes are necessary for staff to be able to implement the trained interventions effectively (van Weert, Kerkstra, & van Dulmen, 2004).

Simple Pleasures Simple Pleasures is a therapeutic recreation activity that is designed to reduce isolation, inactivity, and agitation (Buettner, 1999; Kolanowski, Buettner, Costa, & Litaker, 2001). Simple Pleasures provide age- and stage-appropriate recreational items for nursing home residents, which consist of a variety of sensorimotor recreational items. Some items encourage active engagement (e.g., activity apron, electronic busy box, and look inside purse), which may be more useful for persons in middle stages of dementia, and others may increase comfort (e.g., a muff for hand warming, and a hot water bottle cover). Buettner (1999) found that the items for comfort and heat were very frequently chosen by residents, which may reflect the Need-Driven Dementia Compromised Behavior Model (Algase et al., 1996). Decreased patient agitation and improved family visiting were documented when the residents were given Simple Pleasures (Buettner, 1997, 1999).

Simulated Presence As persons with severe dementia lose interest in, and perhaps become agitated by, familiar television or radio programs or movies, an alternative is homemade audiotapes or videotapes made specifically for the individual with dementia; for example, family members may tape themselves talking to their relative, which provides a "simulated presence" (Woods & Ashley, 1995). A personalized, interactive audiotape that contains references to preserved memories is made by the family, and concentrates on two to three themes, repeated in different ways (e.g., important life events, loved ones, hobbies, and interests). Family members are encouraged to use phrases of affection. The tape is edited and silent pauses are added, so the resident has the opportunity to respond to the tape. Persons in late stages of dementia may not respond, but these pauses may be helpful in allowing enough processing time for the messages in the tape. The familiar voices and messages may increase comfort and quality of life. Woods and Ashley reported decreased social isolation and agitation in the residents who participated, and recommended "simulated presence" for nursing home residents who respond well to family and other familiar people. Alternatively, videotapes could be made by family members, and may also include stories, songs, or activities. A family video could be a useful tool for staff to use to comfort or redirect a confused or agitated resident.

CASE 8.1 ILLUSTRATION OF MEMORY BOOK TO IMPROVE QUALITY OF LIFE AT THE END OF LIFE

Mrs. MacDonald, the spouse of a man with Alzheimer's disease who resided in a long-term care facility, observed that other nursing home residents had memory books and decided that her husband should have one too. The SLP conducted a functional, dynamic assessment. Although she and other team members questioned whether he would benefit from intervention based on the severity of his cognitive deficits, a memory book was constructed using large photos from Mr. MacDonald's childhood and young adult years, accompanied by simple words and phrases in large print. The SLP instructed the staff and the client's wife regarding the use of the memory book. She also instructed them to use Simple Pleasures activities, to which Mr. MacDonald responded positively during assessment. Mrs. MacDonald reported that her husband really liked the book and the Simple Pleasures activities, and that their visits were much more satisfying now. The SLP asked, "How do you know when he likes something?" She reported, "He smiles and hums while we're using them! He makes happy noises!" The SLP learned that even persons with severe cognitive-communicative deficits benefit from skilled services to design quality life enhancing interventions.

REFERENCES

Achterberg, W., Pot, A., Kerkstra, A., Ooms, M., Muller, M., & Ribbe, M. (2003). The effect of depression on social engagement in newly admitted Dutch nursing home residents. *The Gerontologist*, *43*(2), 213–218.

Adkins, E. R. H. (1993). Quality of life after stroke: exposing a gap in nursing literature. *Rehabilitation Nursing*, *18*(3), 144–147.

Aikman, G. G., & Oehlert, M. E. (2000). Geriatric Depression Scale: Long form versus short form. *Clinical Gerontologist*, *22*, 63–70.

Albert, S. M. (1997). Assessing health-related quality of life in chronic care populations. In J. Teresi, M. P. Lawton, D. Holmes, & M. Ory (Eds.), *Measurement in elderly chronic care populations*. New York: Springer.

Albert, S. M, Castillo-Castaneda, C., Sano, M., Jacobs, D. M, Marder, K., Bell, K., et al. (1996). Quality of life in patients with Alzheimer's disease as reported by patient proxies. *Journal of the American Geriatrics Society*, *44*, 1342–1347.

Albert, S. M., Jacobs, D. M., Sano, M., Marder, K., Bell, K., Devanand, D., et al. (2001). Longitudinal study of quality of life in people with advanced Alzheimer's disease. *American Journal of Geriatric Psychiatry*, *9*(2), 160–168.

Algase, D. L., Beck, C., Kolanowski, A., Whall, A., Berent, S., Richards, K., et al. (1996). Need-driven dementia-compromised behavior: An alternative view of disruptive behavior. *American Journal of Alzheimer's Disease*, *11*, 10–19.

Allen-Burge, R., Burgio, L., Bourgeois, M., Sims, R., & Nunnikhoven, J. (2001). Increasing communication among nursing home residents. *Journal of Clinical Geropsychology*, *7*, 213–230.

Allison, P. J., Locker, D., & Feine, J. S. (1997). Quality of life: A dynamic construct. *Social Science in Medicine*, *45*(2), 221–230.

Almeida, O. P., & Almeida, S. A. (1999). Short versions of the Geriatric Depression Scale: A study of their validity for the diagnosis of a major depressive episode according to ICD-10 and DSM-IV. *International Journal of Geriatric Psychiatry*, *14*, 858–865.

Amir, M., Bar-On, D., & Penso, R. (1996). Positive-Negative Evaluation (PNE) scale: A new dimension of the subjective domains of quality of life measure. *Quality of Life Research*, *5*, 73–80.

Andersen, E. M., Vahle, V. J., & Lollar, D. (2001). Proxy reliability: Health-related quality of life (HRQoL) measures for people with disability. *Quality of Life Research*, *10*, 609–619.

Baillon, S., van Diepen, E., & Prettyman, R. (2005). Variability in response of older people with dementia to both Snoezelen and reminiscence. *British Journal of Occupational Therapy*, *68*(8), 367–374.

Baker, R., Baell, S., Baker, E., Gibson, S., Holloway, J., Pearce, R., et al. (2001). A randomized controlled trial of the effects of multi-sensory stimulation (MSS) for people with dementia. *British Journal of Clinical Psychology*, *40*, 81–96.

Baker, R., Dowling, Z., Wareing, L. A., Dawson, J., & Assey, J. (1997). Snoezelen: Its long-term and short-term effects on older people with dementia. *British Journal of Occupational Therapy*, 60, 213–218.

Bédard, M., Molloy, D., Squire, L., Minthorn-Biggs, M-B., Dubois, S., Lever, J., et al. (2003). Validity of self-reports in dementia research: The Geriatric Depression Scale. *Clinical Gerontologist*, *26*(3/4), 155–163.

Berlowitz, D., Du, W., Kazis, L., & Lewis, S. (1995). Health-related quality of life or nursing home residents: Differences in patient and provider perceptions. *Journal of the American Geriatrics Society*, *43*, 799–802.

Bohac, D. L., Smith, G. E., & Rummans, T. R. (1996). Sensitivity, specificity and predictive value of the Geriatric Depression Scale-Short Form (GDS-SF) among cognitively impaired elderly. *Archives of Clinical Neuropsychology*, *11*, 370(A).

Bourgeois, M., Dijkstra, K., Burgio, L., & Allen-Burge, R. (1999, November). Effective communication during care routines: A staff training program. Paper presented at the Gerontological Society of America conference, San Francisco, CA.

Bourgeois, M., Dijkstra, K., Burgio, L., & Allen-Burge, R. (2001). Memory aids as an augmentative and alternative communication strategy for nursing home residents with dementia. *Augmentative and Alternative Communication*, *17*, 196–210.

Bourgeois, M., Dijkstra, K., Burgio, L., & Allen, R. S. (2004). Communication skills training for nursing aides of residents with dementia: The impact of measuring performance. *Clinical Gerontologist*, *27*, 119–138.

Bourgeois, M., Dijkstra, K., & Hickey, E. (2005a). Impact of communicative interaction on measuring quality of life in dementia. *Journal of Medical Speech Language Pathology*, *13*, 37–50.

Bourgeois, M., Dijkstra, K., & Hickey, E. (2005b, November). Assessing quality of life in persons with dementia. Paper presented at the American Speech Language Hearing Association convention, San Diego, CA.

Bradford Dementia Group. (1997). *Evaluating dementia care: The DCM method* (7th ed.). Bradford, UK: University of Bradford.

Brandtstadter, J., & Greve, W. (1994). The aging self: Stabilizing and protective processes. *Developmental Review*, *14*(1), 52–80.

Brod, M. (1998). *Dementia Quality of Life Instrument*. San Francisco: Quintiles.

Brod, M., Steward, A. L., Sands, L., & Walton, P. (1999). Conceptualization and measurement of quality of life in dementia: The dementia quality of life instrument (DQoL). *The Gerontologist*, *39*, 25–35.

Brown, E. J. (1999). SNOEZELEN®. In L. Volicer & L. Bloom-Charette (Eds.), *Enhancing the quality of life in advanced dementia* (pp. 168–185). Philadelphia: Brunner/Mazel.

Browne, J. P., O'Boyle, C. A., McGee, H. M., Joyce, C. R. B., McDonald, N. J., O'Malley, K., et al. (1994). Individual quality of life in the healthy elderly. *Quality of Life Research*, *3*, 235–244.

Browne, J., O'Boyle, C., McGee, H., McDonald, N., & Joyce, C. (1997). Development of a direct weighting procedure for quality of life domains. *Quality of Life Research*, *6*, 301–309.

Buettner, L. (1997). *Simple Pleasures: A multi-level sensory motor intervention for nursing home residents with dementia*. Binghamton, NY: Binghamton University Press.

Buettner, L. (1999, January–February). Simple Pleasures: A multilevel sensorimotor intervention for nursing home residents with dementia. *American Journal of Alzheimer's Disease*, 41–52.

Burke, W. J., Rubin, E. H., Morris, J., & Berg, L. (1998). Symptoms of "depression" in senile dementia of the Alzheimer's type. *Alzheimer's Disease and Associated Disorders*, *2*, 356–362

Butler, R. (2002). Declaration of the rights of older persons. *The Gerontologist*, *42*(2), 152–153.

Calkins, M. (2003). Coming to consensus on "therapeutic." *Alzheimer's Care Quarterly*, *4*(2), 158–159.

Cheng, S., & Chan, A. (2006). Relationship with others and life satisfaction in later life: Do gender and widowhood make a difference? *Journal of Gerontology*, *61B*, P46–P53.

Coen, R., O'Mahony, D., O'Boyle, C., Joyce, C. R. B., Hiltbrunner, B., & Walsh, J. B. (1993). Measuring the quality of life of dementia patients using the Schedule for the Evaluation of Individual Quality of Life. *Irish Journal of Psychology*, *14*, 154–163.

Coon, D., Mace, N., & Weaverdyck, S. E. (1996). Resident Behavior/Life Qualiaty Inventory. In D. Coon & N. Mace (Eds.), *Quality of life in long-term care*. New York: Haworth Press.

Coons, D. H., & Mace, N. L. (1996). *Quality of life in long-term care*. New York: Haworth.

Cunningham, W. E., Burton, T. M., Hawes-Dawson, J., Kington, R. S., & Hays, R. D. (1999). Use of relevancy ratings by target respondents to develop health-related quality of life measures: An example with African-American elderly. *Quality of Life Research*, *8*, 749–768.

Dempster, M., & Donnelly, M. (2000). How well do elderly people complete individualized quality of life measures: An exploratory study. *Quality of Life Research*, *9*, 369–375.

Diener, E., Emmons, R., Larson, R., & Griffin, S. (1985). The Satisfaction with Life Scale. *Journal of Personality Assessment, 4*, 92–101.

Dorman, P., Waddell, F., Slattery; J., Dennis, M., & Sandercock, P. (1997a). Is the EuroQol a valid measure of health-related quality of life after stroke? *Stroke, 28*, 1876–1882.

Dorman, P. J., Waddell, F., Slattery, J., Dennis, M., & Sandercock, P. (1997b). Are proxy assessments of health status after stroke with the EuroQoL questionnaire feasible, accurate, and unbiased? *Stroke*, *28*(10), 1883–1887.

Epstein, A. M., Hall, J. A., Tognetti, J., Son, L. H., & Conant, L. J. (1989). Using proxies to evaluate quality of life: Can they provide valid information about patients' health status and satisfaction with medical care? *Medical Care*, *27*(Suppl. 3), S91–S98.

EuroQoL Group. (1990). EuroQoL: A new facility for the measurement of health related quality of life. *Health Policy*, *16*, 199–208.

Feinberg, L., & Whitlatch, C. (2001). Are persons with cognitive impairment able to state consistent choices? *The Gerontologist*, *41*(3), 374–382.

George, L. K., & Bearon, L. B. (1980). *Quality of Life in Older Persons: Meaning and measurement*. New York: Human Sciences.

Gerritsen, D., Steverink, N., Ooms, M., & Ribbe, M. (2004). Finding a useful conceptual basis for enhancing the quality of life of nursing home residents. *Quality of Life Research*, *13*, 611–624.

Gill, T. M., & Feinstein, A. R. (1994). A critical appraisal of the quality of quality-of-life measurements. *JAMA*, *272*, 619–625.

Goffman, E. (1961). *Asylums*. Harmondsworth, UK: Penguin.

Grainger, K. (1995). Communication and the institutionalized elderly. In J. F. Nussbaum & J. Coupland (Eds.), *Handbook of communication and aging research* (pp. 417–436). Mahwah, NJ: Lawrence Erlbaum.

Hays, R. D., Vickrey, B. G., Hermann, B. P., Perrine, K., Cramer, J., Meador, K., et al. (1995). Agreement between self reports and proxy reports of quality of life in epilepsy patients. *Quality of Life Research*, *4*, 159–168.

Helmes, E., Csapo, K. G., & Short, J. A. (1987). Standardization and validation of the Multidimensional Observational Scale for Elderly Subjects (MOSES). *Journal of Gerontology*, *42*, 395–405.

Hickey, E., & Bourgeois, M. (2000). Health-related quality of life (HR-QOL) in nursing home residents with dementia: Stability and relationships among measures. *Aphasiology*, *14*, 669–679.

Hickey, A. M., Bury, G., O'Boyle, C. A., Bradley, F., O'Kelly, F. D., & Shannon, W. (1996). A new short form individual quality of life measure (SEIQoL-DW): Application in a cohort of individuals with HIV/AIDS. *British Medical Journal*, *313*, 29–33.

Hobson, J. P., & Meara, R. J. (1997). Is the SF-36 health survey questionnaire suitable as a self-report measure of the health status of older adults with Parkinson's disease? *Quality of Life Research*, *6*, 213–216.

Hoe, J., Katona, C., Roche, B., & Livingston, G. (2005) Use of the QOL AD for measuring quality of life in people with severe dementia: The LASER-AD study. *Age and Ageing*, *34*, 130–135.

Hoerster, L., Hickey, E., & Bourgeois, M. (2001). Effects of memory aids on conversations between nursing home residents with dementia and nursing assistants. *Neuropsychological Rehabilitation*, *11*(3/4), 399–427.

Holtkamp, C., Kragt, K., Van Dongen, M., Van Rossum, E., & Salentijn, C. (1997). Effecten van snoezelen op het gedrag van demente ouderen (Effects of Snoezelen on the behavior of demented elderly). *Tijdschrift voor Gerontologi e en Geriatrie*, *28*, 124–128.

Hope, K. W. (1998). The effects of multisensory environments on older people with dementia. *Journal of Psychiatric and Mental Health Nursing*, *5*, 377–385.

Howard, K., & Rockwood, K. (1995). Quality of life in Alzheimer's disease. *Dementia*, *6*, 113–116.

Isella, V., Villa, M., & Appollonio, I. (2005). Screening and quantification of depression in mild-to-moderate dementia through the GDS short forms. *Clinical Gerontologist*, *24*(3/4), 115–125.

Jacelon, C. S. (1995). The effect of living in a nursing home on socialization in elderly people. *Journal of Advanced Nursing*, *22*, 539–546.

Jang, Y., Mortimer, J., Haley, W., & Graves, A. (2004). The role of social engagement in life satisfaction: Its significance among older individuals with disease and disability. *The Journal of Applied Gerontology*, *23*(3), 266–278.

Jette, A., Davies, A., Cleary, P., Callans, D., Rubenstein, L., Fink, A., Kosecoff, J., Young, R., Brook, R., & Delbanco, T. (1986). The Functional Status Questionnaire. *Journal of General Internal Medicine*, *1*, 143–149.

Justice, A. C., Rabeneck, L., Hays, R. D., Wu, A. W., & Bozzette, S. A. (1999). Sensitivity, specificity, reliability, and clinical validity of provider-reported symptoms: A comparison with self-reported symptoms: Outcomes Committee of the AIDS Clinical Trials Group. *Journal of Acquired Immune Deficiency Syndrome*, *21*(2), 126–133.

Kaakinen, J. R. (1992). Living with silence. *The Gerontologist*, *32*(2), 258–264.

Kaakinen, J. (1995). Talking among elderly nursing home residents. *Topics in Language Disorders*, *15*(2), 36–46.

Kane, R. (2001). Long-term care and a good quality of life: Bringing them closer together. *The Gerontologist*, *41*(3), 293–304.

Kane, R. (2003). Definition, measurement, and correlates of quality of life in nursing homes: Toward a reasonable practice, research, and policy agenda. *The Gerontologist*, *43*, 28–36.

Kane, R., Kane, R., Bershadsky, B., Degenholtz, H., Kling, K., Totten, A., et al. (2005). Proxy sources for information on nursing home residents' quality of life. *Journal of Gerontology*, *60B*(6), S318–S325.

Kolanowski, A., Buettner, L., Costa, P., & Litaker, M. (2001). Capturing interests: Therapeutic recreation activities for persons with dementia. *Therapeutic Recreation Journal*, *35*, 220–235.

Kragt, K., Holtkamp, C., Van Dongen, M., Van Rossum, E., & Salentijn, C. (1997). Het eVect van snoezelen in the snoezelruimte op het welbevinden van demente ouderen (Effects of Snoezelen in the Snoezelen room on the well-being of elderly people with dementia). *Verpleegkunde*, *12*, 227–236.

Krause, N. (2004). Lifetime trauma, emotional support, and life satisfaction among older adults. *The Gerontologist*, *44*(5), 615–623.

Kwa, V. I., Limburg, M., & de Haan, R. J. (1996). The role of cognitive impairment in the quality of life after ischaemic stroke. *Journal of Neurology*, *243*(8), 599–604.

Lancioni, G. E., Cuvo, A. J., & O'Reilly, M. F. (2002). Snoezelen: An overview of research with people with disabilities and dementia. *Disability and Rehabilitation: An International Multidisciplinary Journal*, *24*(4), 175–184.

Lawton, M. (1975). The Philadelphia Geriatric Center Morale Scale: A revision. *Journal of Gerontology*, *30*, 85–89.

Lawton, M., Moss, M., Fulcomer, M., & Kleban, M. (1982). A research and service oriented Multilevel Assessment Instrument. *Journal of Gerontology*, *37*, 91–99.

Lawton, M. P. (1991). A multidimensional view of quality of life in frail elders. In J. E. Birren, J. E. Lubben, J. C. Rowe, & D. E. Deutchman (Eds.), *The concept and measurement of quality of life in the frail elderly* (pp. 3–27). San Diego, CA: Academic Press.

Lawton, M. P. (1994). Quality of life in Alzheimer disease. *Alzheimer Disease and Associated Disorders*, *8*(Suppl. 3), 138–150.

Lawton, M. P. (1997). Assessing quality of life in Alzheimer's disease research. *Alzheimer Disease and Associated Disorders*, *11*, 91–99.

Lawton, M. P., Van Haitsma, K., & Klapper, J. (1996). Observed affect in nursing home residents with Alzheimer's disease. *Journal of Gerontology*, *51B*(6), 309–316.

Lawton, M. P., Van Haitsma, K., Perkinson, M., & Ruckdeschel, K. (1999). Observed affect and quality of life: Further affirmations and problems. *Journal of Mental Health and Aging*, *5*, 69–82.

Levesque, S., Cossette, S., & Potvin, L. (1993). Why alert residents are more or less willing to cohabit with cognitively impaired peers: An exploratory model. *The Gerontologisti33*(4), 514–522.

Lewinsohn, P., Mermelstein, R., Alexander, C., & MacPhillamy, D. (1985). The Unpleasant Events Schedule: A scale for the measurement of aversive events. *Journal of Clinical Psychology*, *41*, 483–489.

Liukkonen, A. (1995). Life in a nursing home for the frail elderly: Daily routines. *Clinical Nursing Research*, *4*, 358–370.

Livingston, G., Johnston, K., & Katona, C. (2005). Systematic review of psychological approaches to the management of neuropsychiatric symptoms of dementia: Old Age Task Force of the World Federation of Biological Psychiatry. *American Journal of Psychiatry*, *162*(11), 1996–2021.

Logsdon, R. G., Gibbons, L. E., McCurry, S. M., & Teri, L. (1999). Quality of life in Alzheimer's disease: Patient and caregiver reports. *Journal of Mental Health and Aging*, *5*, 21–32.

Lubinski, R. (1995). State-of-the-art perspectives on communication in nursing homes. *Topics in Language Disorders*, *15*(2), 1–19.

Lubinski, R., Morrison, E. B., & Rigrodsky, S. (1981). Perception of spoken communication by elderly chronically ill patients in an institutional setting. *Journal of Speech and Hearing Disorders*, *46*, 405–412.

Lundh, U., & Nolan, M. (1996). Aging and quality of life. 1: Towards a better understanding. *British Journal of Nursing*, *5*(20), 1248–1251.

Lyketsos, C. G., Gonzales-Salvador, T., Chin, J. J., Baker, A., Black, B., & Rabins, P. (2003). A followup study of change in quality of life among persons with dementia residing in a long-term care facility. *International Journal of Geriatric Psychiatry*, *18*(4), 275–281.

MacPhillamy, d., & Lewinsohn, P. (1982). The Pleasant Events Schedule (#1): Studies on reliability, validity and scale intercorrelations. *Journal of Consulting and Clinical Psychology*, *50*, 363–380.

Magaziner, J., Simonsick, E. M., Kashner, T. M., & Hebel, J. R. (1988). Patient-proxy response comparability on measures of patient health and functional status. *Journal of Clinical Epidemiology*, *41*(11), 1065–1074.

McCallion, P., Toseland, R., Lacey, D., & Banks, S. (1999). Educating nursing assistants to communicate more effectively with nursing home residents with dementia. *The Gerontologist*, *39*, 546–558.

Miller, N. E. (1980). The measurement of mood in senile brain disease: Examiner ratings and self-reports. In J. O. Cole & J. E. Barrett (Eds.), *Psychopathology in the aged* (pp. 97–118). New York: Raven Press.

Mitchell, J., & Kemp, B. (2000). Quality of life in assisted living homes: A multidimensional analysis. *Journal of Gerontology*, *55B*(2), P117–P127.

Moffat, N., Barker, P., Pinkney, L., Garside, M., & Freeman, C. (1993). *Snoezelen: An experience for people with dementia*. Chesterfield: ROMPA.

Mor, V., Branco, K., Fleishman, J., Hawes, C., Phillips, C., Morris, J., et al. (1995). The structure of social engagement among nursing home residents. *Journal of Gerontology: Psychological Sciences*, *50B*, P1–P8.

Neugarten, B. L., Havighurst, R. J., & Tobin, S. S. (1961). The measurement of life satisfaction. *Journal of Gerontology*, *16*, 134–143.

Nordeson, A., Engstrom, B., & Norberg, A. (1998). Self-reported quality of life for patients with progressive neurological diseases. *Quality of Life Research*, *7*, 257–266.

Noro, A., & Aro, S. (1996). Health-related quality of life among the least dependent institutional elderly compared with the non-institutional elderly population. *Quality of Life Research*, *5*, 355–366.

Novella, J. L., Ankri, J., Morrone, I., Guillemin, F., Jolly, D., Jochum, C., et al. (2001). Evaluation of the quality of life in dementia with a generic quality of life questionnaire: The Duke health profile. *Dementia and Geriatric Cognitive Disorders*, *12*(2), 158–166.

Novella, J., Jochum, C., Jolly, D., Morrone, I., Ankri, J., Bureau, F., et al. (2001). Agreement between patients' and proxies' reports of quality of life in Alzheimer's disease. *Quality of Life Research*, *10*, 443–452.

O'Boyle, C. A., McGee, H. M., Hickey, A., Joyce, C. R. B., Browne, J. P., & O'Malley, K. (1993). *The Schedule for the Evaluation of Individual Quality of Life (SEIQoL): Administration manual*. Dublin: Royal College of Surgeons in Ireland.

Ormel, J., Kempen, G. I. J. M., Deeg, D. J. H., Brilman, E. I., von Sonderen, E., & Relyveld, J. (1998). Functioning, well-being, and health perception in late middle-aged and older people: Comparing the effects of depressive symptoms and chronic medical conditions. *Journal of the American Geriatrics Society*, *46*, 39–48.

Ormel, J., Lindenberg, S., Steverink, N., & Verbrugge, L. (1999). Subjective well-being and social production functions. *Social Indicators Research 46*, 61–90.

Parkerson, G. R., Broadhead, W. E., & Tse, C. J. (1990). The Duke Health Profile: A 17-item measure of health and dysfunction. *Medical Care*, *28*(11), 1056–1072.

Paul-Brown, D., Frattali, C., Holland, A., Thompson, C. & Caperton, C. (2004). *Quality of Communication Life Scale*. Rockville, MD: ASHA.

Philp, I., Mutch, W. J., Devaney, J., & Ogston, S. (1989). Can quality of life of old people in institutional care be measured? *Journal of Clinical and Experimental Gerontology*, *11*(1/2), 11–19.

Pierre, U., Wood-Dauphinee, S., Korner-Bitensky, N., Gayton, D., & Hanley, J. (1998). Proxy use of the Canadian SF-36 in rating health status of the disabled elderly. *Journal of Clinical Epidemiology*, *51*(11), 983–990.

Pinkney, L. (1997). A comparison of the Snoezelen environment and a music relaxation group on the mood and behaviour of patients with senile dementia. *British Journal of Occupational Therapy*, *60*, 209–212.

Port, C., Gruber-Baldini, A., Burton, L., Baumgarten, M., Hebel, J. R., Zimmerman, S., et al. (2001). Resident contact with family and friends following nursing home admission. *The Gerontologist*, *41*(5), 589–596.

Porzsolt, F., Kojer, M., Schmidl, M., Greimel, E. R., Sigle, J., Richter, J., et al. (2004). A new instrument to describe indicators of well-being in old-old patients with severe dementia. *Health and Quality of Life Outcomes*, *2*, 10.

Pot, A., Deeg, D., Twisk, J., Aartjan, T., & Beekman, T. (2005). The longitudinal relationship between the use of long-term care and depressive symptoms in older adults. *The Gerontologist*, *45*(3), 359–369.

Rabins, P. V., Kasper, J. D., Kleinman, L., Black, B. S., & Patrick, D. L. (1999). Concepts and methods in the development of the ADRQL: An instrument for assessing health-related quality of life in persons with Alzheimer's disease. *Journal of Mental Health and Aging*, *5*, 33–48.

Radomski, M. V. (1995). Nationally speaking: There is more to life than putting on your pants. *American Journal of Occupational Therapy*, *49*(6), 487–490.

Reed, B., Jagust, W., & Coulter, L. (1993). Anosognosia in Alzheimer's disease: Relationships to depression, cognitive functioning, and cerebral perfusion. *Journal of Clinical and Experimental Neuropsychology*, *15*, 231–244.

Retsinas, J., & Garrity, P. (1985). Nursing home friendships. *The Gerontologist*, *25*(4), 376–381.

Richter, J., Schwarz, M., Eisemann, M., & Bauer, B. (2003). Quality of life as an indicator for successful geriatric inpatient rehabilitation: A validation study of the "Vienna List." *Archives of Gerontology and Geriatrics*, *37*, 265–276.

Richter, J., Schwarz, M., Eisemann, M., & Bauer, B. (2004). Validation of the "Vienna List" as a proxy measure of quality of life for geriatric rehabilitation patients. *Quality of Life Research*, *13*, 1725–1735.

Roos, N. P., & Havens, B. (1991). Predictors of successful aging: A twelve-year study of Manitoba elderly. *American Journal of Public Health*, *81*(1), 63–68.

Ruta, D. A., Garratt, A. M., Leng, M., Russell, I. T., & MacDonald, L. M. (1994). A new approach to the measurement of quality of life: The Patient Generated Index. *Med Care*, *32*, 1109–1126.

Salamon, M. J. (1988). Clinical use of the life satisfaction in the elderly scale. *Clinical Gerontologist*, *8*(1), 45–54.

Sanifort, F., Becker, M., & Diamond, R. (1996). Judgments of quality of life of individuals with severe mental disorders: Patient self-report versus provider perspectives. *American Journal of Psychiatry*, *153*, 497–502.

Sano, M., Albert, S. M., Tractenberg, R., & Schittini, M. (2000). Developing utilities: Quantifying Quality of Life for stages of Alzheimer's Disease as measured by the Clinical Dementia Rating. In S. Albert and R. Logsdon (Eds.), *Assessing Quality of Life in Alzheimer's Disease (pg. 81–94)*. NY: Springer.

Saxena, S., O'Connell, K., & Underwood, L. (2002). A commentary: Cross-cultural quality-of-life assessment at the end of life. *The Gerontologist*, *42*(Special Issue III), 81–85.

Schroll, M., Jonsson, P. V., Mor, V., Berg, K., & Sherwood, S. (1997). An international study of social engagement among nursing home residents. *Age and Aging*, *26*(S2), 55–59.

Selai, C. E., Trimble, M. R., Rossor, M. N., & Harvey, R. J. (2000). The Quality of Life Assessment Schedule (QOLAS): A new method for assessing quality of life (QOL) in dementia. In S. M. Albert & R. G. Logsdon (Eds.), *Assessing quality of life in Alzheimer's disease* (pp. 31–50). New York: Springer.

Selai, C., Vaughan, A., Harvey, R. J., & Logsdon, R. (2001). Using the QoL-AD in the UK. *International Journal of Geriatric Psychiatry*, *16*, 537–538.

Selwood, A., Thorgrimsen, L., & Orrell, M. (2005). Quality of life in dementia: A one-year follow-up study. *International Journal of Geriatric Psychiatry*, *20*, 232–237.

Seman, D. (2005). Defining dignity: A means to creative interventions. *Alzheimer's Care Quarterly*, *6*(2), 111–128.

Sevush, S., & Leve, N. (1993). Denial of memory deficit in Alzheimer's disease. American *Journal of Psychiatry*, *150*, 748–751.

Sheikh, J. A., & Yesavage, J. A. (1986). Geriatric Depression Scale (GDS): Recent findings and development of a shorter version. In T. L. Brink (Ed.). *Clinical gerontology: A guide to assessment and intervention*. New York: Haworth.

Sigman, S. (1985). Conversational behavior in two health care institutions for the elderly. *Institutional Journal of Aging and Human Development*, *21*, 147–163.

Silberfeld, M., Rueda, S., Krahn, M., & Naglie, G. (2002). Content validity for dementia of three generic preference based health related quality of life instruments. *Quality of Life Research*, *11*, 71–79.

Siu, A. L., Reuben, D. B., Ouslander, J. G., & Osterweil, D. (1993). Using multidimensional health measures in older persons to identify risk of hospitalization and skilled nursing placement. *Quality of Life Research*, *2*, 253–261.

Smith, J. P., & Kington, R. S. (1997). Race, socioeconomic status, and health in late life. In L. G. Martin & B. J. Soldo (Eds.), *Racial and ethnic differences in the health of older Americans*. Washington, DC: National Academy Press.

Sneeuw, K. C. A., Aaronson, N. K., de Haan, R. J., & Limburg, M. (1997). Assessing quality of life after stroke: The value and limitations of proxy ratings. *Stroke*, *28*(8), 1541–1549.

Spaull, D., Leach, C., & Frampton, I. (1998). An evaluation of the effects of sensory stimulation with people who have dementia. *Behavioural and Cognitive Psychotherapy*, *26*, 77–86.

Spranger, M. A., & Aaronson, N. K. (1992). The role of health care providers and significant others in evaluating the quality of life of patients with chronic disease: A review. *Journal of Clinical Epidemiology*, *45*(7), 743–760.

Steverink, N. (2001). When and why frail elderly people give up independent living: The Netherlands as an example. *Ageing & Society*, *21*, 45–69.

Teri, L., & Lewinsohn, P. (1982). Modification of the Pleasant and Unpleasant Events Schedule for the use with the elderly. *Journal of Consulting and Clinical Psychology*, *50*, 444–445.

Teri, L., & Logsdon, R. G. (1991). Identifying pleasant events for Alzheimer's disease patients: The Pleasant Events Schedule-AD. *The Gerontologist*, *31*, 124–127.

Teri, L., & Wagner, A. (1991). Assessment of depression in patients with Alzheimer's disease: Concordance among informants. *Psychology and Aging*, *6*(2), 280–285.

Thapa, K., & Rowland, L. A. (1989). Quality of life perspectives in long-term care: Staff and patient perceptions. *Acta Pscyhiatrica Scandinavica*, *80*, 267–271.

Thorgrimsen, L., Selwood, A., Spector, A., Royan, L., de Madariaga Lopez, M., Woods, R., et al. (2003). Whose quality of life is it anyway? The validity and reliability of the Quality of Life–Alzheimer's Disease (QoL-AD) scale. *Alzheimer Disease and Associated Disorders*, *17*, 201–208.

van Straten, A., de Haan, R. J., Limburg, M., Schuling, J., Bossuyt, P. M., & van den Bos, G. A. M. (1997). A stroke-adapted 30-item version of the Sickness Impact Profile to assess quality of life. *Stroke*, *28*(11), 2155–2161.

van Weert, J., Janssen, B., & van Dulmen, A. (2006). Nursing assistants' behaviour during morning care: Effects of the implementation of Snoezelen, integrated in 24-hour dementia care. *Journal of Advanced Nursing*, *53*(6), 656–668.

van Weert, J., Kerkstra, A., & van Dulmen, A. (2004). The implementation of Snoezelen in psychogeriatric care: An evaluation through the eyes of caregivers. *International Journal of Nursing Studies*, *41*(4), 397–409.

van Weert, J., van Dulmen, A., & Spreeuwenberg, P. (2005a). Behavioral and mood effects of Snoezelen integrated into 24-hour dementia care. *Journal of the American Geriatrics Society*, *53*(1), 24–33.

van Weert, J., van Dulmen, A., & Spreeuwenberg, P. (2005b). Effects of Snoezelen, integrated in 24 h dementia care, on nurse-patient communication during morning care. *Patient Education and Counseling*, *58*(3), 312–326.

van Weert, J., van Dulmen, A., & Spreeuwenberg, P. (2005c). The effects of the implementation of Snoezelen on the quality of working life in psychogeriatric care. *International Psychogeriatrics*, *17*(3), 407–427.

Verkaik, R., van Weert, J., & Francke, A. (2005). The effects of psychosocial methods on depressed, aggressive and apathetic behaviors of people with dementia: A systematic review. *International Journal of Geriatric Psychiatry*, *20*(4), 301–314.

Viitanen, M., Fugl-Meyer, K. S., Bernspang, B., & Fugl-Meyer, A. R. (1988). Life satisfaction in long-term survivors after stroke. *Scandinavian Journal of Rehabilitation Medicine*, *20*(1), 17–24.

Volicer, L., & Bloom-Charette, L. (Eds.). (1999). *Enhancing the quality of life in advanced dementia*. Philadelphia: Brunner/Mazel.

Ware, J. E., Kosinski, M., & Keller, S. D. (1996). A 12-item short-form health survey: construction of scales and preliminary tests of reliability and validity. *Med Care*, *34*, 220–233.

Ware, J. E., & Sherbourne, C. D. (1992). The MOS 36-item short form health survey (SF-36): I. Conceptual framework and item selection. *Med Care*, *30*(6), 473–483.

Whitehouse, P. J., Patterson, M. B., & Sami, S. A. (2003). Quality of life in dementia: Ten years later. *Alzheimer Disease and Associated Disorders*, *17*, 199–200.

Williams, L. S. (1998). Health-related quality of life outcomes in stroke. *Neuroepidemiology*, *17*(3), 116–120.

Wood, V., Wylie, M. L., & Sheafor, B. (1969). An analysis of a short self-report measure of life satisfaction: Correlation with rater judgments. *Journal of Gerontology*, *24*, 465–469.

Woodend, A., Nair, R., & Tang, A. (1997). Definition of life quality from patient versus health care professional perspective. *International Journal of Rehabilitation Research*, *20*, 71–80.

Woods, P., & Ashley, J. (1995). Simulated presence therapy: Using selected memories to manage problem behaviors in Alzheimer's disease patients. *Geriatric Nursing*, *16*, 9–14.

World Health Organization Quality of Life Group (WHOQOL Group). (1993). Study protocol for the World Health Organization project to develop a Quality of Life assessment instrument (the WHOQOL). *Quality of Life Research*, 2, 153–159.

World Health Organization Quality of Life Group (WHOQOL Group). (1995). The World Health Organization Quality of Life assessment (WHOQOL): Position paper from the World Health Organization. *Social Science and Medicine*, *41*, 1403–1409.

World Health Organization Quality of Life Group (WHOQOL Group). (1998a). Development of the World Health Organization WHOQOL-BRIEF Quality of Life assessment. *Psychological Medicine*, *28*, 551–558.

World Health Organization Quality of Life Group (WHOQOL Group). (1998b). The World Health Organization Quality of Life assessment (WHOQOL): Development and general psychometric properties. *Social Science and Medicine*, *46*, 1569–1585.

Wu, A. W., Jacobson, D. L., Berzon, R. A., Revicki, D. A., van der Horst, C., Fichtenbaum, C. J., et al. (1997). The effect of mode of administration on Medical Outcomes Study health ratings and EuroQoL scores in AIDS. *Quality of Life Research*, *6*, 3–10.

Wylie, M. L. (1970). Life satisfaction as a program impact criterion. *Journal of Gerontology*, *25*, 36–40.

Wyller, T. B., Holmen, J., Laake, P., & Laake, K. (1998). Correlates of subjective well-being in stroke patients. *Stroke*, *29*(2), 363–367.

Wyller, T. B., Sveen, U., Sodring, K. M., Pettersen, A. M., & Bautz-Holter, E. (1997). Subjective well-being one year after stroke. *Clinical Rehabilitation*, *11*(2), 139–145.

Yesavage, J. A., Brink, T. L., Rose, T. L., Lum, O., Huang, V., Adey, M., et al. (1983). Development and validation of a geriatric depression screening scale: A preliminary report. *Journal of Psychiatric Research*, *17*, 37–49.

Zank, S., & Leipold, B. (2001). The relationship between severity of dementia and subjective wellbeing. *Aging Mental Health*, *5*, 191–196.

Zimmerman, S., & Magaziner, J. (1994). Methodological issues in measuring the functional status of cognitively impaired nursing home residents: The use of proxies and performance-based measures. *Alzheimer Disease and Associated Disorders*, *8*, S281–S290.

9

Caregiver and Family Issues

The purpose of this chapter is to highlight the important role of caregivers in the treatment continuum for persons with dementia, as well as the role of the SLP in advising and supporting caregivers throughout this process. In past years, prior to the explosion of direct interventions for persons with dementia, the SLP's work with caregivers was to provide assistance *indirectly* to persons with dementia through their caregivers, primarily in the form of education about the diagnosis and future planning (Clark, 1997). Research into models of caregiving and interventions for caregivers has increased in the past decade, revealing the need for a menu of training approaches for caregivers based on their unique demographic characteristics, support needs, educational level, and relationship to the care recipient, and a variety of socioeconomic factors. The challenge to professionals in providing advice to caregivers is a range of emotional and psychosocial barriers that interfere with the acceptance and implementation of caregiving recommendations.

SLPs need to understand specific caregiver needs and characteristics in order to match successfully the support and training approach to each unique caregiver. This chapter will begin with a summary of what is known about caregivers, including what different caregivers bring to the situation, their needs and expectations, their emotional and physical health risks, and the types of barriers that prevent them from benefiting from services offered. The types of interventions available to caregivers will be outlined next, ranging from the generic educational and supportive models, to the communication-specific training approaches. At the conclusion of this chapter, it should be evident that the role of the SLP is to provide education, support, and training to caregivers of persons with dementia from diagnosis through the end of life.

Researchers have conceptualized the process of caregiving as shown in Figure 9.1. The stress process model of caregiving (Pearlin, Mullan, Semple, & Skaff, 1990) organizes the many factors that impact the process and outcomes of caregiving. In simple terms, the many types of problems experienced by the caregiver (e.g., objective problems with the care recipient and their own subjective responses to these problems) are **stressors** that contribute to negative and positive

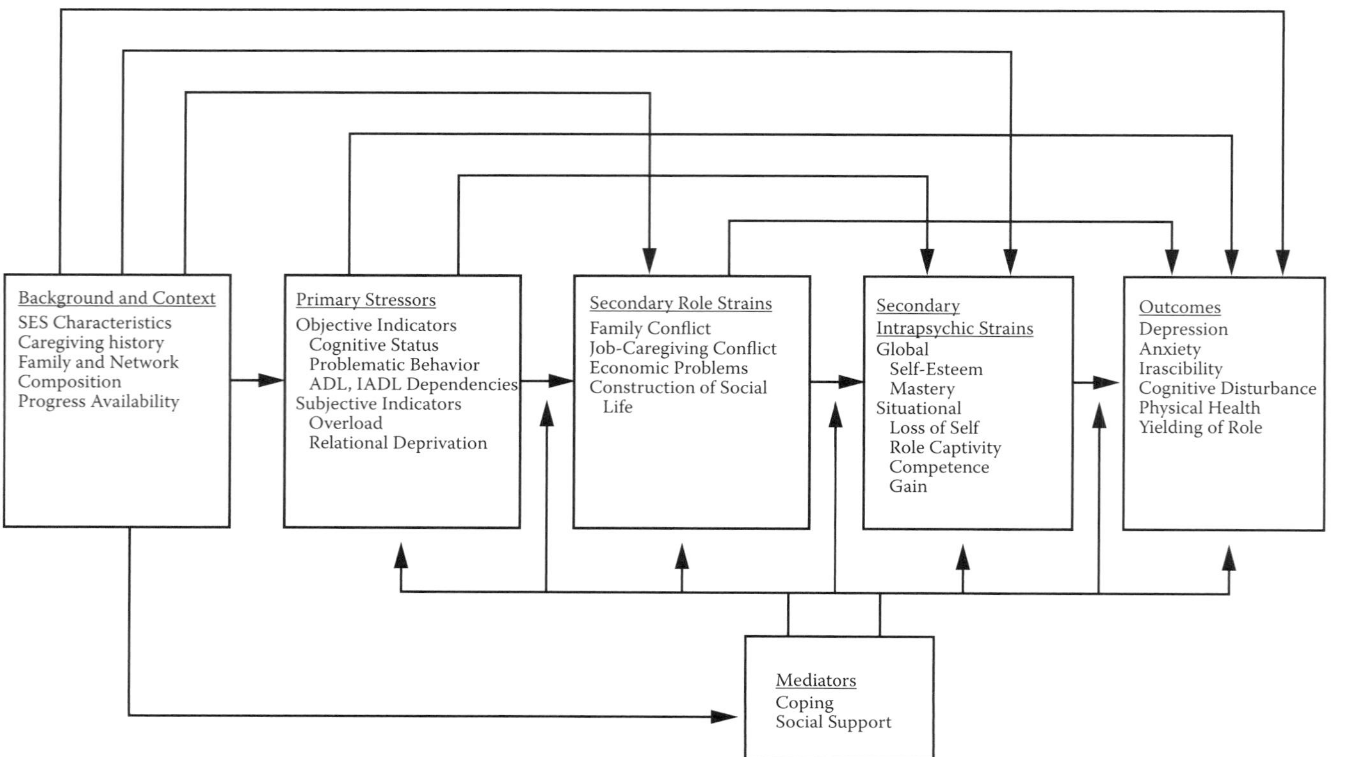

Figure 9.1 Stress Process Model of Caregiving.

caregiver (and care recipient) **outcomes** (e.g., poor health and depression). The resources that modify or regulate the relationship between the stressors and the outcomes are the **moderators** (Aneshensel, Pearlin, Mullan, Zarit, & Whitlatch, 1995). The entire caregiving process operates within the social, economic, and cultural context of the individual caregiver and his or her unique **background and contextual** variables. In the dementia caregiving context, the primary stressors include the patient's health condition and related problems (e.g., cognitive impairment, problem behaviors, and activities of daily living [ADL] dependencies) and the caregiver's emotional responses to these challenges (e.g., perceived stress, role strain and overload, and feelings of deprivation). These stressors lead to the secondary stressors of family conflict and work, employment, and financial strains. Without moderating factors, these stressors can lead to negative caregiving outcomes (e.g., caregiver depression, anxiety, anger, poor health, mortality, and patient institutionalization). However, when caregivers have access to social support (i.e., instrumental and emotional) and to interventions designed to address caregiving challenges, and have effective coping strategies that provide a sense of mastery and self-esteem, these factors tend to moderate the stressors and result in more positive caregiving outcomes. The individual characteristics and situations of each caregiver create an almost infinite array of response possibilities related to variables such as age, gender, race and ethnicity, socioeconomic status, education, relationship, and proximity to care receiver. The following chapter provides a general overview of the many factors to consider when working with patients with dementia and their caregivers.

CAREGIVER CHARACTERISTICS

The most important support for persons with dementia may well be their caregivers. A caregiver is a relative or friend who provides help with personal needs and household chores to another person without payment (National Alliance for Caregiving and the American Association of Retired Persons [NAC/AARP], 1997). This survey estimated that there are 22 million caregiving households in the United States, 18 million of which were White, non-Hispanic families, and 5 million of which included a person with dementia. The number of dementia caregivers continues to increase as the baby boomers age, life expectancy increases, and medical technology advances (Schulz & Martire, 2004). The shift in health care focus from acute to chronic diseases is resulting in more persons requiring caregiving for longer durations and for more types of tasks. A decade ago, 10% of the elderly population (2.97 million persons) required help with ADLs, such as dressing and bathing, and 23.2% of the elderly population (6.26 million) required help with instrumental activities of daily living (IADLs), such as shopping and finances (Van Nostrand, Furner, & Suzman, 1993). These numbers are sure to increase in the coming years.

Family caregivers often have difficulty pinpointing the exact time when caregiving began because the types of care provided are the typical tasks one family member would do for the other, whether or not they had a chronic illness or disability (e.g., cooking meals and doing the laundry; Schulz & Quittner, 1998). When care exceeds the boundaries of what is normal (e.g., help with bathing and toileting), family caregivers may admit that their helping role has changed. Family and friends provide 75% of care, and the remaining 25% of care is purchased (Schulz & Martire, 2004). National surveys of family caregivers reveal the majority of caregivers of a person with dementia are middle-aged, married females who work at least part-time (American Association of Retired Persons and Travelers Companies Foundation [AARP/TCF], 1988; NAC/AARP, 1997). These caregivers provide care primarily to a parent, grandparent, friend, aunt or uncle, or spouse, and many of them have children in the home. Most caregivers live with the disabled person, providing an average of 5 years of care at an estimated rate of approximately 17 hours (*SD* = 17.4) per week; whereas many dementia caregivers reported providing 8 or less hours of care a week, up to 16% reported providing constant care (NAC/AARP). The types of tasks included in caregiving range from IADLs (e.g., medication administration, managing finances, shopping, housework, meal preparation, transportation, and arranging outside services) to ADLs (e.g., dressing, bathing, toileting, and feeding). Caregiving for any disabled individual is burdensome, but the range, frequency, and severity of cognitive deficits and problem behaviors associated with dementia can produce stresses that are physically demanding and unremitting (Ory, Yee, Tennstedt, & Schulz, 2000). As patient function declines and the duration, amount, and intensity of caregiving increase, caregiver perceptions of their own burden and depression become increasingly negative (Schulz & Williamson, 1991). Most caregivers report lower incomes and lower self-reported health, and as a result, most are at risk for psychological distress and burden, psychiatric and physical illness, and economic stressors (Schulz, O'Brien, Bookwala, & Fleissner, 1995).

Factors Related to the Caregiving Experience

Many factors influence the perceptions associated with caregiving, including the relationship of the care provider to the care recipient (i.e., spouse, son or daughter, other relative, or friend), the nature of the relationship (e.g., loving or adversarial), the role of the caregiver (e.g., primary versus secondary), age, gender, education, financial resources, proximity to the care recipient, and ethnicity. In-depth analyses of all of these caregiving variables are beyond the scope of this chapter, but are available in other resources (e.g., Schulz, 2000); below is a summary of some of the factors critical to the understanding of SLPs who provide services to caregivers.

Type of Relationship to Care Recipient: Spouses The relationship of the caregiver to the care recipient is known to influence the caregiving experience (Schulz, O'Brien, Bookwala, & Fleissner, 1995; Yee & Schulz, 2000). Spousal caregivers are thought to provide the most extensive and comprehensive care because of the nature of the marital relationship (Stone, Cafferata, & Sangl, 1987). Rose-Rego, Strauss, and Smyth (1998) found gender differences in psychological, social, and physical well-being in their caregiving sample. Caregiving wives reported more negative feelings, including depression, about caregiving than did husbands. This difference may have been related to differences in women's attentiveness to their emotions, their willingness to report negative symptoms, their use of emotion-focused coping strategies, and the nature of the caregiving tasks. Yet, Brown and Alligood (2004) found that wives often have difficulty accepting help from others, which was thought to be related to needing assistance in recognizing problems, accepting direction from others, and recognizing help needs. In contrast, caregiving husbands expressed feelings of isolation and invisibility in their care work, reported a combined management and nurturing caregiving style, and persevered due to feelings of commitment, responsibility, and devotion to their wife (Russell, 2001). The impact of caregiving on spouses is influenced by the nature of their marital relationship. When spouses report low marital cohesion and satisfaction, they also report more depression (Rankin, Haut, & Keefover, 2001). Their perceptions of the level of marital affection and marital satisfaction are inversely related to their grief responses to the dementia diagnosis (Lindgren, Connelly, & Gaspar, 1999). Disagreement about the effects of caregiving on the caregiver can cause relationship strain between spouses, even when there is little disagreement about the care recipient's needs (Lyons, Zarit, Sayer, & Whitlatch, 2002). Spouses feel more burdened and depressed about their caregiving responsibilities than adult children caregivers, particularly when their spouse has physical impairments and behavior problems (Pinquart & Sörensen, 2003). Problem behaviors, especially emotional lability, were associated with negative well-being in wives and younger (< 65 years old) husbands (Croog, Sudilovsky, Burleson, & Baume, 2001).

Type of Relationship to Care Recipient: Adult Children and Their Siblings In the past decades, much research has focused on understanding adult children caregivers and the effects of a multitude of variables such as family composition, gender, geographical proximity, and marital status on the extent of care being given to their elderly parents (Dwyer, Henretta, Coward, & Barton, 1992; Fulton, 2005; Stoller, Forster, & Duniho, 1992). For example, adult children are more likely to be involved in the caregiving process when the parent is widowed and has functional or cognitive impairment, and if they live nearby (Crawford, Bond, & Balshaw, 1994, Stoller et al., 1992). In fact, even prior to caregiving, adult children who are in good health and have positive family norms for caregiving have increased expectations for primary involvement in caregiving when the time arrives (Franks, Pierce, & Dwyer, 2003); a large network of sisters, however, decreases the expectation for primary responsibility for parental care. Daughters, with or without siblings, are more likely to provide caregiving assistance than sons (Dwyer & Coward, 1991). They also tend to give a wider range of care, such as assistance with ADLs and IADLs (Dwyer et al., 1992; Horowitz, 1985). Daughters' involvement in caregiving is greatest when they are not married (Connidis, Rosenthal, & McMullin, 1996, Lang & Brody, 1983) and when parents are more impaired (Crawford et al., 1994). Widowed mothers prefer the help of daughters to the help of sons if both are nearby (Crawford et al.), especially if more of their assistance is needed (Stoller et al.). Widowed mothers even seem to grow closer to their daughters (Lopata, 1987) and more distant from their sons (Atchely, 1988). Daughters report stronger feelings of attachment, and think their parent(s) to be in greater need of help than sons, which may explain their greater caregiving involvement

(Cicirelli, 1983). Gender role attitudes reflecting higher expectations from daughters compared to sons might be another explanation for their greater involvement in caregiving (Finley, 1989). However, not all studies report differences in feelings of attachment toward parents between daughters and sons (Crawford et al.). Adult daughters report doing more personal care and household chores (Dwyer & Coward, 1991) than sons who help with other chores, such as money management, home repairs, and transportation (Collins & Jones, 1997). This gendered division of labor does not hold for spousal caregivers, who provide more similar types and amounts of care to their spouses than do adult children (Tennstedt, Crawford, & McKinlay, 1993). In summary, the adult child caregiving role is substantially different from the spousal caregiving role; adult children have to acknowledge that they no longer are in a position to receive help and support from, but now must provide assistance and emotional support to, their parents. It can be difficult for children to make this change (Connidis et al., 1996) and maintain feelings of intimacy, interconnectedness, and reciprocity (Kaye & Applegate, 1990). The change in caregiving role has an impact on interpersonal relationships in caregiving dyads; for adult children, the level of affection is a decisive factor in giving care, whereas for spouses, feelings of obligation are important (Connidis et al.).

The impact of siblings on the caregiving equation is also important. For example, the amount and intensity of care provided by siblings to elderly parents are influenced by both their availability and proximity, as well as by their behavior (Fulton, 2005; Matthews). When a sibling starts to provide assistance to a parent, the odds of another sibling initiating assistance increase. However, when a sibling stops providing assistance, the other sibling is more likely to discontinue assistance (Dwyer et al., 1992). Adult children caregivers without siblings perform a role that is similar to the spousal caregiver role because caregiving responsibilities cannot be shared with a close family member (Hooyman & Lustbader, 1986). Adult children without siblings appear to have greater role responsibilities, but also have a more positive reaction to caregiving and a smaller extent of feelings of abandonment than adult children caregivers with siblings (Barnes, Given, & Given, 1992). The availability of siblings to share caregiving responsibilities increases the potential for conflict. Daughters as primary caregivers seem to experience more conflict with sisters than brothers, with sisters feeling guilty about not doing more (Brody, Hoffman, Kleban, & Schoonover, 1989). Adult children with siblings expect their siblings to share the caregiver burden and feel abandoned if they do not receive this help and support. Regardless of the presence of helping siblings, however, caregivers reported a negative impact of their assistance on their health over time. In addition, they reported receiving less affective support and experiencing increased feelings of abandonment over time (Barnes et al., 1992). For daughters, support from their husband or friends was more important and prevalent than that from a sibling due to the potential for sibling conflict (Brody et al., 1989).

The Caregiving Role: Primary Versus Secondary Caregivers In addition to the caregiver's relationship to the care recipient, his or her role as either the primary or secondary caregiver impacts the nature and outcomes of the care provided. Caregiving responsibilities are usually assumed by one person, the primary caregiver; however, secondary caregivers have been reported to provide supplementary assistance with a wide variety of tasks (Pruchno, Peters, & Burant, 1995; Tennstedt, McKinlay, & Sullivan, 1989). As a result of different expectations on either side, there are potential disagreements and divergent perceptions about caregiving. Family conflicts arise between primary and secondary caregivers regarding issues of parental illness and the level of assistance required from the family (Semple, 1992). Often, the advice provided from other family members is experienced as stressful (MaloneBeach & Zarit, 1995). Bourgeois, Beach, Schulz, and Burgio (1996) found that primary and secondary caregivers exhibited 64% disagreement on perceptions of primary caregiver coping efficacy, 51% disagreement on primary caregiver strain, and 46% disagreement on perception of problem behavior, with greater agreement on measures of more objective behaviors. This degree of disagreement between caregivers may account for dissatisfaction in perceptions of support and contribute to higher levels of stress. Instead of reducing burden and stress, disagreement or other upsetting elements of the relationship between primary and secondary caregivers could be stronger than positive effects of support (Pagel, Erdly, & Becker, 1987). Disagreement contributes to feelings of strain and burden among caregivers, thereby increasing the likelihood of placement in a nursing home.

Disagreement about problem behavior can also result in divergent reactions to them by the caregiver, resulting in an increase in problem behavior. Insight into differences in coping behavior among primary and secondary caregivers can help to explain differences in disagreements. According to content analyses of interviews with caregivers (Gottlieb & Gignac, 1996), adult children tend to use wishful thinking as a coping strategy more often than spouses. However, this does not relate closely to actual problem behaviors of their parent, nor does it adequately reflect their caregiving strain. A second difference in coping strategies is that adult female children caregivers seem more optimistic, whereas spouses use humor more to deal with the caregiving burden. Third, adult children seek (outside) help to a greater extent than spouses. In order for coping strategies to be effective for both primary and secondary caregivers and patients, caregivers have to be aware of their coping strategies and coordinate them with those of the secondary caregivers. Primary and secondary caregivers should also decide on a division of caregiving tasks that are complementary. For instance, during a family meeting, the primary and secondary caregivers could set up a realistic and specific schedule for caregiving, encouraging participation without trying to equate types of help (Zarit & Edwards, 1999).

Other Factors That Impact Caregiving: Race, Ethnicity, and Culture As mentioned throughout the previous sections, a multitude of factors impact the caregiving equation, including age, gender, education, health, financial resources, the composition of family networks, the coping skills of the caregiver, the quality of the caregiver–care recipient relationship, and their physical proximity. In our diverse society, however, differences in race, ethnicity, and culture cannot be overlooked when providing services to caregivers. Sensitivity to the different needs and responses to caregiving challenges of minority caregivers will enhance positive outcomes.

In the United States, the four federally designated ethnic minority categories are American Indian/Alaska Native, Asian/Pacific Islander, Black, and Hispanic (Yeo, 1996). Within these classifications, differences in national origin, culture, and language further diversify the groups. For example, Young and Gu (1995) reported their Asian sample to include native Hawaiian, Japanese, Vietnamese, Cambodian, Chinese, and Filipino elders. Factors such as degree of acculturation and ethnic identity, education, income, and religious affiliation, among others, influence the degree to which caregivers access available resources and supports for their family member with dementia. Pinquart and Sörensen (2005) have developed a model representing the many factors influencing ethnic differences in stressors, resources, and outcomes related to caregiving (Figure 9.2).

Medical professionals are challenged to provide appropriate and culturally sensitive services to diverse patients, particularly when (a) the patient does not speak English, (b) the symptoms of dementia (e.g., confusion and memory loss) are viewed as normal aging processes in other cultures, (c) cultural traditions of family responsibility and gender roles preclude the acceptance of outside help, and (d) there are cultural differences in the perception of institutionalization and or health-related and end-of-life decision making (Yeo, 1996). As a result, resources to educate professionals about racial, cultural, and ethnic differences are becoming available (Edgerly, Montes, Yau, Stokes, & Redd, 2003; Santo Pietro & Ostuni, 2003; and see Table 9.1). Efforts are under way to translate diagnostic tests, educational materials about dementia, and caregiver resources into different languages (e.g., Fuh, Wanh, Liu, & Wang, 1999).

To summarize some of the literature on racial and ethnic differences in caregiving and a recent meta-analysis of 116 empirical studies of family caregiving (Pinquart & Sörensen, 2005), non-Whites are 30% more likely to be caregivers; to be adult children, friends, or other family members; to have a lower socioeconomic status; to have worse physical health; to spend more than 13 hours per week in caregiving activities; and to receive more informal support (McCann et al., 2000; Pinquart & Sörensen, 2005); additionally, these responsibilities increase with age for married persons. Minority elders tend to report lower levels of stress, burden, and depression; to hold stronger beliefs about filial support; and to be more likely to use faith, prayer, and religion as coping strategies (Connell & Gibson, 1997; Koenig et al., 1992). African American caregivers' higher religiosity than Whites' contributed to more positive feelings about caregiving, lower anxiety, and lower feelings of bother by the care recipient's behavior (Roff et al., 2004). In fact, feelings of respect for an older family member often lead to "normalization" of problem behaviors and delayed dementia evaluation (Cloutterbuck & Mahoney, 2003). Similarly, Native American populations whose cultural value of idealizing elders for their wisdom and high moral values may explain the cognitive decline in dementia as either part of normal aging or a transition to the next world, and may choose to depend solely on the family for caregiving (Jervis & Manson, 2002). Native families face a multitude of challenges related to poverty, drug and alcohol abuse, and living in rural areas or on reservations, where there are not many formal services or

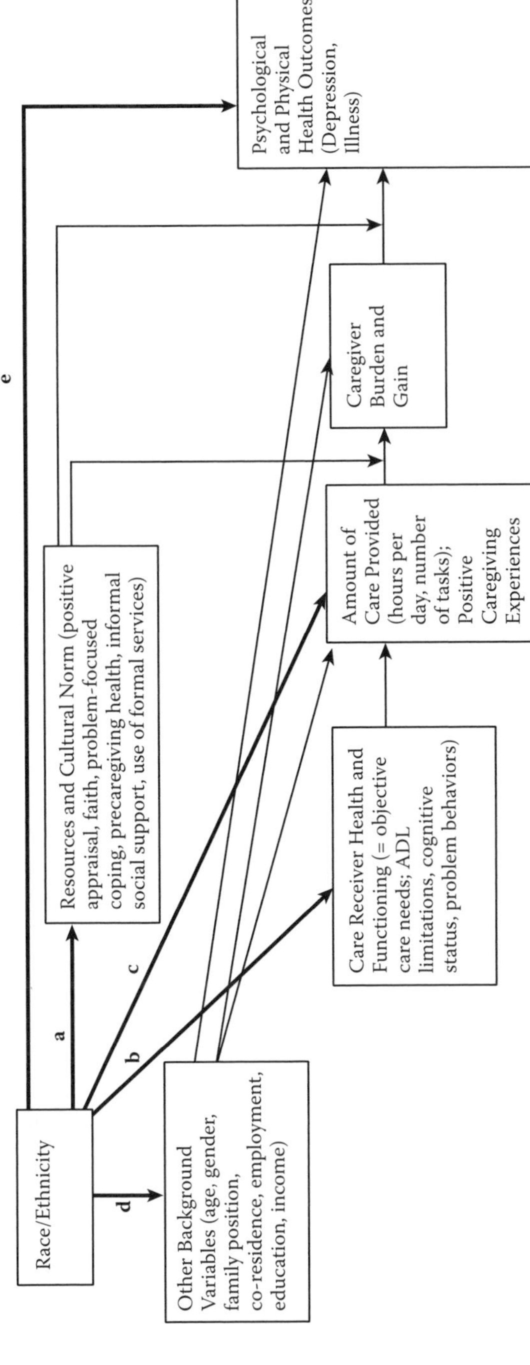

Figure 9.2 Factors Influencing Ethnic Differences in Caregiving Variables. Reprinted with permission: Pinquart and Sörensen (2005).

TABLE 9.1 Resources for Caregivers of Different Ethnicities

Ethnicity	References
American Indian/Alaska Native	Jervis and Manson (2002); Kramer (1996)
	John, Hennessy, Roy, and Salvini (1996)
Asian/Pacific Islander	
• Chinese	Elliot, Di Minno, Lam, and Tu (1996); Teng (1996)
• Japanese	Tempo and Saito (1996)
• Filipino	McBride and Parreno (1996)
• Korean	Youn, Knight, Jeong, and Benton (1999)
• Vietnamese	Yoe, Uyen Tran, Hikoyeda, and Hinton (2001)
	Yee, Nguyen, and Ha (2003)
• Hmong	Gerdner, Tripp-Reimer, and Yang (2005)
African American	Barnes, Mendes de Leon, Bienias, and Evans (2004)
	Dilworth-Anderson, Goodwin, and Williams (2004)
	Lewis and Ausberry (1996)
Hispanic	
• Spanish	Mungas (1996); Taussig and Ponton (1996)
• Mexican	Briones, Ramirez, Guerrero, and Ledger (2002)
	Chiriboga, Black, Aranda, and Markides (2002)
	Gallagher-Thompson, Talamantes, Ramirez, and Valverde (1996)
• Cuban and Puerto Rican	Henderson (1996)

long-term care facilities; these factors and the lack of understanding of dementia may lead to severe caregiver stress, elder neglect, and elder abuse (Paveza et al., 1992; Whitehouse, Lerner, & Hedera, 1993). Latino caregivers, who are mostly females caring for parents or parents-in-law, report high levels of depression, low availability of informal support, and underutilization of formal services (Ayalon & Huyck, 2001); in fact, the highest level of depression was seen in Latino caregivers when compared with Japanese, African Americans, and Whites (Adams, Aranda, Kemp, & Takagi, 2002; Pinquart & Sörensen). Contradictory findings, however, were published by Morano and Sanders (2005), whose adult children Latino caregivers reported less depression, lower levels of role captivity, and higher self-acceptance than White caregivers; their regression analyses revealed that feelings of role captivity were stronger predictors of negative and positive caregiving outcomes than ethnicity. In general, less is known about the caregiving and coping strategies of Asian groups (e.g., Chinese, Japanese, Korean, and Filipino), especially the Vietnamese and Hmong (Thompson, Gallagher-Thompson, & Haley, 2003). However, innovative intervention programs targeting the specific needs and challenges of ethnic minority caregivers are appearing (e.g., Los Angeles' El Portal Latino Alzheimer's project; San Francisco's Japanese Kimochi, Inc.; and the John XXIII Multiservice Chinese Outreach Center; Edgerly et al., 2003).

Research into the barriers to accessing culturally appropriate services for ethnic minority elders is underway; economic, geographic, cultural, and linguistic differences are important factors in the social and health care delivery systems, as well as perceptions of and stigma associated with cognitive impairment (Hinton, 2002; Ortiz & Fitten, 2000). This information will extend the literature on caregiving minority families, their extended social networks, and help-seeking processes in an effort to improve the quality of care and management of dementia in all health care settings.

Risks and Benefits of Caregiving

Caregivers of all types may have different expectations and stresses related to the caregiving responsibilities, which lead to different caregiving outcomes, including physical health and mental health outcomes of the caregiver and the risk of patient institutionalization. Measures of physical health outcomes include self-rated global health, frequency and types of medical conditions, health-related behaviors, medications, and hospitalizations, and physiological changes (e.g., immune functioning, hypertension, and cardiac health; Bookwala, Yee, & Schulz, 2000). Mental health, or psychiatric, outcomes include self-report measures of well-being, depression, anxiety, and psychiatric drug use. In studies comparing the physical health outcomes of caregivers and noncaregivers, caregivers reported lower overall global health (Beach, Schulz, Yee, & Jackson, 1998), more physical health problems (Cochrane, Goering, & Rogers, 1997), less physical activity and sleep (Burton, Newsom, Schulz, Hirsch, & German, 1997), and increased medication use (Schulz & Williamson, 1997). Caregivers have poorer immune functioning (Glaser & Kiecolt-Glaser, 1997), higher cardiovascular risk factors (Vitaliano, Scanlan, Krenz, Schwartz, & Marcovina, 1996), and increased blood pressure (Moritz, Kasl, & Ostfeld, 1992) than noncaregiving controls. With regard to mental health outcomes, dementia caregivers report increased depression and anxiety in comparison to age- and gender-based controls (Schulz & Williamson, 1997). Overall, caregiver physical and mental health, as well as other risk factors (e.g., gender, financial status, and personality variables), predict negative caregiving outcomes (Ory et al., 2000). For example, increased depression and anxiety and limited social support are related to negative physical health (Li, Seltzer, & Greenberg, 1997). Poor physical health increased caregiver-reported depression (Harwood, Barker, Ownby, & Duara, 2000). One of the strongest and recurring findings in this literature is the relationship between patient factors and the mental and physical health outcomes of caregivers. Patient problem behaviors are especially predictive of negative caregiver physical and mental health (Hooker et al., 2002; O'Rourke & Tuokko, 2000). When patients have increased dependency in ADLs in addition to problem behaviors (e.g., disinhibition and limited awareness), there are reports of increased caregiver depression (Neundorfer et al., 2001; Rymer et al., 2002). Informal support from family and friends was found to diminish when patient problem behaviors and functional limitations increased, resulting in more caregiver-reported depression and burden (Clyburn, Stones, Hadjistavropoulos, & Tukko, 2000). Overall, caregiver stress is related to the severity of the dementia of the patient, the type and amount of problem behavior the patient exhibits, the amount of support the caregiver receives, and the fact that these factors change over time as the patient's disease progresses; a well-functioning support system and a high quality of social services to the caregiving dyad have a positive impact on burden and strain (Bass, 1990).

When the caregiver is no longer healthy, mentally or physically, and the caregiver's quality of life diminishes, the person with dementia is at increased risk of institutionalization (Argimon, Limon, Vila, & Cabezas, 2005). Other factors that increase risk of institutionalization include inadequate caregiver coping strategies, caregiver stress, insufficient support for the caregiver, and disagreement among caregivers, as well as having a caregiver with any of the following characteristics: an adult child as a primary caregiver, a relatively young caregiver (e.g., a grandchild), an employed child caregiver, or a caregiver with lower morale (Montgomery & Kosloski, 1994). Additional risk factors for institutionalization include client characteristics such as advanced age, poor health, lower functional status, problems with ADLs, cognitive impairment, and living alone without access to a support group of family or friends.

In general, adult children caregivers with financial resources, who provide substantial care to old parents who are highly dependent on them, are at the greatest risk of institutionalizing their parent (Montgomery & Kosloski, 1994). Although nursing home placement might seem like a good solution to reduce caregiver stress for the caregiver, research has shown that this stress generally does not decrease after institutionalization (Zarit & Whitlatch, 1992) and that the caregivers are not always ready for this step when professionals advise them to put their relative in a nursing home (Zarit & Knight, 1996). In contrast, attention to the caregiver's health risks in the form of increased support (e.g., assistance with patient ADLs, overnight help, and fewer caregiving hours) was found to improve caregiver mental functioning (Markowitz, Gutterman, Sadik, & Panadopoulos, 2003) and decrease the risk of care recipient institutionalization (Gaugler et al., 2000). This portends well for the potential possible impact of intervention on caregiving outcomes.

McKinlay, Crawford, and Tennstedt (1995) found that caregiving is not always perceived as stressful. In fact, NAC/AARP survey caregivers reported the feeling that best described their caregiving experience was happiness (48.9%) and love (17.3%); feelings of burden, obligation, sadness, and anger ranged from 2.5 to 15.2%. There is a growing literature on the positive aspects of caregiving that suggests that some caregivers find satisfaction and rewards in providing care and that this results in reduced reports of caregiver stress and in other improved caregiver outcomes (Miller & Lawton, 1997; Roff et al., 2004). In a study of 978 spouse and child caregivers, Raschick and Ingersoll-Dayton (2004) found that female caregivers experience more caregiving "costs" than do male caregivers, and that adult children caregivers experience more rewards than do spousal caregivers. The care recipient's helpfulness, however, was found to have a greater impact on spousal than adult children caregivers.

Barriers to Obtaining Assistance With Caregiving

Professionals (e.g., social workers and case managers) often express frustration with caregivers who appear reluctant to implement suggested caregiving strategies and recommendations for formal services. In addition to the psychosocial variables that define the caregiver (e.g., relationship, gender, and ethnicity), additional psychological factors have been identified that impact such caregiving situations and outcomes. There appear to be unspoken barriers that prevent the adoption of particular strategies that exist without the overt awareness of the caregiver. Albert (1990) suggested that caregivers may be reluctant to acknowledge the extent of the disruption on the household of the care recipient's illness until they become so stressed that minor problems precipitate catastrophic reactions. Rubinstein (1990) explained that there may be psychological and symbolic meanings of the term *home* that contribute to the commitment to care for the person with dementia at home. For example, issues of control, security, family history, independence, comfort, and protection are all related to the idea that keeping a sick person at home means that the person is not fully "sick." Some caregiving families figure out their own management strategies, such as using routines for caregiving tasks and redefining parent–child roles (Albert), that are effective for a while; other families struggle in a mode of constant crisis management and delay the search for and acceptance of outside help. There is a tendency for families who are more involved in the day-to-day care of the person, and who co-reside, to use fewer formal services (Diwan, Berger, & Manns, 1997; Gill, Hinrichsen, & DiGiusepppe, 1998) until the care recipient exhibits multiple ADL deficits (Diwan et al., 1997). Often, the nonuse of available services is related to the caregiver's feeling of personal competence or caregiving mastery; such caregivers feel good about their ability to provide care for their loved one (Hamilton, 1996).

Other issues that pose often insurmountable barriers to obtaining adequate help include the social stigma and feelings of failure associated with seeking help, the lack of knowledge of the existence of services, the overwhelming array of choices available once identified, the fears of the cost of the services, the possibility of patient refusal to cooperate with services, and lack of transportation. Once the caregiver has been convinced to try a service, new problems arise, including dissatisfaction with the services provided and conflict between caregivers and service providers involving differences in beliefs about the focus and intensity of caregiving tasks (Corcoran, 1993; Weinberger et al., 1993; Zarit, 1990). It may seem obvious that there is a need to understand the lifestyle, values, and goals of the caregiver, as well as his or her caregiving style, in order to provide effective services (Corcoran, 1994), but unless one uses the appropriate assessment tools to determine these caregiving characteristics, they might be overlooked. For example, Corcoran (1994) discovered that most men prefer a task-oriented approach to caregiving, whereas most women prefer a parental model emphasizing the physical and emotional health of the care recipient. Tools such as Communicating With Others: What's My Style or Hidden feelings That Influence Communication (Ostuni & Santo Pietro, 1991) should be helpful in identifying the important factors to be addressed in order to engender a positive, trusting relationship with the caregiver and to increase the possibility of positive caregiving outcomes. Toth-Cohen and colleagues (2001) outlined the four key factors to consider when working with caregivers of persons with dementia in their homes to be (a) understanding the personal meaning of home for the family, (b) viewing the caregiver as a "lay practitioner,"

(c) identifying the caregiver's beliefs and values, and (d) recognizing the demand characteristics of the services provided.

Finally, the most important variable in caregiving interventions may well be time. It is necessary to recognize that it may take more time than anticipated or desired for the caregiver to understand the extent of his or her caregiving challenges, to identify and accept the resources available, and to make the necessary changes in thinking and management styles to create a positive caregiving outcome. Bourgeois and colleagues (Bourgeois, Schulz, Burgio, & Beach, 2002) kept track of how long it took for caregivers to attempt or adopt a suggestion from a professional; in some cases, even with repeated suggestions over time, it took 6–12 months before the caregiver was able to overcome his or her personal barriers to the suggested strategy. Variability in time reflects the complexity of caregiving issues and the continuum of caregivers and caregiving styles; professionals should not become disheartened when caregivers need time to change. Instead, professionals should understand that different people require different amounts of time to be able to accept recommendations that may be in conflict with or differ from their own personal beliefs, family history, and coping styles. We need to trust that most caregivers will eventually be ready to try something new, and when that time comes, we need to be ready to support them in their efforts.

Interventions for Family Caregivers

The past decade has seen a proliferation of interventions developed to improve the psychosocial-emotional responses and patient management skills of family caregivers (Bourgeois, Schulz, & Burgio, 1996; Coon, Gallagher-Thompson, & Thompson, 2003). With few exceptions, the interventions have been applied to a variety of caregivers, including spouses, adult children, siblings, friends, and paid caregivers. A multitude of caregiving interventions, ranging from information and resources, individual and family counseling, support groups, and day care and respite services to caregiver stress reduction and skills training to manage patient behaviors has appeared in the literature since the mid-1980s (Bourgeois et al., 1996; Kennet, Burgio, & Schulz, 2000). The purposes of these interventions have varied widely, and include the following: to enhance the caregiver's knowledge (Brennan, Moore, & Smyth, 1991; Brodaty, Roberts, & Peters, 1994), to increase cognitive skills in problem solving (Labrecque, Peak, & Toseland, 1992), to reduce dysfunctional thoughts (Gallagher-Thompson & Steffen, 1994), to improve coping (Gallagher-Thompson & DeVries, 1994), to increase behavior management skills (Bourgeois, Burgio, Schulz, Beach, & Palmer, 1997; Bourgeois et al., 2002), and to modify positive and negative affect (Teri & Uomoto, 1991; Toseland, Rossiter, Peak, & Smith, 1990). As shown in Schulz and Martire's (2004) model (Figure 9.3), the many different types of intervention are thought to address different stressors and health processes; research is ongoing to better match interventions with desired outcomes.

Other interventions are designed to provide relief from caregiving in the form of respite care or adult day care. In these treatments, time away from caregiving responsibilities is intended to result in positive changes in mood, quality of life, and feelings about caregiving, but this does not always happen (Theis, Moss, &

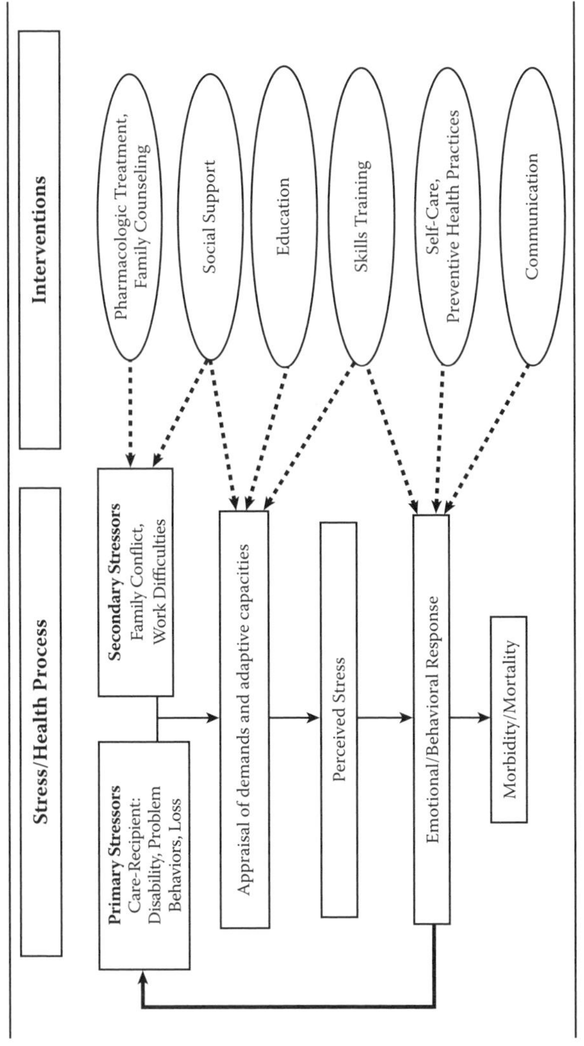

Figure 9.3 The Stress/Health Model Applied to Caregiving and Associated Interventions. Reprinted with permission: Schulz and Martire (2004).

Pearson, 1994; Zarit, Greene, Ferraro, Townsend, & Stephens, 1996). Changes in physical health and sleep improvements have been the result of two studies of short-term institutional respite (Caradoc-Davies & Harvey, 1995; Larkin & Hopcroft, 1993). Caregivers, however, do not take advantage of this intervention as often as it is available. Lawton, Brody, and Saperstein (1989) found that only 58% of caregivers in their study utilized the services. A wide variety of psychosocial treatments report generally positive, but not always durable, outcomes. Similarly, many behavioral interventions produce robust effects with encouraging evidence of maintenance and generalization, but with so few subjects that generalization to the general caregiving population remains problematic. Table 9.2 lists some benefits and limitations of the many caregiving intervention models described in the literature.

TABLE 9.2 Benefits and Limitations of Caregiving Interventions

Intervention Models	Benefits	Limitations and Barriers
Information and education: Brodaty, Roberts, and Peters (1994): classes Brennan, Moore, and Smyth (1991): computer Glueckauf and Loomis (2003)	Increased knowledge and access to resources	Not individualized or personalized; overwhelming
Support groups: Castle, Wilkins, Heck, Tanzy, and Fahey (1995) Chiverton and Caine (1989) Goodman and Pynoos (1990) Martindale-Adams. Nichols, Burns, and Malone (2002)	Increased knowledge Sharing of common feelings and experiences Improved practical problem solving	Individual needs may not be addressed in group setting
Individual and family counseling: Gwyther (1990) Kaplan and Gallagher-Thompson (1995) Toseland and Smith (1990) Rose and DelMaestro (1990) Whitlatch, Zarit, Goodwin, and von Eye (1995)	Increased knowledge Personal needs addressed	Social stigma associated with seeking psychological help Scheduling sessions Family conflicts
Case management: Challis, von Abendorff, Brown, Chesterman, and Hughes (2002) MaloneBeach, Zarit, and Spore (1992) Woods, Wills, Higginson, Hobbins, and Whitby (2003).	Coordination of informal and formal support services Increased service use	Dissatisfaction with services Conflict between caregivers and service providers
Multicomponent interventions: Brodaty, McGilchrist, Harris, and Peters (1993); Demers and Lavoie (1996)	Large menu of services Reductions in negative caregiver outcomes Delayed patient institutionalization	Overwhelming array of choices Cost of multiple services Waiting lists

TABLE 9.2 (Continued)

Intervention Models	Benefits	Limitations and Barriers
Hinchliffe, Hyman, Blizard, and Livingston (1995) Ingersoll-Dayton, Chapman, and Neal (1990) Mittelman et al. (1995); Mittelman, Ferris, Shulman, Steinberg, and Levin (1996); Mittelman (2003); Mittelman, Roth, Haley, & Zarit (2004) Mohide et al. (1990); Oktay and Volland (1990)		
Respite care (adult day care, in-home care, and short-stay institutional): Caradoc-Davies and Harvey (1995) Kosloski and Montgomery (1995) Larkin and Hopcroft (1993) Lawton, Brody, and Saperstein (1989) Theis, Moss, and Pearson (1994) Zarit, Greene, Ferraro, Townsend, and Stephens (1996)	Caregiver has time away from patient Patient benefits from social and cognitive stimulation	Caregiver reluctance to use due to fear of cost, patient refusal and other problem behaviors, and transportation issues
Skills training: Bourgeois, Burgio, Schulz, Beach, and Palmer (1997); Bourgeois, Schulz, Burgio, and Beach (2002) Gallagher-Thompson and Steffen (1994) Gallagher-Thompson and DeVries (1994) Gallagher-Thompson, Arean, Rivera, and Thompson (2001) Glueckauf et al. (2005) Hébert et al. (2003) Kuhn, Fulton, and Edelman (2003) Labrecque, Peak, and Toseland (1992) Logsdon, McCurry, and Teri (2005) Teri and Uomoto (1991) Toseland, Rossiter, Peak, and Smith (1990)	Caregiver learns coping skills and new techniques for managing problems Reductions in negative caregiver and patient outcomes	Skills trained may not reflect caregiver choice Skills trained may not apply to future problems

Source: Adapted from Bourgeois (1997).

Multiple Component Interventions

Many intervention models have a single or primary focus of the treatment provided; the multiplicity of caregiver needs, however, has been addressed in interventions consisting of multiple components. For example, early multicomponent interventions provided a combination of educational sessions, care planning, support groups, or a "buddy" (Ingersoll-Dayton, Chapman, & Neal, 1990); education and respite (Mohide et al., 1990; Oktay &

Volland, 1990); or information, counseling, problem solving, and a support group (Demers & Lavoie, 1996). Counseling on multiple topics, such as problem solving, time management, and stress reduction (Toseland & Smith, 1990), and individual and family counseling designed to increase knowledge and affective responses to caregiving (Mittelman et al., 1995; Mittelman, Ferris, Shulman, Steinberg, & Levin, 1996) have improved caregiving outcomes for a wider range of caregivers. The addition of cognitive and behavioral skills training to intervention models has also contributed to positive caregiving outcomes (Gallagher-Thompson & DeVries, 1994; Gallagher-Thompson & Steffen, 1994).

The only problem with these multipronged approaches is that it is difficult to know which specific component of the intervention contributed most to the caregiving outcome; in these times of fiscal constraint, it is important to provide the best services possible at the least cost. For example, Hinchliffe, Hyman, Blizard, and Livingston (1995) provided drug therapy, behavioral, coping, and cognitive skills training, respite, *and* education to caregivers; it is unknown which aspects of the intervention were helpful, and all components may not be needed. Therefore, it is important to try to match the most effective intervention components to the particular needs of specific caregivers and to avoid providing unnecessary or ineffective service components. Too many choices may overwhelm caregivers or lead to nonuse of services. Yet, a meta-analysis of 30 psychosocial interventions for caregivers (Brodaty, Green, & Koschera, 2003) documented significant benefits in caregiver psychological distress and caregiver knowledge, particularly when the patients were involved in the intervention (i.e., when caregivers learned how to modify patient behaviors), the programs were more intensive, and the programs were tailored to caregivers' needs. Some of the interventions even delayed nursing home admission (Brody et al., 1989; Eloniemi-Sulkava, Sivenius, & Sulkava, 1999; Mittelman et al., 1996; Riordan et al., 1998).

Efforts are now under way to compare treatment components within multicomponent interventions for their relative effectiveness. For example, Bourgeois and colleagues (2002) developed a multicomponent intervention specifically to extend the generalizability of the most promising, state-of-the-art caregiver-focused skills training packages (Lovett & Gallagher, 1988) and patient-focused skills training approaches (Pinkston, Linsk, & Young, 1988; Zarit, Anthony, & Boutselis, 1987). They compared the effects of two well-defined and well-monitored skills training interventions (patient change or self-change) with a control condition in which caregivers received a quasi-treatment (group class, home visits, and patient behavior tracking). Spousal caregivers in both intervention groups demonstrated significant improvements in a variety of caregiver outcome measures such as depression, perceived health, caregiver strain, and self-efficacy as a result of successfully implementing patient change or self-change programs. However, caregivers who were taught to implement patient-focused behavior change programs in this study were highly effective in decreasing problem behaviors, demonstrating maintenance of treatment gains over time; caregivers who were taught to change their own behavior in response to caregiving challenges demonstrated significantly higher self-ratings of mood at the postintervention and follow-up assessments. The effects of the interventions were most evident for the outcomes that directly reflected the skills targeted by the training (i.e., teaching behavior management skills reduced problem behavior; teaching mood-elevating procedures improved mood ratings), and less so for those outcomes that were hypothesized to be related to the skills but not directly trained (e.g., anger and perceived health). These findings suggest that future interventions should assess the individual caregiver's specific training needs and tailor intervention to address directly those issues to maximize the desired outcomes. Differences in acceptability (i.e., implementation) of treatment plans between the two treatment groups suggested that caregivers might have different opinions about the behaviors they wanted to change, as well as perceived difficulty of implementing behavior change programs involving other individuals. Future interventions should be designed to offer a menu of behavior change strategies with therapist guidance in the selection process based on a caregiver needs assessment.

The analysis of different treatment components or treatment packages through a variety of outcome measures is also important for understanding the relationship between treatment components and outcomes. For example, Steffen (2000) compared a home-delivered videotaped Coping With Frustration class plus telephone follow-up with traditional face-to-face Coping With Frustration classes and a waiting list group and found that both treatment groups reported significant improvements in depression, hostility, and confidence in their ability to handle caregiving challenges, whereas the control group did not. Similar results were seen by Eisdorfer et al. (2003) and Mahoney et al. (2003) in their telephone-based cognitive-behavioral interventions; caregivers reduced their stress and depression and increased life satisfaction compared to minimal education and support groups. Glueckauf, Bourgeois, Massey, Pomidor, and Stine (2004) compared Internet-delivered and telephone-delivered Positive Caregiving classes to dementia family caregivers and found substantial increases in self-efficacy perceptions, and reduced caregiver burden post training for both treatment groups. The authors pointed out that these studies have all been conducted with caregivers living in metropolitan and urban areas. Glueckauf, Ketterson, Loomis, and Dages (2004) and Glueckauf et al. (2005) have recently designed a telephone-delivered modification of the Positive Caregiving classes specifically for a rural population; the Alzheimer's Rural Care Healthline (ARCH) program is designed to compare the effects of the telephone-based caregiving classes with a minimal education and support control condition on caregivers' depression, perceived self-efficacy, and burden.

In 1995, the National Institute on Aging and the National Institute on Nursing Research funded six intervention research programs designed to evaluate the effectiveness of different multicomponent interventions for family caregivers of persons with AD (Schulz et al., 2003). Each intervention model aimed to change specific caregiving stressors, and the caregivers' appraisal of and response to the stressors, and to address the specific needs of culturally diverse racial and ethnic majority and minority populations. This unique NIH initiative required adherence to the randomized controlled clinical trial requirements of (a) random assignment to treatment and control conditions, (b) common outcome measures, and (c) identical measurement intervals. As displayed in Table 9.3, the six studies evaluated different multicomponent interventions, with different racial and ethnic populations, and slightly different control conditions. Preliminary analyses of the combined data from these studies revealed that caregivers in intervention conditions reported reduced burden and reduced depression compared to those in control

TABLE 9.3 Characteristics of the Resources for Enhancing Alzheimer's Caregiver Health (REACH) Interventions

Site	Population	Intervention	Control Condition	Findings
Burgio, Stevens, Guy, Roth, and Haley (2003)	African American and White Spouse and nonspouse N = 118	Problem-solving training to change patient problem behaviors and caregiver coping	Telephone support and written materials about dementia and caregiving	African American and nonspouses had greater benefits than Whites and spouses.
Mahoney, Tarlow, and Jones (2003)	White and African American Wife, husband, and child N = 100	Telephone intervention for caregivers (voice-mail, bulletin board, and "ask the expert") and patient distraction calls	Written information about dementia caregiving and referral sources	Wives with low mastery and high anxiety benefited the most from automated telecare.
Burns, Nichols, Martindale-Adams, Graney, and Lummus (2003)	White and African American Spouse and nonspouse N = 167	Written information and skills training in patient behavior change and caregiver stress reduction	Written information about dementia caregiving and referral sources	Education intervention in the primary care setting reduced stress and burden; changing both patient and caregiver was better than either one alone.
Eisdorfer et al. (2003)	Cuban American and White Spouses, daughters, and other relatives N = 225	Family systems therapy and computerized telephone system	Telephone support and written materials about dementia and caregiving	Information technology reduces distress and depression in Whites and Cuban Americans; particularly effective for Cuban husbands and daughters.
Gallagher-Thompson et al. (2003)	White and Latino Wife and daughter N = 213	Psychoeducational class on caregiver coping and mood management	Telephone support and written materials about dementia and caregiving	More improved coping with skills building and support than with support group alone.

TABLE 9.3 (Continued)

Site	Population	Intervention	Control Condition	Findings
Gitlin (2003)	White and African American Spouse and nonspouse $N = 255$	Home environmental skills building to change patient behaviors	Written information about dementia caregiving and referral sources	Less upset with memory-related behaviors and improved affect with intervention; women benefited more than men in mastery and ability to manage daily caregiving tasks.

conditions. Specifically, women and individuals with high school or less education reported lower burden, whereas caregivers who were Latino, had less than a high school education, and were nonspouses reported lower depression than similar caregivers in the control conditions.

Schulz and colleagues (2003) pointed out that although these intervention studies have provided more insight into which strategies are useful for enhancing outcomes for different caregivers, the effects of these interventions on burden, depression, and other indicators of psychological well-being remain small to moderate. They hypothesized that the reason for these disappointing effects may be that caregivers cannot be categorized into single syndromal groups that are the target of a specific intervention. Caregivers may instead have problems of varying intensities in multiple areas and may need different intervention components tailored to address those specific issues. The attempt to find a "one-size-fits-all" intervention remains unsuccessful and most likely unrealistic. This important finding has led to the funding of a second phase of intervention studies, called Resources for Enhancing Alzheimer's Caregiver Health (REACH) II. The purpose of these studies is to evaluate an intervention composed of multiple treatment components (safety, self-care, social support, emotional well-being, and problem behaviors) that is specifically tailored to the individual caregiver. A risk appraisal instrument will determine the intensity of each treatment component a caregiver requires. Those treatments will be delivered using the most promising combination of in-home visits and telephone-based support found in the REACH studies.

Communication-Focused Dementia Caregiver Interventions

Family caregivers of a person with dementia report that attempting to communicate with their loved one can be stressful (Clark & Witte, 1995). This is probably due to not understanding the communication problems associated with dementia, nor having the skills needed to prevent or repair communication breakdowns. As a result, caregivers may develop misconceptions about changes in communication, unrealistic expectations of communicative interactions, and negative communication patterns with their family member with dementia (Ripich, Ziol, & Lee, 1998). Investigations of the relationship between communication problems and caregiving burdens reveal that specific semantic and pragmatic breakdowns in language processing by persons with dementia result in problem behaviors that are stressful to caregivers (Savundranagam, Hummert, & Montgomery, 2005). For example, word-finding difficulties interfere with topic maintenance in a conversation (Ripich, 1994), and misunderstood conversations lead to caregiver frustration (Orange, 1995). Therefore, it follows that caregivers need assistance to understand the progressive decline in communication skills over the course of dementia, the impact on problem behaviors, and strategies to ease the stress and burden of impaired communication.

There are many publications for caregivers concerning the changes in communication behaviors related to dementia. Those written by SLPs describe the communication impairments and preserved abilities across mild, moderate, and severe stages of the disease (e.g., Rau, 1993; Santo Pietro & Ostuni, 2003). Other, more general guidebooks also contain chapters on communication challenges and recommended strategies for improving communication (e.g., Mace & Rabins, 1999; Tappen, 1997). Research on the many commonsense recommendations for caregivers about how best to communicate with persons with dementia has been forthcoming in the literature with mixed results. For example, Hendryx-Bedalov (1999) noted that persons with AD appeared to have more difficulty responding to abstract rather than concrete language during mealtime conversations; however, when caregivers were taught to use more concrete questions, the responses of the person with AD were not much different from when they were asked abstract questions. Similarly, Tappen and colleagues (Tappen, Williams-Burgess, Edelstein, Touhy, & Fishman, 1997) taught caregivers three conversation-enhancing strategies (i.e., closed-ended questions, respecting personhood, and topic maintenance) and documented their increased use of these strategies with relatively little differential effect on the persons with dementia who responded positively to all strategies. Caregivers report dissatisfaction with some recommended strategies that they have tried without much success, such as using a slow rate of speech and short utterances (Orange, 1995).

Small and Gutman (2002) reviewed the literature to identify all the recommended communication strategies for caregivers (see Table 9.4 for a list of the 10 most frequently recommended strategies). Caregivers were then asked to rate the frequency of use and effectiveness of each of these strategies. Similar to other reports in the literature, short simple speech and asking one question or giving one instruction at a time were judged effective techniques (Kemper, Anagnopoulos, Lyons, & Heberlein, 1994; Small, Kemper, & Lyons, 1997; Small et al., 2003). In contrast to Small et al. (1997), these caregivers reported dissatisfaction with paraphrased speech, and they did not use the following strategies very often: slowed speech, eliminating distractions, approaching from the front, and maintaining eye

TABLE 9.4 Rank Order of the Most Frequently Recommended Communication Strategies

1. Use short, simple sentences.
2. Speak slowly.
3. Ask one question or give one instruction at a time.
4. Approach slowly and from the front; establish and maintain eye contact.
5. Eliminate distractions (e.g., TV and radio).
6. Avoid interrupting the person; allow plenty of time for responding.
7. Use yes–no rather than open-ended questions.
8. Encourage circumlocution during word-finding problems.
9. Repeat messages with the same wording.
10. Paraphrase repeated messages.

Source: From Small and Gutman (2002).

contact. As Small and Gutman pointed out, there is still a great need for research on the efficacy of these recommended strategies in real-life situations. Several studies have begun to address these issues directly; for example, caregivers have been taught to use memory aids to enhance conversations (Bourgeois, 1992; Burgio et al., 2001) and to reduce repetitive requests (Bourgeois et al., 1997). In other research, caregivers were taught to improve repair strategies (Orange & Colton-Hudson, 1998). In addition to improving communication, these studies have also found reduced caregiver-reported stress.

Although many of the above-reviewed caregiving interventions addressed communication-related issues in a general way, family caregivers need specific training, such as identifying communication problems and applying communication strategies, to improve communicative interactions. In addition, as mentioned in chapter 3, many problem behaviors exhibited by persons with dementia appear related to communication and cognitive impairments that can be modified successfully with communication- or memory-enhancing interventions designed by SLPs. Therefore, the role of the SLP in working with caregivers is multidimensional. SLPs can teach caregivers about the cognitive and communicative deficits and strengths of the person with dementia as the disease progresses. They can convey specific strategies and techniques for supporting and maintaining satisfying conversations and for modifying related problem behaviors. It is important to note that SLPs can be reimbursed for training caregivers; in chapter 11, examples of caregiver treatment goals will be provided. In addition, SLPs can recognize the other psychosocial and emotional needs of caregivers and make recommendations for other services, including educational materials, Web sites, support groups, and other relevant community resources. Table 9.5 provides a list of the educational topics that are beneficial to caregivers; Table 9.6 is a list of Web sites and Internet resources for caregivers. Finally, SLPs can provide counseling services to caregivers struggling emotionally with caregiving challenges. As discussed in chapter 8, the functional approaches suggested in this book for treating the person with dementia and their caregivers are designed to help maintain a quality life in the face of the many difficulties related to a degenerative disease such as dementia

TABLE 9.5 Examples of Caregiver Education Topics

Dementia: Definition, stages, expected course, and treatment
Understanding Alzheimer's disease and related dementias
Characteristics of Alzheimer's disease and related dementias
Communication skills
Behavior management
Activities of daily living (ADLs); bathing, dressing, toileting, and feeding
Medical care: Diagnostic evaluation, treatment, and drug studies
Nursing and home health care services
Respite and day care services
Residential care and nursing home options
Support groups
Counseling services
Transportation services
Local agency services
Legal issues and services
Financial issues and services

TABLE 9.6 Web Sites and Internet Resources for Family Caregivers

Administration on Aging: http://www.aoa.gov
Source for long-term care ombudsmen: http://www.aoa.gov/prof/aoaprog/elder_rights/LTCombudsman/ltc_ombudsman.asp
Alzheimer Disease Education and Referral Center (ADEAR): http://www.alzheimers.org
Alzheimer's Association: http://www.alz.org
Alzheimer's Foundation of America: http://www.alzfdn.org
American Geriatrics Society: http://www.americangeriatrics.org
Area Agency on Aging: http://www.n4a.org
Source for eldercare local community services: http://www.n4a.org/locator
Family Caregiver Alliance: http://www.caregiver.org
Mayo Clinic: http://www.Mayoclinic.com/health/alzheimers-caregivers
Medline Plus: http://www.nlm.nih.gov/medlineplus/alzheimerscaregivers.html
National Family Caregiver Support program: http://www.fullcirclecare.org
Online Caregiver magazine: http://www.caregiver.com
Source of CD-ROM training materials: http://www.OrcasHealth.com
Source of large-print and adaptive household and leisure materials: http://www.eldercorner.com
Source of Video Respite tapes and other Alzheimer's-related materials: http://www.healthpropress.com

and to assist with end-of-life communication. The interventions described in the remaining sections of this chapter were designed by SLPs specifically for dementia caregivers to improve communicative interactions with their loved one.

The FOCUSED Program Ripich (1994) adapted a communication skills training program developed for nursing assistants (Ripich, Wykle, & Niles, 1995) to address the needs of family caregivers. Based on an interactive discourse model of conversational exchanges, this seven-step program, called the FOCUSED program, teaches caregivers specific conversation skills (**f**ace-to-face, **o**rientation, **c**ontinuity, **u**nsticking, **s**tructure, **e**xchange, and **d**irect). See Table 9.7 for a description of each strategy. This training program is designed to be used in six 2-hour modules and includes a trainer's manual, a caregiver's guide, pre- and postassessments, reminder cards on which are printed the FOCUSED principles, and an instructional videotape (*Alzheimer's Disease Communication Guide: The FOCUSED Program for Caregivers*; Ripich & Wykle, 1996).

Ripich et al. (1998) evaluated this program with 19 caregivers (15 women and 4 men) and a waitlist control group of 18 caregivers (15 women and 3 men). The treatment group attended four 2-hour sessions. Both groups completed an assessment battery, consisting of measures of well-being (positive and negative affect), depression, health, stress and burden (general and communication hassles), and knowledge of AD and communication, in each of four phases: pretraining, immediately, and 6 and 12 months post training. Treatment caregivers demonstrated significant decreases in communication hassles and increases in knowledge about AD and communication in posttraining, which maintained at 6 and 12 months, compared to control caregivers, who did not show these effects. No changes were reported in any of the other measures of affect, depression, health, or general caregiving hassles. This study provides support for the effectiveness of a communication-focused skills training program to produce changes in communicative interactions between caregivers and their family member with dementia. Byrne and Orange (2005) pointed out, however, that this program was "not based on a theoretical framework that justifies its program elements" (p. 196), and as Small and Gutman (2002) found, not all of the recommended strategies have been reported to be

TABLE 9.7 FOCUSED Communication Strategies

Face-to-face	Face the person with AD. Call his or her name. Touch the person. Gain and maintain eye contact.
Orientation	Orient the person to the topic by repeating key words several times. Repeat and rephrase sentences. Use nouns and specific names.
Continuity	Continue the same topic of conversation for as long as possible. Restate the topic throughout the conversation. Indicate that you are introducing a new topic.
Unsticking	Help the person become "unstuck" by suggesting the intended word. Repeat the sentence using the correct word. Ask, "Do you mean …?"
Structure	Structure your questions so that the person can recognize and repeat a response. Provide two simple choices at a time. Use yes–no questions.
Exchange	Keep up the normal exchange of ideas in everyday conversation. Keep the conversation going with comments like "Oh, how nice," or "That's great." Do not ask "test" questions.
Direct	Keep sentences short, simple, and direct. Put the subject of the sentence first. Use and repeat nouns rather than pronouns. Use hand signals, pictures, and facial expressions.

Source: Ripich and Wykle (1996).

effective. SLPs must be sure to monitor the effects of any treatment program that recommends the FOCUSED strategies.

Teaching Caregivers to Use Memory Aids As mentioned in chapter 4, family caregivers have been taught to use memory wallets and memory books to improve conversations with the person with dementia (Bourgeois, 1994). When the perceptions of the caregivers in that study did not match the objective data (i.e., spouses were not impressed with the improvement in conversation about familiar historical content when other behavior problems persisted), Bourgeois and colleagues (1997) explored the benefits of teaching caregivers to use targeted written text to modify caregiver-identified repetitive verbal behaviors that were reported to be disruptive and to prevent satisfying communicative interactions. For example, if the caregiver was distressed that the person with AD repeatedly asked about a deceased relative, then a page was made for the memory book that stated the facts (e.g., "My husband, Jim, was laid to rest in St. Mary's Cemetery on March 14, 2002"). In each case, a written statement and cue format were developed to address the unique concern of the person, ranging from a reminder card that read, "We are going to the grocery store," to an erasable memo board on the refrigerator that read, "Today is Monday. Jane will be home at 3 o'clock." Results revealed that, in addition to caregivers reporting reductions in the frequency of repeated verbalizations with the use of these written tools, they also expressed satisfaction with their own ability to modify a previously frustrating problem.

It must be noted that the caregivers in this study were part of a larger study (Bourgeois et al., 2002) and were asked to keep track of the frequency of the most stressful problem behaviors of their spouse with AD over the course of the study. In some cases, the data sheets revealed that the problems identified as very stressful were in fact very rare in occurrence; it was only those that persisted over time that were addressed with a written memory aid strategy. It was suggested that the recording of data itself might be an effective intervention for helping the caregiver to be more objective about the frequency of particularly challenging behaviors. As Bourgeois et al. (2002) reported, however, control group caregivers who did not receive training in memory aids may have become more objective about the problem behaviors of their spouse with AD because of data recording, but the frequency of the challenging behaviors was not changed as a result of data recording alone. Recording the frequency of problem behaviors is, however, an important precursor to the development of an effective intervention. Appendix 9.1 includes examples of data-recording sheets recommended for caregivers and instructions for their use.

Several other tools for working with caregivers have also been included at the end of this chapter. Appendix 9.2 contains caregiver instructions for making memory aids. Appendix 9.3 has caregiver instructions for having satisfying conversations with the care recipient using a memory aid. Appendix 9.4 contains caregiver instructions for developing and using written cues (in the form of reminder cards).

CASE 9.1 ILLUSTRATION OF A CAREGIVER INTERVENTION

The conference room at the Capital Area Regional Hospital was fast becoming crowded for the monthly meeting of "Caregivers: Education and Support." Mr. and Mrs. Wong; Juanita Hernandez and her sister, Maria; the Johnson family (siblings Jamar, Jerrell, and Jenisha); Mrs. Bernadette Sterling; Burton Hughes; and several other newcomers were chatting quietly. The social worker, Mary Washington, was checking with the guest speaker, Dr. Henry, about the projector and his handouts for tonight's presentation. Within minutes everyone found a seat, and Ms. Washington made some welcoming remarks and introduced the speaker and his topic, "Recent Advances in Dementia Medications." As Dr. Henry began his lecture, Ms. Washington surveyed the assembled group and reflected on their progress in the past months.

Mr. and Mrs. Wong, middle-aged professionals and second-generation Taiwanese, were caring for Mr. Wong's father with dementia. Several months ago, Mrs. Wong had called in distress; her husband expected her to quit her job to care for his father, who was exhibiting uncharacteristic behaviors (e.g., putting clothing in shopping bags, buying cigarettes at the corner grocery, and asking strangers for directions to the bus station). They had sent him to Taiwan to visit his siblings during the summer, but upon his return he denied that he had seen anyone he knew or that he had had anything to eat for the entire 3 weeks. Ms. Washington advised Mrs. Wong to make an appointment with their family physician. Subsequent to Mr. Wong Sr.'s dementia diagnosis, Mr. and Mrs. Wong began attending this group, and over the past few months they had implemented several suggestions: They hired a personal assistant to spend the daytime hours with Mr. Wong, fixing his meals, playing chess with him, and taking him to the Asian Social Club for their afternoon men's group. Mr. Wong Jr. made an appointment with an attorney to discuss financial and medical decision making.

Juanita Hernandez and her sister, Maria, both single mothers with several young children, were sharing responsibility for their mother with dementia. Their mother, Ana Luz, had cared for an extended family of more than 25 foster children over the years, but had been unable to complete any of her routine household activities for many months. She spent hours sitting in a chair on the porch, watching the passersby; she forgot to bathe or change her clothing. On the day when Maria arrived home to hear her young son screaming in his crib, apparently unattended for hours, Juanita and her sister arranged for a medical evaluation. It has been a very difficult 6 months for these sisters, trying to enlist the help of other siblings to share in the care of their mother as well as multiple small children. But Ms. Washington remembers vividly the family meeting she facilitated at Ana Luz' home; several other sisters and two brothers had an emotional time learning that their mother with dementia required such close supervision and assistance. But they were quick to volunteer for a variety of activities at specific times, as Ms. Washington noted these on an erasable monthly calendar; each sister agreed to spend one day a week at their mother's house watching the babies and preparing meals. One brother offered to do the yard work and take out the garbage weekly; the other planned to take Ana Luz to church on Sundays. It has not always gone as smoothly as everyone had hoped, but they have recently started having a family potluck dinner at Ana Luz's after church on Sunday, and that is helping everyone plan for the coming week.

It was rewarding to see the Johnson family all in attendance tonight. Siblings Lamar, Jerrell, and Shaniqua have their own families and many personal challenges, but they have been able to help their beloved uncle Oscar to get diagnosed and moved to an assisted living facility. Last month, they mentioned the facility staff were concerned that Oscar was not attending his usual activity programs and was missing meals; the Johnsons are hoping to get some ideas tonight about how to get their uncle to take his medications correctly.

Mrs. Bernadette Sterling and Burton Hughes are both in their 70s. They met last year at the hospital's adult day care facility, where their spouses spent the daytime hours. Mr. Sterling died a few months ago, but Mrs. Sterling still attends these meetings. Mr. Hughes has come to the meeting tonight for ideas about how to handle his wife's fears about the new day care staff member who has a foreign accent. Mrs. Sterling is remembering when Ms. Washington first suggested adult day care for her husband; she had just dismissed that idea because her husband's illness had made him quick to say anything that came to mind and she was afraid he would say something racist in public. She regrets the many months she waited until she was so worn out from caregiving that day care was her only hope. But she was determined to avoid placing her husband in a nursing home; her fears were put to rest when she watched the staff anticipate potentially difficult situations and carefully redirect him to a positive activity. Mr. Hughes' wife will be fine once he alerts the staff to watch for signs that she is becoming fearful.

As the presentation winds down and Dr. Henry is answering questions from the audience, Ms. Washington notices that a couple of last meeting's newcomers are not present tonight. Seth McCory, a busy young attorney, had asked her at the end of the meeting for other sources of information about dementia; she gave him a list of reputable Web sites and a bibliography of books and pamphlets to get him started learning about his mother's diagnosis. Mary Smith, the freelance photographer, whose only relative was an aunt in another state who was calling her daily with troubling questions, needed the toll-free helpline number for advice when these unexpected calls occurred. As different as each of these caregivers are, there are different solutions for their needs. Ms. Washington is relieved that her hospital and her community have the wealth of resources needed to meet the needs of everyone who is dealing with the challenges of dementia.

REFERENCES

Adams, B., Aranda, M., Kemp, R., & Takagi, K. (2002). Ethnic and gender differences in distress among Anglo-American, African-American, Japanese-American and Mexican-American spousal caregivers of persons with dementia. *Journal of Clinical Geropsychology, 8*(4), 279–301.

Albert, S. M. (1990). The dependent elderly, home health care, and strategies of household adaptation. In J. F. Gubrium & A. Sankar (Eds.), *The home care experience* (pp. 19–36). Newbury Park, CA: Sage.

American Association of Retired Persons [AARP] and Travelers Companies Foundation. (1988). *A national survey of caregiver*. Washington, DC: Opinion Research.

Aneshensel, C., Pearlin, L., Mullan, J., Zarit, S., & Whitlatch, C. (1995). *Profiles in caregiving: The unexpected career*. New York: Academic Press.

Argimon, J., Limon, E., Vila, J., & Cabezas, C. (2005). Health-related quality-of-life of caregivers as a predictor of nursing-home placement of patients with dementia. *Alzheimer Disease and Associated Disorders, 19*(1), 41–44.

Atchely, R. C. (1988). *The social forces in later life*. Belmont, CA: Wadsworth.

Ayalon, L., & Huyck, M. (2001). Latino caregivers of relatives with Alzheimer's disease. *Clinical Gerontologist, 24*(3/4), 93–106.

Barnes, C., Given, B., & Given, C. (1992). Caregivers of elderly relatives: Spouses and adult children. *Health & Social Work, 17*, 282–289.

Barnes, L., Mendes de Leon, C., Bienias, J., & Evans, D. (2004). A longitudinal study of Black-White differences in social resources. *Journal of Gerontology: Social Sciences, 59B*, S146–S153.

Bass, D. (1990). *Caring families: Supports and interventions*. Silver Spring, MD: NASW.

Beach, S., Schulz, R., Yee, J., & Jackson, S. (1998). Negative (and positive) health effects of caring for a disabled spouse: Longitudinal findings from the Caregiver Health Effects Study. *Journal of Psychology and Aging, 15*(2), 259–271.

Bookwala, J., Yee, J., & Schulz, R. (2000). Caregiving and detrimental mental and physical health outcomes. In G. Williamson, P. Parmelee, & D. Shaffer (Eds.), *Physical illness and depression in older adults: A handbook of theory, research, and practice* (pp. 93–131). New York: Plenum.

Bourgeois, M. (1992). Evaluating memory wallets in conversations with patients with dementia. *Journal of Speech and Hearing Research, 35*, 1344–1357.

Bourgeois, M. (1994). Teaching caregivers to use memory aids with patients with dementia. In Caregiving in Alzheimer's disease II: Caregiving interventions. *Seminars in Speech and Language, 15*(4), 291–305.

Bourgeois, M. (1997). Families caring for elders at home: Caregiver training. In B. Shadden & M. A. Toner (Eds.), *Communication and aging: For clinicians by clinicians* (pp. 227–249). Austin, TX: Pro-Ed.

Bourgeois, M., Beach, S., Schulz, R., & Burgio, L. (1996). When primary and secondary caregivers disagree: Predictors and psychosocial consequences. *Psychology and Aging, 11*, 527–537.

Bourgeois, M., Burgio, L., Schulz, R., Beach, S., & Palmer, B. (1997). Modifying repetitive verbalization of community dwelling patients with AD. *The Gerontologist, 37*, 30–39.

Bourgeois, M., Schulz, R., & Burgio, L. (1996). Interventions for caregivers of patients with Alzheimer's disease: A review and analysis of content, process, and outcomes. *International Journal of Aging and Human Development, 43*, 35–92.

Bourgeois, M., Schulz, R., Burgio, L., & Beach, S. (2002). Skills training for spouses of patients with Alzheimer's disease: Outcomes of an intervention study. *Journal of Clinical Geropsychology, 8*, 53–73.

Brennan, P., Moore, S., & Smyth, K. (1991). ComputerLink: Electronic support for the home caregiver. *Advances in Nursing Science*, *13*(4), 14–27.

Briones, D., Ramirez, A., Guerrero, M., & Ledger, E. (2002). Determining cultural and psychosocial factors in Alzheimer disease among Hispanic populations. *Alzheimer Disease and Associated Disorders*, *16*, S86–S88.

Brodaty, H., Green, A., & Koschera, A. (2003). Meta-analysis of psychosocial interventions for caregivers of people with dementia. *Journal of the American Geriatrics Society*, *51*, 657–664.

Brodaty, H., McGilchrist, C., Harris, L., & Peters, K. (1993). Time until institutionalization and death in patients with dementia. *Archives of Neurology*, *50*, 643–650.

Brodaty, H., Roberts, K., & Peters, K. (1994). Quasi-experimental evaluation of an educational model for dementia caregivers. *International Journal of Geriatric Psychiatry*, *9*, 195–204.

Brody, E. M., Hoffman, C., Kleban, M. H., & Schoonover, C. B. (1989). Caregiving daughters and their local siblings: Perceptions, strains, and interactions. *The Gerontologist*, *29*, 529–538.

Brody, E., Litvin, S., Hoffman, C., & Kleban, M. (1992). Differential effects of daughters' marital status on their parent care experiences. *The Gerontologist*, *32*, 58–67.

Brown, J., & Alligood, M. (2004). Realizing wrongness: Stories of older wife caregivers. *Journal of Applied Gerontology*, *23*(2), 104–119.

Burgio, L., Allen-Burge, R., Roth, D., Bourgeois, M., Dijkstra, K., Gerstle, J., et al. (2001). Come talk with me: Improving communication between nursing assistants and nursing home residents during care routines. *The Gerontologist*, *41*, 449–460.

Burgio, L., Stevens, A., Guy, D., Roth, D., & Haley, W. (2003). Impact of two psychosocial interventions on white and African American family caregivers of individuals with dementia. *Gerontologist*, *43*, 568–579.

Burns, R., Nichols, L., Martindale-Adams, J., Graney, M., & Lummus, A. (2003). Primary care interventions for dementia caregivers: 2-year outcomes from the REACH study. *Gerontologist*, *43*, 547–555.

Burton, L., Newsom, J., Schulz, R., Hirsch, C., & German, P. (1997). Preventive health behaviors among spousal caregivers. *Preventive Medicine*, *26*, 162–169.

Byrne, K., & Orange, J. B. (2005). Conceptualizing communication enhancement in dementia for family caregivers using the SHO-ICF framework. *Advances in Speech-Language Pathology*, *7*(4), 187–202.

Caradoc-Davies, T., & Harvey, J. (1995). Do social relief admissions have any effect on patients or their caregivers? *Disability and Rehabilitation*, *17*(5), 247–251.

Castle, S., Wilkins, S., Heck, E., Tanzy, K., & Fahey, J. (1995). Depression in caregivers of demented patients is associated with altered immunity: Impaired proliferative capacity, increased CD8+, and a decline in lymphocytes with surface signal transduction molecules (CD38+) and acytotoxicity marker (CD56+CD8+). *Clinical Experimental Immunology*, *101*, 487–493.

Challis, D., von Abendorff, R., Brown, P., Chesterman, J., & Hughes, J. (2002). Care management, dementia care and specialist mental health services: An evaluation. *International Journal of Geriatric Psychiatry*, *17*(4), 315–325.

Chiriboga, D., Black, S., Aranda, M., & Markides, K. (2002). Stress and depressive symptoms among Mexican American elders. *Journal of Gerontology: Psychological Sciences*, *57B*, P559–P568.

Chiverton, P., & Caine, E. (1989). Education to assist spouses in coping with AD: A controlled trial. *Journal of the American Geriatrics Society*, *37*, 593–598.

Cicirelli, V. G. (1983). Adult children's attachment and helping behaviour to elderly parents: A path model. *Journal of Marriage and the Family*, *45*, 815–824.

Clark, L. (1997). Communication intervention for family caregivers and professional health care providers. In B. Shadden & M. A. Toner (Eds.), *Aging and Communication* (pp. 251–274). Austin, TX: Pro-Ed.

Clark, L., & Witte, K. (1995). Nature and efficacy of communication management in Alzheimer's disease. In R. Lubinski (Ed.), *Dementia and communication* (pp. 238–256). San Diego, CA: Singular.

Cloutterbuck, J., & Mahoney, D. (2003). African American dementia caregivers: The duality of respect. *Dementia*, *2*(2), 221–243.

Clyburn, L., Stones, M., Hadjistavropoulos, T., & Tuokko, H. (2000). Predicting caregiver burden and depression in Alzheimer's disease. *Journal of Gerontology: Social Sciences*, *55B*, S2–S13.

Cochrane, J., Goering, P., & Rogers, J. (1997). The mental health of informal caregivers in Ontario: An epidemiological survey. *American Journal of Public Health*, *87*, 2002–2007.

Collins, C., & Jones, R. (1997). Emotional distress and morbidity in dementia carers: A matched comparison of husbands and wives. *International Journal of Geriatric Psychiatry*, *12*, 1168–1173.

Connell, C., & Gibson, G. (1997). Racial, ethnic and cultural differences in dementia caregiving: Review and analysis. *The Gerontologist*, *37*, 355–364.

Connidis, I. A., Rosenthal, C. J., & McMullin, J. A. (1996). The impact of family composition on providing help to older parents. *Research on aging*, *18*(4), 402–429.

Coon, D. W., Gallagher-Thompson, E., & Thompson, L. (Eds.). (2003). *Innovative interventions to reduce dementia caregiver distress*. New York: Springer.

Corcoran, M. (1993). Collaboration: An ethical approach to effective therapeutic relationships. *Topics in Geriatric Rehabilitation*, *9*, 21–29.

Corcoran, M. (1994, November). Individuals caring for a spouse with Alzheimer's disease: A descriptive study of caregiving styles. Paper presented at the Gerontological Society of America Convention, New Orleans, LA.

Crabtree, J., & Crabtree, D. (1993). *Home caregiver's guide: Articles for adult daily living*. Tucson, AZ: Therapy Skill Builders.

Crawford, L., Bond, J., & Balshaw, R. (1994). Factors affecting sons' and daughters' caregiving to older parents. *Canadian Journal on Aging*, *13*(4), 454–469.

Croog, S., Sudilovsky, A., Burleson, J., & Baume, R. (2001). Vulnerability of husband and wife caregivers of Alzheimer disease patients to caregiving stressors. *Alzheimer Disease and Associated Disorders*, *15*(4), 201–210.

Demers, A., & Lavoie, J. (1996). Effect of support groups on family caregivers to the frail elderly. *Canadian Journal on Aging*, *15*(1), 129–144.

Dilworth-Anderson, P., Goodwin, P., & Williams, S. (2004). Can culture help explain the physical health effects of caregiving over time among African American caregivers? *Journal of Gerontology: Social Sciences*, *59B*, S138–S145.

Diwan, S., Berger, C., & Manns, E. (1997). Composition of the home care service package: Predictors of type, volume, and mix of services provided to poor and frail older people. *The Gerontologist*, *37*, 169–181.

Dwyer, J. W., & Coward, R. T. (1991). A multivariate comparison of the involvement of adult sons versus daughters in the care of impaired parents. *Journal of Gerontology*, *46*, S259–S269.

Dwyer, J. W., Henretta, J. C., Coward, R. T., & Barton, A. J. (1992). Changes in helping behaviors of adult children as caregivers. *Research on Aging*, *14*(3), 351–375.

Edgerly, E., Montes, L., Yau, E., Stokes, S., & Redd, D. (2003). Ethnic minority caregivers. In D. Coon, D. Gallagher-Thompson, & L. Thompson (Eds.), *Innovative interventions to reduce dementia caregiver stress* (pp. 223–242). New York: Springer.

Eisdorfer, C., Czaja, S., Loewenstein, D., Rubert, M., Arguelles, S., Mitrani, V., et al. (2003). The effect of a family therapy and technology-based intervention on caregiver depression. *Gerontologist*, *43*, 521–531.

Elliot, K., Di Minno, M., Lam, D., & Tu, A. (1996). Working with Chinese families in the context of dementia. In G. Yeo & D. Gallagher-Thompson (Eds.), *Ethnicity and the dementias* (pp. 89–108). Washington, DC: Taylor & Francis.

Eloniemi-Sulkava, U., Sivenius, J. S., & Sulkava, R. (1999). Support program for demented patients and their carers: The role of dementia family care coordinator is crucial. In K. Iqbal, D. Swaab, B. Winblad, & H. M. Wisniewski (Eds.), *Alzheimer's disease and related disorders* (pp. 795–802). West Sussex, UK: John Wiley.

Finley, N. J. (1989). Theories of family labor as applied to gender differences in caregiving for elderly parents. *Journal of Marriage and the Family*, *51*, 79–86.

Franks, M., Pierce, L., & Dwyer, J. (2003). Expected parent-care involvement of adult children. *Journal of Applied Gerontology*, *22*(1), 104–117.

Fuh, J., Wanh, S., Liu, H., & Wang, H. (1999). The caregiving burden scale among Chinese caregivers of Alzheimer patients. *Dementia and Geriatric Cognitive Disorders*, *10*(3), 186–191.

Fulton, B. R. (2005). Adult child caregivers of persons with Alzheimer's disease: Social exchange, generativity, and the family. *Dissertation Abstracts International*, *66*(2-B), 1219.

Gallagher-Thompson, D., Arean, P., Rivera, P., & Thompson, L. (2001). A psychoeducational intervention to reduce distress in Hispanic family caregivers: results of a pilot study. *Clinical Gerontologist*, *23*(1/2), 17–32.

Gallagher-Thompson, D., Coon, D., Solano, N., Ambler, C., Rabinowitz, Y., & Thompson, L. (2003). Change in indices of distress among Latino and Anglo female caregivers of elderly relatives with dementia: Site-specific results from the REACH national collaborative study. *Gerontologist*, *43*, 580–591.

Gallagher-Thompson, D., & DeVries, H. (1994). Coping with frustration classes: Development and preliminary outcomes with women who care for relatives with dementia. *The Gerontologist*, *34*(4), 548–552.

Gallagher-Thompson, D., & Steffen, A. (1994). Comparative effects of cognitive-behavioral and brief psychodynamic psychotherapies for depressed family caregivers. *Journal of Consulting and Clinical Psychology*, *62*(3), 543–549.

Gallagher-Thompson, D., Talamantes, M., Ramirez, R., & Valverde, I. (1996). Service delivery issues and recommendations for working with Mexican American family caregivers. In G. Yeo & D. Gallagher-Thompson (Eds.), *Ethnicity and the dementias* (pp. 137–152). Washington, DC: Taylor & Francis.

Gaugler, J., Edwards, A., Femia, E., Zarit, S., Stephens, M., Townsend, A., et al. (2000). Predictors of institutionalization of cognitively impaired elders: Family help and the timing of placement. *Journal of Gerontology: Psychological Sciences*, *55B*, P247–P255.

Gerdner, L., Tripp-Reimer, T., & Yang, D. (2005). Perception and care of elders with dementia in the Hmong American community. *Alzheimer's & Dementia*, *1*(Suppl. 1), S54–S55.

Gill, C., Hinrichsen, G., & DiGiusepppe, R. (1998). Factors associated with formal service use by family members of patients with dementia. *Journal of Applied Gerontology*, *17*, 38–52.

Gitlin, L., Winter, L., Corcoran, M., Dennis, M., Schinfeld, S., & Hauck, W. (2003). Effects of the home environmental skill-building program on caregiver-care recipient dyad: 6-month outcomes from the Philadelphia REACH initiative. *The Gerontologist*, *43*, 532–546.

Glaser, R., & Kiecolt-Glaser, J. (1997). Chronic stress modulates the virus-specific immune response to latent herpes simplex type 1. *Annals of Behavioral Medicine*, *19*, 78–82.

Glueckauf, R. L., Bourgeois, M., Massey, A., Pomidor, A., & Stine, C. (2004, June). *Alzheimer's Rural Care Healthline: Supporting rural caregivers across Florida* (Grant No. 2004103). Tampa, FL: Johnny Byrd, Sr. Alzheimer's Center and Research Institute.

Glueckauf, R., Ketterson, T., Loomis, J., & Dages, P. (2004). Online support and education for dementia caregivers: Overview, utilization, and initial program evaluation. *Telemedicine Journal and e-Health, 10*, 223–232.

Glueckauf, R., & Loomis, J. (2003). Alzheimer's caregiver support online: Overview, lessons learned, and future directions for research and practice. *Neurorehabilitation, 18*, 135–146.

Glueckauf, R. L., Stine, C., Bourgeois, M., Pomidor, A., Rom, P., Young, M. E., et al. (2005). Alzheimer's Rural Care Healthline: Linking rural caregivers to cognitive-behavioral intervention for depression. *Rehabilitation Psychology, 50*, 346–354.

Goodman, C., & Pynoos, J. (1990). A model telephone information and support program for caregivers of Alzheimer's patients. *The Gerontologist, 30*(3), 399–404.

Gottlieb, B., & Gignac, M. (1996). Content and domain specificity of coping among family caregivers of persons with dementia. *Journal of Aging Studies, 10*(2), 137–155.

Gwyther, L. (1990). Letting go: Separation-individuation in a wife of an Alzheimer's patient. *The Gerontologist, 30*, 698–702.

Hamilton, E. (1996). Factors associated with family caregivers' choice not to use services. *American Journal of Alzheimer's Disease, 11*, 29–38.

Harwood, D., Barker, W., Ownby, R., & Duara, R. (2000). Caregiver self-rated health in Alzheimer's disease. *Clinical Gerontologist, 21*(4), 19–33.

Hébert, R., Lévesque, L., Vézina, J., Lavoie, J-P., Ducharme, F., Gendron, C., et al. (2003). Efficacy of a psychoedudcative group program for caregivers of demented persons living at home: A randomized controlled trial. *Journal of Gerontology: Social Sciences, 56B*, S58–S67.

Henderson, J. N. (1996). Cultural dynamics of dementia in a Cuban and Puerto Rican population in the United States. In G. Yeo & D. Gallagher-Thompson (Eds.), *Ethnicity and the dementias* (pp. 153–166). Washington, DC: Taylor & Francis.

Hendryx-Bedalov, P. (1999). Effects of caregiver communication on the outcomes of requests in spouses with dementia of the Alzheimer's type. *International Journal of Aging and Human Development, 49*, 127–148.

Hinchliffe, A., Hyman, I., Blizard, B., & Livingston, G. (1995). Behavioural complications of dementia: Can they be treated? *International Journal of Geriatric Psychiatry, 10*, 839–847.

Hinton, L. (2002). Improving care for ethnic minority elderly and their family caregivers across the spectrum of dementia severity. *Alzheimer Disease and Associated Disorders, 16*, S50–S55.

Hooker, K., Bowman, S., Coehlo, D., Lim, S., Kaye, J., Guariglia, R., et al. (2002). Behavioral change in persons with dementia: Relationships with mental and physical health of caregivers. *Journal of Gerontology: Psychological Sciences, 57B*, P453–P460.

Hooyman, N., & Lustbader, W. (1986). *Taking care: Supporting older people and their families*. New York: Springer.

Horowitz, A. (1985). Sons and daughters as caregivers to older parents: Differences in role performance and consequences. *The Gerontologist, 25*, 5–10.

Ingersoll-Dayton, B., Chapman, N., & Neal, M. (1990). A program for caregivers in the workplace. *The Gerontologist, 30*(1), 126–130.

Jervis, L., & Manson, S. (2002). American Indians/Alaska Natives and dementia. *Alzheimer Disease and Associated Disorders, 16*, S89–S95.

John, R., Hennessy, C., Roy, L., & Salvini, M. (1996). Caring for cognitively impaired American Indian elders: Difficult situations, few options. In G. Yeo & D. Gallagher-Thompson (Eds.), *Ethnicity and the dementias* (pp. 187–203). Washington, DC: Taylor & Francis.

Kaplan, C., & Gallagher-Thompson, D. (1995). The treatment of clinical depression in caregivers of spouses with dementia. *Journal of Cognitive Psychotherapy, 9*, 35–44.

Kaye, L., & Applegate, J. (1990). Men as elder caregivers: A response to changing families. *American Journal of Orthopsychiatry, 60*(1), 86–95.

Kemper, S., Anagnopoulos, C., Lyons, K., & Heberlein, W. (1994). Speech accommodations to dementia. *Journal of Gerontology, 49*, P223–P229.

Kennet, J., Burgio, L., & Schulz, R. (2000). Interventions for in-home caregivers: A review of research 1990 to present. In R. Schulz (Ed.), *Handbook on dementia caregiving* (pp.61–126). New York: Springer.

Koenig, H., Cohen, H., Blazer, D., Pieper, C., Meador, K., Shelp, F., et al. (1992). Religious coping and depression among elderly, hospitalized medically ill men. *American Journal of Psychiatry, 149*(12), 1693–1700.

Kosloski, K., & Montgomery, R. (1995). The impact of respite use on nursing home placement. *The Gerontologist, 35*(1), 67–74.

Kramer, B. J. (1996). Dementia and American Indian populations. In G. Yeo & D. Gallagher-Thompson (Eds.), *Ethnicity and the dementias* (pp. 175–181). Washington, DC: Taylor & Francis.

Kuhn, D., Fulton, B., & Edelman, P. (2003). Powerful tools for caregivers: Improving self-care and self-efficacy of family caregivers. *Alzheimer's Care Quarterly, 4*(3), 189–200.

Labrecque, M., Peak, T., & Toseland, R. (1992). Long-term effectiveness of a group program for caregivers of frail elderly veterans. *American Journal of Orthopsychiatry, 62*(4), 575–588.

Lang, A., & Brody, E. (1983). Characteristics of middle-aged daughters and help to their elderly mothers. *Journal of Marriage and the Family, 45*, 193–202.

Larkin, J., & Hopcroft, B. (1993). In-hospital respite as a moderator of caregiver stress. *Health & Social Work, 18*(2), 133–138.

Lawton, M., Brody, E., & Saperstein, A. (1989). A controlled study of respite service for caregivers of Alzheimer's patients. *The Gerontologist, 29*(1), 8–16.

Lewis, I., & Ausberry, M. (1996). African American families: Management of demented elders. In G. Yeo & D. Gallagher-Thompson (Eds.), *Ethnicity and the dementias* (pp. 167–174). Washington, DC: Taylor & Francis.

Li, L., Seltzer, M., & Greenberg, J. (1997). Social support and depressive symptoms: Differential patterns in wife and daughter caregivers. *Journal of Gerontology: Social Sciences, 52B*, S200–S211.

Lindgren, C., Connelly, C., & Gaspar, H. (1999). Grief in spouse and children caregivers of dementia patients. *Western Journal of Nursing Research, 21*(4), 521–537.

Logsdon, R., McCurry, S., & Teri, L. (2005). STAR-Caregivers: A community-based approach for teaching family caregivers to use behavioral strategies to reduce affective disturbances in persons with dementia. *Alzheimer's Care Quarterly, 6*(2), 146–153.

Lopata, H. (Ed.). (1987). *Widows: Vol. 2. North America*. Durham, NC: Duke University Press.

Lovett, S., & Gallagher, D. (1988). Psychoeducational interventions for family caregivers: Preliminary efficacy data. *Behavior Therapy, 19*, 321–330.

Lustbader, W., & Hooyman, N. R. (1994). *Taking care of aging family members: A practical guide* (Rev. ed.). New York: Free Press.

Lyons, K., Zarit, S., Sayer, A., & Whitlatch, C. (2002). Caregiving as a dyadic process: Perspectives from caregiver and receiver. *Journal of Gerontology: Psychological Sciences, 57B*, P195–P204.

Mace, N. L., & Rabins, P. V. (1999). *The 36-hour day: A family guide to caring for persons with Alzheimer's disease, related dementing illnesses, and memory loss in later life* (3rd ed.). Baltimore: Johns Hopkins University Press.

Mahoney, D., Tarlow, B., & Jones, R. (2003). Effects of an automated telephone support system on caregiver burden and anxiety: Findings from the REACH for TLC intervention study. *Gerontologist, 43*, 556–567.

MaloneBeach, E., & Zarit, S. (1995). Dimensions of social support and social conflict as predictors of caregiver depression. *International Psychogeriatrics*, 7, 25–38.

MaloneBeach, E., Zarit, S., & Spore, D. (1992). Caregivers' perceptions of case management and community-based services: Barriers to service use. *Journal of Applied Gerontology*, *11*(2), 146–159.

Markowitz, J., Gutterman, E., Sadik, K., & Papadopoulos, G. (2003). Health-related quality of life for caregivers of patients with Alzheimer disease. *Alzheimer Disease and Associated Disorders*, *17*, 209–214.

Martindale-Adams, J., Nichols, L., Burns, R., & Malone, C. (2002). Telephone support groups: A lifeline for isolated Alzheimer's disease caregivers. *Alzheimer's Care Quarterly*, *3*(2), 181–189.

Matthews, S., & Rosner, T. (1988). Shared filial responsibility: The family as the primary caregiver. *Journal of Marriage and the Family*, *50*, 185–195.

McBride, M., & Parreno, H. (1996). Filipino American families and caregiving. In G. Yeo & D. Gallagher-Thompson (Eds.), *Ethnicity and the dementias* (pp. 123–135). Washington, DC: Taylor & Francis.

McCann, J., Herbert, L., Beckett, L., Morris, M., Scherr, P., & Evans, D. (2000). Comparison of informal caregiving by black and white older adults in a community population. *Journal of the American Geriatrics Society*, *48*(12), 1612–1617.

McKinlay, J., Crawford, S., & Tennstedt, S. (1995). The everyday impacts of providing informal care to dependent elders and their consequences for the care recipients. *Journal of Aging and Health*, 7, 497–528.

Miller, B., & Lawton, M. (1997). Positive aspects of caregiving. Introduction: Finding balance in caregiver research. *The Gerontologist*, *37*, 216–217.

Mittelman, M. (2003). Community caregiving. *Alzheimer's Care Quarterly*, *4*(4), 273–285.

Mittelman, M., Ferris, S., Shulman, E., Steinberg, G., Ambinder, A., Mackell, J., et al. (1995). A comprehensive support program: Effect on depression in spouse-caregivers of AD patients. *The Gerontologist*, *35*(6), 792–802.

Mittelman, M., Ferris, S., Shulman, E., Steinberg, G., & Levin, B. (1996). A family intervention to delay nursing home placement of patients with Alzheimer disease. *Journal of the American Medical Association*, *276*(21), 1725–1731.

Mittelman, M., Roth, D., Haley, W., & Zarit, S. (2004). Effects of a caregiver intervention on negative caregiver appraisals of behavior problems in patients with Alzheimer's disease: Results of a randomized trial. *Journal of Gerontology: Psychological Sciences*, *59B*, P27–P34.

Mohide, E., Pringle, D., Streiner, D., Gilbert, J., Muir, G., & Tew, M. (1990). A randomized trial of family caregiver support in the home management of dementia. *Journal of the American Geriatrics Society*, *38*, 446–454.

Montgomery, R. J. V., & Kosloski, K. (1994). A longitudinal analysis of nursing home placement for dependent elders cared for by spouses vs. adult children. *Journal of Gerontology: Social Sciences 1994*, *49*(2), S62–S74.

Morano, C., & Sanders, S. (2005). Exploring differences in depression, role captivity, and self-acceptance in Hispanic and non-Hispanic adult children caregivers. *Journal of Ethnic & Cultural Diversity in Social Work*, *14*(1/2), 27–46.

Moritz, D., Kasl, S., & Ostfeld, A. (1992). The health impact of living with a cognitively impaired elderly spouse. *Journal of Aging and Health*, *4*, 244–267.

Mungas, D. (1996). The process of development of valid and reliable neuropsychological assessment measures for English- and Spanish-speaking elderly persons. In G. Yeo & D. Gallagher-Thompson (Eds.), *Ethnicity and the dementias* (pp. 33–46). Washington, DC: Taylor & Francis.

National Alliance for Caregiving and the American Association of Retired Persons (NAS/AARP). (1997). *Family caregiving in the US: Findings from a national survey: Final report*. Bethesda, MD: National Alliance for Caregiving.

National Institute on Aging. (1991). *Bound for good health: A collection of age pages*. Bethesda, MD: U.S. Department of Health and Human Services, Public Health Service.

Neundorfer, M., McClendon, M., Smyth, K., Stuckey, J., Strauss, M., & Patterson, M. (2001). A longitudinal study of the relationship between levels of depression among persons with Alzheimer's disease and levels of depression among their family caregivers. *Journal of Gerontology: Psychological Sciences*, *56B*, P301–P313.

Oktay, J., & Volland, P. (1990). Posthospital support program for the frail elderly and their caregivers: A quasi-experimental evaluation. *American Journal of Public Health*, *80*(1), 39–46.

Orange, J. B. (1995). Perspectives of family members regarding communication changes. In R. Lubinski (Ed.), *Dementia and communication* (pp. 168–186). San Diego, CA: Singular.

Orange, J. B., & Colton-Hudson, A. (1998). Enhancing communicating in dementia of the Alzheimer's type: Caregiver education and training. *Topics in Geriatric Rehabilitation*, *14*, 56–75.

O'Rourke, N., & Tuokko, H. (2000). The psychological and physical costs of caregiving: The Canadian study of health and aging. *Journal of Applied Gerontology*, *19*(4), 389–404.

Ortiz, F., & Fitten, L. (2000). Barriers to healthcare access for cognitively impaired older Hispanics. *Alzheimer Disease and Associated Disorders*, *14*, 141–150.

Ory, M., Yee, J., Tennstedt, S., & Schulz, R. (2000). The extent and impact of dementia care: Unique challenges experienced by family caregivers. In R. Schulz (Ed.), *Handbook on dementia caregiving: Evidence-based interventions for family caregivers* (pp. 1–32). New York: Springer.

Ostuni, E., & Santo Pietro, M. J. (1991). *Getting through: Communicating when someone you care for has Alzheimer's disease*. Vero Beach, FL: Speech Bin.

Pagel, M., Erdly, W., & Becker, J. (1987). Social networks: We get by with (and in spite of) a little help from our friends. *Journal of Personality and Social Psychology*, *53*, 793–804.

Paveza, G., Cohen, D., Eisendorfer, C., Freels, S., Semla, T., Ashford, J. W., et al. (1992). Severe family violence and Alzheimer's disease: Prevalence and risk factors. *Gerontologist*, *32*, 493–497.

Pearlin, L., Mullan, J., Semple, S., & Skaff, M.(1990). Caregiving and the stress process: An overview of concepts and their measures. *The Gerontologist*, *30*(5), 583–594.

Pinkston, E. M., Linsk, N. L., & Young, R. N. (1988). Home-based behavioral family treatment of the impaired elderly. *Behavior Therapy*, *19*(3), 331–344.

Pinquart, M., & Sörensen, S. (2003). Associations of stressors and uplifts of caregiving with caregiver burden and depressive mood: A meta-analysis. *Journal of Gerontology: Psychological Sciences*, *58B*, P112–P128.

Pinquart, M., & Sörensen, S. (2005). Ethnic differences in stressors, resources, and psychological outcomes of family caregiving: A meta-analysis. *The Gerontologist*, *45*, 90–106.

Pruchno, R., Peters, N., & Burant, C. (1995). Mental health of coresident family caregivers: examination of a two-factor model. *Journal of Gerontology: Psychological Sciences*, *50B*, P247–P256.

Rankin, E., Haut, M., & Keefover, R. (2001). Current marital functioning as a mediating factor in depression among spouse caregivers in dementia. *Clinical Gerontologist*, *23*(3/4), 27–44.

Raschick, M., & Ingersoll-Dayton, B. (2004). The costs and rewards of caregiving among aging spouses and adult children. *Family Relations*, *53*(3), 317–325.

Rau, M. T. (1993). *Coping with communication challenges in Alzheimer's disease*. San Diego, CA: Singular.

Riordan, J., & Bennett, A. (1998). An evaluation of an augmented domiciliary service to older people with dementia and their carers. *Aging & Mental Health*, *2*, 137–143.

Ripich, D. (1994). Functional communication with AD patients: A caregiver training program. *Alzheimer Disease and Associated Disorders, 8*, 95–109.

Ripich, D., & Wykle, M. (1996). *Alzheimer's disease communication guide: The FOCUSED program for caregivers*. San Antonio, TX: Psychological Corporation.

Ripich, D., Wykle, M., & Niles, S. (1995). Alzheimer's disease caregivers: The FOCUSED program: A communication skills training program helps nursing assistants to give better care to patients with disease. *Geriatric Nursing, 16*, 15–19.

Ripich, D., Ziol, E., & Lee, M. (1998). Longitudinal effects of communication training on caregivers of persons with Alzheimer's disease. *Clinical Gerontologist, 19*, 37–55.

Rob, C. (1991). *The caregiver's guide: Helping elderly relatives cope with health and safety problems*. Boston: Houghton Mifflin.

Roff, L., Burgio, L., Gitlin, L., Nichols, L., Chaplin, W., & Hardin, J. M. (2004). Positive aspects of Alzheimer's caregiving: The role of race. *Journal of Gerontology: Psychological Sciences, 59B*, P185–P190.

Rose, J., & DelMaestro, S. (1990). Separation-individuation conflict as a model for understanding distressed caregivers: Psychodynamic and cognitive case studies. *The Gerontologist, 30*, 693–697.

Rose-Rego, S. K., Strauss, M. E., & Smyth, K. A. (1998). Differences in the perceived well-being of wives and husbands caring for persons with Alzheimer's disease. *The Gerontologist, 38*, 224–230.

Rubinstein, R. L. (1990). Culture and disorder in the home care experience: The home as the sickroom. In J. F. Gubrium & A. Sankar (Eds.), *The home care experience* (pp. 37–58). Newbury Park, CA: Sage.

Russell, R. (2001). In sickness and in health: A qualitative study of elderly men who care for wives with dementia. *Journal of Aging Studies, 15*, 351–367.

Rymer, S., Salloway, S., Norton, L., Malloy, P., Correia, S., & Monast, D. (2002). Impaired awareness, behavior disturbance, and caregiver burden in Alzheimer disease. *Alzheimer Disease and Associated Disorders, 16*(4), 248–253.

Santo Pietro, M. (1994). Assessing the communication styles of caregivers of patients with Alzheimer's disease. *Seminars in Speech and Language, 15*, 236–246.

Santo Pietro, M., & Ostuni, E. (2003). *Successful communication with persons with Alzheimer's disease: An inservice manual* (2nd ed.). St. Louis, MO: Elsevier Science.

Savundranagam, M. Y., Hummert, M., & Montgomery, R. (2005). Investigating the effects of communication problems on caregiver burden. *Journal of Gerontology: Social Sciences, 60B*, S48–S55.

Schulz, R. (Ed.). (2000). *Handbook on dementia caregiving: Evidence-based interventions for family caregivers*. New York: Springer.

Schulz, R., Burgio, L., Burns, R., Eisdorfer, C., Gallagher-Thompson, D., Gitlin, L., et al. (2003). Resources for enhancing Alzheimer's caregiver health (REACH): Overview, site-specific outcomes, and future directions. *Gerontologist, 43*, 514–520.

Schulz, R., & Martire, L. (2004). Family caregiving of persons with dementia: Prevalence, health effects, and support strategies. *American Journal of Geriatric Psychiatry, 12*, 240–249.

Schulz, R., O'Brien, A., Bookwala, J., & Fleissner, K. (1995). Psychiatric and physical morbidity effects of Alzheimer's disease caregiving: Prevalence, correlates, and causes. *The Gerontologist, 35*, 771–791.

Schulz, R., & Quittner, A. (1998). Caregiving through the life span: An overview and future directions. *Health Psychology, 17*, 107–111.

Schulz, R., & Williamson, G. (1997). The measurement of caregiver outcomes in Alzheimer disease research. *Alzheimer Disease and Associated Disorders, 11*, 117–124.

Semple, S. (1992). Conflict in Alzheimer's caregiving families: Its dimensions and consequences. *The Gerontologist*, *32*, 648–655.

Small, J. A., & Gutman, G. (2002). Recommended and reported use of communication strategies in Alzheimer caregiving. *Alzheimer Disease and Associated Disorders*, *16*, 270–278.

Small, J., A., Gutman, G., Makela, S., & Hillhouse, B. (2003). Effectiveness of communication strategies used by caregivers of persons with Alzheimer's disease during activities of daily living. *Journal of Speech, Language and Hearing Research*, *46*, 353–367.

Small, J. A., Kemper, S., & Lyons, K. (1997). Sentence comprehension in Alzheimer's disease: Effects of grammatical complexity, speech rate, and repetition. *Psychology and Aging*, *12*, 3–11.

Smith, K. S. (1992). *Caring for your aging parents: A sourcebook of timesaving techniques and tips*. Lakewood, CO: American Source.

Steffen, A. M. (2000). Anger management for dementia caregivers: A preliminary study using video and telephone interventions. *Behavior Therapy*, *31*, 281–299.

Stoller, E. P., Forster, L. E., & Duniho, T. S. (1992). Systems of parent care within sibling networks, *Research on Aging*, *14*(1), 28–49.

Stone, R., Cafferata, G., & Sangl, J. (1987). Caregivers of the frail and elderly: A national profile. *The Gerontologist*, *27*, 616–626.

Tappen, R. (1997). *Interventions for Alzheimer's disease: A caregiver's complete reference*. Baltimore: Health Professions.

Tappen, R., Williams-Burgess, C., Edelstein, J., Touhy, T., & Fishman, S. (1997). Communicating with individuals with Alzheimer's disease: Examination of recommended strategies. *Archives of Psychiatric Nursing*, *21*, 249–256.

Taussig, I. M., & Ponton, M. (1996). Issues in neuropsychological assessment for Hispanic older adults: Cultural and linguistic factors. In G. Yeo & D. Gallagher-Thompson (Eds.), *Ethnicity and the dementias* (pp. 33–46). Washington, DC: Taylor & Francis.

Tempo, P., & Saito, A. (1996). Techniques of working with Japanese American families. In G. Yeo & D. Gallagher-Thompson (Eds.), *Ethnicity and the dementias* (pp. 109–122). Washington, DC: Taylor & Francis

Teng, E. (1996). Cross-cultural testing and the cognitive abilities screening instrument. In G. Yeo & D. Gallagher-Thompson (Eds.), *Ethnicity and the dementias* (pp. 77–85). Washington, DC: Taylor & Francis.

Tennstedt, S., Crawford, S., & McKinlay, J. (1993). Determining the pattern of community care: Is coresidence more important than caregiver relationship? *Journal of Gerontology*, *48*, S74–S83.

Tennstedt, S. L., McKinlay, J. B., & Sullivan, L. M. (1989). Informal care for frail elders: The role of secondary caregivers. *The Gerontologist*, *29*, 677–683.

Teri, L., & Uomoto, J. M. (1991). Reducing excess disability in dementia patients: Training caregivers to manage patient depression. *Clinical Gerontologist*, *10*, 49–63.

Theis, S., Moss, J., & Pearson, M. (1994). Respite for caregivers: An evaluation study. *Journal of Community Health Nursing*, *77*(1), 31–44.

Thompson, L., Gallagher-Thompson, D., & Haley, W. (2003). Future directions in dementia caregiving intervention research and practice. In D. Coon, D. Gallagher-Thompson, & L. Thompson (Eds.), *Innovative interventions to reduce dementia caregiver stress* (pp. 299–311). New York: Springer.

Toseland, R. W., Rossiter, C. M., Peak, T., & Smith, G. C. (1990). Comparative effectiveness of individual and group interventions to support family caregivers. *Social Work*, *35*, 209–217.

Toseland, R. W., & Smith, G. C. (1990). Effectiveness of individual counseling by professional and peer helpers for family caregivers of the elderly. *Psychology and Aging*, *5*, 256–263.

Toth-Cohen, S., Gitlin, L., Corcoran, M., Eckhardt, S., Johns, P., & Lipsitt, R. (2001). Providing services to family caregivers at home: Challenges and recommendations for health and human service professions. *Alzheimer's Care Quarterly*, *2*, 23–32.

Van Nostrand, J., Furner, S., & Suzman, R. (Eds.). (1993). *Health data on older Americans, United States: 1992* (Ser. 3). Hyattsville, MD: National Center for Health Statistics.

Vitaliano, P., Scanlan, J., Krenz, C., Schwartz, R., & Marcovina, S. (1996). Psychological distress, caregiving, and metabolic variables. *Journal of Gerontology: Psychological Sciences*, *51B*, P290–299.

Weinberger, M., Gold, D., Divine, G., Cowper, P., Hodgson, L., Schreiner, P., et al. (1993). Social service interventions for caregivers of patients with dementia: Impact on health care utilization and expenditures. *Journal of the American Geriatrics Society*, *41*, 153–156.

Whitehouse, P., Lerner, A., & Hedera, P. (1993). Dementia. In K. Heilman (Ed.), *Clinical neuropsychology* (pg. 603–645). New York: Oxford University Press.

Whitlatch, C., Zarit, S., Goodwin, P., & von Eye, A. (1995). Influence of the success of psychoeducational interventions on the course of family care. *Clinical Gerontologist*, *16*(1), 17–30.

Woods, R., Wills, W., Higginson, I., Hobbins, J., & Whitby, M. (2003). Support in the community for people with dementia and their carers: A comparative outcome study of specialist mental health service interventions. *International Journal of Geriatric Psychiatry*, *18*(4), 2989–307.

Yee, B., Nguyen, H., & Ha, M. (2003). Chronic disease health beliefs and life style practices among Vietnamese adults: Influence of gender and age. *Women & Therapy*, *26*(1/2), 111–125.

Yee, J., & Schulz, R. (2000). Gender differences in psychiatric morbidity among family caregivers: A review and analysis. *The Gerontologist*, *40*, 147–164.

Yeo, G. (1996). Background. In G. Yeo & D. Gallagher-Thompson (Eds.), *Ethnicity and the dementias* (pp. 3–7). Washington, DC: Taylor & Francis.

Yeo, G., & Gallagher-Thompson, D. (Eds.). (1996). *Ethnicity and the dementias*. Washington, DC: Taylor & Francis.

Yoe, G., Uyen Tran, J., Hikoyeda, N., & Hinton, L. (2001). Conceptions of dementia among Vietnamese American caregivers. *Journal of Gerontological Social Work*, *36*, 131–152.

Youn, G., Knight, B., Jeong, H., & Benton, D. (1999). Differences in familism values and caregiving outcomes among Korean, Korean American, and White American dementia caregivers. *Psychology and Aging*, *14*(3), 355–364.

Young, J., & Gu, N. (1995). *Demographic and socioeconomic characteristics of elderly Asian and Pacific Island Americans*. Seattle, WA: National Asian Pacific Center on Aging.

Zarit, S. H. (1990). Interventions with frail elders and their families: Are they effective and why? In M. P. Stevens, J. H. Crowther, S. E. Hobfoil, & D. L. Tennenbaum (Eds.), *Stress and coping in later life* (pp. 147–158). Washington, DC: Hemisphere.

Zarit, S. H., Anthony, C., & Boutselis, M. (1987). Interventions with caregivers of dementia patients: Comparison of two approaches. *Psychology and Aging*, *2*(3), 225–232.

Zarit, S. H., & Edwards, A. (1999). Family caregiving: Research and clinical interventions. In R. Woods (Ed.), *Psychological problems of ageing*. London: John Wiley.

Zarit, S. H., Greene, R., Ferraro, E., Townsend, A., & Stephens, M. (1996, November). Adult day care and the relief of caregiver strain: Results of the adult day care collaborative study. Symposium presented at the annual meetings of the Gerontological Society of America, Washington, DC.

Zarit, S. H., & Knight, B. G. (Eds.). (1996). *A guide to psychotherapy and aging: Effective clinical interventions in a life-stage context*. Washington, DC: APA.

Zarit, S. H., & Whitlatch, C. J. (1992). Institutional placement: Phases of the transition. *The Gerontologist*, *32*, 665–672.

APPENDIX 9.1: DATA-RECORDING SHEETS AND INSTRUCTIONS FOR CAREGIVERS

Day	Count Problem: Cannot Find Room	Count Problem: Asks What Time It Is
Monday		
Tuesday		
Wednesday		
Thursday		
Friday		
Saturday		
Sunday		

1. Ask the caregiver to identify and describe the problem behaviors.
2. Determine which are the most stressful behaviors, and write them on the data sheet.
3. Discuss a time for recording behaviors (use the same time every day, such as after breakfast or dinner, or before bed).
4. Practice recording with verbal role-play.
5. One week later, review the data sheet. Discuss frequencies. Decide on the problem to remediate.

APPENDIX 9.2: MAKING MEMORY AIDS: FAMILY CAREGIVER INSTRUCTIONS

1. Complete a "Memory Aid Information Form" (see Appendices 4.2 and 4.3 for different versions).
2. Make a written list of all possible sentences to include in the memory aid.
3. Choose an appropriate number of written sentences or reproducible pages to include in the memory aid for your family member.
4. Find family pictures that clearly illustrate each of the sentences. Magazine pictures and other souvenirs or familiar items, such as maps, concert programs, ticket stubs, invitations, and greeting cards, can also be included to illustrate the pages.
5. Choose the size of memory aid that you feel is most appropriate for your family member. Memory wallets are recommended for persons who live at home and still go on outings outside of the home; memory books are better for persons who are housebound or in nursing homes, and who may have trouble turning small pages. Wearable memory wallets are also valuable in the nursing home or assisted living setting.
6. Assemble the supplies needed to make the memory aid. Remember the scissors, the glue, and a black ink pen.
7. Print sentences in black ink and large letters, or use your computer to type the words on the pages.
8. Trim and paste pictures onto relevant pages.
9. Slip book pages into clear plastic page protectors or laminated wallet pages. Using a hole-punch, make holes for each wallet page.
10. Put all book pages into a three-ring notebook, and wallet pages into a wallet with 1" rings.
11. Read the "Guidelines for Having a Satisfying Conversation" (Appendix 9.3).
12. Share the memory aid with its new owner.

APPENDIX 9.3: GUIDELINES FOR HAVING A SATISFYING CONVERSATION

1. ***Ask*** them to have a conversation with you.
   "Mary, I'd really like to talk with you today. Would you mind if I sat down beside you?"
2. ***Guide*** the conversation onto specific topics and ***redirect*** the conversation back to the topic when the person begins to ramble.
   "Mary, let's talk about your family now—please tell me all about them."
3. ***Reassure*** them and ***help out*** when they get stuck or can't find the word they want to use.
   "That's OK, Bob; what else can you tell me about your life?"
4. ***Smile*** and ***act interested*** in whatever they're talking about, even if you're not quite sure what they are trying to say.
5. ***THANK*** them for talking with you.

WHAT TO *AVOID* DURING CONVERSATIONS

DO NOT quiz the person or ask lots of specific questions.
"Now who is this person? I know you know: Who is it?"

DO NOT correct or ***contradict*** something that was stated as a fact even if you know it's wrong.
"No, that's not John. That's Jason, remember, your grandson Jason?"

APPENDIX 9.4: REMINDER CARDS: USING WRITTEN CUES IN THE HOME AND NURSING HOME

© Michelle S. Bourgeois, Ph.D.

When a question is repeated a few seconds after you have just answered it, a **reminder card** may help to keep the information in mind. Follow these easy steps for successful remembering:

1. State the answer to the question or concern.
2. Write the answer on an index card or notepad.
3. Read the card aloud with the person, and give it to him or her.
4. When the question is repeated, *do not* say the answer. *Instead*, say, "Read the card."
5. Do this each time the question is repeated.

EXAMPLES

Q: When am I going to the store?
A: **I am going to the store after lunch.** (Write this on the card.)
Q: Where are we going?
A: **We are going to church.** (Write this on the card.)
Q: Where is my paycheck?
A: **My money is safe in the bank.** (Write this on the card.)

HELPFUL HINTS

Print a clear message.
Use large print. Use a few, simple, positive words.
Make the message personal.
Use personal pronouns (*I*, *my*, *we*) in the message.
Read the message aloud.
If there are reading errors, change the message.

10

Impact on Staff
Training and Supervision Issues

Estimates suggest that, by the year 2050, there will be approximately 14 million people with a dementia diagnosis in the United States (Hebert, Beckett, Scherr, & Evans, 2001). When the family can no longer manage the person with dementia at home, or when there is no family to provide care, residential care is the logical option. Thus, approximately 4.6 million persons with dementia will reside in nursing homes (Burgio & Stevens, 1999), where currently 75% of all residents have a dementia diagnosis (Beck, Doan, & Cody, 2002). In this setting, care is provided largely from staff in the nursing department, as well as the activities department. The staff hired to provide care to the frail elderly range from nurses in managerial positions who have advanced degrees to CNAs in paraprofessional positions who often have a high school education. Certified CNAs (CNAs) hold approximately 85% of all positions in long-term care (Beck et al., 2002). The job of a CNA is demanding under the best of circumstances, and the challenges of providing quality care to persons with dementia are many. Accordingly, efforts are under way to develop effective staff training programs and desirable work environments in times of high staff turnover and few staff incentives.

In 1987, the federal government mandated that nursing homes provide a therapeutic, rather than custodial, model of care (Omnibus Budget Reconciliation Act [OBRA] of 1987, 1991). Since then, the nursing home industry has struggled to meet the expectations of lawmakers and families. CNAs are required to receive 75 hours of basic training upon employment and to take 12 hours per year of continuing education (Lescoe-Long, 2000). Yet a report on CNA training, published by the Office of the Inspector General (OIG, 2002), emphasized that staff training has not kept pace with the needs of the nursing home industry. Research efforts have resulted in a better understanding of the personnel who make caregiving their profession, as well as the challenges they face on the job and the types of supports (e.g., training) that help them to provide quality care. Still, CNAs report needing more training, especially in the management of problem behaviors, in information about depression and aggression, and in communicating more effectively with residents with dementia (Grainger, 1995; Harrington et al., 2002; Mercer, Heacock, & Beck, 1993; Nakhnikian, Wilner, Joslin, & Hurd, 2002). The OIG (2002) report identified additional training needs related to teamwork, coping with death and dying, time management, and new technologies. Researchers have found that inadequate training and inadequate staffing were the two main reasons for the perception that nursing homes in the United States are not providing quality care (Harrington et al., 2002; Schirm, Lehman, & Barton, 1996). One must acknowledge the variables that often undermine the desired therapeutic model of care, including the costs of providing these services and the limited resources at every level from federal, to state, to the individual. Nevertheless, progress is being made toward the goal of quality therapeutic care for those in need.

STAFF CHARACTERISTICS

Certified CNAs provide up to 90% of resident care in long-term care facilities (Beck et al., 2002; Beck, Ortigara, Mercer, & Shue, 1999; Harrington et al., 2002). The workforce is predominantly female, non-White, and unmarried, and has children at home (Scanlon, 2001). Most CNAs have a typical workload of 11–12 residents each day or evening shift, but they may be responsible for as many as 45 residents on the night shift. Inadequate staffing patterns, among other employment challenges, result in high turnover. Some national estimates of staff turnover range from 99 to 200% annually (American Health Care Association, 2002; Cohen-Mansfield, 1997). A review of the turnover literature from 1990 to 2003 reported CNA turnover rates ranging from 14 to 346% (Castle, 2006), but with many inconsistencies in the definition of *turnover* in those studies. Therefore, Castle conducted a survey of 529 nursing homes in four states, and included questions about voluntary and involuntary turnover, shifts worked, and part-time and temporary staff turnover. Nursing home administrators reported an overall average rate of 81% annual and 74% 6-month CNA turnover; but when the other turnover factors were considered, the adjusted rates were 119% annually and 107% at 6 months (Castle). Thus, high staff turnover is one of the long-term care industry's biggest challenges, giving rise to issues related to the continuity of care and the expense of constant staff training and retraining.

The reasons for high turnover are many and are often related to job satisfaction. Job characteristics that influence satisfaction include workload, pay and benefits, perceived autonomy, job pride, and professional interactions, among others (Castle & Engberg, 2006; Price, 2000). Workload and staffing patterns are major contributors to job dissatisfaction (Chou, Boldy, & Lee, 2002). In fact, a study conducted by the U.S. Centers for Medicare and Medicaid Services (2001) found that 52–97% of nursing facilities failed to meet staffing threshold recommendations (below 2.4 hours per resident day for nurses' aides) and as a result had poor resident outcomes. Low pay that keeps CNAs below the poverty level and needing a second job is another significant factor in turnover (Brunk, 1997); many CNAs are single heads of household, are immigrants who speak English as a second language, are from disadvantaged backgrounds, and report being abused by boyfriends or husbands. Nevertheless, many express a sincere interest in the job, due to having cared for sick or dying relatives; they report a sense of calling to the profession (Schirm et al., 1996).

The CNA's job is particularly difficult both physically and emotionally. Many residents require assistance with personal care tasks that involve lifting and transferring. A variety of behaviors that are exhibited by persons with dementia, such as verbal abuse, physical agitation, and wandering, can be difficult to manage on a daily basis. The frequent incidence of resident death can cause emotional strain. Burgio and Scilley (1994) reported observing CNAs engaged in resident care activities 53% of the time and nonwork activities 14% of the time; housekeeping and record-keeping chores occupied 33% of the time. CNAs report that their jobs are highly stressful due to resident disruptive behaviors (physical and verbal abuse, and wandering), as well as high staff absenteeism that results in pulling staff from the care of familiar residents to those whom they do not know well. They complain of lack of information during orientation and lack of supervision and performance feedback once they are on the job. CNAs request more supervision, more involvement in the decision-making process for their residents, and more training in behavior management skills, the mental health needs of residents (Burgio & Scilley), and communicating effectively with residents and staff (Mercer, Heacock, & Beck, 1993; Santo Pietro, 2002). It is a hopeful sign that the frontline staff can specify the improvements in their working conditions that would help to elevate the quality of care they could provide to their residents. This is especially important in light of the fact that, given these limitations of their working conditions, the more experienced CNAs have been found to complete their work in a routine, repetitive manner; to tend to ignore individual residents' medical or social needs; and to tend to reinforce residents' dependency behaviors and discourage independent behavior (Burgio & Scilley). CNAs themselves report that they cut corners and cannot provide quality care because of high workloads, lack of time, and inadequate training (Bowers & Becker, 1992; Schirm et al., 1996). The implementation of targeted training in areas of concern should lead to changes in the quality of services provided, and result in residents who are more content and staff who are more satisfied with their jobs. Training has the potential to reduce turnover (Grant, Kane, Potthoff, & Ryden, 1996) and increase job satisfaction (Morgan, 1996).

STAFF TRAINING NEEDS AND MODELS

The evolution of staff training in dementia care has been described as paralleling the increase in knowledge about dementia from simple descriptions of the disease process itself and application to the "medical" model, to behavioral approaches designed to teach specific caregiving strategies, to person-centered models that teach staff to view the world through the eyes of their clients (Ortigara & Rapp, 2004). An early study on staff training for dementia care (Teri, Baer, Orr, & Reifler, 1991) documented improved knowledge of AD and problem-solving skills after a 2-day lecture training program, compared to staff from facilities that did not attend the program. On-the-job skill performance and long-term follow-up data, however, were not reported. The following review of training programs to teach communication skills, behavior management skills, and person-centered care will document the improvements in research and training methodologies that are resulting in better training and resident outcomes.

Communication-Based Models

The focus of training on communication processes stems from the observations of professionals that persons with dementia demonstrate communication deficits related to their illness and that these deficits contribute to impaired conversational interactions with their caregivers (Santo Pietro, 2002). In addition, persons with dementia can have additional communication-related impairments due to comorbid conditions, such as depression, stroke, and hearing loss. Further, many environments in which these persons live have been described as "communication impaired" due to the paucity of available communication partners, the lack of stimuli from the environment that could elicit conversation topics, and the ignorance of potential conversation partners about the communication deficits and needs of the residents (Lubinski, 1995). These factors and others have contributed to a rationale for the communication-based training programs described below. Some examples of communication-focused training programs are shown in Table 10.1.

Koury and Lubinksi (1995) conducted the earliest known studies of the effectiveness of communication-based training with CNAs. They evaluated the types of learning components in staff training programs that would result in greater learning of ways to improve CNA interactions with residents with dementia and their problem-solving skills. One group of CNAs received a traditional 1-hour in-service lecture program, a second group received 1 hour of training through a role-play protocol, and a third group did not receive any training. All CNAs were assessed prior to and post training on the Protocol for Assessing CNAs' Knowledge and Behavioral Intents Toward the Communication Impaired Elderly (Koury & Lubinski, 1995). There were no significant differences between groups in the amount of knowledge learned through the in-services, but the role-play group provided significantly more quality responses. Koury and Lubinski concluded that the hands-on, performance-based individualized training had an advantage over the traditional, classroom, lecture-style training.

Another program, the CNA Communication Skills Program (NACSP; McCallion, Toseland, Lacey, & Banks, 1999), was designed to teach CNAs to communicate and interact more effectively with nursing home residents with

TABLE 10.1 Examples of Communication-Focused Training Programs for Long-Term Care

Boczko and Santo Pietro (1997)	*The Breakfast Club: Program Training Guide*
Bourgeois, Dijkstra, Burgio, and Allen (1998)	*Increasing Effective Communication in Nursing Homes: Inservice Workshop Training Manual, Videotapes, and Documentation Forms*
Bourgeois and Irvine (1999)	*Working With Dementia: Communication Tools for Professional Caregivers* (CD-ROM and videotape in-service training materials)
Santo Pietro and Ostuni (2003)	*Successful Communication With Persons With Alzheimer's Disease: An In-Service Manual*
Toseland and McCallion (1998)	*Maintaining Communication With Persons With Dementia: An Educational Program for Nursing Staff and Family Members*

dementia. The main purposes of the study were to determine whether the training program improved the well-being of the residents and increased CNA knowledge of dementia and caregiving responses, and decreased rates of staff turnover. This study utilized a 2 (Intervention Conditions) × 2 (Nursing Homes) × 4 (Assessment Times) nested partial-crossover control group design with randomization to treatment condition by nursing unit within each nursing home. The NACSP condition consisted of five 45-minute group didactic sessions and four 30-minute individual practice and feedback sessions. The content of the training included knowledge of dementia, verbal and nonverbal communication, memory aids, and problem behaviors; in the individual sessions, project staff observed the CNA implementing the skills learned in each group session and provided performance feedback. Assessment of the outcome measures was conducted prior to training initiation, and at 3, 6, and 9 months posttraining termination. CNAs on the waitlist control group units did not participate in any assessments until the 6-month assessment of the treatment group.

Results revealed that on a measure of well-being (the Cornell Scale for Depression in Dementia), residents in the treatment group demonstrated significantly greater decreases in depressive symptoms at 3 and 6 months post training than did the waitlist control residents, who demonstrated increased symptoms (McCallion et al., 1999). The results were somewhat disappointing for the CNAs. There were no significant differences between treatment group and waitlist CNAs on the knowledge of dementia test as a result of training; there were significant differences in their knowledge about the management of problem and agitated behaviors post training, but these changes were not sustained at the 6-month assessment. However the effect of training on turnover rates revealed significant differences at the 6-month assessment; two treatment CNAs had terminated employment compared to 13 waitlist CNAs. Overall, McCallion and colleagues concluded that NACSP was effective in training CNAs to interact more effectively with nursing home residents with dementia, in reducing depression in residents with dementia, and in reducing the levels of staff turnover.

In 1996, Bourgeois and Burgio were funded by the National Institute on Aging to evaluate a CNA training program ("Increasing Effective Communication in Nursing Homes," R01 AG 13008-04) designed to increase and improve the communicative interactions between residents with dementia and CNAs. The program included a didactic in-service (with a manual and handouts); on-the-job, individualized skills training; personalized resident memory books; and a formal staff management system to evaluate the effects of training CNAs to use communication skills and memory books with their residents with dementia (Bourgeois, Dijkstra, Burgio, & Allen, 1998). In the pilot study (Allen-Burge, Burgio, Bourgeois, Sims, & Nunnikhoven, 2001), each of 12 CNAs received two 1-hour didactic in-services, followed by 2 weeks of individualized on-the-job training. A 12-page personalized memory booklet consisting of biographical, orientation, and daily schedule information was constructed for each resident. By the end of the second week of on-the-job training, 8 of the 12 CNAs had achieved a performance score of 80% accuracy in using the trained skills, including increased use of instructions and positive statements. Residents were observed to be in possession of their memory books during

70% of the observations post intervention and to demonstrate increased rates of speaking compared to baseline observations. In addition, visitors and other residents were observed to be talking more frequently with residents with memory books after treatment implementation. This effect was particularly striking for the rate of positive statements made by any person in the environment post intervention, including the resident. Some of these effects were shown to maintain at the 1-month follow-up assessment.

The subsequent study increased the on-the-job training period to 4 weeks, and specific minor details of the formal staff management system were tailored to the needs of individual nursing homes in the two study locations (Burgio et al., 2001). Trained CNAs talked more, used positive statements more frequently, and provided more specific instructions to residents during care activities, without increasing the total amount of caregiving time. These positive changes in CNA behavior were still evident 2 months after the research staff had left the facilities. The staff management system included training of the licensed practical nurses (LPNs) and registered nurses (RNs) who observed CNAs during care activities and provided immediate verbal performance feedback. In addition, CNAs monitored their own skill performance by completing a self-monitoring form at the end of their shift. These forms were entered into a weekly lottery, with the winner choosing from a variety of incentives (e.g., the opportunity to leave work earlier than scheduled, extra pay, and goodie bags). Other incentives included public recognition of job performance criterion attainment by posting their names on an Honor Roll. An in-depth analysis of the components of the communication skills training program (Bourgeois, Dijkstra, Burgio, & Allen, 2004) revealed that CNAs significantly increased their use of effective skills and instructions, and decreased their use of ineffective instructions (see Table 10.2).

During baseline observations, CNAs displayed low rates of all skills and instructions, with the exception of *announcing care* and *addressing resident by name*, which were used 70–80% of the time (Bourgeois et al., 2004). Treatment group CNAs needed an average of 8.35 sessions of one-to-one training with feedback (*SD* = 2.86; range = 3–15) to achieve job performance criteria. The Communication Skills Checklist (Figure 10.1) was the tool used during care activity observations by

TABLE 10.2 CNA Skills and Instructions During Care Interactions

Effective Skills	Effective Instructions	Ineffective Instructions
Announce care when entering resident's room.	Give short and clear instructions.	Multistep instructions
Address the resident by name.	Give positive feedback when resident follows directions.	Negative statements
Wait 5 seconds before providing physical help.	Talk about resident's life or day.	Unhelpful questions
Introduce self by name.	Use the memory books to explain care.	
Give appropriate announcement for every activity.		

Source: Bourgeois et al. (2004).

ACTIVITIES OBSERVED (MINIMUM = 3)
Toileting Grooming Hygiene Washing
Dressing Transfer Turning

CNA'S APPROACH

CNA approaches within resident's visual field	YES NO
CNA calls resident by name	YES NO
CNA introduces self by name	YES NO
CNA announces activity	YES NO

BEHAVIORAL DISTURBANCE (during this observation):
Verbal Disruption Physical Disruption Physical Aggression None

CNA's Response to Behavioral Disturbance
Use of ComBook Biographical Statements Distraction Soothing Talk Touch

CNA waits 5 sec. for resident to respond Never Sometimes Always

Communication	+	-		Communication	+	-		Communication	+	-		Communication	+	-	
1. S G 2+			C B	31. S G 2+			C B	61. S G 2+			C B	91. S G 2+			C B
2. S G 2+			C B	32. S G 2+			C B	62. S G 2+			C B	92. S G 2+			C B
3. S G 2+			C B	33 S G 2+			C B	63. S G 2+			C B	93. S G 2+			C B
4. S G 2+			C B	34. S G 2+			C B	64. S G 2+			C B	94. S G 2+			C B
5. S G 2+			C B	35. S G 2+			C B	65. S G 2+			C B	95. S G 2+			C B
6. S G 2+			C B	36. S G 2+			C B	66. S G 2+			C B	96. S G 2+			C B
7. S G 2+			C B	37. S G 2+			C B	67. S G 2+			C B	97. S G 2+			C B
8. S G 2+			C B	38. S G 2+			C B	68. S G 2+			C B	98. S G 2+			C B
9. S G 2+			C B	39. S G 2+			C B	69. S G 2+			C B	99. S G 2+			C B
10. S G 2+			C B	40. S G 2+			C B	70. S G 2+			C B	100. S G 2+			C B
11. S G 2+			C B	41. S G 2+			C B	71. S G 2+			C B				
12. S G 2+			C B	42. S G 2+			C B	72. S G 2+			C B				
13. S G2+			C B	43. S G2+			C B	73. S G2+			C B				
14. S G 2+			C B	44. S G 2+			C B	74. S G 2+			C B				
15. S G 2+			C B	45. S G 2+			C B	75. S G 2+			C B				
16. S G 2+			C B	46. S G 2+			C B	76. S G 2+			C B				
17. S G 2+			C B	47. S G 2+			C B	77. S G 2+			C B				
18. S G 2+			C B	48. S G 2+			C B	78. S G 2+			C B				
19. S G 2+			C B	49. S G 2+			C B	79. S G 2+			C B				
20. S G 2+			C B	50. S G 2+			C B	80. S G 2+			C B				
21. S G 2+			C B	51. S G 2+			C B	81. S G 2+			C B				
22. S G 2+			C B	52. S G 2+			C B	82. S G 2+			C B				
23. S G 2+			C B	53. S G 2+			C B	83. S G 2+			C B				
24. S G 2+			C B	54. S G 2+			C B	84. S G 2+			C B				
25. S G 2+			C B	55. S G 2+			C B	85. S G 2+			C B				
26. S G 2+			C B	56. S G 2+			C B	86. S G 2+			C B				
27. S G 2+			C B	57. S G 2+			C B	87. S G 2+			C B				
28. S G 2+			C B	58. S G 2+			C B	88. S G 2+			C B				
29. S G 2+			C B	59. S G 2+			C B	89. S G 2+			C B				
30. S G 2+			C B	60. S G 2+			C B	90. S G 2+			C B				

S = 1-Step Instructions
G = General Instructions
2+ = Multi-Step Instructions
\+ = Positive Statements
\- = Unhelpful/Negative Comments
C = Memory/ComBook
B = Biographical Statements (life/day)

Figure 10.1 Communication Skills Checklist.

research staff and trained LPNs to document skill performance and to share with CNAs for feedback purposes. During posttraining observations, CNAs showed significant improvements over baseline for the effective skills (*address resident by name*, *introduce self by name*, *announce every activity*, and *wait 5 seconds*), for effective instructions (*short and clear instructions*, positive feedback, and talk about resident's life), and ineffective instructions (*multistep instructions* and *unhelpful questions*). At the 3-month follow-up observation, these behaviors maintained or exceeded posttraining rates. Personalized memory books were present during 84.3% of training sessions, but were used during only 26.5% of follow-up sessions. In spite of this, the overall quality of communicative interactions during care interactions improved. Before training, CNAs' communication style was task focused and neutral; after training, CNAs were more positive, and engaged in social and personalized conversations with the residents during care.

The impact of the training program, and memory books in particular, on the communication interactions between residents and CNAs was evaluated in an analysis of pre- and posttraining 5-minute conversations. Quantitative measures (e.g., duration, percentage of time, and frequency) of resident and CNA verbalizations, positive and negative statements, and memory book use and qualitative measures (e.g., content of resident and CNA utterances) were compared pre- and post training (Bourgeois, Dijkstra, Burgio, & Allen-Burge, 2001). Residents and CNAs significantly increased the number of utterances spoken and positive statements in posttraining conversations, and residents made significantly more informative statements when they used their memory books. In addition, posttreatment resident conversations were more coherent and contained fewer empty phrases, and CNAs used more facilitative discourse strategies (i.e., encouragement and cues) compared to control group participants (Dijkstra, Bourgeois, Burgio, & Allen, 2002). The enhanced information sharing and social closeness that were fostered through the use of personalized memory aids were thought to influence CNAs' judgment of residents' level of depression; treatment group CNAs felt their residents with memory aids were less depressed post training compared with control group CNAs, who rated their residents as more depressed over time. Bourgeois and colleagues (2001) concluded that when the CNAs did less talking and more listening to their residents, they appeared to understand them better. There is room for improvement, however. Communication interventions designed to create opportunities for residents and CNAs to discuss topics of a personal nature about their feelings and emotions could further enhance CNAs' understanding of resident feelings.

Other communication-focused staff-training programs developed by speech-language pathologists have been published, but with minimal to no efficacy data. Boczko and Santo Pietro (1997) developed a 12-week training program for CNAs to direct "Breakfast Clubs" with dementia residents using a teaching-by-modeling approach. CNAs first observed the implementation of the program, then they assisted, and finally they directed the activity. The protocol was similar to the one described in chapter 5 that was implemented successfully by speech-language pathologists (Santo Pietro & Boczko, 1998). Bayles and Tomoeda (1998) developed a training videotape, *Improving the Ability of Alzheimer's Patients to Communicate*. Santo Pietro and Ostuni's (2003) comprehensive in-service training manual, *Successful Communication With Persons With Alzheimer's Disease*, addresses a wide variety of topics that affect communication, including (a) the communication challenges in the nursing home environment; (b) communication strengths and problems of patients with Alzheimer's disease and their professional caregivers; (c) multicultural, verbal abuse, and neglect issues; and (d) strategies for successful communication through the end of life. This training program consists of 12 1-hour didactic modules with quizzes, role-play, and group discussion activities that can be spread out in time, and on-site practicing is recommended in between each subsequent didactic session. More research is needed to document the efficacy of these programs to improve the communicative interactions of residents and CNAs, as well as other related behaviors and perceptions.

Santo Pietro (2002), in her review of communication-based training programs, summarized the recommendations gleaned from the literature and her own training experiences. These recommendations include (a) keep lectures to a minimum, (b) present a variety of active learning experiences, (c) present information that CNAs really need, (d) train on-site, (e) follow up the training with booster sessions, (f) use other informational resources and evaluative performance-based feedback, and (g) provide emotional support. For example, the New England Research Institute (1995) has produced a 30-minute video for this purpose: *Working It Out: Support Groups for CNAs.*

Behavior Management and Skills Training Approaches

In a review of behavioral interventions for managing the behavioral deficits and excesses of nursing home residents, Burgio and Stevens (1999) pointed out that this literature helped to establish the observation that the behavior of CNAs can contribute to undesirable resident behaviors. Therefore, CNAs were prime candidates for training in how to modify their own behavior as well as the behavior of their residents. Observational studies conducted in the 1990s helped to identify specific stimulus events and reinforcement contingencies that contributed to the maintenance of undesirable behaviors (e.g., Burgio, 1996; Burgio et al., 1990, 1994; Roth, Stevens, Burgio, & Burgio, 2002). Subsequently, many studies were conducted to demonstrate the effects of specific antecedent and consequence manipulations on targeted behaviors. For example, Burgio, Scilley, Hardin, Hsu, and Yancey (1996) used environmental white noise under headphones to reduce residents' disruptive vocalizations; and Lundervold and Jackson (1992) taught CNAs to use differential reinforcement procedures to reduce residents' aggressive behaviors. Researchers have concluded from these studies that these types of behavioral interventions are effective if the CNAs are trained to use them consistently (Burgio & Stevens, 1999). Unfortunately, many training programs simply present the material didactically, do not follow through with performance-based training and feedback, and do not monitor or supervise the implementation of the trained skills over time. As a result, problem behaviors persist in the nursing home, and CNAs continue to experience dissatisfaction with their job. The following training programs were developed with the above limitations in mind; these researchers attempted to find ways to improve the efficacy of skills training programs for CNAs.

Stevens and colleagues (1998) developed a training program to teach nursing staff basic behavior management skills. Two groups of CNAs received a 5-hour didactic in-service followed by 3 weeks of on-the-job training: One group received conventional (i.e., typical) staff management (CSM), whereas the second group received formal staff management (FSM). The FSM system was based on the earlier Behavioral Supervision program developed by Burgio and Burgio (1990), and includes supervisory monitoring, self-monitoring, and verbal and written performance feedback to maintain long-term use of the trained skills by CNAs. The skills that were trained included (a) identifying environmental factors than affect resident behavior, (b) identifying the antecedents and consequences of behavior, (c) communication skills, (d) positive reinforcement procedures, and (e) distraction and diversion techniques. Observational data revealed that CNAs in both groups demonstrated increased use of the skills after the on-the-job training; however, at the 26-, 38-, and 46-week postintervention assessments, only the FSM group CNAs continued to use the trained skills, and the rate of skills used by the CSM group dropped to baseline levels. The researchers concluded that didactic training was only the first step in increasing CNA knowledge of behavioral skills; on-the-job training was necessary to obtain accurate performance of the skills, and a formal system of staff management was required to maintain skill use over time.

A variety of training programs for CNAs targeting specific problem behaviors in nursing homes have been evaluated. Parks, Haines, Foreman, McKinstry, and Maxwell (2005) designed an educational program to improve the knowledge and attitudes of nursing staff on end-of-life care issues in long-term care. Their program of five in-service lectures with take-home self-study modules, Dignity in Dementia, produced significant changes in staff knowledge and attitudes about end-of-life care, which maintained for one year. Pillemer et al. (2003) described a randomized treatment and control group study of the Partners in Caregiving program designed to increase cooperation and effective communication between family members and nursing home staff. Separate training sessions were held with family and staff, followed by a joint meeting with facility administrators. Results revealed improved attitudes and less conflict among trained family and staff, and a lower reported likelihood of quitting by trained staff.

Landreville, Dicaire, Verreault, and Levesque (2005) evaluated a training program for managing the agitation of nursing home residents. The program of 8 hours of class instruction and 8 hours of weekly supervision by the trainers addressed behavioral skills for assessment, prevention, and reduction of aggressive and nonaggressive agitated behavior. Pre- and posttraining assessments revealed a high degree of staff satisfaction and of staff feeling more effective in managing agitation after training, as well as a reduction in the number and frequency of agitated resident behaviors.

Chang and Lin (2005) reported the effects of a training program to teach feeding skills to CNAs on their knowledge, attitude, and feeding behaviors, and the eating outcomes of their residents with dementia. The treatment group received 3 hours of in-service classes and one hour of hands-on training and demonstrated significantly more knowledge, more positive attitudes, and better behaviors than the control group, who did not receive any training. Residents whose CNA received training had significantly longer total eating times, but this did not result in fewer eating difficulties or increased food intake. The authors suggested that the CNAs' increased knowledge of feeding difficulties after training led to higher scores on the

TABLE 10.3 Examples of Available Dementia-Specific Training Materials

Authors	Resources
Alzheimer's Association (2006)	*Foundations of Dementia Care* (classroom training)
	CARES: A Dementia Caregiving Approach for Direct Care Workers (Web-based training)
	Dementia Care Training for Team Leaders: Successful Supervision (Web-based training)
Andersen (1995)	*Caring for People With Alzheimer's Disease: A Training Manual for Direct Care Providers*
Cohn, Smyer, and Horgas (1994)	*The A-B-Cs of Behavior Change: Skills for Working With Behavior Problems in Nursing Homes* (in-service manual)
Eastern Michigan University (1997)	*Care of the Person With Dementia: A Training Program for Residential Program Staff*
Parks, Haines, Foreman, McKinstry, and Maxwell (2005)	*Dignity in Dementia* (5 in-service modules)
Pillemer et al. (2003)	*Partners in Caregiving*
State of Florida, Department of Elder Affairs (1996)	*Alzheimer's Disease Training Manual*

Edinburgh Feeding Evaluation in Dementia scale (EdFed; Watson, 1994) and the unexpected negative results. Differences between groups on several demographic variables, as well as a small *N*, were also thought to constrain the study results.

There are staff training programs for other problem behaviors, such as bathing problems (Hoeffer, Rader, McKenzie, Lavelle, & Stewart, 1997), dressing (Rogers et al., 1999; Vogelpohl, Beck, Heacock, & Mercer, 1996), and incontinence (Schnelle, Newman, & Fogarty., 1990), to name a few. Consumers must be aware that a multitude of training programs in the form of videotapes, training manuals, books, and other handouts have been developed and marketed to long-term care facilities prior to careful evaluation of their effectiveness. Table 10.3 lists some of the more recently published training materials that are available; few of these programs and materials have published efficacy data, however.

Person-Centered Staff Training Approaches

Kitwood (1997) has developed a person-centered model of nursing home care in which the CNAs are trained to view the resident as the focus of the care process and to understand the entire psychosocial environment surrounding that resident. The Dementia Care Mapping system describes the many needs of the residents, including the need for loving, generous, forgiving, and unconditional acceptance, comfort, attachment, inclusion, occupation, and identity. Person-centered care (PCC) training programs demonstrate how to help residents participate in their own care and make decisions and choices about their daily life, and how to solicit their opinions. Boettcher, Kemeny, DeShon, and Stevens (2004) evaluated the effects of a PCC staff training program that included dementia-specific training content, experiential learning activities, and a mentoring system. CNAs and nurse-mentors participated in five didactic sessions covering knowledge of dementia and the person-centered care approach, communication skills, skills for individualizing care and for responding to need-driven behaviors, and skills related to working with the family. In addition, the nurse-mentors received an additional four sessions on supervisory topics such as observation, feedback, goal setting, and problem solving. All of these skills were then practiced through role-plays and on-the-job coaching. Pre- and posttraining ratings of the seven major skills addressed in the program documented significant changes in four of the seven skills 2 months post training; these skills were nonverbal initiation of PCC, assisting resident with independence-oriented tasks, verbal conversation, and using resident-specific details in conversation. The other three behaviors, initiating lifestyle-oriented activities, responding to calls for help, and person-centered interaction with families, occurred so infrequently during observation periods that statistical analysis was not appropriate. The authors were encouraged that this PCC approach to staff training contributed to a successful culture change in that facility for both the residents and the staff. The goal of creating a positive environment for the person with dementia was realized through meeting *staff* needs for cognitive, affective, and skill learning and effective mentoring.

The idea of improving the quality of care for residents with dementia by enhancing the work environment of the staff has arisen from the literature documenting the relationship between job-related stress, job dissatisfaction, and staff turnover in dementia care facilities (Burgio et al., 2002; Foner, 1994) and the relationship between quality of care and quality of life for residents with dementia (Smyer, Brannon, & Cohn, 1992; Tellis-Nayak & Tellis-Nayak, 1989). McAiney (1998) proposed the Empowered Aide Model, which includes four components: empowerment, organization, education, and teamwork. CNAs are allowed to make decisions about when to wake and bathe residents, staff–resident assignment, and unit rotation schedules. In-service topics include managing stress, problem solving, difficult behaviors, communicating with residents and coworkers, and working together as a team. An evaluation study documenting the effects of this program on decreasing job-related stress and improved perception of the work environment is under way.

In a related study, Gruss, McCann, Edelman, and Faran (2004) compared the job stress of CNAs in empowered and nonempowered units of a long-term care facility. They defined *empowerment* as the "process whereby organizational factors and job characteristics create an environment that may result in employee perceptions of having control and access to power within the organization, resulting in positive employee, organization, and family outcomes" (p. 209). In this study, one of two dementia care units in the facility was modified to include empowering factors such as permanent assignment to a "neighborhood," for which the CNA had control and responsibility for decisions about maintenance and housekeeping, resident care and therapy schedules, resident food selections, and activity programming. The CNAs were expected to develop relationships with residents' family and participate in the care plan meetings. The comparison unit was a traditional dementia care unit on which staff rotated resident and unit assignments, had few opportunities for developing relationships with residents or their families, and did not participate in decision making or care planning for the residents.

Gruss and colleagues (2004) reported that, based on one-on-one interviews with each CNA on both units, the empowered unit was perceived to have five of the six targeted organizational empowering factors, whereas the control unit aides reported the presence of only two empowering factors. Results of the modified Caregiver Stress Questionnaire revealed that CNAs in the empowered unit endorsed more resident-focused stressors, whereas the control unit aides reported more job-focused stressors. The investigators reflected that the culture change effected in the empowered unit helped CNAs to focus more on their residents' concerns and less on the negative aspects of their job. Other researchers who have evaluated the empowerment model of nursing home care and training have found similarly positive effects on job satisfaction and reduced job stress (Laschinger, Finegan, Shamian, & Wilk, 2001; Wilson & Laschinger, 1994) and positive effects on leadership skills (Laschinger, Wong, McMahon, & Kaufman, 1999).

Another dementia-specific training program for staff in assisted living facilities, Staff Training in Assisted Living Residences (STAR), was based on the person–environment fit and social learning theory models (Teri, Huda, Gibbons, Young, & van Leynseele, 2005). The three main priorities of the program are to "(a) reinforce values of dignity and respect for residents, (b) improve staff responsiveness to resident needs, and (c) build specific staff skills to enhance resident care and improve job skill and satisfaction" (Teri et al., 2005, p. 687). Evaluation of training provided to 114 staff through two 4-hour workshops, four individualized on-site consultations, and three leadership sessions revealed that trained staff reported less adverse impact and reaction to residents' problems and more job satisfaction compared with control staff. Furthermore, residents in facilities with trained staff displayed significantly reduced levels of affective and behavioral distress compared with control residents. The training program highlighted the fact that assisted living residents usually have more say in their daily care than nursing home residents, and specific skills in approaching and soliciting their involvement and support in accepting care were needed. Additionally, Teri (1990) developed a videotape-training program to teach the basic concepts in identifying the antecedents and consequences of behavior (ABCs), *Management of Behavioral Disturbance in Dementia: A Behavioral Approach*. On-the-job practice of training skills was provided, but performance data on this component were not reported. Similarly, the three leadership modules were presented in a didactic discussion format, with no assessment of skill mastery or knowledge acquisition.

Technology-Delivered Training Programs: Video Versus CD Versus Internet

In an effort to develop attractive, interesting, and effective staff training programs, a multitude of media options have been explored. Since the 1980s, the educational use of videotape became commonplace, and video-based educational training programs for CNAs and for family caregivers became widespread. Kaplan (1996) included, as an appendix to her article on caregiver training, a list of 14 videotape resources for training purposes; a catalog of additional training materials is available from the Alzheimer's Disease Education and Referral Center (ADEAR; 2006; http://www.niapublications.org). See Table 10.3 for more technology-delivered resources. As Irvine, Ary, and Bourgeois (2003) observed in their review of technology-based training media, although there are many benefits of each medium, there are also limitations. For example, the advantages of videotapes are that they can be viewed at convenient and multiple times, and they can show real-life examples of problem behaviors and models of desired staff behaviors (Lewis, Scott, Bielfeld, & Slabe, 1995; Teri, 1990). Similarly, print materials can be read and reread as desired; low literacy levels, however, make print media challenging for some. In addition, in-services based on videotaped materials may not be tailored to viewers' experiences or training needs, and the material presented can be known or uninteresting, leading to inattention and limited learning. Interactive multimedia (IMM) using the computer, and more recently the Internet, has the potential to overcome some of the limitations of other media. IMM programs can be tailored to individuals and, therefore, more personally relevant and motivating to users (Noell & Glasgow, 1999). In addition, the interactive feature of programs that allow for criterion-referenced mastery of training content has great potential for efficient and effective training and quality assurance. Researchers are documenting the benefits of these new technologies in comparison with more conventional training programs.

Irvine et al. (2003) randomly assigned CNAs to treatment conditions, comparing a videotaped lecture-based training program to an interactive multimedia computer training program on CD-ROM. The CNAs rated videotaped vignettes of caregiving situations before and after training. CNAs who received the interactive computer training demonstrated significantly more correct responses at posttest than did the videotape training participants; they were also more likely to report intention to use the correct strategies and to have increased self-efficacy to use the correct strategies. Similarly, Rosen et al. (2002) conducted a 6-month randomized trial comparing a computer-based interactive video training program to the same content delivered to nursing home staff in a lecture format by a nurse educator. The computer-based training resulted in greater compliance and satisfaction with the training and greater knowledge acquisition when compared to the lecture and control groups.

Ronch et al. (2004) have designed an Internet-based person-centered care training program for staff in long-term care facilities, the Electronic Dementia Guide for Excellence (EDGE). Carefully developed over a period of years to provide clinical guidelines for research-based interventions, this program, modeled on Maslow's hierarchic organization of needs model (Maslow, 1964), contains modules that were field tested in multiple sites, included in a videotape to show in workshops, and eventually adapted for the Internet (http://health.state.ny.us/diseases/conditions/dementia/edge/index.htm). Ronch et al. described the use of the EDGE program by many sites; however, evaluative data are not reported to date.

In 1971, the state of Florida mandated the Teaching Nursing Home pilot project, whose mission was to create a person-centered long-term care system through training, research, and networking. The resulting GeriU Web site (http://www.geriu.org; GeriU, n.d.) provides a variety of training modules on gerontology and geriatric education topics, including a series designed to provide dementia care competencies for CNAs and licensed practical nurses. These modules include written and video-based content on the nature of dementia, communication, distress behaviors, loved ones, activities of daily living, environment, and ethics. Other modules on falls are aimed at the professional medical audience (i.e., medical students and physicians needing continuing education).

In the past 5 years, this technology-driven training industry has virtually exploded. Searching the Internet yields hundreds of training sites that range from state- and federally funded programs, universities, and private industry, to not-for-profit organizations; the obvious need for quality caregiving of our cognitively impaired elders is fueling this creative training industry. Fortunately, many of the authors of these products understand the importance of evaluation and are publishing research to document the effects of their programs. In the years to come, it will become increasingly difficult to choose among the many effective programs that are available, such as those described below.

The Oregon Center for Applied Science develops and evaluates a variety of health and health behavior products related to general health and wellness, parenting skills, teen health, women's health, and children's safety. Their Older Adults product line includes multimedia training programs such as Caregiver's Friend: Sensitive Conversations (communication skills for families caring for an older relative); Caregiver's Friend: Dealing With Dementia; Communication Skills for Family Caregivers of Persons With Dementia; the Family Caregiver's Guide to Dementia/Alzheimer's; and Strategies for Dementia: Communication Skills for Professional Caregivers. Each of these products was evaluated in a randomized clinical trial that compared the multimedia program with a control condition and assessed caregivers' knowledge, intention to use the skills trained, and satisfaction with the program (Irvine et al., 2003). Additional outcomes, such as improved depression, anxiety, stress, self-efficacy, intention to seek help, and positive perceptions of caregiving, were documented for the Caregiver's Friend: Dealing With Dementia program (Beauchamp, Irvine, Seeley, & Johnson, 2005). Each of these products includes video dramatizations, testimonials, quizzes, lesson plans handouts, and certificates documenting skill mastery in print, video, CD-ROM, and Internet formats. These products are available at http://www.orcasinc.com (Oregon Center for Applied Science, n.d.) and http://www.hcimarketplace.com (HealthComm Interactive Marketplace, n.d.).

Mather Lifeways Institute on Aging (http://www.matherlifeways.com; Mather Lifeways, n.d.) is a not-for-profit company with a mission to promote positive aging through education, training, and research. Their programs—Empowering Caregivers, Powerful Tools for Caregivers, Powerful Tools for Caregivers Online, Making Sense of Memory Loss, S.E.L.F. (person-centered care training), and L.E.A.P. (staff development and retention)—are all delivered through a variety of media, including in-service and online classes using print manuals, CD-ROMs, PowerPoint slides, evaluation tools, and templates for handouts and marketing. Each program undergoes rigorous evaluation prior to commercial release, with the research results guiding future program replications. For example, the Making Sense of Memory Loss program was formally evaluated with more than 200 participants in the Chicago area (Kuhn & Mentes de Leon, 2001), and similarly positive results were documented in a follow-up study with 110 caregivers from nine different chapters of the Alzheimer's Association (Kuhn & Fulton, 2004). Improved self-care and self-efficacy of family caregivers were documented in an evaluation of the Powerful Tools for Caregivers program (Kuhn, Fulton, & Edelman, 2003); improved staff retention, job satisfaction, organizational climate, leadership behaviors, and work productivity were outcomes of the L.E.A.P. program (Hollinger-Smith & Ortigara, 2004). Evaluation of the S.E.L.F. program is under way.

The University of Pennsylvania School of Nursing's Hartford Center of Geriatric Nursing Excellence (n.d.) has developed an online learning product, Gero T.I.P.S., for nurses and other health care clinicians. The goal of this free program that translates academic research into practical applications is to **t**each **i**nnovative **p**ractical **s**olutions to clinicians in the field. The two online training programs, (a) Restraint-Free Care and (b) TLC for LTC, present the content in modules that each includes a video, planning materials, presentation tools, participant handouts, and evaluation forms (http://nursing.upenn.edu/centers/hcgne/gero_tips/default.htm).

The American Society on Aging (ASA) has developed a series of Web seminars that use multimedia and interactive distance learning technology to deliver live and stand-alone Web-based training programs on topics of interest to professionals in aging-related fields. General aging issues, such as geriatric assessment, older driver wellness, and risk of falls, are presented to multiple participants simultaneously through a graphics presentation over the Internet and by conversation over a toll-free phone line, fostering interactive audience participation. In partnership with the Positive Aging Resource Center of Brigham and Women's Hospital and Harvard Medical School, the ASA offers a Web seminar series, Alzheimer's Disease: Taking Control, to introduce professional caregivers to a different form of care for persons with Alzheimer's disease, habilitation therapy. This approach actively engages participants in the processes of learning to manage the challenging behaviors associated with the disease by teaching related to the therapeutic domains, critiquing care environments, presenting cases, and developing behavioral plans.

As shown in Table 10.4, other Internet-based training programs for dementia caregivers are available. Again, little research has been conducted to date on the efficacy of training delivered via the Internet.

POST TRAINING: THE CHALLENGE OF SUPERVISION

The recognition that ongoing supervision of staff is needed to keep a successful training program going is one of the biggest challenges to the nursing home industry, as well as to the researchers who develop training programs. The fact that most of the training programs described above included some type of staff mentoring (Boettcher et al., 2004); organizational empowerment strategies, such as support from the unit leader (Gruss et al., 2004) and an emphasis on teamwork (McAiney, 1998); or a structured staff management system including supervisory monitoring, performance feedback, and tangible incentives (Stevens et al., 1998) reinforces the notion that didactic training alone is not sufficient to make permanent changes in the quality of care provided in these settings. As Foster (2004) remembered, when she was first hired to be a unit director of her nursing home's Alzheimer's unit, she had had no training on how to supervise her staff. Fortunately for her, a unit director's certificate course was developed at the Rush Alzheimer's Disease Center that included training on management skills, such as successful ways to recruit, hire, motivate, and terminate staff.

Many of the training programs described in this chapter included components for supervising on-the-job criterion-based performance at the time of training and over time, for developing incentives and other motivation systems, and for fostering leadership skills in their employees. Since Burgio and Burgio (1990) first proposed the behavioral supervision model that included components of self-monitoring, supervisory monitoring, supervisory performance feedback and praise, and tangible lottery-based incentives for achieving skill criteria, the training industry has acknowledged the need for ongoing supervision in order to maintain the benefits of training programs. After a series of studies, Burgio and his colleagues have concluded that although NAs do increase their knowledge of skills through didactic in-services, and on-the-job training components do ensure the use of trained skills, it is the formal system of staff management that is necessary to maintain skill performance over time. For example, Burgio et al. (1990) used FSM to increase

TABLE 10.4 Technology-Based Staff Training Programs and Resources

Administration on Aging, Alzheimer's Resource Room Training Materials (manuals, videos): http://www.aoa.gov/ALZ/Public/Alzprof/resources_prof/training_materials
Care of the Person With Dementia: A Training Program for Residential Program Staff
Caring for People With Dementia: A Training Guide
Dementia: The Power of Nutrition in Care Giving
Hand in Hand: A Start-Up Kit for Dementia Day Services
Handbook for Volunteers: The Friday Club
Home Is Where I Remember Things: A Curriculum for Home and Community Alzheimer's Care
How to Hire and Train Help in the Home (English, Spanish, Russian)
How to Organize and Manage a Support Group (Spanish)
Respite Workers Training Packet (English, Spanish)
Training Curriculum for Law Enforcement Personnel
Alzheimer's Association: http://www.alz.org/qualitycare/training
Classroom training: Foundations of Dementia Care
Web-based trainings: CARES: A Dementia Caregiving Approach™ for Direct Care Workers
Dementia Care Training for Team Leaders: Successful Supervision
Alzheimer's Disease Education and Referral Center: http://www.niapublications.org/adear/
Alzheimer's Disease: Unraveling the Mystery (speaker's kit CD-ROM)
American Society on Aging: http://www.asaging.org/webseminars/
Alzheimer's Disease: Taking Control (Web seminar)
Dementia Solutions: http://www.health.state.ny.us./diseases/conditions/dementia/edge/index.htm
Electronic Dementia Guide for Excellence (Ronch et al., 2004)

(*Continued*)

TABLE 10.4 (Continued)

Mather Lifeways, Inc.: http://www.matherlifeways.com
Empowering Caregivers
Powerful Tools for Caregivers
Powerful Tools for Caregivers Online
Making Sense of Memory Loss
S.E.L.F (person-centered care training)
L.E.A.P. (staff development and retention)
National Institute on Aging: http://www.nia.nih.gov/Alzheimers/caregiving/professional/
The Growing Challenge of AD in Residential Settings (Kuhn, 2006; includes manual, three training modules, PowerPoint presentations, and videotapes; videotapes available at http://www.alzheimers.org/caregiving/challenge.htm):
The Alzheimer's Care Kit: Signs and Symptoms of Alzheimer Disease
Alzheimer's Disease: Inside Looking Out (Cleveland Area Chapter, Alzheimer's Association)
Assessing the Mental Status of the Older Person; Video Press: 1-800-328-7450
Losing It All: The Reality of Alzheimer's Disease
Complaints of a Dutiful Daughter
Oregon Center for Applied Science: http://www.orcasinc.com or http://www.hcimarketplace.com
Caregiver's Friend: Sensitive Conversations
Caregiver's Friend: Communication Skills for Family Caregivers of Persons With Dementia
Caregiver's Friend: Dealing With Dementia
Family Caregiver's Guide to Dementia/Alzheimer's
Strategies for Dementia: Communication Skills for Professional Caregivers
University of Pennsylvania: http://www.nursing.upenn.edu/centers/hcgne/gero_tips/
Gero T. I. P. S. (Teach Innovative Practical Solutions; online training programs)
Restraint-Free Care
TLC for LTC

use of prompted voiding techniques; Stevens et al. (1998) used FSM to maintain behavior management skills; and Allen-Burge et al. (2001) used FSM to increase use of communication skills. The person-centered approaches (e.g., Boettcher et al., 2004; Kitwood, 1997) and other residential models (e.g., the Eden Alternative; Thomas, 1996) are attempting to change the culture of nursing home care through staff empowerment in order to impact the quality of care of the residents and the job satisfaction of the employees. There should be much progress toward these goals reported in the next decade.

The Role of the SLP in Training Nursing Home Staff

Without a doubt, the nursing home SLP plays an important role in training nursing home staff. From the wealth of training materials reviewed above, it is obvious that the importance of communication is recognized by all professionals in the nursing home industry. To the extent that SLPs have specialized training in the identification, assessment, and remediation of communication deficits, they will serve many important roles in service delivery to the residents *and* the staff of the facility. First, they will work with the staff to identify residents who may need direct services from the SLP for specific communications impairments, such as aphasia and swallowing difficulties. When the SLP first arrives at a new facility, offering to conduct an in-service on communication skills and deficits of the nursing home population can be a great way to introduce him or herself, the types of residents and problems the SLP can serve, and the range of information he or she can share in future in-services. The SLP can emphasize the collaborative and consultative roles he or she can serve in helping to solve problems with challenging residents and to contribute to an improved quality of care for the residents.

Once specific clients have been identified for assessment and intervention planning, the SLP can write treatment goals that include the staff in their implementation and ongoing evaluation. As outlined in chapter 11 on goal writing, staff can be included in identifying specific therapy needs for individual residents, in taking some preintervention data on the frequency of specific problems, in suggesting possible treatment strategies, in implementing the treatment plan, and in keeping track of treatment outcomes. Partnering with the CNAs by soliciting their advice and ideas will create an environment of mutual trust, respect, and cooperation.

SLPs can also serve an important role in working with families of residents in the nursing home. They can facilitate interactions between family and staff, who both have the residents' needs in mind but can experience communication breakdowns for many reasons. Some facilities have family support groups that would welcome an occasional in-service on a variety of topics related to communication, swallowing, and engagement in activities. End-of-life communication and hospice and palliative care are other areas where the SLP can provide unique information and support to families and staff. Special workshops can be offered to assist families in creating memory books or to train volunteers to be successful visitors.

REFERENCES

Allen-Burge, R., Burgio, L., Bourgeois, M., Sims, R., & Nunnikhoven, J. (2001). Increasing communication among nursing home residents. *Journal of Clinical Geropsychology*, *7*, 213–230.

Alzheimer's Association. (2006). *Foundations of dementia care (and other training materials)*. Retrieved July 23, 2008, from www.alz.org

Alzheimer's Disease Education and Referral Center (ADEAR). (2006). Retrieved July 23, 2008, http://www.niapublications.org

American Health Care Association. (2002). *Results of the 2001 AHCA nursing position vacancy and turnover survey*. Washington, DC: Author, Health Services Research and Evaluation.

Andersen, A. (1995). *Caring for persons with Alzheimer's disease: A training manual for direct care providers*. Baltimore: Health Professions Press.

Bayles, K., & Tomoeda, C. (1998). *Improving the ability of Alzheimer's patients to communicate* [Videotape]. Tucson, AZ: Canyonlands.

Beauchamp, N., Irvine, A. B., Seeley, J., & Johnson, B. (2005). Worksite-based Internet multimedia program for family caregivers of persons with dementia. *The Gerontologist*, *45*, 793–801.

Beck, C., Doan, R., & Cody, M. (2002). Nursing assistants as providers of mental health care in nursing homes. *Generations*, *26*, 66–71.

Beck, C., Ortigara, A., Mercer, S., & Shue, V. (1999). Enabling and empowering certified nursing assistants for quality dementia care. *International Journal of Geriatric Psychiatry*, *14*, 197–212.

Boczko, F., & Santo Pietro, M. J. (1997). *The Breakfast Club: Program training guide*. Vero Beach, FL: Speech Bin.

Boettcher, I., Kemeny, B., DeShon, R., & Stevens, A. (2004). A system to develop staff behaviors for person-centered care. *Alzheimer's Care Quarterly*, *5*(3), 188–196.

Bourgeois, M., Dijkstra, K., Burgio, L., & Allen, R. (1998). *Increasing effective communication in nursing homes: Inservice Workshop Training manual, videotapes, and documentation forms*. Tallahassee: Department of Communication Disorders, Florida State University.

Bourgeois, M., Dijkstra, K., Burgio, L., & Allen, R. S. (2004). Communication skills training for nursing aides of residents with dementia: The impact of measuring performance. *Clinical Gerontologist*, *27*, 119–138.

Bourgeois, M., Dijkstra, K., Burgio, L., & Allen-Burge, R. (2001). Memory aids as an AAC strategy for nursing home residents with dementia. *Augmentative and Alternative Communication*, *17*, 196–210.

Bourgeois, M. & Irvine, B. (1999). *Working with dementia: Communication tools for professional caregivers* CD-Rom and videotape Inservice training programs]. Eugene: Oregon Center for Applied Science (ORCAS). Award of Distinction from *The Communicator* and Finalist, Telly Awards (2000).

Bowers, B., & Becker, M. (1992). Nurse's aides in nursing homes: The relationship between organization and quality. *The Gerontologist*, *32*, 360–366.

Brunk, D. (1997, July). Random acts of violence: How CNAs cope with abuse from residents. *Contemporary Long Term Care*, 38–42.

Burgio, L. (1996). Direct observation of behavioral disturbances of dementia and their environmental context. *International Psychogeriatrics*, *8*, 343–346.

Burgio, L., Allen-Burge, R., Roth, D., Bourgeois, M., Dijkstra, K., Gerstle, J., et al. (2001). Come talk with me: Improving communication between nursing assistants and nursing home residents during care routines. *The Gerontologist*, *41*, 449–460.

Burgio, L. D., & Burgio, K. L. (1990). Institutional staff training and management: A review of the literature and a model for geriatric long-term care facilities. *International Journal of Aging and Human Development*, *30*, 287–302.

Burgio, L. D., Engel, B. T., Hawkins, A., McCormick, K., Scheve, A. S., & Jones, L. T. (1990). A staff management system for maintaining improvements in continence with elderly nursing home residents. *Journal of Applied Behavior Analysis*, *23*, 111–118.

Burgio, L., & Scilley, K. (1994). Caregiver performance in the nursing home: The use of staff training and management procedures. *Seminars in Speech and Language*, *15*, 313–322.

Burgio, L., Scilley, K., Hardin, J., Hsu, C., & Yancey, J. (1996). Environmental "white noise": An intervention for verbally agitated nursing home residents. *Journal of Gerontology: Psychological Sciences*, *51B*, 364–373.

Burgio, L., Scilley, K., Hardin, J., Janosky, J., Bonino, P., & Slater, S. (1994). Studying disruptive vocalization and contextual factors in the nursing home using computer-assisted real-time observation. *Journal of Gerontology: Psychological Sciences*, *49*, 487–496.

Burgio, L., & Stevens, A. (1999). Behavioral interventions and motivational systems in the nursing home. In R. Schulz, G. Maddox, & M. Lawton (Eds.), *Annual review of gerontology and geriatrics: Vol. 18. Focus on interventions research with older adults* (pp. 284–320). New York: Springer.

Burgio, L., Stevens, A., Burgio, K., Roth, D., Paul, P., & Gerstle, J. (2002). Teaching and maintaining behavior management skills in the nursing home. *The Gerontologist*, *42*, 487–496.

Castle, N. (2006). Measuring staff turnover in nursing homes. *The Gerontologist*, *46*, 210–219.
Castle, N., & Engberg, J. (2006). Organizational characteristics associated with staff turnover in nursing homes. *The Gerontologist*, *46*, 62–73.
Chang, C-C., & Lin, L-C. (2005). Effects of a feeding skills training program on nursing assistants and dementia patients. *Journal of Clinical Nursing*, *14*, 1185–1192.
Chou, S., Boldy, D., & Lee, A. (2002). Measuring job satisfaction in residential aged care. *International Journal for Quality in Health Care*, *14*, 49–54.
Cohen-Mansfield, J. (1997). Turnover among nursing home staff: A review. *Nursing Management*, *28*(5), 59–64.
Cohn, M. D., Smyer, M. A., & Horgas, A. L. (1994). *The ABC's of behavior change: Skills for working with behavior problems in nursing homes*. State College, PA: Venture.
Dijkstra, K., Bourgeois, M., Burgio, L., & Allen, R. (2002). Effects of communication training on the discourse of nursing home residents with dementia and their nursing assistants. *Journal of Medical Speech-Language Pathology*, *10*, 143–157.
Eastern Michigan University. (1997). *Care of the person with dementia: A training program for residential program staff*. Lansing: Author.
Foner, N. (1994). Nursing home aides: Saints or monsters? *The Gerontologist*, *34*, 245–250.
Foster, S. (2004). The Special Care Unit Director's Course: An innovative program to develop and empower individuals to become effective leaders. *Alzheimer's Care Quarterly*, *5*, 184–187.
GeriU. (N.d.). GeriU.org: The online geriatrics university. Retrieved August 8, 2008, from http://www.geriu.org
Grant, L., Kane, R., Potthoff, S., & Ryden, M. (1996). Staff training and turnover in Alzheimer special care units: Comparisons with non-special care units. *Geriatric Nursing*, *17*(6), 278–282.
Gruss, V., McCann, J., Edelman, P., & Faran, C. (2004). Job stress among nursing home certified nursing assistants: Comparison of empowered and nonempowered work environments. *Alzheimer's Care Quarterly*, *5*(3), 207–216.
Gwyther, L. P. (1985). *Care of Alzheimer's patients: A manual for nursing home staff*. Chicago and Washington, DC: Alzheimer's Association and American Health Care Association.
Harrington, C., Kovner, C., Mezey, M., Kayser-Jones, J., Burger, S., Mohler, M., et al. (2002). Experts recommend minimum nurse staffing standards for nursing facilities in the U.S. *The Gerontologist*, *40*(1), 5–16.
HealthComm Interactive Marketplace. (N.d.). HealthComm Interactive: Programs for Better Education and Health. Retrieved August 8, 2008, from http://www.hcimarketplace.com
Hebert, L, Beckett, L., Scherr, P., & Evans, D. (2001). Annual incidence of Alzheimer's disease in the United States projected to the years 2000 through 2050. *Alzheimer Disease and Associated Disorders*, *15*, 169–173.
Hoeffer, B., Rader, J., McKenzie, D., Lavelle, M., & Stewart, B. (1997). Reducing aggressive behavior during bathing cognitively impaired nursing home residents. *Journal of Gerontological Nursing*, *23*, 16–23.
Hollinger-Smith, L. M., & Ortigara, A. (2004). Changing culture: Creating a long-term impact for a quality long-term care workforce. *Alzheimer's Care Quarterly*, *5*(1), 60–70.
Irvine, A. B., Ary, D., & Bourgeois, M. (2003). An interactive multi-media program to train professional caregivers. *Journal of Applied Gerontology*, *22*, 269–288.
Kaplan, M. (1996). Training staff in behavior management. In M. Kaplan & S. Hoffman (Eds.), *Behaviors in dementia* (pg. 47–61). Baltimore: Health Professions Press.
Kitwood, T. (1997). *Dementia reconsidered: The person comes first*. Buckingham, UK: Open University Press.

Koury, L., & Lubinski, R. (1995). Effective in-service training for staff working with communication-impaired patients. In R. Lubinski (Ed.), *Dementia and communication* (pp. 279–291). San Diego, CA: Singular.

Kuhn, D. (2006). *The growing challenge of AD in residential settings*. Retrieved August 4, 2004, from http://www.alzheimers.org/caregiving/challenge.htm

Kuhn, D., & Fulton, B. (2004). Efficacy of an educational program for relatives of persons in the early stages of Alzheimer's disease. *Journal of Gerontological Social Work, 42*, 109–130.

Kuhn, D., Fulton, B., & Edelman, P. (2003). Powerful tools for caregivers: Improving self-care and self-efficacy of family caregivers. *Alzheimer's Care Quarterly, 4*(3), 189–200.

Kuhn, D., & Mentes de Leon, C. (2001). Evaluation of an educational intervention with relatives of persons in the early stage of Alzheimer's disease. *Research on Social Work Practice, 11*(5), 531–548.

Landreville, P., Dicaire, L., Verreault, R., & Levesque, L. (2005). A training program for managing agitation of residents in long-term care facilities: Description and preliminary findings. *Journal of Gerontological Nursing, 31*(3), 34–42.

Laschinger, H., Finegan, J., Shamian, J., & Wilk, P. (2001). Impact of structural and psychological empowerment on job strain in nursing work settings: Expanding Kanter's model. *Journal of Nursing Administration, 31*, 260–272.

Laschinger, H., Wong, C., McMahon, L., & Kaufman, C. (1999). Leader behavior impact on staff nurse empowerment, job tension, and work effectiveness. *Journal of Nursing Administration, 29*, 28–39.

Lescoe-Long, M. (2000). Why they leave: A new approach to staff retention. *Nursing Homes, 49*(10), 70–75.

Lewis, C., Scott, C., Bielfeld, R., & Slabe, T. (1995). Videotapes on geriatric-related topics. *Topics in Geriatric Rehabilitation, 11*(2), 71–77.

Lubinski, R. (1995). Environmental considerations for elderly patients. In R. Lubinski (Ed.), *Dementia and communication* (pp. 257–278). San Diego, CA: Singular.

Lundervold, D., & Jackson, T. (1992). Use of applied behavior analysis in treating nursing home residents. *Hospital and Community Psychiatry, 43*, 171–173.

Maslow, A. (1964). *Toward a psychology of being*. Princeton, NJ: Van Nostrand.

Mather Lifeways. (N.d.). Mather Lifeways: Ways to age well. Retrieved August 8, 2008, from http://www.matherlifeways.com

McAiney, C. (1998). The development of the empowered aide model. *Journal of Gerontological Nursing, 24*, 17–22.

McCallion, P., Toseland, R., Lacey, D., & Banks, S. (1999). Educating nursing assistants to communicate more effectively with nursing home residents with dementia. *The Gerontologist, 39*(5), 546–558.

Mercer, S., Heacock, P., & Beck, C. (1993). Nurses' aides in nursing homes: Perceptions of training, work loads, racism, and abuse issues. *Journal of Gerontological Social Work, 21*, 95–112.

Morgan, L. (1996). The quality of training for nursing assistants: Evaluations of experienced workers. *Gerontology & Geriatrics Education, 16*(3), 53–61.

Nakhnikian, E., Wilner, M., Joslin, S., & Hurd, D. (2002). Nursing assistant training and education: what's missing? *Nursing Homes Long Term Care Management, 51*, 48–51.

New England Research Institute. (1995). *Working it out: Support groups for nursing aides* [Videotape]. Chicago: Terra Nova Films.

Noell, J., & Glasgow, R. E. (1999). Interactive technology applications for behavioral counseling. *American Journal of Preventive Medicine, 17*(4), 269–274.

Office of Inspector General (OIG). (2002). *Nursing aide training* (Publication OEI-05-01-00030). Washington, DC: Department of Health and Human Services. Retrieved July 28, 2008, from http://www.oig.hhs.gov

Omnibus Budget Reconciliation Act (OBRA) of 1987. (1991, October). *The Federal Register*, *56*(48), 865–921.

Oregon Center for Applied Science. (N.d.). Oregon Center for Applied Science: Research, innovation, results. Retrieved August 8, 2008, from http://www.orcasinc.com

Ortigara, A., & Rapp, C. (2004). Caregiver education for excellence in dementia care. *Alzheimer's Care Quarterly*, *5*, 179–180.

Parks, S., Haines, C., Foreman, D., McKinstry, E., & Maxwell, T. (2005). Evaluation of an educational program for long-term care nursing assistants. *Journal of the American Medical Directors Association*, *6*(1), 61–65.

Pillemer, K., Suitor, J., Henderson, C., Meador, R., Schultz, L., Robison, J., et al. (2003). A cooperative communication intervention for nursing home staff and family members of residents. *The Gerontologist*, *43*, 96–106.

Price, J. (2000). Reflections on the determinants of voluntary turnover. *International Journal of Manpower*, *22*, 600–624.

Rogers, J., Holm, M., Burgio, L., Granieri, E., Hsu, C., Hardin, J., et al. (1999). Improving morning care routines of nursing home residents with dementia. *Journal of the American Geriatrics Society*, *47*(9), 1049–1057.

Ronch, J., Bradley, A. M., Pohlmann, E., Cummings, N., Howells, D., O'Brien, M. E., et al. (2004). The electronic dementia guide for excellence (EDGE): An Internet-based education program for care of residents with dementia in nursing homes. *Alzheimer's Care Quarterly*, *5*(3), 230–240.

Rosen, J., Mulsant, B., Kollar, M., Kastango, K., Mazumdar, S., & Fox, D. (2002). Mental health training for nursing home staff using computer-based interactive video: A 6-month randomized trial. *Journal of the American Medical Directors Association*, *3*(5), 291–296.

Roth, D., Stevens, A., Burgio, L., & Burgio, K. (2002). Timed-event sequential analysis of agitation in nursing home residents during personal care interactions with nursing assistants. *Journals of Gerontology: Psychological Sciences*, *57B*, P461–P468.

Santo Pietro, M. J. (2002). Training nursing assistants to communicate effectively with persons with Alzheimer's disease: A call for action. *Alzheimer's Care Quarterly*, *3*(2), 157–164.

Santo Pietro, M. J., & Boczko, F. (1998). The Breakfast Club: Results of a study examining the effectiveness of a multi-modality group communication treatment. *American Journal of Alzheimer's Disease*, *13*, 146–159.

Santo Pietro, M. J., & Ostuni, E. (2003). *Successful communication with persons with Alzheimer's disease: An in-service manual* (2nd ed.). St. Louis, MO: Butterworth Heinemann.

Scanlon, W. (2001). *Nursing workforce: Recruitment and retention of nurses and nurse aides is a growing concern* (GAO-01-75OT). Washington, DC: Government Accounting Office.

Schirm, V., Lehman, C., & Barton, K. (1996). A new view: What nursing assistants think about caregiving. *HealthCare in Later Life*, *1*(2), 97–104.

Schnelle, J., Newman, D., & Fogarty, T. (1990). Management of patient continence in long-term care nursing facilities. *The Gerontologist*, *30*, 373–376.

Smyer, M., Brannon, D., & Cohn, M. (1991). Improving nursing home care through training and job redesign. *The Gerontologist*, *32*, 327–333.

State of Florida, Department of Elder Affairs. (1996). *Alzheimer's disease training manual*. Tallahassee: Author.

Stevens, A. B., Burgio, L. D., Bailey, E., Burgio, K., Paul, P., Capilouto, E., et al. (1998). Teaching and maintaining behavior management skills with nursing assistants in a nursing home. *The Gerontologist*, *38*, 379–384.

Tellis-Nayak, V., & Tellis-Nayak, M. (1989). Quality of care and the burden of two cultures: When the world of the nurse's aide enters the world of the nursing home. *The Gerontologist*, *29*(3), 307–313.

Teri, L. (1990). *Managing and understanding behavior problems in Alzheimer's disease and related disorders* [Training program with videotapes and written manual]. Seattle: University of Washington.

Teri, L., Baer, L., Orr, N., & Reifler, B. (1991). Training nursing home staff to work with Alzheimer's disease patients. *Gerontology & Geriatrics Education*, *11*(3), 77–83.

Teri, L., Huda, P., Gibbons, L., Young, H., & van Leynseele, J. (2005). STAR: A dementia-specific training program for staff in assisted living residences. *The Gerontologist*, *45*, 686–693.

Thomas, W. H. (1996).

Toseland, R. W., & McCallion, P. (1998). *Maintaining communication with persons with dementia: An educational program for nursing home staff and family members*. New York: Springer.

University of Pennsylvania School of Nursing, Hartford Center of Geriatric Nursing Excellence. (N.d.). Welcome to Gero T.I.P.S. Online. Retrieved August 8, 2008, from http://www.nursing.upenn.edu/centers/hcgne/gero_tips/default.htm

U.S. Centers for Medicare and Medicaid Services. (2001). *Appropriateness of minimum nurse staffing ratios in nursing homes: Phase II final report*. Cambridge, MA: Abt Associates.

Vogelpohl, T. S., Beck, C. K., Heacock, P., & Mercer, O. (1996). "I can do it" dressing: Promoting independence through individualized strategies. *Journal of Gerontological Nursing*, *22*(3), 39–42.

Watson, R. (1994). Measuring feeding difficulty in patients with dementia: Developing a scale. *Journal of Advanced Nursing*, *19*, 257–263.

Wilson, B., & Laschinger, H. (1994). Staff nurse perception of job empowerment and organizational commitment: A test of Kanter's theory of structural power in organizations. *Journal of Nursing Administration*, *24*, 39–47.

11

Treatment Settings, Goals, and Documentation Issues

This chapter will discuss the range of institutional and community settings in which speech-language pathologists (SLPs) will find potential treatment candidates. We provide information about how SLPs can support individuals with dementia as they transition through different service delivery settings (e.g., home to assisted living to nursing home), as well as information about funding issues and available resources. The differences in functional behaviors, the environment, and communication partners will be outlined for each setting in order to develop logical treatment goals. The aim of the interventions we recommend is to maximize communicative and memory functioning to increase or to maintain activities, participation and engagement, and quality of life for people with dementia across the disease progression. The recommended interventions may also increase the quality of life and decrease the stress of family and professional caregivers of individuals with dementia. Multiple examples of a range of functional goals and ways to document treatment progress will be provided.

This chapter will also address a variety of issues with respect to documentation in various settings so that SLPs are more likely to be reimbursed for their services. Among health care providers, there is ongoing consternation over reimbursement issues. We want to make it clear that SLP services for cognitive-communicative deficits ARE reimbursable (Hopper, 2003; Kander, 2005, 2006; Petty, 2002). Of course, documentation issues and third-party payer regulations change frequently, so the guidelines described here will be fairly broad. Recommendations of Web sites will be provided so that clinicians may maintain current knowledge on these important issues. As most clinicians deal with denials from third-party payers at some point in their careers, strategies for appealing claims will also be provided.

Before getting into specifics of the settings, goals, and documentation, the reader is reminded of some general principles of intervention for dementia. Use of the World Health Organization's (WHO) *International Classification of Functioning, Disability, and Health* (2001) will assist clinicians in addressing a wider variety of treatment targets beyond those designed to reverse impairments.

This model supports the increased focus on maintenance of independence for as long as possible and on enhancing quality of life of persons with dementia as well as their caregivers, who are an essential component of the intervention process. Because behavioral, cognitive, and language changes in dementia interact across the disease progression, caregivers should be provided with information regarding the causes of communication breakdowns and specific strategies to compensate for those deficits. In many cases, they will need specific skills-based training to learn positive interaction styles, behaviors, and appropriate cueing strategies, and to inhibit negative, nonproductive behavior patterns. In chapter 5, we proposed that clinicians consider adopting the following three principles of dementia intervention: (a) The primary goals of intervention should be to maintain independent functioning for as long as possible, (b) and to maintain quality of life through supported participation and engagement in desired activities; (c) these goals should be achieved through procedures that are personally relevant to the client and are trained within functional contexts.

TREATMENT CONSIDERATIONS IN A VARIETY OF SETTINGS

Implementing Memory and Communication Supports Across Settings

Home and Community Most persons with dementia will experience the full course of their illness while living at home and participating in the community (Schulz, 2000). Many persons will adopt memory supports (e.g., planners, calendars, written notes, shopping lists, and maps) for typical age-related changes during the prediagnosis phase. In the early stages of the disease process, overt memory supports will need to be implemented to maintain everyday activities in the home and community. For some persons in the early stages, the goal may be to provide strategies that will allow the individual to maintain work status as long as possible. This may include education and training with employers and/or coworkers and family members. As the disease progresses, caregivers assume responsibility for daily activities, and a range of memory and communication supporting systems can be implemented to maintain participation, engagement, and quality of life. The extent to which these memory supports maintain satisfactory functioning in the home will largely depend on the caregiver's attitude, skills, and health. Caregivers who are willing and able to seek advice and implement suggestions for addressing problem behaviors will be successful in keeping their loved ones at home for the duration of the illness. These caregivers will be able to learn strategies for maintaining functional behaviors and to modify techniques as their loved ones decline. Memory books and interest albums will keep their loved ones conversing about familiar people and activities; memo boards and reminder cards will provide some independence in remembering important facts and reducing repeated questions; and activity modifications will keep the person engaged in familiar lifelong hobbies. See Figure 11.1 and the figures in chapter 5 for examples of these types of memory aids.

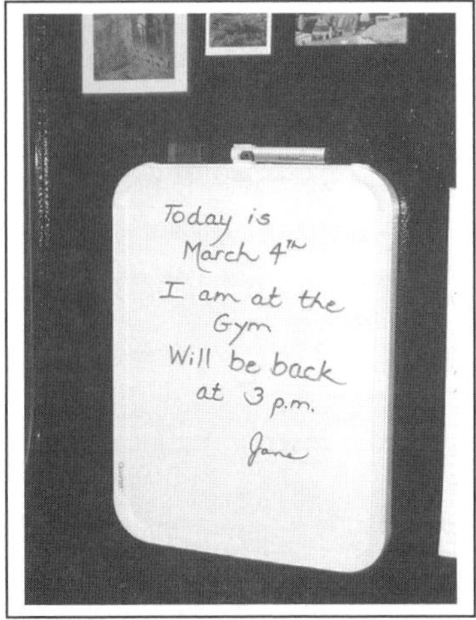

Figure 11.1 Memory Supports for Home and Community Settings.

Day Care When the caregiver begins to experience the stressors of providing continuous care, adult day care can provide a welcome respite. In this setting, the person with dementia has the opportunity for social interaction and participation in stimulating activities that supplement those that are available in the home. Staff is trained to recognize the signs of memory impairment and to respond in appropriate ways; activities are designed to provide opportunities for engagement at the appropriate level of cognitive ability. Some caregivers, however, do not take advantage of day care respite opportunities because of fears that the person will refuse to participate or will be fearful of abandonment. Written memory supports can be very useful in helping the person (and his or her caregiver) transition to this new setting. Reminder cards that state, "I am spending the day with friends. My wife will pick me up at 4:30," or a memory wallet with pages that describe the facility and activities (e.g., "I enjoy my time at Joe's Place," "I play pool with Fred and Sam," and "The meals are delicious") can help prepare people with dementia for their day at the center. Staff can prompt individuals with dementia to read their card or memory wallet when they ask questions about leaving. People who have a memory book should be encouraged to bring them to the center to share with other individuals; activity staff often design group discussions around common topics in memory books, such as "Let's talk about our parents," or "Where did everyone go to school?" Volunteers in adult day care centers may make memory books for persons with dementia and use them for group activities (Bourgeois & Mason, 1996). Another useful suggestion for day care staff is to prepare a simple, large-print list of the day's activities at the center that can be copied and sent home with each person. When the caregiver asks the person about the past day, instead of the typical response, "We didn't do anything," the person can read the list of activities and comment about each one. This memory-supporting tool is particularly useful for alleviating the guilt many caregivers feel about having others care

Today's Schedule of activities:

Tuesday, January 16, 2007

8:00 Arrival and coffee time
8:30 Calendar time
9:00 Today's Program: Therapy Pets
10:00 Snack: Sliced apples and caramel dipping sauce
10:30 Seated Exercise with PT students
11:30 Bathroom
12:00 Lunch: Meatloaf, mashed potatoes, green beans, Cornbread, brownies
1:00 Quiet time: Music students playing the harp
2:00 Conversation groups: Remembering the Civil Rights Era
3:00 Snack: Tea and crumpets
3:30 Bathroom
4:00 Movie time: The Graduate
5:00 Going home

Figure 11.2 Memory Supports for Day Care.

for their family member. Figure 11.2 shows examples of memory supports for adult day care, including an example of a daily schedule to prompt conversation about the day's events at day care.

Assisted Living Residents of assisted living facilities are usually transitioning from the totally independent living environment of their own homes to the semi-independent and semisupervised situation of a private room or apartment in a communal living situation. Some people welcome the comforts, safety, and social benefits of living with other people and transition easily. Others resist the limitations imposed by a reduced living space, the periodic monitoring of their activities, and the privacy issues that accompany residential living. Personal losses can also create barriers to successful acclimation to a new living arrangement; some residents grieve for lost possessions, their deceased partners, their former home and neighborhood, and their independence. They may withdraw from socialization, avoid communal meals, and decline invitations to participate in activities. If individuals are also suffering from memory loss and cognitive decline, they may experience periods of disorientation and confusion in their new surroundings.

The focus of intervention in this setting is on environmental engineering to create a positive, supportive communication environment to assist the person in maintaining or increasing activities and participation and ensuring safety. SLP interventions should be functional and contextualized. Caregivers should be trained to facilitate the use of external cognitive and communication aids. Several memory-supportive tools can ease a difficult transition. A memory album that illustrates the home that has just been left, including pictures of the different rooms with the personal objects, furniture, and memorabilia, can be a comfort (see Figure 11.3). It is helpful to include some written text explaining the circumstances of the move: For example, "My heart condition worries my family. I will be safer living close to other people," and "I was often lonely at home alone. Here I will make many new friends." Staff can suggest that people read their memory book when they get confused or ask to be taken home. Other repetitive requests, such as wanting to drive their car, can be redirected with a memory book page that states, "I enjoyed driving my car around town, but now I don't

Figure 11.3 Memory Supports for Assisted Living.

have to worry about the gas and insurance. Whenever I need to go somewhere, my son drives me in his car."

Assisted living facilities typically support residents in their daily functions with written text in various formats. A quick stroll through an assisted living facility will uncover writing in the form of identification signs on resident rooms and staff offices, newspapers and magazines, menus posted near the dining room, activity schedule boards, and staff name tags. Clinicians working in this environment can encourage their clients to read and respond appropriately to these written cues. When the text is too small or too complex, suggestions for modifying these written supports can be made to the activity staff, who may have the needed supplies for making suggested changes. For example, visually enhancing the day on an activity calendar with a colorful frame can increase the likelihood that residents will be able to find the day's activities. Some clinicians have been successful in convincing the local newspaper to publish a large-print insert of news and announcements once a week for subscribers who used to enjoy reading the paper but now have visual and cognitive limitations (Lou Eaves, October 2000, personal communication); adult literacy resources are also useful (e.g., http://www.news-for-you.com; News-for-You.com, n.d.). Printed invitations to attend a specific facility activity may make the reluctant resident feel welcome, and a daily printed menu slipped under the resident's door may entice him or her to try a meal in the dining room. A large-print directory of important telephone numbers by the telephone in the person's room, with notes about when specific family members are at work or home, can help the person feel it is possible to contact family when needed. Figure 11.3 illustrates some useful memory aids for assisted living settings.

Long-Term Care When medical needs necessitate the move to long-term care, this transition can be facilitated with written supports similar to those used in the assisted living facility. The focus continues to be on environmental engineering. Memory books and wallets, reminder cards, and memo boards can all include text explaining the move to the new facility (e.g., "My new home is Magnolia Manor. I am safe here"). A memory book containing personal biographical information and pictures, or an interest album about a favorite hobby, can be useful for quiet times when staff are busy and the person can review the book independently. Repeated requests for the family can be answered truthfully if the resident has a guest book

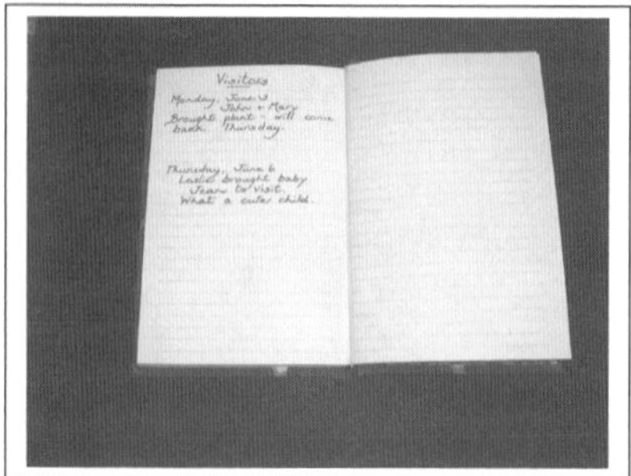

Figure 11.4 Memory Supports for Long-Term Care.

in which family members write notes about their visits and when they will be back: "I see here that your son writes he will be back to visit on Tuesday; that's tomorrow." Family photos and other personal memorabilia should be labeled in large print; it is the experience of many long-term care staff that when they ask about the people in the photos, the resident either cannot remember the accurate names or makes mistakes in naming them. As noted in chapter 6, staff can use a family video to comfort or redirect a confused or agitated resident. Clinicians can suggest to family that they videotape themselves and other family members having a conversation with their relative; or for those residents who do not have family to make a personal videotape, Video Respite tapes can be used (Caserta & Lund, 2002; Lund, Hill, Caserta, & Wright, 1995). Finally, in assisted living and long-term care facilities, the SLP may also promote socialization with other residents for persons with dementia. As noted in chapter 6, this may alleviate some of the social isolation that is prevalent among those with cognitive or communication disorders in nursing homes. Figure 11.4 provides some examples of memory supports for long-term care settings.

Acute Care When a person with dementia enters an acute care setting, it is often because of a medical condition that required anesthesia, is painful, or is treated with strong medications. In all of these cases, the effects of impaired cognition and the consequences of the medical intervention compound the patient's inability to function appropriately or at premorbid levels. The change in environment, which may be confusing in and of itself, may also compound these problems. Persons with dementia are likely to be disoriented, to have difficulty communicating basic needs, and to have needs in social closeness in the acute care setting. Nurses often provide medical instructions verbally (e.g., "The call button is right here. Use it when you feel you need to get up") with the expectation that their patients understand and will remember later in the day. Unfortunately, most patients with impaired cognition prior to the medical intervention are even more impaired immediately afterward and are therefore unable to respond appropriately. When the nurses exhaust their patience with repeated instructions, family members are often called upon to monitor their loved ones around the clock. Figure 11.5 provides some examples of memory supports for the acute care setting.

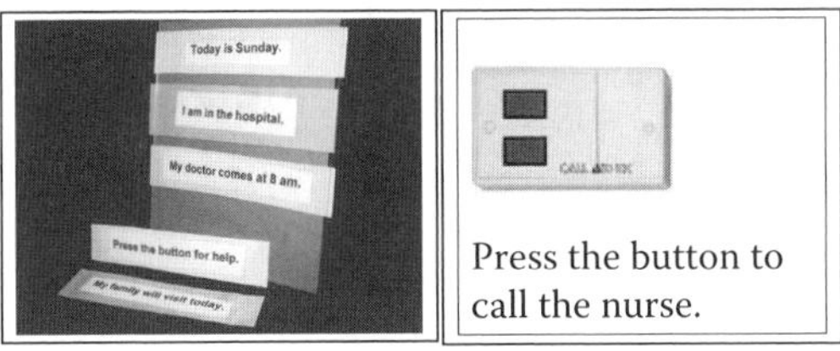

Figure 11.5 Memory Supports for Acute Care.

The role of the SLP is often thought to be solely to evaluate and manage swallowing disorders, but the SLP should also be involved in evaluating and managing cognitive-communicative disorders, including those that may affect safe swallowing. The SLP may be involved in staff education and training in the use of cognitive-communicative strategies that will enhance care and quality of life. SLPs must keep in mind that persons with dementia in the acute care setting may fatigue more quickly and may have high anxiety levels; therefore, treatments need to be efficient and strategies must be easy to implement by other staff and family members. Some simple written tools can facilitate comprehension of nursing instructions and increase orientation in the acute care setting. However, these cues are often provided ineffectively, such as by writing too much or not making the cues portable. Alternatively, large-print statements, posted on the patient's bedside tray and within eye range, can help patients to remember where they are, how to call for help, and other important messages relevant to their medical condition (see Figure 11.5). Thus, staff in-services are important for teaching nurses how to make appropriate written cueing systems for the particular care needs of an individual and how to implement them for maximum effects. Family caregivers should also be taught strategies that will enhance communication for medical needs as well as social and emotional needs.

Rehabilitation and Skilled Nursing The patient in rehabilitation or skilled nursing is, by nature of the medical condition that necessitated this placement, in a temporary situation that can be disorienting and disagreeable. Coming from acute care, the effects of pain medications and the residual effects of anesthesia may still be contributing to increased cognitive dysfunction. If the medical condition (e.g., hip fracture) and the rehabilitation are painful, the person will not be in the best frame of mind to cooperate with therapy. In these situations, the patient's care planning is usually conducted by a team of professionals, including the physician, social worker, SLP, OT, PT, and nursing staff. Therefore, the therapeutic intervention plan must address the patient's need to understand and cooperate with demands from multiple therapists and nurses. As in the acute care setting, SLPs have a role in this setting to provide consultation services to the other professionals in the form of advice about the cognitive, communicative, and cueing needs of the patient. In rehabilitation, however, the treatment plan is likely to be more intensive, with more active involvement of all therapists. The SLP may initiate individual cognitive-communication goals related to medical, social, and emotional needs, as well as to enhance the achievement of goals in other disciplines.

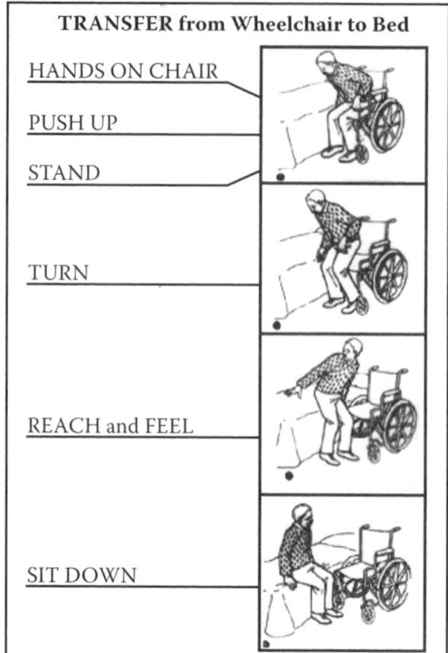

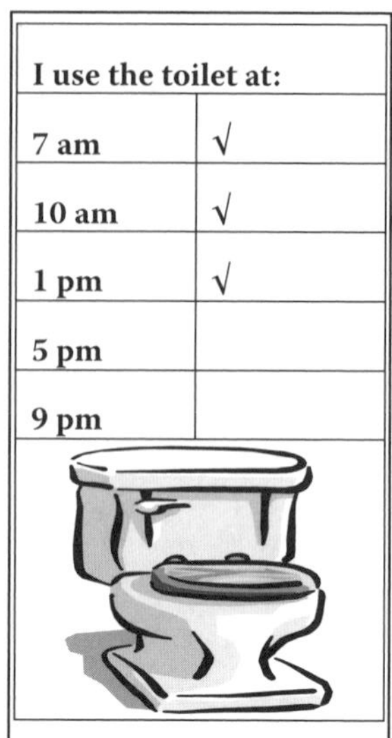

I use the toilet at:	
7 am	√
10 am	√
1 pm	√
5 pm	
9 pm	

Figure 11.6 Memory Supports for Rehab Settings.

Whenever opportunities for cotreatment exist, the needs of the patient will dictate the particular therapeutic routines undertaken. For example, if the primary focus of rehabilitation is physical recovery, the SLP can best serve the client's needs by ensuring that the PT's instructions are presented in a format that the patient can understand and remember. Consultation about length of verbal commands, repetition of the same verbal command, and the use of written commands with picture supplements should be offered. Figure 11.6 illustrates examples of memory aids used for physical therapy. The objective of the consultation should be the enhancement of therapy outcomes and most independent placement possible upon discharge.

Hospice Care When a person has a life-limiting illness, hospice care may be instituted. Hospice uses the principles of palliative care. The purpose of hospice or palliative care is to facilitate the best possible quality of life through relief of suffering and control of symptoms, as well as death with dignity, using a multidisciplinary approach (Last Acts Palliative Care Task Force, 1997). Caregivers must also "remain sensitive to personal, cultural and religious values, beliefs and practices" (Last Acts Palliative Care Task Force). The Task Force also identified the following principles of palliative care: (a) respecting patient goals, preferences, and choices; (b) comprehensive caring (physical, psychological, social, and spiritual support); (c) utilizing the strengths of interdisciplinary resources; (d) acknowledging and addressing caregiver concerns; and (e) building systems and mechanisms of support (http://www.lastacts.org).

The principle regarding caregiver concerns should not be overlooked. Markowitz, Gutterman, Sadik, and Papadopoulos (2003) found that disruptive patient behaviors, perceived poor quality of patient medical care, and lack of caregiver support were associated with decreased mental and physical functioning among caregivers. The caregiver's QoL should be monitored in addition to that of the patient. Interventions that improve the symptoms of the illness have the potential to improve both the patient and caregiver's QOL.

Hospice care is funded by Medicare Part A, if the prognosis for life span is 6 months or less. A dilemma exists for providers of persons with dementia: determining at what point the 6-month prognosis can be made for end of life. There are Medicare guidelines for characterizing this point, but this determination is not that clear cut (Covinsky, Eng, Lui, Sands, & Yaffe, 2003; Hurley & Volicer, 2002; Schonwetter et al., 2003). Severe declines in functional status (swallowing, mobility, communication, and continence) are associated with the beginnings of the terminal stage. Schonwetter et al. reported that, of those meeting Medicare guidelines for hospice care, only about three fourths died within the 6-month time period. Based on other literature, Allen, Kwak, Lokken, and Haley (2003) suggested that dementia may be a contributor to death far more than is recognized, and that criteria for providing hospice care be expanded. One suggestion by Allen, Kwak, et al. (2003) was to determine the typical and atypical behavioral features of end-stage dementia so that family members may be educated on what to expect and so that caregivers may know when intervention is necessary. Thorough assessment is needed to determine the cause of atypical behaviors and to provide appropriate need-based and strength-based interventions. Some of the atypical behaviors may be indicators of pain. Given that pain management is one focus of palliative care, hospice should be instituted more frequently and sooner with persons in the late stages of dementia (Allen, Kwak, et al.).

Pain Management

An important role for the SLP in the medical settings is to help nurses to interpret the nonverbal communicative attempts of patients with cognitive-communicative impairments. Those with severe cognitive impairments may not be able to participate in reliable self-report of pain or discomfort in the assessment process, such as following surgery or during an illness. Assessment of the presence and severity of pain is one of the main responsibilities of nurses, so that they may assist physicians with pain management. Typically, pain assessment is done verbally, by self-report. Nurses ask patients if they have pain, and if they respond affirmatively, they are asked to rate the severity. In the presence of language deficits, such as word-finding and comprehension difficulties, patients may not be able to explain their pain adequately. Instead, patients with cognitive impairments are known to express pain in nonverbal ways, such as crying out or yelling, restlessness, rocking, rubbing a body part, grimacing, and other aggressive or resistive behaviors (Feldt, Warne, & Ryden, 1998; Marzinski, 1991). Disruptive vocalization is often ignored and fails to be interpreted as an expression of pain (Ryden & Feldt, 1992). In fact, persons who were vocally disruptive received less analgesic medication than nondisruptive patients (Carriaga et al., 1991).

The importance of attempting to accurately assess pain in persons with cognitive impairment arises from the many studies reporting the inadequate pain treatment of persons with painful conditions who are unable to communicate their pain. Hospitalized cognitively impaired patients were found to receive significantly less analgesic medications postoperatively compared with cognitively intact patients (Bell, 1997; Feldt, Ryden, & Miles, 1998; Fisher et al., 2002). Similarly, pain is poorly managed in persons with dementia in long-term care (Parmelee, Smith & Katz, 1993). Even when nurses used a visual analogue pain-rating scale to assess pain in patients with potentially painful conditions (e.g., arthritis, osteoporosis, and cancer), cognitively impaired residents received significantly fewer scheduled pain medications than cognitively intact residents (Horgas & Tasi, 1998; Kaasalainen et al., 1998).

Attention to this problem in assessing and treating pain in persons with cognitive and communicative impairments has been a focus of nursing educators in recent years, with good results. Feldt and Finch (2002) found similar amounts of analgesic medications administered during hip fracture recuperation to both cognitively impaired and intact residents who reported similar pain intensity ratings. However, Feldt and Finch cautioned nurses in long-term care that residents with cognitive impairment may not anticipate the need for pain medication and may not request "prn" (as-needed) pain medications; as a result, nursing staff may need to schedule routine medication administration in anticipation of expected periods of pain fluctuation. Use of pain tools that persons with cognitive impairments are able to complete would also be recommended.

Ferrell, Ferrell, and Rivera (1995) evaluated the ability of cognitively impaired nursing home residents to complete five different pain intensity tools and found that 83% of 217 subjects with a mean MMSE score of 12.1 were able to complete at least one of them; however, only 17% could complete all five of the instruments. Given the challenges of obtaining reliable self-report, observational tools (Abbey et al., 2004; Feldt, 2000; Hurley, Volicer, Hanrahan, Houde, & Volicer, 1992; Warden, Hurley, & Volicer, 2003) are sometimes used to determine if there are nonverbal signs of pain. For example, the Checklist of Nonverbal Pain Indicators (CNPI; Feldt) is an observational tool nurses can use to indicate the presence of a variety of verbal and nonverbal behaviors to communicate pain. Huffman and Kunik (2000) reported, however, that the available assessment tools for persons with dementia who are noncommunicative require improvements in accuracy and facility. Likewise, Snow et al. (2004) warned that these scales are not comprehensive enough for an accurate assessment of pain.

There are many versions of pain-rating scales; some simply require the patient to provide a number from 0 to 10, with the instructions that 0 means *no pain at all* and 10 means *the worst pain possible*. Tools such as the Verbal Descriptor Scale (Feldt, Ryden, et al., 1998) require the patient to endorse one of seven brief pain severity descriptions (from *no pain* to *pain as bad as it could be*). In a review of the literature, Huffman and Kunik (2000) found that persons with dementia who were communicative were able to report pain as validly as persons who were cognitively intact. Moreover, Fisher, Burgio, Thorn, and Hardin (2006) developed and examined an explicit procedure for obtaining self-report pain data from nursing home residents with varying levels of cognitive ability. They documented consistent and reliable self-report pain assessments with residents who had a mean MMSE of 15 (SD = 7). Residents were provided with adequate time and assistance (e.g., verbal prompts) to respond in yes–no and Likert scale response formats using a 17-item modified version of the Geriatric Pain Measure—Modified (GPM-M; Ferrell, Stein, & Beck, 2000; Simmons, Ferrell, & Schnelle, 2002), which was referred to as *GPM-M2*. Evidence for psychometric properties was good, including validity, internal consistency, and stability.

Given the documentation of significant difficulty in adequately assessing and managing pain in persons with cognitive deficits, a role for the SLP in working with persons with dementia is to facilitate communication for pain assessment and management. Snow et al. (2004) made several useful suggestions for comprehensive pain assessment in persons with dementia so that all four components of pain (i.e., sensory, behavioral, emotional, and cognitive) are considered. These recommendations include the following: (a) Use multiple measures and multiple raters, (b) adapt existing measures so that persons with communication impairments may complete them, and (c) adapt those instruments that were designed for persons with dementia so that they may be used to assess pain (e.g., the Affect Rating Scale; Lawton, Van Haitsma, & Klapper, 1996). SLPs could provide valuable assistance in this process by interpreting nonverbal expressions of pain for nursing staff when residents are exhibiting problem behaviors such as agitation. SLPs may act as one of the raters of nonverbal communication, or may assist in adapting existing tools so that persons with cognitive impairments are able to use them. For example, Lasker (2006), working with nursing staff at a local hospital, revised a visual pain scale to graphically depict facial features associated with different severities of pain (Figure 11.7). Finally, SLPs must keep in mind that "everyone can communicate, everyone does communicate" (Beukelman & Mirenda, 1998), and that it is our job to assist other caregivers to figure out what and how people with dementia, who are labeled as "noncommunicative," are communicating.

PAIN SCALE

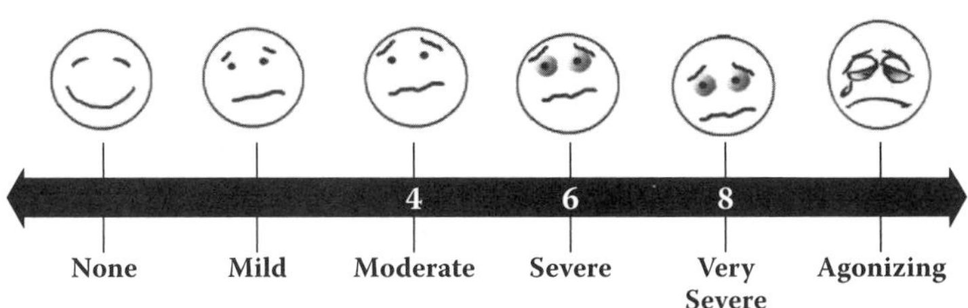

Figure 11.7 Visual Pain Scale. Source: Laster (2006).

Advance Directives

Another role of the SLP in medical settings (hospital, home and community, and nursing home) may be to assist dementia patients with advance care planning for future medical treatment and end-of-life care. During every hospital admission, patients are asked to sign a document consenting to the planned treatment; they are also asked if they have completed an advance directive form and have a copy with them, or to complete one during the admissions process. For most people, the solicitation of their desired wishes in the event of unplanned medical complications is disconcerting and often surprising. It is not common for most people to have considered all of the potential outcomes of their hospitalization, especially the negative ones. Very few people prepare advance directive documents specifying their treatment preferences prior to hospital admission.

Most recently, the tragic case of Terri Schiavo (Annas, 2005) highlighted the difficult choices and controversy inherent in the decisions that family and medical staff have to make when a person becomes incapacitated medically and cannot express his or her own treatment wishes. In an ideal world, everyone would prepare an advance directive document specifying treatment preferences for a variety of medical conditions and end-of-life care. Although various population surveys document support for advance care planning, in actuality, very few people have executed advance directives; those who have are typically older, White, well-educated, and of higher socioeconomic status (Bravo, Dubois, & Pâquet, 2003). In their Canadian survey, Bravo et al. (2003) documented prevalence rates ranging from 7.4% for formal advance directives for research to 42.3% for informal advance directives for health care in older women who knew someone with a cognitive impairment.

Perrin (1997) described the most common types of advance directives: (a) A *living will* communicates patient's refusal of treatment when terminally ill, (b) a *medical directive* communicates patient's treatment preferences (to be provided or withheld) in the event of incapacity, and (c) a *durable power of attorney for health care* appoints a proxy to make health care decisions in the event of incapacity. Attorneys, and in particular those specializing in elder care law, can assist in preparing and notarizing advance directive documents. Several nonprofit agencies have developed documents and procedures for the general public who recognize the need for advance planning. One consumer education initiative (http://www.midbio.org) sells book designed to promote meaningful conversations among family members about preparing for end-of-life decisions. The Partnership for Caring organization (n.d.) makes available advance directives forms for all 50 states and the District of Columbia, as well as a toll-free number for information and counseling (http://www.partnershipforcaring.org). The Aging With Dignity organization (n.d.; http://www.agingwithdignity.org) has developed an advance directive document, *Five Wishes*, designed to help individuals identify (a) the person to make care decisions for you when you can't, (b) the kind of medical treatment desired and not wanted, (c) the degree of comfort desired (including pain management), (d) desired personal interactions, and (e) personal statements to loved ones about important topics (e.g., asking forgiveness, desired funeral details, and other final wishes). This consumer-friendly document is particularly useful to families and professionals as a tool for initiating conversations about these important topics.

Advance care directives need to be initiated and executed while the patient still has decision-making capacity (Mezey, Mitty, & Ramsey, 1997). SLPs may be involved in competency evaluations when patients present with signs of incompetence and incapacity. Competence is a legal judgment made only by a judge; the person has to comprehend the nature of the action in question and understand its consequence. Capacity is a clinical judgment that (a) the patient understands that he or she has the right to make a choice; (b) the patient understands the medical situation, prognosis, risks, benefits, and consequences of treatment or no treatment; (c) the patient must be able to communicate the decision; and (d) the decision is consistent over time (Roth, Meisel, & Lidz, 1977). Because different kinds of decisions require different levels of decisional capacity and most decisions are situation specific, the evaluation team needs to understand not only the extent of the decisions required and the potential ramifications of each decision but also how to communicate the choices effectively to the person with impaired cognition. The SLP on the team can serve an important role in determining the extent of comprehension, make suggestions for appropriate assessment tools, and offer support strategies (i.e., visual and written cues).

Allen, DeLaine, et al. (2003) developed some objective measures of capacity in their study of correlates of advance care planning in nursing homes. Based on a sample of 78 nursing home residents with a mean MMSE score of 14 (SD = 6.5), they found that these residents were able to state a treatment preference but did not understand the treatment situation or the consequences of the treatment choice. Residents who verbally interacted with others were more likely to understand and appreciate treatment choices; in addition, cognitive supports and prompts (Allen & Shuster, 2002) and different response options (yes–no versus scaled responses; Fisher et al., 2006) appear to increase the likelihood of participation in treatment planning discussions.

Moye, Karel, Azar, and Gurrera (2004) found that adults with mild dementia could participate in medical decision making at acceptable legal standards, but the focus of the process should be on having the person describe the reasons for specific medical choices and the implications of those choices on future outcomes, and not to require comprehension of the meaning of specific diagnostic and treatment procedures. Similarly, Widdershoven and Berghmans (2001) proposed using advance directives in dementia care as communication tools, to assist the person with dementia in structuring communication about care plans and treatment options to physicians and other medical personnel.

Obtaining Referrals

In many medical facilities, speech-language pathologists spend at least 80% of their time working in the area of dysphagia. For many SLPs, they are simply going along with usual practice in that facility and are kept busy enough with dysphagia referrals that they do not go out of their way to look for communication-related referrals. Although this is understandable, the result is that many individuals with reduced communication abilities are then at risk for decreased activities, participation, and quality of life. As we have delineated in this book, the SLP's role is to work with persons with cognitive-communication disorders, even if those disorders result from degenerative diseases. The SLP may solicit these referrals by educating the staff regarding the role of the SLP with persons with cognitive-communicative disorders. See Appendix 11.1 for an example of a handout for a "Speech Therapy In-Service" that could be adapted depending on the setting. Also, some tips for doing this, based on the second author's clinical experience in a wide variety of nursing homes and hospitals were presented in chapter 6.

REIMBURSEMENT AND DOCUMENTATION ISSUES

Obtaining funding for rehabilitation services, particularly in skilled nursing and long-term care facilities, can be quite overwhelming. To complicate matters, there are many misconceptions about whether SLPs can be reimbursed for working with persons with dementia. Although it may be challenging to obtain reimbursement for these services in some instances, it is possible (Kander, 2006). As stated elsewhere, the OBRA of 1987 mandated communication-related service provision for residents with dementia. However, it is up to the SLP to conduct evaluation and intervention for functional cognitive-communicative behaviors, and to document needs, goals, and deficits in a way that is acceptable to the local intermediary. More recent legislation has impacted the way that services are delivered and/or reimbursed. There are some general principles that clinicians can keep in mind that will increase their success in obtaining reimbursement. Some common problems with documentation were described by Caniglia (2003): unclear skilled versus unskilled services, incomplete documentation, lack of functional goals, unreasonable amount of time to set up functional maintenance program, inappropriate reason for evaluation or client not appropriate for therapy, and "best practice" standards not represented in treatment plan. Swigert (2002) also provided examples of reasons for denials for reimbursement, such as treatment goals being too ambitious, treatment goals met but treatment continued, or goals not being met and a reevaluation was not completed. In all cases, clinicians must follow the ethical standards established by the American Speech-Language-Hearing Association (ASHA) or other professional associations when documenting and billing services. These and other issues will be discussed below.

Navigating the Maze of Third-Party Payers

Most clinical services are paid, at least in part, by third-party payers, or insurers. The landscape of these insurers has changed significantly over the past few decades, and continues to evolve. Clinicians must learn about the types of Medicare programs that are available to reimburse for rehabilitation services, as well as other private insurance companies. The clinician must also learn about the types of insurance companies that result in different types of coverage plans, such as fee-for-service versus health maintenance plans or preferred provider plans. This chapter is not meant to provide a thorough accounting of the evolution of all of these plans.

Significant information is available on the Internet and through ASHA. Luckily, most facilities or rehabilitation companies have staff that has primary responsibilities of keeping up with third-party payer regulations, particularly Medicare regulations in the case of skilled nursing and long-term care facilities; this does not alleviate the SLP of the responsibility for knowledge related to documentation and reimbursement. Because of the focus on dementia care, the emphasis of the discussion will be on Medicare. Furthermore, many insurance companies follow the lead of Medicare in determining definitions and documentation requirements. Medicare policy states that speech-language pathology services must be necessary for the diagnosis and treatment of speech and language disorders resulting in communication disabilities, and for the diagnosis and treatment of swallowing disorders (Olshin, Ciolek, & Hwang, 2002).

Of particular significance to clinicians is the distinction between Medicare Part A and Part B coverage. Medicare Part A is the coverage that is provided for in-patient medical care, which may be provided in acute care or acute rehabilitation hospitals, skilled nursing facilities, or home health care. Medicare Part B is the coverage that is provided for out-patient medical care, which may be provided in out-patient departments of hospitals, clinics, or long-term care (Petty, 2002). Some of the reason for confusion is that Medicare recipients may move between different levels of care, which may be covered under Part A or Part B. For example, there are times when a long-term care resident has the onset of a new illness or the exacerbation of a current condition that requires hospitalization. As long as the hospital stay is at least 3 days long, the resident may be able to obtain rehabilitation services in the skilled nursing unit, under Medicare Part A. When that person either regains prehospitalization status or plateaus before reaching that point, then he or she will be moved back to long-term care, which is not covered by Medicare. The U.S. Senate Committee on Aging (2000) stated that long-term care does not have a goal of curing an illness; long-term care, rather, is designed to promote an optimal level of functioning in the face of a chronic illness or disability (Petty). Medicare does not consider many of the services provided in long-term care or in home health care as medically necessary, and therefore does not reimburse these services; this level of care is referred to as *custodial care* and includes assistance with basic activities of daily living (ADLs; e.g., bathing, grooming, dressing, and meal preparation) or social support. Medicare will cover only services that are considered "skilled" services, as will be described in more detail below, whether covered by Part A or Part B. Thus, the important distinction is "in-patient" versus "out-patient" services.

The significance of whether a person is covered by Medicare Part A or Part B is the reimbursement scheme. In rehabilitation or skilled nursing facilities, Medicare Part A now reimburses under a scheme called the Prospective Payment System (PPS), which allocates a certain amount of funding depending on the level of services being provided, or resource utilization groups (RUGs). The RUGs are defined by the number of services being provided (e.g., by the PT, OT, and SLP) and the amount of time per week that the client receives those services. Thus, the rehabilitation team must quickly evaluate a client and determine prognosis, functional treatment goals, and estimated duration of services (time, days, etc.).

Medicare Part B has been in a state of flux for the past decade; part of the Balanced Budget Act of 1997 directed Part B services to be capped at $1,500 per year for occupational therapy, and another $1,500 for physical therapy and SLP services combined (Olshin et al., 2002). This was implemented in 1999, but then a moratorium was placed on the cap in the Balanced Budget Reform Act of 1999. As of January 1, 2006, the Deficit Reduction Act resulted in the therapy cap being reinstated, but with an increased allowance of $1,780; however, Congress has authorized providers to request exceptions to this cap based on individual needs for medically necessary services (ASHA, 2006; Center for Medicare and Medicaid Services [CMS], 2006a,b). According to CMS, providers may exceed the cap, using an automatic process exception, if they are able to justify the therapy cap exception. This justification may include issues such as the patient's condition, including complexities and severity; the type, frequency, and intensity of services provided; or the interaction of current conditions and complexities that may cause treatment to be needed that exceeds the cap. CMS has suggested that clinicians consult the Medicare policies specifically, as well as their professional literature, to determine if clients have medically complex needs or if treatments that exceed cap amounts are medically necessary and justifiable. Furthermore, legislation allows providers who report quality measures (e.g., ASHA's National Outcomes Measurement System, or NOMS) to obtain a 1.5% bonus in reimbursement.

The moratorium on the therapy cap was a welcome relief to clinicians, as well as to the Medicare recipients whose services were cut short by the cap. A study by Olshin et al. (2002) revealed that the therapy cap policy may have unintended consequences for the people who were most likely to receive inadequate services (those who are older, female, minority, and in certain geographic areas; require institutional care; and/or have complex medical conditions). This study also revealed that few Medicare recipients actually receive outpatient therapy services (8.6%), and that among those most likely to use rehabilitation services are those with neurological disorders. Furthermore, other research has found that the cost of care for persons with Alzheimer's is high, but that this is not due to a higher intensity of care; rather, persons with dementia have more adverse health events, such as hip fractures, strokes, and pneumonia (Sloan & Taylor, 2002). Consequently, in addition to the dementia, persons with Alzheimer's are quite likely to require rehabilitation services. Efforts at cost containment and reduced hospitalization for nursing home residents, such as implementation of primary care teams in nursing homes (Joseph & Boult, 1998), may result in those residents needing more services under Part B, as they will not meet the 3-day minimum hospital-stay policy.

Accordingly, an additional role of SLPs who work with persons with dementia is to advocate for the provision of services that will improve their functional abilities and quality of life. ASHA has been engaged in significant advocacy efforts and maintains suggestions on its Web site for SLPs to participate in these efforts. Whereas strides have been made in the recognition of the skilled services that SLPs provide to those with cognitive-communicative deficits, problems remain. In a recent issue of the *ASHA Leader* ("Crisis in Health Care Reimbursement," 2006), two private practitioners reported that actual reimbursement for services has decreased over the years, and that the time and effort that are involved in obtaining reimbursement are very time-consuming and costly. Thus, clinicians must remain active in advocating for their clients to be able to receive much-needed and valuable services.

Goal Writing for Reimbursement

Treatment goals should clearly specify a functional skill or behavior that is targeted. Goals should also focus on enhancing communication and swallowing activities and participation (Caniglia, 2003; Hopper, 2003; Logemann, 2003). These goals should not be aimed at restoring function when a client has a progressive dementia; rather, they should be targeted toward training in the use of compensatory strategies with the client as well as the caregivers. One important aspect of your documentation, including goal writing, for funding is the correct use of acceptable terminology. We are not going to give "hard-and-fast" rules for terminology use, because this changes across intermediaries and over time. There are a few constants, however: You must document that communication (or swallowing) is a factor in providing services, and you must document that you provided *skilled* services (i.e., your services required special training and could not be done by someone without that training). The initial evaluation, treatment plan, progress notes, and discharge paperwork must all reflect skilled speech-language pathology services.

BOX 11.1 LIST OF SKILLED SERVICES FOR DEMENTIA REIMBURSEMENT

Skilled services include the following:

1. Diagnosing and assessing communication and cognitive skills
2. Designing treatment programs
3. Establishing compensatory skills
4. Analyzing and modifying behaviors to improve functional abilities
5. Conducting task analyses to establish a hierarchy of tasks and cues to direct a client toward a goal
6. Training the client and staff and family caregivers to implement a *restorative* treatment program (i.e., skills can improve) or a *functional maintenance program* (FMP)
7. Reevaluating the client based on a change in condition (i.e., either an increase or a decrease in status)

There should be a staff member or supervisor within the hospital or rehabilitation company that can keep you up to date on acceptable terminology. The *ASHA Leader* is another good resource for tips on Medicare documentation. Communication goals for people with dementia must be written so that they reflect skilled services and address communication needs. Below are examples of goals written to reflect (a) skilled versus (b) unskilled services:

The bottom line is that when requesting reimbursement for SLPs, treatment goals should never use the word *practice* and should always focus on a functional communication need.

BOX 11.2 EXAMPLES OF REIMBURSABLE COGNITIVE-COMMUNICATION GOALS

1. a. "Client will initiate communication at the sentence level using memory cards with a photo and written sentence to communicate social/medical/nursing needs."
   b. "Client will practice reading sentences on memory cards."
2. a. "Client will demonstrate comprehension of yes/no questions at the phrase level, when shown related picture stimuli, to increase understanding of questions related to medical/nursing needs."
   b. "Client will practice answering yes/no questions."
3. Client will increase ability to express basic needs using multimodality communication with minimal staff cues 80% of the time.
4. Client will increase ability to indicate meaningful information about pain and body function to staff using multimodality communication with minimal cues 90% of the time.
5. Client will make comprehensible requests for basic needs using written and visual cues with minimal staff cues 80% of the time.
6. Client will increase ability to participate in conversation and activity programs using written cues and pictures with minimal staff cues 80% of the time.
7. Client will produce comprehensible language in conversation related to basic, social, and emotional needs using written cues 90% of the time.
8. Client will decrease occurrence of agitation and abusive verbal behavior through increased functional communication using written and visual cues to less than two episodes of agitation per shift.
9. Client will decrease repetitive questions related to (*going home*) using written cue cards with minimal to no verbal cues to fewer than two times per hour (*fewer than five times per day*, etc.).
10. Client will increase recall of daily schedule using a written cue card and minimal to no verbal cues 80% of the time.
11. Client will use a memory logbook to increase recall of personal and facility information with minimal to no verbal cues 80% of the time.
12. Client will increase recall of hip precautions using a written cue card independently with > 90% accuracy.
13. Client will decrease sundowning behaviors in response to Simulated Presence audiotapes of family members played by staff members every afternoon.

The same principles apply to documentation and goal writing for feeding and swallowing goals. The goals should be measurable and functional and indicate the level of support and types of strategies being utilized to increase self-feeding and/or swallowing abilities to increase nutrition and hydration and/or safety. Self-feeding and swallowing goals should refer to the following types of issues: ability to self-feed, amount and type of assistance required, environmental changes, supervision, use of adaptive equipment, food textures and liquid consistencies, temperature and placement of food, order and rate of presentation of foods and liquids, and/or specific swallowing strategies utilized (Logemann, 2003; Thayer, 2006). The diet levels that are ordered for a person with eating and swallowing disorders should be the least restrictive levels that are safe (e.g., if a person may safely consume soft finger foods, a puree diet would be unduly restrictive). Please note that conducting oral motor exercises with clients is not considered skilled services, and may be particularly inappropriate for those with degenerative neurological diseases. Logemann noted that, if used, exercises must be stated in terms of functional outcomes in order to be reimbursable. The SLP can target the use of specific strategies by the client, through the use of caregiver assistance and supervision and/or cueing systems, as shown in the examples below. The SLP should not spend inordinate amounts of time actually feeding a client. The SLP should conduct therapeutic trials of various food textures, liquid consistencies, adaptive equipment, swallowing strategies, and cueing techniques to determine the safest manner in which a client should be fed or may self-feed. Once this is established, the SLP should train the family or staff caregivers to implement these recommendations.

BOX 11.3 REIMBURSABLE SWALLOWING GOALS

Reimbursable swallowing goals will include statements regarding safe swallowing and/or increased nutrition and hydration using a variety of functional behaviors or strategies:

1. Client will increase safe swallowing by using ... strategy given caregiver cues less than 50% of the time during meals and snacks.
    - Thermal stimulation: Alternate hot and cold temperatures of foods and drinks.
    - Positioning: Use chin tuck, head rotation, or tilt.
    - Strategies: multiple swallows per bolus, alternate liquids and swallows.
    - Equipment: use of adaptive cups or silverware for safe amounts and positioning.
2. Client will be free of signs and symptoms of aspiration 100% of the time when fed a puree diet with honey-thick liquids by a caregiver with the use of an adaptive cup and safe swallow strategies.

Reasonable Expectation for Progress

Another important aspect of documentation in the plan of treatment is the statement of reasonable expectation for progress. As discussed above, you must identify a client's *strengths* as well as *needs* in an evaluation. This understanding of your client's strengths will help you to state a reasonable expectation for progress, and can be listed on the initial evaluation and plan of treatment. This should also be documented in the Minimum Data Set (MDS) evaluation section, "Functional Rehabilitation Potential." The SLP can be involved in the MDS evaluation and can educate other health care professionals, particularly nurses, regarding the documentation of preserved strengths, such as preserved implicit memory and oral reading. Hopper (2003) noted that two positive prognostic indicators should be noted, such as potential to learn, family support, or prior level of function. Some other examples of strengths to document include the following:

- Intact auditory comprehension and ability to follow directions
- Adequate attention skills for your treatment tasks and strategies
- Ability to generalize from a structured learning environment
- Intact skills that allow the patient to compensate for specific deficits (e.g., oral reading ability)
- Intact orientation to time, place, and medical situation
- High level of motivation

BOX 11.4 EXAMPLES OF DOCUMENTING REASONABLE EXPECTATION FOR SIGNIFICANT PROGRESS

- "Understanding of conversational speech improved when shorter sentences with simple vocabulary were used, background noise was reduced (e.g., radio and television turned off), and client was alerted to attend to conversation before speaking to him. This suggests that training and instruction to the client and his caregivers will help the client to understand conversation related to his medical care and social and emotional needs."
- "The client displays intact reading skills, which suggests that she could benefit from use of external aids, such as written and photo cueing systems, to increase her ability to follow directions in therapy, to use compensatory strategies for specific deficits and medical precautions, and to maintain attention for task completion."
- "Given graphic cueing systems (written sentences and photos), the client was able to produce appropriate verbal language at the phrase/sentence level. This suggests that training the client to use these types of compensatory strategies would allow him to become a functional communicator for basic, social, and emotional needs."

- Intact reasoning and judgment
- Preserved social skills
- Demonstrated desire to interact with others in the environment (Holland, 1998)

Coding for Documentation and Billing

Another aspect of reimbursement and documentation that clinicians should be aware of is that of coding systems that may be used. For Medicare and most insurers, clinicians must use codes for diagnoses using the International Classification of Diseases, 9th ed. (ICD-9); for supplies, equipment, devices, and some procedures using the Healthcare Common Procedure Coding System (HCPCS); and for health care procedures and services using the Current Procedural Terminology (CPT; ASHA, 2006b; CMS, 2006a,b). The SLP must identify the ICD-9 codes for the medical diagnosis and for the communication and/or swallowing diagnosis. For example, a person with dementia may have a medical diagnosis of Alzheimer's disease (331.0), a communication diagnosis of symbolic dysfunction (784.6), and a swallowing diagnosis of dysphagia (787.2).

The ICD-9 codes must be recorded on the initial evaluation and plan of treatment as well as the discharge paperwork, and any relevant monthly summaries and continuation plans. The ICD-9 codes may also be used to justify the exception to therapy caps that were noted above; some ICD-9 codes trigger an automatic exception due to the complexity of the diagnosis or of the treatment needed. For example, ICD-9 codes 330.0–337.9 (hereditary and degenerative diseases of the central nervous system), codes 340–345.91 and 348.0–349.9 (other disorders of the central nervous system), and codes 430–438.9 (cerebrovascular disease) allow for an automatic exception to the therapy caps for all three rehabilitation disciplines. Codes for specific communication diagnoses (784.3–744.69, aphasia, voice and other speech disturbance, and other symbolic dysfunction) and dysphagia (787.2) allow exceptions to the therapy cap for SLP services only. Additionally, codes for diagnoses such as memory loss (780.93) may allow for an exception when used in combination with another ICD-9 code (e.g., dysphagia). Again, the services that exceed the cap must be medically necessary, or the claim will likely be denied. Documentation must support the exception, and in the case of communication and swallowing disorders, the use of ASHA's NOMS has been recommended by CMS to document functional improvements (ASHA, 2007a).

CPT codes are used across all health care providers, but there are certain categories that may be used by speech-language pathologists. See Table 11.1 for examples of CPT codes used by SLPs. The codes allow billing that is either time based or procedure based, and these are based on relative value units (RVUs) developed by CMS policy makers. Time-based codes are billed in 15-minute increments, and procedure-based codes are billed per procedure. Note that 92506, or speech-language evaluation, is a procedure-based code, and CMS determined that a typical amount of time that an SLP should spend on this procedure is 156 minutes. Additional guidelines, including times for each 15-minute increment, can be found in the ASHA report on 2007 Medicare Fee Schedule for Speech-Language

TABLE 11.1 Communication and Swallowing CPT Codes Used by SLPs

CPT Codes*	Code Descriptors
Communication Codes	
92506	
procedure-based	Speech and language evaluation: evaluation of speech, language, voice, communication, and/or auditory processing; includes cognitive-communicative disorders and multimodality communication (non-speech-generating device use)
92597	Evaluation for use and/or fitting of voice prosthetic device to supplement oral speech
92626	Evaluation of auditory rehabilitation status; first hour
92627	Evaluation of auditory rehabilitation status add-on (each 15 minutes)
92607	Evaluation for prescription for speech-generating device, first hour (if less than 1 hour, use –52 modifier)
92608	Evaluation for speech-generating device, each additional 30 minutes; may be used on following days until evaluation is completed.
96105	Assessment of aphasia by standardized tests with interpretation and report, per hour (use –52 modifier if less than 30 minute segment)
92507	Individual treatment of speech, language, voice, communication, and/or auditory processing; includes training and modification of use of voice prosthetics; includes treatment of cognitive-communicative disorders, multimodality communication (non-speech-generating devices), and aural rehabilitation by SLPs
92508	Group treatment of speech, language, and hearing disorders (two or more individuals)
97532	Development of cognitive skills (each 15 minutes): may be used in place of, but not in addition to, 92507 for development of skills to improve attention and memory. Note that 92507 is the preferred code by many intermediaries.
92609	Programming, modification, and training for use of speech-generating device services
Swallowing Codes	
92610	Clinical "bedside" swallowing evaluation
92612	Fiberoptic endoscopic evaluation of swallowing (FEES)
92616	Fiberoptic endoscopic evaluation of swallowing and sensory testing (FEEST)
92611	MBS or videofluoroscopy swallow evaluation: the SLP portion of the procedure.
92526	Treatment of swallowing dysfunction and/or oral function for feeding

All CPT codes are © 2006, American Medical Association.
Source: ASHA (2007c).

Pathologists (ASHA, 2007c), which can be found at the ASHA Web site: http://www.asha.org/members/issues/reimbursement/medicare.

Also of importance is that speech-language pathologists are not recognized as independent providers by CMS. SLPs must bill under the institutional code for hospitals and facilities, or under the code of the physician with whom they work. The amount that Medicare can be billed for SLP services (and all other services) is determined by the Medicare Fee Schedule, which is compiled by CMS. Insurance companies may either use this fee schedule or create their own. SLPs may not bill third-party payers more than the allowable amount according to these schedules. Clients who self-pay may not be restricted to these allowable amounts. SLPs should be aware that they may not set prices in collusion with colleagues, as this is illegal (ASHA, 2006c).

Documenting Progress

SLPs must also keep careful records of their treatment services on an ongoing basis, not just at evaluation and discharge. Daily notes should be kept, and weekly progress notes should be written. From the outset, the SLP should be mindful of keeping data using objective measurements. Weekly and monthly progress notes must demonstrate that the client is progressing and that short-term goals are being advanced accordingly. If the client is not making progress, then there must be documentation of a reevaluation and modification of goals to make them more appropriate. Thus, your behavioral objectives should indicate this progression. Some examples of how to modify behavioral objectives over time include changing the level or complexity of the behavior, changing the level or types of cueing or assistance required, changing the context in which the behavior will be performed,

BOX 11.5 MODIFYING SHORT-TERM OBJECTIVES TO SHOW PROGRESS IN FUNCTIONAL BEHAVIORS

Level of complexity of the behavior:

- Words, phrases, sentences, and conversation
- Copy written words, write to dictation, and spontaneously write
- Find sections in memory book, find specific information, make entries, and use book independently

Level and types of cueing, assistance, and prompts:

- Minimal, moderate, or maximum
- Tactile, verbal, or visual

Context:

- In treatment sessions
- In one-on-one conversation with another resident or staff member
- In conversation with family caregivers
- In group conversation or activity

Time intervals and immediacy of responses:

- Recall after 5-minute delay, 1-hour delay, and 24-hour delay
- Respond within 30 seconds, 15 seconds, and 5 seconds

Percentage of accuracy/frequency of occurrence (# of repetitions/# of trials): ____________

revising the timing of stimuli and responses, and increasing the percentage of accuracy or frequency of occurrence of a behavior. Below are examples of these aspects of the behavioral objectives that can be modified.

Functional Maintenance Programs

Functional Maintenance Programs (FMP) are a means of providing short-term, consultative interventions for persons with dementia in long-term care (Hopper, 2003). An FMP might be initiated when a client plateaus during treatment and there is not reasonable expectation for continued improvement, or when a short-term treatment is established specifically to establish an FMP for a client who does not have substantial restorative potential given skilled treatment services (ASHA, 2001). The FMP is developed from the results of a comprehensive evaluation of the functional strengths and needs of the person with dementia. The point of the FMP is to train caregivers to implement the intervention in order to maintain the highest level of skills possible in the person with dementia. According to the Health Care Finance Administration (HCFA) policies, a resident is eligible for the development of an FMP under the following conditions: (a) a documented change in condition (either an increase or decrease), (b) a medical condition associated with loss of function, (c) discharge from skilled services with the need for intervention to maintain rehabilitation outcomes, and (d) the need to update an established program through skilled services (Hopper). The SLP typically trains nursing assistants to follow through with the interventions in the FMP, and these should be listed in the resident's plan of care (see Appendices 11.2 and 11.3 for examples of care plans for communication strategies and swallowing safety). The plan of care details the care to be provided on a daily basis for each resident. In addition to nursing staff, other departments may be responsible for following through with the FMP, such as the activities department (Hopper).

The Appeals Process

Some clinicians avoid working on goals other than for dysphagia due to fears of reimbursement denials. Fortunately, clinicians around the country are reporting success in obtaining reimbursement for interventions designed to improve the cognitive-communicative functioning of patients with dementia across the severity continuum and in a variety of settings. This is due to the fact that clinical researchers are publishing more reports of successful treatment strategies for persons with dementia and that clinicians who have been denied reimbursement for these clients have appealed the decision with positive outcomes. In many cases, intermediaries may not be aware of effective interventions, other than dysphagia treatments, for persons with dementia. Clinicians must keep in mind that Congress has mandated rehabilitation services for persons with dementia (ASHA, 2005); thus, it is illegal for intermediaries to automatically deny all claims for persons with Alzheimer's, as has been done in some regions (Kander, 2006; O'Boyle, 2001). The appeals process can serve an educational function and increase reviewers' knowledge of effective treatments. In the appeals process, clinicians must provide new information regarding medical necessity or other details that were omitted in the original documentation, rather than simply citing Medicare regulations (Caniglia, 2003).

Reporting Results to Family Caregivers

In addition to supplying documentation to third-party payers, SLPs should provide results of evaluations and interventions to family caregivers. There are several things to keep in mind when providing this information. First, the SLP should be aware of the client's and family's cultural background and educational levels and provide information in a way that is respectful of their knowledge and perspectives. Be cautious in providing information to family members; for example, if you are not sure of an answer, be honest about that. Be sensitive to the impact of your judgments regarding the client and the care being providing. Emphasize that you are describing what you see now and that you may be missing important information that they may provide. Always highlight strengths in addition to reporting weaknesses, and focus on what is important to know for immediate care as well as for helping the family to plan for the future. Finally, be collegial and collaborative in developing and implementing a plan of care; reinforce family efforts to follow through with treatment strategies, and gently encourage those who are less involved. Keep in mind that family caregivers often have an overwhelming amount of responsibilities; stress that the recommended strategies are meant to facilitate their communication or to make caregiving less stressful and their family member's quality of life better.

RESOURCES FOR FAMILY CAREGIVERS AND CLINICIANS

Resources for Advance Directives

Five Wishes: advance directive for medical, personal, emotional, and spiritual needs; http://www.agingwithdignity.org

Last Acts: consumer and family resources for end-of-life care; http://www.lastacts.org

Partnership for Caring: advance directives for all 50 states and Washington, D.C.; http://www.partnershipforcaring.org

General Information on Medicare Regulations and Plans

American Association for Retired Persons: http://www.aarp.org, or call 1-800-424-3410

Center for Medicare Advocacy: http://www.medicareadvocacy.org, or call 1-860-456-7790 or 1-800-262-4414

Medicare: http://www.medicare.gov, or call 1-800-MEDICARE (1-800-633-4227)

Medicare Rights Center: http://www.medicarerights.org, or call 1-888-466-9050 (HMO appeals hotline)

Information on Best Practices, Treatment Efficacy, and Reimbursement Issues

American Speech-Language-Hearing Association (ASHA): http://www.asha.org

American Speech-Language-Hearing Association *Access SLP Health Care*, a bimonthly e-newsletter: http://www.asha.org/about/publications/access-slp-hcare/ASLP0306.htm, or e:mail join-access-slphealthcare@lists.asha.org

Communication Aids Manufacturing Association: http://www.aacproducts.org

Speech-generating devices—evaluation and report protocols: http://www.aac-rerc.com

Information on Coding Systems

CPT codes: http://www.ama-assn.org/ama/pub/category/3113.html

HCPCS codes: http://www.cms.hhs.gov/MedHCPCSGenInfo/

ICD-9 codes: http://www.cdc.gov/nchs/about/otheract/icd9/abticd10.htm

APPENDIX 11.1: SPEECH THERAPY IN-SERVICE: COGNITIVE AND COMMUNICATION DISORDERS AND TREATMENT

I. **Most residents have some type of communication impairment**, and many have some combination of communication impairments, including the following:
   - A. **Hearing loss**
   - B. **Word-finding difficulty**: slower speed of thinking of the words to express ideas, or inability to come up with the right words
   - C. **Dysarthria**: speech problem caused by stroke, Parkinson's disease, and other neurological problems—weakness, incoordination, and reduced range of motion of muscles used to speak
   - D. **Aphasia**: language problems usually caused by stroke—including difficulty understanding what others say and difficulty expressing needs and thoughts
   - E. **Cognitive-linguistic deficits**: difficulty understanding others, and difficulty expressing oneself due to decreased attention and memory—may result from multiple transient ischemic attacks (TIAs), stroke, brain tumor, Alzheimer's dementia, Parkinson's dementia, and other types of dementia

II. **Strategies for improving communication:**
   - A. Approach the resident from the front.
   - B. Speak at a comfortable loudness level for each resident.
   - C. Speak slowly and clearly.
   - D. Introduce yourself each time you approach the resident: "My name is Grace, and I'm your nursing assistant today."

E. Prepare the resident for what you plan to do: For example, "It's time to take a shower," and "I'm going to help you eat your breakfast."
F. Give simple, specific, one-step instructions: For example, when eating, instruct the resident to do one step at a time, such as "Open your mouth," "Chew," and "Swallow," and give the resident time to do each step before instructing him or her to do the next step.
G. When repeating, say the same thing two times, then rephrase if the resident still doesn't understand.
H. Make positive comments: "You look nice today," and "I enjoy talking with you."
I. **Use many different ways to communicate** with residents with aphasia, dementia, and/or hearing loss, especially using visual cues:
   1. **To improve** the resident's **understanding**:
      – **Supplement what you say** with **writing**, **gestures**, **drawing**, or **pointing** to the communication boards or objects to assist his or her understanding of your messages.
      – Say, "Let's talk about your family," and write, *Family*.
      – Say, "Did you watch the baseball game last night?" and gesture swinging a baseball bat and throwing a baseball.
      – Say, "I'd like to know more about your family," and show a communication board or photo with her children.
   2. **To improve** the resident's ability to **respond**:
      – Give **written choices** to questions (e.g., "What kind of juice would you like?") and then provide written choices (e.g., Orange, Apple, and Cranberry). Write in big letters with the words spaced apart enough to be able to interpret where she is pointing.
      – Show her a **communication card**, and ask her to point to what she wants or needs.
      – Confirm her choice: "You want …?"
      – Show her the photo album with family members, and **pay attention to her words as well as gestures and facial expressions** to learn more about the photos.

III. **More on using memory books and communication boards:**
A. Uses of memory books and communication boards … they can be used to help residents:
   1. To converse about their families and their lives, fulfilling important **social and emotional needs**
   2. To increase **orientation** to place and people in the facility—nurses, activities, schedule, and room number
   3. To **create a diversion** when residents are agitated, bored, or displaying problem behaviors.
B. How to use memory books and communication boards:
   1. Show the resident the book and say, "Let's look at this book about you."
   2. Help the resident read the sentences as necessary.

3. Refer the resident to the orientation information: "This is a picture of your room where you live now."
4. Show the resident a picture of his or her nurse to reassure him or her that people are here to take care of him or her.
5. Make comments and give compliments about the photos: "What a nice house!" or "You have such a nice-looking family," or "You made beautiful quilts."
6. Ask open-ended questions that do not have a right or wrong answer, and encourage the resident to tell you more about the photos and sentences.

C. Keeping memory and communication boards with the resident:
  1. A bag and plastic pocket will be attached to the resident's wheelchair or walker, if the resident has one. Be sure to put the book in the bag and pocket each day, just as you give the resident glasses, hearing aids, and other necessities each day.
  2. For ambulatory residents, small portable books, cards, or calendars will be given if the resident is able to see small print and photos. A small book can be carried by the resident, attached to a belt loop or carried in a waist pack.
  3. Alternatively, the book can be kept in the resident's room or at the nursing station and handed to an ambulatory resident as necessary.

APPENDIX 11.2: CARE PLAN: COMMUNICATION STRATEGIES

Problem No.	Date	Problems and Strengths	Goals	Approach	Discipline	Goal Analysis
1	01/13/2007	Mrs. Smith has cognitive-linguistic deficits that impact:	1. Mrs. Smith will be able to indicate pain by pointing to a FACES scale and answering yes–no questions with verbal prompts.	1. Use visual aids, including memory and communication cards, visual scales, reminder cards, a calendar, name tags, and signs.	All	
		1. ability to communicate medical, basic, social, and emotional needs	2. Mrs. Smith will be able to indicate basic needs during care routines by pointing to written and/or pictured choices.	2. Encourage Mrs. Smith to respond to questions related to care routines and medical needs; use written cues as needed.	All	
		2. orientation to place	3. Mrs. Smith will increase ability to converse about personally relevant topics related to social and emotional needs.	3. Encourage Mrs. Smith to discuss personally relevant information related to social and emotional needs with use of conversation books.	All	
		3. recall of daily activities	4. Mrs. Smith will be oriented to place with visual aids and verbal cues.	4. Use a multiple-choice format to increase response to questions related to meals and basic needs (e.g., "Do you want juice or water?").	All	
			5. Mrs. Smith will decrease repetitive questions with use of reminder cards and graphic schedules.	5. When conversing, ask open-ended questions that do not have a right or wrong answer, and make comments and positive statements related to Mrs. Smith's interests.	All	
			6. Mrs. Smith will increase participation in everyday activities with cues to look at activity schedule and reminder cards.	6. Provide praise and meaningful communication when Mrs. Smith is engaging in appropriate behavior.	All	
				7. Speech therapy for cognitive-linguistic deficits.	SLP	

APPENDIX 11.3: CARE PLAN: DYSPHAGIA STRATEGIES

Problem No.	Date	Problems and Strengths	Goals	Approach	Discipline	Goal Analysis
2	01/13/2007	Mrs. Smith has dysphagia and receives a mechanically altered diet.	1. Mrs. Smith will be free of signs and symptoms of aspiration with the least restrictive diet and liquids.	1. Diet as ordered.	Dietary	
			2. Mrs. Smith will use safe swallowing techniques.	2.Dysphagia evaluation and treatment with SLP.	SLP	
			3. Mrs. Smith will maintain adequate oral intake for nutrition and hydration needs.	3. Cue Mrs. Smith to sit upright for all p.o. intake.	SLP, nursing	
				4. Cue Mrs. Smith to alternate liquids and solids—use verbal cues and written cue cards.	SLP, nursing	
				5. Cue for oral clearance as needed—provide models and verbal cues.	SLP, nursing	
				6. Cue to clear throat and cough if Mrs. Smith has wet voice quality—provide models and verbal cues.		

REFERENCES

Abbey, J., Piller, N., De Bellis, A., Esterman, A., Parker, D., Giles, L., et al. (2004). The Abbey pain scale: A 1-minute numerical indicator for people with end-stage dementia. *International Journal of Palliative Nursing, 10*, 6–13.

Aging With Dignity. (N.d.). *Five wishes*. Retrieved August 1, 2008, from http://www.agingwithdignity.org

Allen, R., DeLaine, S., Chaplin, W., Marson, D., Bourgeois, M., Dijkstra, K., et al. (2003). Advance care planning in nursing homes: Correlates of capacity and possession of advance directives. *The Gerontologist, 43*(3), 309–317.

Allen, R., Kwak, J., Lokken, K., & Haley, W. (2003). End-of-life issues in the context of Alzheimer's disease. *Alzheimer's Care Quarterly, 4*(4), 312–330.

Allen, R., & Shuster, J. (2002). The role of proxies in treatment decisions: Evaluating functional capacity to consent to end-of-life treatment within a family context. *Behavioral Science and the Law, 20*, 235–252.

American Medical Association. (2006). *Current procedural terminology* (CPT®, 4th ed.). Retrieved August 1, 2008, from http://www.ama-assn.org/cpt

Annas, G. (2005). "Culture of life" politics at the bedside: The case of Terri Schiavo. *New England Journal of Medicine, 352*(16), 1710–1715.

American Speech-Language-Hearing Association (ASHA). (2001, November 30). Model medical review guidelines for dysphagia services. *DynCorp Therapy PSC, 23*, 1–13.

American Speech-Language-Hearing Association (ASHA). (2005, December 23). *Medicare coverage of cognitive therapy by speech-language pathologists*. Retrieved January 12, 2007, from http://www.asha.org/members/issues/reimbursement/medicare/cognitive/

American Speech-Language-Hearing Association (ASHA). (2006a, December 11). *Congress extends therapy cap exception process & halts scheduled fee cuts*. Retrieved January 12, 2007, from http://www.asha.org/about/legislation-advocacy/2006/CngressExtndExcp/

American Speech-Language-Hearing Association (ASHA). (2006b, October 30). *Introduction to billing code systems*. Retrieved January 12, 2007, from http://www.asha.org/members/issues/reimbursement/coding/code_intro/

American Speech-Language-Hearing Association (ASHA). (2006c). *Representation of services for insurance reimbursement, funding, or private payment*. Retrieved January 12, 2007, from www.asha.org/policy

American Speech-Language-Hearing Association (ASHA). (2007a, January 4). *CMS Issues guidance on therapy cap exceptions process: ASHA's NOMS recommended to satisfy documentation requirements*. Retrieved January 12, 2007, from http://www.asha.org/about/legislation-advocacy/2006/CMScapexcept07/

American Speech-Language-Hearing Association (ASHA). (2007b, January 12). *Coding for reimbursement FAQs: Speech-language pathology*. Retrieved January 12, 2007, from http://www.asha.org/members/issues/reimbursement/coding/coding_faqs/

American Speech-Language-Hearing Association (ASHA). (2007c). *Medicare fee schedule for speech-language pathologists*. Retrieved January 12, 2007, from http://www.asha.org/NR/rdonlyres/11796FF2-5814-4754-9B8C-5A0BA91447F0/0/2007MPFSSLP.pdf

Bell, M. (1997). Postoperative pain management for the cognitively impaired older adult. *Seminars in Perioperative Nursing, 6*(1), 37–41.

Beukelman, D. R., & Mirenda, P. (1998). *Augmentative and alternative communication: Management of severe communication disorders in children and adults* (2nd ed.). Baltimore: Brookes.

Bourgeois, M., & Mason, L. A. (1996). Memory wallet intervention in an adult day care setting. *Behavioral Interventions: Theory and Practice in Residential and Community-Based Clinical Programs, 11*, 3–18.

Bravo, G., Dubois, M-F., & Pâquet, M. (2003). Advance directives for health care and research: Prevalence and correlates. *Alzheimer Disease and Associated Disorders, 17*(4), 215–222.

Caniglia, J. (2003, January–March). Documentation pitfalls—and how to avoid them. *The ASHA Leader Online*. Retrieved January 12, 2007, from http://www.asha.org/about/publications/leader-online/archives/2003/q1/030218e.htm

Caserta, M., & Lund, D. (2002). Video Respite in an Alzheimer's care center: Group versus solitary viewing. *Activities, Adaptation, & Aging, 27*(1), 13–26.

Centers for Medicare and Medicaid Services (CMS). (2006a, December 29). *Outpatient therapy cap exceptions process for calendar year (CY) 2007* (Pub 100-04, Medicare Claims Processing, Transmittal 1145). Washington, DC: Department of Health and Human Services.

Centers for Medicare and Medicaid Services (CMS). (2006b, November). *Rehabilitation therapy information: Resource for Medicare*. Medicare Learning Network. Retrieved January 12, 2007, from http://www.cms.hhs.gov/MLNGenInfo

Covinsky, K. E., Eng, C., Lui, L. Y., Sands, L. P., & Yaffe, K. (2003). The last 2 years of life: Functional trajectories of frail older people. *Journal of the American Geriatrics Society, 51*, 492–498.

Crisis in Health Care Reimbursement. (2006, September 5). *ASHA Leader, 11*(10), 10–11, 27.

Feldt, K. S. (2000). The checklist of nonverbal pain behaviors (CNPI). *Pain Management Nursing, 1*, 13–21.

Feldt, K., & Finch, M. (2002). Older adults with hip fractures: Treatment of pain following hospitalization. *Journal of Gerontological Nursing, 28*(8), 27–35.

Feldt, K., Ryden, M., & Miles, S. (1998). Treatment of pain in cognitively impaired compared with cognitively intact older patients with hip fracture. *Journal of the American Geriatrics Society, 46*, 1079–1085.

Feldt, K., Warne, M., & Ryden, M. (1998). Examining pain in aggressive cognitively impaired older adults. *Journal of Gerontological Nursing, 24*(11), 14–22.

Ferrell, B. (1995). Pain evaluation and management in the nursing home. *Annals of Internal Medicine, 123*, 681–687.

Ferrell, B., Ferrell, B. R., & Rivera, L. (1995). Pain in cognitively impaired nursing home patients. *Journal of Pain and Symptom Management, 10*(8), 591–598.

Ferrell, B., Stein, W. M., & Beck, J. C. (2000). The Geriatric Pain Measure: Validity, reliability, and factor analysis. *Journal of the American Geriatrics Society, 48*, 1669–1673.

Fisher, S. E., Burgio, L. D., Thorn, B. E., Allen-Burge, R., Gerstle, J., & Roth, D. (2002). Pain assessment and management among cognitively impaired nursing home residents: Association of Certified Nursing Assistants pain report, MDS pain report, and analgesic medication use. *Journal of the American Geriatrics Society, 50*, 152–156.

Fisher, S. E., Burgio, L. D., Thorn, B. E. & Hardin, J. M. (2006). Obtaining self-report data from cognitively impaired elders: Methodological issues and clinical implications for nursing home pain assessment. *The Gerontologist, 46*(1), 89–96.

Holland, A. (1998, May). Management of behavioral, memory, and other cognitive/linguistic disorders in individuals with dementia. Paper presented at the National Rehabilitation Services Continuing Education Seminar, Dallas, TX.

Hopper, T. (2003). "They're just going to get worse anyway": Perspectives on rehabilitation for nursing home residents with dementia. *Journal of Communication Disorders, 36*, 345–359.

Horgas, A., & Tasi, P. (1998). Analgesic drug prescription and use in cognitively impaired nursing home residents. *Nursing Research, 47*, 235–242.

Huffman, J. C., & Kunik, M. E. (2000). Assessment and understanding of pain in patients with dementia. *The Gerontologist, 40*(5), 574–581.

Hurley, A., Volicer, B., Hanrahan, P., Houde, S., & Volicer, L. (1992). Assessment of discomfort in advanced Alzheimer's patients. *Research in Nursing and Health*, *15*(5), 369–377.

Joseph, A., & Boult, C. (1998). Managed primary care of nursing home residents. *Journal of the American Geriatrics Society*, *46*(9), 1152–1156.

Kaasalainen, S., Middleton, J., Knezacek, S., Hartley, T., Stewart, N., Ife, C., et al. (1998). Pain and cognitive status in the institutionalized elderly. *Journal of Gerontological Nursing*, *24*(8), 24–31.

Kander, M. (2005, September 6). It's about time. *The ASHA Leader*, *3*, 15.

Kander, M. (2006, May 23). Medicare covers cognitive therapy. *The ASHA Leader*, *11*(7), 3, 14.

Lasker, J. (2006). Visual Pain Scale. Unpublished scale, used with permission. Florida State University, Tallahassee.

Last Acts Palliative Care Task Force. (1997, December). *Precepts of palliative care*. Retrieved January 12, 2007, from www.lastacts.org:80/docs/profprecepts.pdf

Lawton, M. P., Van Haitsma, K., & Klapper, J. (1996). Observed affect in nursing home residents with Alzheimer's disease. *Journal of Gerontology: Psychological Sciences*, *51B*, P3–P14.

Logemann, J. (2003, January–March). Dysphagia and dementia: The challenge of dual diagnosis. *ASHA Leader Online*. Retrieved January 14, 2007, from http://www.asha.org/about/publications/leader-online/archives/2003/q1/030218g.htm

Lund, D. A., Hill, R. D., Caserta, M. S., & Wright, S. D. (1995). Video Respite: An innovative resource for family, professional caregivers, and persons with dementia. *The Gerontologist*, *35*(5), 683–687.

Markowitz, J. S., Gutterman, E. M., Sadik, K., & Papadopoulos, G. (2003). Health-related quality of life for caregivers of patients with Alzheimer disease. *Alzheimer Disease and Associated Disorders*, *17*, 209–214.

Marzinski, L. (1991). The tragedy of dementia: Clinically assessing pain in the confused nonverbal elderly. *Journal of Gerontological Nursing*, *17*(6), 25–28.

Mezey, M., Mitty, E.., & Ramsey, G. (1997). Assessment of decision-making capacity: Nursing's role. *Journal of Gerontological Nursing*, *23*(3), 28–35.

Moye, J., Karel, M., Azar, A., & Gurrera, R. (2004). Capacity to consent to treatment: Empirical comparison of three instruments in older adults with and without dementia. *The Gerontologist*, *44*(2), 166–175.

News-for-You.com. (N.d.). News for You. Retrieved August 6, 2008, from http://www.news-for-you.com

O'Boyle, R. (2001). *Medicare coverage for dementia patients clarified*. Retrieved August 4, 2008, from http://ec-online.net/Knowledge/Articles/medicaredementia.html

Olshin, J., Ciolek, D., & Hwang, W. (2002). Study and report on outpatient therapy utilization: Physical therapy, occupational therapy, and speech-language pathology services billed to Medicare Part B in all settings in 1998, 1999, and 2000. *AdvanceMed, 500-99-0009, 1–123.* Columbia, MD: AdvanceMed PSC CERT Therapy Services Error Rate Study.

Parmelee, P. A., Smith, B., & Katz, I. R. (1993). Pain complaints and cognitive status among elderly institutionalized residents. *Journal of the American Geriatrics Society*, *41*, 517–522.

Partnership for Caring. (N.d.). Partnership for caring. Retrieved August 5, 2008, from http://www.partnershipforcaring.org

Perrin, K. (1997). Giving voice to the wishes of elders for end-of-life care. *Journal of Gerontological Nursing*, *23*(3), 18–27.

Petty, D. (2002). Explaining Medicare to caregivers. *Center for Medicare Education Issue Brief*, *3*(7), 1–8. Retrieved January 15, 2007, from http://www.MedicareEd.org

Roth, L., Meisel, A., & Lidz, C. (1977). Tests of competency to consent to treatment. *American Journal of Psychiatry, 134*(3), 279–284.

Ryden, M.B., & Feldt, K.S. (1992). Goal-directed care: caring for aggressive nursing home residents with dementia. *Journal of Gerontological Nursing*, 18(11), 35–41.

Schonwetter, R. S., Han, B., Small, B. J., Martin, B., Tope, K., & Haley, W. E. (2003). Predictors of six-month survival among patients with dementia: An evaluation of hospice Medicare guidelines. *American Journal of Hospice Palliative Care*, 2, 105–113.

Schulz, R. (2000). *Handbook on dementia caregiving: Evidence-based interventions for family caregivers*. New York: Springer.

Simmons, S. F., Ferrell, B. A., & Schnelle, J. F. (2002). The effects of a controlled exercise trial on pain in nursing home residents. *Clinical Journal of Pain, 18*, 380–385.

Sloan, F. A., & Taylor, D. H., Jr. (2002). Effect of Alzheimer disease on the cost of treating other diseases. *Alzheimer Disease and Associated Disorders, 16*(3), 137–143.

Snow, A. L., O'Malley, K. J., Cody, M., Kunik, M. E., Ashton, C. M., Beck, C., et al. (2004). A conceptual model of pain assessment for noncommunicative persons with dementia. *The Gerontologist, 44*(6), 807–817.

Swigert, N. (2002). *Managing Medicare: Documenting what you do is as important as doing it*. Retrieved January 14, 2007, from http://www.asha.org/about/publications/leader-online/archives/2002/q1/

Thayer, K. (2006). *Establishing an effective dysphagia program in a long term care facility*. Retrieved January 8, 2007, from http://www.speechpathology.com/articles/article_detail.asp?article_id=38

U.S. Senate Committee on Aging. (2000). Report 106-229. In *Developments in aging: 1997 and 1998* (Vol. 1). Washington, DC: Author.

Warden, V., Hurley, A. C., & Volicer, L. (2003). Development and psychometric evaluation of the pain assessment in advanced dementia (PAIN-AD) scale. *Journal of the American Medical Directors Association, 4*, 9–15.

Widdershoven, G., & Berghmans, R. (2001). Advance directives in dementia care: From instructions to instruments. *Patient Education and Counseling, 44*, 179–186.

World Health Organization. (2001). *International classification of functioning, disability, and health*. Geneva: Author.

Subject Index

Note: locators for figures are in italic, and tables are in bold

B

D

F

N

O

S

Author Index

A

B

D

E

F

G

H

I

J

K

M

N

O

T

X

Y

Z